The Prophetic Call
to
Love and Justice

The Prophetic Call to Love and Justice

Rediscovering the Old Testament

The Amsterdam Way of Interpreting Scripture

ARNOLD H. DE GRAAFF

RESOURCE *Publications* · Eugene, Oregon

THE PROPHETIC CALL TO LOVE AND JUSTICE
Rediscovering the Old Testament; The Amsterdam Way of Interpreting Scripture

Copyright © 2025 Arnold H. De Graaff. All rights reserved. Except for brief quotations in critical publications or reviews, no part of this book may be reproduced in any manner without prior written permission from the publisher. Write: Permissions, Wipf and Stock Publishers, 199 W. 8th Ave., Suite 3, Eugene, OR 97401.

Resource Publications
An Imprint of Wipf and Stock Publishers
199 W. 8th Ave., Suite 3
Eugene, OR 97401

www.wipfandstock.com

PAPERBACK ISBN: 979-8-3852-4836-0
HARDCOVER ISBN: 979-8-3852-4837-7
EBOOK ISBN: 979-8-3852-4838-4

To my parents:

Jan de Graaff, 1900–1982
Jannetje Verwey, 1899–2002
For their constant care during difficult times

Contents

Preface xi

Introduction to the Amsterdam way of interpreting the scriptures xv

Chapter 1: The forerunners and founders: Palache, Buber and Rosenzweig, Miskotte, Beek, Breukelman, Deurloo 1

Chapter 2: A Third Alternative 9
    2:1 An uncharacteristic outburst 9
    2:2 Deurloo's and Breukelman's critique and use/appreciation of the 'critical historical method' 13
    2:3 Historical situation and cultural context 15
    2:4 The prophetic call to love and justice 19

Chapter 3: The challenge of secularization in interpreting scripture for today 21
    3:1 Secularization: a case study 21
    3:2 Dis-enchantment and re-enchantment 27

Chapter 4: First impressions 34
    4:1 Deurloo's specific exegetical method for Bible Study 35

Chapter 5: The general approach of the Amsterdam way of interpretation 37
    5:1 Main characteristics 37
    5:2 Translating from the Hebrew into a common language of the day 39
    5:3 The historicity of the scriptures 42
        a) Talstra's view of 'religious language' 42

CONTENTS

      b) Ahlstrom's view of 'religious language' 45
      c) Religious language that gives expression to ecstasy and suffering 47
  5:4 Deurloo's exegetical method: four examples 52
      a) Jacob fleeing Esau 53
      b) Patriarchal Lies 59
      c) Jesus' temptations 61
      d) Sodom and Gomorrah 66

Chapter 6: Re-reading Genesis –through Genesis all of the Old and New Testament 72

  6:1 'Introduction' to Genesis: general perspective 72
  6:2 Breukelman and Deurloo's interpretation of Genesis 82
  6:3 Genesis 1:1–2:3 The creation of the earth: a good home for humanity 84
  6:4 Genesis 2:4–25 The 'second' creation story could have as a title, 'This is the one' 97
  6:5 Genesis 3 An impossible possibility: wanting to be like God 103
  6:6 Genesis 4:1–16 The human and his brother 108
  6:7 Genesis 5:1–11:26 The generations of Adam; the second 'toledot' 116
  6:8 Genesis 6:9–11:26 Living before and after the flood; ten generations from Noah to Abraham 119
  6:9 Genesis 11:27–25:11 The Terah 'toledot'; the centre of the 'toledot' cycles 125
  6:10 Genesis 12:1–25:11 'Go from . . . to the land I will show you' 129
  6:11 Genesis 13:1–14:24 Two ways of seeing, Abram and Lot 132
  6:12 Genesis 18:16–19:38 Sodom and Gomorrah 135
  6:13 Genesis 25:19–35:29 The Isaac 'toledot'; Rebecca; Jacob and Esau. 138
  6:14 Genesis 22:1–14 The offering of Isaac 139
  6:15 Genesis 24:1–67 History continues; Rebekah 145
  6:16 Genesis 27:1–35:29 Esau and Jacob, the stolen blessing 147
  6:17 Genesis 29:15–31:32 Jacob and Laban, the deceiver deceived 151
  6:18 Genesis 32:1–33:14 Jacob meeting Esau Face to Face 153
  6:19 Genesis 37: 1–50:26 The Jacob 'toledot', the Joseph (Novella) 155

CONTENTS

Chapter 7: Re-reading Joshua 166
- 7:1 Introduction to Joshua 166
  - a) The described history and the history and time of the author 171
  - b) Joshua, a prophetic book 174
  - c) The Extermination of the Canaanite peoples 177
  - d) Moses and Joshua, their mission 185
  - e) A place for the Torah 186
  - f) An inheritance forever 186
- 7:2 Joshua 2 The confession of Rahab in solidarity with Israel 193
- 7:3 Joshua 3–4 Crossing the Jordan and entering into a new period 197
- 7:4 Joshua 5 Circumcision and the Passover 200
- 7:5 Joshua 6 The conquest of Jericho 202
- 7:6 Joshua 7–8 All the people; Ai and the ban 204
  - a) The ban 208
  - b) An interruption? A second dedication ceremony 211
  - c) Religious geography and chronology *vs.* physical geography and chronology 214
- 7:7 Joshua 9 The strategy of the Gibeonites 218
- 7:8 Joshua 10:12–15 The sun standing still 220
- 7:9 Joshua 10, 11 The conquest 225
- 7:10 Joshua 13–21 The division of the land 227
- 7:11 Joshua 22 The Jordan is not a border 228
- 7:12 Joshua 23,24 Joshua's last words; God the giver and the gods 229
- 7:13 Concluding remarks 232
- 7:14 *Excursion: Israel and Palestine* 240
  - a) Introduction 240
  - b) Scriptural witness: the appeal to the 'destruction of the Amalikites' 242
  - c) The New Testament witness 246
  - d) The promise of the land 250
  - e) Christianity's anti-Semitism 253
  - f) Zionism and especially American Zionism 254
  - g) Deurloo's vision 255
  - h) The promise of the 'land' today 261
  - i) Dr. Andrew Judge's account of the land 262
  - j) Billy Gauthier's account of the land 263

CONTENTS

    k) Alternatives for today: regenerative agriculture, fishing and forestry 265

Chapter 8: A new God-image?! 268
  8:1 Introduction: a preamble 268
  8:2 The god of the scriptures 271
  8:3 Yahweh's love affair with all people and the earth 275
  8:4 Yahweh's anger and wrath 278
  8:5 Yahweh as Father, Mother, Parent, Friend and Lover 280
  8:6 Yahweh's forgiveness and compassion 282
  8:7 Yahweh's holiness 284
  8:8 The New Testament witness 285

Chapter 9: The nature of Biblical Theology 290
  9:1 Exodus and (return from) Exile belong together (2003) 299
  9:2 King and Temple (2004) 319
    a) A Biblical theological perspective: King and Temple 319
    b) Kingship 328
    c) Temple 332
  9:3 Barren Women and Unexpected Sons (2006) 343
    a) Introduction 343
    b) The death and resurrection of a son 356
    c) Mother Mary 360
  9:4 Creation from Paul to Genesis (2008) 371
    a) Introduction 371
    b) Creation and nature 373
    c) Wisdom 377
    d) Job 383
    e) Ecclesiastes 386
    f) Yahweh's creating and 'maintaining' are of one piece 387
    g) Miskotte's view of God's 'for-seeing' 401

Chapter 10: Conclusion: The Amsterdam Way of Exegesis 404
  10:1 Karl Barth's influence? 406
  10:2 Once more; the question of 'historicity' of the scriptures 414
  10:3 A summary of the Amsterdam approach 417

Chapter 11: Psalms and liturgy 419
Bibliography 425

Preface

THIS STUDY IS THE result of a lifelong journey to understand the scriptures. See my *Understanding the Scriptures* together with Seerveld of 1968. Even after I became a fulltime psychotherapist, I continued my search for a different understanding that could serve as an alternative to my 'indoctrination' both by my family and my religious community in the Dutch Calvinist tradition. The work of Deurloo and others came as an unexpected surprise and as a gift. It has been a moving and rewarding journey that brought many tears of joy. Finally I was able to take distance to my strict religious upbringing as well as to much of modern, critical theological scholarship. For the first time the scriptures opened up and began to shine. I am sure it is not the last word about exegesis, but it does provide a crucial new basis. Surprised by joy!

When I left Toronto and the Institute for Christian Studies, I also left behind my original training in the Amsterdam Philosophy of Dooyeweerd and Vollenhoven and followers, which in many ways perpetuated the more negative sides of the Calvinist tradition.

This book offers an in-depth presentation of the Amsterdam way of interpreting the scripture, particularly through one of its main representatives, Karel Deurloo. It is not intended to be an academic analysis and critique of the Amsterdam tradition. Rather it is meant to inspire others with this rich tradition.

My father never found a different understanding of the scriptures and comfort during his difficult life, although he struggled and searched. Yet, I am grateful to both my parents for exposing me to the old Calvinist tradition, in spite of all the distress it caused me and a life-long search for an alternative. Without them I would not have had any exposure to the scriptures, however limited and skewed. I am dedicating this book to their memory for their care during many difficult years. Even though my

PREFACE

father never seemed to approve of me and I had to cope with my mother's intense emotional reactions and possessiveness, I continued to struggle and search.

I regret that I was not able to share this vision with my children when they were young. My hope is that they might find my own spiritual struggle through many decades, illuminating. This study has made me more keenly aware of my failures as a father, for which I am sorry.

Primarily the book offers a *third alternative* to liberal, critical historical interpretations on the one hand and fundamentalist or literalistic interpretations on the other.

This book is intended primarily as a starting point for adult bible study groups. With the decline of many denominations and churches there will be a great need for small bible study groups to come to a new understanding of the scriptures in their prophetic meaning for today. My hope is that the richness of the scriptures will shine through again in the many passages discussed and thus take on new meaning as they did for me. As well, it can serve individuals to reacquaint themselves with the core message of the Bible.

I am grateful for the encouragement I received from the Rev. Dr. Marco Visser and Dr. Joep Dubbink. The many publications of the Amsterdam tradition showed me the way. My hope is that more of those publications will be translated into English.

A special thanks to Dr. Rinse Reeling Brouwer for his gracious offer to read the manuscript and for his careful reading, and thoughtful, encouraging comments. He saved me from making crucial errors in interpreting the Amsterdam tradition. I have also been enriched by his many articles and books.

I am grateful for the writings of Dr. Lambert Zuidervaart, emeritus professor from the Institute of Christian Studies, the University of Toronto, and Calvin University. After I left Toronto, someone gave me a copy of Lambert's *Social Philosophy after Adorno* (2007). After that I read his, (2004), *Artistic Truth: Aesthetics, Discourse, and Imaginative Disclosure*, followed by many of his other volumes. It provided me with a genuine alternative to the Amsterdam philosophy to which I was exposed. I am grateful for his insights and support.

One of the great benefits of the Amsterdam approach to exegesis is the wholesome effects it can have on an alternative to the traditional understanding of many doctrines, which awaits further implementation. It has a profoundly affirming potential for re-directing away from the many unfortunate and negative results of old doctrines and all the rationalistic and dualistic tendencies as they were lived in the conservative, religious community in Holland and elsewhere.

Most of all I am thankful for the support and encouragement of my partner, Rita Reitsma, who read earlier drafts of the book, which tremendously enhanced its quality.

All the biblical references are from the Revised Standard Version, 1952.

> He has shown you, O man, what is good;
> and what does the Lord require of you
> but to do justice, and to love kindness,
> and to walk humbly with your God?
>
> MICAH 6:8

Introduction to the Amsterdam way of interpreting the scriptures

ORIGINATING IN THE TURMOIL of the nineteen twenties and nineteen forties in the Netherlands, the Amsterdam way of interpreting scripture continues to make history for its profound work. Extending beyond the Netherlands, it has become a 'school' or new tradition.

Throughout, its emphasis has been on the proclamation or prophetic nature of scriptures. The key to interpreting and understanding the purpose of the Bible is not in its literary stories, political propaganda, ideologies, historicity, moralistic lessons or touching psychological tales.

Instead the scriptures in their given-ness and unity are a prophetic proclamation or revelation. They are about God's call to love and justice. They speak to us very directly and personally, and give rise to joy and thanksgiving. They address us, confront, comfort and guide us. They speak to us at the core of our being, our hearts, in which we give direction to our lives.

In view of either a critical liberal or a fundamentalist understanding of the scriptures, an alternative was sorely needed. Various forms of historical criticism dominated the interpretation of the Bible for centuries and linger on. It left the church and pastors with fragmented texts that obscured the religious meaning of the words and their prophetic power.

Introduction

For many decades and until today scholars and pastors had to deal with the results of this type of historical, critical exegesis and commentaries. Instead of fragmented small parts of a text rooted in different traditions and edited together by later scribes, the Amsterdam school emphasizes the unity of the texts and their inter-connectedness as they are given in the whole of the scriptures.

Although the primacy of the critical historical method is generally minimized today, it is still a strong force in exegetical studies that lingers on in many commentaries and biblical studies. These are used by clergy and lay persons to prepare sermons, catechism lessons and Bible studies. More recently, it is more and more displaced by the critical literary method, which approaches different books of the bible as works of art to be appreciated for their literary beauty to be studied like Homer and Shakespeare. Although it emphasizes the unity of the scriptures, unfortunately this newer approach did little to recover the prophetic message.

The exegetical tradition that developed in Amsterdam made a radical break with the dominant critical historical approach of the time as well as a strictly literary approach. At times that put them on the defensive. At least some, if not many, suffered from unjust criticisms of being unscholarly, or were simply ignored. Reading their many publications shows how unfair those criticisms have been.

As well, it would be a mistake to interpret the Amsterdam way of exegesis as a (more elaborate) form of literary analysis or criticism. All the literary structural givens like, 'plot, actors, time, space, context, story teller, heroes, themes, repetitions, polar opposites, framework, concentric symmetry, key words, points of view, climax, etc.' as well as the 'geographical and historical' references are in the service of the prophetic message. These literary structural categories can be applied to any (ancient) writing. For a general interpretive guideline, it is not sufficient to search for a combination of "historical, literary and theological' meanings. Rather the historical and literary givens are for the purpose of elucidating the message. The title of this book could be, "The Primacy of the Prophetic Message". In this context, the words 'prophetic message' is more appropriate and has priority over 'theological message'. 'Theological' soon has the connotation of abstract, theological statements or doctrines. In contrast, 'prophetic message' has the meaning of being personally addressed and engaged, challenged, judged, guided, called, reassured, comforted, liberated and led to joy and thanksgiving. Together

Introduction

these words point to the faithful testimony of the scribes, prophets and wise men to the living word of God as witnessed in the scriptures.

There is certainly lots of room for discussion and debate. Any specific aspect of interpretation can be challenged. No interpretation is final and can always be re-examined. Yet neither the historical nor the literary approach should serve as the key to interpreting the scriptures for reasons that will be carefully shown in the chapters that follow. Against this background the rediscovery of the unity and prophetic message of the scriptures was like a breath of fresh air. People again felt personally addressed and found new unexpected meaning.

After introducing the main originators of the Amsterdam school and four concrete examples of their exegetical method, comes the issue of secularization and its influence on interpretation. Then there follows a close re-reading of both Genesis and Joshua. The interpretation of Joshua has come into the spotlight again today because of the political situation in Palestine and the annihilation of the Palestinian people in Gaza (and the West Bank). The promise of the land to the fore-fathers and the conquest of Canaan by Joshua are misused to justify the destruction of Gaza and killing tens of thousands of Palestinians. For this reason I have added an *Excursion about Israel and Palestine.*

Out of the close reading of both Genesis and Joshua a new God image arose for me. At least, new to me, having been 'indoctrinated in the Calvinist view and way of life' with its emphasis on the eternal council of God, election, reprobation, total depravity, original sin and the absolute antithesis between Christians and non-Christians, which has taken me all my life to escape. My first publication as a professor was, *Understanding the Scriptures*, (1969). Now, 56 years later, it feels like I have finally found a satisfactory answer to my life-long quest that has given me great joy and satisfaction. My new understanding of the 'God image of the scriptures' has been the key factor in this search.

At different points I have translated the titles of various publications by the Amsterdam writers. Unfortunately very few have been translated into English. Any Dutch quotes have been translated by the author. Throughout the book I have tried to summarize and elucidate the meaning from the Dutch publications. This was another compelling reason for writing this book.

CHAPTER 1

The forerunners and founders
Palache, Buber and Rosenzweig, Miskotte, Beek, Breukelman, Deurloo

A NUMBER OF LEADING scholars, Palache, Buber and Rosenzweig, Beek, and Miskotte prepared the way for this new approach. Much of their writing and teaching related to the growing emergence of Nazism and the collaboration of many theologians with the Nazi ideology. Although this approach to exegesis became known as the 'Amsterdam School', it was promoted by many scholars in the Netherlands from many different public universities with theology departments and in Eastern European universities.

1) J.L. Palache, (1886–1944)

Palache, was a Jewish professor at the University of Amsterdam in biblical exegesis. He wrote a crucial article that was republished in *Voices from Amsterdam*, called "The nature of Old Testament narrative."[1] He examined the narrative literature of Arabic, Syriac, and Talmudic traditions.

Summing up, Palache concluded:

> We have found the following characteristics of *narrative* in the Semitic literatures:
>
> 1) Narrative is a preferred means of framing thoughts or to persuade. It provides (often unhistorical) answers to all sorts of questions, not only in the Bible, but also in the Haggadah (as

---

1. Kessler, *Voices from Amsterdam*, 3–22.

in the Arabic Hadith). These stories incline toward visualization and concrete representation.

2) The truth question must be reversed from the usual perception. The story is not told because it happened, but becomes real by the telling. The telling creates tradition in generations that follow, supported by the belief of the pious.

3) It draws, if necessary, in a poetic manner on free fantasy and is not bound to reality, nor to older models, nor to historical tradition, nor even to a holy scripture. Mutually divergent representations exist side by side and initially do not give cause for critique.

4) In a longer or shorter period of time the narrative becomes tradition and tradition becomes reality.[2]

According to Palache, this means we cannot force our logic or our modern sense of history on these narrative accounts. We would be inclined to make everything too smooth and make them more consistent representations than the ancients had thought for themselves. The ancients had a far more independent attitude toward the material and the tradition and composed much more themselves than is commonly assumed. His studies had a profound effect on the writers of the Amsterdam school and relativized many discussions about the historicity of specific biblical stories and their references to dates and place names.

One 'hears' the voice of faith in relating to tradition in the words of the psalmist: "O God, with our ears we have heard, our fathers have told us . . ." (Psalm 44:2), in which "with our ears we have heard it" (which for us has the emotional value of: "we have seen it with our own eyes.")[3] His advice is that we ought to develop a delicate feel for this literature.[4] Palache illustrated his thesis with many examples. Tragically, as a Jewish person, he was fired from the University of Amsterdam. He and his wife were deported and murdered in 1944 by the Nazis.

Palache's main thesis makes an important contribution to the ongoing discussions about the historicity of the scriptures. In particular he alerted us to the specific nature of *narrative* genre in the Bible.

---

2. Kessler, *Voices from Amsterdam*, 3, 4, 18.
3. Kessler, *Voices from Amsterdam*, 21.
4. Kessler, *Voices from Amsterdam*, 22.

2) M. Buber (1878-1965) and F. Rosenzweig (1886-1929)

Along with other professors at the Jerusalem University, Buber and Rosenzweig made a new beginning in the interpretation of the Hebrew Bible. They strongly emphasized the role of *key* words and *core themes* or motifs as well as the basic structure of larger literary units (over against all fragmenting and atomizing of texts according to their sources or redactions). Their approach cut through the generally accepted critical historical and literary methods. The analysis of the 'use' of words, (style and structure) was their main concern. The Hebrew bible was created for proclamation (for sounding out) and not for its beauty as a work of art. The characteristics of a text or a literary unit were all in the service of the prophetic message. Their aim was to persuade and change the hearer.

Buber and Rosenzweig put all these guidelines into practice in their translation of the Bible in ordinary German, staying very close to the original meaning of the key words in Hebrew, entitled *Die Schrift und ihre Verdeutschung*, (1936). This work is still a source of inspiration for many members of the Amsterdam tradition.

3) Miskotte, K.H. (1894-1976)

One of the most important founders of the Amsterdam tradition was Miskotte. He was born in a conservative Reformed family in the Netherlands. After attending a Christian high school he studied theology at the university in Leiden from 1914-1920 during the first World War. He became a socialist and was deeply inspired by the Old Testament. In 1923 he started a correspondence with Karl Barth (1886-1968). During his first pastorate, he earned a doctorate in theology at the University of Groningen in 1932, entitled *The Essence of the Jewish Religion*. In 1937 he made a trip to the Dutch East Indies. A few years later, in 1940, Holland was invaded by the German army. He became involved with a resistance group. The Nazis banned his war time book, *Edda and Torah*. In 1941 he published his well-known *Biblical ABCs*. He was appointed to a professorship in theology and ethics at the University of Leiden in 1941.

In 1956 he published his major work, *When the Gods are Silent*, which was translated in both German (1963) and English (1967). At the age of 65 he retired from his professorship, but remained very active till his death in 1976. Karl Barth died in 1968, which ended their long friendship. His radio sermons gained him national prominence. He became known as a major proponent of Barth's theology in the Netherlands. He started his own journal, *In the Waagschaal*.

In his dissertation he had already engaged in an intensive study of Judaism, which became a trusted introduction to Jewish philosophy within the Jewish community. To him Judaism was a form of humanism in which humanity became its own savior, following Rosenzweig. The danger he saw was that humanity would no longer need God or his Son. The Torah he saw as entirely positive, calling the people of Israel away from heathen veneration in the here and now. In the 1930's, he became known as a major opponent of National Socialism (Nazism). He called it a new heathenism.

He left behind a large collection of diaries, letters, sermons and articles. This archive is located at the University of Leiden. In 2012 the Miskotte/Breukelman chair for theological hermeneutics at the Protestant Theological University was established in order to promote the study of Miskotte. Presently that chair is occupied by Prof. Dr. R.H. Reeling Brouwer. His legacy will continue on and inspire many generations to come. It is difficult to adequately summarize the richness and depth of the contribution he made and the legacy he left.

4) M.A. Beek (1909–1987)

Beek was appointed in 1946 to the chair vacated by Palache's forced dismissal based entirely on his being Jewish, and was appointed professor of Hebrew Language and 'Faculteit der Letteren' at the University of Amsterdam. At his retirement in 1974 he gave a farewell lecture, which was republished in *Voices from Amsterdam*, titled "Saturation points and unfinished lines in the study of Old Testament literature."[5] Beek was not dogmatic about his own interpretation of the scriptures. In this lecture he strongly encouraged his doctoral students to follow their own exploration of the text. He highlighted the dead end of much exegetical scholarship and the need to explore new approaches. He made them aware of the work of Buber and Rosenzweig and the Midrash tradition. Initially he studied with B.D. Eerdmans in Leiden who charted an independent course away from the popular 'documentary hypothesis' of Graf-Kuenen-Wellhausen ('bronnen theorie').

---

5. Kessler, *Voices from Amsterdam*, 23–35.

5) F. Breukelman (1916–1993)

Breukelman was a prolific writer and interpreter. He was also a very emotional person that could react with vehemence and intensity, shouting and crying. He had such a strong sense of perfectionism that it prevented him from publishing. He used to provide his students with stenciled notes that would be changed and corrected the next time. It is only because of the persuasion and work of his friends that his lifelong projects on Genesis and Matthew were finally published.

He had a difficult childhood. His family was under the threat of Huntington's disease (an incurable hereditary disease) that affected several members of his family. Breukelman himself was not affected, but he lived under the threat of this disease for many years, never knowing whether or not he would develop the disease. His mother suffered from severe depression, as well as did Breukelman. He was aware that he was a very emotional person, subject to uncertainty, despair, and doubts. Miskotte commented once on 'your depressive moments and euphoria and manic reactions', and recommended that he see a doctor.

He grew up in a liberal family, both theologically and socially. He was a member of a socialist party. His parents considered it important that he get some exposure to the Christian religion. Once he graduated from the Christian Lyceum he was persuaded to study theology at the University of Leiden. He soon became dissatisfied

Through Miskotte he also became acquainted with Buber and Rosenzweig. These two sources inspired him throughout his life. From them he took in that every literary style in the Bible is tied to the message of the texts. Form and content are inseparably connected. They form the biblical message. These factors, from Barth and Buber influenced him throughout his theological career. He was deeply affected by the destruction of the war and particularly by the bombing of the dykes of an island in Zeeland, where he was a minister, that caused an environmental disaster and in which thousands of people died.

In 1948 he became a minister in Simonshaven, in Zeeland. During that time he broke with the critical historical methods of interpreting the scriptures and chose to base his exegetical work on the Bible texts handed down instead of the assumed sources out of which the texts were constructed. In 1968 he was appointed as academic assistant at the University of Amsterdam. At first he devoted a lot of attention to the translation of the Bible, since a new translation was being proposed in Holland.

He became very critical of it and offered many examples and alternative translations. His critical and vehement tone alienated him from most other biblical exegetes that were involved in the new translation.

In van Zanden there is an interesting section on Breukelman's 'pietism' ("bevindelijkheid"). He compares it to Miskotte's view of 'the objective side' of a person's faith as a personal response to the great deeds of God that is called forth by the redemptive facts, but comes from the perspective of the human and therefore is 'subjective' in nature, *and* the subjective inner experience of life before the face of God, in which all our life experiences and situations play a role (the horizontal dimension). The first is the most important. In many orthodox communities the 'subjective side' often dominated, giving rise to a preoccupation with inner feelings. It often became a self-absorbed attitude that resulted in depression, passivity, guilt, fear, uncertainty and anguish, that could dominate an entire community. Van Zanden related Breukelman's piety and inner struggles more to Miskotte's views. His pietism was deeply grounded in the revelation of the Name. They were not just part of his inner feelings. Generally, his intense feelings were a burden that he carried throughout his life, but they did not stop him from his life-long exploration of the scriptures that came to fruition in his biblical theological studies.

6) K.Deurloo (1936–2019)

Deurloo grew up in Amsterdam. In his youth he listened to the inspiring sermons of Miskotte, whose way of preaching was very intense and made the stories come alive. It inspired Deurloo enough that he decided to study theology, because he wanted to become a preacher like Miskotte. He studied theology at the University of Amsterdam and wrote his dissertation under the guidance of M.A. Beek. It was entitled *Cain and Abel: an investigation of the exegetical method with regard to a small literary unit of the TeNaK.* (1967). After his graduation he became youth minister in Eindhoven and in 1971 he became a student pastor in Amsterdam. Following his teacher Prof. Dr. Beek he was appointed professor of Old Testament at the University of Amsterdam and lectured there from 1975–1996. From 2003–2006 he occupied a special position (the Dirk Monshouwer chair) in Biblical Theology at the Free University of Amsterdam. He became a great inspiration to many students, pastors and theologians. He also attracted many foreign theology students, including from Germany and Hungary.

From early on, together with his colleague Nico Bouhuijs, student pastor in Leiden, starting during the 1960's, Deurloo presented at least nine television programs called, *'Closer to...Genesis'; Prophets; Paul;* etc. The presentations later became written publications due to popular demand. Along with Breukelman, he became one of the most important representatives of the 'Amsterdam school'. From 1980–1997 he served as the editor of the series, *'Amsterdams Cahiers for Exegesis and Biblical Theology'*. Each year a new volume of exegetical articles was published in these *Cahiers* by many different theologians. One of his concerns was to bring the Bible close to ordinary people again, including faithful churchgoers and to give them a new understanding of the prophetic message of the scriptures, especially of the Hebrew Bible.

He had a special talent and concern for telling Bible stories to children without moralizing and intellectualizing. He created delightful accompanying songs. See his *A Child May Stand in the Centre*, with an Appendix of songs and music (1982), and his, together with Hanna van Dorssen and Karel Eykman: *That is Seven; Seven ways to tell Children from the Bible.(2001),*

I regret that during the time I spent at the Free University from 1960–1966 and the many short visits during the late eighties, the nineties, and early two thousands that I did not get to know him or even know about his work. His concern for children and youth would have fit well with my own interests in *The Educational Ministry of the Church*. As it was, I had to leave the practical outworking of my thesis for later. (See my *The Joy of Learning*, together with Jean Olthuis, a master teacher and her *Teaching with Joy in Learning*, and several other curriculum guides).

Deurloo became known for his careful exegesis of the scriptures, in which the uniqueness of the Hebrew language stood out. The focus was on the narrative character of many stories and the literary characteristics of the text, (as well of other genres in the Bible: psalms, proverbs, prophecy, gospels, letters and apocalyptic writings). In 2004 a new translation in the Netherlands of the Bible was published with which he took issue together with Nico ter Linden, a well-known Amsterdam minister. See his *It Counts Closely*, (2008),

His slogan and guideline was: 'the text must have its say'. See the title of the book by Joep Dubbink (2020), *The Text Must Have Its Say, Reading scripture according to Karel Deurloo* (1984). Also see Deurloo's, together with R. Zuurmond, *The Bible makes school; an Amsterdam way in the exegesis,* He wrote over thirty books and many articles. He published separate studies or expositions on Genesis, Joshua, Judges, Jonah, Ruth, and the Psalms as well as numerous articles. Several of his books were translated into German.

    I will present four concrete examples of his way of interpreting the scriptures in chapter 5. These examples could be multiplied by numerous other ones and have been most inspiring and edifying to me. One after the other they light up. It has left a glow around many Bible stories that daily lights my way, even when the going is difficult and discouraging.

CHAPTER 2

A Third Alternative

Right from the beginning the founders of the Amsterdam approach articulated a third alternative. They emphasized the unity of the scriptures and its prophetic message. Following are two examples of Deurloo's rejection of the (literalistic, fundamentalistic) approach of the evangelical tradition and the alternative to the historical critical, interpretations. His third alternative also serves as a self-criticism of the more traditional, rationalistic and moralistic tendencies of the (older) Reformed position in the Netherlands. It is a welcome and liberating alternative. Breukelman and Deurloo, together with many co-workers, made a fundamental contribution to a new understanding of the scriptures.

In Deurloo's and Bouhuijs', *A Stranger in Our Midst*, 1980; as well as other places, Deurloo is uncharacteristically critical of the evangelical (literalistic) understanding of the gospel of Jesus Christ, separated from its Old Testament roots.

2:1 *An uncharacteristic outburst*

Deurloo was a peaceable man. Yet when it comes to interpretations of the gospel he was often grieved in his spirit. Perhaps his frequent television presentations made him even more acutely aware of the evangelical distortion of the gospel in the media. The evangelical reduction of the gospel to "Jesus saves us from our sins" and moral lessons, dominated the media. In view of his own understanding of scriptures he could become angry and discouraged. His reaction is all the more relevant on the North American continent.

As he writes (translated freely):

> Have you ever been to a funeral, where a well-meaning minister was busy ruining his audience's spiritual health? It seems that you are supposed to be for God and belong to a special club, or even more nastily, you have to have 'Jesus in your heart', because otherwise, after your death, you will end up smoking a nasty pipe (face eternal damnation). Such funerals seem to be good places to really rub it in good and proper. We hope that many can smile pitifully about such situations. We, instead, become very angry... Better a clear atheism than such seemingly friendly cruel Christianity. Unabashed atheism is to be preferred above evangelical sermons on radio and T.V.[1]

This uncharacteristic 'outburst' by Deurloo presumably was prompted by a sincere question from a young girl having heard the story of young Samuel in the tabernacle with Eli, the priest, about God's existence and presence (1 Sam 3:1-9). She asked, "What if he called me by my name during the night, like Samuel? That would really scare me." This was from a young girl afraid of the existence of a god who after your death takes revenge and will do you in. Deurloo's whole "spirit" would be grieved and incensed to the core, because he experienced it as a violation of her spirit.

This touched him deeply since he spent so much time presenting the scriptures to children in stories and songs, without dumbing down its meaning and without moralizing and intellectualizing. See his, *And that is Seven! Seven ways to tell children the bible stories* (2001). As well, there is his *A child may stand in our midst; exegetical stories for young ears.* (1982)), and *A humble and down to earth King; David and Saul in prophetic perspective*, (1984). It is a booklet with plays for the children to enact. All of them contain many songs together with accompanying music.

It is a cry from the heart that is pained and discouraged by the distortions of the gospels and especially its separation from the Hebrew Scriptures. It reminds me of children that would be converted year after year during their daily Vacation Bible school experience, or Sunday school years, until they would outgrow the experience, often leaving them with doubt, anger and skepticism or outright rejection of God and the Bible. Over the decades I have always been surprised by the intense

---

1. Deurloo, *Een Vreemdeling*, 10–11.

anger of many clients about their Sunday school, catechism, communion, or church experiences.

I quoted Deurloo here, at the beginning, to highlight the difference between the Amsterdam tradition and the evangelical approach that dominates the media and public awareness on this continent. The prophetic witness of the scriptures cannot be captured by slogans or billboards along the highway of "Jesus saves us from our sins," or, "Believe in the LORD Jesus Christ and you will be saved" or other variations.

As a counter-point, the other night we happened to watch a documentary during Black History Month, which was the history of gospel songs and singers. The energy and exuberance of the singers and soloists was heartwarming, even though the gospel message may be very limited. They understood something of the ecstasy David experienced when he danced before the Lord with all his might, "I will make merry before the Lord." (2 Sam. 6:13-21) It highlights what was missing in the orthodox tradition with its inner piety, self-doubts, intellectualism and doctrinal correctness, even though in Holland the popular hymns of Johannes de Heer compensated somewhat for that one-sided rationalistic emphasis. Vice versa, the conservative understanding of the gospel could have enriched the gospel singers' evangelical tradition.

An intense debate has developed on the internet about evangelical politics in support of Donald Trump, their savior and authoritarian leader. Recently (1/4/24) Dr. Lambert Zuidervaart wrote a *blog* entitled, "Saving Democracy from its Evangelical Foes." He refers to a presentation by two scholars in Grand Valley, Michigan on March 15, 2024. There was an hour long discussion, sponsored by Eerdmans Publishing Company, by K. Kobes Du Mez, author of *Jesus and John Wayne; how white evangelicals corrupted a faith and fractured a nation* (2020) and D. Gushee, author of, *Defending Democracy from its Christian Enemies* (2023).

Each, strongly oppose the political authoritarianism and the reactionary nationalism of white evangelicals that is fuelled by fear. It is a similar cry from the heart and full of anguish because of the distortion of the gospel of Jesus Christ and its national witness. However challenging and fragile democracy may be in the U.S., it calls all evangelicals back to an inclusive view of democracy and the rule of law, opposing all authoritarianism and reactionary views. Then, Zuidervaart added a new blog (April 16, 2024) called "Rejecting White Christian Racism," in which he reviews Jim Wallis' book, *The False White Gospel* (2024). It is another cry from the heart and a call to repentance. The evangelical political stance has its roots in the distortion of the gospel, separated from the Old Testament, as well as the ideology of America as the chosen people and as the Promised Land.

Breukelman with his intense emotions had a very different personality than Deurloo's, with intense emotions. When talking about misinterpretations of critical biblical scholars or misguided translations that would obscure the meaning of texts, he was reported to cry and yell at the violation of the scriptures. He too could become very grieved in his spirit. Many were put off by his reactions at lectures and popular presentations, while others were attracted by his deep concern and challenging interpretations. Students, ministers and many others would flock to his 'lectures' in his parsonage to hear his interpretations and translations.

Today the situation is not much different or maybe even more acute. Social media, radio, television and college campuses are more and more dominated by the evangelical misunderstanding of the gospel, ('a non-Jewish-Jesus who saves us from our sins', especially in its disconnection from the Old Testament). Evangelical television ministers, ever since Billy Graham's presentations, dominate public awareness on this continent. University students who generally are not required even in their doctoral studies to reflect on the foundations and history of their discipline have long since abandoned an interest in religion and the scriptures, assuming it to be outdated and reflecting a primitive and mythological stage of humanity and a Christianity that we have overcome that is historically unreliable. Campus crusades, other evangelical approaches and many leading appointments in colleges and universities have not been able to stop this tide.

All the years that I have studied theology did not bring me any closer to an understanding of the scriptures as the witness to the living Word of God. In this climate, where does one start and break through centuries and decades of misunderstanding? There is no lively discussion in the Canadian media about theology and religion as there is in Holland. What a professor presents in Vancouver is not necessarily discussed or responded to in Toronto or Montreal or in the leading theological or church journals. Very little makes the evening news, unless it is a scandal.

In the end, in spite of the many distortions and overlays, both by Protestant theology and evangelical revival meetings and campus crusades, I can only trust the power of the Word to come through.[2]

---

2. See Deurloo and Bouhuijs, *De Stem in het Gebeuren*, 87–91.

2:2 Deurloo's and Breukelman's critique and use/appreciation of the 'critical historical methods'

Deurloo's accounts are always very open and un-dogmatic. He presents his studies in an open-ended way ("could it be . . ."; "let's assume for a moment"). His interpretations are always open to change and correction. A strong example is his plea for a 'late dating' of the actual writing of the Bible books. It is a liberating approach that makes room for future discoveries. At the same time it does not take away from his presentations of the prophetic proclamation. See his *Grown Scriptures; closer to the origin of the books of the Bible*, (1982, 2nd edition). This emphasis delivers orthodoxy from changing modern scholarship or new archeological discoveries. In upholding the truth of the scriptures, it often seems that the trustworthiness of the Bible depends on its historicity. Otherwise all is lost. We will come back to this issue in chapter 5.

With regard to the critical historical methods, from the beginning Deurloo examined and consulted many of the main studies and commentaries. For example, his study of Genesis as shown in his doctoral dissertation on *Cain and Abel; Research with regard to an exegetical method with regard to a small 'literary unit'* (1967), illustrates this point. Likewise, in a later study on the book of Ruth, written together with Kees van Duin, he quotes many of the key commentaries on Ruth. The same is true for his book on *The Human as Riddle and Secret; proclaiming anthropology in Genesis 2–4*, (1988). Rather than debating their presuppositions and misguided conclusions, he checks their interpretations and suggestions against the actual text in its unity and total context. The same is true with his account of Jonah, Ruth, Saul, David, and the Psalms in which he gives an extensive account of the sources he consulted (*Better than seven sons; the book of Ruth as messianic reference. 1996* and *Jonah, Exposition of the Hebrew Bible, Commentary for Bible study, education and preaching. 1995.*) He expresses his gratitude for the many exegetical studies, and pleads for the freedom of theology as a separate academic discipline.

As a working method one can appreciate his positive approach. Rather than engaging in a negative critical debate, he 'simply' takes their results and checks them against the actual text as it has been handed down to us over the centuries, together with its inter-textual references and its place in the whole of the canon, including the Writings (the third major group after the Torah and the Prophets). Focusing on the unity of the text and highlighting the many details of the text, he comes to very different interpretations that allow its central message and witness to come through, speaking to our hearts.

In contrast, Breukelman in his Biblical theological study of Genesis enters into an intense debate with many different exegetes. See his *Biblical Theology: The firstborn Israel in the midst of the peoples on the earth as the theme of 'the book of the generations of Adam, the human or earthling'*. On page 24, he presents a brief account of how his approach differs from other commentaries by Dillman, Gunkel, Driver, Skinner, Procksch, Von Rad, and Westermann.

> In their interpretations the book of Genesis disappears in the mist and as a unity of composition disappears entirely outside the scope of the vision of the researchers, with the result that not even one part of their exposition can be interpreted meaningfully.[3]

In an "Intermezzo" on page 94 and following, he enters into a discussion with a number of other exegetes, like Benno Jacob, U. Cassuto, A. Van Selms, and von Rad. Of von Rad he will say, "What he does with this small pericope, Genesis 11:27–32, is really terrible."[4] Finally on p.175 in a small "Interruption," he enters into discussion with van Selms, Calvin, Goeters, Gunkel, Procksch, von Rad, and Westermann, followed by extensive notes.

In view of the spiritual significance and the negative effect on individual believers and the Christian church as a whole, their reactions are understandable. Deurloo seems to go back and forth between outright appreciation of biblical scholarship, deep pastoral concern and outrage about the damage and alienation it has brought about among believers. Given my own experience in childhood and as a life-long student of theology, I am inclined to favor Deurloo's pastoral concerns that are still very relevant today, especially on this continent with its right-wing nationalistic, evangelical Christianity that catches the headlines and dominates the media, reflecting a simplistic, distorted, de-contextualized and opportunistic use of scripture.

---

3. Breukelman, *Bijbelse Theologie; het Eerstelingschap van Israel*, 1/2, 24.

4. Breukelman, *Bijbelse Theologie; het Eerstelingschap van Israel*, 1/2, ("Wat von Rad met de kleine pericope Genesis 11: 27–32 doet is ronduit verschrikkelijk") 94.

2:3 Historical situation and cultural context

Exegesis does not happen in a vacuum. It is deeply influenced by the dominant events of the day. As an example, below is a brief sketch of the years before and during the two world wars. Europe was in ruins after WW I. About forty million soldiers and civilians had been killed or wounded, almost one million by gas warfare. In the midst of this disastrous and despairing situation, Karl Barth wrote his *Commentary on the letter to the Romans,* 1919 (1st edition) and 1922 (2nd edition). It hit like a thunderbolt in the theological community and churches in Europe. Barth called for a radical break with the liberal theology of his time and the old traditions that supported the Nazi regime. Barth's commentary was a clarion call for a new beginning and for a reformation.

Soon afterwards, during WW II, Europe had to cope with even more massive destruction and the death and injury of 75 million people, which accounted for about 3 percent of the world population. After the war, Holland too was flooded in popular magazines with the accounts and pictures of the Nazi extermination camps. These images are engraved in my mind as a twelve year old boy. In the extermination camps more than six million Jewish people were murdered along with hundreds of thousands of political prisoners, homosexuals, Gypsies, and Jehovah's Witnesses. In my mind I can still see the group of citizens led away from our street during a general round-up to the railroad station to the concentration camps, never to return. Ingrained in my mind also are the pictures and documentaries of Jewish families unloaded at Auschwitz or Dachau or elsewhere and the look on the faces of the children, boys and girls, soon to be gassed and murdered. It remains forever an incomprehensible and impossible possibility!

For Barth faith could not come from the human psyche (Schleiermacher), history (Troeltch), or morality (Ritschl). Knowledge of God, according to Barth was only possible because of God's gracious initiative to reveal himself. God speaks to us through the witness of the scriptures. He emphasized the radical nature of God's sovereignty and grace. He highlighted again that this sovereign God chose to reveal himself and to make his Name known to us, making humanity the object of his love and grace. This astounding fact, according to Barth, as testified to in the scriptures, confronts and addresses us very personally. It is not us that need to interpret the Word, but the Word interprets us. It is a powerful force that emanates from the words. They are the powerful word of Yahweh. It is a force that has the power to convince and overpower.

After Auschwitz nothing could be the same, including theology and ethics. After Auschwitz the world vowed, "Never again." However, the genocides have continued unabated from the killing fields of Cambodia, the Congo, Rwanda, East Timor, Sarajevo, Srebrenica, Kosovo, Darfur, and many others, and not to forget, the nuclear destruction and horror of Hiroshima and Nagasaki. Wars have followed one another, from the cold war to the Korean War to Vietnam, to Iraq, to Afghanistan, to Syria and countless other conflicts, and with it, the on-going threat of terrorism, nuclear war and now the devastating war in Ukraine and the horrendous war in Gaza, (a new genocide committed by the Jewish government and army and condoned by many Israelis.). It makes it hard to continue writing this study, for every scripture passage stands as a witness against the killing of over fifty thousand Palestinians, including thousands of children; and the killing goes on unabated, daily adding to the number of civilians killed and injured and the destruction of their homes, hospitals, schools, universities, museums and all other infrastructure.

During this time global capitalism, with its neo-liberal ideology of unlimited growth and its need for endless consumption, gained the day and has become the global driving force and power. It is the new global ideology or religion, the new world power. It had its start in the Enlightenment and the Industrial Revolution with its efficient, mass production and with its colonialism that conquered the globe, dispossessing and killing people and confiscating lands and resources.

With these economic developments came the degradation of the environment: the pollution of the soil, water and air; deforestation; global warming; an increase in violent storms and 'natural' disasters; droughts; floods; increasing desertification; the erosion, destruction, and salinization of the soil; a worldwide decline in fresh water; air pollution; the disappearance of countless species of plants and animals; the plastic pollution of the oceans and the earth; rising sea levels; declining fish stocks; threatening epidemics among chickens, pigs, goats, horses, and cows, and now, humans. In short, we have created severe environmental degradation and a climate emergency.

This degradation of the environment ('the sixth extinction') challenges our traditional view of God and the earth. It makes us cry out, 'LORD, do you see what is happening to your creation and humanity?' When all this is happening, while we are in the midst of it, we can retreat in despair and hopelessness or we can wait upon the LORD our Redeemer and Creator. We can hold hands in solidarity and protest.

With global capitalism also came the growing gap between the rich and the poor, between the (over)developed countries and the (pillaged) impoverished countries with widespread corruption everywhere. One (small) part of the world's population struggles with obesity, diabetes and addictions, the other (large) part with hunger and death from preventable diseases (16,000 children a day). Children sorting through garbage dumps for discarded electronics with poisonous elements; increasing slums around overcrowded cities along the ocean and river deltas, threatened by rising sea levels; homeless people, over-populated jails and a growing world population are all well-documented and for all to see on social media. Mass media and communication technology of every kind bombard us daily with images of these events, often in a sensationalized, disconnected way that keeps the reality far from us.

There is a long caravan of millions of war and climate refugees travelling from the middle Americas to North America and from Africa and the Middle East across the ocean to Europe. They are trying to escape the horrors of war, extreme floods and droughts, and hoping for a new life. Many are abused and exploited along the way and pushed back when they are in sight of the 'promised land' or tragically or 'conveniently' drown in the sea. The refugee crisis is just in its beginning. With more and more wars and a changing climate it is promising to become an 'insoluble crisis' with hardened positions and piecemeal solutions, giving rise to extreme nationalism and dictatorships. Democracy seems to be declining, even in so-called developed countries. The perplexing nature of this global situation has left many people with an overwhelming sense of powerlessness and pessimism.

Differently from the ideology of the 1920's and 1940's, today we are confronted by the neo-liberal ideology (religion) of global capitalism with its belief in unlimited growth and profit for the few and exploitation suffering and austerity programs for the rest of humanity. The call for a renewed understanding of the scriptures is as relevant today as it was in the 1920's and 1940's, if not more so. We live in a 'critical decade' and a 'climate emergency', to which many have reacted with protest and action. We are witnessing the world-wide failure of capitalism. It is unable to deal with climate change and the disintegration of communities (the lack of adequate housing, sanitation, water, sufficient economic resources, education and healthcare) for many segments of the world population.

By contrast, we seldom hear and see what millions of people are doing to create a different life for themselves or just to make a difference, in big and small ways. For this we are mostly dependent on the alternative press, the internet and local actions. It takes a conscious effort to become aware of what countless courageous people are doing to change their situation, or return to a healthy and more meaningful way of life, or simply to protest and to bear witness at the risk of their lives.

We constantly need to remind ourselves of this context and history in trying to understand the scriptures anew. In 2016, I wrote *The Gods in Whom They Trusted; the Disintegrative Effects of Capitalism; a Foundation for Transitioning to a New Social World*.[5] It is in this situation and environment that we are to sound the words of the scriptures and are called to bear witness and take action.

When we see the extent of the destruction of neo-liberal capitalism, we can ask ourselves, if we do not put our trust in those gods, which god can we trust? This question rises, since we are not able to live without a sense of some higher power and ultimate meaning. And how does this god reveal himself? A new understanding of the scriptural God-image and his revelation to humankind is crucial. There are many distorted images that are the result of decades, if not centuries, of misdirected Sunday school and catechism teaching, and misguided preaching and exegesis. (See chapter 8.)

It is within this context that the Amsterdam way of interpreting the scriptures with its focus on the prophetic message came into being. Miskotte, one of the founders of the Amsterdam School of Exegesis, wrote his challenging articles and books. I was delighted to find out that one more of Miskotte's books were translated. It was given the promising title, *Biblical ABCs: The basics of Christian Resistance* (2022). The translators Eleonora Hof and Collin Cornell, especially Collin hopes it can be a powerful instrument in the church's (educational) ministry to oppose rightwing Christian propaganda with its white supremacy, racism, homophobia, misogyny, anti-abortion, the right to bear arms and extreme nationalism with a misguided appeal to freedom and democracy. Ironically the only freedom they seem to embrace is the authoritarianism of dictators, no matter how corrupt. Resistance to these forces is what connects Miskotte's time and our time. The other popular book by Miskotte translated in English is his *When the Gods are Silent* (1967).

---

5. Freely available at www.foundationalissues.com.

2:4 *The prophetic call to love and justice*

The Amsterdam school of exegesis and biblical theology began as a counter protest to the Nazi ideology by Miskotte and others. He wrote his *Biblical ABCs, The basics of Christian resistance*, about the key words and themes that unify all of scripture. The Amsterdam school was born from a crisis and was a response to a crisis. More than that, its approach to exegesis and that of the Amsterdam school in general, provide all the basic givens for a truly renewed, understanding of the scriptures. The text became foremost and must have its say and not the origin of the text over many centuries or its purely literary structure. I consider this a fundamental presupposition and contribution of the Amsterdam school.

Secondly, the focus throughout is on the prophetic ('theological') meaning of the text and not just on its religious, historical, political, sociological, or economic context. A text may manifest all these aspects but none of them can be considered the fundamental meaning of a text. Any of these dimensions may contribute to our understanding of the prophetic meaning but cannot serve as the hermeneutic key. This emphasis on the prophetic meaning of biblical texts, I consider the second presupposition and contribution of the Amsterdam school.

Making the text first and foremost, placing the text in the centre with its prophetic meaning, makes the Word of God once again present in our midst, as a powerful force especially in our present global crisis and suffering. The texts speak for themselves both then and now. They hold us in their grip. It directly addresses us. The initiative comes from Yahweh. He speaks and it is. To speak with Miskotte, the Bible is 'anti' the established order, and anti our conservatism. It is a critical voice that also leads to self criticism. It is anti our systems and anti our religiosity. It questions our securities and our sense of reality.

In the 1940's the clarion call of Barth's *Commentary on the letter to the Romans* still echoed through the streets of Amsterdam and was taken up by several scholars. Different Bible study groups developed in Amsterdam, that were attended by Jews, non-Christians and Christians alike. These early Bible classes focused on reading and listening to the scriptures in a new way, to hear again the meaning of the Name of this mysterious God and his actions for humankind. In time these Bible study groups became the inspiration for the Amsterdam school of exegesis and biblical theology.

It is heartwarming and encouraging that this tradition has been taken up again by the New Bible School (De Nieuwe Bijbel School) with new groups starting up throughout Holland. They hold the promise of a further return to the scriptures.[6]

During the last few decades more than fifty booklets or Cahiers and Supplements (See the bibliography) of the Amsterdam School have been written by exegetes and biblical scholars, more or less committed to the same principles of interpretation. Each Cahier contains between half a dozen to a dozen exegetical articles, providing a wealth of insights into the different parts of the bible, as well as many separate studies on individual Bible books. They were written by scholars from the main universities and theological schools in Holland, both Reformed, Catholic and Jewish. Since all the main public universities in Holland, in Groningen, Utrecht, Leiden, and Amsterdam and others, used to have a theological department, until recently, scholars from all over the Netherlands have contributed to their publications.

In 2022 the latest in the series of Supplements was published. This study by Marco Visser, called *Pars Pro Toto, (Part for the Whole)* is exemplary of the Amsterdam tradition of studying the Bible. We can only hope many more will follow. The 'Amsterdam school' stands for all of Holland, 'pars pro toto', and for all those who have and will contribute in the future. Many may have trouble locating Holland or the Netherlands on the map, but most everyone knows about Amsterdam.[7]

To summarize, what is unique about the Amsterdam school? Two things: foremost is the general approach or working method to exegesis, to give voice to the primacy of the text as it has been given in its unity and interconnectedness with all of scripture. Secondly the emphasis is on the prophetic message of the scriptures: the prophetic call to love and justice.

---

6. See https://www.denieuwebijbelschool.nl/, and https://podcastluisteren.nl/pod/De-Nieuwe-Bijbelschool.

7. See https://www.societashebraica.nl/ for a list of publications.

CHAPTER 3

The challenge of secularization in interpreting the scripture for today

3:1 Secularization: a case study

As a prophetic witness, the scriptures can serve as a guide or touchstone to the ups and downs and perplexities of life today and our global situation. The contemporary *Accra Confession* of the ecumenical councils of the Reformed churches illustrates how closely the prophetic message, a lived faith and daily actions, ought to be and can be intertwined. It is the opposite of a 'pietistic faith' with its conservatism that exists, to whatever degree, separate from daily life.

It is striking that the socialist party in Holland both before the war, right after the war and presently has in actuality implemented the prophetic witness more clearly than the Christian political parties. Centuries of a more or less dualistic and moralistic vision and way of life takes its toll. Writing about these issues is a part of my own personal journey with the Christian faith and seeking an alternative. We know that the traditional Christian view no longer speaks to millions of people that have been alienated from the Christian church, including myself.

Any branch of Old Testament studies has become a highly specialized field of research. This highly specialized, academic study of the scriptures removed many exegetical studies and commentaries even further from the people and their churches.

After an extended exploration of the historical and cultural situation in chapter 1, it is helpful to trace the process of secularization further. Again, it is within this context that we are called to sound out the words of scripture for our time and in our situation. The failure of global capitalism is becoming more and more evident by the day in its inability to deal with damaging environmental and social realities. It is clearly unable to provide wholesome food, education, healthcare and other social services for the majority of people in the world (austerity programs whenever the gross national product is declining or inflation is rising). It is helpful to elaborate on global capitalism and its impact on our very way of thinking. It is not enough to translate the scriptures in modern English, since the words themselves have been 'colonized' by the powerful dominant class.

Many of the same changes that took place in Dutch society have happened in Canada as well, but they do not seem to be as much a part of our consciousness as in Europe. Moreover, the gap between orthodoxy and liberalism are much greater in Canada than in Holland with its wide range of viewpoints.

All in all, the country's size, the density of the population, the tradition of intense discussion and as a result, the close interactions makes for an interesting "case study." The largest protestant church in Holland was the Reformed Church (Hervormde Kerk). It came into existence during the time of the reformation. During the great synod of Dordt in 1618–1619 three forms of unity were adopted that formally unified the churches. In 1834 and in 1886, two groups split off from the national protestant church in protest against its "liberalism" and "critical" view of the scriptures. In 1892 they came together and formed the Christian Reformed Churches (de Gereformeerde Kerken in Nederland). During the last fifty years a serious attempt was made to re-unite the reformational churches in Holland. In 2004 three denominations, the Reformed Church, the Christian Reformed Church and the Evangelical-Lutheran Church, finally were able to join together to form the Protestant Church of the Netherlands (de Protestantse Kerk in Nederland).

This United Church has about 1,800,000 members, which is about 11 percent of the Dutch population. Meanwhile, several groups and individual congregations did not go along with the new united church. As a result there are still several smaller Reformed denominations and church groups in Holland. These divisions among the churches remained a lifelong stumbling block for many. For them the Church does not exist, only an endless array of separate churches that disagree, excommunicate one another, or break formal ties with each other.

THE CHALLENGE OF SECULARIZATION

During the turbulent years of the 60's and 70's Dutch society was shaken to its roots. Fundamental changes took place in every aspect of society. People no longer "blindly" accepted the authority of the church and political leaders. They became independent and found their own voice. This new found *emancipation* and *independence*, along with the *economic prosperity* and the *social security* led to fundamental changes.

At the same time there was the postwar disillusionment with the past, the split within the reformed churches during the war, the government policies with regard to the (former) Dutch colonies, the threat of a nuclear war, the peace movement, public protests, counterculture, feminism and a new role for women. There was a radical change in morality with regard to sexuality, dancing, movies, Sunday observance, drugs, drinking, gambling, birth control, abortion, homosexuality, divorce, civil disobedience, as well as many other aspects of life. All these changes led to a wide-spread "secularization" process.

Sunday used to be the most boring day of the week for me, since we were not allowed to ride our bikes, have friends over, play soccer, or buy some candies or an ice cream in the store. My father had sense enough to take us on long walks in the country and visit relatives. I still remember how guilty I felt the first time I bought something on a Sunday. My brother had to return from a 'summer camp' of the sea cadets because he felt too guilty about sailing on Sunday and not going to church that day. I was only allowed to join the boy scouts in our town because it was, unofficially, a protestant group with a Christian scout leader. All of that would not make one long for 'the good old days'.

The change from a predominantly religious society to a secular society was not a big loss. Before the war, Holland was very divided, religiously, and as a consequence, socially and politically. As a child the Roman Catholic kids on our street were not allowed to play with us, protestant kids. We were considered heathens that had forsaken the Mother church. During the war I was suddenly not allowed to play any longer with my best school friend because my family was not part of the newly separated church. I was aware how heavily the Christian morality weighted upon my family. Participating in the Lord's Supper (communion) was a precarious event ("drinking judgment to one self"). Popular music and programs on the radio were forbidden as ungodly. Divorce and birth control were not acceptable. Homosexuality was an 'unknown' issue and not talked about. Women often had too many children, because birth control methods were considered an interference with God's intention for life.

Rather than just "secularization," it is probably more helpful to see these changes in society in terms of *emancipation, individualization* and an emphasis on *economic prosperity* and *consumption*. With these developments, the mindset and worldview of people was transformed and changed drastically. Television images and news items from around the world reached even the smallest villages in Holland that had been relatively isolated before the war. Issues and conflicts from every part of the globe, religious practices and local customs, space exploration and the expanding image of the universe, rapid developments in the sciences, new archaeological discoveries, the increasing number of nature programs, etc., became part of the daily news and entered and changed peoples' consciousness. What my parents and grandparents could not have imagined (airplanes, radios, televisions, refrigerators, freezers, toasters, coffee makers, new foods and fruits, French fries, hot dogs, ketchup, coca cola, popular music, and today computers and cell phones, etc.) became the common awareness of the generation that came of age after the war. The world had changed forever, including people's worldview, and there was no going back.[1]

Sixty years later, our situation is not much different from that of the 1960's and the following decades, except that we may have grown more numb to it. After the war Holland was flooded by images of the concentration camps. People vowed, "Never again." But since then wars have followed one another, and with it, the ongoing threat of terrorism and nuclear war.

The changes in worldview and self-awareness deeply affected the Christian community in Holland as well as the rest of the Western world. Up to the present, orthodox Christianity has hardly begun to incorporate these fundamental changes in their view of life. An increased

---

1. Geert Mak, *De Eeuw van Mijn Vader*. Amsterdam: Atlas, 1999; Geert Mak, *Hoe God Verdween uit Jorwerd.*. See the references to the many sociological studies by G. Dekker in the bibliography of *The Gods in Whom They Trusted*. Dekker, G. *De mens en zijn godsdienst*; Dekker, G. *Godsdienst en samenleving: inleiding tot de studie van de godsdienstesociologie*; Dekker, G. *De stille revolutie: De ontwikkeling van de Gereformeerde Kerken in Nederland tussen 1950 en 1990*; Dekker, G., Luidens, D.A. & Rice, R.R., eds. *Rethinking secularization: Reformed reactions to modernity*; Dekker, G. "De ontwikkeling van godsdienst sociologie in Nederland," in *Nederlands Theologisch Tijdschrift*, 55, (2001) 13–30; De Vriese, H. & Gabor, G., eds. *Rethinking secularization; philosophy and the prophecy of a secular age*; Dobbelaere, K. *Secularization: An analysis at three levels.*

understanding of the slow development of the earth over billions of years became an important part of the changing worldview. As more and more information and images penetrated people's consciousness, it began to challenge the traditional understanding of creation as portrayed in the book of Genesis. It became evident that humans were latecomers – very late – in the development of the world.

Moreover, there were several "trial balloons" (humanlike apes and ape-like humans) before a truly Homo sapiens people, our modern human species, became established. At the same there were Neanderthal people whose existence intermingled with Homo Sapiens before they became extinct. None of these givens could be harmonized with the creation story in Genesis, including the creation of the first humans, Adam and Eve, at least not in the way they were traditionally understood. The appearance of the Hebrew people in the northern part of Palestine took place even much later. Many peoples and civilizations preceded them, both in the Ancient Near East and on other continents.

This new knowledge and wide-spread awareness threw more and more doubt on the historicity of the Bible stories. Did things really happen the way they are reported in the Bible? Following these early stories, was there really a worldwide flood which only Noah and his family and all the animals survived? Were these just mythological stories like so many other creation and flood stories of the surrounding people? Was all of Genesis 1–11 a mythological account to provide an origin for the Hebrew people and all the other nations, tracing it right back to the beginning of time?

Christians, believing in the trustworthiness and historicity of the Bible, started to wonder if the six days of creation should be understood as long periods of time. It was an attempt to harmonize the historicity of the Bible with new knowledge about the origin and development of the world and yet not hold to a literal interpretation of Genesis. Even today in some orthodox Reformed churches on this continent, this same kind of approach is followed. There it is acceptable to believe that God used the evolutionary process to create the world including humans. However, each stage of development involved a distinctive creative act of God. In their view, to believe otherwise would not be acceptable.

As the many popular booklets published during the sixties and seventies indicate, the inspiration and authority of the Bible began to be doubted and questioned. To stem the tide and to bring the congregations up to date with what was happening in biblical research, both Roman

Catholic and Protestant churches added their own official booklets to the stream of publications about the interpretation of the Bible. Many specific questions were raised about errors and discrepancies as well as difficult to understand texts.[2]

How could Abraham have owned and be given camels when they were not domesticated till much later? What was the date of the exodus of the people of Israel from Egypt? Many biblical scholars today question whether there was even such a mass exodus and a forty year journey through the desert before they entered and settled in Palestine. Did they conquer the entire land under the leadership of Joshua, as it says in the book of Joshua, or was it more like the account in the book of Judges, that they occupied the land only piecemeal and over a (long) period of time? Did the sun actually stand still when Joshua commanded it, so that the people could continue to pursue the fleeing enemy? How could Jericho be captured, when the city did not exist as a fortified city during that time period?

The change from a religious society to a secular one does mean that the words of the scriptures have to be sounded out anew, just as they would have if the old ways had continued. It is understandable that part of the Amsterdam way of interpreting also had to come to terms with the remnants of the old views of 'historicity' and the traditional views of 'morality'. For example, Deurloo with his keen concern for children made a point to describe masturbation "as a healthy normal sexual activity" and "onanism" as a violation of the obligation in the ancient world to produce off-spring for a deceased brother that had nothing to do with masturbation. His treatment of homosexuality in relation to Sodom and Gomorrah speaks for itself. He was not afraid to describe what circumcision is like in his children's stories. Likewise in his description of nakedness a little later on, "they were both naked, and were not ashamed." His main concern is to oppose, from out of the scriptures, all sexual moralism. Instead he celebrates the gift of sexuality and eroticism that continues on after the 'fall'. One of his ways to describe Sunday was to state that Sunday means that "God has time for us," which immediately changes its meaning from a burden and something boring to one of liberation, joy, and celebration. His emphasis on the "un-historical" nature of many stories is also a reaction to the old view of scripture that obscured the meaning of the scripture. Again and again he opposed any form of "historicizing"

2. De Graaff, "Reading the Hebrew Scriptures Backwards," freely available at www.foundationalisssues.com.

and "a history of ancient Israel," or the 'history of redemption'. Instead of history, his emphasis is on the prophetic message, that is, the present and the future and not just on the past.

3:2 Dis-enchantment and re-enchantment

There has been a long tradition of describing the results of 'secularism' in terms of the "dis-enchantment" of life, of everything. It is only one way that people have taken note of the effects of secularization. In itself the word 'secular-ization' (in contrast to the 'sacred' or 'supranatural') does not solve anything, since it is rooted in global capitalism, which is founded on corrupt systems, individualization, commercialization, privatization, and consumption.

Dr. Ad Van Dussen, in his "God's providence," ("God's voorzienigheid") highlights this problem and asks, why it may be harder today to experience God's presence in the world. "It has to do with secularization, that powerful movement that has pushed God out of our lives."[3] This secularized worldview has deeply penetrated our consciousness, our outlook, our frame of reference, our way of thinking, our language and words, our perceptions, and our feelings.

According to him, we daily experience the pressure of "living in a closed worldview."[4] "The world has become dis-enchanted, without deeper meaning; we no longer search for supernatural causes for hard to understand events like freak accidents. Much can be explained in a naturalistic way without taking recourse to the hypothesis of 'God'.[5] In case of an unforeseen and tragic accident with deadly consequences, we tend to speak about a 'stupid coincidence' rather than 'the Lord took our dearly beloved son home'.

He echoes the concerns of Dr. E. Talstra in his *Between Old and New Readers*, 2002, of how to relate the un-self-conscious, immediate way the scriptures talk about God's presence and actions in life to our modern view of the world.[6] The biblical world and our world do not touch. He also talks about the difficulty of hearing the Word of God speaking in our secularized view of life. As he states: "Creation is not nature, in the sense

---

3. Van Dussen, "God's voorzienigheid," 3.
4. Van Dussen, "God's voorzienigheid," 14.
5. Van Dussen, "God's voorzienigheid," 3.
6. Talstra, *Tussen Oude en Nieuwe Lezers*, 42, 69, 81.

of a neutral material environment, but the stage of God's artistry that is regularly celebrated and sung about in the worship service."[7]. Our ability to speak in an uninhibited way about everyday human experience as the scriptures do has greatly diminished.

The distance between religious language and our day to day human experience has become so great that there is hardly a point of contact anymore. Scriptural language and daily language are miles apart. There needs to be room for religious language to speak about themes like creation and history, humankind and evil. When creation is nothing more than matter and history is seen as just chance, fate, or an evolutionary process, there is nothing to communicate.[8] In looking for help from the systematic theologians, Talstra could not find a different view.[9]

Secularization has not only obscured our understanding of the scriptures but has also taken its toll on church membership. Based on present statistics and trends it is estimated that by 2040 (in less than 15 years) the Anglican Church will no longer exist as a separate denomination. The United Church of Canada is not far behind. It loses one church every week. A possible coalition between the Anglican and the United Church may postpone the inevitable for some years. The average age of United Church members is 65 years. The Presbyterian, Lutheran, and Roman Catholic churches and others closely follow this general trend. When the last church closes its doors, all that will be left are the Books of Praise and the Bibles. We trust that new small household gatherings and Bible study groups will emerge from these declines.

Every exegete, minister and reader is confronted with this difficulty: how can the scriptures sound and speak within a secular understanding of life. In general, the Amsterdam way of interpreting can help a lot to bridge this gap by highlighting each specific key word or expression, and bringing the scriptures close to our experience. It motivated Miskotte, Deurloo, Kuitert and others to write "vocabulary lists." (for example: *Do You Understand What You Read?* and *Signals from the Bible*, both by Kuitert). These explanations of key words that have their own distinct meaning in the scriptures add an element of surprise by highlighting its immediacy. Often I have to ask myself, 'is that what it really says', especially of passages I thought I knew really well. Each time I listen to one of the presentations of the New Bible School in Amsterdam, I have that

---

7. Talstra, *Tussen Oude en Nieuwe Lezers*, 95.
8. Talstra, *Tussen Oude en Nieuwe Lezers*, 82.
9. Talstra, *Tussen Oude en Nieuwe Lezers*, 69, 70.

same experience. We can only expect this process of secularization to increase, which distances modern people even more from the direct and uninhibited way the scriptures talk about God and life. We have lost the vocabulary list and the grammar book.

Many First Nations people as well as many indigenous tribes still relate to creation in this deeply respectful and spiritual way with thanksgiving and care.[10]

Over against a 'secular worldview' stands a 'scriptural view of the world'. See the introduction to Genesis chapter 6. For a further development of such a 'scriptural view' see Deurloo's and Hemelsoet's discussion in *Over Mountains and through Valleys; biblical geography: the place where it is written.* 1988.[11]

The 'biblical view of the world' itself is never fixed and static. Rather it is *prophetic*. God is talked about spatially. Every time he is present on certain mountains and in specific valleys. It is a call that needs to be responded to by each generation anew. As insights in many scriptural references grow, so will our understanding of the 'world image of the scriptures'. In turn this would be even more so for any 'Christian systematic theology' and an articulated 'Christian philosophy'. All human articulation stands under the judgment of this prophetic vision, whether exegesis, theology or philosophy.

The word 'disenchantment' does describe the effects of secularization well, in which all things are robbed of their mystery and meaning. The poetry of life, with its depth of meaning or its sacredness is disappearing. Things that are not quantifiable or reducible to scientific analysis do not count, especially when increasing profits is god.

Very generally, for our purposes here, such an alternative vision to a secularized worldview would be to embrace an integrated (phenomenological) view of reality in which everything and all creatures have their rightful place. It is the opposite of a world of brute facts, of pure physicality and a reductionistic, one-dimensional view of nature, without time, place or context. Such an empiricistic view is the opposite of an interrelated open view of reality, in which all creatures are meaningfully and inseparably interconnected. In a reductionistic view there is no room for any of this nor God's presence or actions and his call to love.

---

10. De Graaff, *The Gods in Whom They Trusted*, 193
11. Deurloo and Hemelsoet, *Over Mountains and through Valleys,* 13.

Forests are a good example. In a reductionistic view a forest is *nothing more* than a 'stand of two-by-fours' or so many 'containers of wood chips' or 'biomass' for generating electricity. At most, within a neoliberal reductionistic perspective it has a legal, political, and economic dimension, but these are not inherent to the functioning of a forest. That the biological, ecological, emotional, recreational, aesthetic and spiritual dimensions are *inherent* to the very nature of a forest and its life-giving totality seems like the Romanticism of a previous century. Within a reductionistic view clear cutting forests seems like the only logical thing to do. It is efficient and economical. What is there against it, if they are only stands of two-by-fours? In disputes, most often the forests and its people tend to lose out to economic interests.

There are any number of books that talk about the re-enchantment of life over against a reductionistic vision and practices. For some of the rich literature on this subject, see: Gordon Graham, *The Re-enchantment of the World; Art versus Religion*, (2007); Morris Berman, The *Re-enchantment of the World*, (1981); which is my favorite study because it connects W. Reich's insights (a pupil of Freud), with a part of my therapy training which was in bioenergetic psychotherapy; Thomas Moore, *The Re-enchantment of Everyday Life*, (1996); Bruna Bettleheim, *The Uses of Enchantment; the meaning and importance of fairy tales*, (1977); Gregory Bateson, *Steps to an Ecology of Mind*, (1972); and finally, Carol H. Lankton and Stephen R. Lankton, *Tales of Enchantment*. (1989). All the books, include many other references.

There are many books that explore such an integral view. They are astounding in their richness of how a forest really functions even on a chemical, physical, biological, and ecological level.[12] In these accounts we are far removed from the 'brute facts of pure physicality, and 'a forest is nothing more than',

"The real forest, however, has many different sides of which the economic side is only one dimension and needs to be seen in the light of all the other sides. Only then can we truly relate and respond to a particular forest that exists in a particular place, that is of concern to a particular people, and, ultimately, to all of life on the earth. To relate to a forest only as an economic object, we need to close ourselves off from the richness

---

12. See Suzanne Simard's, *Finding the mother tree; discovering the wisdom of the forest*, (2021); and Peter Wohlleben, *The hidden life of trees;* and Diana Beresford-Kroeger, *Our Green Heart: The Soul and Science of Forests* (2024); and David Suzuki's T.V. presentation on the secret life of forests.

and diversity of the forest and the ecology within which it is embedded. In the process we distort ourselves as well as that forest."[13]

Only within such a context can we understand something of the wonder and surprise of Isaiah,

> For you shall go out in joy, and be led back in peace;
> The mountains and the hills before you shall break forth into singing,
> and all the trees of the field shall clap their hands.
> Isaiah 55:12 cf. 44:23 (cf. Isa 44:23)

All creation rejoices with joyful songs and clapping of hands at the miraculous return of the Lord's exiled people. Through death (the exile) they have returned to life, to the Promised Land, just like before through the Red Sea and the Jordan.

Ultimately trees exist to praise the Creator and to be there for humankind, even as they feed, care for and communicate with each other. It is its religious, spiritual or prophetic dimension that shows us its basic meaning. Forests are sacred. Forests are not only a source of beauty and wonder (its aesthetics, an inspiration for music, poetry and painting) or a source of quiet and rejuvenation. It is not easy to convey this core meaning of forests, to praise the Creator and to serve all humankind. A Buddhist monk simply wrapped a yellow robe around a tree to convey that trees are sacred. It takes the eyes of faith to see both the forests' beauty and agony (in the face of its destruction globally). Ultimately forests are holy, that is our confession.

The next time I walk through the forest, I will pause and remember the vision of the ancient prophet Ezekiel and live in hope.

> And wherever the river goes, every living creature that swarms
>   will live . . .
> On the banks, on both sides of the river, there will grow all kinds
>   of trees for food.
> Their leaves will not wither nor their fruit fail, but they will bear
>   fresh fruit every month . . .
> Their fruit will be for food, and their leaves for healing.
> Ezekiel 47:9–12 (cf. Revelation 22:1–2)

The earth's forests too, along with the rest of creation, will be delivered from futility from their death sentence and be restored to their original calling to be of service to all.

---

13. De Graaff, *The Gods In Whom They Trusted*. 204.

THE PROPHETIC CALL TO LOVE AND JUSTICE

> God said, 'See I have given you every plant yielding seed that is upon the face of all the earth, and every tree with seed in its fruit; and you shall have them for food. And to every beast of the earth, and to every bird of the air, and to everything that creeps on the earth, everything that has the breath of life, I have given every green plant for food. And it was so. God saw everything that he had made, and behold, it was very good.
> Genesis 1:29–31

This is the forest's basic calling and task, just as the Light's task was to be Day and the Darkness to be Night, and the Firmament's and Dry Land's task was to be a boundary to the primal waters, so the Forest's task is to praise the Creator and provide food and be a source of healing and blessing. The curse will be lifted and the forests will join in the celebration of the liberation of the sons of God. We live in hope, so forests can start practicing clapping their hands, awaiting their deliverance from futility. Or, which is the same thing, save and restore a piece of forest in hope of a final restoration. That is our hope . . . the re-enchantment of all of life.

We are all called to restore language to its rightful place, to name and to disclose the depth of meaning of everything and all relations. Through poetry, music, prose, songs, drama, we are to rediscover the richness of all creatures and all things around us. Nothing is just a pure object or subject but functions in a rich context of many inter-relationships and depth of meaning. Everything needs to be restored from its "nothing but" characterization, its reductionism and restored to its fullness of meaning, like the forest. The commercialization of language and empiricism has reduced all things, events and relationships to "nothing but" objects of pure factuality and physicality without context, history, time or place. When truth and factuality in public discourse no longer seem to matter on this continent and in the speeches of many leaders, it leaves us with a bewildering world that we have difficulty naming and understanding. The media invites us each day to normalize lies and distortions. In the face of this daily onslaught, distortion of experience and colonization of our language, we are called to recapture the meaning of our lives.

The scriptures address us in the *fullness of everyday life* and relationships. It has its own poetic and literary structure and depth of meaning that relates to all of life. That is how we are addressed, confronted, comforted, guided and reassured. If we listen to the scriptures with this new openness and expectation, we will be able to hear again the living words of God that can inspire and redirect us.

CHAPTER 4

First impressions

A UNIFIED GENERAL APPROACH to exegesis is another unique feature of the Amsterdam school. The various parts cannot be isolated from one another. It is as a total unified approach that these guidelines make their impact. It implies an eclectic approach with regard to various exegetical methods. If they contribute to the understanding of the prophetic meaning of the text, they should be considered and tried out, in spite of misguided presuppositions. This approach brings any particular passage closer to ordinary believers.

Academic exegesis has become a highly specialized and scholarly enterprise. This does not mean that the more specialized technical linguistic and historical work of exegetes is unnecessary or is not essential. On the contrary, it is of vital importance to the church. Since, the texts we have in our Bibles went through a long history and because there are many textual traditions, that have to be considered (Talstra), the orthodox Christian community cannot excuse itself from the responsibility of doing this painstaking, historical, academic work.

The Amsterdam approach has been severely critical of the historical methods, especially in the beginning (see chapter 1). They were primarily reacting to the damage done by the historical methods to the understanding of the scriptures during many decades and even centuries. The effects of fragmenting and obscuring the prophetic message may, unfortunately, linger on for many decades to come. Exegetes may have even moved on to a more literary analysis, but not the average minister and church member. Interpretations do not only determine an individual's faith but also that of entire religious communities. This fact cannot be underestimated. Again and again we have to return to the simplicity, unity and directness of the scriptures.

Most, if not all, of the contributors to the Amsterdam approach have taken the historical (political, economic, social) context seriously. Considering the historical context of a text is very different from analyzing changes within a particular text over time that may instead be due to different textual traditions or editorial revisions from a later period. Even if there are linguistic cues (Talstra) for such changes, it is not always possible to establish the time or importance of later revisions. Such analyses depend on a careful, detailed exegetical analysis, which is a more professional and scholarly task, beyond the scope of many ministers and priests. It is also a potential source of speculation and fragmentation by exegetes that see a new revision with every change (see Noort).

Any Bible study group that has access to a concordance or even an annotated study Bible with maps, references, and various translations makes a good start, and can aid in tracing the meaning of key words and themes. Most helpful would be if a number of members of a Bible study group read along from other Bible translations taking note of losses and gains, like the *Jewish Study Bible; TeNaK Translation; Jerusalem Bible; The New English Bible, with the Apogrypha; The New Testament in Modern English for Schools*, as well as the *Revised Standard Version* and others. At the same time it would be helpful if some followed other references from a study Bible or a concordance to get a sense of inter-textual references. Discussing what stands out for each member and how each member relates the passage to their own life situation will be a critical element.

4:1 *Deurloo's specific exegetical method for Bible Study*

In his *The Bible makes 'School'*, he gives a brief summary of his own very practical exegetical approach in point form:

- choose a small pericope; make an initial translation
- writing the Hebrew text on a separate page; consult a grammar; indicate tense
- writing subordinate clauses one line lower; indent direct speech; and changes in tense
- make a second sheet and write the Hebrew in a colometric way (units of breath)

- following Buber's colometric representation; we read the text out loud
- indicate sections according to word repetitions, associations, chiasms
- next to that subjects and their role,
- word meanings, opposites, displacements, told time and time of the author
- all the while asking ourselves how the parts relate to the whole
- now is the time to consult a concordance and lexicon; what colour does a specific word have in a specific context?
- is it used in a specific way? In what other kind of texts does it occur? (prophetic etc.)
- could it be a motif, or a theme, in a book or section?
- does it concern key words that are determinative for the TeNaK?
- are there conscious references to other Bible books? or an 'echo'?
- we take note of the specific place of the pericope in its immediate context
- is there information of a social-cultural, historical, etc. nature?
- all information is welcome if it is placed under the critique of the text
- now a conversation can start with other readers and exegetes...[1]

Deurloo engages first of all in a thorough lingual and literary structure analysis of the text. Only then will he consult other commentaries and studies.

---

1. Deurloo and Zuurmond, *De Bijbel Maakt School*.

CHAPTER 5

The general approach of the Amsterdam way of interpretation

THE FOLLOWING 'METHODS' of the Amsterdam way must be understood as an 'integral general approach' or 'way of reading'. Together, as a basic approach or as a 'very practical working method' it can help elucidate and highlight the prophetic meaning of the texts. This approach is not the same as the 'critical historical methods' or the 'literary methods' or any of the other established methods. Every aspect of this new approach is geared to show the Bible's central message and bring it close to the reader and listener.

5:1 Main characteristics

Here are some of the key aspects of this approach point by point:

- The text is first and foremost; the text must have its say; the focus is on the final text as it has been handed down to us
- The emphasis is on a careful, close reading of the text
- Inter-textual reading or the unity of the scriptures of the Old Testament as well as the New Testament with references back and forth
- A rediscovery of the importance of the Old Testament for the church; the unique voice and central place of the Hebrew Scriptures for the whole of theology

- One focus is on key words (motif) and repetitions of words and phrases; an analysis of word use; the idiom, the distinctive characteristics of the texts are important

- Another focus is on structure and style; the framework of larger literary units; its stylistic form; depth structure of a text compared to the surface structure;

- The focus on core themes and key words that serve as a basis for biblical theology; the biblical theological themes serve as a framework for the interpretation of individual texts and vice versa. Biblical theology is oriented to the words, concepts and structure of the Old Testament.

- Using colometric representation. Writing out the text in separate sentences that reveals its structure. Sentences that can be spoken in one breath; emphasis is on the spoken word as it addresses the hearer;

- or a 'diagrammatic' representation of the text that can present a visual picture of the text, taking note of changes in actors, addressees, gender, singular or plural, primary and subordinate sentences, writing each change on a new line (Talstra). Such a diagrammatic picture of the text is a helpful and essential tool for the exegete. It would be interesting to compare the two approaches in more detail.

- The importance of an 'idiolect' translation, that is, staying close to the original Hebrew, Aramaic, Greek; a translation is always an interpretation.

- Focus on larger units; place of a particular pericope (segment) in the whole of a Bible book.

- Texts are neither primarily historical nor literary works. The scriptures are 'non-historical' books; they are prophetic proclamations ('history that proclaims'). They do have a 'historical context', which cannot always be established. The so-called 'historical books' (Joshua through II Kings) are not history books. The focus is not on the assumed different sources or transmission history. Not the history of the text (different manuscripts and translations) is central but the actual text that has been handed down to us. They are 'narrated proclamations'. And they are in the service of the proclamation, to persuade and change the hearer (Palache).

- The Jewish interpretations (including the rabbinic traditions) are important and helpful in understanding specific texts
- A 'theological' approach is not the same as an ideological, sociological, political, economic, or cultural interpretation, although each one may contribute to the understanding of the text.
- Archeological givens too are in the service of and can elucidate the message; there is often a schematic geography and time lines (prophetic geography, locations and times, Noort).
- Feminist, inter-cultural, liberation theology approaches can all aid in the interpretation of texts.

It is only *together* and in interaction that these different ways of approaching interpretation take on their meaning. It is a more 'eclectic' approach rather than based on one particular method. The one description that could catch Deurloo's approach is the phrase, "the text must have its say," with its prophetic meaning.

5:2 Translating from the Hebrew into a common language of the day

The suggestions for a new translation of the Bible by the Dutch Bible Association gave rise to intense discussions about the merits of the new proposed translation. In 1952 the new translation ('Nieuwe Vertaling') of the Bible was presented to the Protestant churches in the Netherlands. Right from the beginning there was a strong critical reaction by Breukelman. Three of his original articles in a magazine edited by Miskotte, (In de Waagschaal) are reprinted in the *Amsterdam Cahiers, (3, 4, 5, 6.)*. His vehement criticisms were not well-received and gave rise to many negative reactions. He alienated himself from many of his fellow exegetes that had worked hard at the new translation. Later on many of his suggestions were considered and many of his main concerns and principles were honored. His approach was deeply influenced by Buber's and Rosenzweig's, *Die Schrift und ihre Verdeutchung* (1961).

The intense debates around new translations illustrate once more the great distance between biblical language and the language of today. Some translations can indeed sound too archaic and many modern translations lose significant aspects of the original message, like the *Good News for Modern Man*. The Amsterdam 'school' has made an important contribution to closing this gap between the ancient languages and present day languages. They did so by a close reading of the text, highlighting inter-textual references, the unity of the text and its place in the whole of a segment, chapter and book; always conscious of key words and themes that unify the text, so that they would not be obscured by a different translation each time a key word occurred.

Deurloo also offered his evaluation of the new translation. He did it in a unique way. Together with the well-known Amsterdam minister, Nico ter Linden, they published, *It counts close,* (2008). The second part in the book was called: "Not this way, but that way." More than 180 pages are devoted to alternative translations of specific passages to the ones in the *New Translation*. In that way they presented many positive alternative translations. From their presentation of these scripture passages, it is evident how deeply they were grieved about these modern translations of the Bible because it distorted and covered over the richness and power of the prophetic message. The often intense critique of the new translation expresses their deep concern to let the living word of God sound out clearly.

The old 'Staten Vertaling' from the sixteen hundreds commissioned by the Dutch government is still favored by many conservative church communities. I just passed on my large copy from the seventeenth century to my daughter. It was the family Bible on my mother's side. It may be comparable to the English St. James translation. It stayed more closely to the original language. Many of its phrases have penetrated the Dutch language and became common expressions that are treasured by many older Christians. The New Translation is written in more modern Dutch and may be more accessible to younger persons, even though many of the key words and inter-textual connections were lost.

Dubbink, in his, *The Text Must have its Say*, follows up on this point by highlighting the difference between 'dynamic-equivalent' translating (in more modern Dutch) and 'idiolect' translating (staying as close to the original Hebrew or Aramaic as possible). (p.66). Dubbink also supervised Eleonora Hof's Masters thesis: *Principles of Translating by the 'Amsterdam School' and the 'Statenvertaling'; a qualitative and theological comparison.* (2009). It is a very helpful and careful account of the differences and agreements between the two traditions, which is still evident today. Right from the beginning, she provides a summary of the forerunners and founders of the Amsterdam 'school': (Palache, Beek, Breukelman, Miskotte, Buber), different organizations and publications,(Deurloo,

Oussoren, Dubbink), and different emphases, liturgical reading (Boendermaker and Monshouwer), and political reading, (Barth, Miskotte, Reeling Brouwer, and Boer).

What stands out in her description is that 'historicizing' is strongly opposed by Deurloo, who promotes an 'actualizing' translation (pp.21–22), including a focus on 'unhistorical texts' (62, 67–69). Instead of using the past tense, he consistently uses the present tense to emphasize its meaning for today in our lives. The scriptures are not just about the past as historical documents that have no meaning for us today.

In three earlier publications many of the details of the Amsterdam way of interpreting the scriptures were elaborated: K. Deurloo and F.J. Hoogewoud, eds. *Starting with the letter Beth; essays about Biblical Hebrew and the Hebrew Bible; dedicated to Dr. A. G. Van Dalen*, 1985, K. Deurloo and R. Zuurmond, *The Bible makes 'school' (history) ; an Amsterdam way in the exegesis*, 1984,; Supplement Series 1, *The Rediscovery of the Hebrew Bible*, 1999; as well as many articles in the Cahiers. In 2005 another volume was published that elaborated on various issues of translating, H. Blok, et.al. eds, Supplement Series 4, *To be read out loud, Miqra; Anniversary volume for Frits Hoogewoud*, 2005, which includes the twenty propositions by Dr. Maria de Groot (with English summaries) that were published earlier in Cahier 1, edited by Deurloo, et.al. J. Van Dorp in an article in #22 *of the ACEBT,* 2005, "A few remarks by the translation of Jonah 1:1" as well as T. Driehuizen, "Jonah repeated," in the same volume.

In an article by Everett Fox, "A Buber-Rosenzweig Bible in English," Fox presents a very helpful overview of Buber's translation, giving several striking examples.[1] His explanation of the oral reading is convincing. I look forward to be able to consult his: *The five books of Moses* and Buber's and Rosenzweig's, *Die schrift und ihre Verdeutschung*.

From the beginning Breukelman articulated a Biblical Theological frame of reference for the exegesis of particular texts, which in turn served for the further development of Biblical Theological themes. F. Breukelman, *Bibblical Theology 1; Introduction, Reading the scriptures*, 1980. It served as the hermeneutic presupposition for translating individual texts and 'pericopes'. The other way around, the interpretation of specific texts served as a constant correction or enrichment of the fundamental 'hermeneutic horizon' or frame of reference.

---

1. Deurloo et al., *Cahier #2*, 8–22.

5:3 *The historicity of the scriptures*

The question of historicity needs further attention. Deurloo has said the scriptures contain "unhistorical history." Many critics have jumped on this expression as well as Rev. Nico ter Linden's expression, "the Bible stories are true, but they did not really happen." For Deurloo the term "unhistorical history" is an expression he treasured. The important question is why did he treasure this expression? As I understand him, he was constantly concerned that the miracle of Yahweh's dealings with Israel did not get lost or absorbed by some general history of Ancient Israel, or more broadly, the general history of the Ancient Middle East.

For him the term 'unhistorical history' could convey something of the mystery of Yahweh's gracious and merciful actions with Israel and all humanity. The expression pointed to the presence and working of the Name, always in a surprising and miraculous way. "I shall be with you." Other times he uses the words "prophetic history." Perhaps that term, *'history that proclaims'*, is the most helpful designation that creates the least tension between revelation and creation, without undermining the miracle of Yahweh's presence. "Prophetic history' makes a claim upon us and invites us to join in and act accordingly. In these words he tried to capture something of the miracle that God can speak through human language, through human words and stories. He wanted to capture something of the basic meaning of Israel's journey with this mysterious God. It is a journey that cannot be expressed in the 'annals of the king's' or by ordinary general historical concepts of cause and effect, of verified documents, or of fate and chance.

5:3a) Talstra's view of 'religious language'

First, it may be helpful to look at Deurloo's description within a larger context, by considering Talstra's use of the word "religious language" and some other descriptions by Barton, Barr, Berkouwer, and Ahlstrom.

Talstra in his book *Old and New Readers*, frequently and freely uses the words "religious language," (pp. 21, 25, 29, 38, 42, 48, 54, 55, 61, 69, 70, 74, 81, 94, 95, 103 and others). He distinguishes the uniqueness of religious language (and knowledge) from other kinds of language, like political, economic, social, or cultural language and knowledge. Religious language must not be seen as a special form of the language of art, morality or politics, but as an authentic form of the use of language that has its own legitimacy (p.43). With his strong emphasis on the priority of linguistic analysis before all other forms of analysis, Talstra's use of 'religious language' is firmly rooted in the actual language we experience. It is not some supernatural language.

Language has its own irreducible characteristics that must be honored as well in exegesis. This does present the difficulty of how to relate the unique religious nature of language to all other forms of language and knowledge. Does this mean there is a natural point of contact in human nature for the proclamation of the scriptures without the need of the power of God's revelation in the scriptures?

Language also has its own general structure or regularity (grammar, syntax, tense, semantics, rhetorical effects, etc.), that comes to expression in the actual language used by a particular people in a particular time and culture. There is a distinction, therefore, between the general linguistic connections and built-up or architecture of a text and the specific (historically and culturally determined) way in which people express themselves and communicate through their language, their typical way of thinking and speaking, as it unfolds over time. In his Old and New Readers, Talstra outlines step by step, with many concrete biblical examples, his approach to exegesis. The English study by Young Bok Park, *Restoration in the book of Ezekiel; a text-linguistic analysis of Ezekiel 33–39, 2013*, provides an excellent and helpful example of his approach.

Language certainly has its historical, cultural, social, political, psychological, aesthetic, etc, sides, but it cannot be reduced to any of these dimensions of life. Religious language is not ideological or political language, or the language representing a certain social class or power elite, etc., even though it can also be studied from any of these points of view. Religious language is uniquely colored or determined by a person's or a community's core beliefs or convictions. Talstra refers to this fact often when he asserts the irreducible nature of religious language. We could say, in religious language the basic elements, or structure, of a language plays the "basic role" and the "religious" or "belief" aspect gives it its ultimate and unique meaning.

One could compare religious language to "church music." To compose, play or sing religious music one must first of all be a good musician. One must know something about notes, pitch, rhythm, melody, harmony/dissonance, volume, speed, etc. to make a good composition. In turn, it is these basic structural elements that a composer imaginatively uses to give expression to religious feelings and experiences of hope, love, faith, sorrow, remorse, joy, renewal, fellowship, and so on. The music has to resonate deeply, emotionally and bodily, and move us if it is to make an impact and give expression to our deepest convictions. Through music a composer imaginatively discloses something of the meaning of a lived faith and living according to that faith.

The same is true for church or temple architecture, religious education, pastoral counseling, diaconal services, and so on. To engage in any of these activities, one must first of all be a good architect, educator, communicator, counselor, social worker, etc. His insistence on the irreducible and unique nature of religious language is one of Talstra's major contributions that have far-reaching consequences. The word has truly become flesh and entered into human history and life. Religious language is deeply rooted in the fabric of creation.

Religious language compared to the everyday language and culture of today is a good example of how totally the scriptures are anchored in human experience and history. This natural connection between a lived faith and life is also one of Talstra's concerns. All one needs to do is let scripture speak because as religious language it speaks to all of life. In that view one does not have to search for a connection between religion and experience, religion and culture, religion and society, religion and art. This insistence on the integral connection between the religious language of the scriptures and life is another of Talstra's major contributions, perhaps his most important contribution, given the pervasive dualism within the Christian tradition.[2]

Such an approach to the priority and irreducibility of language in interpretations, requires a more total view of life, or, as I call it, a more integral or holistic view of life. They are the functions and regularities that we all depend on each day. I take it that is what Barton, in his book Reading the Old Testament (1984), refers to when he states that ultimately exegesis requires a view of religion and life.[3]

Although Barton does not take his starting point in a philosophical discussion of hermeneutics (theories of interpretation), he is aware that methods of interpretation need a broader frame of reference about the nature of existence and reality. Exegetes start from a pre-understanding of scripture and a unifying perspective ("a theory of religion and reality").

---

2. For a more elaborate account of Talstra's view see my essay "Reading the Hebrew Scriptures Backwards; the Old Bible is Dead, a New Scriptures is Emerging," freely available on line, www.foundationalissues.com.

3. R. Morgan with John Barton, *Biblical Interpretation*, 278,279.

At the same time they need to let the text speak for itself. This hermeneutic circle is unavoidable and acceptable as long as the one keeps informing and correcting the other.

James Barr, having distanced himself from a fundamentalist, evangelical viewpoint, struggled with the same issue in his *Biblical Faith and Natural Theology* (1993). In opposition to Karl Barth, he tried to establish, in different ways, how scripture is embedded in life.

Berkouwer too in his contribution *The Resurgence of Natural Theology*, 1974, and his dogmatic studies on general revelation, providence and scripture never found his way out of this dilemma and as a result this tension between faith and human experience colors his systematic theology.

It is not surprising that when Talstra looked for a more integral view of "providence," "history" and "general revelation" in relation to Psalm 67 he could not find any Dutch theologian (neither Berkouwer, Berkhof, and he could have added, Schillebeexkz (R.C.), or any other theologian) that presented a different view. Yet he notes that as a result of this tension, there is a growing distance between faith and life.[4]

This approach to the nature of religious language that speaks to all of life also provides an important perspective with regard to the historicity of certain events and persons in the Bible. 'Historical', or 'geographical', references, for example, can only provide a plausible focus or context. They are in the service of the prophetic meaning of the passage. By themselves they do not 'prove' anything about the historicity or actuality of places and names. A mere historical account can provide interesting background information about the history of Israel, but nothing more.

Deurloo was moved to write a separate booklet about geographical references, K. Deurloo and B. Hemelsoet, *On mountains and in valleys: biblical geography: the place where it is written.* 1988. (*Op Bergen en in dalen; bijbelse geografie: de plaats waar geschreven staat.*). They wanted to show the prophetic meaning of many references to places and dates.

5:3b) Ahlstrom's view of 'religious language'

Most authors recognize that the Hebrew Scriptures are a religious book that contains religious history writing. Many call it "theological" historiography without meaning to imply that the scriptures contain theological

---

4. Talstra, *Oude and Nieuwe Lezers*, 68–71.

concepts and theories. Some call it "confessional," "faith" history writing, and so on. The only other person I have come across that talks specifically about "religious history" in the same way as Talstra does with regard to 'religious language' is G.W. Ahlstrom. In his *The History of Ancient Palestine* (1993) he describes 'religious historiography', which according to Ahlstrom has a special purpose, it wants "to proclaim and persuade."

To do so it ". . . can use literary patterns, make adaptations, corrections and sometimes fictional writings, as well as include exact events and exclude others . . . " And again, ". . . religious historiography does not per se need to build upon any reality, because religion makes its own reality . . . "[5] This description reminds us of Palache's account of narrative writings.

It is only in the context of recognizing scripture as religious writing that research in the historical background of the Hebrew scriptures and proposals for reconstructing the past (when possible) are meaningful. It allows the Ancient Near Eastern historian to be an historian and not keep one eye on the 'historical' givens of the scriptures. At times the Bible can serve as a secondary source, but only if there are at least two or more primary other sources (Becking; Smelik). A historian that is focused on the period of history reflected in the scriptures can provide a possible or plausible historical context for certain stories as we have indicated in Genesis and Joshua. More often than not, such historical contexts emphasize even more the basic difference between religious history and other kinds of history.

Religious texts, of whatever kind, always address us personally. They convey deep convictions or ultimate beliefs; they confront, appeal, invite, direct, warn, encourage, comfort, and so on. That is the nature of religious texts. As a lived faith they involve a way of living, and as such they invite us to join in and do accordingly. Core beliefs about life are not just some general religious ideas. As basic testimonies about life they want to be lived. We can make them our own or reject them, but we cannot avoid the encounter, in this case, with the religious text. They want to be taken to heart and lived. It is up to us to ponder the message, and to take it to heart. These authors of long ago remind us and point us back to that life-giving way of the scriptures. In this way the scriptures present us with a prophetic conviction and witness. Prophetic history is history that proclaims and invites us to join in, confess and celebrate.

---

5. Ahlstrom, *The History of Ancient Palestine*, 43.

THE AMSTERDAM WAY OF INTERPRETATION

5:3c) Religious language that gives expression to ecstacy and suffering

Religious texts can also give expression to our highest ecstasy and deepest anguish. "And David danced before the Lord with all his might" (2 Sam 6:14; cf. 1 Chr 15:1–29). He was clothed only in a linen ephod. "So David and the elders of Israel . . . to bring up the ark of the Lord . . . with shouting, to the sound of the horn. . . ." (1 Chr 15:25-28) Michal, Saul's daughter, looking down from the window of her palace, was greatly offended. She said, "How the king of Israel (dis)honored himself today before the eyes of his servants' maids, as one of the vulgar fellows shamelessly uncovers himself." And David said "It was before the LORD . . . and I will make merry before the LORD." (2 Sam 6:20-22)

Although he was not allowed to build a temple for the LORD, he was allowed to bring the ark up to Zion, to the city of Jerusalem. He was in ecstasy because the Lord would dwell among his people again, God-with-us. The court annals of the kings might have just recorded that on December 25 in the year 728 B.C. that the ark of the Lord was brought to Jerusalem, but they might not have recorded what David experienced.

For David it was a matter of ecstasy, he was beyond himself. He had experienced something of the miracle and mystery of God dwelling among his people. He had pleaded with God to let him build a temple. "I will not give sleep to my eyes or slumber to my eyelids, until I find a place for the Lord, a dwelling place for the Mighty One of Jacob." (Psalm 132:4, 5) Just as Moses knew that he could not go on without the Lord being with his people, even after the golden calf idolatry, he pleaded with God and the Lord conceded and said, "My presence will go with you." (Exodus 33:14) Miriam, when Moses had finished his song, had danced after the crossing of the Red Sea. "Then Miriam, the prophetess . . . took a timbrel in her hand; and all the women went out after her with timbrels and dancing. And Miriam sang to them: 'Sing to the LORD, for he, has triumphed gloriously; the horse and his rider he has thrown into the sea.'" (Exod 15:21) The women had experienced the wonder and miracle of God-with-us, God dwelling among us.

When the shepherds saw the star above Bethlehem, "They rejoiced exceedingly with great joy." (Matt 2:10) They too were beyond themselves. "The glory of the LORD had shone around them." (Luke 2:9) and they had heard the angels sing. And Mary sang her song, "My soul magnifies the LORD, and my spirit rejoices in God my Savior." (Luke 1:46, 47) And Zechariah, the father of John the Baptist, "was filled with the Holy Spirit,

THE PROPHETIC CALL TO LOVE AND JUSTICE

and prophesied, saying, 'Blessed be the LORD God of Israel, for he has visited and redeemed his people.'" (Luke 1: 67–68). Simeon in the temple "took up Jesus in his arms and blessed God and said, "LORD, now lettest thou thy servant, depart in peace . . . for my eyes have seen thy salvation." (Luke 2–30) All of them, experiencing God-with-us, could not hold back and burst out in song and ecstasy.

In the gospel of John it is stated most succinctly. "And the Word became flesh, and dwelt among us full of grace and truth . . . the glory as of the only Son from the Father." (John 1:14) "No one has ever seen God; the only Son, who is in the bosom of the Father, he has made him known." (John 1:18) David is still dancing and invites all of us to dance with him and celebrate the miracle of the Word that has become flesh and dwelt among us, God with us. And Moses, Miriam, Elizabeth, Zechariah and Simeon are all still singing and prophesying and invite us to join in with all the women of Israel. The Psalmist commands a whole orchestra and all living creatures to join in this praise (Ps 150).

Religious knowing can also express the opposite experience, that of ultimate anguish and despair, that of near death, as David knew so well.

> My God, my God, why hast thou forsaken me?
> Why art thou so far from helping me, from the words of my groaning?
> O my God, I cry by day, but thou dost not answer; and by night,
>   but find no rest.
>
> I am poured out like water,
> and all my bones are out of joint;
> my heart is like wax,
> It is melted within my breast;
> my strength is dried up like a potsherd,
> and my tongue cleaves to my jaws;
> Thou dost lay me in the dust of death.
>   Psalm 22:1, 2 and 14, 15. cf. Psalm 88

It is the agony and cry of all those who have been massacred and perished for the sake of the Name. Their cry has not been silenced and echoes through the heavens and across the centuries. Their voices still speak and that of all those suffering. They wait for deliverance of the sons of God along with all of creation.

In all their vulnerability these words convey the power of the Word and the appeal to take them to heart. The encounter with this text presented the first readers and now us, as present day readers, with a choice:

Whom will we serve? Is it the idols of the day or following a life-giving way? The scriptures continually encourage us to walk humbly with our God and be comforted, guided and encouraged along the way. Human language is truly taken up in God's revelation and provides a natural point of contact. That does not mean for a moment there is no need for proclamation and the Word becoming flesh and dwelling among us. Hearts and barren wombs need to be opened for the miracle of the Son to be born. The uniqueness of God's speaking finds no parallel in human experience. In opposition to all godless powers it needs to be maintained. Yet there is no dualism between creation and revelation.

For our purposes it is enough to say that scripture contains 'history that proclaims, invites, challenges, judges, confronts, reassures, and provides hope, meaning and perspective.' It happened, but not in documentary fashion. We cannot reconstruct a 'history of Israel' or the 'historical Jesus' from the scriptures. The events recorded in the gospels, for example, cannot be harmonized. They each present a distinct message or proclamation. The various 'historical references', (dates, names of places, etc.), are taken up for the proclamation. Even when it comes to the resurrection stories, they present many variations that cannot be harmonized. They must be interpreted in the light of each evangelist's emphasis and witness. The scriptures do not present a 'past history' but a reality out of which and by which we can live. The storytellers and others have to take recourse to language that the historian does not have. As Deurloo put it in *It Truly Happened*,

> The language of the bible teaches us to be done with the western-Christian prejudice that only what is historically true is really true. Or vice versa, the bible is true and therefore historical. According to scriptural standards that is heresy. In itself not such a big one, but what is terrible is that this heresy has caused many to lose contact with the bible and the church. They could no longer hold the bible to be true and dependable. The opportunity to learn anew and understand the language of the bible had been taken away. Stupid books like 'the Scriptures are true after all' could not stop this process in breakdown of understanding. The story of Israel itself will have to break through these misunderstandings.[6]

---

6. Duerloo, *Waar Gebeurd*, 29.

He quotes von Rad as saying, "We with our historical-critical science, try to establish, what minimally can be assumed to be historical. Israel's story wants something different. It wants to convey a maximum of proclamation." (p, 30)

> No doubt we need to say that Israel founded its faith on and anchors it in history. But when we do we need to let go of any modern sense of history writing, which holds to the relativity and transitoriness and inaccessibility of all history. God's great deeds in Israel's history created the community of Israel and 'creates' that fellowship of believers each time again as the stories are told. They did not become past tense . . . the voices that are heard, tell and sing in such a way, that we can live with their words in the present.[7]

Most ministers and pastors, I dare say, at least, on this continent have a hard enough time preparing their weekly sermons and catechetical teaching. They simply would not have the time next to their many other duties in a congregation. Moreover as 'frontline' workers, they have to deal with all the questions of our secularized and stressful times. They need all the (readymade) help they can find. Many pastors flocked to the expositions by Miskotte, Breukelman and Deurloo in the past. It was the need of the hour. Just as today The New Bible School (in the Netherlands de Nieuwe Bijbel School) presentations are the need of our day. It is interesting to note that a group of ministers gather once a week in Amsterdam as they did long ago, to establish a good translation together of a particular passage or unit and to explore its meaning for today to help them with their sermonizing.

There are several issues that may benefit from further elucidation or changes in formulation. We will come back to these in the final evaluation in the last chapter. Some of those issues relate to the historicity of scriptures that we have already touched on. As I have mentioned earlier, the misunderstanding of the doctrine of providence and maintaining the creation (Heidelberg Catechism), and the changed 'God-image' need further attention. Some have expressed the desire that more attention could be given to the apocalyptic literature. This is both for clarification, and to save those passages from literalistic, biblicistic and speculative evangelical interpretations. Other issues that may arise as we move along

---

7. Duerloo, *Waar Gebeurd*, 30.

are, for example, how we understand and respond to other religions, especially those of Indigenous peoples.

How are we to deal with some of the major other obstacles to understanding the scriptures? We no longer understand the language of the scriptures. It often sounds quaint and old-fashioned. What are we to make of a 'righteous scale' or a 'righteous path' for example compared to other expressions like a 'righteous man'?

That is why one of the first things a Bible Study Group needs is a study Bible, like the Harper Study Bible (1952–1972) with a concordance and maps in the back. Even better is if one of the participants has a more elaborate concordance to check out the many inter-textual references. Next to these aids are what I call the 'vocabulary lists', like Kuitert's *De Spelers en het spel* (1964, yes, 'even' Kuitert, from his earlier period translated in English, *Signals from the Bible*, 1972); Miskotte's, *Bijbels ABC* (1966/1992; *Biblical ABCs, The Basics of Christian Resistance* 2022); and Deurloo's (with Bouhuijs) and his *Ways of Language and Errors of Language*, (*Taalwegen en Dwaalwegen* 1967/1985) and his book with Hemelsoet, *Over Hills and in Valleys; biblical geography: the place where it is written*, 1988); (*Op Bergen en in Dalen; biblical geographie: de plaats waar geschreven staat*), and other similar studies.

We have lost the vocabulary lists and can no longer decipher the grammar. We all need to go back to Bible study groups. It is interesting that in the new Bible classes an equal amount of time is devoted to try to understand a particular text in its meaning for today. We can all learn to listen again to the text and read very closely to discover its meaning for us. Noting the many details in a text already tends to bring it closer to the hearers. I was struck again by the brief exposition of the gospel of Mark by B. Hemelsoet, a Roman Catholic New testament theologian, who from the beginning contributed to the Amsterdam tradition of interpretation. By noting the many details of the text, he succeeds in conveying something of the mystery and surprise of the step by step revelation of the names 'Son of Man' and 'Messiah' in the gospel of Mark, B. Hemelsoet, *Mark; Exposition of a part of the scriptures*, (1977). See his many articles in Cahiers 1 through 16.

Besides establishing a good translation of a text there is the additional challenge of how these stories and words can speak to our modern world. We all face the problem of how to sound out the words of scripture in a secularized world that has deeply influenced our view of reality and that of our hearers. Almost every word and critical human issue and concern has been taken up and perverted by modern advertising. Our language needs to be decolonized, since it is inseparably connected to global capitalism with its 'scientistic' and 'technisistic' concepts, ('Science-based facts and policies'). Deurloo and followers give several examples of words that are radically distorted, like "cosmos, nature, time, days, names, etc. by social and philosophical concepts.

The misuse of language, or, better, the commercialization of language is perhaps most evident in the names of many stores and the products they sell (as any trip to any large shopping mall will tell you). One interesting one is: 'Pink is life and life is Pink', which sells women's lingerie. These could be multiplied by the hundreds). In order to increase sales, some small thing needs to be added every few years to maintain their market share. Toothpaste is one of my favorite examples; every few years something 'new' is added that is 'recommended by the dental association' to make your teeth whiter, prevent cavities, or protect your gums. The increased cost presumably guarantees its quality.

We are daily bombarded by hundreds of advertisements in a relentless assault on our sensibilities. Human language is commercialized and robbed of depth of meaning and mystery. Our language and concepts have been 'colonized'. Every human need and experience, no matter how personal and intimate, is used to serve an increase in consumption. It seems only poetry and music (and other forms of art) are left to convey the mystery of human experience.

5:4: Deurloo's exegetical method: four examples

Having set the stage and provided the background and the main characteristics of the Amsterdam way of interpreting the scripture, as well as the secular and disenchanted climate in which the words of scripture have to be sounded out and interpreted anew, it may be helpful at this point to give some concrete examples of Deurloo's own exegetical method. In one booklet (*It Truly Happened, Waar Gebeurd*) he gives four examples of his interpretations and counters some of the criticisms of different passages, (passages that seem to make use of fairy tales, legends, sagas, myths, geographical references, etc. and so-called inaccuracies and anachronisms). He does so, not by directly countering these interpretations or engaging in a defense of the faith (apologetics). Instead he takes the criticisms seriously and checks them out against the details of the text. In all four instances he comes to a very different conclusion than the critical historical approach.

In the first example of a passage that seems to have a 'fairy tale' origin or character, Jacob fleeing from his brother Esau, who had vowed to kill him after his deceit and deprive him of the rights of the blessing of the first-born (Gen 28,29), Deurloo counters this interpretation by checking out the details of the passages. In that context he directly challenges one of the main exegetical approaches of the critical historical method that was very dominant for a long time. According to this 'Documentary Hypothesis' or the 'splitting-of-sources', which analyzes the assumed origin of any passage, whether or not they have their origin in a particular use of the God name tradition. The result of this approach is a basic fragmentation of any text, especially in the first five books of the Bible, (Gen, Exod, Lev, Num, and Deut)

He gives examples of how the second series of stories about the Jacob cycle are divided or split-up and which passages belong to each tradition; he lists which verses and parts belong to J (Jawist), E (Elohim), P (priestly), or D (Deuteronomist), according to the theory. If we follow this analysis we soon realize we are left with fragments and skeletons.[8]

His approach does not depend on a scholarly exegetical knowledge of the passages considered. For him they depend on a close reading of the passages. It is the texts themselves that reveal their true meaning. For example, he makes it clear why suddenly there is a reference to the name Jahweh in the middle of an E (Elohim) section and how it adds to the meaning of the passage. It is the actual interpretations of many scripture passages by Deurloo that are most convincing and moving, and a constant source of inspiration, for they witness to the living word of God. It is worth following Deurloo's four examples closely to appreciate his main exegetical approach.

5:4a) Jacob fleeing Esau

This is the story of Jacob fleeing from his brother Esau and his dream along the way, known as the 'Jacob's ladder' dream.

It is one unified account that is framed by two sentences at the beginning and the end, "Jacob left Beersheba, and went to Haran." (Gen

---

8. Deurloo, *It Truly Happened*, 32–48.

28:10) and "Then Jacob went on his journey, and came to the land of the people of the east." (Gen 29:1), the land of his relatives. Right from the beginning it highlights this momentous event of leaving the promisedland.

In the story as seen through the eyes of the 'source-splitters' it is clear that the Jawist and Elohim god names are interwoven. Deurloo examines this approach by first reproducing the text with the E parts printed cursively, and the J parts in regular script. Later additions are placed in brackets. The first task of this form of interpretation is to take note of tensions and repetitions. To follow and appreciate Deurloo's interpretation, we need to read and follow the story along in the Bible.

We are immediately struck by the use of Elohim (name of God) next to Yahweh. At the end of vs. 22 the tense changes from the third person (God, Yahweh) suddenly to the second person (You). It seems that the piece about Elohim is a relatively complete story in itself. Within it there is just a small fragment of J who uses the name Yahweh for God. How must we interpret this account of E with its fragment of J and what are the consequences for the historicity of the story?

The 'source-splitter' holds that the E piece is a typical sanctuary story that tells us how Bethel became a cultic place and that a sense of holiness surrounds this place and what the meaning is of the stone that is placed upright (a 'holy stone', called, a Massebe) upon which Jacob pours oil as an offering and an act of worship. It explains why this place is called Bethel instead of its previous name Luz. "Surely the LORD is in this place; and I did not know it. How awesome is this place! This is none other than the house of God, and this is the gate of heaven." (Gen 28:16–17). There is nothing especially Israelite about this story. They originate from pre-Israelite times. When Bethel was taken over by the Israelites as a sanctuary (I Kings 12:29), Jacob as the tribal ancestor and his encounter with God were simply inserted here. The entire focus is on the general 'religious' meaning and the national tribal father Jacob who plays a general role. There is no clarity about a proclamation here.

In the fragment about the Jawist the emphasis is just the opposite; the emphasis is not on the sanctuary but on the promise that Jacob and his descendants will inherent the land on which he is sleeping. Almost in passing the reference is connected to Bethel. The old God of Bethel, Elohim, is suddenly called Yahweh. The real message appears to be an emphasis on the promises to Jacob by Yahweh. From the 'source-splitter's' account all historicity has disappeared. It is just an allusion to an ancient story about the origin of a cultic place. It may be interesting but nothing more. So why bother with this story?!

The Jawist speaks very directly and addresses Jacob as "you." There is clearly a personal relation between God and Jacob. How telling to let a dream become a place for the encounter with God on that precarious journey fleeing from his brother that is out to kill him. In this way the God-revelation becomes a very special encounter and personal experience. Jacob becomes devout and worships God, because he knows that his life is guided by God. However such a conclusion and sermon would still be much too general, for that kind of sermon you don't need Gen. 28.

When we assert that such an interpretation (of a god experience) does not do justice to the account, which does not mean that we doubt that some ancient givens are incorporated in the text. The cultic place Bethel is much older than when it was given a function much later within Israel (I Kings 12:29). Many details from ancient times are incorporated in the biblical stories. Not their ancient origin is crucial, nor even how they have functioned within historical Israel, rather the function they were given in a particular biblical story is crucial.

When we read the story again we will not just focus on some irregularities and tensions in the text, even though they may play a fitting role. We will first of all focus on certain key words and phrases that call for our attention and give it a focus. Then Deurloo quotes the story once more and underscores several key words and phrases, namely: 'place', 'took a stone', 'a ladder set up on the earth', 'the Lord stood above him', 'Yahweh in this place', 'heaven', 'took the stone'.

He quotes J. Fokkelman who asserted that the words in Genesis 28 are placed in a particular scheme, a 'mirror image' (chiasm). Gen 28:10–13a and 16–19 are placed around the speech by Yahweh, 13b–15. The storyteller plays with this scheme or pattern. This structure should prevent us from too quickly assuming a 'two-sources theory'. We recognize the pattern: (1) 10–13a is the introduction; (2) 13b–15 the discourse by Yahweh; (3) 16–19 Jacob's response in word and deed; (4) 20–22 Jacob's promise. 1 and 3 correspond with each other and 3 and 4 relate to each other. This division runs right through the assumed different sources. In this way we can trace the unity of the story, by tracing each part of the story. In the following account we will closely follow Deurloo's interpretation.

We are already familiar with the family connections and itinerary from Gen 27:41–46; and 28:1–5. Jacob's mother instructs him, saying,

"Behold, your brother Esau comforts himself by planning to kill you. Now therefore, my son, obey my voice; arise, flee to Laban my brother in Haran, and stay with him for a while, until your brother's fury turns away ..." Then Rebekkah said to Issaac ..." If Jacob marries one of the Hittite women such as these, one of the women of the land (like Esau), what good will my life be to me?" Then Isaac called Jacob and blessed him and charged him ..." Arise, go to Paddan-aram to the house of Bethuel your mother's father; and take as wife from there one of the daughters of Laban your mother's brother ... Thus Isaac sent Jacob away ..."

So Jacob left Beersheba and went to Haran. It seems like a very ordinary account. But is it? Haran is the place that Abraham left to go to the land that the Lord would show him. Is this journey of Abraham, the new history in the land of promise not being undone by Jacob? For that reason the storyteller makes this crucial moment of Jacob leaving the land a very special moment: "And he came to a certain place, and stayed there that night, because the sun had set." (Gen 28:11) The sun goes under, it is a night scene, messengers of God travel up and down a ladder, and then there is an encounter with Yahweh who blesses him. We not only read the story as a unity but also as a part of a coherent series, the Jacob cycle.

Here Deurloo emphasizes that the word 'place' is mentioned three times without a name. Later the name 'place' is mentioned three times again. By then the name of the place can be mentioned, 'the house of God'. Many givens are already provided in this introduction that will play a role in the rest of the story. It is very imaginative, as if the reader is right there. Both the actual reading out loud and the literary devices put the listener right in the middle of the story: a ladder, a staircase, like that of a Babylonian temple, with messengers going up and down. First our view goes down and then up, where it is placed on the land and then up, where its top reaches heaven. We see the movement between heaven and earth, of the messengers of God going up and down, to end with the LORD's activity. From the earth (the land Canaan), the staircase we see reaches into heaven and on top of the stairs Yahweh is placed. It is a Babylonian dream vision in the land of Canaan that Jacob experiences, before he leaves to go to the east, to Babylon. Not there, but here in this land the secret of God's presence opens up to him. The secret is hidden in the name Yahweh, and therefore that name has to sound here.

The second part is the speech of Yahweh. We will remember for a moment that he is going the opposite direction Abraham went. Will Abraham's journey and the new vision be undone? Jacob is confronted with Yahweh, "I am the Lord, the God of Abraham your father, and the God of Isaac." Yes, also the God of Isaac, and as becomes clear in this speech, now also the God of Jacob. In distinction from Isaac, Abraham is explicitly called "your father" and with his blessing you Jacob are blessed. You laid yourself down in this place; this is the land I will give you and your seed.

Look around; eastward to the west, the south and the north, the whole country, I will give to you and your descendants. With your descendants all the peoples of the earth shall be blessed. Jacob receives the complete blessing of Abraham. It is about the land of promise and many descendants, about humanity and all the peoples of the future. Jacob's journey has become a sign of his return. In this land he will be named by his new name, "Israel" (Gen 32:28), which also happens in a night scene, when he wrestles with a messenger of God. He will become the father of a great nation. The new history, which started with Abraham, will continue with Jacob, now called Israel. ("Your name shall no more be called Jacob, but Israel,' for you have striven with God and with men, and have prevailed' . . . So Jacob called the name of the place Peniel, saying, 'For I have seen God face to face, and yet my life is preserved'. The sun rose upon him as he passed Peniul, limping because of his thigh." Gen 32:28–31)

The third part is Jacob's reaction. The big words Jacob heard from God penetrate in two steps, "I am the God of your father Abraham and I will also be your God." He first realizes that God has appeared to him. In the second place he is suddenly overcome by fear because of the great secret of this place. It is repeated twice, "This place"! Now he knows what he is leaving. This is the place where Yahweh reveals himself. "Surely the LORD is in this place." This is the house of God, the gate of heaven. Just as in the dream, the view looks down and then up. In this place heaven and earth hold hands. Here Yahweh will be for and with his people.

Jacob's reaction is to erect, to 'stand up' a 'massebe', a 'holy stone'. It is mentioned in several places in the scriptures as well as in Canaanite religion, but here it becomes a sign. This stone on which he had laid his head to sleep becomes an erected sign over which Jacob pours oil. It is not a holy stone in itself, but a visible sign and seal, like a sacrament that points to this history between Yahweh and Jacob on the earth. Finally we hear the name of the place, Beth-el, house of God. It has become a special place, at first without a name, simply the place on which he laid down. This is the land which I promised to Abraham. House of God stands for the whole of the Promised Land, which in this story Jacob is leaving.

The fourth part is Jacob's promise. We need to place his words next to those of Yahweh. Most translators make it into a condition, "If God will be with me . . . then I will give." Grammatically that is incorrect and from the point of view of Biblical theology, even less so. "If God gives me bread and clothing and makes me return to my father's house, then I will . . . give ten percent back." Such an interpretation would be totally in contrast with this entire history of Jacob and the entire Bible. It is more to the point to see this promise as a solemn acknowledgment of what Jacob heard from Yahweh, "I am Yahweh, the God of Abraham . . . see, I will be with you." Jacob repeats these last words, "If God will be with me . . . and will keep me in this way that I go." This way that I have to go, the first thing I will need is bread and clothing. Yahweh will bring me back to my father's house in peace." (We remember Esau's threat to kill him).

That will be enough. Jacob repeats very modestly, what Yahweh has said. For now he relates it to his present desperate situation. If Yahweh is my God, then this stone here will indeed be a sign of a God-house, as a sacramental sign of what has happened in this place. In his final response to God Jacob speaks in the second person singular and with that he enters into a relation initiated by God, "of all that thou givest me . . . a tenth I give to thee," Gen 28:22. (It is like Abraham did before in Gen 14:20 and it is how faithful Israel will do it according to the Torah in their offerings.)

These are some of the historical givens of an 'unhistorical' story. Deurloo conveys that in itself we have nothing against source-splitting. ('documentary hypothesis') If the text gives occasion for that, it is even fun to try to re-construct the sources. It becomes even more exciting if it helps to understand the text better. There was a scribe who put the pieces (of the sources) together. He didn't do that just for fun. He must have found that combining these sources was meaningful. He wanted to say something and that is what we have in the scriptures. The story of Jacob, his God experience, only as a whole can convey the mystery of God's presence. It becomes proclamation.

Not in the historical indications in the Jacob story, but in the 'unhistorical' parts we find the meaning. Not the pre-Israelite Bethel-god, the holy place, the stone from a long ago past can tell us anything and not even the probable tribal ancestor Jacob can tell us something, but only the story itself, which so freely and creatively uses these ancient givens, can carry the proclamation.

It does not matter a lot if this story in its present form came into existence around 750 BCE or only during the exile between 600 and 500 BCE. The latter view is more probable. The difference in style of Genesis, which gave rise to the 'source-splitting' theory could point to older written materials which the scribes used. On the other hand, they can also point to different scribal circles from Jerusalem and northern Israel which were deported as well, and which during the exile have contributed to the writing of Genesis. The name of the place Bethel cannot be found exactly on a map. Instead Bethel itself becomes a reference to the promised land of Abraham. Something is done with the old givens and motifs. The final writing is late Judaic. We can enter the story only if we pay attention to the functional whole, in which all the details have their place. It would be instructive at this point to follow the story of Jacob's return and his meeting with Esau for the first time. (Gen 32:1–21), but we will save that for the account of Genesis in chapter 6.

This interpretation by Deurloo is a good example of his way of interpreting the scriptures. He takes note of the historical-critical interpretations, engages in a close reading, provides his own translation, considers the old traditions, the key words and phrases in a particular story, the interconnections with other books of the Bible, and how they all add up to the proclamation.

5:4b) Patriarchal lies

Next, we will examine once again one of the most widespread and esteemed methods of interpretation, the 'documentary hypothesis.' It is also called the 'source-splitting' theory (the documentary hypothesis). To remind us, this means that any text is considered to be made up of different parts or sources that can be identified in the text and that have their origin in different traditions. Deurloo's critique of the 'source-splitting' theory is very clear: in this view the text is split into three parts or more, according to whether their origin is in the Jahwist, the Elohim, or the Priestly tradition, or the Deuteronomist. In his view, however, the story does not appear to be an 'artificially-put-together-collage' or composition. Again and again he illustrates how these so-called split-off ' parts' give meaning and are essential to the whole impact of the passage. He turns the historical analysis or hypotheses upside down. Rather than distracting from the meaning of the text and invalidating it, the so-called 'split-off segments' actually enhance the meaning of a passage. When he takes issue with this approach he does not deny that the storytellers used ancient sources and literary motifs. Rather, an exegete needs to focus first of all on the given unity of the book, which is not done enough in Old Testament exegesis (*Waar Gebeurd*, p.35).

In the following examples of his exegetical approach, we will let Deurloo speak for himself. We will look at his interpretations of stories that seem to have a 'fairy-tale' character, or that read like a 'legend' and so on. All the examples are from his booklet, *It Truly Happened; about the un-historical character of Biblical stories*, (1981).

In the following example, there are three similar events of the patriarchal fathers lying about their wives. Usually they are attributed to different sources (the documentary hypothesis). Yet, they are not just repetitions. In these examples we can see the effects of a source-splitting analysis: the text is broken up in three different parts. In a discussion in *It Truly Happened*, 1981, pp. 51–53), he examines the three quite similar stories of Abraham and Isaac lying about their wives, claiming them to be their sister with disastrous results, risking everything (Gen 12:10–20; 20:1–18; 26:1–11). The same motif of the threatened ancestral mother is used three times in a different way. In each instance, there is a famine. The tribal ancestors end up in a strange country in which they are 'sojourners' dependent on the hospitality of the city dwellers. In each instance, the husband claims that his beautiful wife is his sister and not his wife for fear she will be taken into the ruler's harem and they themselves will be killed. In each instance, a plague erupts and the patriarchal father receives his wife back again.

Deurloo calls it typical male stories told around the campfire. The flocks have been watered and taken care of, the children are sleeping and the women are in their own quarters. The half-nomadic people travel along the edges of the cultivated land and cities, exchanging goods. The stories are told about how clever the tribal fathers were and how they fooled the mighty city dwellers and rulers.

He checks the splitting of the three assumed sources against the text in its unity. He makes a convincing case for three different emphases and proclamations. They are not mere repetitions. The first time the emphasis is from the threat of Egypt and in preparation of the exodus of the people to the Promised Land, "But the LORD afflicted Pharaoh and his house with great plagues because of Sarai, Abram's wife" (Gen 12:17). It alerts the reader to what is to come and points ahead to the ten plagues before the Exodus.

The second time (Gen 20:1–18) the emphasis is on the special plague of barrenness that hits the court of Abimelech, "and God also healed his wife and female slaves so that they bore children. For the LORD had closed all the wombs of the house of Abimelech because of Sarah, Abraham's wife." It points ahead to the promised son that introduces the following story of the miraculous birth of Isaac from the barren Sarah.

The third time (Gen 26:1–33) again there is a famine. But this time Isaac is forbidden to go to Egypt. The emphasis is on the special place in the land of promise and protection for Isaac. The story is followed by an account of Isaac's riches and a dispute about the wells. "For now the LORD has made room for us, and we shall be fruitful in the land . . . We see plainly that the LORD is with you; so we say, let there be an oath between you and us . . . that you will do us no harm, just as we have not touched you . . . You are now the blessed of the LORD and have sent you away in peace . . ." It alerts the reader to the coming conquest and inheritance of the land under Joshua.

Each of the three seeming 'repetitions' alerts the reader to the coming liberation from slavery in Egypt, from the world powers of oppression and the special child that will carry the blessing and will become a great nation in the promised land. Deurloo's examples add meaning to the text.

In an earlier paper, "Lost Faith," I closely followed Becking's account, together with Smelik of the same three stories, *A Patriarchal Lie*, 1989, and the use of the splitting of the three sources theory. I found Deurloo to be the most convincing and prophetic account. Although I did appreciate and learn from Becking's careful and more elaborate way he dealt with the 'splitting of sources theory' ('documentary hypothesis' or 'sources theory').

5:4c) Jesus' temptations

They are seen as 'legendary' stories to proclaim something crucial about Jesus' ministry. Here we do not encounter giants and speaking animals. As before, Deurloo starts by giving his own translation including the references in the text to the Hebrew Scriptures (Deuteronomy 8:3; Psalm 91:11, 12; Deuteronomy 6:16; 6:13). He wonders, is this story an (eyewitness) account of the evangelist, or one of the followers about Jesus' first ministry? It shows all the characteristics of a 'legendary story' as a form of folklore, recounting human actions that are believed to have taken place in history. Again Deurloo will make the point that such 'legendary characteristics' are used from the very beginning of his ministry to proclaim something essential about Jesus. Again we need to follow the story along in the scriptures.

Who is this tempter, that devil? He brings Jesus through the air to the pinnacle of the temple. Did Jesus literally stand there at a certain moment? Then there is that very high mountain, from which you can see all the kingdoms of the earth (the earth was seen as flat). But where can we find such a mountain in Palestine? Such things only happen in legends, about saints and heroes for example. It is a visionary event. Did Jesus have such visionary experiences? If so, how did Matthew come to know these givens? This 'legend' is by Jesus followers and in this form, by Matthew, put in story form, just as the story about David and Goliath is told in I Samuel 17. There it is a 'fairy tale' literary motif, here a 'legendary motif', but in both they are not just 'made-up stories' in the negative sense of the word.

Mark has only a two verse reference to the temptations, directly following the baptism by John the Baptist, "The Spirit immediately drove him out into the wilderness. And he was in the wilderness forty days, tempted by Satan; and he was with the wild beasts; and the angels ministered to him." (Mark 1:11, 12).

Matthew elaborates on this account to characterize the whole of Jesus' ministry. "And he fasted forty days and forty nights, and afterwards he was hungry. And the tempter came and said to him, "If you are the Son of God, command these stones to become loaves of bread." But he answered, "It is written, man shall not live by bread alone, but by every word that proceeds from the mouth of God." (Matt 4:2–4)

Matthew too speaks in an 'unhistorical' way about real events. Right at the beginning of his ministry he summarizes everything about who Jesus is and what he does. During his entire life he had to resist the temptation to succeed as the Son of God through his miraculous powers. Imagine, making bread out of stones! In one mighty gesture, he would have solved the question of famine and hunger. Just like that, the bread question solved! But he can only be called God's Son, because he hungers with the hungry and suffers with the sick, the naked, the thirsty, the strangers, and the imprisoned. The first part of Matthew's gospel takes place in Galilee, where the question of bread was a pressing problem. This issue is summarized in the first temptation.

It would not have been impossible for God or Jesus to turn stones into bread, as we read earlier from John the Baptist in his condemnation of the hypocrisy of the Pharisees and Sadducees wanting to be baptized by him, "Bear fruit that befits repentance, and do not presume to say to yourselves, 'We have Abraham as our father'; for I tell you, God is able from these stones to raise up children to Abraham." (Matt 3:8, 9)

We are reminded instead of Jesus feeding great crowds of people because he had compassion on them. In Matthew 14:13-21 is the account of feeding five thousand people, and in Matthew 15:32-39 the feeding of four thousand, "He saw a great throng; and he had compassion on them, and healed their sick . . . When it was evening the disciples came to him and said, 'This is a lonely place, and the day is now over; send the crowds away to go into the villages and buy food for themselves'. Jesus said, 'They need not go away; you give them something to eat' . . . And those who ate were about five thousand men, besides women and children." From this we can understand Jesus saying, "for I was hungry and you gave me food, I was thirsty and you gave me drink, I was a stranger and you welcomed me, I was naked and you clothed me, I was sick and you visited me, I was in prison and you came to me . . . Truly I say to you, as you did it to one of the least of these my brethren, you did it to me." (Matt 25:31-46) Compare Luke 9: 10-17; Mark 6:30-44; Matt 6:31-34; John 6:22-40.

Another temptation occurs in Jerusalem; to jump off the roof of the temple, and at the last moment be saved by the angels. Jesus faces the threat of death in Jerusalem. "Then the devil took him to the holy city, and set him on the pinnacle of the temple, and said to him, 'If you are the son of God, throw yourself down . . .'" (Matt 4:5, 6) "Jesus said to him, 'Again it is written, 'you shall not tempt the LORD your God'" (Matt 4:7). Similarly, when he is crucified he hears the satanic voice, ". . . If you are Son of God come down from the cross." (Matt 27:40) But as this cursed, dying man, the least of all people, that is how he is the Son of God.

"Again, the devil took him to a very high mountain, and showed him all the kingdoms of the world and the glory of them; and said to him, "All these I will give you, if you will fall down and worship me." Then Jesus said to him, "Be gone, Satan! for it is written, 'You shall worship the LORD your God, and him only shall you serve.'" (Matt 4:8-10). "Then the devil left him . . . ." (Matt 4:11) "Now the eleven disciples went to Galilee to the mountain to which Jesus had directed them . . . (Matt

28:16) Here, at the end of Matthew, Jesus is presented again on a mountain not as needing to prove himself to the devil as though the devil has the ultimate authority, rather as the real ruler of the world, "And Jesus came and said to them, 'All authority in heaven and on earth has been given to me . . . and lo, I am with you always, to the close of the age.'" (Matt 28:18–20) That is how he proved himself to be God's Son, entering Jerusalem as a lowly servant riding on a donkey to be murdered like a common slave and revolutionary and appearing to the disciples on the mountain in Galilee as the risen Christ. "And when the devil had ended every temptation, he departed from him until an opportune time."

The history of the temptations, in the beginning of the gospel, with its themes of hunger, fear of death, and, later, the high mountain from which to rule, summarizes the entire gospel. All the temptations Jesus had to endure during his ministry take form in the figure of the tempter, the devil. Is it only a legendary story? No, the Bible does not just tell 'fairy tales' or 'legends'. The gospel writer uses these givens of widespread literary forms for his proclamation, to convey to us the great event with which they were confronted. They do so with a lot of freedom; for they are themselves taken up into the service of telling us the Word of God that took place in the midst of our human history. The overwhelming power of these events makes these givens suitable to convey the prophetic message.

In the Apostolic Confession the church confesses that "on the third day he arose from the dead." They intended to say nothing more and nothing less than that it truly happened. Can we reconstruct this event in historical, documentary, eye-witness accounts of the resurrection? Could hidden cameras, if they had existed at that time have recorded this event? It is an event that can only truly be conveyed as a confession of faith. It proclaims, no more and no less. It is a confession of a miracle to be celebrated with thanksgiving.

The quest for the 'historical Jesus' is as fruitless as the search for 'the history of Israel'. The gospel writers do not tell us about the resurrection; what they do tell is that they confessed the resurrection, each in their own way. The resurrection stories cannot even be harmonized in any sequence of events. They tell of the event, not as some past happening, but as a future that has started and opened up. "Do not be amazed; you seek Jesus of Nazareth, who was crucified. He has risen, he is not here; see the place where they laid him." (Mark 16:6) Jesus cannot be found among the dead. In Galilee, they will see him and from there they proclaim the gospel to all nations.

Matthew tells the same event very differently. The stone the women saw was rolled away, not before their eyes but for the ears of the readers ("there was a great earthquake"). The soldiers that had to guard the grave, fled in fear. Thus the witnesses are out of the way, in order to leave free room for the women to tell about the resurrection to the others. They entered into the grave, only to be sent away by a messenger of God to tell about the empty grave. "He is not here; for he has risen, as he said. Come and see the place where he lay. Then go quickly and tell his disciples that he has risen from the dead, and behold, he is going before you to Galilee; there you will see him . . . So they departed quickly from the tomb with fear and great joy . . . " (Matt 28:6–10)

In the story of Luke we hear still other accents. It highlights the disciples' lack of faith who are only convinced later by Jesus' exhortation on the way to Emmaus. The women are told, ". . . .Why do you seek the living among the dead? Remember how he told you, while he was still in Galilee, that the Son of man must be delivered into the hands of sinful men, and be crucified, and on the third day rise. And they remembered his words . . . and they told the apostles, but these words seemed to them like an idle tale, and they did not believe them." (Luke 24:1–11) Along the way to Emmaus Jesus explained, ". . . beginning with Moses and all the prophets, he interpreted to them in all the scriptures the things concerning himself . . . their eyes were opened and they recognized him . . . " (Luke 24:27–31) They returned to Jerusalem and told the others, "The Lord has risen indeed, and has appeared to Simon!" (Luke 24:34)

John's account might be even more puzzling, ". . . for as yet they did not know the scripture, that he must rise from the dead." (John 20:9). So they just went home. To really see, the disciples have to know the scriptures. The evangelist lets them enter the scene. Now Peter and the beloved disciple (John) can play a role at the grave. (John 13:23; 19: 26, 27) They are part of the proclamation about following and going ahead, looking and really seeing, seeing and believing. Later on Jesus will say to Thomas, "Unless I see . . . I will not believe." (John 20:25) "Thomas answered him, 'my LORD and my God!' Jesus said to him, 'Have you believed because you have seen me? Blessed are those who have not seen and yet believe.'" (John 20:28, 29)

All four of the evangelists leave a place for the final mystery and secret of the resurrection. Their 'unhistorical' and free way of telling, is in the service of this secret, this reality. They can barely find language to witness to what has happened.

In the midst of us, it happened and took place. The past is not accessible to us as regular validated history, or as a documentary, but only as an encounter which has changed us and continues to change us, each time again, when we hear the story in the midst of the history in which we live. It is the realty in which we become involved and in which the barrier of death (the stone is rolled away) brought about this witness.

5:4d) Sodom and Gomorrah

Deurloo discusses the destruction of Gomorrah in *It Truly Happened*.[9] It is telling that Abraham's rescuing of Lot is not mentioned by the prophets which were probably written before Genesis. The grotesque erotic scene of Genesis 19:4, 5 is not mentioned anywhere else in the scriptures. According to the story, presumably the whole population "the men of Sodom, both young and old, all the people to the last man," all of them, grey-haired old men and youngsters were inflamed by lust to sexually violate the two messengers that were staying with Lot. The impossibility of this description (all, both young and old) already makes it clear for Deurloo that this story has nothing to do with homosexuality. Yet how much damage has been done within the Christian tradition with this and other stories!

Zuurmond, one of the frequent contributors to the Cahiers, in a carefully documented article has questioned the age-old interpretation of Genesis 19:5.[10] According to Zuurmond the emphasis is on the violence of the people of Sodom and not on their presumed 'homosexuality'. Genesis 19:5 says, "And they called to Lot, 'Where are the men who came to you tonight? Bring them out to us, that we may know them.'" The comparison to Judges 19:22, is instructive. In that horrible story the emphasis is on the violent mal-treatment of the concubine. "They knew her and abused her all night." By morning she was dead. "The emphasis is on the violence, without mercy destroying a human being who can't defend herself against the sexual assault of the neighbor."[11]

---

9. Deurloo, *Waar Gebeurd*, 53–58.
10. R. Zuurmond, "Sodom, the history of a prejudice," *Cahier #5*, 27–40.
11. Zuurmond, *Cahier #5*, p.29.

Earlier already in Genesis 13:13, we read "the men of Sodom were wicked, great sinners against the LORD." At most we can say the threat of the Sodomites could include sexual violation. More likely, the author used a well-known motif in storyform to give expression to the violent abuse of the inhabitants against defenseless travelers. The wickedness of the Sodomites is focused on the horrendous violation of the right of strangers. Whatever sexual aspects there may have been, it is subordinated to the violence toward and violation of the right of strangers. The misinterpretation of this passage has simply been repeated from one commentary to another over the centuries, without carefully examining the text, as Zuurmond illustrates. This has and continues to create much pain and tragedy for many people.

Back to Deurloo, who highlights the inter-textual context of passages referring to Sodom and Gomorrah is very revealing. Let's assume for a moment that Genesis did not exist yet. Can we come to know more about the tradition of Sodom and Gomorrah from other, earlier parts as a literary motif? Let us start with a prophet that is usually assumed to be the oldest of the later prophets. Amos proclaims the disasters that will come over Israel in order to bring about a total 'turn over'. There will be hunger, thirst, and plant diseases. He summarizes it in the well-known threefold disasters, hunger, pests, and the sword.

> I gave you cleanness of teeth in all your cities,
> And lack of bread in all your places, yet you did not return to me . . .
> And I also withheld the rain from you
> When there were yet three months to the harvest . . .
> Yet you did not return to me . . .
> I smote you with mildew;
> I laid waste your gardens and your vineyards
> Your fig trees and your olive trees the locust devoured;
> Yet you did not return to me . . .
> I sent among you a pestilence after the manner of Egypt;
> I slew your young men with the sword . . .
> Yet you did not return to me.
>
> I overthrew some of you,
> As when, God overthrew Sodom and Gomorrah . . .
> yet you did not return to me.
> Therefore thus I will do to you, O Israel;
> Because I will do this to you,
> Prepare to meet your God, O Israel.
>   Amos 4:6–12

It will be a total catastrophe, an all-consuming fire! A few stumps of not yet burned wood will be left. A similar image of total destruction, turning everything upside down, is called forth by Isaiah, "Your country lies desolate, your cities are burned with fire . . . If the LORD of hosts had not left us a few survivors, we should have been like Sodom, and become like Gomorrah (Isaiah 17:9). Apparently that is the situation in the year 701 BCE. The Assyrians have destroyed everything. Only the city of Jerusalem is left, which has yet escaped total destruction.

Next to the image of a total catastrophe, there is another point of comparison with Sodom and Gomorrah. In the next verse Isaiah addresses the rulers and their subjects. "Hear the word of the LORD, you rulers of Sodom! Give ear to the teachings of our God, you people of Gomorrah!" (Isa 1:10) This pair of cities also stands for the inhabitants. There is anarchy, the leaders and the people are corrupt. "Their partiality witnesses against them; they proclaim their sin like Sodom. They do not hide it. Woe to them! For they, have brought evil upon themselves." (Isa 3:9) In their corrupt ruling they are like Sodomites. Jeremiah too uses both meanings, "they commit adultery and walk in lies; they strengthen the hands of evildoers, so that no one turns from his wickedness; all of them have become like Sodom to me, and its inhabitants like Gomorrah." (Jer 23:14, 15) Later on he too will use the image of the cities being turned upside down. "As when Sodom and Gomorrah and their neighbor cities were overthrown, says the LORD, no man shall dwell there, no man shall sojourn in her." (Jer 49:18)

And the judgments on the Chaldeans is portrayed in a similar way, "As when God overthrew Sodom and Gomorrah and their neighbor cities, says the LORD." (Jer 50:40) The prophet Zephaniah adds, "Moab shall become like Sodom, and the Amorites like Gomorrah, a land possessed by nettles and salt pits, and a waste forever." (Zeph 2:9) In Lamentations we read, "For the chastisement of the daughter of my people has been greater than the punishment of Sodom, which was overthrown in a moment, no hand being laid on it." (Lam 4:6) In a somewhat strange application of this motif Jeremiah says when he curses the day of his birth and someone having to bring the good news of the birth to his father, "Cursed be the man who brought the news to my father, a son is born to you, making him very glad. Let that man be like the cities which the LORD overthrew without pity." (Jer 20:15, 16)

Once we have this witness and imagery about Sodom and Gomorrah before us, a text from Deuteronomy, an earlier writing, catches our attention. When Israel is thrown out of the country, and vomited out,

> the whole land brimstone and salt, and a burnt-out waste, unsown, and growing nothing, where no grass can sprout, an overthrow like that of Sodom and Gomorrah, Admah and Zebuiim, which the LORD overthrew in his anger and wrath – yea all the nations would say, 'Why has the LORD done thus to this land?'"
> Deuteronomy 29:23, 24

The author of Deuteronomy knows the tradition of Sodom and Gomorrah and those of the two other cities who faced a similar judgment. The other two cities can even be mentioned by themselves, "How can I give you up, O Ephraim! How can I hand you over, O Israel! How can I make you like Admah! How can I treat you like Zeboiim! (Hos 11:8)

Instead the Lord's heart is turned upside down; it continues with, "My heart recoils within me, my compassion grows warm and tender." Instead of a catastrophe of the turning upside down of cities, God's heart is turned upside down. Nothing is said in all these passages about Lot who escaped the judgment and nothing about the sexual threat to the two messengers. These sins are missing in the catalogue of sins against Sodom and Gomorrah, according to the prophets.

Ezekiel lists the following sins, "Behold, this was the guilt of your sister Sodom: she and her daughters had pride, surfeit of food, and prosperous ease, but did not aid the poor and needy. They were haughty, and did abominable sins before me; therefore I removed them, when I saw it." (Ezekiel 16:49, 50) According to one commentator these accusations are surprising given the story of Genesis 19. It is assumed that this tradition about Sodom and Gomorrah was well known and were applied in different situations. Assume further that the text of Genesis is not older but younger than most of the prophets. Could not the author of Genesis have applied this well-known tradition in his own special way? It is only a small part of Genesis 19 that corresponds to the previous materials.

> Then the LORD rained on Sodom and Gomorrah brimstone and fire from the LORD out of heaven; and he overthrew those cities, and all the valleys, all the inhabitants of the cities, and what grew on the ground.
> Genesis 19:24, 25

Most important is how the author wove this story into the whole of the Abraham cycle, we read that after Lot has chosen to live around Sodom, "And Lot lifted up his eyes, and saw the Jordan valley was well watered everywhere like the garden of the Lord, like the land of Egypt, in the direction of Zoar; this was before the Lord destroyed Sodom and Gomorrah... Now the men of Sodom were wicked, great sinners against the Lord." (Gen 13:10, 13) It is an ominous warning. This sinfulness comes out in Genesis 19 as the total lack of hospitality, which was the highest virtue in the Near East. The erotic lust by all, both young and old is a caricature, boys and old men, all consumed by lust. This is not a moral condemnation about sexual behavior. It is a symbol of their total attitude, a catalogue or summary of their wickedness. It gets a function in this story against the threatened messengers who have to defend themselves against the mob. They struck them with blindness so they could not find the door, even though they kept groping for it. Both 'small and great' is repeated.

The storyteller lets us know where Sodom and Gomorrah are located, in the Valley of Siddim, which cannot be found on the map, because the Valley of Siddim (that is the Salt Sea), that is the Dead Sea, did not exist yet at that time. "And all these joined forces in the valley of Siddim (that is the Salt Sea)" (Gen 14:3). In this story of chapter 14, the kings of Sodom and Gomorrah, of Admah and of Zeboiim and others are all gathered together to fight in the valley of Siddim to subdue the surrounding peoples.

The LORD had decided to let Abraham know of his plans to destroy Sodom and Gomorrah after he had visited with him. "Because the outcry against Sodom and Gomorrah is great and their sin is very grave." (Gen 18:20)

Abraham pleaded with the LORD to save the life of Lot and his family. "Far be that from thee! Shall not the Judge of all the earth do right?" Gen 18:25. In a daring dialogue he bargains with God. If there are only fifty, forty, thirty, twenty, and finally, "if there are only ten righteous people, will you destroy the cities?" The LORD answered, "For the sake of ten I will not destroy it." And the LORD went his way.

"And Abraham went early in the morning to the place where he had stood before the LORD; and he looked down toward Sodom and Gomorrah and toward all the land of the valley, and beheld, and lo, the smoke of the land went up like the smoke of a furnace... God remembered Abraham and sent Lot out of the midst of the overthrow, when he overthrew the cities in which Lot dwelled." (Gen 19:27–29) It reminds us of Gen 8:1, after the great flood, "But God remembered Noah and all the beasts and all the cattle that were with him in the ark." The story continues.

The story of the destruction of Sodom and Gomorrah follows directly upon Abraham entertaining three guests that passed by his tents. He immediately invited them to stay, wash their feet, and rest themselves under a tree, "while I fetch a morsel of bread" Gen 18:5. Then Sarah and the servants prepared a sumptuous meal: cakes, a calf, tender and good, curds and milk. He offered the height of hospitality. Lot does likewise when the two messengers appear in the city, "spend the night and wash your feet . . . and he made them a feast, and baked unleavened bread, and they ate." (Gen 19:2, 3) In Judges 19:16–26 we find a terrible 'anti-story' of hospitality. "And he went in and set down in the open square of the city; for no one took them into his house to spend the night." (Gen 19:15) No one cared, except for an old man, even though he could not prevent the abuse of his guest's concubine. (Gen 19:15, 20) As it says repeatedly, in those days when there was no king in Israel, everyone did what seemed right in their own eyes. (Gen 19:1, 21:25)

CHAPTER 6

Re-reading Genesis

*through Genesis all of the Old Testament
and the New Testament*

6:1 'Introduction' to Genesis: general perspective

'INTRODUCTIONS' TO ANY PARTICULAR Bible book usually deal with questions of origin, date, authorship, different editions (redactions), difficult texts, time described and the time of the author, and the main divisions. Both Breukelman and Deurloo have written extensively about the book of Genesis. This re-reading of Genesis closely follows their exposition. Primarily my intention is to trace how Deurloo, (together with Bouhuijs, his co-author in many of his booklets and television programs) interprets each part of Genesis as 'prophetic literature' or 'narrative proclamation' as it is given in the texts and makes that the priority of their exposition. Their aim was to bring the scriptures as near to ordinary hearers and readers as possible. They would do so by a close reading of the text, highlighting inter-textual references, key words, recurring themes, and so on. All was in an attempt to have people hear the living Word of God again.

This introduction became quite long, since the book of Genesis has a long history of interpretation from a literalistic, fundamentalist approach to liberal, critical interpretations. It requires a different introduction that sets the stage for the actual account of Genesis in contrast to traditional interpretations and commentaries.

Consulting many commentaries on Genesis, Joshua, and Judges, I was seldom edified. See the overview of commentaries and studies of

Genesis in *Cahier 27* (2012); "The book Genesis in recent research," ("*Het boek Genesis in recent onderzoek*," by W. Hilbrands.), which provides an elaborate and scholarly overview. Either the historical questions of the (assumed) different traditions of the origin of the text dominates the exegesis, or the exegetical analysis stopped halfway, leaving the 'application' or 'theological' meaning' to pastors and priests to decipher. On any specific exegetical issue there is seldom a consensus. Many different hypotheses dominate the exegesis. The same could be said of the summaries of recent research of Joshua, Numbers, Deuteronomy, Jonah, and Hosea. Although helpful in developing an alternative interpretation of these Bible books, pastors and priests would have been helped more by summaries of the prophetic vision and themes of each book. The state of recent research does not exactly motivate a person to rush to a theological library, on the contrary, they prompt one to look elsewhere for helpful materials.

Generally these overviews to the different Bible books illustrate significant limitations or 'poverty' of exegetical studies, even though each one may provide some valuable insights. They are helpful in as much as they provide an overview of the literature and the history of interpretation. For any pastor it would take a lot of time to sort out these exegetical issues and controversies. Since exegesis has become a highly specialized academic enterprise, ministers are more and more dependent on overviews and non-academic studies. We can appreciate the studies by the Amsterdam tradition that sort out various hypotheses that have been suggested and provide alternative interpretations as we saw in chapter 5 in the examples provided by Deurloo.

Deurloo, together with Hemelsoet, in their *Over Hills and through Valleys; biblical geography; the place where it is written*, (1988) highlights some major themes about time and space. The opening sections are not so much about specific locations or place names, but about key words or themes that characterize the scriptures as a whole. They are like basic pre-understandings or 'word horizons'. When Deurloo makes a point, he does so by referring to many scripture passages that together form basic themes that guide us every time we read about times, days, years, places, spaces, and the land.

Geographical references and names are prophetic references. When the scriptures speak in terms of these spatial images in stories and poetry Deurloo inspires us to ask ourselves when the scriptures make reference to a spatial image, or a geographical reference, a specific time and place, or a name of a person, to ask ourselves what prophetic meaning these references may have. After the initial chapter he goes through the scriptures step by step highlighting geographical references and their distinct prophetic meaning in the total context of the passage and the rest of the scriptures. We will comment on these references as we come across them in the rest of the book.

It is in this context of the 'secularization' of all of life and its 'disenchantment', the 'colonization' or 'commercialization' of our language, that we are called to sound out the words of scripture as the living Word of God. Let us see what that may sound like from the books of Genesis and Joshua. The following introductory comments serve as such a thematic horizon for the study of Genesis. For Deurloo too, Genesis, including the creation stories, must be understood from out of the redemption of Jesus Christ and not as a separate topic or doctrine, which explains the titles of his other two booklets about Genesis in *The beginning in our midst; aspects of Biblical creation-faith*, (1972) and *Creation from Paul to Genesis; small Biblical theology*, (2008). Both books are Christ centered. They start from the Christ-event looking back to the beginning. It is only from out of redemption that we can understand the creation accounts. One of his articles summarizes Breukelman's study of Genesis: "The Simplicity of Genesis" ("De eenvoud van Genesis," *Interpretatie* Januari 1993). Inspired by Breukelman and Deurloo, at least fifty articles and booklets have been published about Genesis by them and many of their followers. *(Genesis, Cahier 27,* 2012). This view of Genesis is characteristic of the Amsterdam school. It led, as we will see, to a very different view of creation, providence, God's presence, the image of God, humankind, (original) sin, (substitutionary) atonement, and the nature of Biblical Theology.

If Breukelman's and Deurloo's interpretation of Genesis 1–11 and his followers is correct, as I believe it is, that God's creating is an inseparable part of the stories of the patriarchs, then his creating a safe and good place for humans to live before his presence has radical implications for our faith. It means that from the very beginning God wanted a people for his very own companionship, to walk and talk with in the cool of the evening in the Garden of Eden. Even when humans turned their backs to him again and again, he remained true to his intention by restoring his relationship. God continues to be with us even through judgment and death and even by taking on our human form through his

Son. All of the scriptures from the beginning are about God's love affair with humankind.

Genesis is a book of narratives with a 'theological' message written for the faith community. It is literary and 'theological' in orientation. It narrates the story of God who created the world as a good and safe place to live on the earth under the heavens for the people he chose and through them for all humanity. In the telling it elucidates who this God is. Genesis shifts our attention away from any questions about the origin of the world and relates everything to God and Israel and humanity. The first chapter culminates in the crown of creation, the creation from the earth of the 'earthling', Adam,

Many may have listened to an animated storyteller, at a campfire or in school, or even a puppet show as I did on the market once a week following the antics of Jan Klaassen and Katrijn (that was before the Saturday morning television cartoons for children). All the children sitting on the cobblestones would shout to warn them that something dangerous was about to happen or would loudly comment on the events. The suspense was intense and the outcome a sigh of relief. I also vividly remember the stories our fourth grade teacher told about the reformation, about people gathering illegally in the dark of the evening to read the scriptures and worship, all the while in fear of informers and the police. We would sit at the edge of our seats, living the experiences.

Following the storyteller of Genesis closely, Deurloo trusts we can live into the events as if we were there to make them our own.

> You've gone to the theatre. You've taken your place and you're waiting for the great moment when the lights go out, the voices become silent and the curtains rise. It can happen, as we are listening that we become one with the figures in the story and experience the events with them, like a play. Can we listen to the scriptures in this manner as co-participants, co-actors?[1]

Genesis 1-11 is not the story of the creation of the world and the early beginnings of humankind. It is not about how everything came into being. It is not about the how, the where and when, or what was before, but about the fact that Yahweh created the heavens and the earth for a purpose: that is, to have communion with humankind and to create a safe and good place for them to live in his presence. All of Genesis 1 finds its culmination in the creation of humanity. It is not a mythological

---

1. Deurloo, *Closer to Genesis*, 9.

account, but Israel's reflection on the past in narrative form and in narrative time.

"In the beginning God created the heavens and the earth." (Gen 1:1) Right from the first verse of the scriptures we hear this astounding confession of faith. It is not a scientific statement but a prophetic or confessional statement. It can be compared to a 'birth announcement', "God gave us a baby girl," (Olthuis), which tells us about a true historical event. But it says nothing about the fact that the parents had sexual intercourse nine months before when the wife was fertile and could conceive, or whether they had been struggling a long time to become pregnant. It says nothing about where the birth took place and how mother and baby are doing. It only tells us about the most important thing that happened. God blessed the couple with a baby girl. On their part, the announcement is a confession of their faith. It certainly tells us that it happened, that it is real, a 'historical event', to be celebrated with thanksgiving. In this manner we might conceive of Genesis 1 as a birth announcement. It may not satisfy our curiosity about the origin of the universe and how it all came about, but it does relate the most important thing to us. To study how, when, and where, we have to consult the scientific theories. These are continually updated and revised many by Christian scientists.

This confession keeps us from asking a host of other questions. As a confession of faith it prevents us from absolutizing the forces of nature, as independent powers, like the oceans, storms, fertility, political powers, or any other aspect of creation. Right from the start, all of creation is 'demythologized', in view of the 'nature religions' of the time. All creatures are creatures of the LORD. Creation does not exist independently. They depend on the LORD for their existence. This confession also prevents us from seeing 'the laws of nature' as independent forces that function by themselves. There are no 'natural laws' that need to be broken through in crucial circumstances, in a supernatural way like the miracles in the scripture. They are all God's laws that he upholds and uses for his purposes. This too is a liberating perspective for anyone who struggles with or doubts the many miracles told in the Bible, culminating in the resurrection of the LORD.

Genesis 1 does provide a fundamental perspective for scientists and engineers that accept the confession of Genesis 1. The regularities of creation can be abstracted and investigated independently. However, at some point the results of scientific experimentation and research need to be reintegrated in our total 'scientific' understanding of the world and 'natural' history. Along the way, there are many 'ethical questions' that need to be faced about the use of our scientific or technical insights and results, whether they serve 'the enhancement of all of life', or its 'destruction'.

Given this perspective on Genesis as confession and poetry, there is no basis in Genesis 1 and 2 for big debates about evolutionism versus creationism, about whether each day is to be interpreted as long periods of time, maybe millions of years, or that God made use of the evolutionary process to create all species excluding humans. Such views are based on the idea that Genesis 1 and 2 provide us with a mythological or scientific or historical account of the creation of the universe. Likewise other creation myths of those times cannot be explained by the 'scientific' views of ancient times. Nor is Genesis 1–11 a primal history of the origin of nations.

All such questions are based on the assumption that Genesis 1–11 is separated from the rest of Genesis, which is a widely held theory. According to this view, the general primal world history comes first (1–11) and then the history of the patriarchs (12–50). This view is based on the presuppositions of the critical historical method and source analysis that Genesis 1–11 has a different origin. The texts of Genesis themselves give no basis for such a view. Genesis forms a unified whole.

This prophetic confession motivates us to join hands with all those who relate to all creatures, both big and small, and all lands and seas with care and respect. We are to hold hands, especially with many aboriginal peoples that still live in harmony with creation and have a respectful attitude to all creatures.   Those of us brought up with a colonial, scientistic attitude, have a lot to learn from our aboriginal brothers and sisters. As I detail in chapter 10, we need to learn from the critiques and contributions of all other religions. (Also see: "The radical witness of the religions to the neoliberal ideology; a.The Christian religious critique of neoliberal economic policies; b. The work and witness of the world religions; faith-based organizations," pp. 266–73) in my, *The Gods in Whom They Trusted; the Disintegrative Effects of Capitalism; the Foundation for Transitioning to a New Social World* (2016) which is freely available on line.

Genesis narrates the story of the beginnings of God's acts on behalf of his chosen people, Israel. It is not just an archaic tale or myth about an ancient people. It is about Israel's place in the world that God created, namely that Israel is the first-born among the nations for the benefit of all peoples. The story of the other nations is interwoven with that of

Israel (the table of the nations in Gen 5 and 10). The primary question is who will be the 'firstling' (not necessarily the first-born) among the nations, who carries the blessing of the first-born? Via Noah, Shem, Terah, Abraham, Isaac, and Jacob it ends with the twelve tribes of Israel, Joseph (Ephraim and Manasse (the Northern and Southern kingdoms), in Egypt, with Judah emerging as the primary heir.

Genesis is written as a narrative. Through its many stories it proclaims a prophetic message. It is a book of 'generations', or rather of 'generating' or becoming. It looks forward to what is to come and not only backward. The focus is not on any strictly historical questions but on the message and its meaning. Genesis was written by and for the faith community, for the synagogue but also for Christians for whom these stories are the foundation of the New Testament. It 'only' tells us the most important fact that Yahweh created the heavens and the earth for humankind; it says nothing about the how, or the when. In story form, it is confessional history, or history that proclaims and that invites to confess and to celebrate as so many Psalms do when reciting the creation of the earth, like Psalm 104–106.

The New Testament starts with: "The book of the genealogy of Jesus Christ, the son of David, the son of Abraham. Abraham was the father of Isaac, and Isaac the father of Jacob..." (Matt 1:1) and so on. These words echo the headings of Genesis, "These are the generations of..." Throughout the New Testament there are constant references to the Hebrew Scriptures. Mark starts his gospel with, "The beginning of the gospel of Jesus Christ, the son of God. As it is written in Isaiah the prophet, "As it is written in Isaiah the prophet, 'Behold, I sent my messenger before thy face...'" (Mark 1:2) Without these narratives it is impossible to understand the New Testament.

From the New Testament perspective all of the Old Testament could be summarized by "Moses and the prophets." As Jesus said to the rich man who pleaded with Jesus to send a warning to his five brothers of the coming judgment; Jesus responded with, "They have Moses and the prophets; let them hear them," and, "if they do not hear Moses and the prophets, neither will they be convinced if someone should rise from the dead." (Luke 16:19–31) On the way to Emmaus, Luke narrates, "And beginning with Moses and all the prophets, he (Jesus) interpreted to them in all the scriptures the things concerning himself." (Luke 24:27) In Luke 16:44, Jesus adds, "These are my words which I spoke to you, while I was still with you, that everything written about me in the law of Moses and the prophets and the psalms must be fulfilled."

A close reading of the scriptures reveals the depth of Genesis 1 and 2. It is the story of God who created the earth to provide a good home for the people he chose, and through them, for all humanity. They are not an account of the origin of the world in itself. Genesis is very carefully constructed. It is not only the first book in the Bible, but it sets the stage for all of the Old Testament and New Testament.

The accounts of the patriarchs end with Joseph in Egypt. This set the stage for the exodus, the liberation from slavery in Egypt, through the waters of death (The Red Sea), to the Promised Land, across the waters of the Jordan. Canaan was 'conquered' by Joshua, followed by a period of decline. Judges ends with, "in those days there was no king in Israel. All the people did what was right in their own eyes." (Judg 21:25). The people called for a king. So Samuel anointed first Saul and then David as king. (1, 2 Samuel). The stories of the decline of the kings end with the Exile to Babylon. (1, 2 Kings and Chronicles). After 40 years, a remnant returned to the Promised Land (Ezra and Nehemiah).

At each stage of their journey and experiences with Yahweh, the four major prophets, (Isaiah, Jeremiah, Ezekiel and Daniel) and the twelve minor prophets called them to repentance and pronounced judgment on them along with the promise of liberation and forgiveness if they repented and changed their ways. In principle, Genesis contains all of the scriptures, just as Mathew contains all of the New Testament.

It starts with "In the beginning..." now something is about to happen: an event that takes place in a specific time and a specific place. The Bible tells a history; the story has a plot, a beginning middle, and an end. It is a story between concrete figures. The main characters are God and humans. Not God in a general generic sense because he does not exist as a general god and not humanity in general as we know them, because according to the Bible that is not the human he intended in his covenant call to love and justice.. It is about the LORD, the God of Israel and Israel the people of God. These are the two main figures of the story that follows.

To understand the particularity of this story, we need to understand the "pars pro toto" (a literary figure: a part that stands for or is representative of the whole) character of the scriptures. Applied to Israel, these people stand pars pro toto for all of humanity, and the land stands for all the earth. Looked at historically it is just a miniscule nation in the midst of the great empires of the world at that time. And this land, looked at geographically is just a dot on the world map. It stands pars pro toto for the whole earth. In this way the particular story of the God of Israel with his people, represents world history. The particular is universal and the universal is represented by the particular. It becomes our story. At the end of chapter 7 in the Excursion, I have detailed the change from the particular (the Jewish people) to the universal (the gentiles).

And we, as non-Jews are invited to participate in this history. Only in this way does it make sense to listen to and live according to the scriptures. Whoever does not belong to the people of Israel (as most of us reading this are not children of Abraham, Isaac and Jacob) is a 'gentile' (goyim), but as 'gentiles' we are called to join in and identify with this history. Where does this history take place? In and around the land of Canaan, it occurs between about fifteen hundred years before Christ and 100 years after Christ.

This does not mean we are called to identify with the present Israeli government and military and the West Bank radical orthodox nationalists with their land claims. On the contrary, we can only witness against and oppose such destructive policies and practices that are resulting in the genocide of an entire people, the Palestinians. We can only mourn and repent from our complicity and that of our governments in this genocide that will haunt Israelis for decades to come. For a more elaborate account see the Excursion, chapter7 (after Joshua), "Israel and Palestine." Both peoples, the Israelis and the Palestinians have a right to a safe homeland where they can live in peace.

We become involved in this story not because we are so good at living into a situation and are able to identify ourselves with it, but because the LORD, the God of Israel lives himself into our human situation. He, from his side, pulls us into this story of liberation and fulfillment. Let us listen to this God who in the beginning is not just there but is busy creating. In the two creation accounts the human stands central. He is the partner in this history. He has a context, the stage for the narratives. Therefore the story has to start with the context, the earth.

In the account of Genesis 1–11, I have followed closely, verse by verse, Deurloo's earlier exposition from 1967. His earlier work and articles catch more of the flow of the Hebrew text and are more personal, pastoral and warm in tone. His later book on Genesis (2004, together with Kessler) has more of a teaching focus with summaries and overviews. I have benefited from this latest version as well as his many articles. Many stories may seem (overly) familiar to us, but the surprise is in the details, inter-textual connections, key words and themes that give new meaning to the stories and most importantly the prophetic message.

One way to 'use' these stories of Genesis in a Bible study group, for example, is to read the Scripture story out loud, perhaps from different translations, read the explanation, and open it up for discussion and hear how different people respond to each story, all the while following the narration closely and looking up the many references and its place in the whole of the scriptures by using a concordance. This summary of the stories can serve as an initial indication of the prophetic message and as a guideline for discussion. The title for this section could be, "Reading Genesis for the first time, again." It is not a commentary, but a summary of the prophetic message that leads to worship.

The stories need to be sounded out in the context of worship and resonate in song and prayer. In relation to this it is exhilarating to read how Deurloo would write songs and music for the children's services in Amsterdam with the help of poets and musicians, which the adults would sing along in followup to the scriptural story. (See the conquest of Jericho in chapter 7).

All the while we will remember, the prophetic witness of Genesis comes in storied form, keeping in mind Palache's account of narratives. Narratives that have a literary form (plot, characters, etc.) take place in narrative places (geography and characteristics) and narrative time. "Now it happened when . . ." We get some sense of that when we watch the campfire of some aboriginal peoples after the hunt (perhaps of several days) when the storytellers start to tell of the hunt with great exuberance and excitement. Everyone is spellbound, clapping their hands and shouting in approval. Of course, the hunt happened, but not exactly the way it is described (like "by the bend in the river by the great tree on the third day of the hunt . . .") all to heighten the tension of the story. The geographical details may be different and the details of the account may vary. Imaginative places and imaginative times may be hard for us to envision if all we know is chronological, physical and factual, historical time. 'Imagined time' is not untrue or fabricated. They are not fairy tales. The narrators used this form of writing to convey the prophetic message. The story is the message. So we will read closely and carefully to catch the message and the meaning.

6:2 Breukelman and Deurloo's interpretation of Genesis

Both, Breukelman and Deurloo, as well as many of their followers pay a lot of attention to historical research by other commentators and Biblical theologians, even when they reject their basic pre-suppositions that violate the textual givens and become speculative. The only one I found that followed a different approach was Talstra's account of different passages in his *Old and New Readers*, 2002. At each point where the more technical (linguistic, literary, historical) exposition was completed, he would indicate that he had reached the end of his exegetical work where we are left with the prophetic word of God that makes a personal appeal and speaks to all people. Then he asks if we can identify ourselves with ancient Israel and the church of all ages today in our situation.[2]

Such a view and appeal to our participation only makes sense in a 'reenchanted' world (over against a one-dimensional, impoverished view of reality as pure physicality, history as pure factuality, and causation). In a one-dimensional view there is no room for God, faith or religion, as Talstra himself indicates. In contrast, in an integrated view, God's word indeed speaks to all of life and all people in their total life situation.

Breukelman too has written extensively about the book of Genesis. Although Breukelman's detailed study was not published until 1992, throughout his academic career he focused primarily on Genesis and his other major interest, the gospel of Matthew, which, in his mind served as the introduction to the whole of the New Testament. These two interests kept him preoccupied until his retirement. The results of his decades' long study and lecturing were circulated by him in stencil form, which were revised repeatedly. He was never quite satisfied. He loved teaching but remained reluctant to publish. Under the urging of colleagues he finally agreed to the publication of his insights. The book was entitled, *Biblical Theology; The Theology of the book of Genesis; Israel, the first one ('firstling') among the nations; in the midst of the peoples of the earth as the theme of the generations of Adam, the human;* (1992), Volume I, 2, Together with his extensive and detailed study of Mathew it became his life's work.

Breukelman starts his study of Genesis with the following heading, "The book Genesis as the book of the generations of Adam, the human; about the becoming of Israel in the midst of the peoples of the earth. An analysis of the composition of the book" *(Volume 1, 2, p.11)*.

---

2. Talstra, *Oude en Nieuwe Lezers*, 117–204; 193–198; 301–309.

He considered Genesis a grand composition, revealing the secret of Israel's beginning, its origin, in story form. He called it the overture to the whole of the Hebrew Scriptures. Each part can only be understood in light of the whole of Genesis and vice versa. The structure as a whole explains how the various themes are developed and the place and function they have in the whole. From his close reading he concluded that Genesis must be understood as a fundamental unity. Even the first eleven chapters, which are usually considered to have a separate origin and theme (the primal history of the becoming of the nations of the world), he considered to be an inseparable part of the story of the patriarchs. The 'toledot' (the generations or becoming of) structure (10 times) of Genesis emphasizes this unity even more as well as the many key words and motifs that unify the separate stories.

Deurloo followed In Breukelman's footsteps. Already in 1967 he wrote about *Genesis, Closer to Genesis, (Dichter bij Genesis)* together with his co-author Bouhuijs. The booklet was the result of a popular T.V. series called, *Closer to the prophets; Closer to Paul.* and many other booklets. *Closer to Genesis* went through many editions, (sixth edition in 1985). Together with his colleague, Zuurmond, (1991) he wrote another booklet about Genesis. It was called, *The days of Noah; the stories around the flood in scripture and oldest tradition.* Before that he had written his doctoral thesis, (1967) *Cain and Abel,* under his promoter M.A. Beek. Finally, in his book *The Human as Riddle and Secret; biblical anthropology in story form, in Genesis 2-4,* (1988), he presents a very detailed and inspiring exegesis, verse by verse and line by line, of this small segment of Genesis 2-4, which is incorporated in the re-reading of Genesis. It could also have served as the fifth volume of his biblical theological studies.

Together with Martin Kessler he published a more extensive commentary in English, *A commentary on Genesis: the book of beginnings.* (2004).These studies were summarized in his biblical theology series, K. Deurloo, *Small Biblical Theology: Exodus and Exile (2003); Temple and King (2004); Our beloved mother gives birth to a son (2006); Creation from Paul to Genesis 2008);* Throughout his career he published many articles (at least 13) about Genesis in the Cahier series of the Amsterdam school of exegesis and biblical theology. In honor of Deurloo's 60th birthday (1995) *Still Closer to Genesis,* was published with over 28 contributions from different scholars.

His biblical theological studies provide the hermeneutic or thematic horizon (perspective) for individual studies, which, in turn, enrich and correct the thematic understanding and structural unity of the texts. They are like 'word horizons', or word vistas. The many separate articles by Deurloo in the Cahiers on Genesis serve as detailed, exegetical studies, usually in conversation or in contrast to many leading interpreters of Genesis. They serve as a validation or elaboration of his earlier booklet, *Closer to Genesis*, (1967) See *Cahiers*, 1, 2, 5, 6, 7, 8, 9, 10, 11, 14; and sections in most of his other booklets. There are also two volumes of children's stories and songs about Genesis.

6:3 Genesis 1:1–2:3 *The creation of the earth: a good home for humanity*

"In the beginning . . ." serves as a superscription of what is to follow, like in John 1:1 "In the beginning was the Word, and the Word was with God and the Word was God. He was in the beginning with God; all things were made through him, and without him was not anything made that was made. In him was life, and the life was the light of man. The light shines in the darkness, and the darkness has not overcome it." The heading of verse Gen 2:4, "These are the generations of the heavens and the earth when they were created." is a subscription for the entire section. Gen 5:1 "This is the book of the generations of Adam" starts a new section.

There are two creation stories at the beginning of the Bible. (Gen 1:1–2:4 and Gen 2:4–2:24). In both stories the creation of the 'earthling', the human, stands central. He is the partner in this history of Yahweh, the God of Israel. The human needs a context, a setting. That is why we have a creation story of the earth on which the human lives. You can work your way from the context to the central figure. That's what happens in the first creation story. After the creation of everything else the story culminates in the creation of the earthling. It can also be told by starting with the creation of humans and in the process tell of their context. That is the approach of the second creation story.

The creation stories are 'young' stories. Most likely they were composed around the sixth century before Christ or later, during the exile. By that time the God of Israel and his people already had a long history behind them: the patriarchs, slavery in Egypt, the Exodus, the long journey through the desert, the gift of the Torah, the entry into the Promised Land, the period of the judges and kings, ending in the Exile. All this had happened before the creation stories were written. Then they had time to pause and reflect. Besides despair and anguish there was also time for reflection upon their past and for wonder and praise. Genesis 1 and 2 can be seen as a confession and a song of praise. It also served as a great overture to what was to come between this God of Israel and his people and through them with all humanity.

The word 'create' appears 6 times in this first section (Gen 1:1–2:4):

> In the beginning God created...
> Genesis 1:1.

> Then created God the great sea monsters
> Genesis 1:21.

> So God created man in his own image, in the image of God he created him;
> male and female he created them.
> Genesis 1:27

> And God blessed the seventh day and hallowed it,
> because on it God rested from all his work which he had done in creating.
> Genesis 2:3

Between the words 'create' at the beginning and end, the story takes place. They form the frame around what the narrators want to tell, the creation of heaven and earth. The threefold repetition of the word 'create' in verse 27 emphasizes the focus of the story, the creation of the human. "So God created man in his own image, in the image of God he created him; male and female he created them." The creation of heaven and earth is for the sake of humans.

In Gen 1:2 the "earth" comes first, for the earth is the future home of humanity. It is the first subject and is described as a jumble or chaos (tobu wa-bohu), and as darkness over the (mythical) deep. It prepares us for the significance of the creation of light 'In the beginning' he prepared a habitable place to live.

The earth ('erets') means both the land of Canaan and the whole earth. The part stands for the whole, pars pro toto. "The earth was without form and void and darkness was upon the face of the deep." Void and empty is like a primal cry of anguish. Like a desert where there is no water, no roads, no settlements, only emptiness and darkness. It is threatening and chaotic. This is the worst that can happen. When the prophet Jeremiah has to pronounce judgment, he uses the same words:

THE PROPHETIC CALL TO LOVE AND JUSTICE

> I looked on the earth, and lo, it was waste and void; and to the
> heavens, and they had no light.
> ... I looked, and lo, there was no man, and all the birds of the
> air had fled.
> I looked, and lo, the fruitful land was a desert,
> and all its cities were laid in ruins before the Lord, before his
> fierce anger.
> For thus says the Lord, 'The whole land shall be a desolation; yet
> I will not make a full end.
> For this the earth shall mourn, and the heavens above be black'
> ...
>
> Jeremiah 4:23–28.

The same words are used here, void and empty, primal chaos and darkness upon the face of the deep. It is an unbearable reality in which human life is impossible. There is nowhere to hide or to go. But, the Spirit of God was moving over the face of the deep, over the primal waters. That is the first signal, the Spirit of God moving over the waters. Could this void ever become a habitat for humanity? It is the first signal that in the midst of this uninhabitable situation there is a promising future for humanity. In Deuteronomy 32:11 that word 'moving over' is used to describe the eagle hovering over its nest, ready to bear up any of its young in case they falter.

> Like an eagle that stirs up its nest, that flutters over its young,
> spreading out its wings, catching them, bearing them on its
> pinions...
> Deuteronomy 32:11

That is how the Spirit of God hovers over the void and the primal darkness. This text is full of promise about what is to come. "By the word of the Lord the heavens were made and all their hosts. (Psalm 33:6). The spirit, the breath of God, was already present. He was preparing to speak. God's spirit or breath is in contrast to the darkness and changes the (threatening, primordial) deep to waters. 'And the Spirit of God was moving over the waters' Gen 1:2, as if they are already demythologized. It sets the stage for what is coming.

> And God said, 'let there be light', and there was light. And God
> saw that the light was good; and God separated the light from
> the darkness. God called the light Day, and the darkness he
> called Night. And there was evening and there was morning,
> one day.
> Genesis 1:3–5

That is how the spirit of God hovers over creation. Then, God speaks and commands. That is what makes everyone sit up and take note. It is an astounding declaration.

> I form light and create darkness,
> I make weal and create woe,
> I am the Lord, who does all these things...
> I made the earth, and created man upon it;
> it was my hands that stretched out the heavens....
> All of them are put to shame and confounded,
> the makers of idols go in confusion together,
> but Israel is saved by the LORD with everlasting salvation;
> you shall not be put to shame or confounded to all eternity
> For thus says the LORD, who created the heavens (he is god),
> who formed the earth and made it
> (he established it; he did not create it a chaos, he formed it to
>   be inhabited!)
> I am the LORD, and there is no other...
> Assemble yourselves and come ...
> you survivors of the nations!
> They have no knowledge who carry about their wooden idols,
> and keep praying to a god that cannot save.
>   Isaiah 45:7–20. (cf. Isa 44:9–20 and 57:13; Jer 10:11–15)

The darkness and the waters remain as a threat to humanity. Darkness means death like in Psalm 88:6 "Thou hast put me in the depths of the Pit, in the regions dark and deep." And the waters are a threat to life, "They surround me like a flood all day long; they close in upon me together." (Ps 88:17). Both chaotic powers are pushed back by God's speaking. In the midst of the silence of the gods, God commanded and it was. It is a command, "light become," and the light became. There was light all around. And God saw the light that it was good. First God separated the light from the darkness and called out its name and said your task is to be the Day and to the darkness, your task is to be the Night and together, the Sun, Moon and the Stars are to be the timekeepers to mark the seasons and the days of our life.

God gives them their place. "Thine is the day, thine also the night; thou hast established the luminaries and the sun. Thou hast fixed all the bounds of the earth; thou hast made summer and winter." (Ps 74:16–17). The night must always give way to the daylight, each morning again. The threat of the darkness will finally be totally undone. In the New Jerusalem there will be no temple,

> ... For its temple is the Lord God Almighty and the Lamb. And the city has no need of sun or moon to shine upon it, for the glory of God is its light, and its lamp is the Lamb ... Then he showed me the river of the water of life ...
> Revelations 21:22 and 22:1

"Let there be light; and there was light ..." One can only imagine what those words must have sounded like to the exiled people in Babylon. God speaks and it happens. It is a confession (as in Isaiah and Jeremiah) and hymns of praise are the response, like Ps 104 and Ps 148,

> Bless the LORD, O my soul!
> O LORD my God, thou art very great!
> Thou art clothed with honor and majesty,
> who coverest thyself with light as with a garment,
> who has stretched out the heavens like a tent,
> who hast laid the beams of thy chambers on the waters,
> who makest the clouds thy chariot,
> who ridest on the wings of the wind,
> who makest the winds thy messengers,
> fire and flame thy ministers.
> Psalm 104:1–4 (cf.Ps 148:1–6)

And to us in the midst of environmental disintegration, how do we hear those words? The story continues,

> And God said, 'let there be a firmament in the midst of the waters, and let it separate the waters from the waters. And God made the firmament and separated the waters which were under the firmament from the waters which were above the firmament. And so it was ...
> And God called the firmament Heaven. And there was evening and there was morning, a second day.
> Genesis 1:6–8

Here the storyteller borrows and adapts the ancient worldview of a three layered universe with waters above and under the earth and a flat earth resting on pillars in the midst of the world's oceans. The writer uses the images of his day. With that image he does not want to tell us how the world is constructed. He wants to tell us something very different.

From that moment on, the dome has the task to be Heaven. God calls the dome or the firmament Heaven. Heaven is the boundary of our human experience, the boundary between God's abode and the earth.

The first day God called the light, Day. Now there is time for us, time to be his people. On the second day God called the firmament, Heaven. Now there is space in which we can breathe, because the chaos that threatens humankind from above is banned by the firmament. The Heavens are the divine guarantee that we can live on this earth. He has set a boundary to the chaos and the threatening waters.

Without this boundary of the firmament, the earth would be flooded as in the days of Noah. When "On that day all the fountains of the great deep burst forth and the windows of the heavens were opened." "But God remembered Noah and all the beasts and all the cattle that were with him in the ark . . ." (Gen 7:11) "and the fountains of the deep and the windows of the heavens were closed." (Genesis 8:2) Unless God maintains the boundary between heaven and the primal waters there will be chaos and darkness. The firmament guarantees that life can flourish upon the earth. It provides protection.

> And God said, 'Let the waters under the heavens be gathered together into one place, and let the dry land appear.' And it was so. God called the dry land Earth, and the waters that were gathered together he called Seas. And God saw that it was good. And God said, 'let the earth put forth vegetation, plants yielding seed, and fruit trees bearing fruit in which is their seed, each according to its kind upon the earth.' And it was so . . . And God saw that it was good. And there was evening and there was morning, a third day.
> Genesis 1:9–12, 13

After the third day we hear 'and there was evening and there was morning'. A new day starts in the evening after sun down for the Hebrews. And again we hear like after the first day 'it was good', which was missing after the second day, for there was still one separation to come, the threat of the primal seas.

Another separation happened, the dry land (Earth) was separated from the waters, (Seas), the dangerous waters. All through the scriptures the sea remains a symbol of a primal threat, until a boundary is set and the sea is no more.

> Then I saw a new heaven and a new earth; for the first heaven and the first earth had passed away, and the sea was no more. And I saw the holy city, New Jerusalem, coming down out of heaven from God, prepared as a bride adorned for her husband;

> Behold, the dwelling of God is with men. He will dwell with them, and they shall be his people, and God himself will be with them.
> Revelations 21:1–3

Now there is time to be God's creatures as he intended. There is space under the protection of the firmament. There is solid ground under our feet without the threat of the primal waters. What happens next, is directly related to the first, second and third day.

First day	light	Fourth day	sun, moon and stars
Second day	heaven, (waters under the heavens)	Fifth day	birds and fish
Third day	earth, dry land	Sixth day	the animals of the land and the human

Again a separation occurs. The day is separated from the night. The sun is called the greater light to rule the day and the moon to rule the night along with the stars to indicate the seasons and the days and years of our life. Neither the sun nor the moon are gods (as they were for the surrounding peoples; it is a 'protest' against all sun, moon and star worshippers). They are creatures of God that have their assigned place and name, Day and Night. All things exist for Yahweh and Israel, for God and his people. Heaven is only mentioned in relation to the earth. Heaven is hidden from us; we can only see the great dome above us. We live under the protection of God's Heavens. "The heavens are the LORD's heavens, but the earth he has given to the sons of men." (Ps 115:16)

God cares for all his creatures, including the stars, like a shepherd watching over his sheep, as they are drawn along the dome of Heaven; and not one goes missing.

> He determines the number of the stars,
> he gives to all of them their names.
> Great is the LORD and abundant in power;
> his understanding is beyond measure.
> Psalm 147:4, 5

> Lift up your eyes on high and see: who created these?
> He who brings out their host by number, calling them all by name;
> by the greatness of his might, and because he is strong in power not one is missing.
> Isaiah 40:26

As my mother used to sing in her falsetto voice:

Weet gij hoeveel sterren schitteren	Do you know how many stars are blinking
In het ruime hemelrond? . . .	in the outstretched heavens?. . .
Al die duizenden tezamen,	All those thousands together
Roept de Heer bij hunne namen.	The Lord calls by their names.
En niet een ontglipt zijn oog.	Not one escapes his eye.

It was one of the many Johannes de Heer's popular evangelical hymns that used to comfort her during the difficult pre-war depression, WWII years, and immigration as a displaced person, along with such songs as "Ga niet alleen door het leven. Laat een uw leidsman zijn." (Don't go through life alone. Let one be your guide) and "Daar ruist langs de wolken een liefelijke naam" (Amidst the clouds there echoes a lovely name), and others. They gave expression to her simple faith in her Savior and LORD. Unlike my father, who lived by K. Schilder's sermons, his former minister in Zuidland. These are the words and melodies I remember, and not my father's long and intense discussions with my uncles at birthday parties about election, baptism, the church and ministers. Not once did we have a discussion about the Bible passages he read at the table or a minister's sermon on Sunday. Yet I have dedicated this book to them in the trust that they would be edified and comforted by it as I am, even though he always seemed deeply disappointed in me and my mother had her intense moods and possessiveness.

In the day of fulfillment there will no longer be a need for the sun and moon. "The sun shall be no more your light by day, nor for brightness shall the moon give light to you by night; but the LORD will be your everlasting light, and your God will be your glory" (Isa 60:19). Until that day the sun and the moon and the stars will give light and make life possible on the earth. "The light shines in the darkness and the darkness did not overcome it." (John 1:5). Humans live under God's protection as God's partners.

On the fifth day, in correspondence with the second day, God brings life to the two danger zones, the heavens and the sea. Both regions begin to swarm with living creatures in great variety. There they are: birds and fishes. The word 'fishes' is not mentioned until verse 26. Instead we hear of God creating the great sea monsters and every living creature that moves, with which the waters swarm, according to their kinds . . ." But what about those powers of chaos? Here they are represented by the great sea monsters. The chaotic powers are there, the primal monsters of the sea, the Leviathan, they are also part of God's creation. To the surrounding people they represented unmanageable forces of chaos and evil. But He created them. They do God's bidding.

> Yonder is the sea, great and wide,
> which teems with things innumerable,
> living things both small and great.
> There go the ships,
> and Leviathan which thou didst form to sport in it.
> These all look to thee,
> to give them their food in due season...
> When thou sendeth forth thy Spirit,
> they are created;
> and thou renewest the face of the ground.
> Psalm 104:25–30 (cf. Job 41:1–34).

> In that day the LORD with his hard and great and strong sword
>   will punish
> Leviathan the fleeing serpent,
> Leviathan the twisting serpent,
> and he will slay the dragon that is in the sea.
> Isaiah 27:1 (cf. Isa 51:9–11)

The threatening forces of chaos and evil, they are not a counterforce over against God. He created them and they do his bidding. He sets their boundaries, until the sea monsters are no more and there is only "the water of life" (Rev 21:6; 22:17).

On the sixth day animals and humans are created. Humans and animals co-exist and are often mentioned together in the scriptures. They were created together and share the same food. "Let the earth bring forth living creatures according to their kinds. And God made the beasts of the earth according to their kinds, and the cattle according to their kinds and everything that creeps upon the ground according to their kind. And God saw that it was good." After this repetition, we expect 'according to their kinds'. Instead we read, "let us make man . . . in our image, after our likeness." (Gen 1:26)

The teller uses the plural, instead of a direct command like before, we hear, "Let us." It is as if God pauses for a moment to focus solely on the creation of the human. We hold our breath. The word "create" is used three times to emphasize that everything is concentrated on this special creature, the human. The plural reminds of a king like a 'royal we'.

With this act of creation everything concentrates on the creation of the human as the crown or fulfillment of everything that went before. The earth provides the setting or context for man's actions. "So God created man in his own image, in the image of God he created him, male and female he created them." (Gen 1:27). He is commanded to fill the earth and subdue it; and to have dominion, that is, to be God's caretaker or representative on earth; to rule as God rules. Some interpreters have said, that only holds for before the fall. After the fall humans (partially) lost that image. Yet, even after the fall, the narrator repeats "Whoever sheds the blood of man, by man shall his blood be shed; for God made man in his own image. (Gen 9:6) Humans are not to kill one another because they remain image bearers of God. They have a calling: to be caretakers and to look after the earth and all living creatures: the plants, the trees, the birds, the insects, the fishes and their co-humans.

In the beginning God created the heavens and the earth. What is the purpose? It is so that a common history may take place between God and humanity. God as the focal point of all that is in the heavens now concentrates on the focal point of all that is on the earth. What is the earthling's task? It is to be responsible for what is on earth. Just as God is responsible for what takes place in heaven. "The heavens are the LORD's heavens, but the earth he has given to the sons of man." (Ps 115:16) Or as the Lord's Prayer has it, "Thy will be done, on earth as it is in heaven." (Matt 6:10). Three times the word 'create' is used to emphasize that this is the core of the creation story. To be created in God's image means to be a human, and to care for everything on the earth. That is their responsibility to rule in a way that reflects the way God rules the earth.

Finally, He created them male and female. "So God created man in his own image, in the image of God he created him; male and female he created them. And God blessed them." (Gen 1:27) Together as male and female they are image bearers. The image is not something in them (a divine spark or soul, or an eternal spirit in an earthly body), but the image becomes reality every time humans become engaged and realize their responsibility for the earth. Image bearing is not an inner quality or status symbol but a history of responsible actions. It is not a characteristic but it describes a relationship and acting accordingly. Image bearing is a verb. It realizes itself in the doing of caretaking and in the relation of male and female.

> Be fruitful and multiply, and fill the earth and subdue it; and have dominion over the fish of the sea and over the birds of the air and over every living thing that moves upon the earth. And God said, 'behold, I have given you every plant yielding seed which is upon the face of all the earth, and every tree with seed in its fruit; you shall have them for food. And to every beast of the earth, and to every bird of the air, and to everything that creeps on the earth, everything that has the breath of life, I have given every green plant for food.' And it was so. And God saw everything that he had made, and behold, it was very good. And there was evening and there was morning, a sixth day.
> Genesis 1:28–31

The text itself explains the meaning of the image of God. It consists of two parts. First of all, it is to have dominion over the fish, the birds, the cattle, and over all creeping things, "and over all the earth" (Gen 1:26). Secondly, it is to be "to be fruitful and multiply and fill the earth." (Gen 1:8) God's image is equal to male and female. "In the image of God he created him, male and female he created them." Gen 1:27) God addresses man in the plural, as male and female. They are the only creatures God speaks to directly. What does male and female mean? What does being fruitful mean as an expression of the essence of God's image? As mysterious as it sounds here in Genesis 1, it becomes full of promise in Genesis 5.

> This is the book of the generations of Adam. When God created man, he made him in the likeness of God. Male and female he created them, and he blessed them, and named them Man when they were created. When Adam had lived a hundred and thirty years, he became the father of a son in his own likeness...
> Genesis 5:1–5

The bearing of a son, Seth, is followed by the all the generations of Adam until Noah, ten generations (all of chapter 5); and then ten generations from Noah to Abraham (Gen 10, 11). The command to have dominion over the animals becomes secondary compared to this central theme, the becoming of the firstborn son, as the blessed one that is to carry the blessing for all people. The birth of a son becomes the main theme of the book of Genesis. They are blessed, bear a son and his name is called out, which indicates his function upon the earth. To bear a son will result in the becoming of Israel in the midst of all the nations. Just as the functions of the Day, Night, Heaven, Earth, and Seas are called out, so is the name, Man. The secret of Man becomes evident in Israel. Israel's proclamation of the basis of its history represents all history. With the proclamation of his name history can start. For this purpose heaven and earth are created to serve as the setting of human history. It is not a 'primal history' that is told in Genesis 1. It is the beginning of Israel's history and all human history.

There is still one day to come, the seventh day. Yahweh stops his work on the seventh day. "Thus the heavens and the earth were finished." Israel will follow Yahweh's example in the celebration of the Sabbath. The narrator wants to tell us that God takes time. He has time for us. And that is why Israel rests on this day and celebrates what holds for every day, that God has time for us. With one sentence Deurloo breaks through all the moralisms and legalisms of Sunday observance of my childhood. God has time for us, and so we can take time for God. With this surprise the story is completed. God blessed and hallowed the seventh day.

> Thus the heavens and the earth were finished, and all the host of them. And on the seventh day God finished his work which he had done, and he rested on the seventh day from all his works which he had done. So God blessed the seventh day and hallowed it, because on it God rested from all his work which he had done in creation.
> Genesis 2:1–3

What are we to do with this creation story? Is it a mythical account of the creation of the world like other ancient near eastern myths? Although the narrator uses mythological images from the surrounding peoples, he has a different purpose. We are simply asked to listen carefully to what the storyteller has to tell us in his way, using some of the materials of their time about God and humans. Crucial is what they wanted to do with their story, their proclamation. God created the heavens and the earth to make a good place for humans to live with him in communion.

This is written for the people in exile that are mourning and longing for their homeland. (Ps 137) The big questions they struggled with were: where are we and why are we in Exile and what will happen to us? In that situation in exile, prophets, scribes and narrators arose who heard the voice again that called out to the people, "Hear, oh Israel, The LORD your God" is a unique God. He is the God of Israel. He who has liberated you before, He is present here in Babylon as well. And then the stories came ... They are truly in darkness, in the midst of the powers of darkness and they tell of God who in the midst of the powers of chaos and commanded, "let there be light."

They not only tell how it was and how he was for his people, but also how it will be. People rise up that felt called to tell that the God of Israel is the same today as yesterday; that He keeps covenant forever and does not forsake the works of his own hands. To tell history is not just telling how it was, but how he was for his people. Prophets and scribes rose to tell of the past, which at the same time is the story of the present. It is not the crisis in which they find themselves. It is the starting point for what they have to say. Their trust comes to expression in retelling the great deeds of Yahweh. They find themselves in a desperate chaotic situation and they tell of God who in the beginning, in the midst of the void and darkness proclaimed, "Let there be light." And light means life, life for humanity. His Spirit hovered over the darkness and breathed life in all living creatures.

If we want to know more about how everything came about we need to turn to science. There are many discussions of this issue also in orthodox circles. In Genesis the storyteller has another purpose. In the beginning God created the heavens and the earth, not the universe. Heaven and Earth is the backdrop of the history of God with his people. If we want to know what the purpose of everything is, we need to listen to our storytellers because everything, the large picture, is in the service of the small, namely the history of God and his people. The vast universe is a space limited and protected by God. The seventh day, the last day is the day of the LORD. The remarkable part is that Israel celebrates the seventh day in the midst of the exile. They confirm that the last day is the day toward which we live, the day of the LORD, our future.

I can think of no better way to close this first chapter of Genesis than by quoting the prophet Isaiah. "The people who walked in darkness have seen a great light; those who dwelt in a land of deep darkness, on them has a light shined." (Isa 9:2; cf. Matt 4:15–16) And "Comfort, comfort my people, says your God. Speak tenderly to Jerusalem." (Isa 40:1, 2) "And the glory of the LORD shall be revealed, and all flesh shall see it together, for the mouth of the Lord has spoken." "He will feed his flock, like a shepherd, he will gather the lambs in his arms . . ." (Isa 40:5, 11) "Speak tenderly to Jerusalem," God's abode where he dwells among his people as it is celebrated in Handel's Messiah.

The Hebrew Scriptures conclude with "But for you who fear my name the sun of righteousness shall rise, with healing in its wings . . .

Behold, I will send you Elijah the prophet..." (Mal 4:2, 5), which is taken up by John, "There was a man sent from God, whose name was John. He came for testimony, to bear witness to the light, that all might believe through him. He was not the light, but came to bear witness to the light." (John 1:6) Jesus is also called the "bright morning star" (Rev 22:16) and the light of the world. "I am the light of the world; he who follows me will not walk in darkness but will have the light of life." (John 8:12)

The story of Genesis, as interpreted by Breukelman and Deurloo, is very different from what most of us have learned in Sunday school, church school or the Christian school. It may go something as follows: "Long ago before anything, God decided he wanted friends he could talk to and take a walk with in the cool of the evening in the Garden of Eden. So, first of all, he decided to create a good home for his friends. He created an earth that was a good place to live with fruit trees and lots of plants and many animals and fishes . . . Later on, it is said that Methuselah walked with God and that Abraham and David were called "god's friends." The Bible is the love story between Yahweh and his people and through them with all the people of the world." The secret of humanity becomes apparent in Israel's history. It is the story of all mankind.

6:4 Genesis 2:4–25 The 'second' creation story could have as a title, 'This is the one.'

Genesis 1 serves as an overture in which all the main themes are announced and incorporated. It is an overture to the story about adam, the 'earthling'. The one for the many; pars pro toto; Israel and all humanity on the earth under heaven in the presence of the LORD; the one that will carry the blessing of the first-born for the benefit of all humanity. The book of Genesis is representative of the whole of the message of the Old Testament. It tells of a group of 'called out ones' who interpret their people's history as a liberation movement and with prophetic vision tell us, how it was, and how it will be.

Let us look at Genesis 2. In verse 4 we read: "These are the generations of the heavens and the earth when they were created. In the day that the Lord God made the earth and the heavens, when no plant of the field was yet on the earth and no herbs of the field had yet sprung up . . ." In verse 4 the order is reversed, the earth comes first and then the heavens, which calls attention to the Earth. In the following chapters the word Earth is heard twenty times. Humans can only live if the earth is fertile, and becomes cultivated land and if the human is there to tend the Garden.

Will the earth really become fertile soil with fields to grow crops and pastures to feed the animals? For that to happen, there first has to be water, "... a mist went up and watered the whole face of the ground." Secondly there have to be earthlings to work the ground, "and there was yet no man to till the ground"

Then the Lord God formed man of dust from the ground, and breathed into his nostrils the breath of life:

> ... and man became a living being. And the LORD God planted a garden in Eden, in the east, and there he put the man whom he had formed.
> Genesis 2:7, 8

The LORD God becomes a gardener, planting a beautiful garden with fruit trees "that were pleasant to the sight and good for food." Later the serpent uses this given to deceive and tempt Eve, "the woman saw that the tree was good for food, and it was a delight to the eyes." The earthling lives to till the ground in paradise, his calling.

The superscription to this section reads, "These are the generations of the heavens and the earth when they were created." (Gen 2:4) It is the first of the 'toledot' sections that structure the book of Genesis. It is future orientated and focuses on what is generated and for what purpose. What comes forth out of Heaven and Earth, (the superscription)? What makes its appearance on the Earth under Heaven? Unlike in ancient creation mythologies, Heaven and Earth are not divine productive powers in themselves that create and produce all the other creatures (Father Heaven and Mother Earth). Rather they are creatures made by the LORD God to provide a good home for the earthling. God created and said, "Let there be light." And light means life, life for humanity. His Spirit hovered over the darkness and breathed life in all living creatures. This counters also pagan sexual mythology (the Heavens, Male, and the Earth, Female).

The Garden of Eden lies between four rivers of which Palestine is the 'middle'. It was the then known cultural world, the world of the Bible. That is where the earthling is placed by God "the LORD God took the man and put him in the Garden of Eden to keep it, to till the earth." The earth is his 'life ground', his source of life. The earth is not yet the pastures that surround the cultivated land. It is still a lifeless desert where nothing can grow, "when no plant of the field was yet in the earth and no herb of the field had yet sprung up." There is a progression of plants to herbs and the sign of what is to come, "not yet." What is needed is water, "for the LORD God had not caused it to rain upon the earth," therefore the alternative, "a mist went up from the earth and watered the whole face of the ground." (Gen 2:15) It underscores the miracle of the life giving water. It prepared the way for the miracle of the creation of man. Apart from water, one more thing is needed to make the earth (the dry, desert-like ground) into cultivated land and fields in order for the earth to give rise to bushes and many plants to grazing.

More is needed for the earth to become fertile. There needed to be humans to till the ground, "and there was no man to till the ground." Then comes the great surprise and miracle, "then the LORD God formed man of dust from the ground, and breathed into his nostrils the breath of life; and man became a living being." There is a strong connection between 'adam', the earthling and the ground, 'adama'. The soil is there for the sake of the earthling, the human, and not the other way around. "And out of the ground the LORD God made to grow every tree that is pleasant to the sight and good for food, the tree of life also in the midst of the garden, and the tree of the knowledge of good and evil." (Gen 2:9) Man and the earth belong together. It is his source of life. This was unlike how it was in Egypt, with its regular flooding of the fields, and irrigation that required a lot of work. Instead it will depend on the early and late rains provided by the LORD God, and not by the rain and storm god, Baal. At each step in their relationship with Yahweh that will be the crucial issue! (See: 1 Kings 17 and 18 re: Elijah and the Baal priests on Mount Carmel).

"Then the LORD God formed man of dust from the ground and breathed into his nostrils the breath of life; and man became a living being." (Gen 2:7) These last verses have often created misunderstanding. The meaning is not that the human is made up of two substances: an earthly (body) and an immortal (soul). We are not two substances. Body and soul are two aspects of the total human looked at from two different points of view. What is the earthling, totally dust, nothing, from the ground? On the other hand God blows the breath of life in his nostrils, which simply means that he can breathe, that he is a living creature. The question is not how things and human are put together, but what is important for the whole to function.

It is a mistake to interpret these words about humans as having two substances, which is a Greek notion. The earthling is dust, but he lives by the grace of God. He becomes a living being. Theologians used to debate whether the soul entered the embryo at conception, at six weeks, three months, or at birth, when the living organism (the fetus) can live outside the womb. In biblical times that is when his name would be called out, and after seven days an offering could be brought. (Lev 12: 2–6; Ex 13:2, 12)

The 'pro-life' movement mistakenly assumes that a 'living organism', such as an 'embryo' is a human being, a person. In the Reformed community in which I grew up, any birth control method was considered interfering with God's will. One of my father's relatives had 19 children, and many couples had 8 or 10 children. Many of the newborns died at birth or in infancy, including in my father's family.

"And the LORD God planted a garden in Eden, in the east; and there he put man whom he had formed." (Gen 2:8) The name Eden signifies beauty, abundance, and joy. The description of the Garden of Eden reflects known images from the prophets,

> For the LORD will comfort Zion;
> he will comfort all its waste places,
> and will make her wilderness like Eden,
> Her desert like the garden of the Lord;
> joy and gladness will be found in her,
> thanksgiving and the voice of song.
> Isaiah 51:3 (Ezek 36:34–36

To till and keep the garden, that is their calling and responsibility, to be gardeners, caretakers of the earth. The human environment is the garden of God. "The LORD God took the man and put him in the garden."

> A river flowed out of Eden to water the garden, and there it divided and became four rivers . . .
> Genesis 2:10

The water of the rivers, illustrate the abundance of life given by the Lord.

> They feast on the abundance of thy house,
> and thou givest them drink from the river of thy delights.
> For with thee is the fountain of life; in thy light we see light.
> Psalm 36:8, 9

Rivers and trees belong together. A blessed man is like . . .

> He is like a tree planted by streams of water,
> that yields its fruit in its season . . .
> Psalm 1:3 (cf. Jer 17:8)

The inseparable relationship between the man and the field stands central. It is put in the framework of a living relationship with the LORD God. But now another relationship demands attention. "Yahweh God said: "It is not good . . ." in contrast to the repeated phrase, "It was good." Unlike the animals, the earthling lacks something, a partner like the animals he had named. The LORD decided and said: "I will make for him a helpmeet, as his opposite."

The LORD put him in a deep sleep, like a narcosis, and made him a helper fit for him. He awakes and calls out, "This at last is bone of my bones and flesh of my flesh; she shall be called Woman, because she was taken out of Man." He had named all the animals and the birds, but had not encountered a companion of his kind. Now he can exclaim, "This is the one, this one, this one and no other." This one provides a true meeting and relationship. It is an expression of deep connection and bond. We belong together. We are partners and a team. When Laban meets Jacob, he embraces him and exclaims, "Surely you are my bone and my flesh!" (Gen 29:14) This is the one. With this description all human relationships are characterized. We belong together. This is the norm, to be a co-human with all other humans.

A 'helpmeet' is not just a maid or a nanny, but a helper is someone we need to remain standing. Without her help we fall flat on our face. We can compare her help to the help of the LORD. In Ps 121 we read,

> I lift up my eyes to the hills.
> From whence does my help come?
> My help is from the LORD,
> who made heaven and earth
>
> The LORD will keep your going out
> and your coming in
> from this time forth and for evermore.
>   Psalm 121

If that help does not come, we are done for. That kind of help must be created for the earthling. I will make a "helper fit for him." (Literally, "I will make him a helper, who is over against him.") A helper and one who at the same time can challenge him; "and . . ." She remains totally herself and is a helper. Maybe that is the tension in a good relationship. When the Bible talks about a helper that is someone we need to remain standing, like God is a helper to humanity. "My help is from the LORD, who made heaven and earth." Without such a helper that can face him, he cannot manage. The secret of his humanness is not in his physical labor (tilling the ground) or even his 'cultural' activity (naming the animals), however important. After calling out the animals' names, he can now call out another name, Woman. (Gen 2:23).

The Hebrew word for man is isj, and for woman isja. For this reason she shall be called Woman, because she was taken out of man. "Therefore a man leaves his father and his mother and cleaves to his wife, and they become one flesh. And the man and his wife were both naked, and were not ashamed." (Gen 2:25) That is how it was in the beginning and that is how it can be today. When the relationship is good, couples are not ashamed. When a relationship is broken, nakedness becomes an embarrassment.

Why this 'second' creation story? The simple answer is that we can talk about the creation in many different ways as the scriptures do. The psalmist (Ps 104, or 74 for example) does it in a different way than Isaiah (45:8, 18, 19; 43:1, 7, 15) or Jeremiah (31:35, 36) or Paul (Colossians 1:15–20).[3] Just as Mark, Matthew and Luke each tell the same story about Jesus in a different way. In the text there is another reason. Genesis 1 connects with Genesis 5:1 ("This is the book of generations of Adam") and 2, 3, 4 are also an interconnected unit. Genesis 2–4 tells us who this human is and how he was intended by God, namely the human in the presence of God and as aid to his fellow humans.

The first scene is dominated by man becoming a 'name caller' of all the animals. Male and female are mentioned right next to 'men and the land.' This is equal in importance. "This at last is bone of my bones and flesh of my flesh." She is the one! The one name that needs to be called out is Woman, "She shall be called Woman because she was taken out of Man." Genesis 3:20. She is brought to him to enter into a relation with her, "Therefore a man leaves his father and mother and cleaves to his wife." It is a bodily connection, "and they become one flesh." To her he cleaves. It indicates the concreteness of the relationship and celebrates the gift of eroticism. We are in the neighborhood of the Song of Solomon. "I am my beloveds and his desire is for me.." (Song 5:10). To be man before the face of God is to be man and wife together, before each other's face. The relationship is focused on becoming one flesh and so the "it is not good that the man should be alone," culminates in the relation of male and female. Before the two play their role, and especially the wife who stands

3. Beker and Deurloo, *The beginning in our midst; aspects of the biblical creation faith*, and Deurloo's, *Creation from Paul to Genesis*,

central, a short sentence follows. The man had intercourse with his wife. (4:1).This sentence, with all its erotic glow, cannot go unnoticed.

It is touching and heartwarming the way these two are presented to us. "And the man and his wife were both naked, and were not ashamed." (Gen 2:25) Some argue that this only applies to before the 'fall' and that after that everything changed. After their disobedience we read that "they knew that they were naked; and they sewed fig leaves together and made themselves aprons." Man and wife recognize each others' nakedness and cover themselves. They have become self-conscious. They have to hide their sexuality from each other: guilt-shame-negative sexual relations seem the new reality. The lovers in the Song of Solomon are not bothered by such feelings, as well as in this mini-story. Glorious nakedness that Solomon sings about is without shame for each other. How good is their encounter? It is a narration, not the description of a 'primal state', of a past event. The meaning is clear, their relationship is good. "It is not good" that humans are alone. That becomes concrete in this relation, in which a man and his wife unselfconsciously encounter each other sexually and in their nakedness, "now Adam knew Eve his wife," (Gen 4:1). The miracle and goodness of two human beings freely encountering each other sexually remains, also after the 'fall'. The narrator continues with his theme, who is this human? First of all, man is twofold, together, male and female, they become one flesh. Next to this basic given other aspects need to be dealt with in the following accounts.

6:5 Genesis 3 An impossible possibility: wanting to be like God

Genesis 3 tells us how it went. The human does not want to live by the grace of God. Instead he wants to be like god and apart from God. Genesis 4 describes that the earthling does not want to be a neighbor to his brother, and how he becomes a murderer. So from the earthling before God he wants to be like God, and from being of aid to his neighbor he becomes a murderer of his fellow-human.

Genesis 3 tells how things unfold, particularly in relation to God. Genesis 2 and 3 form a painful contrast to the idyllic harmony in the garden. That is how the people in exile are comforted with a vision of the garden of the LORD, of Eden. All they might remember was that their land was laid waste and became a wilderness. Those waste lands will become like the Garden of Eden. That is the promise. That is also how Lot saw the Jordan valley, "the Jordan Valley was well watered everywhere like the garden of the Lord." (Gen 13:10) This is the kind of fruitful garden that the LORD grants the earthlings. "And the Lord God planted a garden in Eden, in the east; and there he put the man he had formed. And out of the ground the LORD God made to grow every tree that is pleasant to the sight and good for food . . . the tree of life also in the midst of the garden, and the tree of the knowledge of good and evil." Gen 2:8, 9). The tree of life in the midst of the garden represents all the trees. "You may freely eat of every tree of the garden . . ." (2:16) and "behold, I have given you . . . every tree with seed in its fruit; you shall have them for food." (1:29)

The serpent in his deceptiveness will distort these words and insinuate, ". . . did God (really) say, you shall not eat of any tree of the garden?" leaving out the other half of the message. Eve responds with, "We may eat of the fruit of the trees of the garden." Instead of, "we may freely eat of every tree" and "I have given you every tree with seed in its fruit." She accepts the deceptive serpent words which leaves out the rest of the words and gives the impression that God is not truthful with her. Ultimately they give in to the serpent's manipulation acting on his claims that the tree's fruit would not make her die and that instead it would open her eyes "your eyes will be opened, and you will be like God, knowing good and evil." (3:5)

This tree sets limits. Of all the other trees you may eat freely to your heart's content . . . "But of the tree of the knowledge of good and evil you shall not eat, for in the day that you eat of it you shall die" receives the emphasis "you may freely." The human lives under the protection of the commandment not to eat of that one tree. It is the one commandment the Lord gives to the earthlings. It summarizes all the commandments, which enables the good life and leaves the humans their freedom. "You may freely eat from every tree." Eating means life. But eating of that one tree would destroy their relationship with the LORD. Breaking that relationship of trust and dependence means death. "Knowledge of good and evil" in this context means breaking with the God of the covenant to live independently without Yahweh, wanting to become like God.

There is a change. After their disobedience "then the eyes of both were opened, and they knew they were naked." "And the Lord God made for Adam and for his wife garments of skins, and clothed them." The word 'garments" is used both for a priestly tunic (Lev 8:7, 13; Ex 29:4–6) or a royal robe (like Joseph's coat, Gen 37:3, and a royal princess, (2 Sam 13:18). They were afraid to come into God's presence in their estrangement. Before, they were not ashamed of their nakedness with each other. Now they are not only ashamed but also afraid. But God comes to their aid and makes them more of a complete body covering, made of animal skins. They can stand once more before him, before a holy God with a priestly robe that was worn on the Day of Atonement. ("You shall be holy; for I the Lord your God am holy," Lev 18:2). The LORD himself comes to the rescue. Their eating of the one forbidden tree has corrupted their relation before the face of God. It is this relation that carries all the other relations.

They have taken an independent position over against God. Now they can once again appear before the face of God. He himself covers their 'nakedness'. Their nakedness has become a symbol of their estrangement from God. Nevertheless, life continues. Liberating words sound out, "The man called his wife's name Eve, because she was the mother of all living." And, "Now Adam knew his wife, and she conceived." In Genesis 5, we get to hear all the generations of Adam, "This is the book of the generations of Adam." (5:1) The Song of Salomon still sounds out and love continues. Again Deurloo makes use of this context to counter all moralistic attitudes toward sexuality and nudity.

It would be a mistake to think that this happened long ago in the primal history of humanity that does not have a lot to do with us. That would be a misunderstanding about this account of Genesis 3. That would be like, 'it seems that everything was good at first, then came the fall, and we living after the fall, we can't do much about that. Then the story of Genesis 3 becomes something like, 'you know that story about Adam and Eve with that apple and the snake', paradise lost, end of story.

We need to approach this story differently. When this is written the people are in exile in a foreign land. Our scribe looks back on the whole history of Israel with its God and all that happened between them. A God who knows what is good for his people. At the same time it is a story of a people that turned their back to God to go their own way and serve idols. The storyteller is stuck with that question. How is that possible? How could they choose this option? It seems an impossible possibility. He searches for an answer. He is a storyteller, not a philosopher or theologian.

So he starts to tell . . . it is like a play. The players are from the same act as before, God and his people, the hymn of praise about the creation.

He has to interrupt that song and show the other side. The set is the same. We already met it in the previous act, the two trees. They lived in the time of the great empires of the struggle between Mesopotamia and Egypt.

It may be hard for us to understand the appeal of their pagan vision and way of life. In that vision everything had its place. There was no other side. Everything had its place in the cosmic order, life and death, light and darkness, gods and people, all of which becomes manifest in the mystery of the rising sun each day. The rising sun overcomes the darkness and life conquers death each day. In the east where the sun rises is the garden of the gods. In that garden there is a tree.

The tree of Babylonian myth unifies the two worlds, the world of life and the world of death. Here mysteriously life conquers death each day again. The night is the darkness of the under-world, which is symbolized by the snake. It is all about the two powers, which together represent the cosmic unity of the two worlds of cosmic life. Together they represent the unity of the cosmos and together they represent daily the conquest of death by the rising of the sun. Whoever dies participates in this life. Humans are fed by the fruit of the tree of life. They are encapsulated by the unity of these two worlds of death and life. The small earthling is taken up in the cosmic harmony of the spheres. This tree determines our lives.

The storyteller of Genesis 3 does something with those two trees. In exile he no longer experienced the harmony of the spheres. It is a trap. The earthling is not a part of the great harmony of the cosmos. But the 'cosmos' (better heaven and earth) is the setting of the history between this special God and his special people, these 'unharmonious' people. That is what our storyteller is stuck with, the earthlings who no longer want to play their role. Then he continues to tell . . .

On the stage he sets two trees: the tree of life and the tree of the knowledge of good and evil. Good is what makes life possible and evil is the opposite. God knows what is good for the earthlings. That is God's issue. Who told us all that? Who whispered that in our ears? We don't know. The storyteller does not know either. He takes recourse to the image of the snake that slithered into paradise. It is clear from the story that evil cannot be attributed to God and is not explained. And what about that one tree they are not to eat from?

The earthlings go beyond their ability and stature; they want to be like god, knowing good and evil. They eat from the fruit of the tree. The result is clear, they indeed become familiar with good and evil, but without clearly distinguishing. They live in a compromised state. Their eyes are opened and they see they are naked. They don't know where to hide. "And they heard the sound of the LORD walking in the garden in the cool of the day, and the man and his wife hid themselves from the presence of the LORD among the trees." The LORD called them to account and said, "Where are you?" "Have you eaten of the tree of which I commanded you not to eat?" Adam blames his wife and the wife blames the snake. God cursed the snake, the woman, the man and the land. In this way we can get a sense of the double side of God's creation, its ambiguous state.

The whole creation, the good creation gets a double meaning of joy and hardship. With toil you shall work and with toil you shall bear children. The humans have chosen the impossible and brought judgment upon themselves. In chapter 2 we heard that the earthling is from the earth, dust, but living by the grace of God. He can breathe. Once more we hear ". . . you are dust, and to dust you shall return." (Gen 3:19) The story has ended.

But the storyteller has one more concern. Imagine that they have to live for all eternity in this compromised state, torn between good and evil. "Then the LORD God said, 'Behold, the man has become like one of us, knowing good and evil; and now, lest he put forth his hand and take also of the tree of life and eat, and live forever; therefore the LORD God sent him forth from the garden of Eden, to till the ground from which he was taken . . ." (Gen 3:23)

An angel guarded the way to the tree of life. That way will not be closed forever. In and through the judgment there will be an end to the curse. In the book of Revelation we read, "Then he showed me the river of the water of the tree of life . . . on either side of the river, the tree of life, with its twelve kinds of fruit, yielding its fruit each month; and the leaves of the tree were for the healing of the nations. There shall be no more anything accursed . . ." (Rev 22:1–3) Then the curse shall be lifted. Till that day the "whole creation has been groaning in travail together until now; but not only the creation but we ourselves, who have the first fruits of the Spirit, groan inwardly as we wait for the adoption as sons . . . For in this hope we were saved." (Rom 8:22–24) Yet the story goes on.

They are liberated from slavery in Egypt and led to the Promised Land, flowing with milk and honey. There are on-going blessings and hardships. This account is not about eternal doom because of 'original sin" at the dawn of history. The curses are signs of the human's break with Yahweh. They are signs of a disturbed relationship, a fundamental break. Yet it is not without hope. Life continues and awaits the birth of the first-born who will carry the blessing. Instead of death, we read that "the man called his wife's name Eve, because she was the mother of all living." (Gen 3:20) This is followed by, "Now Adam knew Eve his wife and she conceived and bore Cain." (Gen 4:1) There is a new beginning. Even after the great flood we read, "I will never again curse the ground because of man . . . neither will I destroy every living creature as I have done." (Gen 8:21)

These common givens from daily life ('in the sweat of your brow' and 'pain in child bearing', 'the snake, upon your belly you shall go' (who unexpectedly can bite you in the heel') are lifted up to signs and symbols of the mystery of human life. The daily burden of life is used to explain the riddle of human life. They do not function as an eternal doom over life, like a dark cloud, because of this one wrong decision at the beginning of time that has not a lot to do with us. Instead it emphasizes what and who man is his inclination toward good and evil, his ambivalence. There is no 'original sin' that happened at the dawn of history apart from us, instead there is a description of humanity's tendencies, his ambivalent nature toward good and evil.

6:6 Genesis 4:1–16 The human and his brother

The next small unit of Gen 4:1–16, followed by two genealogies of Cain, (4:17–24) and Seth, (4:25–26) is an integral part of chapters 2-3-4 and must be interpreted in the light of the whole of Genesis and the whole of the Hebrew scriptures. Chapter 5 connects to chapter 1. Gen 5:1–2 reads, "This is the book of the generations of Adam. When God created man, he made him in the likeness of God. Male and Female he created them, and he blessed them and named them Man when they were created." connects directly with 2:4 ("These are the generations of the heavens and the earth when they were created"). This verse in chapter 5 briefly summarizes the creation account.

The story of Cain and Abel is an integral part of (under the heading) "these are the generation of the heavens and the earth when they were created." (2:4) Often it is read separately from Genesis 2 and 3, which tells of the first humans. This story stands on its own and shows a coherent whole. It is very compact and different in style, different from chapter 1 and 2. Yet it is closely connected to Gen 2, 3. The story opens with the same characters of Genesis 2, 3, Adam and Eve. The events described happened in or near the Garden of Eden. There are similarities in themes and words. In both stories the relation between human and the earth plays an important part. "And now you are cursed from the ground" (4:11) is similar to "Cursed is the ground because of you." (3:17) In 2 and 3 God is referred to as Yahweh Elohim. In 4:1–16 he is referred to as Yahweh. There is coherence or continuity and difference between Genesis 2, 3 and 4:1–16. There is a redactional (editorial) unity to Gen.4. Between the story of the creation of the earth in Genesis 1 and the history of the development of humanity in Genesis 5, chapters 2–4 form a unity with its own title and intention. The real genealogy of Adam does not start until Genesis 5:1, with the 'toledot' formula "This is the book of the generations of Adam."

In this separate section of Gen 2–4 the scriptures present a 'biblical anthropology-in-story-form'. It describes the fundamental pattern of the relation between God and the human, the human and his co-human, and the human and the earth. Already during the first generation, after the creation of humans (Gen 2) follows the break and alienation with Yahweh and in the second generation the break with the co-human. In the very details Genesis 3 and 4 are attuned to each other. There is a progression or deepening in the break and estrangement. All the big questions of humanity are raised in Genesis 2–4: life and death, work, sexuality and violence, strength and weakness, family history and world history, they all flow together. The prototypes are also archetypes. The words and deeds of specific individuals at the beginning are of significance for all of humanity. They mirror the fundamental patterns of human existence. Beyond the particularity of Genesis 4, the main concern is about the universality of violence and alienation.

The consequences of the break between Yahweh and humanity become increasingly evident. There is a progression. It ends with the great flood, "And the LORD was sorry that he had made man on the earth, and it grieved him to his heart," (Gen 6:6). Afterwards Noah built an altar to the LORD. "And when the LORD smelled the pleasing odor, the LORD said in his heart, 'I will never again curse the ground because of man, for the imagination of man's heart is evil from his youth.'" (Gen 8:21) There is a new beginning even after the judgment of the great flood.

Soon (Gen 11) we will hear the story of the generations of Terah, the father of Abraham, the father of Isaac, the father of Jacob and his special son Joseph. At that point the people of Israel and the Promised Land are in sight. Gen 5:1 "This is the book of the generations of Adam" sets the stage for the many generations to come, from Adam to Seth to . . . Noah and from Noah to Shem to Terah, to Abraham, Isaac and Jacob, and ending with Joseph in Egypt. Through these generations we come to know the basic theme of Genesis: the becoming of the people of Israel in the midst of all the nations on the earth. It is about the human in the presence of God and as aid to his fellow humans. The special human, Adam takes on sharper contours. All the generations from Adam on culminate in this special one, the first-born, Seth, who carries the blessing for all. The creation story serves as an introduction.

Through their disobedience and the murder, the relationship with God, the brother and the land is broken; they are cursed and driven from the garden. (Gen 3:23), But the story does not stop with being banished from the garden of Eden. It continues, and it came to pass, "Now Adam knew Eve, his wife." (Gen 4:1). The earthling had given her the name, Eve, "because she was the mother of all living." (Gen 3:20). She would bear sons and daughters. This is the first time we hear of the procreation of a child by Adam and Eve, it follows directly upon their expulsion from the garden. The story continues after being banned from Paradise. "The man knew Eve his wife and she conceived" and bore sons and daughters. Even though the relationship between the LORD God and the earthlings was disturbed, their relationship continues. God remains faithful to his intention. He continues to reveal himself. The outcome is painful, even though they are graced by continuing to live.

Right from the beginning Yahweh takes an active part in the birth of Cain. Eve achieves giving birth to a man "with the help of the LORD." (Gen 34:1) It is the first act of Yahweh in relation to Cain. There is coherence between God's creating and the procreation of woman and man, (as we will see in the rest of Genesis). Right from his beginning Yahweh has a relationship with Cain. Yahweh gives life to Cain together with his mother Eve. In contrast, his brother Abel is only mentioned in passing, "and again, she bore his brother Abel." From there on Abel is primarily "his brother." He is hardly visible as his name indicates, 'wind, breath or vapor.'

Chapter four is dominated by God's three speeches that take up most of the verses. Yahweh's speaking and questioning determines the entire story. Cain is the central figure in the story. He is introduced with some detail. He is conceived, born and given a name. His actions too are given a great deal of attention. Cain is linked to the earth; he is a 'tiller of the soil,' a farmer. He follows in his father's footsteps, and brings an offering of the fruits of the earth. In doing so he acknowledges Yahweh as the Creator and the close relation between Yahweh, humans and the earth. At the end, this positive tie is completely broken.

In time Cain and his brother Abel each bring an offering from their work, "of the fruit of the ground" and Abel "of the firstlings of his flock and of their fat portions." (cf. Lev 3:15–16) The offerings they present to Yahweh seem to be equal in quality. There is no indication that one is better than the other. Cain offers first and Abel follows his brother's initiative. Many suggestions have been given in the commentaries why "the Lord had regard for Abel and his offering, but for Cain and his offering he had no regard," but none of them is supported by the account. All we can gather from the account is that Cain is not a brother and does not want to behave like a brother. The only indications we are given is that Cain is very angry and refuses to look up "So Cain was very angry, and his countenance fell." (Gen 4:5)

Yahweh gives Cain a warning (his first speech), "Why are you angry, and why does your countenance fall?" He is both warned and encouraged, "If you do well, will you not be accepted? And if you do not do well, sin is couching at the door; its desire is for you, but you must master it." (Gen 4:6, 7) Cain does not look his brother in the face, but lies in ambush for him like a wild animal looking for prey. Yahweh's speech reveals Cain's anger and bad intention and encourages him to do well and lift up his face and look his brother in the face. He warns Cain to master his desire to lie in wait for Abel. He reproaches him for not looking at his weaker brother, the 'wisp of air' or a nothing, we might say.

Cain talks to his brother. The translations usually fill in with "Let us go out to the field," which is missing in the Hebrew but which makes sense in the flow of the story. We do not know what is said. What follows is a most concise account of a murder. "And when they were in the field, Cain rose up against his brother Abel, and killed him." (Gen 4:8) After this Yahweh spoke for the second time, "Where is Abel your brother?" These words call Cain to give account of his deed. At first he refuses to answer and take responsibility, "I do not know. Am I my brother's keeper?" (Gen 4:9) It is the one thing Cain does not want to do, be his brother's keeper and take responsibility for him as the older brother.

Then the LORD confronts him directly, "What have you done?" "The voice of your brother's blood is crying to me from the ground." (Gen 4:11) Abel's blood speaks louder than all his other actions. His spilt blood cries out. The word used for 'crying out' is the cry of all the oppressed, the afflicted, strangers, widows and orphans. Like that of the oppressed Israelites, the LORD said, "I have heard their cry because of their task masters; I know their sufferings . . . to deliver them and to bring them out of that land to a good and broad land, a land flowing with milk and honey . . ." (Exod 3:7, 8) It reflects an opposite kind of response by God to their 'crying out': deliverance instead of judgment. The earth is like a wide-open mouth to drink in Abel's blood. It expresses the relation between Yahweh, the earth and blood.

In Genesis 4 follows the third speech by the LORD, "And now you are cursed from the ground, which has opened its mouth to receive your brother's blood from your hand. When you till the ground, it shall no longer yield to you its strength; you shall be a fugitive and a wanderer on the earth." (Gen 4:11, 12)

Yahweh offers some protection for Cain when he expressed his fear that anyone who would find him would kill him. "Then the LORD said unto him, 'Not so! if anyone slays Cain, vengeance shall be taken on him sevenfold.' And the LORD put a mark on Cain." (Gen 4:15) Sadly we read at the end that, "Cain went away from the presence of the LORD and dwelt in the land of Nod, east of Eden." (Gen 4:16) He consciously separated himself from Yahweh, the covenant God and became a wanderer, a fugitive.

Yet in the next section we read that "Cain knew his wife, and she conceived and bore Enoch. (Gen 4:17) There is a new beginning, even for Cain. There was a postponement of judgment and death. We are not told why and should not speculate. Evil is not explained. This bitter reality is present and must be opposed. All we know is that it does not happen outside of God, outside his power. The origin of evil is not explained. It will be crucial to see how this event is built into a larger biblical theological perspective. Genesis does not only present us with a very specific and different God-image but also a specific image of the earthlings. It is not presented in an abstracted theoretical way but by way of narratives. It calls attention to the human condition. "Behold, the man has become like one of us, knowing good and evil." (3:22)

In Genesis 4 we are confronted by the contrast of the human, how he was intended by God and the way he showed himself. In Genesis 4 we hear how he showed himself to be a murderer of his fellow human. In Genesis 2 the concern is the relation between men and women. In Genesis 4 it is the relation between man and his brother. The storyteller is talking about the human, his true nature and how that comes out in his relation to his partner and brother. It is the human who ignores his brother and ends up killing him. It anticipates the main concern about Abraham and Sarah, their relationship and their barrenness, while the unit about Esau and Jacob reflects the relation between the oldest son and the younger one.

The author takes a familiar theme and an historical figure and makes it to stand for the main figure in a way that goes far beyond a historical figure. Hamlet in Shakespeare, for example, stands for an historical figure, a prince from Denmark. What that prince of Denmark meant is not important. The most important thing is what that prince of Denmark does, that is the key. Hamlet as a general human figure tells us a lot. Something like this is what the storyteller does in Genesis 4. The Cain figure is a familiar one, but the historical background does not tell us that much. The story is exemplary. Just as Abel functions primarily as a secondary figure whose role it is to be murdered. His name means, a 'wisp' or 'breath' of air. Before you have a good look, it is gone. Seven times Abel is called Cain's brother without his name. So Cain is presented as an exemplary figure.

Yet it is helpful to know where that Cain figure may come from. In the scriptures we encounter a lot of Cain figures. The name Cain may mean blacksmith. And there may be an association with the nomadic tribe 'the Kenites'. They may stand as a model, a half-nomadic tribe, who as blacksmiths roam the deserts, looking for work. Already at the beginning of Genesis they played an important role in the history of Israel. When Israel left Egypt they came along. (Judg 1:16) They were a mysterious people to the settled Israelites, never settling down in one place. Their patron saint was the god of fire; fire for mining metals and forging farm implements and weapons. Because of this they were feared and looked at with wonder and suspicion. It is not surprising that Cain and his brother's story was seen as an 'etiological story' (explanatory story) that explained why Cain's descendents were a wandering tribe looking for work from one tribe to another, both needed and feared. Although this approach to Cain has been abandoned, it lingers on in some studies. It may still be valid, though the evidence is not conclusive.

This story is as relevant today as it was then. People can be incredibly caring and helpful as well as commit unimaginable and unspeakable crimes, and everything in between. Where does evil come from? The author doesn't say, he does not know either. He can only tell a story in a very concise form, "And Cain talked to Abel his brother." The account in

Hebrew does not tell us what was said. "And when they were in the field, Cain rose up against his brother Abel and killed him.'" It was an impossible possibility.

The doctrine of 'original sin' (Adam and Eve eating from the forbidden tree) has hovered as a dark cloud over the Reformed community. 'Our best works are like filthy garments before God' and 'we are 'totally unable to do any good and inclined to all evil'. 'Our natural tendency is to hate God and our neighbor'. 'We increase our guilt every day'. Such is the perspective of the Heidelberg Catechism, used to teach children in the Christian faith. No wonder this perspective on human nature has given rise to a lot of despair and sense of doom, especially when combined with the doctrine of God's eternal council, reprobation and election. Doubt, fear, hopelessness, and uncertainty as well as melancholy and sadness were the order of the day. Those attitudes characterized many Christian communities. This is how a, fearful and full of guilt, ten year old boy was indoctrinated in the Reformed faith. I don't think my parents participated in the Lord's Supper (communion) very often; they had too many doubts about their faith.

The belief that sin entered the world through the woman is equally reprehensible. In this section the woman speaks and acts also on behalf of her husband. It is a story about both men and women. His eating shows his agreement with her. They both were not ashamed of their nakedness before their rebellion, and together they sowed fig leaves to cover their genitals after their break with God. The break with God also gave rise to their self-consciousness toward each other. Independence from God creates distance. They feel exposed to each other's views. Their guilt is not first of all related to sexual desire and shame. Their awareness of their nakedness is first of all related to the moment of meeting with God. They stood naked before him. It is this relation that carries all the other ones. Adam did not listen to the voice of God when he should have. The male and the female together are responsible for the break with God.

The judgments upon their violation are signs of the riddle of their existence after their rebellion against God. The fundamental break is with God, claiming their autonomy and independence from the Creator. That is the theme of these chapters. Their new awareness of guilt and shame stands next to their delight in their sexual closeness and culmination, not in the place of it. This narrated anthropology does not explain how it turned out this way with humanity. Evil is not explained. From the beginning humanity is characterized by ambivalence. They can turn either to good or evil. It emphasizes what is going on with humanity's ongoing journey in history. The secret of humanity that comes to the fore in these narratives, is that God continues his journey with humanity. Instead of death, there is judgment and a new beginning, even for Cain. Adam called his wife's name Eve and the Lord clothed them. The riddle of humanity is its ambivalence toward good and evil. There is a new beginning. There are signs of God's goodness throughout history. Reformed theologians had to invent the idea of 'common grace' to account for the good in the world, of loving kindness, and solidarity, of justice and faithfulness, "he makes his sun rise on the evil and the good, and sends rain on the just and the unjust." (Matt 5:45)

". . . At that time men began to call upon the name of the LORD." (Gen 4:26) That is how this section ends, with hope. Adam and Eve receive another son and call out his name, Seth. Abel is not forgotten, "God has appointed for me another child instead of Abel, for Cain slew him." (4:25) Then, and in the midst of this, men began to call upon the name of the LORD. This is not about the origin of religion in ancient times. They 'call out' the name of Yahweh. Israel is called to listen to Yahweh and in many stories, songs and prophecies to call out his Name. In these few stories the essence of humanity is told. With this human, the great adventure with Yahweh begins.

From here on there are two lines in human history. The first is those living in the presence of the LORD, following his life-giving directions, and calling upon his Name. The second line of people have turned away from the LORD God, and boasted of their achievements (musicians and metal workers as well as farmers) and power, their revenge on anyone who should dare to oppose them. The first genealogy mentioned is that of Cain and his off-spring. (Gen 4:17–24) The second line is that of Seth. (Gen 5) There will be a development of nations, the different peoples and the descendents of Seth that will give rise to the Son. In a few pages Deurloo gives a very detailed exegesis (In: *The Human as Riddle and Secret*, pp. 126–36) of the names and additional information in the genealogies. It would take us too far afield to follow all the details of his genealogical explanations. The connections he makes are intriguing.

In exactly the middle of the country Abraham will call out the name of the LORD (Gen 12:8) and again after his detour to Egypt, in that same place. (Gen 13:4) The calling of the Name fulfills itself in Israel. The concept Israel rises out of the biblical tradition and as such it is not a 'historical concept'. The question about Israel is not first of all 'historical' but must be understood as proclamation. The writings of Israel as they are heard and told in the Old Testament, read in the church, are not just as literature, but as living words. What does the story say? Thus Christians 'taking over' the stories of the Hebrew Scriptures, is a sign of obedience to Jesus who commanded his disciples to proclaim the book of Israel to all peoples.

6:7 Genesis 5:1–11:26 The generations of Adam; the second 'toledot'

In Genesis 5 a new section starts. It is the second 'toledot', the generations of Adam. In chapter 2:4 it summarizes the story of the generation of the heavens and the earth. Gen. 5:1 could have continued right from there, if it had not been for what had to be told in chapters 2 to 4. The narrator first had to tell us something different. He first had to tell us about the contrast between God's intention for humans and the way humans chose their own dead end way. After that he could continue with chapter 5. Now, the real history of the human, adam, can begin. The whole creation is there for the sake of the human in the presence of the LORD. It is the reverse of how we usually think. First there is the creation, and then humanity. The narrator could have continued right after Genesis 1 by telling us how that human made history. But we saw that chapter 1 could not make a direct connection with chapter 5.

> This is the book of the generations of Adam. When God created man, he made him in the likeness of God. Male and female he created them and he blessed them and named them Man when they were created. When Adam had lived a hundred and thirty years, he became the father of a son in his own likeness, after his image, and named him Seth. The days of Adam after he became the father of Seth were eight hundred years; and he had other sons and daughters. Thus all the days that Adam lived were nine hundred and thirty years; and he died.
> Genesis 5:1–5

Who enters history again and again in a surprising manner? The storyteller is primarily interested to tell us who appears one after the other by having offspring. However, it is not just a book of generations, of a succession of descendants, or of a family genealogy. The verse that was skipped in our earlier discussion reads. "These are the generations of the heavens and the earth when they were created." (Gen 2:4) What appears first? It is heaven and earth. They are indeed generated. It adds, "... when they were created."

They did not just appear by a natural process like that of nature mythologies (heaven, male, copulating with earth, female), or of evolution. They are created by God. He spoke and it was. It is first of all in opposition to all fertility cults of the surrounding peoples. Secondly it makes a connection with Genesis 5:1. Placing the two one after the other, they read, "These are the generations of the heavens and the earth when they were created" and "This is the book of the generations of Adam, when God created man ..." (The first and second toledot sections) shows the similarity and connection.

The ten toledot (generations) headings, structure the entire book of Genesis from beginning to end. Most commentators tend to divide Genesis in two basic parts, namely a primal mythical history of mankind (the universal) (Gen 1:1–11:27) and the history of the patriarchs (the particular), (Gen 11:28–50:26). However, the first eleven chapters are as much a part of the stories of the patriarchs as the rest. From the beginning the concern is the becoming of the people of Israel, the place of Israel in the midst of all nations. The universal "all the peoples of the earth" is enclosed by the particular, Israel. The creation story culminates in the creation of humans made in God's image as men and women with the joint calling to be caretakers of the earth and to fill the earth.

The main emphasis in all the toledot sections is on the 'first one', 'firstling' (not necessarily the firstborn) that carries the blessing for all the brothers and sisters of his father's house, and through them for all the peoples of the earth. This basic structure is brought out and reinforced in each section by several main themes and key words. The book of Genesis manifests a very integral structure that highlights its prophetic meaning.

This structure starts with the heading of "These are the generations of the heavens and the earth when they were created" (Gen 2:4) and continues with "This is the book of the generations of Adam" (Gen 5:1) and then, "these are the generations of Noah" and so on. It functions as the head of each main section. Genesis is the book of beginnings or the 'coming into being'. The question is not how and when did everything start or what was before everything, but what is its purpose and meaning and how did it unfold?

The first ten generations are introduced with the familiar formula: so and so ... bore a son. He lived so many ... years and died. For the next ten generations the formula changes to: "These are the descendants of Noah . . . and Noah had three sons, Shem, Ham, and Japheth." (Gen 6:9) and later on it is repeated with: "These are the generations of Noah's sons; sons were born to them after the flood." (Gen 10:1) Now there is a before and after the flood.

Of the sons of Noah it is said that "These are the families of the sons of Noah, according to their genealogies, in their nations; and from these the nations spread abroad on the earth after the flood." (Gen 10:32). The first promise to Abraham is "And I will make of you a great nation, and I will bless you, and make your name great, so that you will be a blessing . . . and by you all the families of the earth shall bless themselves." (Gen 12:1, cf. 22:18; 26:4) The ten toledot divisions go back and forth between the main line, and the origin and development of Israel in the midst of the nations, side by side. It reinforces the main thesis that Genesis narrates the becoming of Israel among the nations.

In this last section (Gen 5) the main concern was the firstborn. In a series of ten generations, it is the firstborn that stands central. The LORD chooses a people with whom to make history. This history, according to the story tellers, contains the secret of world history. Everything is concentrated on this God with this people.

The narrator wants to emphasize once more. The creation of heaven and earth happened because of the great event: that the humans can make their appearance in history. He very briefly summarizes all the key words of Gen. 5:1. There is no continuity of a people except on the basis of the creative act of the Lord God (of Israel). The formula becomes, Seth lives a number of years, he became the father of a son, the first-born; he lived so many years; and he died. The author tells us with such emphasis about the first-born, because he represents the whole family, even though there are many other sons and daughters. So it continues, from Seth to Enoch, to Methuselah, to Lamech and ends with Noah. In the chapters that follow it continues with Abraham, Isaac and Jacob. We are being prepared for the key theme, Israel, the first-born of all the families of the earth; Israel as the representative of all humanity.

Adam in his own sin reflects sin as a human phenomenon, just as Israel points beyond itself, men in the image of God.

We heard it all in Genesis 1 except this one phrase, "male and female he created them, and he blessed them and named them Man when they were created." (Gen 5:2) God called out their name, just like he had called out the name of the Day and the Night, the Heavens, the Earth, the Dry Land and the Seas. With their naming, the earthlings receive both permission and responsibility to care for the creation in the name of the LORD in the midst of all the other creatures. Not to lord it over the creation; not to be 'uber-mensch' or 'super-man' and not to be a lesser being; not to be god, but to be truly human, caring for the earth and fellow humans.

Everything was about the oldest son, the firstborn, in the previous chapter. Through a chain of ten generations (toledots), every time the first-born appears upon the scene. This history of the becoming of the first-borns contains the secret of world history. The LORD chooses a people with whom to make history. On this, everything is concentrated, Yahweh together with his people. How did it go after that? Did the humans come to their senses, joining Seth in calling on the name of the LORD? No, they didn't call on the covenant LORD God (of Israel). Yet the Psalmist invites:

> O give thanks to the LORD, call on his name,
> make known his acts among the peoples!
> Sing to him, sing praises to him,
> Tell of all his wonderful works!
> Glory to his holy name;
> Let the hearts of those who seek the Lord rejoice!
> Psalm 105:1–3

Call out his name and recite all his great deeds of redemption and creation; and then the psalmist recites all his great deeds with Abraham, Joseph, of Israel in Egypt, of Moses, of the exodus, and of the land of Canaan. This psalm is followed by Psalm 106:1–5, which recites all the Lord's great acts in even more detail.

6:8 Genesis 6:1–11:26 Living before and after the flood; ten generations from Noah to Abraham

There are two themes that illustrate the increase in corruption and violence. After the story of the daughters of men marrying the sons of God (Gen 6:4) and later on, (Gen 1:1–9) the sons of men attempting to build a tower that reached to the heavens, we read, " . . . the LORD was sorry that he had made man on the earth, and it grieved him to his heart." (Gen 6:6) Was that the end of the peoples and the nations, of humanity? "But Noah found favor in the eyes of the LORD." (Gen 6:8) There will be a new beginning after the destructive flood. Here a new toledot starts, the one about the generations of Noah, (number 3) to be followed by the toledot of Noah's son, Japheth, (Gen 10:1–11:9) (Number 4); the toledot of Shem (Gen 11:10–26) (number 5) and that of Terah (Gen 11:7–25:11) (number 6).

How did it unfold after Adam and Eve were driven from the garden and Cain was cursed and becoming a wanderer? The storyteller is very blunt about what happened next. "The wickedness of man was great," there was "corruption" and "violence" everywhere.

> The LORD saw that the wickedness of man was great in the earth, and that every imagination of the thoughts of his heart was only evil continually. And the LORD was sorry that he had made man on the earth, and it grieved him in his heart. So the LORD said, 'I will blot out man whom I have created from the face of the ground, man and beast and creeping things and birds of the air, for I am sorry that I have made them'.
> Genesis 6:5–7

What follows is the story of the great flood, of Noah. Is that the end of the religious pride and arrogance of those other nations and people, blotted out from the earth? Right after the story of the great flood follows the story of the tower of Babel. They want to be gods and reach for the heavens. (Gen 11:1–9). It is not totally over. The story of the nations continues as well.

The narrators have told us what happened to the sons and daughters. It sounds like pure (Greek) mythology. But the storytellers use some of these mythological givens to describe the peoples in their religion. They use old well-known mythological materials when people reached a very high old age ("the mighty men that were of old, the men of renown"). They had heard of giants who lived to be very old; of sons of god who mixed with the earthlings. Within the religion of the surrounding people that was possible. Half-gods appeared on the scene, powerful men that made a name for themselves. (Gen 6:4) See Breukelman's article in the first publication of the *Amsterdamse Cahiers for Exegesis and Biblical Theology*, # 1 (1980), "The story about the sons of God who married the daughters of men" (as part of "the book of the generations of Adam, the human. Gen 6: 1–4. It forms a contrast between the real humans the generations of God's people amidst the other peoples and a protest against the pagan myths of the deification of humans.

Everything becomes mixed together, gods and humans, heaven and earth. The earthlings forget that they are flesh, that they are human. Human is the name that was called out by God. But the human that is described here wants to be more; he reaches beyond his powers and enlarges himself to be superhuman. They became very old and forgot they are flesh. They are giants, no longer earthlings. When they try to erase the boundaries between God and the human, between heaven and earth, then what happens?

> When men began to multiply on the face of the ground, and daughters were born to them, the sons of God saw that the daughters of men were fair; and they took to wife such of them as they chose. Then the LORD said, 'My spirit shall not abide in man forever, for he is flesh, but his days shall be a hundred and twenty years'. The Nephilim (giants) were on the earth in those days . . . These were the mighty men that were of old, the men of renown.
> Genesis 6:1–4

The third toledot follows with the generations of Noah. At the beginning of the flood story, Noah is already described as a "righteous man, blameless in his generation; Noah walked with God. And Noah had three sons, Shem, Ham, and Japheth." Whatever is about to happen, will happen within the context of Noah "who found favor in the eyes of the Lord." (Genesis 9, 10)

> Now the earth was corrupt in God's sight, and the earth was filled with violence. And God saw the earth, and behold, it was corrupt; for all flesh had corrupted their way upon the earth. And God said to Noah, 'I have determined to make an end of all flesh; for the earth is filled with violence through them; behold, I will destroy them with the earth. Make yourself an ark . . . For behold, I will bring a flood of waters upon the earth, to destroy all flesh in which is the breath of life from under heaven; everything that is on the earth shall die. But I will establish my covenant with you . . .
> Genesis 6:11–18

Noah is instructed to build an ark with the same comparative proportions of a coffin as Moses' small 'ark' (coffin) and store enough food for the animals and themselves. Noah did "all God had commanded him." Then he was told to go into the ark with his entire family. They did and God shut the door behind them. What follows is the disaster, the great catastrophe. Is that the end of humanity and their religious pride?

Right after the story of the flood, we hear again about the heathen. It is not the end of their striving to be like God. "Now the whole earth had one language and few words. And they said to one another . . . 'Come let us build ourselves a city, and a tower with its top in the heavens.'" (Gen 11:1, 7)

The people were not only one in religion but also one in language that would enable them to build a high tower. The storyteller has in mind the many familiar towers of the time, the 'ziggurats'. These giant towers express the religious tendency of the human to reach the heavens and become like god. They had not learned anything. But the LORD puts a stop to it. "Come, let us go down . . . " We remember the "us" from Gen. 1, "Let us make man . . . " God seems to ponder for a moment what he is about to do. Then he confuses their language, so that they can no longer continue to build their tower. So they stopped building the city with its mighty tower, "and from there the LORD scattered them abroad over the face of the earth." (Gen 11:8)

The narrator uses this given of the confusion of language to tell us something different than the origin of the many languages. We are not called to stick together in a 'safe' place, together safely on the way to heaven. That is not our calling. We are called to be truly human on this earth and to develop the ground for the benefit of all, especially the vulnerable. So the Lord scattered them all over the earth. The mighty city of Babel, (with a play on words, is called, 'confused', 'balal'). We would say, 'babble'. The scriptures oppose all attempts by human's to make their own name great. In the Bible, the Lord makes the humans' name great. In the humanity of the people God's name is made great.

Earlier we asked ourselves what happened, to the sons and daughters. The storytellers have told us: in Genesis 6, the daughters of men and in Genesis 11, about the sons of men. In between there is the story of the flood. How did it go with the nations? The nations live 'before and after the disaster'. They continue as if nothing has happened. They continue with what occupied them before the flood, corruption and violence. It is the fate of the peoples to live without meaning and purpose, just before and after, no real change or history.

In the midst of the story of the disaster, a human appears on the scene. It is Noah, the first born, a righteous man, who did what he was commanded, to be truly human before the face of the LORD. Noah, as the first born, represents God's people. The LORD remains true to his creation. He does not abandon the works of his hands, but keeps covenant forever. How do the nations live? They live 'before' or 'after' the flood in endless succession. Yet after the flood and the new beginning they continue as usual, as if nothing has happened. They continue on with what they were doing before the flood, 'business as usual', or making themselves or their nation, 'great again'.

It is a future without meaning. If the meaning of history is 'to live before and after the disaster', the catastrophe, then history is truly senseless. Today we have two big catastrophes (WWI and II) behind us, and many other wars and disasters. What is our destiny? Will it be another new, (last) disaster? In the middle of the story of the catastrophe, a man comes to the fore: Noah. He did what he was called to do, to be truly human in the presence of God. Noah, the first born, represents God's people. The LORD remains true to his people. That is what the history of this God with his chosen people shows. God did not give up on humanity.

"Let us make man in our image, male and female" Those words from Genesis 1 could be the theme of the whole Bible. It is God's initiative, even if the heathen rage and people make themselves 'great'.

> Why do the nations conspire,
> and the peoples plot in vain?
> Psalm 2:1

> God is our refuge and strength,
> A very present help in trouble,
> Therefore we will not fear though the earth should change,
> Though the mountains shake in the heart of the sea;
> Though its waters roar and foam,
> Though the mountains tremble with its tumult,
> The nations rage, the kingdoms totter;
> He utters his voice, the earth melts.
> The LORD of hosts is with us;
> The God of Jacob is our refuge.
> Psalm 46:1–7

If this were the meaning of world history, that we only live 'before' and 'after' the disaster, then is an endless succession of 'before' and 'after'. Then history would be completely meaningless. The meaning of history is either living before and after the disaster or living before and after *the* first-born, Jesus the Messiah. Matthew describes it as follows:

> As were the days of Noah, so will be the coming of the Son of man. For as in those days before the flood they were eating and drinking, marrying and giving in marriage, until the day when Noah entered the ark, and they did not know until the flood came and swept them all away, So will be the coming of the Son of man.
>
> Matthew 24:37–39 (cf. Luke 17:26)

The LORD commands Noah to build an ark. "For behold, I will bring a flood of waters upon the earth, to destroy all flesh . . . everything that is on the earth shall die. But I will establish my covenant with you." (Gen 6:17) When the ark was ready, again the LORD said to Noah, "Go into the ark, you and your household, for I have seen that you are righteous before me in this generation." (Gen 7:1) "And Noah did all that the LORD had commanded him." (Gen 7:5) Then the flood came. "On that day all the fountains of the great deep burst forth and the windows of the heavens were opened. And rain fell upon the earth forty days and forty nights." (Gen 7:11, 12) The firmament is no longer a boundary between heaven and earth and the deep is no longer separated from the dry land. The primal waters cover everything. It is creation in reverse.

After many days "God remembered Noah and all the beasts and all the cattle that were with him in the ark. And God made a wind blow over the earth, and the waters subsided; the fountains of the deep and the windows of the heavens were closed, the rain from the heavens was restrained." Gen 8:1, 2) It is like a new creation. When the waters had receded and the earth was dry, (a dove had returned with a new olive leaf), God said to Noah, 'Go forth from the ark and your whole family and all the animals'. When he stepped out on the earth, the first thing Noah did was to build an altar to the LORD. "And when the Lord smelled the pleasing odor, the Lord said in his heart, 'I will never curse the ground because of man . . . neither will I ever again destroy every living creature as I have done. While the earth remains, seedtime and harvest, cold and heat, summer and winter, day and night, shall not cease.'" (Gen 8:22) And a bow in the clouds appeared to confirm the promise.

How did it go after the flood? As we saw earlier, it did not go well. The nations carried on as before. At the same time a new generation appeared on the scene: The generations of the sons of Noah (Gen 10:1–32), the fourth toledot, and more specifically the generations of Shem (11:10–26), the fifth toledot, came to the fore.

The first ten generations from Adam to Noah show a declining line. But God gives Adam and Eve another son, Seth, "God has appointed for me another child instead of Abel, for Cain slew him." (Gen 4:25) He provides comfort through Noah, a new and different Adam. We can compare the commandment to Adam and Eve in paradise, in the good creation with the commandment to Noah. It gives expression to the bitter secret of the good creation. Along with Noah the animals have been saved from the flood, only to live in fear of man.

> The fear of you and the dread of you shall be upon every beast of the earth, and upon every bird of the air, on everything that creeps on the ground and all the fish of the sea; into your hand they are delivered. Every moving thing that lives shall be food for you; and as I gave the green plants, I give you everything.
> Genesis 9:2, 3

Now the animals live in fear and dread of humans. From vegetarians, humans become omnivores and carnivores. The peace of Eden is replaced by war, violence and death in creation. Given the decline and extinction of millions of species today, we can only say, 'animals beware of humans!'

These are the generations of Noah . . . " (Gen 6:9) "After the flood Noah lived three hundred and fifty years. All the days of Noah were nine hundred and fifty years; and he died." (Gen 9:28) Thus Noah continues the line of Adam, as the second Adam. Through the accumulation of all the names of the generations, the origin of Israel slowly becomes evident.

6:9 Genesis 11:27–25:11 *The Terah 'toledot'; the center of the 'toledot' cycles*

Before we start with the story of Abram and his offspring, it is helpful to remember the connection with the previous accounts. We have followed the becoming of God's people (one line) in the midst of all the other peoples (the other line).

From the beginning the theme is the becoming of Israel in the midst of the nations. Abraham and Israel are still hidden among the sons of Shem and the nations that will most directly surround Israel: Lot, in Moab and Ammon (19:37–38); Ishmael, the desert peoples to the south of Israel (21:14–21; 25:12–18) and especially Esau, in Edom (25:23, 30). This is underscored in the framework around this chapter,

> These are the generations of the sons of Noah, Shem, Ham and Japheth; sons were born to them after the flood.
> Genesis 10:1

> These are the families of the sons of Noah, according to their genealogies, in their nations; and from these the nations spread abroad on the earth after the flood.
> Genesis 10:32

We need to take note especially of the words, "After the flood." In Genesis 5, the heading is "The generations of Adam" (the human). They are characterized by "he became the father of a son." (Gen 5:3) The birth of a representative of humans is decisive. With Abraham this miracle of the birth of a son determines his entire life. It is the miracle of Israel that appears in the midst of the nations. This is why the secret is hidden in the "before and after," the generation of that one son. Who they are is summarized in Genesis 10. Every time it is mentioned, almost as an aside, and he had "sons and daughters." Who are these? Genesis 10:32 gives the answer, "the nations."

Who they are is summarized in this chapter 5. How can they be characterized these sons and daughters that are mentioned like a refrain in Genesis 5? In two sentences they are introduced, to our surprise, first of all by the daughters. "When men began to multiply on the face of the ground, and daughters were born to them . . ." (Gen 6:1) and to them, the sons of Noah "sons were born after the flood." (Gen 10:1) The daughters are characterized with a 'near-eastern myth'. They intermarried with the 'sons of God'. And the sons are characterized by their desire to eradicate the boundary between heaven and earth. (Gen 11:1–9) Together they live before and after the flood. With that, the history of the nations is determined, "living before and after the flood," without a future.

In chapter 10 we get a view of the "nations after the flood." Deurloo suggests that these lists may be derived from ancient trade lists. The Japheth list mentions two generations. "From these the coastland peoples spread . . . in their lands, each with his own language, by their families, in their nations." (Gen 10:5). The Ham list has three generations and the Shem list four. In chapter 11 the generations of Shem is continued. (11:10). The most threatening are the list of Ham, the traditional enemies of Israel, Egypt (10:13) and the Philistines (10:14). Two other threatening names are mentioned, Babel (10:10) and Assyria (10:11). With a broad geographical sweep, from "the coastland" people (10:5) to "the hill country of the east" (10:30), the peoples are indicated. They are like the ends of the earth.

One more area is described in quasi geographical terms, the land of the Canaanites: "from Sidon, in the direction of Gerar, as far as Gaza and in the direction of Sodom, Gomorrah, Admah and Zeboiim" (Gen 10:19). They are the cities that we know from the Abraham story. It is like a square that encompasses the land of Canaan, the land of promise. Abraham has not appeared yet, but the land is already there, waiting for the miraculous birth of the son. Genesis 4 ended with, "At that time men began to call upon the name of the LORD." (Gen 4:26) Is it an event without a place? Here in the midst of the land of Canaan both moments, the land and the son will be connected.

Earlier, we highlighted the structure of Genesis 1–4 (the creation; Adam and Eve, their striving to be like God; Cain, not wanting to be responsible for his brother) the narrator shows how the promised son, in a surprising manner, appears among the brothers and sisters. In chapters 5–11 both are mentioned together, Israel and the peoples of the earth.

The separation from the other nations comes later. The narrator can follow these two themes at the same time. Now Israel must separate itself from the surrounding peoples and starts its own history. Slowly the first-born separates from his family. That is essential, because Israel needs to take centre stage.

First of all, by way of introduction, they tell the story of Terah, the first-born (the sixth toledot). The introduction to Genesis at the end of chapter 11 reads:

> Now these are the descendants of Terah. Terah was the father of Abraham, Nahor, and Haran; and Haran was the father of Lot. Haran died before his father Terah in the land of his birth, in Ur of the Chaldeans. And Abram and Nahor took wives; the name of Abram's wife was Sarai, and the name of Nahor's wife, Milcah, the daughter of Haran the father of Milcah and Iscah. Now Sarai was barren; she had no child.
> Genesis 11:27–30

Terah took Abram his son and Lot the son of Haran, his grandson, and Sarai his daughter in law, his son Abram's wife,

> ... and they went forth together from Ur of the Chaldeans to go into the land of Canaan; but when they came to Haran, they settled there.
> Genesis 11:27–31

Abraham goes through the entire breadth of the biblical world, from Mesopotamia to Egypt. They left Ur of the Chaldeans, that is, the land of Nebuchadnezzar, the land of exile, and Egypt, the land of exodus, to go to the land of Canaan. The verbs "Go" and "seeing" appear twice in a special way. The first time it relates to the land (Gen 12:1) and the second time to the son (Gen 22:2). They correspond to each other. "Go ... to the land I will show you" and, "Go ... to the land Moriah" (seeing). The first sentence characterizes the chapters 12–14, the second 15–22. The whole history is framed by two genealogical notes at the beginning and the end, Gen 11:27–32 and 22:20–24. The first mention is coupled with the promise, "with you all the families of the earth will be blessed." The second one, "with your seed shall all the nations of the earth bless themselves." Between those two points lies Abraham's history.

It is not Abraham's initiative to leave Ur of the Chaldeans. The place name itself is an anachronism. The Chaldeans are the neo-Babylonians, the people that led the people of Israel into exile. The name Ur of the Chaldeans refers historically to the time of king Nabunid, the cultural and religiously interested neo-Babylonian king that restored the old Ur. Out of this area, a remnant of the exiled people returned to the Promised Land. Abram already left, and returned to the land of promise. Pharaoh lets him go, even before the exodus is foretold. (Gen 12:19, 20) "They set him on the way, with his wife and all that he had." The Babylonian place and the motif of the exodus are combined here (Gen 15). God reveals himself to Abraham with the familiar formulation of the exodus from Egypt. In Gen 15:7 we read, "I am the Lord who brought you from Ur of the Chaldeans, to give to you this land to possess." (cf. Lev 25:38; Neh 9:7)

They came to Haran and settled there. Maybe this relates to the way of wandering Bedouins, or in memory of Terah's oldest son, Haran, who died there. Deurloo is inclined to think that this topographical detail has a confessional meaning. Namely that the narrator is preparing us for the great event of Genesis 12, Abram's call. Those who want to go to the land without a particular reason don't get there. They leave for Canaan but settle in Haran, and "they settled there." How then did Abram get to the Promised Land? This is where Abram's story starts.

6:10 Genesis 12:1–25:11 'Go from ... to the land I will show you'

> Now the LORD said to Abram, 'Go from your country and your kindred and your father's house to the land that I will show you, And I will make of you a great nation, and I will bless you, and make your name great, so that you will be a blessing'.
> So Abram went, as the LORD had told him, and Lot went with him. And they set forth to go to the land of Canaan ... Abram passed through the land to the place at Shechem, to the oak of Moreh. At that time the Canaanites were in the land. Then the LORD appeared to Abram, and said, 'To your descendants I will give this land.' So he built there an altar to the LORD, who had appeared to him. Thence he removed to the mountain on the east of Bethel, and pitched his tent, with Bethel on the west and Ai on the east; and there he built an altar to the LORD and called on the name of the LORD. And Abram journeyed on, still going to the Negeb.
> Genesis 12:2, 4–9

Abram separates himself from his father's house. He went with his entire household, his nephew Lot and his many belongings. In today's language, he became an 'immigrant' or a 'refugee', "a wandering Aramean." Almost in passing it mentions that Sarai was barren and had no child. In contrast the same section mentions the word 'son' four times. A little further on we read, "And Abram took Sarai his wife, and Lot his brother's son, and all their possessions which they gathered, and the persons that they had gotten in Haran; and they set forth to go to the land of Canaan." (Gen 12:5) This time Abram himself takes the initiative. They leave the place of fatherly authority behind and their entire clan. "So Abram went, as the LORD had told him" in the hope that he would get to see a land. "Then the LORD appeared to Abram." (Gen 12:7)

This is the land of the theophany, where the LORD shows himself to him. A notable place is reached, namely Bethel in the west and Ai in the east. That is the border between Northern (Joseph: Ephraim and Manassah) and Southern Israel (Judah and Benjamin). The book of Joshua draws the same borders. With this indication we are exactly in the middle of the land. With Abram we arrive at this place. Here, in this special place, Abram builds an altar "and called on the name of the LORD" (Gen 12:8). These are the words with which Genesis 2–4 ends in such a hopeful way. In the midst of the 'Canaan-human', who is nowhere, the storytellers highlight for a moment the place where 'God' and the 'murder' are not forgotten. "At that time, the Canaanites were in the land." (Gen 12:6)

Deurloo in *Closer to Genesis*, p.88, muses whether Abram was an actual historical figure. He suggests that the storyteller uses the figure of a tribal head of roaming Bedouins to tell the story of the origin of the people of Israel. The teller was aware that the tribal head of Israel was originally from the Euphrates, the land of the two rivers. "A wandering Aramean was my father" (Deut 26:5) is a text that was recited at the presentation of the first-fruits of the harvest.

By interpreting the history of Abram in this light in exile they confessed their faith in the LORD the God of Israel and Israel's miraculous origin among all the nations of the earth. We are inclined to ask, are the events true; did they happen? 'Confessions-of-faith' stories are true. Of course they are true. Just as the birth announcement, "God gave us a girl!" is true. It happened. One way Deurloo likes to answer those kinds of questions is by saying, 'Israel exists, does it not?! (Then so does Abraham', or David, or Joseph, or Joshua, or . . .) Our way to describe such events is very limited, it is either factual or fiction. As Palache pointed out the narrators' or storytellers' time and truth are hard for us to imagine.

We can be grateful to Deurloo that he was not afraid to consider critical scholarship with regard to the origin and authorship of Genesis. Rather than immediately rejecting these critical theories as was often done within conservative circles, he engaged in what can be called 'a critical retrieval' of current scholarship. Not for a moment did it take away for him from the trustworthiness and meaning of the scriptures, as is clear from all his writings. In doing so, he did us a great service. Where many of us might have been afraid to seriously (re-)consider alternative answers, and venture a different viewpoint, he looked for what we might learn from other theories and scholars in spite of their often objectionable presuppositions (hence the 'critical').

Rather than outright rejection, he inspired us also to engage in a 'critical retrieval'. It made him consider many geographical references as etiological marking points (like famous stones, caves, hills, pillars of salt, etc.), or aetiological stories and exemplary stories. More often than not he would express appreciation, or if the text demanded a different view, he would not hesitate to reject the view. It left many discussions openended or undecided. During his entire life he kept searching the scriptures for their meaning. Such an approach is liberating. Many questions remain open and challenging. By contrast, it is sad to see when prospective doctoral students, for example, have to be defensive or rationalize their insights to their supportive conservative community to avoid severe condemnation and rejection.

Other authors have used the words; this is an 'exemplary story or figure' or 'cautionary tale for our edification 'Noort). Expanding on that notion, Deurloo suggests that a well-known historical figure, like 'the head of a Bedouin tribe' stood as a model for the figure of Abram. At times there are givens in the text that point to the fact that we are dealing with an idealized figure or story. Later on someone else may come up with a different interpretation. That is what open-ended means. It is an honest engagement with the text and the history of interpretation. These considerations usually add to the prophetic meaning of a text, inviting us to join in the confession of faith and celebration. During the process of interpreting we constantly need to keep in mind the 'narrative' character of large parts of the scriptures, as explained earlier by Palache.

Abram travelled through the land to see his inheritance from one end of the country to the other. At crucial points he built an altar like a 'beachhead', there to call on the name of the LORD like in the days of Seth. The only guarantee he had was the voice that said, "Go from your country" and "Go to the land I will show you." Is it such a great country, 'flowing with milk and honey'? (Gen 3:8)

The first thing we hear in the same chapter is that there was a famine in the land, and in the next chapter, war. Abram must travel to a land of famine and war. In spite of this, it is a great land because that is where the LORD will appear, where he will show himself. Because of that it is a great land. "And I will make of you a great nation and bless you." (Gen 3:12) In turn you, Israel shall bless all the nations. And cursed are those nations who do not join in. Israel knows all about them, the mighty rulers, emperors and kings, nations that do not bless Israel, they are banned.

The word 'bless' appears many times in these first few verses of chapter 12. When two people meet each other, look each other in the eyes, embrace, and give gifts, they are truly united. When two people truly give themselves to the other and for the other and make the encounter into a festive occasion, the Bible uses the word 'bless'. That is what it means to bless your neighbor. Of old the high priest would lift up his arms and lay the blessing on the people.

The LORD bless you and keep you:
The LORD make his face to shine upon you, and be gracious to you:
The LORD lift up his countenance upon you, and give you peace.
So shall they put my name upon the people of Israel, and I will bless them.
    Numbers 6:24–27 (cf. Psalm 67)

and if you obey the voice of the LORD your God . . .
The LORD your God will set you high above all the nations of the earth.
And all these blessings shall come upon you and overtake you . . .
Blessed shall you be in the city, and blessed shall you be in the field . . .
    Deuteronomy 28:1–6

If we encounter the LORD God in this way and call on his name, we are blessed. And if Israel responds in this way to the blessing of the LORD, by blessing all the peoples, then by way of summary the narrator can say, "And with you all the families of the earth shall be blessed." Then there will be peace on earth.

6:11 Genesis 13:1–14:24 Two ways of seeing, Abram and Lot

But not all is peace. Before long there is famine in the land and Abram has to move further south with his herds and people, all the way to Egypt. It becomes a shameful journey. Afraid to be murdered because of his beautiful wife, he lies, claiming that she is his sister. She ends up in Pharaoh's harem. Abram prospers (Gen 12:15–16). He will have his own exodus. "But the LORD afflicted Pharaoh and his house with great plagues because of Sarai, Abram's wife." (Gen 12:17) It pre-figures the exodus to come. Pharaoh discovers his lie and sends him away. "Now then, here is your wife, take her, and be gone" (Gen 12:19). And they send him on his way, "So Abram went up from Egypt, he and his wife, and all that he had, and Lot with him, into the Negeb." (Gen 13:1)

He travels north as far as Bethel ". . . to the place where he had made an altar at the first; and there Abram called upon the name of the Lord." (Gen 13:2–4) He is back where he needs to be and calls out what he needs to call. His journey to Egypt has not been in vain in spite of his shameful deception and risking everything. He may prefigure a great tribal ancestor but he is not a saint.

Meanwhile Lot had travelled with Abram to the Promised Land and to Egypt. What role does he play in the Abram cycle? His uncle Abram had taken him under his wing, since his father had died. Lot is a contrasting figure to Abram in a way that makes Abram stand out all the more strongly. It is the one remaining tie to his past that Abram needs to leave behind. Israel has to go its own way. Abram represents Israel and Lot the other peoples. They were both very rich with large flocks.

There was not enough land to accommodate both large households, "Now Abram was very rich in cattle, in silver, and in gold." (Gen 13:2) "And Lot, who went with Abram, also had flocks and herds and tents, so that the land could not support both of them dwelling together; for their possessions were so great that they could not dwell together." (Gen 13:6) "And there was strife between the herdsmen of Abram's cattle and the herdsmen of Lot's cattle. At that time, the Canaanites and the Perizzites dwelt in the Land." (Gen 13:7) The earth could not accommodate both.

"Then Abram said to Lot, 'Let there be no strife between you and me . . . for we are kinsmen. Is not the whole land before you? Separate yourself from me. If you take the left hand, then I will go to the right . . .'" (Gen 13:8, 9) And just like Abram had looked over the land that the LORD would show him, Lot "lifted up his eyes" and saw a "valley well watered everywhere like the garden of the LORD," the Jordan valley, like paradise. He saw fertile pastures and prosperity. We might say: "He saw dollar signs." This is the valley Lot chose . . . Lot journeyed east, thus they separated from each other. Abram dwelt in the land of Canaan, while Lot dwelt among the cities of the valley and moved his tent as far as Sodom." (Gen 13:11, 12) The storyteller alerts us to what is to come, "Now the men of Sodom were wicked, great sinners against the LORD." (Gen 13:12, 13)

After they had separated, Abram is encouraged by the LORD. "Lift up your eyes, and look" in every direction . . ." Gen. 13:14, 15). "For all the land which you see I will give to you and to your descendants forever." Both men look and see, but one sees prosperity in the lush valley among the wicked Sodomites and Abram sees the uninhabitable highlands to the west.

But Abram sees more, he sees the Promised Land. By faith he journeyed on to the oaks of Mamre, near Hebron and there he built an altar to the LORD. There are two ways of seeing. Abram sees what he has heard. Lot sees only what is before him. Israel sees what it has heard. The peoples see just what is before them. Israel separates itself for all generations to come from the other nations. When Israel starts to tell its history, it starts to tell about the great acts of the LORD in the gift of land, the land, because it has been given to Israel by the LORD as a heritage. The 'earth land' is where history will be made; a history which is representative for the whole world will take place here, in Canaan. It is a place where humanity can live and thrive. It is the land where the LORD will show himself.

The coming disaster already rumbles in the distance. The narrator has alerted us to it twice. First in Genesis 13: 10, "this was before the LORD destroyed Sodom and Gomorrah" and Genesis 13:13, "now the men of Sodom were wicked and great sinners against the LORD." Four kings of the region rebelled and made war against five other kings, including the kings of Sodom and Gomorrah. The battle did not go well for the five kings. Some fled and fell into the bitumen pits of that area, others fled to the mountains. The conquerors took all the goods and food of Sodom and Gomorrah, including Lot and his goods. One escapee told Abram what had happened to Lot. So Abram came into action. He took all his trained men and defeated the enemy by means of a clever military strategy. He brought back Lot with everything he had acquired. He accepted no reward from the king of Sodom.

In the midst of the peoples, stands the disaster. They live from disaster to disaster. That is how the narrator depicts world history, as a meaningless history, from one disaster to another, from one war to another, from one famine to another. "Living before and after the flood" remains the theme of this episode.

After this disaster, the LORD reassured Abram again, "Fear not, Abram, I am your shield; your reward shall be very great." He has seen the land, but Sarai was barren, we read earlier. He had no son, so how could he become a great nation? Abram expressed his concern to the LORD. "O LORD God, what wilt thou give me, for I continue childless." Will my trusted slave and overseer be my heir? And the LORD said, No, your own son, your first-born, shall be the heir. The LORD asked him to look at the stars and number them. Then he said to him, "So shall your descendants be." "And he believed the LORD; and he reckoned it to him as righteousness." (Gen 15:6) In every respect Abram could only live by faith in spite of famine, war, being landless and without children.

Abram was not without doubts. The LORD said to him, "I am the LORD who brought you from Ur of the Chaldeans, to give you this land to possess." But Abram replied, "... how am I to know that I shall possess it?" Then the LORD made a solemn covenant with him and repeated, "To your descendants I give this land . . ." (Gen 15:18) an enormous land as far as you can see, from the north to the south and from the east to the west, an idealized size. That settled the promise of the land once more, but what about an heir?

After ten years in the land of Canaan, Sarai has a solution and takes matters in her own hands. She had a slave woman from Egypt and told Abram to take her as his wife and have a child with her. "The LORD has prevented me from bearing children; go in to my maid; it may be that I shall obtain children by her." (Gen 16:2) And Abram did and Hagar bore a son, Ishmael. But Hagar looked with contempt at Sarai. Sarai complained to Abram. But Abram said, "Behold your maid is in your power; do to her as you please. Then Sarai dealt harshly with her, and she fled from her." But the LORD told her to go back to her mistress with the promise that her son too would become a great nation and be blessed.

The becoming of Israel in the midst of the nations will not happen in a natural way, that is, what is 'natural' among the surrounding peoples. It will take a miracle. Once more the LORD reassured Abram with the promise of the Land and a multitude of offspring. (Gen 17) The sign of the covenant was the circumcision of all the males. All the men including Ishmael were circumcised as a sign and confirmation of the covenant.

His name would no longer be Abram, but Abraham, "for I have made you the father of a multitude of nations." And Sarai's name will be Sarah, "I will bless her, and she shall be a mother of nations." After hearing all this Abraham "fell on his face and laughed, and said to himself, 'shall a child be born to a man who is a hundred years old? Shall Sarah, who is ninety years old, bear a son?'" (Gen 17:17)

6:12 Genesis 18:16–19:38 Sodom and Gomorrah

Once more the Lord appeared to Abraham. He showed himself to him. Three men appeared and Abraham invited his guests to stay and refresh themselves and have a meal, as was customary law with regard to strangers. And they prepared a great meal, a 'morsel of bread' as the text reads. He joined them as they ate. Again they told Abraham that Sarah would have a child by the time they would return in the spring. Sarah heard what the men had said and laughed. "Now Abraham and Sarah were old, advanced in age; it had ceased to be with Sarah after the manner of women . . . after I have grown old, shall I have pleasure?" She was caught out laughing even though she denied it. But the LORD said, "Is anything too hard for the LORD?" and we could add, "Is anything too hard for the Creator of heaven and earth, who made male and female together as his image bearers?" This is not a proof text that tells us that God is almighty. It simply says, is there anything that the Lord says he will do that will not come to pass? God does what he has said.

Two of the men went on their way and Abraham accompanied them for a while. They wanted to share with Abraham that they were going to destroy Sodom and Gomorrah. Remembering his nephew, he pleaded and bargained with the LORD. "Wilt thou indeed destroy the righteous with the wicked? . . . Far be it from thee! Shall not the Judge of all the earth do right?" (Gen 18:23-25) The LORD had said, "Because the outcry against Sodom and Gomorrah is great and their sin is very grave, I will go down to see whether they have done altogether according to the outcry which has come to me; and if not, I will know." "For the sake of ten I will not destroy it." The LORD went his way and Abraham returned to his place. The storytellers say nothing about the angels. We are not informed what the angels were like. The teller only informs us what they said and did. An angel is no more than a messenger. He says and does what he has been commanded. Different figures can play this role in the scriptures.

The two angels came to Sodom and Lot persuaded them to come and stay with him for the night, knowing that it was not safe for them to stay in the city square. It is a first warning that the 'rights' of strangers will not be honored. He extended the customary hospitality to the two men. During the night, all the men of the city, both young and old, to the last man, surrounded the house and demanded that Lot bring out the two men "to know them."

We need to be very reserved in our response to this story. It is not about a general judgment against homosexuality. "The men of Sodom were wicked, great sinners against the LORD." Even the children had joined the men. Are we to think that all the children and the old people were burning with desire to have sexual intercourse with the two men? This is not what is being told here, it is something different.

In describing the situation in Sodom, the storyteller wants to let us know that all the relations between the people were disturbed. He uses sexuality, or rather sexual abuse and violence, as an illustration of how all the interpersonal relations were broken. In the East it was of crucial importance to extend hospitality to strangers. This was so important that Lot would even give his own flesh and blood, his two virgin daughters, before he would violate that norm. If that norm is violated, then all human relations are at risk and broken. To be a hospitable person, that is, to be truly human as is expected, you must do everything in your power to defend it and welcome strangers in your house. "When a stranger sojourns with you in your land, you shall not do him wrong. The stranger who sojourns with you shall be to you as the native among you, and you shall love him as yourself; for you were strangers in the land of Egypt: I am the LORD your God." (Lev. 19:33) The angels struck all the men with blindness so that they could no longer find the door. Again we hear, "both small and great, so that they wearied themselves groping for the door."

Then they said to Lot to gather his entire family. But his sons in law, betrothed to his two daughters thought that he was joking. "He seemed to his sons in law to be jesting." When morning came, they were urged to flee the city. "Flee for your life; do not look back or stop . . ." After they had left the city, Lot and his wife and two daughters were allowed to stay in a little place close by, in Zoar. But Lot's wife looked back and became a pillar of salt. She could not separate herself from her surroundings. The narrators have chosen the setting of the landscape for their story. In the salt pillars and mountains on the southwest side of the Dead Sea there are many of those pillars. Every guide can show you Lot's wife in one of those salt pillars. Lot's wife has become a part of the decor. She could not let go. Lot too cannot separate himself from the city. He stayed in a cave close to Zoar, because he was afraid to enter the city. With Zoar we are already in the direction of Moab and Ammon.

"So it was that, when God destroyed the cities of the valley, God remembered Abraham, and sent Lot out of the midst of the overthrow." (Gen 19:29) When the LORD remembered Abraham he spared Lot and his family. How did it go with Lot after the disaster of the destruction of Sodom and Gomorrah? We remember that after the flood the people continued to do what they had been doing before the disaster. 'Business as usual', we would say. This theme returns to describe how Lot continued to live. 'Without his knowledge', he becomes the father of two sons by his two daughters, called Moab and Ammon, who became the fathers of the Moabites and the Ammonites.

The people living after the flood also knew nothing. The contrast between Lot and Abraham could not be greater. Lot an old man, with his two 'grandsons', rather sons, on his knees, and Abraham laughing in his tent. When we come closer to Abraham's tent, we can already hear the laughter. In his tent a son is born. His name is Isaac, which means "God has made laughter for me, everyone who hears will laugh over me." "And she said, 'Who would have said to Abraham that Sarah would suckle children? Yet I have borne him a son in his old age.'" Abraham was a hundred years old when Isaac was born. And Abraham circumcised Isaac when he was eight days old. By a miraculous birth, the promised son appeared.

This concludes the first of the three great stories of Genesis, those of Abraham, Isaac, and Jacob, and the becoming of Israel in the midst of the nations.

6:13 Genesis 25:19 –35:29   *The Isaac 'toledot'; Rebecca, Jacob and Esau*

The Isaac cycle is the 8th toledot. Just before that it relates the generations of Ishmael which is the 7th toledot, (Gen. 25:12–18). It is very short, but it emphasizes that Ishmael too shall be a great nation with many descendents, as was promised to Hagar. (Gen 16:7–14) "Behold you are with child, and shall bear a son; you shall call his name Ishmael (that is 'God hears'); because the LORD has given heed to your affliction." He too will become a great nation." Ishmael will share in the blessing of Abraham, "I will so greatly multiply your descendants that they cannot be numbered for multitude." This is almost identical to the promise to Abraham. And Hagar confessed, "Thou art a God of seeing . . . Have I really seen God and remained alive after seeing him?" The well where she found water was called, Beer-lahai-roi, that is, the well of one who sees and lives.

Again and again we hear that God hears the voice of the distressed. ("And now behold, the cry of the people of Israel have come to me, and I have seen their oppression . . . " (Exod 3:7, cf. Exod 22:23; and many Psalms) Earlier when Hagar was sent away, ". . . Abraham rose early in the morning, and took bread and a skin of water, and gave it to Hagar, put it on her shoulder, along with the child, and sent her away. And she departed, and wandered in the wilderness of Beersheba." When the water ran out, she despaired for the life of her child. Not to have to hear her child crying and watch him dying, she sat a 'long' distance away from him. (Gen 21:15)

"The child lifted up his voice and wept." and God heard the voice of the lad" dying of thirst in the desert. "Arise, lift up the lad, and hold him fast with your hand; for I will make him a great nation . . ." (Gen 21:16–18) "Then God opened her eyes, and she saw a well of water; and she went ... and gave the lad a drink. And God was with the lad and he grew up ..." (Gen 21:19, 20) Ishmael became a real nomad of the desert, an expert with the bow, "a wild ass of a man." (Gen 16:12) The list of his generations will say, "These are the sons of Ishmael and these are their names, by their villages and by their encampments, twelve princes according to their tribes." Ishmael too shares in the blessing, just like Esau later on.

Hearing these stories and promises again or anew, we are encouraged to look at the stars, each time my mother would hear these stories she would be inspired and sing, "Do you know how many stars ..." That is how great Israel will become.

6:14 Genesis 22:1–14 *The offering of Isaac*

In the life of the peoples the disaster stands central "before and after the flood." In the life of Abraham everything is about the birth of the first-born, Isaac, 'all who hear will laugh'. And now, of all things, he is asked to offer his dearly beloved son as a burnt offering. It is a repulsive story. There lies the boy, the promised son and Abraham is ready to slaughter him in an offering ritual. This is no longer his son. The body of the boy has become an animal; an animal whose head is pulled back to cut its throat. At the last moment God intervenes and stops Abraham. In the nick of time ... it turns out alright. But we still stay fixated on that raised knife and the body of the boy and the gruesome moment to come. However that kind of image leads us astray in our understanding of this story.

How did this story of child sacrifice enter the scene? It is simply because it was a reality at that time. In the land of Canaan, among the people with whom Abraham lived, child sacrifice happened. When building a house or a wall, they would offer a child to the gods to secure that the house or wall would be solid and dependable. The body would be cemented in the wall. The scriptures talk about this religious practice with great repulsion.

> In his days Hiel of Bethel built Jericho; he laid its foundation at the cost of Abiram his first-born, and set up its gates at the cost of his youngest son Segub, according to the word of the Lord, which he spoke by Joshua the son of Nun.
> 1 Kings 16:34.

THE PROPHETIC CALL TO LOVE AND JUSTICE

At the re-building of Jericho two child sacrifices were brought. Surrounded by this practice it would not be strange if the Israelites also asked themselves whether or not they too should offer children to God. To this concrete question the prophet Micha, among other references to the practice, answers very clearly and strongly,

> And they have built the high place of Topheth, which is the valley of the son of Hinnom, to burn sons and their daughters in the fire, which I did not command, nor did it come into my mind.
> Jeremiah 7:31.

> You shall not give any of your children to devote them by fire to Moloch, and so profane the name of the LORD: I am the LORD.
> Leviticus 18:21; 20:2–5

> He (king Ahaz) even burnt his son as an offering, according to the abominable practices of the nations whom the LORD drove out before the people of Israel.
> II Kings 16:3. (cf 21:6)

> Shall I give my first-born for my transgression, the fruit of my body for the sin of my soul?
> He has showed you, O man, what is good; and what does the LORD require of you
> but to do justice, and to love kindness, and to walk humbly with your God?
> Micah 6:7, 8

It is clear the LORD does not want this extreme devotion. We are asked to go with God, believing and trusting that God does what he has promised. We are asked to go with God on our journey through life. Walking humbly with our God and doing justice. In Genesis 12 we heard, "Go" and Abraham went but now the son, "Take your son." Will Abraham continue to walk with God? Abraham does. "And He believed the LORD; and he reckoned it to him as righteousness." (Gen 15: 6) Abraham had to take leave of his natural surroundings, his kindred, Lot his nephew, and now he is asked to surrender his only son, his assurance for the future. Here it is clear that the future is not determined by natural ties, but that they are determined by what God says and does.

Take your son ... and go ... and he went. The parallel with Genesis 12 is the key to this episode. "After these things God tested Abraham." With that phrase we know the outcome of the story. When God called him, Abraham answered, "Here am I." Even when his son asks, 'we have wood, the knife and the fire, but what about the sacrifice? He simply answers, "Here am I, my son . . . God will provide himself the lamb for a burnt offering, my son." He gently reassures his son. Twice it says, "So they went both of them together." "Abraham believed and trusted." "And by your descendents shall all the nations of the earth bless themselves, because you have obeyed my voice." (Gen 22: 18)

Traditionally any first-born son is to be redeemed by a burnt offering, (Exod 13: 2, 12, 15; Num 3: 13; 8:17) as also happened with Jesus when his parents presented him in the temple and they sacrificed a burnt offering, "a pair of turtledoves, or two young pigeons." (Luke 2:22–24)

With this motif of 'child sacrifice' the narrators tell us how Abraham becomes directly involved with God in the history that he had in mind. He trusted in a future which God sees. The storytellers want to tell us the story of the route God wants to go with his people. He takes the initiative again and again, but not without involving his people; and not without the answer of the human partner who travels along with God. In this way he wants to be God and in no other way.

In an earlier and separate article, Deurloo examined the details of the story. "Because you have listened to my voice (Genesis 22)."[4] Here he calls attention to all the details of the story and the key words together with his own translation. The story starts with the words, "After these things . . ." (Gen. 22:1) After all the following has happened: Abraham and Sarah's questionable actions, taking matters in their own hands, giving her slave woman to Abraham, the birth of Ishamel and sending him away, having to separate from Lot, whose life was saved with his family during the destruction of Sodom and Gomorrah, and sojourning "many days in the land of the Philistines." "And Abraham hearkened to the voice of Sarai." (Gen 16:2) Together with Gen 22:20 ("Now after these things . . ."), it frames the story. The previous cycle (15–22) was primarily focused on the land "After these things . . ." (Gen 15:1). The focus is now on the birth of a son. God called Abraham and said, "Take your son, your only son Isaac, whom you love, and go to the land of Moriah, and offer him there as a burnt offering upon one of the mountains of which I shall tell you." (Gen 22:2)

These two relations in which Abraham acts are described as the love for his son (Genesis 22:2) and the fear of God (Gen 22:12) echoes the

---

4. Deurloo, *Cahier #5*, 41–60.

words of Genesis 12, "Go, you, from your country and your kindred and your father's house . . ." That call comes at the beginning of the stories of the land and signifies the break with his 'natural' past, his family and kinsmen, to become a sojourner, a stranger. This new call, "Take your son . . ." comes at the end of the stories about the birth of a son, and indicates a break with a 'natural' future that is personified by his son Isaac. Abram has to go to "a land that I will show you," here to the land of Moriah. 'Seeing' becomes a key word in chapter 22 as well as in the beginning.

Isaac is the only one, he is the son. The words "the only one" appears together with "so they went both of them together." In Genesis 22:2, 6, 8, 12, the 'only one" and "together" is a thematic word as a part within the whole. The call is to go "to the place of which God had told him." Abram "saw the place from afar off," "we will go yonder," "when they came to the place of which God had told him." There Abram built an altar. The place remains unnamed here, "a mountain." Because of its repetition we are inclined to think of Jerusalem, the place of which Yahweh had said, "But you shall seek the place which the LORD your God will choose . . . thither you shall bring your burnt offerings . . ." (Deuteronomy 12: 5–7) Here he will offer a ram. The three words, 'take', 'go', and 'burnt offering,' become the building blocks of the story. They are repeated in Deuteronomy 12:3–10 and remain in a tension with vs.2. Abraham went to the place for the burnt offering. They form a circle around the story.

At the beginning of this cycle, we read to "Go" and he went, but here we read "Take" and then Isaac, followed by "wood for the burnt offering." It places the emphasis on the sacrifice. "On the third day Abraham lifted up his eyes and saw the place from far off." "On the third day" is the day on which it is going to happen. It announces a new time period. The same words are used in Genesis 13:14 "Lift up your eyes." They show the special nature of the seeing. With emphasis Abraham says, "I and the boy" he says to his two young men and added, we will return to you, "we come again to you." And it is not until verse 19 that we read, "So Abraham returned to the young men."

"So they went both of them together." "And Abraham took the wood for the burnt offering and laid it on Isaac," which intensifies the story. For Isaac it is to undergo his destiny, for Abraham it is the deed. That is how the two together go their way. The route is not described further, only the essence of their conversation. "'My father . . . behold the fire and the wood, but where is the lamb for a burnt offering'?" Abraham answered and said, 'God will provide himself the lamb for a burnt offering, my son.' So they went both of them together." (Gen 22)

Abraham trusts entirely on what God sees and has shown him. Then Abraham put forth his hand and took the knife to slay his son." There are two kinds of taking. "And laid the wood in order, and bound Isaac his son, and laid him on the altar, upon the wood." In this story he does what had been lacking in the previous accounts (Gen 16–21), his total trust in the LORD. "Then Abraham put forth his hand, and took the knife to slay his son . . ." (Gen 22:10) With painful precision the story is told in cultic-technical terms. He stretched out his hand, took the knife, to "slay" his son. This journey is a break with the future for Abraham, which he had envisioned in Isaac, whose name means "to laugh." He trusted that what God sees. Then the angel of Yahweh called Abraham "from out of heaven." Twice his name is repeated. "Abraham, Abraham! . . . Do not lay your hand on the lad or do anything to him." "Now I know you are a God-fearing, a righteous man, seeing that you have not withheld your son, your only son, from me." His raised hand is the deed that will confirm his word and is the core of the story.

The scene is frozen in mid air, as it were. The only son he has, Abraham, as a god-fearing man, surrenders his son to the God who sees. It is the secret of Israel's existence. All burnt offerings look to this offering of Abraham. Two additions are added by the author, "So Abraham called the name of the place, 'the LORD will provide.'" A ram caught in a thicket presents itself. "On this mountain of the LORD it shall be provided." With this actualizing formula the importance of this story is underscored. It points ahead to the beginning of a new beginning (Gen 37:1), which starts the toledot of Jacob, ending in Egypt followed by the novelette of Joseph, awaiting the exodus and the return to the Promised Land. From out of Egypt I called my first-born son. In Isaac, the whole seed of Abraham is at risk.

It sets the stage for two more events that need to happen: finding a wife for Isaac from his kinsmen in Haran and a gravesite for the burial of Sarah. "Now after these things it was told Abraham" that his brother Nahor had eight children. What follows is the story of the death and burial of Sarah.

What is good? When is there shalom? "He has shown you, Oh man, what is good . . ." (Micah 6:8) He tells us what he will do and he does what he has said. By that trust we can recognize the people of God that travel through the world. With this story of Abraham as representative of Israel,

THE PROPHETIC CALL TO LOVE AND JUSTICE

and through Israel all of us, we are taught about faith, what it means to trust and believe; to take the LORD at his word. "Go and leave" and "Go and take your son."

In the sixth century before Christ in exile the storytellers paint a picture of Abraham, who stands as model for all of Israel in its obedience and its waywardness and through Israel for us. At the beginning of the Abram cycle God set this whole history of Abraham in motion, "Go from your country and your kindred and your father's house to the land I will show you." "And Abram went, as the LORD had told him and Lot went with him." And in Genesis 22, the last part of the story of Abraham, go to the mountain of Moriah, "Take your son, your only son Isaac, whom you love . . . and offer him there as a burnt offering." "So Abraham . . . went." (Gen 22:1–6) Land and a son, Abram's life is one of living before and after the first-born. "By faith Abraham obeyed when he was called to go out to a place . . . and he went out, not knowing where he was to go. By faith he sojourned in the land of promise, as in a foreign land, living in tents with Isaac and Jacob, heirs with him of the same promise . . . by faith Abraham, when he was tested, offered up Isaac, and he who had received the promises was ready to offer up his only son, of whom it was said, "through Isaac shall your descendants be named." (Hebrews 11:8, 9:17, 18)

Did the story continue? Is there still a future for Israel now that it has been deported to Babylon? As the story about Abraham comes to a close the next episode of the becoming of Israel among the nations is already announced. Abraham receives news of his family back in Haran. His brother had no less than eight sons. "Now after these things it was told Abraham, behold, Milca also has borne children to your brother Nahor," eight sons as well as daughters. Separately the narrators mention, "Bethuel became the father of Rebekah." (Gen 22:23) The narrator wants to alert us to what is to come. Does the story go on that has been started by the LORD?

But first we hear about Sarah's death. He had lived with her for many decades and now he must leave "from before her face." Abraham bought a piece of land with a cave from the Hittites, at Machpelah, near Mamre and Hebron in the land of Canaan, as a burying place, as a first installment on the land. See the touching account by Deurloo about Sarah's death in *Cahier #1*, 'Sarah's grave."[5] From before his tent Abraham has

---

5. Deurloo, Het graf van Sara; 22–32.

a clear view of his wife's grave. There he can remember her life and all the years they had lived together; "Sarah lived a hundred and twenty-seven years; these were the years of the life of Sarah." (Gen 23:1) After the contract was successfully negotiated, "After this, Abraham buried Sarah his wife," before the face of the cave of Mamre (that is Hebron), in the land of Canaan. The patriarchs lived and died toward the future; that cave is a sign of the Promised Land. The story of Abraham is told as the relation between a man and his wife and their son. (In the Jacob story, it is the relation between the man and his brother.) The story of the 'child sacrifice' is lifted up to proclaim a new beginning for the people of Israel in exile to encourage them that a new beginning is possible.

"Remember Abraham, Isaac, and Israel, thy servants, to whom thou didst swear by thine own self, and didst say to them, 'I will multiply your descendants as the stars of heaven, and all this land that I have promised I will give to your descendants, and they shall inherit it forever" (Exod 32:13) "And the LORD repented of the evil which he thought to do to his people," (after the episode of the golden calf).

6:15 Genesis 24:1–67 History continues: Rebekah

The news comes at the right time. He has received the son of the promise as his seed in Gen 22. The story goes on. Having heard the news from his family, Abraham makes his oldest, trusted servant swear that he will go to his country and family and bring back a bride for Isaac. Don't let her marry one of the daughters of the Canaanites, and do not take my son back to Haran. The LORD, the God of heaven who has taken me from my father's house, who has spoken to me, his angel will go before you. The servant hesitated and said, 'What if she is not willing to come?' Abraham responded and said, 'then you are free from your oath'. The narrators highlight an important theme in this long account of finding a bride for Isaac. To settle among the Canaanites and make themselves at home there among the inhabitants with their religious customs was an ongoing temptation for Israel. Abraham radically rejects this temptation. His son must not marry a Canaanite woman. The people of Israel would no longer exist and instead become absorbed by the surrounding peoples.

Each generation anew has to learn that the LORD wants to be the God of his people and that each generation will have to show its faithfulness and solidarity. At the same time the storytellers want to emphasize that a woman will appear on the scene that dares to follow the same route as Abraham, and that is also willing to leave her family. But if she is not willing, "must I then take your son back to the land from which you came?" the servant asked. Abraham emphatically says no to this option and trusted the LORD to guide his servant to find a bride for his son there. "So the servant put his hand under the thigh of Abraham his master, and swore to him. (Gen 24:1–9). Will Rebekah be willing to follow and go to Canaan and will her family be willing to let her go? Will she be ready to follow the same route as Abraham?

As the servant had prayed for, Rebekah offered the servant a drink from her jar and then also offered to give water to the camels. When she did this, he gave her presents of gold and silver and asked who she was and if they could lodge at her place. When he heard who she was, the daughter of Bethuel, the servant bowed his head and worshiped the LORD, and blessed the LORD, the God of his master Abraham, who had led him the right way. She ran back to her family and told them all about the visitor and what he had said. Her brother Laban went to meet the caravan by the well and invited them to come with him. They were offered hospitality and an elaborate meal, but the servant refused to eat until they had shared the purpose of their visit.

The family agreed to the request and said, "Behold, Rebekah is before you, take her and go, and let her be the wife of your master's son, as the LORD has spoken." Upon hearing these words, the servant bowed his head again and then took out all the presents for Rebekah and the rest of her family. The men ate and drank and they stayed the night. The next morning the servant wanted to go back, but the family wanted them to stay a little while, at least ten days. But the servant said, "Do not delay me, since the LORD has prospered my way; let me go that I may go to my master." They decided to ask the maiden, "Will you go with this man?" She said, "I will go." They let her go and blessed her. She did the same thing as Abraham, she went. They left and went on their way.

Isaac was meditating in the field and he looked up and saw the caravan. Rebekah too lifted up her eyes and saw Isaac. She covered her face with her veil. The servant told him all about what had happened. Then we simply hear that Isaac met her and took Rebekah to his tent "and she became his wife, and he loved her so Isaac was comforted after his mother's death." Gen 24:12–67) Now Rebekah can truly take Sarah's place, as the mother of Israel. History continues. The LORD's faithfulness and solidarity with his people is realized by the willingness and trust of his people. The LORD does not forsake the works of his hands, each generation anew. All the way, the LORD and his angel guided Abraham's servant's mission. It is not a heavy confessional issue. The storyteller simply relates how a young man and a young woman came to love each other and became part of Israel's future.

The story continues with Isaac's two sons, Jacob and Esau that were born to Rebekah. Each time the story is about the 'becoming of Israel in the midst of the peoples of the earth'. The story of Abraham is completed. Now the story of Isaac can begin. Each time next to the main figure, the narrator places a counter figure. Lot, Ishmael and Esau are representative of the surrounding peoples. Israel literally lives among the peoples, surrounded by the Moabites, Ammonites (Lot), Edomites (Esau) and the southern nomads (Ishmael). We tend to ask, where does he come from, what is his origin? We have to change our perspective, because the scriptures ask, who comes to the fore again and again in history in a surprising and miraculous way? This is illustrated in a remarkable way in this story about Esau and Jacob.

6:16 Genesis 27:1–35:29 *Esau and Jacob, the stolen blessing*

The first thing we hear about Rebekah is that she is barren. Isaac prays to the LORD and the LORD granted his prayer, and Rebekah his wife conceived. Even before they are born the two "children struggled together within her." She asked the LORD, why is this happening to me? The LORD responded and said, "Two nations are in your womb, and two peoples, born of you, shall be divided; the one shall be stronger than the other, the elder shall serve the younger." (Gen 27:23). Even at birth the struggle continued. The first of the twins came out reddish and hairy. So they called him Esau. After that Jacob came out, holding on to Esau's ankle. They called him Jacob.

With this designation of Esau, the storytellers want us to know where he will live: in the rough country south of the Dead Sea, the land of Edom. Edom, Seir, (Gen 36:9) 'hairy', because of the rough mountainous area. 'red' because the reddish-brown earth (Gen 25:25). It may explain the century long connection and hostility between Israel and Edom. The narrators use this given to indicate the basic theme of the becoming of Israel and its relation to the surrounding peoples.

In this story, Esau comes to the fore first and not Jacob, the 'ankle holder', the 'deceiver'. Jacob/Israel is not portrayed very positively. The two brothers are characterized as a hunter, a man of the field, Esau, and Jacob as a 'homebody', living in tents. For good measure, the narrator adds, "Isaac loved Esau, because he ate of his game; but Rebekah loved Jacob," which set up the conflict from the beginning.

In a few verses (five) the basic theme of the right of the first-born is decided. There are many key words that heighten the account. Each key word is repeated twice (pottage, red, famished, sell, right away today, swear, birthright, four times). With red lentils, we are reminded again of the red-brown earth of the land of Edom. Esau came back from the field, exhausted and dead tired. "Give me something to eat, Jacob." And Jacob immediately exploits the opportunity, "Sell me, today, your birthright." Esau responded and said, "Look, I am starving, what good is my birth right?" At that moment it meant nothing.

About Seth, we read that he lived so many years, became the father of Enosh, and had other sons and daughters ... and he died. This is what Jacob heard. He heard the big event, the many firstborns, out of whom Israel would emerge. Esau only heard the last words, 'and he died'. Esau only knows about the rhythm of nature, of being born, becoming old and dying. Let us eat and drink and be merry, for tomorrow we die. Jacob knows the secret of history, the becoming of a great nation.

This story ends with, "he swore to him and sold his birthright to Jacob. Then Jacob gave Esau bread and a bowl of lentils, and he ate and drank, and rose and went his way. Thus Esau despised his birthright." (Gen 25:33, 34) What has he done, selling his birthright, despising the secret of history? Everything turns around the first-born which concerns all of us. This manipulation and despising will be followed by a more elaborate account in Genesis 27, of Jacob's second deception. Jacob becomes (the firstborn) what Esau is by nature. The oldest shall serve the youngest. It is not a 'natural' following of the generations. Israel is the firstborn only because of God's words and actions. It took many miracles and much weeping.

A short note from the narrators before the next episode is sufficient to disqualify Esau from the blessing of the firstborn. Esau did what Abraham had strictly forbidden Isaac to do (24:3). Esau married two Canaanite women, which gave both Isaac and Rebekah a lot of grief. (26:34) The storytellers portray Esau with a certain amount of sympathy in spite of his blatant disregard of the right of the first-born. Nor did it not prevent

Isaac from wanting to bless his first-born son. Rebekah had forgotten the divine word that the older shall serve the younger. Both mother and son know that the deception they are to engage in deserves a curse. (27:12) However, the blessing cannot wait, even though Isaac's death is not recorded until chapter Genesis 35:29, after Esau and Jacob have reconciled and bury their father together.

The years went by. Isaac had become old and blind. He called Esau and said, "My son, behold I am old; I do not know the day of my death." Go out and hunt some game and prepare it the way I love, and bring it to me so that I may bless you before I die. Rebekah, his mother had heard everything so she told Jacob to quickly get some lambs from the flock so I can prepare them the way your father likes. Then bring them to your father so that he can bless you before he dies. But Jacob had his doubts. 'Perhaps my father will feel me' and realize I am deceiving him. "For Esau is a hairy man and I am smooth." He will curse me instead of blessing me." (Gen 27:1–17)

Rebekah knows what to do. The "curse will be on me," so go and fetch the lambs and I will prepare them. Jacob did what his mother had told him. She prepared the food. Then she took Esau's best garments that were with her and put them on Jacob and the skins of the lambs she put on Jacob's hands and around his neck. Jacob took the food his mother had prepared and brought it to Isaac.

He called out, "My father," Isaac answered and said, "Here I am; who are you, my son?" Jacob answered, "I am Esau your first-born. I have done as you told me; now sit up and eat of my game, that you may bless me." Isaac did not quite trust it and asked how it was that he came back from the hunt so quickly. "The LORD your God granted me success." But Isaac still did not trust it and wanted to touch Jacob. "Come near, that I may feel you, my son, to know whether you are really my son Esau or not." Jacob came close to his father who felt him, and said, "The voice is Jacob's voice, but the hands are the hands of Esau." Isaac did not recognize him because the hands were hairy like Esau's. For a last reassurance he asked right out, "Are you really my son Esau?" Jacob answered, "I am," so Isaac blessed him. Then Isaac ate and drank. "Come near and kiss me, my son." He came close and Isaac smelled the garments. Then he spoke his blessing, May God give you lots of rain, grain and wine. Let peoples serve you... The blessing ends with, "Cursed be everyone who curses you, and blessed be everyone who blesses you!" (Genesis 27:18–29) This is like the blessing of Abraham. (Gen 12:3)

Jacob had just left, when Esau returned from his hunt. He prepared a delicious meal and brought it to his father. Rise up, my father and eat. Isaac answered, "Who are you?" Esau responded with, "I am your son, your first-born, Esau." Isaac was terribly shook up when he realized what had happened. He told Esau of Jacob's deceit. When Esau heard it he was enraged, "He cried out with an exceedingly great and bitter cry." It was a cry of hatred and anguish. Even though Esau had brought it on himself, we can enter into his reaction, "Bless me, even me also, O my father!" Isaac said, "Your brother came with guile, and he has taken away your blessing." Esau responded with, "Is he not rightly named Jacob?" Jacob, the smooth one, we would say, the smooth operator and talker, "For he has supplanted me these two times". He has taken away my birthright and now the blessing."

Again Esau pleaded with his father, "Have you not reserved a blessing for me?" But Isaac had to tell him, "I have made him your lord, and all his brothers I have given to him for servants, and with grain and wine I have sustained him. What can I do for you, my son?" Once more Esau cries out with a heart-breaking cry, "Have you but one blessing, my father? Bless me, even me also, O my father." (Gen 27:22–38) Then Esau cried out and wept. Isaac blessed him as well. You will live in the desert and you will survive with your sword and in time you will break free from your brother.

Although they knew of the divine word that 'the older shall serve the younger', Jacob and Rebekah took matters in their own hands, with deceit, while Isaac ignored those words. Abraham too had taken the initiative in his own hands and took Hagar as his wife to bear a son. Abraham had to learn about having faith. Jacob has to learn about history, the meaning of the first-born. Jacob will learn over time and after much heartache. First of all Jacob will get his just rewards and will be deceived in turn by his uncle, Laban.

Esau hated Jacob for this treacherous deceit, taking his birthright and stealing the blessing from him. Just wait, when your father is dead and the days of mourning are finished, then I will kill you. Rebekah heard about Esau's intentions to kill Jacob as soon as Isaac was dead. Again she has a plan. You have to flee to my brother Laban in Haran until his rage has subsided and he forgets what you have done to him. When he has settled down I will send for you.

Rebekah involves Isaac as if nothing has happened. She told him that she is tired of Esau's wives, "I am weary of my life." If Jacob too marries one of the Hittite women 'what good will my life, be to me'? Hearing this Isaac called Jacob and blessed him and charged him, "You shall not marry one of the Canaanite women. Go to Laban and take a wife from one of his daughters." "God Almighty, bless you and make you fruitful and multiply you that you may become a company of peoples. May he give the blessing of Abraham to you and your descendants with you, that you may take possession of the land of your sojournings which God gave to Abraham!" (Gen 27:41–46; 28: 1–4) So Jacob left (fled) and went to Haran with Isaac's blessing.

A sad commentary is added by the storytellers. When Esau heard about Jacob going to look for a bride among his family in Haran, He looked for a third wife among the descendants of Ishmael, thinking that was the problem all along. He knew Isaac was not pleased that he had married two Canaanite women. In his mind that was easily fixed.

Jacob left for Haran. Along the way when it had become dark, Jacob had a dream, in which there was a ladder on the earth and the top of it reached to heaven. Angels of God went up and down on it and God stood at the top and re-assured Jacob.

> I am the LORD, the God of Abraham your father and the God of Isaac; the land on which you lie I will give to you and to your descendants ... Behold, I am with you and will keep you wherever you go, and will bring you back to this land; for I will not leave you until I have done that of which I have spoken to you.
> Genesis 28:13–15

'Yahweh will be there' was the message, wherever he would go and he would bring him back to the land of promise. Jacob is overtaken by surprise and wonder and called the name of the place, Bethel, house of God and gate of heaven. Here Yahweh the God of heaven will be the God of men on earth. Jacob made a vow and a promise.[6]

6:17 Genesis 29:15–31:32 Jacob and Laban: the deceiver deceived

Jacob travelled on and when he arrived at a watering well, he met shepherds waiting to give their flocks water to drink. Jacob asked where are you from? And they said, Haran. Then, do you know Laban? They said, yes. There is Rachel, his daughter coming with the sheep to water her

---

6. Deurloo, *Waar Gebeurd*, 32–48 and Deurloo, *It Truly Happened*, 28.

flock. It was still early in the day and Jacob said, you could pasture your sheep for a while yet. She responded, we need all of us to roll away the stone from the well, then we can water the flock. Jacob went up and rolled the stone from the well's mouth. Jacob could no longer contain himself. He kissed Rachel and wept aloud. Then he told her that he was her father's kinsman and that he was Rebekah's son. She immediately ran off to tell her family. Laban came to meet them, "he embraced him and kissed him and brought him to their house. And Laban said, "Surely you are my bone and my flesh." (Gen 29:14) He stayed with them for a month.

Laban asked him what he wanted for wages and Jacob said, "I will serve you seven years for your younger daughter Rachel. All agreed and after seven years there was a feast and in the evening Laban brought the oldest daughter to Jacob's tent. In the morning, "behold it was Leah." The deceiver is deceived. He served Laban another seven years for Rachel. After another seven years he married Rachel as well. After that Jacob wanted to leave, but Laban persuaded him to stay on.

Laban's sons became afraid that Jacob would take away all their father's possessions. Jacob noticed a change in Laban's attitude. Then the LORD spoke to him, "Return to the land of your father's and to your kindred, and I will be with you." Jacob talked to Rachel and Leah and together they decided to leave. "And Jacob outwitted Laban the Aramean." So they snuck away to "go to the land of Canaan to his father Isaac. Laban with all his men came after them, and berated him, "Why did you flee secretly and cheat me, and did not tell me, so that I might have sent you away with mirth and songs, with tambourine and lyre? And why did you not permit me to kiss my sons and daughters farewell?" (Gen 31:27, 28)

Finally Jacob became angry at the accusations and told Laban, "These twenty years I have been in your house; I served you fourteen years for your two daughters, and six years for your flock, and you have changed my wages ten times. If the God of my father, the God of Abraham and the fear of Isaac, had not been on my side, surely you would have sent me away empty-handed. God saw my affliction and the labor of my hands, and rebuked you last night." They made a covenant together. Early in the morning Laban got up and kissed his grandchildren and his daughter and blessed them. He departed and returned home.

6:18 Genesis 32:1–33:14 Jacob meeting Esau Face to Face

Jacob went on his way as well, back to the Promised Land, after all those years in Haran. He was very afraid to go back and meet his brother Esau. But the "angels of God met him; when Jacob saw them, he said, 'This is God's army!' He was encouraged and sent messengers to Esau his brother to announce his coming. 'I have sojourned with Laban and stayed until now . . .'" (Gen 32:4) When the messengers came back, they told him that Esau was coming to meet him with four hundred men. Jacob was very scared.

He decided to divide his people in two groups. If Esau kills the one group, the other might escape, forever the schemer. He started to pray and appeal to God for help and protection. "Deliver me, I pray thee, from the hand of my brother, from the hand of Esau, for I fear him, lest he come and slay us all, the mothers with the children." Still taking matters in his own hand, he sent several groups of servants ahead with animals as a present to Esau. "I may appease him with the present that goes before me, and afterwards I will see his face; perhaps he will accept me." He sent everyone and all his flocks and goods across the river Jabbok. Jacob stayed behind, in the night, alone.

Then a man appeared that wrestled with Jacob until morning. In spite of all his efforts, he could not prevail. Then he touched Jacob's thigh, which put it out of joint, and said, "Let me go for the day is breaking." By now Jacob realized he was not dealing with an ordinary man but with God. Jacob responded with, "I will not let you go, unless you bless me." (Gen 32:26) The man asked him for his name. He said, Jacob, from now on your name is changed from Jacob to Israel, "for you have striven with God and with men, and have prevailed." And God blessed him. Jacob called the name of the place Peniel, "For I have seen God face to face, and yet my life is preserved." (Gen 32:30) He cannot enter the Promised Land until he has come face to face, first with God and then with his brother Esau. "The sun rose upon him as he passed Peniel." Apparently God wants to make history with this Israel and journey on with Jacob the liar, now the blessed one. This Jacob must represent Israel in this land.

Deurloo suggests that 'the day is breaking and morning is coming' may be a reference to a river demon that shies away from the light and only has power during the night. The narrators may have used this motif to place their story in the night, by the river, alone. Slowly it becomes clear that the person Jacob is encountering is not just an ordinary man, or Esau, or a river demon. It is a messenger from God, an angel of the LORD, God himself. Jacob can only enter as the blessed one. Not the blessing he had stolen from his brother, but as one blessed by God. He was afraid of Esau, but first he had to come face to face with God, the God of Israel. Jacob becomes aware that he has been overcome, "I won't let you go unless you bless me." Jacob realizes that he needs God's protection-blessing more than anything else in facing Esau.

There he goes, as a marked man, to meet Esau. Once more he tries to be smart and avoid disaster. He put the two maids of Rachel and Leah up front, then Leah with her children and finally Rachel and Joseph at the end. He went before everybody in front and bowed down seven times, until he came close. Esau on the other hand "ran to meet him, and embraced him, and fell on his neck and kissed him, and they wept." Instead of lord, Esau called him brother. When Esau saw the women and the children, he asked, who are all these with you? Jacob replied, "These are the children God has graciously given me. They all bowed down before Esau, the women and all the children."

Esau asked, 'What about all the gifts, all the animals you sent me?' Jacob answers, "To find favor in the sight of my lord." Esau first refused the gifts. He had enough of his own but Jacob insisted, he needed to know whether his brother was really accepting him, "If I have found favor in your sight, then accept my present from my hand; for truly to see your face is like seeing the face of God, with such favor you have received me." (Gen 33:10) Esau's face, like that of an enemy, is diffused as it were with God's face, so that now he can recognize the face of his brother, who runs to embrace him. 'I have seen your face just like God has seen my face'. The encounter between God, human and co-human or brother flow into each other. He gives Esau, as it were, the stolen blessing back, because he himself has become a blessed one. He is no longer Jacob, but he is Israel, God's warrior. What nation is there with whom the LORD has struggled face to face as with Israel?

The New Testament can express it as follows, "If any one says, 'I love God', and hates his brother, he is a liar; for he who does not love his brother whom he has seen, cannot love God whom he has not seen. And this commandment we have from him, that he who loves God should love his brother also. (1 John 4:20, 21) Whoever loves God also loves his brother. It reminds us of Cain not lifting up his face and refusing to look his brother in the face. "Why has your countenance fallen?" (Gen 4:5, 6)

The generation of Isaac has come to a close. This cycle of Isaac is sandwiched in between Abraham the central figure of Genesis and Jacob, the father of the twelve tribes of Judah and Israel. Isaac is an interim person who does not get a lot of attention. The generations of Terah are a narrative dealing with the relationship between man and wife and their son. The generations of Isaac are a narrative of the relation between a man and his brother.

6:19 Genesis 37:1–50:26 The Jacob 'toledot'; the Joseph (Novella)

With the end of the "generations of Isaac" (Gen 25:19–35:29), the book of Genesis could have been *concluded. Esau and Jacob have reconciled. After his struggle with the angel of the Lord, Jacob receives a* new name. He will be called "Israel" ("you have striven with God and with man and have prevailed"). He has become a new man and is blessed by Yahweh. (Gen 35:9) The basic theme of Genesis, the becoming of the people of Israel in the midst of the nations, in the land that the LORD, the God of Israel has given them to possess is now complete. The burning question of whether there will be a ('firstling') son that carries the blessing has now been answered, step by step, from Abraham to Isaac, to Jacob with his twelve sons and Israel with its twelve tribes.

First after chapter 35, there is the toledot (the ninth) of Esau and his descendents. He too is blessed and has become a great nation. (Gen 36:1–43) "... and he (Esau) went into a land away from his brother Jacob. For their possessions were too great for them to dwell together; the land of their sojourning could not support them because of their cattle. So Esau dwelt in the hill country of Seir; Esau is Edom." (Gen 36:7, 8) The account of the generations of Esau end with, "These are the kings who reigned in the land of Edom, before any king reigned over the Israelites." and "These are the names of the chiefs of Esau, according to their families and their dwelling places . . ."

We read that "And Isaac breathed his last; and he died and was gathered to his people, old and full of days; and his sons Esau and Jacob buried him." (Gen 35:28)

Then follows the last toledot (the tenth) of Jacob, (Gen 37:1–50:26) which does not start as usual with 'so and so' was the father of 'so and so' and he married and had sons and daughters... The Jacob/Joseph cycle

THE PROPHETIC CALL TO LOVE AND JUSTICE

(Gen 37:1–50:26) starts immediately with "This is the history of the family of Jacob. Joseph . . ." Without any further introductions, Joseph, being seventeen years old, was sent to his brothers, who were shepherding the flocks. He was a teenager with the sons of Bilhah and Zilpah, his father's wives,

Genesis is about the patriarchs, the founding fathers of Israel, about who will carry the blessing and through whom the promise will be fulfilled. The following book, Exodus is about the liberation from Egypt. The question is how did the people of Israel end up in Egypt when all the forefathers dwelt in Canaan? The Jacob/Joseph cycle gives the answer to that question. The history of Joseph is the link between Genesis and Exodus.

Many exegetes doubt whether that question requires such a long drawn out story (13 chapters). They assume that the whole Jacob/Joseph cycle did not belong to the book of Genesis and was added later. They hold that the Joseph cycle belongs to the wisdom literature, like Proverbs. The wisdom literature wants to instruct in the practical wisdom of living. In the story of Joseph this is done in narrative form. However correct that may be, first and foremost the great theme of Genesis unfolds once more. The theme is summarized with the word "blessed." It is all about Joseph, the blessed one and through him all of Israel and all nations. Far from being an unnecessary story the Joseph cycle forms an integral part of the book of Genesis. It explained how the people of Israel ended up in Egypt and prepares for the transition to the Exodus.

A first reading of this short story about Joseph may give the impression, in today's terms, that it is a story about a very 'dysfunctional family'. Every step of the way, there is envy, hatred, competition, unbearable heartbreak and in the end, many tears of joy.

It all started with Laban's deception of Jacob. Thinking he had married Rachel, he woke up in the morning only to discover it was Leah next to him, the oldest daughter. But Jacob loved Rachel. She was "beautiful and lovely" in contrast to Leah, whose "eyes were weak." And Jacob said to Laban, "What is this you have done to me? Did I not serve with you for Rachel? Why then have you deceived me? Laban's 'lame' answer was, "It is not done in our country, to give the younger before the first-born." After serving seven more years, "Laban gave him his daughter Rachel as a wife." And Jacob "loved Rachel more than Leah."

The stage is set for rivalry, envy, and hatred. "When the LORD saw that Leah was hated, he opened her womb; but Rachel was barren."

After the birth of her first son, Leah said, "Surely now my husband will love me." And after her second son, "Because the LORD has heard that I am hated, he has given me this son also." Again she conceived and said, "Now this time my husband will be joined to me, because I have borne him three sons." She conceived again and called him Judah, ("This time I will praise the LORD) . . . then she ceased bearing.") Thus Reuben, Simeon, Levi and Judah were born, but she still did not feel loved. We can feel her pain, "surely now my husband will love me." But since she ceased bearing, she had no other means to win Jacob's love.

Meanwhile Rachel "envied her sister." In desperation she gave Jacob her personal maid Bilhah (given to her by Laban) as a wife. And Bilhah bore Jacob a son Dan (God has judged me, and also heard my voice and given me a son). Bilhah conceived again and called him Naphtali (With mighty wrestling I have wrestled with my sister and have prevailed). With Dan, and Naphtali Jacob now has six sons.

When Leah is no longer able to bear children, not to be outdone, she gives Jacob her personal maid Zilpah to Jacob as his wife (given to her by Laban). She still does not feel loved. Zilpah bore Jacob two more sons, Gad (Good fortune), and Asher (Happy am I! For the women will call me happy).

Desperate for a child Rachel asks Leah for her son's mandrakes (a fertility stimulant) so she might have a child. But Leah responded by saying, "Is it a small matter that you have taken away my husband? Would you take away my son's mandrakes also?" But Rachel insists and promises Leah that in return she can sleep with Jacob that night. So she does. "And God hearkened to Leah" and, surprisingly Leah herself bore Jacob two more sons and a daughter, Issachar, God has given me my hire because I gave my maid to my husband." And she conceived again and gave birth to a sixth son and she called him Zebulun, "God has endowed me with a good dowry; now my husband will honor me, because I have borne him six sons") and a daughter, Dinah." Now there are twelve sons, which pre-figures the twelve tribes of Israel. There are six sons by Leah, two by Zilpah her maid; and two sons by Rachel's maid Bilhah, (and finally two sons by Rachel herself).

The birth of Joseph does not happen until after another tragedy. Dinah went to visit the women of the land, where she was raped by Shechem, son of Hamor the Hivite, the prince of the land. He loved her and asked his father to give him the young woman for his wife. His father spoke with Jacob and said, "Make marriages with us; give your daughters to us, and take our daughters for yourselves. You shall dwell with us; and the land shall be open to you; dwell and trade in it, and get property in it." The sons of Jacob responded and said that "We cannot do this thing, to give our sister to one who is uncircumcised, for that would be a disgrace to us." All the men of the city agreed to be circumcised along with Hamor and Shechem his son. On the third day when all the men were still in pain, Simeon and Levi took revenge and killed all the males of the town.

Earlier we read that Jacob had bought a piece of land on which he had pitched his tent from Hamor, Shechem's father for a hundred pieces of money. There he erected an altar and called it El-Elohe-Israel (God, the God of Israel) There was really no need for a treaty with Hamor and Shechem. Once again the LORD reassures him of his new name after his struggle with the angel before meeting Esau. His new name is Israel, the father of all twelve tribes of Israel. And God said to him, "I am God Almighty; be fruitful and multiply; a nation and a company of nations shall come from you, and kings shall spring from you. The land I gave to Abraham and Isaac I will give to you, and I will give the land to your descendents after you." (Gen 34:11)

And finally (we would say), "Then God remembered Rachel, and God hearkened to her and opened her womb. She conceived and bore a son and called his name Joseph ("God has taken away my reproach; may the Lord add to me another son!").

But the tragedies continue. When they traveled further, Rachel was about to give birth to the son she for which she had wished. She was "in her hard labor." The midwife tried to comfort her, "Fear not, for now you will have another son." Just before she died in childbirth she called his name, Benoni (son of my sorrow), but Jacob called him Benjamin (son of the right hand). Benjamin was the only one born in Canaan and his mother was buried in the region (Bethlehem) which was later assigned to Benjamin.

One more evil happened, Reuben, trying to take control of his father's household slept with Jacob's concubine, Bilhah, Rachel's maid, and Israel heard about the shame and disgrace. When Jacob blesses his sons at the end of his life, (Gen 49) he disqualifies Reuben, the firstborn, because he had 'defiled' his father's bed. Simeon and Levi are disqualified as well, because of the violent slaughter of all the men of the city of Hamon and Shechem. Thus the blessing of the first born went to Judah. "The scepter shall not depart from Judah, nor the ruler's staff from between his feet, until he comes to whom it belongs; and to him shall be the obedience of the peoples." (Gen 49:10) Not only Reuben is disqualified from the blessing of the first-born, but also Simeon and Levi.

Jacob also blesses Joseph's two sons. "Your two sons, who were born to you in the land of Egypt before I came to you in the land of Egypt, are mine. Ephraim and Manasseh shall be mine, as Reuben and Simeon are," Jacob blessed them in reverse order. Joseph said to his father, "Not so my father, for this one is the first-born; put your right hand upon his head. But his father refused, and said, "I know my son, I know; he also shall become a people, and he also shall be great." So, "By you Israel will pronounce blessings, saying, God make you as Ephraim and as Manasseh." (It is a reminder of Jacob's own deception and that the blessing does not automatically go to the first-born.) Although born and raised in Egypt they will fully belong to Israel.

The final evil that took place in this narrative, about Jacob's family, is his favoring of Joseph. "Now Israel loved Joseph more than any other of his children, because he was the son of his old age . . . But when his brothers saw that their father loved him more than all his brothers, "they hated him, and could not speak peaceably to him." (Gen 37:3, 4) Right from the start, the family discord is stated, "and Joseph brought ill report of them to their father. Now Israel loved Joseph more than any other of his children . . . and he made him a robe with long sleeves."(a royal robe) As a result of this favoritism, the brothers "hated him." The stage is set, for conflict.

To add to the discord, Joseph had two dreams in which he ruled over his brothers and his entire family. "So they hated him yet more for his dreams and for his words." Although Jacob rebuked him for his dreams, his "father kept the saying in his mind" but his brothers "were jealous of him."

When the brothers see an opportunity to get rid of Joseph, they do so and sell him as a slave to a caravan of Ishmaelites "with their camels bearing gum, balm and myrrh on their way to Egypt" (the ingredients for embalming). In turn they sell him to Potiphar, an officer of Pharaoh, the captain of the guard, an Egyptian. The brothers show Jacob his blood soaked long robe with sleeves. Jacob concludes that a wild animal must have killed Joseph. Jacob rent his garments and mourned for his son for many days, and he would not be comforted. "No, I shall go down to Sheol to my son, mourning."

At this point the story about Joseph is 'interrupted' by the account of Judah's unknowing violation of Tamar, his daughter-in-law. (Gen 38)

He had refused to give her his third son in marriage, after the first two had died. Onan, the second son had spilled his seed on the ground because he knew that the offspring would not be his. Judah promised her his youngest son but in the end refused to do so. She outwitted him and dressed up like a prostitute and wheedled a special pledge out of him that he could not deny. Tamar became pregnant. She conceived and Judah had to acknowledge his injustice. The deceiver was deceived, just like Jacob. Reuben had acted intentionally, but Judah unintentionally. Judah was not unpardonable. He knew Tamar without knowing who she was. (38:16) He remained a questionable figure until his conversion when he became a surety for his younger brother, Benjamin. (44:33) Finally, he is blessed by Jacob. (Gen 49:10) The blessings, of Joseph's two sons, prefigure the Northern and Southern kingdoms.

In Egypt, Joseph is blessed. "The LORD was with Joseph, and he became a successful man . . . and his master saw that the LORD was with him, and that the LORD caused all that he did to prosper in his hands." (Gen 39:2, 3) "So he left all that he had in Joseph's charge; and having him he had no concern for anything but the food which he ate." (Gen 39:6)

But all did not go well. Joseph was "handsome and good looking" and the master's wife took a liking to him and wanted to have an affair with him. He refused her and said, "Lo, having me, my master has no concern about anything in the house, and he has put everything that he has in my hand; he is not greater in this house than I am; nor has he kept back anything from me except yourself, because you are his wife; how then can I do this great wickedness, and sin against God?." (Gen 39:8–10).In this answer Joseph by example shows the calling of a true ruler (king). He practices righteousness in the name of the LORD and in keeping with his commandments. My master has entrusted everything to me. He has not withheld anything, "except yourself because you are his wife."

This part of the story is not about a chaste young man that is daily tempted by a seductive woman, but it is about ruling his master's house in the name of the LORD, prefiguring all true kings. (Deut 17:14–20; Josh 1:8; I Sam 8:4–22; Ps 24:1–10) But she does not take no for an answer and accuses him of trying to rape her, holding his robe as evidence. His master is furious and has him thrown in the king's jail.

Again we read, "But the LORD was with Joseph and showed him steadfast love, and gave him favor in the sight of the keeper of the prison." As with his previous master, the keeper left everything to Joseph, "because the Lord was with him; and whatever he did, the LORD made it prosper." After two whole years, when he successfully interpreted the pharaoh's dreams and giving his advice Joseph is appointed as Pharaoh's overlord. "Since God has shown you all this, there is none so discreet and wise as you are; you shall be over my house, and all my people shall order themselves as you command; only as regards the throne will I be greater than you. And Pharaoh said to Joseph, 'Behold, I have set you over all the land of Egypt.'" (Gen. 41:44) Then Pharaoh gave him his signet ring and garments of fine linen and a gold chain for around his neck. Joseph will rule over everything according to his plan (to save up grain during the years of plenty for the seven lean years) except he is not to aspire to the throne itself.

When the severe famine arrives in Canaan, as well as in Egypt, Joseph's brothers are forced to come to Egypt to buy grain for the whole family, because of the severity of the famine. (Gen 42:1–5) Coming before Joseph they bowed down before him with their faces to the ground. "Joseph remembered the dreams which he had dreamed of them." They did not recognize Joseph. When they appeared before Joseph he spoke roughly to them and accused them of being spies. He put them in prison for three days to test them and commanded them to bring their younger brother to prove they had spoken the truth about their father and their family and especially their younger brother, Benjamin.

He overheard them talking among themselves and they did not know he could understand them, "In truth we are guilty concerning our brother, in that we saw the distress of his soul, when he besought us and we would not listen; therefore is this distress come upon us." Reuben chimed in with this and said, "Did I not tell you not to sin against the lad? But you would not listen. So now there comes a reckoning for his blood." After this confession of their guilt, Joseph had to go to another room where he wept.

When they returned home Jacob was utterly distressed and adamant about not taking Benjamin back with them to Egypt. It will be my death. Finally when the famine was severe, Judah said he would be a surety for Benjamin. Back in Egypt they had to have dinner with Joseph. They told him their father was still alive and well and presented Benjamin. When Joseph saw his younger brother, he said, "God be gracious to you, my son! Then Joseph made haste, for his heart yearned for his brother, and he sought a place to weep." As a final test, he had his silver cup placed in

Benjamin's sack. The soldiers caught up with them and returned them to the palace.

Joseph wanted to keep Benjamin as a slave as he had said because the cup was found in his sack of grain. When they appeared again before Joseph, Judah spoke up and said that if Benjamin does not return with us, our father will die, "as his life is bound up in the lad's life." I became surety for the lad to my father, "therefore, let your servant, I pray you, remain instead of the lad as a slave to my lord." After hearing this, Joseph could no longer contain himself. He ordered all the servants to leave them alone. Then Joseph made himself know to them. "And he wept aloud, so that the Egyptians heard it, and the household of Pharaoh heard it." (Gen 45:1) All the pain and all the grief of all those years came out. "I am Joseph; is my father still alive?" Joseph was over thirty years old by then. Such a long, long journey and so much pain and suffering . . .

The brothers became frightened and "could not talk." But Joseph said, "Come near to me, I pray you. They came near. And he said, "I am your brother, Joseph, whom you sold into Egypt. And now do not be distressed, or angry with yourselves, because you sold me here; for God sent me before you to preserve life . . . God sent me before you to preserve for you a remnant on earth, and to keep alive for you many survivors. So it was not you who sent me here, but God; and he has made me, a father to Pharaoh, and lord of all his house and ruler over all the land of Egypt." Gen 45:4–8)

The LORD used this 'dysfunctional' family to preserve his chosen people, this was Joseph's confession. By faith in the God of his forefathers, of Abraham, Isaac, Joseph confessed that the evil his brothers committed against him, the LORD used to save his people from famine and death.

He continued talking to his brothers and said, "Make haste and go up to my father and say to him, "Thus says your son Joseph, God has made me lord of all Egypt; come down to me, do not tarry . . . and there I will provide for you . . . With your own eyes you have seen that it is me and my brother Benjamin can see it is me that is speaking to you." Then he could no longer contain himself and he "fell upon his brother's Benjamin's neck and wept; and Benjamin wept upon his neck. And he kissed all his brothers and he wept upon them; and after that his brothers talked with him." (Gen 45:14)

The brothers returned to Canaan, including Benjamin, with many gifts and provisions. And they told Jacob, "Joseph is still alive, and he is ruler over all the land of Egypt. And his heart fainted, for he did not believe them." But when they told him everything Joseph had said, ". . . the spirit of their father Jacob revived; and Israel said, "It is enough; Joseph my son is still alive; I will go and see him before I die." So Israel set out on the journey with his entire household, seventy persons (then follows a genealogy of all Israel's descendents).

On the way, at Beersheba, he offered sacrifices. "And God spoke to Israel in visions of the night, and said, 'Jacob, Jacob.' And he said, 'Here I am.' Then he said, 'I am God, the God of your father; do not be afraid to go down to Egypt; for I will there make of you a great nation. I will go down with you to Egypt, and I will also bring you up again; and Joseph's hand will close your eyes." (Gen 46:3–4) God reassured him, going down to Egypt does not mean the end of the promise of the Promised Land, (in contrast to Isaac, who was forbidden to go to Egypt). (Gen 26:2)

When he arrived in Egypt, Joseph in his chariot met his father in Goshen. "And he presented himself to him, and fell on his neck, and wept on his neck a good while . . ." "Thus Israel dwelt in the land of Egypt, in the land of Goshen; and they gained possessions in it. And were fruitful and multiplied exceedingly. And Jacob lived in the land of Egypt seventeen years . . ." (Gen 47:27, 28) When he was about to die, he made his son Joseph swear, "'. . . put your hand under my thigh, and promise me . . . Do not bury me in Egypt, but let me lie with my fathers; carry me out of Egypt and bury me in their burying place.' He answered, 'I will do as you have said.' And he said, 'Swear to me'; and he swore to him." (Gen 47:29–31) After Jacob had blessed his sons, including Ephraim and Manasseh, "blessing each with a blessing suitable to him," he died. "When Jacob finished charging his sons, he drew up his feet into the bed, and breathed his last, and was gathered to his people." (Gen 49:33)

"Then Joseph fell on his father's face, and wept over him, and kissed him." And they buried him in the Promised Land, alongside Abraham and Isaac and Jacob. Joseph returned to Egypt with all his brothers. Now that their father was dead, they were afraid that Joseph would hate them and pay them back for all the evil which they did to him. They said to Joseph, "And now we pray you, forgive the transgression of the servants of the God of your father." Hearing this, Joseph wept once more. His brothers fell down before him and said, 'behold we are your servants.'

Once more Joseph reassured them and said, "Fear not, for am I in the place of God? As for you, you meant evil against me; but God meant it for good, to bring about that many people should be kept alive, as they are today. So do not fear; I will provide for you and your little ones. Thus he reassured them and comforted them." Joseph, the blessed one, acting royally, pre-figuring the great king to come, David, who also created a terrible 'dysfunctional' family.

In my work, many people over the years have told me they have regrets about their past, wishing they would have done things differently. But this story reminds us not to judge too quickly. We are not God and he is a righteous God. Joseph was able to confess to the hand of God in his life. As we take the story of Joseph to heart, no matter what our past, we can share in the hope of the promises made then and later, and will be able to confess with God's people of all ages, "I believe in God the Father Almighty, Maker and Maintainer of heaven and earth. And I believe in the forgiveness of sins, the resurrection of the body; and the life everlasting, (even though the whole creation groans for deliverance . . .) (the Apostles Creed).

"So Joseph dwelt in Egypt, he and his father's house . . . and Joseph saw Ephraim's children of the third generation; the children also of Machir the son of Manasseh were born upon Joseph's knees." When Joseph was about to die he made the sons of Israel swear to carry his bones to the Promised Land. "God will visit you, and bring you up out of this land to the land that I swore Abraham, to Isaac, and to Jacob." (Gen 50: 24) So Joseph died. He was hundred and ten years old. And they embalmed him with the same kind of spices that the Ishmaelites had carried with them to Egypt along with Joseph. He was put in a coffin in Egypt. The coffin stood as a silent witness to his faith and the hope of the Israelites for many years, waiting for the day of liberation and entry into the Promised Land . . .

Jacob's family history is truly a tragic story of being hated, of envy, of competition, of death in child birth, of selling a brother into slavery, indifferent to his cries and pleading, and deceiving their father about his death. Joseph will do a lot of crying (more than seven times we read, ". . . he wept") at the reconciliation, meeting his younger brother again after many years (since he was seventeen) and his father, such a long, long journey that is ending in joy. Many of us can probably identify with this severely 'dysfunctional family' and shed many tears with them, though not all stories of alienation and dysfunction have such a happy ending and reconciliation. Joseph's experience ends with tears of happiness. They all embrace, weep and kiss.

What a distortion if all that theologians mention about the Joseph's story is a favorite 'proof text' for the doctrine of divine providence. (Gen

45:5-8; 50:20) "As for you, you meant evil against me; but God meant it for good, to bring it about that many people should be kept alive, as they are today." (Gen 50:20; cf. Gen 22:8, 14) God provided a lamb for an offering thus Abraham called the place, "The LORD will provide..."

In, *The guidance of our existence; questions and references about providence, (Het beleid van ons bestaan; vragen en verwijzingen rondom de voorzienigheid* (1978), Beker and Deurloo, cut off any misunderstanding of such favorite passages. These were often quoted in defense of the doctrine of providence. They write about how it has functioned (was misused) within the Christian community to create a sense of passivity, longsuffering and fatalism, as it was in my own family. Instead they provide a rich 'bouquet of passages' with which we can approach God's maintenance of his creation and history, and the things we cannot understand about evil, accidents, illness, war and the threat of a nuclear disaster.

"The bones of Joseph which the people of Israel carried from Egypt to Canaan were buried at Shechem, in the portion of ground which Jacob bought from the sons of Hamor the father of Shechem for a hundred pieces of money; it became an inheritance of the descendants of Joseph." (Josh 24:2) Joseph, the blessed one, is remembered throughout Israel's history (Deut 33:13; Ps 105:17-22) and the Christian community "By faith Joseph, at the end of his life, made mention of the exodus of the Israelites and gave directions concerning his burial." (Heb 11:22) Joseph is the blessed one in the midst of his brothers and sisters. They too share in his blessing. With this story the authors tell us the story of Israel (the blessed one) of being repressed by the surrounding nations. Likewise they will share in the blessing.

This is how the book of Genesis comes to a close, a single coffin with an embalmed body, standing there, waiting for the fulfillment of the promise to the forefathers, waiting to be buried with his ancestors, waiting for a new leader Moses who would soon be floating in a little 'coffin' in the river Nile, waiting for the "fulfillment of all promises..." (Josh 21:45)

CHAPTER 7

Re-reading Joshua

7:1 Introduction to Joshua

ONCE AGAIN AS IN Genesis, rather than considering the usual introductory questions of author, time, different editions, divisions, difficult texts, etc. it seems important to switch our perspective to more biblical theological themes. These typical introductory issues primarily reflect the exegetes' presuppositions that do not arise from the givens of the text but from other philosophical, historical and theological considerations. This rereading of Joshua starts from the presupposition that each part of Joshua is 'prophetic literature' or 'narrative proclamation' as it is given in the texts, in their unity.

In 1981 Deurloo published his exposition of the book Joshua, *Joshua: exposition of a part of the Bible*. In two articles that followed in 1983 during Israel's military assault on Lebanon, including two refugee camps in which thousands of Palestinians died, he gave a more 'radical' interpretation of Joshua, or, more accurately, he drew out the consequences of his earlier interpretation of Joshua in 1983 with (1) "In solidarity with Israel: reading the Tenach," (pp.23-27) and (2) "With Joshua into the land," (pp.37-48) in, *No place to lay their heads; Israel and the Palestinians, theological clarification of a political conflict*. The various authors of this book present a helpful, challenging, theological-biblical overview and response to the Israeli-Palestinian conflict, including the publications of the World Council of Churches and the Dutch Council of Churches. Later in 2009 in *Cahier (24)*, Deurloo published another article on Joshua, edited by P.J. van Midden. It contained eleven articles by various authors including Deurloo, "'At that time . . .' the liturgical framework of circumcision in the book Joshua. He makes a point that the words 'land', 'Jerusalem', 'Canaan', and 'Israel' do not have a fixed, literal meaning. Instead, in each new situation, these words need to be interpreted again and again. They need to be 'concretized'. He writes these articles in strong opposition to a fundamentalist or literalist interpretation. To the accusations that he is 'spiritualizing' these key words, he responds with, if not 'literal', what then is the opposite of 'literal', is it spiritualizing? Or is it 'historicizing'? His answer is a clear, no! It is 'actualizing' or 'application'.

According to Deurloo, we are dealing with a prophetic book, not a 'historical' book (in the sense of a 'verified-facts-chronological' history). Each time, in a new situation and time, the meaning of these words need to be reinterpreted or actualized. They cannot be fixed geographically or historically. The book of Joshua is a dangerous book in the hands of fundamentalists and literalists. It can easily be used as a political weapon both by Jews and Christians and a rationalization to displace and kill Palestinians and destroy their homeland. The authors make use of geographical and historical references, but these are taken up in the prophetic account. Joshua is the first of the earlier prophetic books (Joshua, Judges, I and II Samuel and I and II Kings) after the five books of the Torah (Genesis, Exodus, Numbers, Leviticus and Deuteronomy).

At this stage, I am only able to highlight certain key themes in Joshua. To give a more coherent and integrated account of a biblical theological perspective would take more time and study. However, right from the beginning, it is important to switch our focus away from these typical introductory questions that immediately prejudice the approach to the book of Joshua and focus instead on the primacy of the prophetic message as proclaimed in this book.

This rereading of Joshua closely follows the exposition of K. Deurloo's, *Joshua, an exposition* (1981). My intention is to trace how Deurloo interprets each part of Joshua as 'prophetic literature' or 'narrative proclamation' as it is given in the texts and makes that the primary focus of his interpretation. At the same time he asks himself throughout how each of the books of the Bible fit into the whole of the scriptures and its core themes. His aim, together with Bouhuijs, in all his booklets and TV programs was to bring the scripture as close to ordinary hearers and readers as possible. They would do so by a close reading of the text, highlighting inter-textual references, core themes, key words, etc. All of this was done in an attempt to have people, again, hear the living Word of God.

These larger contexts, interconnections and core themes are explored in depth by both Breukelman and Deurloo in their Biblical Theological studies. Deurloo's four Biblical Theology studies cover a wide range of topics and themes. Breukelman made the study of Genesis and Matthew his life-long interest. Building on Breukelman's insights, Deurloo was especially keen to discover the key structures and themes of the various Bible books and their inter-connections and the Old Testament as a whole.

We will come back to the nature of Biblical Theology (compared to Systematic Theology) in chapter 9. For now it is sufficient to note that Biblical Theology does not 'abstract' and present a 'systematic account of theological concepts'. Rather it attempts to summarize the core structure and inter-connections of each Bible book. These arise from many biblical texts, in short, its inner structure or perspective. Vice versa, it addresses how the living words continue to correct and deepen our understanding of each part and the whole. Deurloo states: "For me, Biblical theology was always already the necessary horizon for exegesis."[1]; The core words and themes in their inter-connections unite all the different genres of the scriptures, like the large narrative sections, laws, prophetic writings, psalms, wisdom literature, apocalyptic writings, etc.

The Amsterdam Cahiers published a special *Cahier (24)* on *Jozua*, (2009) with eleven contributions by various scholars. It contains an annotated summary of the various commentaries, and different theological studies of the last ten years by Klaas Spronk (pp.1–10). I have benefitted from these contributions as well as Beek's, (1981), Woudstra's (1981), and Spronk's (1994) commentaries on Joshua. Spronk provides a helpful overview of the history and diversity of interpretations. I have also benefitted from many articles on Joshua by Ed Noort.

When consulting many other commentaries on Joshua in the theological libraries of the different theological colleges of the University of Toronto, I was often disappointed and seldom edified or inspired. Writing a commentary or an article on some aspect of Joshua involves a very painstaking process of analysis and comparison. It is an academic enterprise. Either historical questions of the (assumed) different traditions of the origin of the text or its history dominated the exegesis. Or, the exegetical analysis stopped halfway, leaving the 'application', 'interpretation' or 'theological' meaning' to pastors and priests to decipher. That

---

1. Deurloo, *Exodus en Exil*, p.7.

is not to say these commentaries do not contain valuable grammatical, linguistic, historical or sociological insights, yet, usually the key to the whole of the text or the book is missing.

From the beginning Deurloo follows a different order than the Christian Bible. He takes his point of departure in the Palestinian canon, which follows the order of the Law of Moses or the Torah the former or earlier prophets (Joshua, Judges, Samuel, Kings), the later prophets (Isaiah, Jeremiah, Ezekiel and the twelve minor prophets), and the Psalms which represents all the Writings (Psalms, Job, Ruth, Esther, etc.). Together they can be shortened to TeNaK, which represent the beginning letters of the Torah, the teaching of Moses, the Nebiim, the early prophets and the later prophets, and the Psalms, the Ketoebi, TeNaK.

This is the formula and order we find back in the New Testament: "Moses, and the prophets." For Jesus, the disciples and the apostles, these were the authoritative scriptures. There are many references in the gospels and letters that quote or refer back to the Hebrew Scriptures. Without the Hebrew Scriptures we cannot understand the gospels and the apostolic letters. That is why the subtitle of this study reads, "Rediscovering the Old Testament."

If we want to know who God is, read the stories about him in his dealings with his people and through them, with all the nations of the world. Jesus gives the same answer to two of the disciples on the way to Emmaus. If you want to know who I am, read Moses and the prophets. "And beginning with Moses and all the prophets, he interpreted to them in all the scriptures the things concerning himself." (Luke 24:27) His parting words to the disciples were, "These are my words which I spoke to you, while I was still with you, that everything written about me in the Law of Moses and the prophets and the psalms must be fulfilled." (Luke 24:44) These are the same words he said in the parable about the rich man and Lazarus. "They have Moses and the prophets, let them hear them." (Luke 16:30) From the New Testament perspective all of the Hebrew Scriptures could be summarized by "Moses and the prophets and the psalms." This is the shorthand way of referring to the entire Hebrew Scriptures, which was Jesus' and Paul's authoritative Bible. In spite of all its different genres, there is a fundamental unity to the witness of the scriptures. If we want to know who Jesus is, read Moses and the prophets and the responses in the Psalms.

Is there a centre or middle ('het midden') to all of the scriptures and each book? This question about the centre of the scriptures has given rise to longstanding debates. Within the Reformed tradition the 'history of the covenant' was often seen as the key to all of the scriptures. Deurloo provides a different answer. However true that central idea of the covenant may be, he wanted to give a more detailed account of the core theme of each book and the interconnecting themes with the whole of the scriptures.

The Torah is all about the exodus from Egypt and the later prophets about the exile from slavery and the miraculous return from Babylon. The centre of the early or former prophets is David, or more precisely, the king and temple. His exposition is described in his four Biblical Theology volumes. He does not start with the usual (perfect) creation and then the fall into sin (total depravity), redemption (substitutionary atonement) the fulfillment (the resurrection) and the final judgment at the end of time.

The five books of the Law of Moses are centered in the Torah, which is the focus of Exodus, Leviticus, and Numbers. They are framed by Genesis and Deuteronomy. The Torah is centered in the exodus from slavery in Egypt and the former prophets around the kingship (David), and the temple. The focus of the later prophets is the exile and the miraculous return from captivity of a remnant from Babylon.

Deurloo presents this order as a simple and canonical formula. Hence the titles of his Biblical Theology books: *Exodus and Exile, King and Temple, Our dear mother gives birth to a son*, and *Creation from Paul to Genesis*.

Instead, he starts with the Name, Yahweh, the unique God of Israel and his journey with his chosen people Israel, in the midst of all the nations; this particular God in his deeds; his liberating them from slavery and death (from both Egypt and Babylon), his mysterious turn about and the return of his people, (redemption); creation as the setting or theatre for this revelation of his Name, centered in Jesus Christ, the first-born of all creation and the final fulfillment in the birth of the Son, Jesus in the fullness of time, the true, end-time king.

Does he have a name? If so, what is it and what is special about this god? The scriptures do not really answer these questions, at least not in the way we would expect. When Moses is sent to the enslaved Israelites and Pharaoh in Egypt, Moses said, the people won't believe me and will ask me for your name. He was told to answer and say: "God said to Moses, 'I am who I am', and he said, 'I am has sent me to you' The God of your fathers has sent me to you." (Exod 3:13) God also said to Moses "Say this to the people of Israel: 'The Lord, the 'God of your fathers, the God of Abraham, the God of Isaac, and the God of Jacob, has sent me to you; this is my name forever, and thus I am to be remembered throughout all generations.'" (Exod 3:15). We might be inclined to say, that is not much of an answer. There is a further explanation, "God said to Moses, "I am who I am," I will be with you as I am.' Say this to the people of Israel, 'I am has sent me to you.'" (Exod 3:14) "The God of your fathers" or the "God of Israel" become standard phrases to designate the God of Israel. This mysterious God is indicated with the four letters, YHWH, which were not pronounced or spoken.

We cannot possess or control this God or contain him in a philosophical formula or a general theological concept, like the All-knowing, All-seeing, All-present, All-mighty, or a universal power or consciousness. Israel's God can only be known by his deeds. That is why stories must be told about what he did, does and will do.

7:1a) The described history and the history and time of the author

According to biblical chronology, the story of the conquest of Canaan under the leadership of Joshua took place sometime during the 1200's BCE. There is no archaeological nor historical evidence that the conquest of Canaan happened as described in the book of Joshua. In the biblical described time (between 1230–1220), Jericho and Ai did not exist as flourishing and fortified cities, nor did the other city states of the Canaanites and the Philistines. That does not mean these stories are purely mythological. As with the stories of the patriarchs and the exodus, there is a general historical context and archaeological givens that are reflected in the book of Joshua.

During the late Bronze Age (1550–1200 BCE) there was indeed a great upheaval in the whole Mediterranean region. There is evidence that suggests this dramatic change was caused by invasions of mysterious and violent Sea Peoples that devastated everything they encountered. Others point to sudden climate changes that destroyed agriculture and caused widespread famine. Still others point to the breakdown of palace economies of the city states that could not adapt to economic change or social stress. These are all theories to account for this upheaval over a number of decades.

These stories do reflect a general historical context, consciousness and communal memories of violent conquests. Throughout, from century to century, Palestine had been overrun by armies of one empire after the other. Vassal city states that violated their treaties, rebelled, refused to pay tribute or made alliances with other states were severely punished. Cities were burned to the ground; city walls, palaces and temples were destroyed; kings, priests and the elite were killed and their heads displayed on the ruins or they were hanged, impaled, tortured or carried off as slaves; countrysides were ravished; supplies, weapons, women, children, treasures and idols were taken as booty. Monuments and stiles recorded the great deeds of the conquerors and the triumphs of their gods over the gods of subjugated people. It is this general background of brutal and violent conquests in Palestine that are reflected in the conquests described in Joshua.

The authors made use of legends, heroic tales, fables, folk memories, local myths, sagas of territorial conquests, divine warrior narratives, city lists and stories around famous landscapes. These givens can be seen as the basis for the highly structured prophetic composition of Joshua perhaps written after the destruction of Samaria (722 BCE) and before the destruction of Jerusalem (597–587, BCE), or later. The boundaries and names of towns of the tribe of Judah described in Joshua 15:1–63, correspond to expanded borders of Judah during the reign of Josiah (640–609 BCE). The place names also correspond to the settlement pattern during that period. Many of the cities like Jericho, Ai, Bethel, Lachish, Eglon, Hazor, and Naphot Dor and others played a crucial role in Josiah's expansion and reform. King Josiah is like, a second Joshua.

With regard to the time Joshua might have been written, there are several indications that point to a period after the destruction of Samaria (723/722 BCE) and the exile of the ruling class to Assyria. Many people may have fled to the south and to Jerusalem. The time of the reforms of King Josiah (around 620 BCE and following) is past. The conquest and destruction of Jerusalem (from 597–587 BCE) has not yet happened. The people might be frightened. Will the same thing happen to them as to the people of the northern kingdom? Possibly it is in this context that the first readers of the book of Joshua (a first edition?) can be found. The book served both as an encouragement and a warning. There is still time to mend their ways, to put away their idols and to follow the Torah and in this way to keep their covenant with Yahweh. Yahweh will still keep all his promises if they repent, change their ways and trust in him and not in alliances with foreign powers or their arms. A new beginning is possible. These cautionary tales and memories of a time long ago could reassure and comfort the people in their present situation. Others prefer a time of during or after the exile, like Deurloo and Spronk (the North 722 BCE, the South 597 BCE and Jerusalem 586 BCE).

Joshua reflects a multi-layered tradition that in the end formed a carefully structured, coherent literary whole that was closely connected to Deuteronomy and sets the stage for Judges. Without going into all the exegetical questions, there are later redactions that reflect new situations, like the period of the exile and the restoration during the Persian occupation and beyond. Whatever the exact origins and situations, these stories were written for the guidance, the confrontation, and the encouragement of the first and later hearers after Josiah's reign. The retreat of the Egyptian and Assyrian empires during Josiah's reign, allowing for the expansion of Judah's territory gave hope that their fortunes may be restored and the threat of war and conquest may be avoided.

In the whole of the prophetic 'Deuteronomistic history', Joshua constitutes a crucial link in the development of Israel's identity. It is a sequence from the beginning (creation), to the forefathers (Abraham, Isaac, Jacob), the exodus and the law-giving (Moses), the conquest (Joshua), the decline (Judges), the first kings (Saul and David), the building of the temple with its elaborate worship, the ups and downs of the kingship (of Israel and Judah) and to the exile of Israel and Judah.

The conquest story as a whole served to reinforce the belief that they were rightful inheritors of the land that was promised to Abraham, Isaac, and Jacob. The authors used familiar legends from the near eastern world to reassure the people. Coming in from outside to take possession of the land, a warrior god fighting for them, the land as a gift and inheritance, were all part of a common theme or motif in the establishment of a people's identity. Throughout much of Israel's and Judah's history their possession of the land had been at risk. Over centuries, they had been threatened from every side by the Moabites, Amalekites, Edomites, Ammonites, Philistines, Syrians, and the great empires of Egypt, Assyria, and Babylon. There was nothing certain about the promise and possession of the land and their inheritance. It could be taken away.

The conquest stories could reassure the people during the time of King Josiah that they would have peace from their enemies. About both Joshua and David we read, "And the land had rest from war" (Josh 11:23) and "... I will appoint a place for my people Israel, and I will plant them, that they may dwell in their own place, and be disturbed no more; and violent men shall afflict them no more, as formerly ... I will give you rest from all your enemies." (2 Sam 7:10, 11) Both themes are present in Joshua. The enemies are totally conquered and completely destroyed and they are only partially conquered and form a constant danger and temptation. The first is a testimony to Yahweh's faithfulness, fulfilling all his promises, and the second reflects the penalty for the people's disobedience.

The final text, as is often the case, has a complex structure. More could probably have been said by Noort about the linguistic and literary givens of these two accounts (the changes from singular to plural; the diagrammatic picture of the text according to who is speaking and who is being addressed as well as the narrative segments; etc.). However, the key point is clear. Reading other commentaries on these passages, there is also a warning not to speculate and not to fragment the text. With his dry humor, Noort will say at times: "He knows too much!" when with every change an exegete sees a new redaction or when a new source is identified. The whole text can become fragmented into several pieces and small segments. Later, we will yet consider how a sociological-political interpretation (the self-interests of the dominant group, the king, the elite, the priests, the returnees, etc.) can also elucidate or distort (in a reductionistic way) the religious meaning of these exemplary stories.

7:1b) Joshua, a prophetic book

Right from the start Deurloo begins by recalling the refrain of a little children's song he composed for a series of sermons on Joshua (for adults and children). Afterwards it was sung outside on the streets of Amsterdam as well and in demonstrations against missiles with nuclear war heads being placed in Holland in the sixties. When the children sang the refrain, the adults joined in with great abandon. The refrain is simple but profound,

> The liberation is starting.
> Here in the Promised Land.
> All people may enter;
> The liberation is beginning
> It is placed in our hands.

Can we echo that sentiment and join in the protests in our time and our critical situation? Can we sing it with the joy and anticipation (or fear and doubts) of entering the 'promised land'. The land on which we are standing is 'holy ground', dedicated land, the soil, the water, the air, the forests, the animals, birds and fishes, the whole of our 'headwaters region' where I live (the start of many rivers). They are all 'holy' because they belong to the Creator as we highlighted before. They are given to us to protect and to maintain, as caretakers of the creation (Gen 1).

When Joshua was near Jericho before it was conquered, he was confronted by the angel of the Lord ("the commander of the army of the Lord"), "Put off your shoes from your feet; for the place where you stand is holy. And Joshua did so." (Josh 5:15) Jericho stands for the whole land that was dedicated to the Lord. It is holy ground. (Therefore also the 'ban' if anyone violated what was devoted to the Lord.) It is like Moses' encounter with Yahweh and the burning bush in Exodus 3:2–5.

Can we sing our songs of protest and witness because the liberation has started? It is put in our hands in joyful anticipation. Can we sing today in protest against the confiscation of native lands, the murder of countless native women and the separation of thousands of native children from their families? Can we compose our own songs and placards? How would we sing today in protest against the poisoning of our lands and people, of paving over our productive farmlands for more and more highways and sprawling suburbs that violate community, of increasing burning fossil fuels adding to the CO_2 in the atmosphere, scorching the earth and creating violent storms and floods, and poisoning the earth with plastic particles and many other toxic chemicals.

> The liberation is starting.
> Here on this holy ground . . .

Yahweh, the LORD of heaven and earth repeatedly encourages Joshua, ". . . Be strong and of good courage; be not frightened, neither be dismayed; for Yahweh your God is with you wherever you go." (Josh 1: 9). 'Murmuring the words of the Law' (Josh 1:8) they took their first steps into the river Jordan, step by step, keeping their eyes on the ark of the covenant (of the LORD's presence) that would go ahead of them, leading the way, just as before they had crossed the Red Sea with the Egyptian army in pursuit. It was the LORD who would give them the land.

Joshua has often been characterized by the words "promise and fulfillment." That characterization sees the book too much from a historical point of view as just another chapter in the history of redemption. "Promise and miraculous salvation" would be more appropriate. At every stage the 'fulfillment' was in jeopardy and not a foregone conclusion. At every stage there is a miraculous 'salvation' by Yahweh (an opened womb, an heir, the exodus, the re-entry after the exile). The former prophets end with the exile, being led into captivity and the miracle of the partial restoration of Israel. The promise of fulfillment was kept alive by the later prophets in their apocalyptic writings. It gained a crucial step with Jesus' coming. The final fulfillment is still waiting as it speaks to us in the end-time prophecies in the gospels, the letters of Peter and the book of Revelation.

As the first book of the earlier prophets, Joshua has an important place in the whole of the Old Testament. It connects the last book of Moses (Deuteronomy) with the next book (Judges through Samuel and Kings). There are countless references back and forth. These inter-textual references give Joshua its distinct place in the whole of the canon. It is the second group of books of the Hebrew Scriptures, after the Torah.

The 'teaching of Moses', the Torah, comes first. The former prophets (Joshua to Kings) are second. The last book of the later prophets (Isaiah, Jeremiah Ezekiel, and the twelve Minor Prophets) ends with the words, "Remember the law of my servant Moses, the statutes and ordinances that I commanded him at Horeb for all Israel. Behold, I will send you Elijah the prophet . . ." (Mal 4:4, 5)

Joshua is a prophetic book. It is the first of the former prophets. If anything it can be characterized as a 'liturgical' book. Starting with the ceremonial procession through the Jordan; the circumcision and Passover ceremonies; the seven day procession around the city of Jericho and seven times on the seventh day, the blowing of the trumpets (of the year of Jubilee); the writing of the law of Moses on the uncut stones of the altar (Josh 1-8); circumcision of the second generation; the celebration of the Passover; and finally the division of the land at Shiloh at the tent of meeting by casting lots for the inheritance of each tribe, clan and family and the appointment of the cities of refuge to secure justice throughout the land (Joshua 13–21). The book closes with the last messages of Joshua. (Josh 23, 24) Joshua does not just continue the stories of Abraham, Isaac and Jacob, even though there are many references to these five books. With Joshua and crossing the Jordan, there is a transition, a new beginning.

7:1c) The Extermination of the Canaanite peoples

Right from the beginning it is important to address the issue of the annihilation as well as the miracle of the 'sun and moon standing still'. Some pacifists believe that Joshua should not really be in the Bible. Yet the promise of a land and a great people started with Abraham as an oath sworn by Yahweh.

> I am the LORD who brought you from Ur of the Chaldeans, to give you this land to possess.
>
> Know of a surety that your descendants will be sojourners in a land that is not theirs, and will be slaves there, and they will be oppressed for four hundred years . . . and they shall come back here in the fourth generation; for the iniquity of the Amorites is not yet complete. To your descendants I give this land, from the river of Egypt to the great river, the river Euphrates. . .
>
> Now there was a famine in the land, besides the former famine that was in the days of Abraham. And Isaac went to Gerar, to Abimelech, king of the Philistines. And the Lord appeared to him and said, 'Do not go down to Egypt . . . Sojourn in this land, and I will be with you; for to you and to your descendants I will give all these lands, and I will fulfill the oath which I swore to Abraham your father . . . and by your descendants all the nations of the earth shall bless themselves.
>
> Genesis 15:7, 13, 16, 18; 26:1,3, 4 (cf. 17:8; 22:15–18)

These two are inseparably connected, the promise to the patriarchs and the 'conquest' of Canaan. They belong together. We cannot have the one without the other. It also anticipates slavery in Egypt, the exodus, the liberation, and making the connection with Joshua.

> Behold, I have set the land before you; go in and take possession of the land which the LORD swore to your fathers, to Abraham, to Isaac, and to Jacob, to give to them and to their descendants after them.
>
> Deuteronomy 1:8.

It is a story about a sovereign God who chooses a people for his own possession and through them to bless all humanity; it is about God's love affair with humanity, in spite of all odds.

Is Joshua a violent book that encourages war and the killing of indigenous people? It certainly has been used that way historically in order to justify annexation of lands and forcing indigenous people out of their homelands into reservations without adequate resources. For, biblicists and literalists, for whom every word from beginning to end is considered the literal, infallible Word of God, Joshua is indeed a very dangerous book. They can come to dangerous conclusions as happened in the past by justifying colonialism, confiscating lands, enslaving people; defending illegitimate authority and power, etc. Tragically, it still happens today in spite of "Truth and Reconciliation."

The book of Joshua is easily misunderstood, especially the conquest of Jericho (Josh 6) and the two military campaigns in chapters 10 and 11. They need to be seen in the light of the ban and God's holiness. Nothing can take away the horror of war and annihilation of peoples as we are reminded each day by the war in Ukraine and Gaza. Scripture places the annihilation of the Canaanites in a specific context. It is only within that context that we can hear the prophetic word in Joshua, of history that proclaims.

The inter-textual references, especially from Deuteronomy, provide a basic perspective for the book of Joshua. The overall perspective of scripture is that of a holy God dwelling among a holy, consecrated people, living in a holy, uncontaminated land. He chose a people for his own delight to relate to, the descendents of Abraham, Isaac and Jacob.

> Now therefore, if you will obey my voice and keep my covenant, you shall be my own possession among all peoples; for all the earth is mine, and you shall be to me a kingdom of priests and a holy nation.
> Exodus 19:5–6

> Our brethren have made our hearts melt, saying, 'The people are greater and taller than we; the cities are great and fortified up to heaven; and moreover we have seen the sons of the Anakim there'. Then I said to you, 'Do not be in dread or afraid of them. The LORD your God who goes before you will himself fight for you, just as he did for you in Egypt before your eyes, and in the wilderness, where you have seen how the LORD your God bore you, as a man bears his son, in all the way that you went until you came to this place.'
> Deuteronomy 1:28–31

The conquest of Canaan is promised and commanded by the LORD himself. The seven surrounding peoples or nations are to be exterminated because of their abominable practices culminating in the sacrifices of their children and the fertility rites of Baal and Astarte. The prophet Micah also strongly condemns these practices of child sacrifice.

> But in the cities of these peoples that the LORD your God gives you for an inheritance, you shall save alive nothing that breathes, but you shall utterly destroy them, the Hittites and the Amorites, the Canaanites and the Perizzites, the Hivites and the Jebusites, as the LORD your God has commanded; that they may not teach you to do all their abominable practices which they have done in the service of their gods, and so to sin against the LORD your God.
> Deuteronomy 20:16–18

> You shall not give any of your children to devote them by fire to Molech, and so profane the name of your God: I am the LORD.
> Leviticus 18:21

> The graven images of their gods you shall burn with fire; you shall not covet the silver or the gold that is in them, or take it for yourselves, lest you be ensnared by it; for it is an abomination to the LORD your God. And you shall not bring an abominable thing into your house, and become accursed like it; you shall utterly detest and abhor it; for it is an accursed thing.
> Deuteronomy 7:25–26 (cf. Lev 18:24–28)

> Shall I give my first-born for my transgression, the fruit of my
>   body for the sin of my soul?
> He has showed you, O man, what is good; and what does the
>   LORD require of you
> but to do justice, and to love kindness, and to walk humbly with
>   your God?
> Micah 6:7–8

It is not because the people of Israel were such upright and blameless people. On the contrary, repeatedly the scriptures summarize the sins of the people after their liberation from Egypt. They are a sinful and stubborn people. It is only because of the Lord's love and promises that they can cross the Jordan and possess the land. It is only because of God's love affair with his people that they can inherit the land.

> Do not say in your heart, after the LORD your God has thrust them out before you, 'It is because of my righteousness that the LORD has brought me in to possess this land; whereas it is because of the wickedness of these nations that the LORD is driving them out before you. Not because of your righteousness

or the uprightness of your heart are you going in to possess their land; but because of the wickedness of these nations the LORD your God is driving them out from before you, and that he may confirm the word which the LORD swore to your fathers, to Abraham, to Isaac and to Jacob Know therefore, that the LORD your God is not giving you this good land to possess because of your righteousness; for you are a stubborn people. Remember and do not forget how you provoked the LORD your God to wrath . . .
    Deuteronomy 9:4–7

Twice the LORD had to be persuaded not to destroy his people, first by Moses after the incident with the golden calf and once by Joshua after the defeat at Ai. Only after their pleading, does the LORD consent to travel with them and battle for them. It is the miracle of a holy and mighty, liberating God, the Creator of heaven and earth, wanting to dwell among his people. His Presence or glory is like unbearable light. The whole earth cannot contain his glory. As the psalmist put it,

The heavens are telling the glory of God;
and the firmament proclaims his handiwork.
Day to day pours forth speech,
and night to night declares knowledge.
    Psalm 19:1–2

A beautiful psalm, as I later recognized, but every week I was in dread of having to recite a verse from one of the psalms at the 'School with the Bible'; afraid I would not remember or stumble and be shamed. Psalm 19 was the first verse I had to recite with the result I always hated that psalm. The teacher had no way of explaining that these kinds of texts proclaim God-in-action, that from moment to moment He upholds his creation, all his creatures, the heavens and the earth by his mighty word. I could have been comforted and encouraged to risk saying those words, even if I stumbled. God's faithfulness and glory are inseparably connected. All the heavens and the earth loudly proclaim God's faithfulness and glory, his love for humanity and the earth, each morning as the sun rises.

"The heavens proclaim his righteousness; and all the peoples behold his glory." (Ps 97:6) Righteousness and glory go together. All the earth cannot contain it. Salomon prayed, "Behold, heaven and the highest heaven cannot contain thee; how much less this house which I have built." (I Kings 8:27). Ezekiel, the prophet sees the 'glory of the Lord' depart from the temple and then from Jerusalem. (Ezek 10:18; 11: 23) Later, after the return of a remnant, he sees 'the glory of the LORD' returning to Jerusalem and then filling the temple. "And the name of the city henceforth shall be, 'The LORD is there'" (Ezek 48:3), God dwelling among his people.

The book of Micah ends with the words,

> Who is a god like thee, pardoning iniquity and passing over transgression
> for the remnant of his inheritance?
> He does not retain his anger for ever because he delights in steadfast love.
> He will again have compassion upon us, he will tread our iniquities under foot.
> Thou wilt cast all our sins into the depth of the sea.
> Thou wilt show faithfulness to Jacob and steadfast love to Abraham,
> as thou hast sworn to our fathers from the days of old.
>   Micah 7:18–20

The judgment, of the Canaanites, reminds us of the words before the flood, "Now the earth was corrupt in God's sight, and the earth was filled with violence. And God saw the earth, and behold, it was corrupt." "And the Lord was sorry that he had made man on the earth, and it grieved him to his heart" (Genesis 6: 6) Likewise with the destruction of Sodom and Gomorrah, "because the outcry against Sodom and Gomorrah is great and their sin is very grave . . ." (Gen 18:20–21)

In spite of this judgment there was a man, Noah, he was a righteous man, blameless in his generation; Noah walked with God. ". . . Noah found favor in the eyes of the LORD." (Genesis 6:8) And so, by miracle, there is a new future for Noah and God's people and the earth. From afar, Abraham watched the destruction of the two cities Sodom and Gomorrah and their surroundings, "and he looked down . . . and lo, the smoke of the land went up like the smoke of a furnace." "So it was that, that when God destroyed the cities of the valley, God remembered Abraham." (Gen 19:28, 29) Now, faced with overwhelming odds, the LORD appointed a new leader after Moses, Joshua. In spite of these reminders, the Israelites became intermingled with the people of Canaan,

> They did not destroy the peoples,
> as the LORD commanded them,
> But they mingled with the nations

> and learned to do as they did.
> They served their idols,
> which became a snare to them.
> They sacrificed their sons and their daughters to the demons;
> They poured out innocent blood,
> the blood of their sons and daughters,
> Whom they sacrificed to the idols of Canaan;
> and the land was polluted with blood.
> Thus they became unclean by their acts,
> and played the harlot in their doings.
>> Psalm 106:34–39

> When you come into the land, which the LORD your God gives you, you shall not learn to follow the abominable practices of those nations. There shall not be found among you any one who burns his son or his daughter as an offering, anyone who practices divination . . .
>> Deuteronomy 18:9, 10

The blood of their children is crying out from the land, just like Abel's blood in Genesis 4. Only when they stay away from those abominable practices and only when they do not defile the land, will the LORD God dwell among them. Later, when the tabernacle was completed, "then the cloud covered the tent of meeting, and the glory of the LORD filled the tabernacle . . ." When Solomon dedicated the temple ". . . fire came down from heaven . . . and the glory of the LORD filled the temple."

> And the LORD said to Moses, Say to all the 'congregation of the people of Israel, You shall be holy; for I the LORD your God am holy.
>> Leviticus 19:1, 2

> For you are a people holy to the LORD your God; the LORD your God has chosen you to be a people for his own possession, out of all the peoples that are on the face of the earth. It was not because you were more in number than any other people that the LORD set his love upon you and chose you, for you were the fewest of all peoples; but it is because the LORD loves you, and is keeping the oath he swore to your fathers . . .
>> Deuteronomy 7:6–8; (cf. 14:2)

> And now, Israel, what does the LORD your God require of you, but to fear the LORD your God, To walk in all his ways, to love him, to serve the LORD your God with all your heart and with

all your soul, and to keep the commandments and statutes of
the LORD, which I command you this day for your good? Behold, to the LORD your God belong heaven and the heaven of
heavens, the earth with all that is in it; yet the LORD set his
heart in love upon your fathers and chose their descendants
after them, you above all peoples, as to this day. Circumcise
therefore the foreskin of your heart, and be no longer stubborn.
For the LORD your God is God of gods and LORD of lords, the
great, the mighty, and terrible God, who is not partial and takes
no bribe. He executes justice for the fatherless and the widow,
and loves the sojourner, giving him food and clothing. Love
the sojourner therefore, for you were sojourners in the land of
Egypt.
Deuteronomy 10:12–19

The LORD God needs a holy land to dwell with his people. Purified, cleansed from the abominations of the surrounding seven nations, which culminated in child sacrifice and the fertility rites. It is holy ground and if it is contaminated by idolatry, it must be cleansed. He wanted a people dedicated to him, living in partnership with him, and not serving other gods.

Therefore, before the chosen people can take possession of the Promised Land, they must be circumcised as a symbol of their purity and dedication and celebrate the Passover as a symbol of their liberation and their commitment to Yahweh, the god of Israel, and listen again to all the life-giving ordinances written on the altar after they crossed the Jordan. Only then can they appropriate the Promised Land and execute the ban upon the surrounding peoples. The land is a gift from Yahweh.

This is the context and perspective for understanding the book of Joshua, Many more inter-textual references could be sighted as we will see as we read Joshua. Nothing can take away the horrors of war and annihilation, but the scriptures own perspective and witness helps us to understand the conquest of Canaan. It is a limited conquest. It is not an arbitrary act of violence, like that of the great empires against innocent peoples at a particular time in history. Not an example that is to be followed. By miracle and the LORD fighting for them, the Israelites are saved from the real threat of the practices of the Canaanite people. The 'Canaanization' of Israel, losing their identity as a people dedicated to Yahweh the God of Israel, became an ever-present threat.

The command to conquer the land of Canaan, the extermination of the enemy population and putting all the cities and people under the ban is not normative for us today, even though the story itself of the conquest is normative. (Woudstra, p. 30) The story of Yahweh "fulfilling all his promises" to Abraham, Isaac and Jacob and to all their descendants, and giving his people rest, remains for our edification. This is a God to whom we can entrust ourselves. In and through judgments he fulfills all his promises and leads us into the Promised Land.

We will close this section with a quote from the prophet Isaiah and Ezekiel. It is an abiding message of God's desire and intention for humanity. Israel too was vomited out of the land because of their idolatry and contamination of the land and yet God had mercy on them.

> Comfort, comfort my people, says your God.
> Speak tenderly to Jerusalem, and cry out to her
> that her warfare is ended, that her iniquity is pardoned . . .
> . . . In the wilderness prepare the way of the LORD,
> make straight in the desert a highway for our God . . .
> And the glory of the LORD shall be revealed . . .
> He will feed his flock like a shepherd,
> he will gather the lambs in his arms,
> he will carry them in his bosom,
> and gently lead those that are with young.
> Isaiah 40:1–3, 5, 11.

> As I live, says the LORD God, I have no pleasure in the death
> of the wicked, but that the wicked turn from his way and live;
> turn back, turn back from your evil ways; for why will you die,
> O house of Israel?
> Ezekiel 33:11; cf 18:23, 30–32

> Arise, shine; for your light has come,
> and the glory of the LORD has risen upon you.
> For behold, darkness shall cover the earth,
> and thick darkness the peoples;
> But the LORD will rise upon you,
> and his glory will be seen upon you.
> And nations shall come to your light,
> and kings to the brightness of your rising.
>
> The sun shall be no more your light by day,
> Nor for brightness shall the moon give light to you by night;
> But the LORD will be your everlasting light,
> and your God will be your glory.
> Your sun shall no more go down,

nor your moon withdraw itself;
For the LORD will be your everlasting light,
and your days of mourning shall be ended.
Your people shall all be righteous;
they shall possess the land for ever,
The shoot of my planting,
the work of my hands,
that I might be glorified.
      Isaiah 60:1–3; 19–21

This inter-textual perspective on Joshua's conquest calls for a different God-image, different from what many of us have been taught or have absorbed from our families or church. (See "A new God-image?!" chapter 8). The episode dealing with the miracle of the 'sun and the moon standing still' will be addressed later.

7:1d) Moses and Joshua, their mission

Moses' life task was to go up Mount Sinai and receive the Torah from Yahweh. He did so at a very loud blast of the trumpet. The trumpet sound also summoned the people to the mountain to hear the word of Yahweh. "And as the sound of the trumpet grew louder and louder, Moses spoke and God answered him in thunder" (Exod 19:19). The people were not to touch the Mountain at the risk of death. It was holy ground.

Joshua's life task was to bring the Torah into the Promised Land. The Torah had to take root in the lives of the people, each in their own inheritance. As soon as they cross the Jordan, the words of the law are engraved on the stones of the altar. "Every place that the sole of your foot will tread upon I have given to you, as I promised to Moses" (Josh 1:3). So do not walk thoughtlessly, the land is the LORD's. They are not to take one step into the Promised Land without the Torah, that is, without doing justice and practicing loving kindness.

Jericho is holy ground. Jericho stands for all of Canaan, its idolatry and all that is destructive. "Go view the land, especially Jericho. And … for they have come to search out all the land." (Josh 2:1, 3) Jericho stands for the whole country, 'pars pro toto'.

The battle for Jericho and Canaan is a spiritual battle. On the seventh day, seven priests sounded seven trumpets with a long blast, and the walls fell down flat and they took the city. Yahweh had fought for them (Joshua 6). Ten of the twelve spies had thought that it was impossible to conquer Canaan. (Num 13 and 14) Later two spies could report to Joshua that "the LORD has given all the land into our hands; and moreover all the inhabitants of the land are fainthearted because of us." (Joshua 2:24) As Rahab, the harlot, had confessed to the spies, "as soon as we heard it our hearts melted, and there was no courage left in any man, because of you; for Yahweh your God is he who is God in heaven above and on earth beneath" (Josh 2:11).

7:1e) A place for the Torah

From the beginning of the conquest to the very end, the Torah was to travel with them every step of the way. "Be careful to do all the law which Moses my servant commanded you . . . this book of the law shall not depart out of your mouth, but you shall meditate on it day and night, that you may be careful to do according to all that is written in it." (Josh 1:7, 8) Before they can pass over the Jordan, they were to renew their covenant and commit themselves to serve Yahweh only. And once more after they have crossed the Jordan, the Law of Moses had to be written on the stones of the altar. Possessing the land and living by the Torah belong inseparably together. The Torah is to be their guide for living in prosperity in the land and having peace from their enemies.

At the end of his life, Joshua once more gathered the people at Shechem, the ancient sanctuary of the Canaanites, challenging the people to serve Yahweh only. The people responded by saying, "Far be it from us that we should forsake the LORD, to serve other gods" (Josh 24:16). Long before, at Shechem, Jacob had commanded his whole household to put away the foreign gods that were among them. Jacob took the idols and hid them under the oak which was near Shechem. (Gen 35:2–4) Yahweh will only travel with his people and bless them in the new land if they follow the life-giving words of the Torah and put away their idols. It is to be their guide for living well.

7:1f) An inheritance forever

Inheritance in this context does not mean that the land can be 'possessed' and be considered "private property." Rather, inheriting this land means becoming good caretakers of the land. The land will always belong to Yahweh, he is the Landowner. As the Psalmists exclaim, "The earth is the

Lord's and the fullness thereof, the world and those that dwell therein" (Ps 24:1); and, "The heavens are thine, the earth also is thine; the world and all that is in it, thou hast founded them. The north and the south, thou hast created them; Tabor and Hermon joyously praise thy name." (Ps 89:11, 12) Already long ago, the storyteller reminds them, Moses said to Pharaoh, "I will stretch out my hands to the LORD; the thunder will cease, and there will be no more hail, that you may know that the earth is the LORD's." (Exod 9:29)

This view of the land as Yahweh's possession was not only a deep conviction but it was to be put into practice, caring for the land and for each family. Every seven years the land was to lay fallow (so the poor could gather the ears) and every fiftieth year they were not to sow nor reap, the year of Jubilee. "For six years you shall sow your land and gather in its yield; but the seventh year you shall let it rest and lie fallow, that the poor of your people may eat; and what they leave the wild beasts may eat." (Exod 23:10,11; Lev 25:1–7) "And you shall hallow the fiftieth year, and proclaim liberty throughout the land to all its inhabitants; it shall be a jubilee for you, when each of you shall return to his property and each of you shall return to your family ... for it is a jubilee and it shall be holy to you." (Lev 25:10,12) Even if the land had been sold, in the year of jubilee it was to be returned to the original family. "The land shall not be sold in perpetuity, for the land is mine; for you are strangers and sojourners with me. In all the country you possess, you shall grant a redemption of the land." (Lev 25:23)

Right from the start the book of Joshua shows an inseparable connection to the Torah. ("Being careful to do according to all the law which Moses my servant commanded you." Josh 1:7) and the following books ("After the death of Joshua . . . to the people of Israel." Judg 1:1) Moses can only see the Promised Land from afar, from the top of the mountain, but he cannot enter it.

Faithfulness to the Torah stands central in the former prophets (Joshua through Kings). Crossing the Jordan is compared to the crossing of the Red sea. Joshua is commissioned to take the place of Moses.

> And the LORD showed him [Moses] all the land . . . And the LORD said to him, 'This is the land of which I swore to Abraham, Isaac, and to Jacob, I will give to your descendants, I have let you see it with your eyes, but you shall not go over there . . . And Joshua the son of Nun was full of the spirit of wisdom, for Moses had laid his hands upon him . . . And there has not arisen

> a prophet since in Israel like Moses, who the LORD knew face to face, none like him for all the signs and the wonders which the LORD sent him to do in the land of Egypt, to Pharaoh and to all his servants and to all his land, and for all the mighty power and all the great and terrible deeds which Moses wrought in the sight of all Israel.
>
> Deuteronomy 34:1–12; cf. Numbers.27:12–23.

> On that day the LORD exalted Joshua in the sight of all Israel; and they stood in awe of him, as they had stood in awe of Moses, all the days of his life (after the crossing of the Jordan).
>
> Joshua 4:14.

There is a direct inter-connection between the books of the Law of Moses and the earlier prophets. Joshua fills the gap between Judges and the Torah. Joshua is described as a true savior with the 'help of the Lord'. Joshua means "Yahweh, the LORD liberates." He had liberated the whole nation, all the people under one Torah, gathered under the protection of Yahweh and in obedience to him.

In Joshua something new is started. The instruction of Moses, the Torah, is past. The entry into the Promised Land was the first installment of Yahweh's promise to Abraham. It is about receiving the gift of the land and accepting and actively taking the gift in spite of overwhelming enemies with horses and chariots and strongly defended cities with mighty warriors. The Torah is to go with them every step of the way. 'From Moses to Joshua' presents the thematic framework of the whole book.

> After the death of Moses, the servant of the LORD, the LORD said to Joshua, the son of Nun, Moses' minister, Moses my servant is dead; 'Now therefore arise, go over this Jordan, you and all this people, into the land which I am giving to them, to the people of Israel. Every place that the sole of your feet will tread upon I have given to you, as I promised to Moses.
>
> Joshua 1:1–3

> No man shall be able to stand before you all the days of your life; as I was with Moses, so I will be with you; I will not fail you or forsake you. Be strong and of good courage; for you shall cause this people to inherit the land which I swore to their fathers to give them. Only be strong and very courageous, being careful to do according to all the law which Moses my servant commanded you; turn not from it to the right hand or to the left, that you may have good success wherever you go. This book of

> the law shall not depart out of your mouth, but you shall meditate on it day and night, that you may be careful to do according to all that is written in it...
> Joshua 1:5-8

The death of Moses is like a framework around the central figure, Joshua. Moses' death closes the period of the Torah. With Joshua there is a new start, "Now therefore..." Just like Moses Joshua will also be called 'a servant of Yahweh' (Num 12:7). He represents the generation that still knew all the great deeds Yahweh had done in Egypt, crossing the Red Sea and leading them through the wilderness. Joshua had stood at Moses' side with the frightful incident of the golden calf when the future of Israel was in jeopardy, and later, taking exception to the other spies with their unfavorable report. (Exod 24:13; 32:17; Num 11:28)

> And Israel served the LORD all the days of Joshua, and all the days of the elders who outlived Joshua and had known all the work which the LORD did for Israel.
> Joshua 24:31

> ... Joshua and Caleb said, 'The land, which we passed through to spy it out, is an exceedingly good land. If the LORD delights in us, he will bring us into this land and give it to us... men who brought up an evil report of the land died by plague before the LORD. But Joshua the son of Nun and Caleb the son of Jephunneh remained alive, of those men who went to spy out the land.
> Numbers 14:6-38.

Crossing the Jordan serves as the inauguration to living in the land.

> But when you go over the Jordan, and live in the land which the LORD your God gives you to inherit, and when He gives you rest from all your enemies round about, so that you live in safety,
> The LORD your God himself will go over before you...
> Be strong and of good courage; for you shall go with this people into the land which the LORD has sworn to their fathers to give them; and you shall put them in possession of it. It is the LORD who goes before you; he will be with you, he will not fail or forsake you; do not fear or be dismayed.
> Deuteronomy 12:10; 31:3, 7, 8

Joshua signals the beginning of a new stage in the prophetic history and prophetic geography. The prophecy is narrated by means of Israel's

THE PROPHETIC CALL TO LOVE AND JUSTICE

history in the land. It is a story that starts well but ends in the last of the earlier prophets (Kings) with the exile. As was predicted in Leviticus,

> ... and you shall not do as they do in the land of Canaan, to which I am bringing you. You shall not walk in their statutes.
>
> Do not defile yourselves by any of these things, for by all these the nations I am casting out before you defiled themselves; and the land became defiled, so that I punished its iniquity, and the land vomited out its inhabitants.
>
> But you shall keep my statutes and my ordinances and do none of these abominations ... lest the land vomit you out, when you defile it, as it vomited out the nation that was before you.
>
> Leviticus 18:3, 24–26, 28

Between entry and exile, stand the former prophets (Joshua through Kings). They bear witness to what happened to Yahweh's own people. The land vomited them out. It is reminiscent of Genesis 2, from the earth to the garden, out of the garden back to the barren land.

The liberation stories threaten to end in chaos and anarchy, Judges, "In those days there was no king in Israel; every man did what was right in his own eyes. " (Judg 17:6; 19:1; 21:25). It cried out for a true kingship like David's. That story of David's kingship is told in great detail in 1 and 2 Samuel. His kingship is a sign of the future. In 1 and 2 Kings it is all downhill, except for the reform under king Josiah. There, miraculously, the book of the Torah is found (II Kings 22:11, 13), the book with which Joshua entered the land. (Josh 1:6, 7)

The former prophets not only start and end with the Torah, but it also starts and ends with a celebration of the Passover. Before the people can take possession of the Promised Land they have to rededicate themselves by celebrating the Passover and reading the Torah. Just before the exile the people again celebrate the Passover (II Kings 23:21–23), "as it was not celebrated since the days of the Judges."

"Land out," being led into exile is a judgment, but also an historical reality. "Land in," entry into the Promised Land, in as much as it is historical, is first of all a promise and remains a promise. A Passover people only has a future gathered around the Torah of Moses and can look forward to a new entry into the land in which God's servant David shall be their king.

> Behold I will take the people of Israel from the nations among which they have gone, and will gather them from all sides, and

bring them to their own land; and I will make them one nation in the land, upon the mountains of Israel; and one king shall be king over them all; and they shall be no longer two nations and no longer divided into two kingdoms... My servant David shall be king over them; and they shall all have one shepherd...
Ezekiel 37:21–24

These prophetic books do not only describe how it was, but implicitly they tell how it will be. Joshua is not only a prophetic book but also follows a prophetic schematic geography. In a straight line, the land is conquered, from east to west and south to north. They go from Shittim, across the Jordan, to Gilgal and then in one move east and south and with an even briefer description north. In two short chapters of Joshua (10, 11), the whole land is conquered. Chapters 12–22 narrate the division of the land. While the last two chapters, record the final instructions of Joshua to the people.

Chapters 3–8 are more liturgical in nature: the circumcision and rededication of the people; the celebration of the Passover; the crossing of the Jordan with the ark and priests standing in the middle until all the people have crossed; the ceremonial walk around the city Jericho for seven days; the failure to conquer Ai and the execution of the ban; the forbidden covenant with the Gibeonites. Only then are the people ready to receive their inheritance. All the while it is Yahweh that battles for them, enlisting the sun and moon and great hailstones to defeat the enemies. These narrations are exemplary, miracle stories, (Noort).

The Jordan is not as much a geographical divide as a moment in the prophetic proclamation. The Jordan flows between the Torah and the Prophets and will stop flowing for a moment to let the people pass over. 'In three days', this inauguration of the gift of the land put the entry on the same level of importance as the exodus from Egypt. Step by step they may whisper "given," "given by Yahweh."

> 'This day I will begin to exalt you (Joshua) in the sight of all Israel, that they may know that, as I was with Moses, so I will be with you' ... And Joshua said to the people of Israel, 'Come hither, and hear the words of the LORD your God'. And Joshua said, 'Hereby you shall know that the living God is among you ...' 'Behold the ark of the covenant of the LORD of all the earth is to pass over before you in the Jordan ... And when the soles of the feet of the priests who bear the ark of the LORD, the LORD of all the earth, shall rest in the waters of the Jordan,

THE PROPHETIC CALL TO LOVE AND JUSTICE

> the waters of the Jordan shall be stopped from flowing, and the waters coming down from above shall stand in one heap'
> Joshua 3:7–13

Is this a divinely sanctified permission for confiscating new territories? The storyteller does not paint a picture of Israel as one of the great empires that is committed to a program of expansion and extermination, aided by chariots and horses. The country to be possessed is presented as of a surrealistic size, larger than David's kingdom ever was. (Joshua 1:4) It is like Paradise one is inclined to say. It is written for a newly enslaved people liberated for the second time and for their encouragement. Joshua's name is central, 'Yahweh liberates'. He may be the person that leads the people to inherit the land, as promised to Abraham.

> Every place that the sole of your foot will tread upon, I have given to you, as I promised to Moses. From the wilderness and this Lebanon as far as the great river, the river Euphrates, all the land of the Hittites to the Great Sea toward the going down of the sun shall be your territory.
> Joshua 1:3,4

There is lots of room to live for a people that have been liberated from slavery in Egypt and have left the forty year journey through the desert behind them, lots of room to live peacefully. It is pictured in idealistic terms and yet presented in very realistic terms on the map. That land is here. This movement, the Exodus, which has been started by Yahweh, goes on. Before the face of Joshua, 'Yahweh liberates' no one can stop this movement of liberation. In Joshua the name of God is recognized, Yahweh is with him.

We can only read this story liturgically and prophetically. Whoever wants to make these narratives into an unholy war in history, even today, is a dangerous person who corrupts the best into something evil. The reader is invited to identify him/herself with the people and see a future perspective dawning, liberation again and again. These narratives written after the exile are addressed and passed on to a hearing community. There it is read on the Sabbath and on Sunday for the people to be encouraged and prepared for the journey, for a witness and concrete actions, for liberation.

After passing the Jordan the whole country was open before them, including the trans-Jordan. The trans-Jordan tribes (Ruben, Gad and half Manasseh) could only receive their inheritance after crossing the

Jordan along with all the other tribes. They commit themselves to keep the brotherhood and swear not to return to their inheritance until all the tribes have received their portion. In three days it will happen.

7:2 Joshua 2 The confession of Rahab in solidarity with Israel

After the schematized introduction, this story about Rahab the prostitute is perhaps the most captivating. Rahab's story frames the conquest of Jericho, before and after. The first city to be captured is Jericho following the line from Shittim to Gilgal right through the middle of Benjamin's territory dividing the northern from the southern kingdom. Whatever can be said about Jericho historically, geographically and archeologically is less important. It is the first city the Israelites will encounter when crossing the Jordan. (Noort) This city will play an important role. Within three days. "Prepare your provisions; for in three days you are to cross over the Jordan." (Josh 1:11) Joshua sends out two spies that can bring reports and witness. They are to spy out Jericho and the land. "Go view the land, especially Jericho." (Josh 2:1)

Rahab, she knows,

> Who is like thee, O LORD, among the gods? Who is like thee, majestic in holiness, terrible in glorious deeds, doing wonders? ... Thou hast led in thy steadfast love the people whom thou hast redeemed, thou hast guided them by thy strength to thy holy abode. The peoples have heard, they tremble; pangs have seized on the inhabitants of Philistia. Now are the chiefs of Eden dismayed; the leaders of Moab, trembling seizes them; All the inhabitants of Canaan have melted away. Terror and dread fall upon them; because of the greatness of thy arm, they are as still as a stone, till thy people, O LORD, pass by ...
> Exodus 15:11–16

And that is how the king of Jericho understood the spies' mission. Word had come to the king. "Behold certain men of Israel have come here tonight to search out the whole land" (Joshua 2:2). Apparently Jericho stands for the whole country in this context, pars pro toto. From out of Jericho the whole country lies open, to the east, the south and the north. Later on Rahab will say, "I know that the LORD has given you the land, and that the fear of you has fallen upon us, and that all the inhabitants of the land melt away before you. We have heard ... (Josh 2:8–10) The non-Israelites have seen clearly, they know, but instead of surrendering, the city kings conspire together with great fear to fight Israel, while Rahab stays calm and wants to join in with God's people. She is mentioned in the genealogy of Jesus in Matthew 1:5, along with Tamar, Ruth, and David.

The spies found shelter and protection with Rahab, the harlot, who had a house on the city wall. She played her role well with the king and the soldiers, full of 'innocence'. She answered the questions by saying, "true, the men came to me but I did not know where they came from . . . where the men went I do not know pursue them quickly, for you can overtake them." (Josh 24:7) It was like saying I have many clients and I don't ask anything. Meanwhile she hid the spies on the roof under stocks of flax that were drying on the rooftop. After the exchange with the soldiers, she went up to the roof to talk to the men and there she makes an astounding and remarkable confession in words from the song of Moses and the Psalms. Apparently she was familiar with the escape from Egypt and their miraculous escape through the waters of the Red Sea. She has heard and she knows, she truly knows what is at stake.

> For we have heard how the LORD dried up the water of the Red Sea before you when you came out of Egypt, and what you did to the two kings of the Amorites that were beyond the Jordan, to Sihon and Og whom you utterly destroyed. As soon as we heard it, our hearts melted, and there was no courage left in any more of us because of you. The LORD your God is he who is indeed God in heaven above and on the earth beneath. Now then, swear to me by the LORD that as I have dealt kindly with you, you also will deal kindly with my father's house and give me a sure sign . . .
> Joshua 2:10–12

Compare Psalm 135 and 136,

> For I know the LORD is great, and that our LORD is above all gods . . .
> He it was who smote the first-born of Egypt, both of man and beast;
> Who in thy midst, O Egypt, sent signs and wonders against Pharaoh and all his servants;
> Who smote many nations and slew mighty kings,
> Sihon king of the Amorites, and Og, king of Bashan, and all the kingdoms of Canaan,
> and gave their land as a heritage, a heritage to his people Israel.
> Ps 135:5, 8–12

Rahab is familiar with Israel's history. When she says, "we have heard," she does not only speak for the inhabitants of Jericho but for the whole country, "all the inhabitants of the land melt in fear before you." She represents all the nations. Their hearing ends with dread, especially the last event with the two kings of the Amorites which took place "in the plains of Moab beyond the Jordan from Jericho." (Num 22:1) Her statement ends in a confession. She not only has heard, but she knows (in her heart). She recites from the song of Moses.

> Then Moses and the people of Israel sang this song to the LORD, saying, 'I will sing to the LORD, for he has triumphed, gloriously; the horse and his rider he has thrown into the sea. The LORD is my strength and my song, and he has become my salvation; this is my God, and I will praise him, my father's God, and I will exalt him.
> Exodus 15:1–2

With Rahab's recitation, the storyteller wants to proclaim and involve us in the deeds of the one, universal God. Because of this God, Israel has a future in the land and humans have a future on the earth. For Rahab the city Jericho is already conquered now that she has seen all the new and liberating events that happen with Israel. She wants to be part of that, "Now then, swear to me by the LORD . . ." that you will show the same solidarity as I did with you. Be faithful to me and my family as I have shown good faith and solidarity with you." So they promise. The sign will be the red cord hanging from the window, maybe a sign of her profession before. All the inhabitants of that house will be saved. Now it becomes a sign of the covenant they made with her.

Rahab represents all the surrounding nations. "All the inhabitants of the land" (Josh 2:9) have heard. They have panicked and recoiled with fear and loss of courage. Rahab responds with courage and faith. And later, all the kings of the city states band together to fight Israel. Rahab receives a place within Israel as a representative of all the peoples. Her background in a pagan people is not a hindrance for belonging to God's people. At the same time, belonging to the Israelites does not automatically mean belonging to God's people (Achan, Josh 7). As an outsider, a stranger, she makes an astonishing confession. It reminds us of Matt 8:5–13 and 15:21–28 "Truly I say to you, not even in Israel have I found such faith . . ." (Matt 8:10–13) and so the Centurion's servant was healed, and "O woman, great is your faith! Be it done for you as you desire. And her daughter was healed instantly." (Matt 15:21–28)

As to her 'white lie', ('emergency lie'), Woudstra rightly quotes Holwerda stating that "truth in Israel is something different from "agreement with fact." It means "loyalty toward the neighbor and the LORD." (p.71, footnote 14)[2] It reminds me of when I heard a German soldier ask my father if there were any Jews or other eligible men hidden in our house. They went from door to door that day, a 'razzia', searching for people hiding, bringing them outside and herding them to the railroad station, never to return. My father answered with a clear and strong "No!" What he was really saying was, 'there are no sub-humans or slave laborers hidden in our house. After looking around in the workshop downstairs, the soldiers finally left. They never went upstairs. But I always remember that incident sitting there halfway on the steps in fear. It was a concrete lesson in practicing solidarity with our neighbor who was hidden in a space between the ceiling and the floor, on the third floor under my bed. It was one of the occasions that gave rise to my nightmares about being chased and almost caught by soldiers as I defended myself fiercely; as my wife can testify when I thrash around and kick away in my sleep, even till the present. War memories die out very slowly.

The author of the letter to the Hebrews can later say,

> By faith the people crossed the Red Sea as if on dry land; but the Egyptians, when they attempted to do the same, were drowned. By faith the walls of Jericho fell down after they had been encircled for seven days. By faith Rahab the harlot did not perish with those who were disobedient, because she had given friendly welcome to the spies.
> Hebrews 11:29–31

After Jericho has fallen, we read,

> But Rahab the harlot, and her father's household, and all who belonged to her, Joshua saved alive; and she dwelt in Israel to this day, because she hid the messengers whom Joshua sent to spy out Jericho.
> Joshua 6:25

She had practiced solidarity with the spies and the God of Israel and her desire to belong to God's people and they, in turn welcomed her and her family in their midst.

---

2. Woudstra, *The Book of Joshua*, 71.

Each step of the way the Israelites had to show their trust in the LORD their God, 'their God in heaven above and on the earth beneath'. That is how they actualized their faith. In the doing they entered the Promised Land. When they took the first step into the Jordan their eyes focused on the Ark of the Covenant. They joined the liturgical procession walking around Jericho behind the priests with the ark. The big theme of Joshua has become evident in this first great event, the gift of the land and actively receiving the gift.

Because of her faithfulness and solidarity Rahab could join with all God's people. Her prophetic words are summarized by the spies in Joshua 2:25 "truly the LORD has given all the land into our hands; and moreover all the inhabitants of the land are fainthearted because of us." With this expression of faith and solidarity the Israelites are ready to prepare to cross the Jordan.

7:3 Joshua 3-4 *Crossing the Jordan and entering into a new period*

The importance of crossing the Jordan shows in the amount of preparation that is taken. Early in the morning Joshua woke up and told the people to ready themselves to travel from Shittim to the Jordan. From Deuteronomy 31:3-6 they knew what to expect, "The LORD your God himself will go over before you; he will destroy these nations before you . . . Be strong and of good courage, do not fear or be in dread of them . . . for it is the LORD your God who goes with you; he will not fail you or forsake you." They know that once they cross the Jordan they are in enemy territory. There will be no way back. Just as when they took their first steps into the Red Sea. While they were still in the desert, the LORD had commanded Moses to teach the people a song of warning and deliverance (Deut 32), which ends with "For it is no trifle for you, but it is your life; you shall live long in the land which you are going over the Jordan to possess." (Deut 32:47)

At the Red Sea the enemy was behind them and catching up with them. Here the enemy is in front of them. They waited and camped there for three days. After three days the elders went through the camp and told the people, be ready, when you see the priests with the ark follow them. They will show you the way. "When you see the Ark of the Covenant . . . then you will follow it, that you may know the way you shall go, for you have not passed this way before. Yet there shall be a space between you and it (the ark).... Do not come near it." (Josh 3:4) It seems like a strange command, "that you may know the way you shall go."

The Jordan could have easily been crossed at one of the fords like the spies did. But the people need to learn something important. A unique way had to be acknowledged and experienced by them, a way through the waters of death to new life. "Joshua said to the people, 'sanctify yourselves; for tomorrow the Lord will do wonders among you.'" This is not an ordinary crossing. It is a rite of passage, it will be a miracle. Then they will know that the LORD is with Joshua as he was with Moses.

> For the LORD your God dried up the waters of the Jordan for you until you passed over, as the LORD your God did to the Red Sea, which he dried up for us until we passed over, so that all the peoples of the earth may know that the hand of the LORD is mighty; that you may fear the LORD your God forever."
> Joshua 4:23–24.

This is exactly what happens, after the crossing "When all the kings of the Amorites that were beyond the Jordan to the west, and all the kings of the Canaanites that were by the sea, heard that the Lord had dried up the waters of the Jordan for the people of Israel until they had crossed over, their heart melted, and there was no longer any spirit in them, because of the people of Israel." (Josh 5:1) "And the LORD said to Joshua, 'this day I will begin to exalt you in the sight of all Israel, that they may know that, as I was with Moses, so I will be with you.'" (Josh 3:7 cf. 4:14)

The stage has been set for an extraordinary event to happen. Shall not the Creator of heaven and earth, who gathered together the waters and called them Seas, shall he not be able to make a path through the Sea for the people to escape death by Pharaoh's horses and chariots to find liberty? Shall he not be able to make the Jordan to reverse its course to let all the people pass on dry ground? Thus the poet in Psalm 89 can exclaim, "Thou dost rule the raging of the sea; when its waves rise, thou stillest them ... the heavens are thine, the earth also is thine; the world and all that is in it, thou hast founded them. The north and the south, thou hast created them..." (vs. 9–12) and the great king (David) is given power over the sea and rivers, "I will set his hand on the sea and his right hand on the rivers." (vs. 25) Given this confession it is no surprise that the poet in Psalm 114 can say and ask,

> The Sea looked and fled, Jordan turned back.
> The mountains skipped like rams, the hills like lambs.
> What ails you, O Sea, that you flee?

O Jordan, that you turn back?
O Mountains, that you skip like rams?
O Hills, like lambs?
Tremble, O Earth, at the presence of the LORD,
at the presence of the God of Jacob,
who turns the rock into a pool of water,
the flint into a spring of water.
      Psalm 114:3–8).[3]

A miracle has happened. Did you ever see the sea flee or the Jordan reverse its course? What is the matter with you Sea and Jordan? Did you forget your Creator and Ruler that you flee and tremble? It sounds unbelievable to our western, reductionistic, disenchanted and secularized ears. The 'regular' course of 'nature' is changed by the Creator in order to liberate his people. 'Nature' retreats before the history of God's people. It is a prophetic history in which God creates life in the midst of death. This not a report of a natural phenomenon, that is broken through miraculously. Rather it is a description of a liberating history that engages and enlists the hearer to participate and join in.

So it happened as soon as the priests' feet touched the water of the Jordan. It is a decisive moment. A new prophetic history can get started. The priests will stand still in the middle of the Jordan until all the people have passed by, warriors, women and children. "The waters coming down from above stood and rose up in a heap ... the waters were wholly cut off and the people passed over opposite Jericho." They went through the waters of death to a new life, to a land flowing with milk and honey . . . The miracle shows God's power to save his chosen people and through them all peoples of the world. Sometimes the chronology of the story is disrupted in order to complete one sequence and then to come back to it later. Often an event is mentioned and then interrupted to be completed later on.

Characteristics in the landscape are used by the storyteller to explain particular 'geographical' references, like the stones set up like a memorial in the midst of the night camp at Gilgal and in the Jordan. "And they are there until this day" is a familiar formula to indicate a peculiar geographical phenomenon that is used by the storyteller to highlight the prophetic message. These are not references to 'holy stones' (masabes). In this story they become signs that the priests had stood still in the middle

---

3. cf. Deurloo, K., *What is it with you, sea, that you flee? Psalms read, heard and told.*

of the Jordan. There were plenty of such stones around in the rugged landscape around the Jordan and in the Jordan itself.

7:4 Joshua 5 Circumcision and the Passover

Through the procession across the Jordan we become aware that it is a liturgical procession rather than a military march. Even in this section there will be no indication of warfare. Instead there is a cultic and liturgical celebration. The battle of Jericho is postponed. First something else needs to happen that will put the battle in the right perspective. The dating of the crossing receives a special significance. "The Jordan overflows all its banks throughout the time of the harvest." We read, the Jordan was full of water at the moment of the crossing. It emphasizes the miracle. The Jordan is full all the days of the harvest, which happens in spring. The date is specified, ". . . the people came up out of the Jordan on the first day of the first month . . ." (Josh 4:19)

This is not just a historical announcement, but a liturgical one. "Tell all the congregation of Israel that on the tenth day of this month, they shall take every man a lamb . . . It is the Lord's Passover." (Exod 12:1–28). Who may sit at the table of the covenant people? Only those can who are circumcised. That separation becomes even more distinct with the circumcision as described in Genesis 17:12–14. All those who by birth do not belong to the covenant community can join through this sign. Strangers, sojourners that live among you and slaves that you have bought can be taken up in this community. All those who show solidarity like Rahab receive a place in their midst.

Among uncircumcised people like the Philistines it was probably a sign of manliness and vitality. In Israel circumcision takes on another function, like belonging to the covenant community. Just as the harvest celebration takes on a new function as a celebration of the exodus and the entry into the Promised Land. The context may be that in Babylonian captivity the celebration of the Sabbath, circumcision, in the midst of the uncircumcised Neo-Babylonians secured their identity. That may also be the background of Genesis 17 and Joshua 5, but that does not say anything about its prophetic function as a sign in the flesh of belonging to the covenant community.

In Joshua, it is more than a sign of identity. It is assumed that the people that left Egypt that were circumcised as a disobedient people failed to circumcise the next generation. What happened in the desert?

When the spies came back with their discouraging report, except for Caleb and Joshua, the people cried out, "The people wept that night. And all the people of Israel murmured against Moses and Aaron; the whole congregation said to them, 'Would that we had died in the land of Egypt! Or that we had died in this wilderness... Our wives and little ones will become a prey; would it not be better for us to go back to Egypt?' And then the LORD said to Moses, 'How long will they not believe in me, in spite of all the signs which I have wrought among them?'" (Num 14:11). That whole generation was doomed to die in the desert. "So it was their children, whom he raised up in their stead, that Joshua circumcised; for they were uncircumcised, because they had not been circumcised on the way." (Josh 5:7)

Joshua makes specific mention of the men of war. " For the people of Israel walked forty years in the wilderness, till all of the nation, the men of war that came forth out of Egypt, perished, because they did not hearken to the voice of the LORD... (Josh 5:6, cf. Deut 2:14) They were replaced by the new generation whom they had failed to circumcise in the desert.

The first time the Israelites tried to defeat the Amalikites and Canaanites they were defeated for the Lord was not with them nor was the ark of the covenant in their midst. (Num 14:39–45). It was only later they were able to defeat Sihon and Og because the LORD was with them. Moses had interceded for the people, "Now if thou dost kill this people as one man... Then the Egyptians will hear of it... and say, Because the LORD was not able to bring this people into the land which he swore to give to them, therefore he has slain them in the wilderness..." (Num 14:5) Moses appealed to God and said, "The Lord is slow to anger, and abounding in steadfast love, forgiving iniquity and transgression, but he will by no means clear the guilty... Pardon the iniquity of this people, I pray thee, according to the greatness of thy steadfast love, and according as thou hast forgiven this people, from Egypt even until now." (Num 14:18, 19)

Now they had three days rest before Passover must be celebrated. Before all the people could participate all the males had to be circumcised. (Josh 5:2–8) It took away the reproach of Egypt. "This day I have rolled away the reproach of Egypt from you. And so the name of that place is called Gilgal to this day." (Josh 5:9) A new generation has arisen that has taken the place of the older disobedient people that died in the wilderness. By being circumcised and celebrating the Passover in the

Promised Land, the 'reproach of Egypt was rolled away'. The LORD had proven himself to be victorious in spite of a rebellious and doubting people. Their first steps into the Jordan on dry ground, was an act of faith, actively participating in God's liberation in contrast to the older generation.

Passover was celebrated three days later. Although originally a harvest feast, it celebrated the liberation from Egypt. Symbols of the harvest continue to characterize the feast. New, unleavened bread is eaten. A new harvest is starting and they can eat the produce of the land of Canaan. This is also the moment when "the manna ceased on the morrow when they ate the produce of the land; and the people of Israel had manna no more." (Josh 5:12) The crossing of the Jordan is only now complete. A new period has started. The liturgy forms the introduction to the gift of the land (Jericho) and taking possession of the land (Ai). Another kind of liturgy would be celebrated on mount Ebal with a copy of the Law of Moses written on the altar. (Josh 8:32)

Passover will not be celebrated again until the reforms of King Josiah. (2 Kings 23:21–23) Passover is celebrated at the beginning when they entered the land and when they are about to be led into captivity. The prophetic history from Joshua to Kings takes place between these two celebrations and can be read as signs of the exodus. Whoever reads the Torah can do nothing else but cross the Jordan and with the circumcised, covenant people celebrate Passover. The congregation reads this history in this manner, 'until this day.'

7:5 Joshua 6 The conquest of Jericho

Even after the circumcision and Passover the gift of the land (Jericho) does not happen right away. First there is a mysterious encounter between Joshua 'by Jericho' and a man with a drawn sword. 'By Jericho' is not a topographical indication. At that time, Jericho is no more than a pile of ruins from previous centuries. This assumed city may function as representative of the whole country. Are you for us, or for our adversaries Joshua asks? The man answers, "No; but as commander of the army of the Lord I have now come." (Josh 5:14)

Again the narrator assumes that the hearers know the Torah, for it immediately reminds us of the encounter between Moses and the Presence in the 'burning bush', which is a word for the mountain god, Horeb. "Don't come near; put off your shoes from your feet, for the place on which you are standing is holy ground. (Exod 3:5) So here too, "Put off your shoes from your feet; for the place where you stand is holy. And Joshua did so." (Josh 5:15) A messenger of God, the commander of the army of the LORD, had confronted him. Whoever wants to enter the Promised Land has to deal with the LORD of the land and his power.

But the commander of the army of the LORD has also come to remind Joshua that Yahweh himself will battle for Israel. "Hear, O Israel, you draw near this day to battle against your enemies: let not your heart faint; do not fear, or tremble, or be in dread of them; for the LORD your God is he that goes with you, to fight for you against your enemies, to give you the victory." (Deut 20:3, 4) Joshua does not get instructions for the battle, but instead is told to take his sandals off his feet because the ground on which he stands is holy ground. Just as with Moses before he gets his call to free his people. This land too is holy ground (Jericho), a place where Yahweh is Lord and Master. It is a special place of Yahweh. In Joshua 1:2, 3 we read, "Now arise, go over the Jordan, you and all this people ... every place that the sole of your foot will tread upon I have given to you, as I promised to Moses." The conquest is not a foregone conclusion. It will indeed be given by the mighty acts of Yahweh.

The liturgical procession around the city seven times will emphasize that the Lord gives the land to the people. "Now Jericho was shut up, from within and from without because of the people of Israel; none went out, and none came in . . . See, I have given into your hand Jericho, with its king and mighty men of valor." (Josh 6:1, 2) It is God's holy city and holy land. For that reason do not take any of the dedicated things 'But you, keep yourselves from the things devoted for destruction' for yourselves and 'make the camp of Israel a thing for destruction'(Josh 6:18–20). The defilement by one defiles all the people.

Just as with crossing the Jordan, they have to keep their eyes on the ark of Yahweh and the priests as they walk around the city. The walls of the city will not crumble until the sound of the trumpets. Just like at the time of Moses, the people were not to touch the holy mountain of the Lord until they heard the sound of the trumpet. "When the trumpet sounds a long blast, they shall come up to the mountain." (Exod 19:13) For Moses it was a sign that God would be with him and that Israel will serve God at this mountain. (Exod 3:12) The trumpets are of a special kind. According to Leviticus 25:1–12, they are to be blown in the year of Jubilee. "On the day of atonement you shall send abroad the loud trumpet throughout all your land. And you shall hallow the fiftieth year, and proclaim liberty ... when each of you shall return to his property and each of you shall return to his family ... and you shall eat what it yields out of the field."

The narrative suggests that the account in Joshua refers back to this original story in Leviticus. The land is holy but he gives it for a place to live. Only what is dedicated to Yahweh will go back to the temple but "a field, when it is released in the Jubilee, shall be holy to the LORD, as a field that has been devoted; the priest shall be in possession of it." (Lev 27:21) A field that is devoted to the LORD and not part of the family inheritance will go back to the LORD to be used by the priests. The same will be true for Jericho, the devoted things are "all silver and gold, and vessels of bronze and iron, are sacred to the LORD; they shall go into the treasury of the LORD." (Josh 6:19). The people shouted, and the trumpets were blown ... and the walls fell down ... But Rahab, and all her family, were saved and she dwelt in Israel to this day." Rahab is saved from the ban.

7:6 Joshua 7-8 All the people; Ai and the ban

The Jordan is passed, the people have been taken up in the covenant again through their circumcision and Passover observance, (Josh 5:2-11) Jericho is given in Israel's hand. The ark of the covenant of Yahweh stands central in the story around the Jordan and Jericho. Everything took place within the unspoiled sphere of the covenant. Israel has acted like a holy nation. That is how Israel ought to behave, but is that so.

The beginning of Deuteronomy 31 is continually referred to as the measure of the book of Joshua. God called Moses and Joshua to the tent of meeting and said,

> For when I have brought them into the land flowing with milk and honey ... and they have eaten and are full and grown fat, they will turn to other gods and serve them, and despise me and break my covenant. And when many evils and troubles have come upon them, this song (of Moses) shall confront them as a witness ... So Moses wrote this song the same day, And taught it to the people of Israel.
> Deuteronomy 31:20-22

This situation will become acute in the book of Judges. But even in Joshua a counter picture is given in the exemplary story of Ai. "But the people of Israel broke faith in regard to the devoted things . . ." (Josh 7: 1) A part of the people was to capture Ai, but they fled and there were casualties. ". . . And the hearts of the people melted, and became as water." (Josh 7:5) This same expression was used to describe the inhabitants of the land. But now Israel itself has no heart and no courage anymore. That can only mean that Yahweh has turned against his people. In the beginning the tribes of Ruben, Gad and half of Manasse on behalf of all the people had said to Joshua, "Whoever rebels against your commandment and disobeys your words, whatever you command him, shall be put to death." (Josh 1:18) Chapter 7 starts with, "But the people of Israel broke faith . . ." Through the one, Achan, all Israel had sinned. Achan equals the people of Israel. He had not just taken from the spoil and hid it in his tent. In doing so he had broken the covenant and jeopardized the future of all Israel. "Israel has sinned; they have transgressed my covenant which I commanded them; they have taken some of the devoted things; they have stolen, and lied. And put them among their own stuff." (Josh 7:11)

To break faith with regard to the devoted things directly concerns Yahweh. The devoted things are the things that are dedicated to the LORD. Something is wrong with Achan, but that comes a little later. Something is wrong with 'all the sons of Israel'. The people thought that just a small contingent of warriors was enough to take Ai, but they lost the battle and fled. "Let not all the people go up, but let about two or three thousand men go up and attack Ai." (Josh 7:3) In their overconfidence they had forgotten that Yahweh battles for them and gives the victory. Joshua prays in words that are reminiscent of Moses' prayer, "Would it not be better for us to go back to Egypt? (Num 14:3) and Joshua responded, ". . . Alas, O LORD God, why hast thou brought this people over the Jordan at all, to give us into the hands of the Amorites, to destroy us? Would that we had been content to dwell beyond the Jordan!" (Josh 7:7) "For the Canaanites and all the inhabitants of the land will hear of it, and will surround us, and cut off our name from the earth; and what will thou do for thy great name?" (Josh 7:9)

Joshua had warned the people,

> But you, keep yourselves from the things devoted to destruction, lest when you have devoted them you take any of devoted things and make the camp of Israel a thing for destruction and bring trouble upon it."
> Joshua 6:18

This is what happened. Achan's sin put the whole nation under the ban, 'all the sons of Israel'. The community gave rise to an Achan; the whole nation transgresses the covenant and Achan is the expression of that sin. ("Israel has sinned ..." Josh 7:11) Achan expresses an attitude of all the people, contrary to what they are called to be, God's people, as if the conquest of Ai was a trifle and could be done with a few people and not the whole nation and without Yahweh leading the people. This person must be banned from their midst. Achan is the opposite of Rahab. She is also one for the many (of those who want to belong to God's people).

The Lord said to Joshua, "why have you thus fallen upon your face? Israel has sinned; they have transgressed my covenant... Up, sanctify the people..." and Yahweh himself will point out the guilty person. Achan is pointed out and taken outside the camp and stoned, he and all those that belong to him (like Rahab, 'all her family'). The continuation of Israel is a matter of life and death. In past times this was the custom, also outside of Israel. Of a Moabite king it is said he also conducted a holy war, fought by his god and he boasted and applied the ban.

Afterwards, "the LORD said to Joshua, 'Do not fear or be dismayed; take all the fighting men with you and arise, go up to Ai ...'" (Josh 8:1). Ai is defeated and all the inhabitants were slaughtered. It remains a gruesome story, but it is told in the context of an enslaved people, a people who had been liberated from slavery to live in freedom in a land that was sworn to Abraham. What is given from above, the people may possess. Jericho and Ai are exemplary stories for a people in captivity in Babylon. It is not a call to engage in a 'holy war'.

It is past tense. It is a literary motif that has been given a new meaning. In the holy war and the ban the concern is to maintain the identity of the people and against mixing with other destructive peoples. They are to give people hope and proclaim that there is a future for them, that Yahweh will make space to live and to fight against all that threatens that life of abundance in a land flowing with milk and honey. The scribes have given the book of Joshua a liturgical setting, so that it can be read and heard in the liturgy of the congregation today, each Sabbath and Sunday again.

The warfare is not just a wild and gruesome adventure, but a command given by Yahweh. It has to be engaged in on the basis of God's promises. It has to be a movement in which all God's people participate. "The land is given in your hands." Joshua's held up his spear until all the inhabitants of Ai were slain. Like Moses did in the battle with the Amalekites (Exod 17:8–16). Such wars are only successful if Yahweh battles for the people. As in Psalm 46,

> God is our refuge and strength,
> a very present help in trouble.
> Therefore we will not fear
> though the earth should change,
> though the mountains shake in the heart of the sea;
> though its waters roar and foam,
> though the mountains tremble with its tumult . . .
> Come, behold the works of the LORD,
> how he has wrought desolations in the earth.
> He makes wars cease to the end of the earth;
> he breaks the bow, and shatters the spear,
> He burns the chariots with fire!
> Be still, and know that I am God . . .
> Psalm 46:1–10

The part that is conquered until now is only a small part of Canaan. But thematically everything has been accomplished. The detailed narratives of Jericho and Ai can be closed liturgically, just as they were opened liturgically with circumcision and Passover. The end of chapter 8 describes a worship situation. All the people stand together with the ark and the priests in their midst, over against the altar and listen to the reading of the Torah. This scene is typical for the worship situation in the temple in Jerusalem, but that name is withheld until later when Jerusalem is conquered by David. Lacking that central place, now the people have to celebrate elsewhere. The place that is chosen is a place near Sichem, which is probably an old cultic place of worship, as Moses had commanded,

> And Moses and the Levitical priests said to all Israel, 'Keep silence and hear, O Israel: this day you have become the people of the LORD your God. You shall therefore obey the voice of the LORD your God . . . When you have passed over the Jordan, these shall stand upon Mount Gerizim to bless the people: Simeon, Levi, Judah, Issachar, Joseph, and Benjamin. And these shall stand upon Mount Ebal for the curse: Reuben, Asher, Zebulon, Dan, and Naphtali . . .
> Deuteronomy 27:9–13

It is a double mountain because here the blessings and curses of keeping the covenant will be read.

> Then Joshua built an altar in Mount Ebal to the LORD, the God of Israel, as Moses the servant of the LORD had commanded the people of Israel, as it is written in the book of the law of Moses, 'an altar of unhewn stones, upon which no man has lifted an iron tool'; and they offered on it burnt offerings to the LORD, and sacrificed peace offerings. And there, in the presence of the people of Israel, he wrote upon the stones a copy of the Law of Moses, which he had written. And all Israel . . . stood on opposite sides of the ark before the Levitical priests who carried the ark of the covenant of the Lord, half of them in front of Mount Gerizim and half of them in front of Mount Ebal . . . that they should bless the people of Israel . . .
>
> There was not a word of all that Moses commanded which Joshua did not read before all the assembly of Israel, and the women, and the little ones, and the sojourners who lived among them.
>
> Joshua 8:30–35

The people can be at rest, "Thus you shall bless the people of Israel: you shall say to them, 'The LORD bless you and keep you; The Lord make his face shine upon you, and be gracious to you; The Lord lift up his countenance upon you, and give you peace So shall they put my name upon the people of Israel, and I will bless them." (Num 6:23–27) After, the debacle of Ai, Israel can be at rest. All of Israel is gathered together around the altar listening to the instruction of the Torah. To the list of listeners we can add Rahab's name. A reading of the Torah like this does not come back until the end of the earlier prophets (2 Kings 23:1–3, cf. Neh 8:18). After Jericho and Ai we have come to a provisional closing. What the book of Joshua has to proclaim is presented in exemplary narratives. What follows is Joshua's task. After taking the whole country, he has to oversee the division of the land, the inheritance of each tribe, clan and family.

7:6a) The ban

More could be said about the idea of the divine 'ban'. It is a classification like the category "holy" and "unclean." If something or someone falls in the category of the "ban," it is a possession of Yahweh and therefore not to be used by humans. It would contaminate a person or a people and be dangerous (Lev 27:21, 28, 29; Num 18:14; Ezek 44:29). In Joshua executing the ban is an indication of exemplary obedience to Yahweh's commands, "So Joshua defeated the whole land . . . he left none remaining, but utterly destroyed all that breathed, as the Lord God of Israel commanded," (Josh 10:40) "and smote them with the edge of the sword, utterly destroying them, as Moses the servant of the Lord had commanded." (Josh 11:12) The complete ban in warfare has a very particular context in Joshua, Yahweh battles for Israel and conquers the enemy, therefore all the spoil belongs to him. He provides the land.

The whole conquest is told in images that are familiar in the Near Eastern world, a people coming in from the outside, conquering a land, brought about by their warrior god. Added to all this is the fact that the conquest of Jericho, Ai and the rest of the land did not happen the way it is told, which highlights that we are dealing with exemplary stories not historical accounts. When these questions and perplexities are seen as divine revelation about God's nature and an endorsement of just wars, they fail to recognize the influence of Near Eastern imagery and sagas, which are told here within the context of religious history incorporated and taken up in the prophetic message.

What do we stumble over in reading Joshua? First of all, it is the imaginative story of the conquest of Jericho. "They took the city. Then they utterly destroyed all in the city, both men and women, young and old, oxen, sheep, and asses, with the edge of the sword." (Josh 6:20–21) Jericho is placed under the ban. It is a 'religious-history-given' that we repeatedly encounter in the TeNaK. The conquered city as a whole is placed under the ban and dedicated to the god who gave the victory. The fighters are in the service of God as the holy conqueror. To him belong the honor and the spoil. The warriors and their commanders are not to go plundering through the city. With a king of Moab in the ninth century that also seemed to be the case (the Mesa stone). We don't need to doubt that in Israel God was honored with the same kind of holy war. These are seen as 'established facts' relevant for today for fundamentalist and historicist interpreters to make their point. What do they do with this given of the ban? Is it legitimate to be concretized in our times? The answer is a clear "no."

In the time that Joshua chapter six was written, the ban was no more than a past memory of a long bygone era. However much it repulses us, the authors saw no problem in using this motif in their stories. The ban is a given in which the seriousness and intensity of the battle is characterized as the business of Israel's God. Jericho with all its inhabitants must radically disappear. Who may live or not exist in the Promised Land? Not those who corrupt life and make life unlivable. We can just fill in, that in the Promised Land no Hitler can settle. The inhabitants are representative of the seven nations that must be driven out. Cursed is anyone who takes up their practices again, says Joshua. It will be at the cost of human lives yes, even of their own children. (Josh 6:26)

Whoever fights for the future and the freedom of humanity needs to know that they will encounter ruthless opponents that take by force, kill if necessary or initiate 'SLAPP suits'. Their practices have no right to exist. Whoever, Christians included, thinks that there has to be murder and extermination has not read Joshua according to its prophetic intention within the framework of the TeNaK. If anywhere, here it becomes apparent how dangerous the Old Testament stories can be if they are applied literally today in specific circumstances. If the Israelis are Joshua's people and the Palestinians the seven nations to be driven out, then the horrors have no end, the sound of rockets and exploding bombs will have no end and all the land will be devastated and the people killed (50.000 and counting; almost half of them children). If the land is simply the territory of Israel and they repeat the story of Joshua, we soon encounter Palestinians. God forbid when the prophetic character of Joshua is forgotten.

There are many theological and ethical studies that question and debate the description of Yahweh's anger, wrath, the use of violent images, and the accounts of total extermination of entire populations, of men, women, children and animals (the 'ban'), especially in Joshua and Judges. Many of these discussions are misdirected and inappropriate, because they do not take into account the meaning and context of each of these stories. Generally they are the result of a (literalistic) understanding of these references as divine revelation. For example, the conquest of Jericho is first of all a cautionary tale to reassure and comfort the people after Josiah's time and beyond. It is Yahweh's battle, he guarantees the outcome. He provides the gift of the land and an inheritance to each tribe and family, rest from their enemies and peace in the land. Shalom and well-being to all of us as we too follow the divine guidelines (You shall not kill, steal, or covet).

Theologizing about Yahweh's wrath whether towards Israel's enemies or Israel itself, or use of the ban is just as inappropriate as to theologize about patriarchy, miraculous births, the role of women, slavery, the place of widows and orphans, divine monarchy, absolute rule, liberation, miracles, agricultural practices, etc. on the basis of any of these stories. The Hebrew Scriptures are prophetic books with religious directives and not an ethical, historical, sociological, cultural, political, economic, environmental, or geographical book with specific guidelines for those areas of life. These stories in Joshua and elsewhere are not theological accounts of the nature of God or of ethical warfare. Such questions and debates like, "Is God a god of wrath or love? Are there holy wars or just wars?," however well intended, are misguided and tragic because of the struggles, damaging actions, agony and fears they have given rise to in millions of believers down through the ages. More will be addressed about Yahweh's anger and judgment at the end of Joshua, in the following chapter about 'A new God Image?!' The question at this point is how the ban is taken up in this account of the failure to take Ai. How is it taken up in the prophetic message?

The conquest of Jericho and the entire land would be God's battle and victory. Jericho was conquered and after the violation of the ban (taking God's spoils) was settled, they could conquer Ai (Josh 6:1; 8:29). The story continues with the treaty of the Gibeonites (Joshua 9), the conquest of southern Canaan (Joshua 10), the conquest of northern Canaan (Joshua 11) and finally a list of the conquered kings (Joshua 12). The rest of Joshua is devoted to the partition of the Promised Land (Josh 13-22) with two closing chapters of Joshua's farewell speech (Josh 22-23). At the end of chapter 12 we read, "So Joshua took the whole land, according to all that the Lord had spoken to Moses; and Joshua gave it for an inheritance to Israel according to their tribal allotments. And the land had rest from war" (Josh 11:23). This is reiterated later on in Joshua 21:4345. However, there is a discrepancy about how much land was actually conquered, because we also read that the Canaanites were not totally defeated and driven out (Josh 13:1,16:10, 17:12, 18:2,3).

7:6b) An interruption? A second dedication ceremony

The whole story of the conquest of the city of Jericho is cast in the form of a "cautionary tale." The basic theme is about the gift of the land and God is the one fighting for them. After Jericho and the initial failure to take Ai comes this cautionary tale. It is like a warning, like the conquest of Canaan is not a foregone conclusion. It involves their complete cooperation and obedience to the Torah. If it gets violated it will not go well. It is a gift from Yahweh to his people. For that reason possession of the land is dependent on serving Yahweh and not other gods. It can also be taken away again (as the first or second or third readers know so well). Keeping the Torah and being caretakers of the land are inseparably connected. For example, the failure to take the next city, Ai emphasizes this point, inheriting the land remains a promise.

This theme about the land and the Torah is presented in story form. Everything in the story emphasizes this theme: the rededication (circumcision and the Passover); the commander of the army of Yahweh that came to Joshua; the impenetrableness of the city (no one can go in or out); its mighty warriors; the presence of the ark and the priests; walking around the city seven times in silence and seven times on the seventh day; and then the miraculous crumbling of the walls. This is not an ordinary battle. The city is given in Joshua's hand by Yahweh. It is Yahweh's conquest and his city. For that reason too the "ban" is an absolute one. The city is completely dedicated to Yahweh (perhaps like a burnt offering). The city and all its inhabitants are to be destroyed. Therefore they must not make any treaty with the surrounding people, for that will lead to worship of their gods and the distortion of life.

Immediately following the conquest of Jericho and the debacle with Ai and subsequent victory at Ai, the first thing that happens is that Israel makes a treaty with the Gibeonites. Later we read that many Canaanites remained in the land. In Joshua 23 they are called a snare and a scourge that will tempt the Israelites to serve their idols. In the book of Judges all this becomes even more evident. The angel of Yahweh tells the people that they have made a covenant with the inhabitants of the land and not broken down their altars. Then we read, "What is this that you have done?" (Judg 2:2). When the people heard these words they lifted up their voices and wept." The place was called, Bochim, a place of weeping.

What may seem surprising in this text is that after the conquest of Jericho and Ai there is an unexpected brief interlude of 5 verses (Josh 8:30–35). They actually interrupt the flow of the story of the conquests, starting with Jericho, then Ai, then all the southern towns, then all the northern cities, ending with a list of the defeated kings (Josh 12:1–6).

In the midst of these conquests comes a story of a second dedication ceremony. We expected this new rededication right after the crossing of the Jordan, along with the circumcision and the celebration of the Passover in chapter 5. Why was the ceremony in this retelling postponed and placed here in the middle of all the conquests? Did the final editor make a mistake? Was it a later insertion that was misplaced? Or did he have a special reason for placing it here in the middle of the conquests? Deut 11:26–32 and 27:1–14 gave clear instructions when, where and how the ceremony was to be conducted, including writing the law on the stones of the altar. "Now Moses and the elders commanded the people saying . . . on the day you pass over the Jordan to the land which the LORD your God gives you, you shall set up large stones . . . and you shall write upon them all the words of this law, when you pass over to enter the land (Deut 27:1–4) . . . and then follow all the detailed instructions for the dedication ceremony.

The reading of the law written down by Moses and kept in the ark could have come at an earlier point in the story (Josh 4 and 5). *They are not to be in the Promised Land for one moment without a reminder and reaffirmation of the blessings and curses of living or failing to live by the life-giving way of the Torah* (Deut 11:27,28,31). However, the reading of the law does not happen until after the conquest of Jericho and the failure to capture the next city, Ai, because of the violation of the ban with Achan taking some of the spoils dedicated to Yahweh. Only then comes the account of this second dedication to Yahweh in the new land, and before they make a covenant with the Gibeonites, a Canaanite people, who will be "a snare" for the Israelites. (Joshua 9)

The ceremony was elaborate. An altar had to be made of unhewn stones for burnt and peace offerings. Joshua had to write a copy of the Law of Moses on the stones of the altar. The people stood on opposite sides of the ark carried by the Levitical priests; half of them in front of Mount Gerizim and half in front of Mount Ebal. After hearing the Torah being read to them, the people made a solemn promise to follow the Torah and serve only Yahweh, and they were blessed.

Besides the change in the time of the ceremony (right after the crossing, ch.5), there is also a change in location. Instead of this ceremony taking place near where they were camped at Gilgal, it takes place between mount Ebal and Gerizim. These two mountains are about 40 km away from where the people crossed the Jordan. This was much too far for the whole encampment, men, women, children, sojourners and the armed men (40,000) of Reuben, Gad and half of Manassah, and the eastern tribes, to travel for the ceremony. The 'final editor' obviously took a lot of liberty and placed the ceremony in far-off (enemy) territory, close to Shechem (a place of worship), instead of some hillsides near Gilgal.

Deuteronomy makes it clear that this part of the ceremony was to take place right after and close to where they crossed the Jordan, near Gilgal. Why did he make those changes? Why this interruption in the conquests?

As the story goes, after a long journey through the desert, the people of Israel finally crossed the river Jordan near Gilgal close to Jericho to enter the Promised Land. After the waters of the Jordan parted, the priests with the Ark of the Covenant stood in the middle of the river until all the people had passed by to the other shore. This was much like when a previous generation had crossed the Red Sea. Joshua set up twelve stones as a memorial of their crossing in the middle of the Jordan. Twelve men representing each tribe set up another memorial of twelve stones where they camped near Gilgal. All the people "stood in awe of Joshua as they had stood in awe of Moses." (Josh 4:14) The kings of the Amorites and Canaanites, however, hearing about the miraculous crossing became very afraid "their hearts melted" and there was "no longer any spirit in them." (Josh 5:1)

Now they were ready to conquer all the land. Coming from the east, and given the geography of the land, Jericho was the logical entry point. From the point of view of religious history, there was no way around the conquest of Jericho. From there the land is wide open to the west and from there to the north and the south. Given the lay of the land, the geography of the hills and valleys, it is the gateway to Canaan. Jericho is the orientation point. But again, this is not physical geography rather it is geography in the service of the proclamation.

When Joshua came near Jericho, an angel of God appeared to Joshua who called himself "commander of the army of God." This was an indication that God would be the real commander, giving them the victory. Meanwhile, according to the ascribed time given by the author, there is no evidence Jericho and Ai existed as fortified cities at that time.

7:6c) Religious geography and chronology vs. physical geography and chronology

Compared to Deuteronomy, the time and place of the ceremony is changed to a later time and a different place to make a religious point. They are to be wholly dedicated to Yahweh, and they are not to make any covenants with the Canaanites and be tempted to serve their idols. If they fail to do so, it will not go well with them. Not only the time but the geography is changed as well. The reading of the blessings and curses is to take place with the people standing at the foot of two opposite mountains and answering with "amen." In Deuteronomy the people received the gift of the law at Mount Sinai (Deut 5:6) and the promise that if they followed all the words of the law they would be blessed (Deut 28:1). By placing the ceremony at Mount Ebal and Gerizim, all the words of the law were "very plainly" written on the stones of the altar in their new land.

The law from Mount Sinai had been transferred to the Promised Land itself, written on stone. Sinai had truly come home. Now Israel had everything they need to live peacefully in the land in the presence of Yahweh. Therefore there was to be no coalition with the Canaanites, nor to be serving their idols. This dedication ceremony is after the stories of Jericho and Ai and before the treaty with the Gibeonites and following conquests. They are cautionary tales or exemplary stories to teach the people what happens when they follow Yahweh's instructions (the blessing, Jericho) and when they fail to do so (the curse, Ai) and the 'snare' they set for themselves when they make alliances with the Canaanites (the treaty with the Gibeonites). These are not historical events, but admonitions in story form. The possession of the land depends on their faithfulness to Yahweh! Yahweh will fulfill all his promises, but the people have to live up to their part of the covenant agreement. The total conquest reported in the first twelve chapters is evidence that Yahweh has kept all his promises made to their forefathers.

These five verses (Josh 8:30–35) are not misplaced; rather they serve as a hinge or connection between Jericho and Ai and the rest of the conquests. It is as if the author wants to say, 'people, take note, just because Yahweh battles for you, the victory and the possession of the land is not automatic, it is not a foregone conclusion. Look what happened at Ai. Take note what happened right after their new commitment, their forbidden covenant with the Jebusites.' The story of the miraculous capture of Jericho and the failure to capture Ai are examples for the first and later readers of what happens when a people follow or violate the covenant with Yahweh. Both the blessings and the curses hold, just as they are spelled out in great detail in Deuteronomy, chapters 27 through 30. They end with,

> See, I have set before you this day life and good, death and evil. If you obey the commandments of the LORD your God . . . by loving the LORD your God, by walking in his ways, and by keeping his commandments and his statutes and his ordinances, then

> you shall live and multiply, and the LORD your God will bless you in the land which you are entering to take possession of it. But if your heart turns away, and you will not hear, but are drawn away to worship other gods and serve them, I declare to you this day, that you shall perish, you shall not live long in the land which you are going over the Jordan to enter and possess. I call heaven and earth to witness against you this day, that I have set before you life and death, blessing and curse; therefore choose life, that you and your descendants may live, loving the LORD your God, obeying his voice, and cleaving to him; for that means life to you and length of days, that you may dwell in the land which the LORD swore to your fathers, to Abraham, to Isaac, and to Jacob, to give them.
> Deuteronomy 30:15–20 (cf. Deut 30:11–14)

Where will they stand in their new land, under the blessings of Mount Gerizim or the curses of Mount Ebal? "Therefore choose life" is the urgent appeal. If they do, they shall be a people for Yahweh's "own possession," a holy people, sons of God. And whenever they stray, repent and mend their ways, Yahweh will gather them from the ends of the earth, restore their fortunes and have compassion upon them. He will circumcise their hearts, so that they will love the LORD their God with all their heart and with all their soul (Deut 30:1–10). The blessings of land and fertility are dependent on following the Torah, Yahweh's life-giving commandments.

In both Deuteronomy and Joshua, living by the guidelines of the Torah stands central. Without it there can be no rightful worship (that is the ritual with its offerings and liturgy of praise and thanksgiving). The book of Judges tells us what happens when the people forget the Torah and serve the idols instead of Yahweh. "And the people of Israel did what was evil in the sight of the Lord and served the Baals . . . and the Ashteroth. So the anger of the LORD was kindled against Israel, he gave them over to plunderers . . . and he sold them into the power of their enemies round about, so that they could no longer withstand their enemies." (Judg 2:11–14) Serving the idols means death. Deifying and worshipping a part of life instead of the Creator of life, distorts life and enslaves people. Then there is no shalom, only suffering and death. Living by the Torah, worshipping Yahweh only, the promise of the land and many descendants, are inseparably connected, and in that order. Yahweh's faithfulness is not conditional, but it can only be experienced if they actually follow his life-giving directions. He is only present in their living the Torah. Outside of that there is darkness and death.

The Torah is a blueprint for a way of living that is life-enhancing, bringing peace, justice, solidarity, equality, resourcefulness, care and wisdom. If the people follow its directions then everything will do what it is supposed to do, then the heavens will answer the earth, then the rains and the dew will provide the moisture for the olive trees, the vineyards, barley and grass for the flocks. (Hos 2:21–23). There will be abundance and shalom. The patriarchs had already paved the way to the Promised Land. Abraham built an altar at Shechem, Bethel, and at Mamre near Hebron, after being promised the land and many descendants. Isaac built an altar at Beersheba and Jacob at Shechem. The promise of the land and descendants, building altars, worshipping Yahweh only, belong inseparably together. Beersheba and Hebron to the south and Bethel and Shechem, more to the north, are like so many beachheads in the Promised Land. A place where living by the Torah can have free reign.

In this whole religious context, physical geography and chronology must yield to the religious message. Mountains can be moved freely and time sequences can be changed as needed. The mountains that are intended were those close to Gilgal. Geographical and chronological references are in the service of the message, in this case, the cautionary tales about Jericho, Ai, and the Gibeonites. What better way to bring home the message of the blessings and curses, of life and death than by means of these stories. It was a reminder that the land belonged to Yahweh and was a gift for an inheritance to each family and the wellbeing of all.

The highly structured nature of Joshua, as well as many other books of the scriptures illustrates that each separate passage and section needs to be seen as part of a whole. That does not mean that a particular passage cannot be studied for its specific historical, sociological or anthropological background. However, after such detailed study it needs to be reintegrated into the whole of a section or book. It is one of the fundamental shortcomings of theological studies that specific texts are lifted out of their context and compared to other equally isolated texts. Such abstracting leads to very speculative results. Many systematic theological studies used to be of this nature. This approach is all the more debatable considering that the scriptures are of an experiential nature. They do not theorize or speculate about the nature of god, faith, sin, atonement, and so on. The scriptures are of a religious nature that speak to the heart and want to be followed.

If the scriptures are read as prophetic history, they can be a powerful source of inspiration for today. To put it somewhat simplistically, then the message is clear also for our lives in our circumstances: do not absolutize or deify any part of life; if you do, it will not go well, life will become distorted; and if you have, it is never too late to turn around and make a new beginning; you can count on it. Such was the insight and wisdom and deep conviction of the ancient prophets, priests and scribes. The history of the people of Israel and the history of the Christian church (as well as that of Judaism and Islam), may be a story to weep about, but these stories written by a small minority have a lasting significance.

We can read in the book of Judges how it went from there, "... the people lifted up their voices and wept ..." (Judg 2:4) The story goes on.

7:7 Joshua 9   The strategy of the Gibeonites

The taking of the whole country is also interrupted by a very colorful story about the Gibeonites. Gibeon is inhabited by 'untouchables' according to Samuel. "Now the Gibeonites were not of the people of Israel, but of a remnant of the Amorites; although the people of Israel had sworn to spare them, Saul had sought to slay them in his zeal for the people of Israel and Judah. (II Sam. 21:2). Another indication comes from Deuteronomy "... and the sojourner who is in your camp, both he who hews your wood and he who draws your water" ... (Deut 29:11). These words are not included in the list of Joshua 8:33. The least of the sojourners are not mentioned anywhere else in the Old Testament. It is not until chapter 9 of Joshua that they play a role with their trick.

> When all the kings who were beyond the Jordan in the hill country and in the lowland all along the coast of the Great Sea toward Lebanon, the Hittites, the Amorites, the Canaanites, the Perizzites, the Hivites and Jebusites heard of this, they gathered together with one accord to fight Joshua and Israel. But when the inhabitants of Gibeon heard what Joshua had done to Jericho and to Ai, they on their part acted with cunning ...
> Joshua 9:1–3

All seven kings gathered together because they had heard. In contrast to Rahab who also had heard, they decided to fight Israel. With an appeal to a law in Deut 20, the Gibeonites thought they could outsmart Joshua. "When you draw near to a city to fight against it, offer terms of peace to it. And if its answer to you is peace and it opens up to you, then all the people who are found in it shall do forced labor for you and shall serve you ... thus you shall do to all the cities which are very far from you, which are not cities of the nations here ..." (Deut 20:10–15)

So they pretended to be from a very far city and did so with great cunning. Even though there were some doubts, they evaded Joshua's questions and were able to convince the leaders to make a covenant. 'We have come from a very far land, look at our clothes and shoes and here eat some of our bread; we heard what your God did to Egypt and the two Amorite Kings; your servants we will be'. What they mentioned is a caricature of what Rahab confessed.

It worked, but when they were found out, the consequences became clear. They were cursed by Joshua, "Now therefore you are cursed." They had agreed without asking Yahweh. The covenant was sealed with an oath. Joshua kept the oath even though the people of Israel murmured. "But Joshua made them that day hewers of wood and drawers of water for the congregation and for the altar of the LORD, to continue to this day, in the place which he should choose." (Josh 9:27) As cursed people they were nevertheless dedicated to Yahweh, just like the valuables of Jericho. These, the least among the 'strangers in your midst', point forward to the temple in Jerusalem, 'the house of my LORD', which is not mentioned by name yet ...

The Gibeonites belong to the Hevites, one of the seven peoples that needed to be driven out and destroyed, because they represented the defiling of the land with their inhumane religion. They are to be put under the ban, "... you shall utterly destroy them, as the LORD your God has commanded, that they may not teach you to do according to all their abominable practices which they have done in the service of their gods, and so to sin against the LORD your God." (Deut 20:18) This practice of the ban would apply equally to Israel if they violated their covenant with Yahweh.

> And the generation to come, your children who rise up after you, and the foreigner who comes from a far land, would say, when they see the afflictions of that land and the sicknesses with which the LORD has made them sick– the whole land brimstone and salt, and a burnt-out waste, unsown, and growing nothing, where no grass can sprout, an overthrow like that of Sodom and Gomorrah ... yea, all the nations would say, 'Why has the Lord done thus to the land? ... It is because ... they

went and served other gods and worshipped them ... and the LORD uprooted them from their land in anger and fury and great wrath, and cast them into another land, as to this day.
Deutereonomy 29:22–28

The Gibeonites are exemplary of the remaining nations that will lead Israel astray. In the book of Judges this theme will come back in many variations. It is a theme that has also been announced by Joshua in his final admonitions.

> For if you turn back, and join the remnant of these nations left here among you, and make marriages with them so that you marry their women and they yours, know assuredly that the LORD your God will not continue to drive out these nations before you; they shall be a snare and a trap for you, a scourge on your sides, and thorns in your eyes, till you perish from of this good land which the LORD your God has given you.
> Joshua 23:12–13

What happens to these nations in a literary 'unhistorical' way, that is, in a confessional way, is a reality for Israel. In this book the seven nations are a token and warning that only within the covenant with Yahweh there is a future. Even the Gibeonites can belong to the sojourners that engage in 'hewing your wood and drawing your water', that they may all enter a sworn covenant of the LORD your God and establish you as his people, and that he may be your god. (Deut 29:10) Being excluded or included is not a foregone conclusion (Rahab and Achan).

After the Gibeonites our view is turned to the south and after that to the north, which is the focus of Joshua chapters 10 and 11.

7:8 Joshua 10:12–15 The sun standing still

There is another story in this entire miraculous cycle of the conquest of Canaan (Josh 6–12) that is worth highlighting. It is a very brief part of these cautionary tales. The 'sun and moon standing still' is not only a miracle story but this time it has cosmic proportions. The sun and the moon are enlisted in Yahweh's battle.

Yahweh threw down great hailstones from heaven and more enemy soldiers died from hailstones than were killed by the sword (Josh 10:11). All the numinous forces of the cosmos, the Sun, Moon, Stars and all the host of heaven are in the service of Yahweh. They are part of God's creation, God said, "let there be lights in the firmament of the heavens... and it was so." (Gen 1:14) They are creatures and not gods. For this reason people are not to make a graven image of anything that is in heaven above and worship it, "And beware lest you lift up your eyes to heaven, and when you see the sun and the moon and the stars, all the host of heaven, you be drawn away and worship them and serve them" (Deut 4:19; 17:3). For the Canaanites the Sun, Moon and the Stars were the personification of the numinous powers that controlled the cosmos and the events of humankind. In the confrontation with the Canaanite view of the cosmos, the people of Israel were tempted to put their ultimate trust in the mysterious, cosmic forces, including during Josiah's time. Of Manaseh (king of Judah) it is said, that he "worshipped the host of heaven in the two courts of the house of the LORD." (2 Kings 21:5; 23:5)

Especially in the Psalms and Job the sun, moon and stars are celebrated as creatures of Yahweh that follow Yahweh's commands (Job 9:6-8;38:12,31, Ps 104:19, 136:7-9, 147:4-8). Yahweh directs the storms, lightening and the rains (Job 37:1-13). The heavenly bodies are de-sacralized, for they are creaturely and not divine. At the same time they are re-enchanted; the morning stars can sing together and join the sons of God shouting for joy. (Job 38:7). In this cosmic battle between Yahweh and the idolatrous Canaanite people, the hailstones, the sun, the moon and the stars follow God's command. The Storm god, the Sun god and the Moon god are helpless. The hosts of heaven battled alongside Israel against their enemies. Later on, when Deborah, a prophetess and judge, celebrated the victory over the Canaanites, she recounts how the stars fought alongside Israel's soldiers (Judg 5:20). How foolish to look for new gods (Judg 5:8), when the LORD of hosts was battling for them. No Canaanite armies with their hundreds of chariots were able to stand up against the Israelites, because Yahweh fought for Israel. (Josh 11:6, 9) Given this background we can understand the poem that is put in Joshua's mouth. The poem (Josh 10:12-15) plays a pivotal role at the end of the first part of the conquest of southern Canaan (Joshua 10: 1-11) and before the final victory over the coalition of the five kings (Josh 10:16-43).

> Then spoke Joshua to the LORD in the day when the LORD gave the Amorites over to the men of Israel; and he said in the sight of Israel," Sun, stand thou still at Gibeon, and thou Moon in the valley of Aijalon.' And the sun stood still, and the moon stayed, until the nation took vengeance on their enemies. Is this

not written in the Book of Jashar? The sun stayed in the midst of heaven, and did not hasten to go down for about a whole day. There has been no day like it before or since, when the LORD hearkened to the voice of a man; for the LORD fought for Israel. Then Joshua returned, and all Israel with him, to the camp at Gilgal.
Joshua 10:12–15

These four verses could have been skipped and the reader would not have experienced any interruption in the account. It is like the connecting verses of the second ceremony at Mount Gerizim and Ebal in Joshua 8:30–35, although there they seemed more like an interruption in the story.

As the story goes, Joshua's army had marched all night from Gilgal to come to the aid of the Gibeonites and they took the enemy soldiers of five kings camped before the city by surprise (Josh 10: 9,10). The LORD threw them into a panic and Israel slew them and pursued them all the way to Beth-horon. However, on the same day from out of the camp at Makkedah they conquered the city states of Libna, Lachish, Hebron and Debir and the five kings of the coalition. Only then was it evening. (Josh 10:26–27) This was a miraculous campaign starting with a night-long march to Gibeon (twelve km), pursuing the enemy via Beth-Horon to Makkedah and Azeka (eighteen km) and then, from their camp at Makkedah, on to the conquest of the other city states. If this was an ordinary account of a whirlwind campaign, marching dozens and dozens of kilometers, conquering one city after the other, without the aid of 'armored vehicles and airplanes', we would say, 'those soldiers, how did they do it, and all in one day; what a miracle; it must have been a long, long day?' We can visualize the extensiveness of the march: from Gilgal to Gibeon, to Beth-Horon, to Jarmuth, to Makkedah, to Libna, to Lachish, to Hebron, to Debir and back to Gilgal, one long march.

Not only is the account of the campaign interrupted in the middle by the poem cycle about the sun and moon standing still, but it ends with a very implausible reference. In verse 15 we read, "Then Joshua returned, and all Israel with him, to the camp at Gilgal." (Josh 10:15) It indicates that in the middle of the campaign they returned to Gilgal only to go back again to conquer the rest of southern Canaan. Several commentators consider this verse a misplaced later insertion and put it between brackets.

Although factually, Joshua 10:15 is impossible, it is an integral part of the poem intermezzo. The poem has an introduction; a quote of part of the poem; a citation of the source; a further explanation by the storyteller and an epilogue. The narrator inserted the total quotation just as it was, without worrying about the exact fit of verse 15. There are other examples of similar citations of songs, the song of Moses and Miriam (Exod 15:1-21); the song of Deborah and Barak; (Judg 5:1-31) David's song of mourning (2 Samuel 1:17-27) and others. These songs were sung to celebrate great victories and events as in Psalms 78 and 105. Most likely this poem in Joshua 10 with its introduction and epilogue was quoted in its entirety, including verse 15, to celebrate Joshua's astounding victories and the prophetic meaning it gives to the conquests.

The emphasis is on the astounding whirlwind campaign, and all in one day, a 'blitzkrieg'. It makes the Jewish commentator, Michael Hattin state in his *Joshua: The challenge of the Promised Land*,

> In other words, the miracle was not that the sun actually stood still, but rather that the people of Israel succeeded in thoroughly trouncing the southern kings in such a short time, before the sun completed its course and began to set. The physical motion of the sun did not slow, but rather Israel was able to inflict a crushing defeat that should have taken a much longer period of time to accomplish. God acceded by granting them a swift and utter victory because,"God waged war for Israel."[4]

The author fully acknowledges God's utter mastery over the most popular Canaanite gods.

> Taken together with the sudden downpour of hailstones that initiated the rout, perhaps the text here seeks to emphasize God's utter mastery over the most popular Canaanite gods: Thus Baal the storm god bent to the will of the transcendent Creator while Shemesh and Yerah showed their devotion to Him. How unlike their limited abilities was his omnipotence, his closeness and immediacy wholly distinct from their indifference and remoteness! Israel stood witness as the sun, moon, and whirlwind complied, like loyal servants obeying their master . . .[5]

The narrator, during the time of Josiah, or later, remembered the poem recorded in the book of Jashar along with many other songs. We can imagine that he could not hold back any longer and inserted it here. As the commentary to the poem explains, "There has been no day like it before or since, when the LORD hearkened to the voice of a man."

---

4. Hattin, *Challenge*, 156.
5. Hattin, *Challenge*, 154-55.

(Joshua 10:14) At the same time this exclamation of wonder brings home the central message of all the conquests recorded in chapters 10–12. The land they are to possess is God's gift. It is God's doing. God is the Creator and Liberator, "for the LORD fought for Israel" (Josh 10:14), even enlisting the sun and moon to give total victory.

What is recounted here in Joshua 10, is not an ordinary battle of an invading army, rather it is a cosmic, spiritual battle between two powers. It is the Creator god over against the deified powers of God's creation. In the process of conquests the sun and moon have shown their creatureliness, light bearers that are directed by Yahweh. "Thou hast made the moon to mark the seasons; the sun knows its time for setting." (Ps 104:19) "He commands the sun, and it does not rise; and he seals up the stars" (Job 9:7). The Sun and Moon gods have been tarnished and debunked; they have lost their power. It makes the question all the more urgent, who will people serve? It is a question of life versus death, of living in the land flowing with milk and honey or being exiled. The Creator is present in the rising and setting of the sun to the smallest creatures. They can count on it, for he is behind it. The creation and conquest is a miracle and a gift. Following the Torah brings harmony and peace.

There are many miracle stories in the scriptures, in both testaments. But this miracle story about Joshua commanding the sun to stand still is probably one of the more outstanding ones. For many people it may also be the most incredulous one and a stumbling block. How can the solar system be stopped even for one second and not result in the total destruction of this part of the universe? Even drastic changes in temperatures on the earth resulted in the coming and going of ice ages. Likewise, with the impact of a meteor striking the earth resulting in annihilation and destruction, wiped out millions of species. As a literal story about the physical universe and astronomy, it is an unbelievable story, a mythological account allowing Joshua to pursue and destroy his enemies. The swift campaign in one day is the miracle.

Many have tried to explain this event by attributing it to the ancient Ptolemaic geo-centric world view in which the sun was thought to turn around the earth. This view would need to be updated and translated into a Copernican helio-centric view, the earth turning around the sun. None of these kinds of arguments however would make any difference in understanding this passage. Both stay on the level of physical (scientific) worldviews. Josh 10 is not about one scientific worldview over against another. Nor is it about our common experiential way of talking about the sun rising and the sun going down. Any of these explanations would involve a fundamental misunderstanding of this account. A literalistic interpretation of these passages violates the prophetic nature of the scriptures.

It is interesting to note at this point that Alex Brinkman in his survey of many commentaries and 10,000 sermons on Josh 10 could not find even one sermon on the miracle of the sun and the moon standing still (*Deadly Silence.*2019). Beek has a brief section on the "The proclamation of Joshua" 10:12–15), in his commentary, *Jozua*.

7:9   Joshua 10, 11   The conquest

All the nations are divided by north and south. What all the peoples have 'heard' we hear right at the start of chapter 10,

> When Adonizedek king of Jerusalem heard how Joshua had taken Ai, and had utterly destroyed it, doing to Ai and its king as he had done to Jericho and its king, and how the inhabitants of Gibeon had made peace with Israel and were among them, he feared greatly, because Gibeon was a great city, like one of the royal cities, and because it was greater than Ai, and all its men were mighty. So Adonizek king of Jerusalem sent to Hohum king of Hebron, to Piram king of Jarmuth, to Japhia king of Lachish, and to Debir king of Eglon, saying, 'come up to me, and help me, and let us smite Gibeon; for it has made peace with Joshua and with the people of Israel'. Then the five kings of the Amorites . . . went up with all their armies and encamped against Gibeon, and made war against it.
> Joshua 10:1–5

> And the men of Gibeon sent to Joshua at the camp at Gilgal . . . So Joshua went up from Gilgal . . . and the LORD said to Joshua, 'do not fear them, for I have given them into your hands . . . so Joshua came upon them suddenly, having marched up all night from Gilgal. And the LORD threw them into a panic before Israel . . . and as they fled before Israel . . . the LORD threw down great stones from heaven upon them . . . and they died; there were more who died because of the hailstones than the men of Israel killed with the sword.
> Joshua 10:6–11 (cf. Ps 149:5–9)

All the kings of the area came together to battle against Israel. Joshua does not have to initiate the battle. He becomes involved because of

Gibeon and their covenant with them. Kings in the scriptures are highly regarded, but only if they exercise their kingship in the name of Yahweh and establish justice and mercy and protect the widow, orphan and the stranger in their midst, the vulnerable ones. The first kings mentioned all embody the horror of world history (Gen. 31:14, Judges 3:8, Judges 9:5). All the kings that came up against Israel are of the same kind. All the kings are put in a row in Joshua 12 and counted, thirty one of them. This list is prophetic literature.

> Let the faithful exult in glory;
> let them sing for joy on their couches.
> Let the high praises of God be in their throats
> and the two-edged swords in their hands,
> to wreak vengeance on the nations
> and chastisement on the peoples,
> to bind their kings in chains
> and their nobles with fetters of iron.
> to execute on them the judgment written!
> This is glory for all his faithful ones.
> Praise the Lord!
>   Psalm 149:5–9

A possible etiological reference, or a reference to a local folklore tradition, is made with regard to a cave with five trees in front of it. Five kings had hidden in the cave of Makkedah. When Joshua heard about it, he had great stones rolled against the opening. Later they were brought out and put to death and hung on five trees. By evening their bodies were taken down and thrown in the cave with the stones covering the opening, which 'remain till this day'. The narrator also uses parts of an old poem that he uses to describe the miracle of the sun and the moon standing still as an indication of the heavenly bodies being used as servants of Yahweh, just like the hailstones earlier and the stars in Judges 5:20. It was a miraculous and exceptional battle on that day. "There has been no day like it before or since, when the LORD hearkened to the voice of a man; for the LORD fought with Israel." (Josh 10:14)

In the North Country, the mighty king of Hazor stands out. Hazor is along the caravan route in the north and it is the deciding battle. Jabin of Hazor gathered a great army together, "and they came out, with all their troops, a great host, in numbers like the sand of the sea that is upon the seashore, with very many horses and chariots. And all these kings joined their forces . . . to fight against Israel." (Josh 11:4, 5) It reminds us of Deut. 20:1, "When you go forth to war against your enemies, and see horses and chariots and an army larger than your own, you shall not be afraid of them; for the LORD is with you."

So Joshua is encouraged by Yahweh, "And the LORD said to Joshua, "do not be afraid of them, for tomorrow at this time I will give over all of them, slain, to Israel; you shall hamstring their horses, and burn their chariots with fire." (Josh 11:6) The weapons of war need to be dismantled. Horses and chariots are the main symbols of military power. They need to be banned from Israel. During the Exodus, Egypt's horses and wagons are thrown by Yahweh into the Red Sea and drowned. Israel is not to put its trust in horses and wagons. In Micah 5:10 we read, "And in that day, says the LORD, I will cut off your horses from among you and I will destroy your chariots."

Micah is only one of the many prophecies against relying on horses and chariots. Israel is not to be a war nation with great weapons of war. Over against the onrushing horses and chariots of Sisera, Yahweh enlists the help of the stars to battle him. (Judg 5:20–21) "From heaven fought the stars, from their courses they fought against Sisera. The torrent Kishon swept them away, the onrushing torrent, the torrent Kishon. March on, my soul, with might!" Yahweh battles for Israel and Joshua only needs to come 'suddenly' and the battle is already decided.

7:10 Joshua 13–21 *The division of the land*

The kings have fallen. Now Joshua can undertake his final task, to oversee the division of the land. Ruben, Gad and the half-tribe of Manasseh have already received their portion and may now return to their inheritance. The land is divided in the south for 'Judah' (Josh 15 and 18:5) and in the north for 'Joseph' (Ephraim and Manassah) (Josh 16). The Levitical cities and the cities of refuge are also appointed. In the middle of the country at Shiloh the 'tent of meeting' was set up.

> Thus the LORD gave to Israel all the land which he swore to give to their fathers; and having taken possession of it, they settled there. And the LORD gave them rest on every side just as he had sworn to their fathers . . . Not one of all the good promises which the LORD had made to the house of Israel had failed; all came to pass.
> Joshua 21:43–45

The book Joshua is all about the whole Torah, all the land and all the people. The completion of all God's gifts is still to come, but is already present in these last words, 'all came to pass'. In the book of Revelation we read, "Behold the dwelling of God is with men. He will dwell with them, and they shall be his people, and God Himself will be with them . . . and he said, 'Write, for these words are trustworthy and true, and he said to me, "It is done!"' (Rev 21:3–6)

7:11 Joshua 22 *The Jordan is not a border*

As the story of the trans-Jordan tribes illustrate, the Jordan is not a geographic border or divide that separates Rubin, Gad and half Manasseh from the other tribes. They showed solidarity with all the other tribes and crossed the Jordan at the head of all the people and stayed until the whole land was conquered. Their solidarity and faithfulness is once more underscored in the incident of the complaint of the tribe of Joseph about the building of an altar of thanksgiving and peace across the Jordan. (Josh 17:14–18 and 22:10–34) "The Rubenites and the Gadites called the altar Witness, for, they said, it is a witness between us and that the Lord is God." The suspicion of the people is without ground. The priest, Phinehas the son of Eleazar, and twelve elders from Shiloh came to check it out and bring a favorable report to the people. It turned out they are not like Achan "and wrath fell upon all the congregation of Israel." And the people were satisfied. They did not want to set up their own sanctuary away from the other tribes. It was 'only' to be a witness.

> Nay, but we did it from fear that in time to come your children might say to our children, 'What have you to do with the LORD, the God of Israel? Or swear by them, or serve them, or bow down yourselves, For the LORD has made the Jordan a boundary between us and you, you Reubinites and Gadites; you have no portion in the LORD. So your children might make our children cease to worship the LORD. Therefore we said, 'Let us now build an altar . . . as a witness between us and you, and between the generations after us, that we do perform the service of the LORD . . . lest your children say to our children in time to come, 'You have no portion in the LORD'.
> Joshua 22:24–25.

The Jordan is not to be a border between the trans-Jordan tribes and the rest of Israel. They are to be one people, worshipping one god in one sanctuary.

7:12 Joshua 23, 24 Joshua's last words; God the giver and the gods.

The storyteller has been mentioned several times as if one historical figure is responsible for the whole book. Historically speaking it might have been that several scribes have contributed to the book, maybe a scribal collective. Yet the book is not fabricated from many sources. It has form, structure and unity. There are parts, like chapter 19 that are very diverse and have incorporated material that does not always seem necessary. But the main lines, the recognizable themes, striking details that connect via words and expressions, present a lot of structure. Different scribes, perhaps many, created a work that recreated old traditions and created new materials. Especially the references to the books of Moses make for a unity. They were moved by one spirit. That spirit from a literary-technical point of view is the author, the storyteller of the book.

Sometimes the narrator has fun telling his story. Other times he becomes very serious like in the telling of the sermons of Joshua. The hearer in the service is addressed. It is us that are addressed. We have heard the story. It was not told to tell us some interesting facts about a time long past; not to pleasantly engage us or confront us with shocking events to make us recoil, but to place us in the story in which the gravity of the Torah calls us to a new prophetic orientation to Yahweh the God of the covenant. Do we understand what the aging Joshua is saying?

> ... I am now old and well advanced in years; and you have seen all that the LORD has done to all these nations for your sake, for it is the LORD your God who has fought for you. Behold I have allotted to you as an inheritance for your tribes... Therefore be very steadfast to keep and do all that is written in the book of the law of Moses, turning aside from it neither to the right hand nor the left, that you may not be mixed with these nations, left here among you, or make mention of the names of their gods, or swear by them, or serve them, or bow down yourselves, but cleave to the LORD your God as you have done to this day. ...
>
> And now I am about to go the way of all the earth, and you know in your hearts and souls, all of you, that not one thing has

failed of all the good things which the LORD your God promised concerning you; all have come to pass for you, not one of them has failed. But just as all the good things which the LORD your God promised concerning you have been fulfilled for you, so the LORD will bring upon you all the evil things, until I have destroyed you from all of this the good land which the LORD your God has given you, if you transgress the covenant of the LORD your God, which he commanded you, and go and serve other gods and bow down to them. Then the anger of the LORD will be kindled against you, and you shall perish quickly from off the good land which he has given you.
Joshua 23:2-8, 14-18

The hearer is involved in 'all the good' that is already been realized in the story. In this proclamation of the history of God with his people has come to its end. Liturgically we answer, "Amen, that is how it was and will be." The threat of Joshua 23:16 the congregation reads on in the former prophets, in Judges, which is a book that calls for repentance.

With the gift of the land and actively receiving the gift, the conquest is completed.

> ... it was not by your sword or by your bow. I gave you a land on which you had not labored, and cities which you had not built, and you dwell therein; you eat the fruit of vineyards and olive yards which you did not plant. Now, therefore fear the LORD, and serve him in sincerity and in faithfulness; put away the gods which your fathers served beyond the River, and in Egypt, and serve the LORD. And if you be unwilling to serve the LORD, choose this day whom you will serve, whether the gods your fathers served in the region beyond the River, or the gods of the Amorites in whose land you dwell; but as for me and my house, we will serve the LORD.
> Joshua 24:12-15.

God's speaking has come to an end. Yahweh has presented himself with his deeds in their history that culminated in the gift of the land that the people had not conquered, planted or built. It was pure grace. The people are confronted with the one god whose name is explained in his deeds.

The question 'who is god?' is the most fundamental question. There may be many gods and many lords, on the other side of the river in Egypt and the land of the Amorites. There are many gods to choose from for Israel, but Israel is what it is through Yahweh the giver. For Joshua there is only one conclusion for those who have ears to hear, the reality in which god's people stand. Choose then, this day, whom you will serve. The people respond with "Far be it from us that we should forsake the lord, to serve other gods; for it is the LORD our God who brought us and our fathers up from the land of Egypt, out of the house of bondage, and who did great signs in our sight . . . therefore we also will serve the LORD, for he is our God." (Josh 24:16–18)

> And they said, 'We are witness'. He said, 'Then put away the foreign gods which are among you, and incline your heart to the LORD, the God of Israel'. And the people said to Joshua, 'the LORD our God we will serve, and his voice we will obey'. So Joshua made a covenant with the people that day, and made statutes and ordinances for them at Shechem.
> Joshua 24:22–25

This God, stands up for the repressed and the dispossessed, for the widow, the orphan, and the sojourner or stranger in their midst. He cares for his people like a jealous lover, so that his loved ones can be at peace in this covenant. With this god of life, in the intensity of a love story, it is not only their identity but their very existence, their not-being that is at stake. The congregation reads Joshua as a parable of its own existence, and as a promise that is still outstanding.

> And Israel served the LORD all the days of Joshua, and all the days of the elders who outlived Joshua and had known all the work which the LORD did for Israel.
> Joshua 24:31

Judges 2 repeats these words but ends with,

> And all that generation also was gathered to their fathers; and there arose another generation after them, who did not know the LORD or the work which he has done for Israel.
> Judges 2:6–10

From beginning to end Joshua is a prophetic story, in which mountains can be moved, time sequences changed, cities and conquests invented, and in which hailstones, the sun and moon come to the aid of the warriors. All these aspects of the stories are in the service of the prophetic message. In this case a cautionary tale about the sun and moon as his light bearers, that through Joshua, follow Yahweh's command. Right in the middle of the conquests of the city states and their kings, a reminder by way of a fragment of a poem, that Yahweh gives the victory.

Yahweh fights for Israel and Yahweh keeps his promises. The land is Yahweh's gift and their inheritance, if they worship Yahweh only, and not the idols. What better way to bring home this message of the true God than by means of this interlude. This part of a poem highlights the prophetic meaning of this cosmic miracle. It proclaims and wants to persuade us to put our ultimate trust in the Redeemer and Creator and it will go well with us.

7:13 *Concluding remarks*

If we start with the exiled families and children gathered together in Babylon around the campfire with a storyteller, it is not hard to imagine how these stories could be shared with today's children during Sunday school. Joshua itself gives occasion to ask questions by the children like 'what do these stones mean?' (Josh 4:19–23) The many dialogues (Josh 2:24), and vivid descriptions of events lend themselves to good storytelling. By means of imaginary dialogues and interactions, conversations and questions by exiled kids, these events could be brought close to children today. Contemporary children can be asked to share what they know about wars, injustice, poverty, migrants, caring for the earth, etc. What are these struggles about? In the end, the main "lessons" need to be the same as those for the adults: the conquest is about finding a place for the Torah to flourish with its life-giving ways. The land as an inheritance to be cared for is as crucial today as it was then, even though our circumstances seem quite different.

The main theme in Joshua is the land as Yahweh's gift to his people for an inheritance for each tribe, clan and family. The name Joshua means, 'Yahweh is salvation'. In keeping with that, the command to Joshua is, "Go . . . to the land which I am giving to them, to the people of Israel." (Josh 1:2) "You shall cause this people to inherit the land which I swore to their fathers to give them." (Josh 1:6) The story teller presents it as a huge country, stretching from the south to the north as far as the river Euphrates. (Josh 1:4) The territory has ideal proportions. It's an inheritance for each family for generations to come. Not surprisingly, nine chapters of Joshua's twenty four chapters are devoted to the division of the land, and each tribe's inheritance. When we remember that Joshua was written for the soon-to-be-exiled or exiled people, we can understand this concern about every tribe and family's inheritance. What will they find if they are allowed to go back and how will they know which land belongs to whom? First Chronicles devotes the first nine chapters to the genealogy of each family. In Ezra 8 and Nehemiah 7 we find lists of returning families. Their inheritance is of primary importance.

The oral tradition with its storytelling provides unique opportunities to enter into the stories. One drawback may be that it can perpetuate an image of a 'personal' God directly intervening in the lives of a people and directing their affairs. (See the section on God's providence in chapter 9:4). This was the common view of all the ancient near eastern people. At some point it will be helpful (essential) to compare that god-image to another image. The image of Mother Earth of the First Nations, for example, may be familiar enough to children and young people for comparison. Mother Earth is in and behind everything but not identical with the earth, trees, rivers, animals, birds and people. Mother Earth pulsates with life and calls for respect for all creatures if they are to prosper. If not, if the earth is violated, things do not go well.

This is essentially not different from the view of the Hebrew Scriptures. Only by following the life-giving directions of the Torah for all of life can the people find well-being for all with justice, solidarity, resourcefulness, and equality, in short, shalom. Not following those road signs leads to disintegration, to injustice and the violation of the land and all creatures. It is critical to understand that the point is not the dispossession and extermination of others. Rather it's following Yahweh's life-affirming direction, in terms of whom or what we worship and our life-calling.

In coming to terms with these difficult passages in Joshua (God commanding the genocide of the Canaanites), we need to go back to the perspective presented earlier. There we highlighted two requirements for interpreting ancient scriptures. First of all we need an understanding of them as prophetic writings which are integral to all of life, history that proclaims. Secondly, we need to have an understanding of a peoples' way of living and their values.

These healing directives include guidelines for: ultimate convictions, commitment, solidarity, inclusiveness, tolerance, restorative justice, fairness, equality, integrity, respect, tolerance of all peoples, community, resourcefulness, provisioning for all, expressiveness, creativity, and emotional, physical and sexual well-being for all. Our understanding of these ethical demands, have grown over many generations in response to God's good order for life and will continue to deepen.[6] God's love for his creation and humanity comes to expression in the many guidelines that impinge upon us daily.

'General' revelation in creation, society and history adds to our understanding of 'special' revelation. (See the quotations by Zuidervaart in chapter 10) To deepen and grow in that understanding as a faithful community is our common responsibility. No appeal to Jesus' teachings, as is often done in orthodox and evangelical circles, when confronted by difficult passages can absolve us from that responsibility. That is our calling in life. Such an approach does not make our reading of scripture arbitrary and subjectivistic. Over time and having learned from other peoples we understand better, for example that (economic) providing means providing for all people and that doing justice means restorative justice for the whole community, etc. Our 'world views' can easily be limited and misused or plain wrong as well, and become an ideology ('out of sync with reality').

We can only encounter God in this world. His good order for life does not come to us in eternal, a-historical ordinances. There is no absolute, eternal, infallible Word of God from heaven that relieves us of the responsibility to interpret and respond to the scriptures. In the scriptures we can read what God's good intention is for humanity and for the earth, and how that intention was understood and obeyed in a particular time of history and culture by the Israelites. In as much as scripture contains the deposit of the ancient Israelites confession of faith, they can at times be wrong and misguided. Sometimes those misunderstandings are corrected by the scriptures themselves in later books but not always. There are debatable passages in the New Testament as well.

Signposts, in the midst of life, can never be possessed or made into eternal and absolute human laws, even though that has often happened during the course of history. We cannot find ultimate security in eternal, unchanging 'creation ordinances', however tempting. They can only be experienced and recognized by an open heart and spirit. These road signs remain a revelation of God's intention for his creation and humanity.

This interpretative approach becomes crucial as we encounter the many texts of terror in the scriptures. For example in the book of Judges we have to come to terms with Samson's exploits ending his life as a 'suicidal terrorist'; or the gang rape and murder of a Levite's concubine; or

---

6. De Graaff, *The Gods in Whom They Trusted*, Chapter 11.

the abduction of virgins and their forced marriages to the Benjamites; as well as many other examples. At times the scriptures seem to endorse or uncritically present a view of women as economic objects (Deuteronomy), having no rights or voice, of concubines, polygamy, victims of rape (Numbers), slavery, economic injustice, divine rights of kings, miscarriage of justice by the elders in the city gates, etc.

Feminist and liberation writings and cultural interpretations continue to alert us that our understanding of scripture may be limited or distorted. When faced with incongruities between the scriptures and our worldview, the scriptures keep calling us back to greater congruity in our lives. Worldviews can become ideologies that distort reality. In our worldview we give an account or a justification of our life's direction. It conveys a trust that this is what life is about. This means that as our experience deepens and changes, our worldview is challenged as well.

During the last decades it has increasingly become clear that the 'historical critical method' of interpretation is only one of many methods. It has its place but nothing more. The historical critical method still plays an important but limited role in understanding the development and editing of a Bible book, which may help to understand its 'historical' context, as it is taken up in the message. The Bible is not an historical book. It is a profoundly religious book with a prophetic message: the prophetic call to love and justice.

Slowly we have been delivered from the dominance and reductionism of the critical historical method and its pre-suppositions. There are new spaces for other interpretations, like the 'inter-cultural readings' and reading 'from the margins', from feminist, and liberation theology, and from queer readings, etc. These different approaches and concerns can only deepen our understanding of scripture and life, if we don't lose sight of the prophetic message and our distorting pre-suppositions.

The expressions of Judah being God's "chosen people" and the "promised land" as Yahweh's gift to them as their possession, are part of Israel's identity and belief system (ideology). During the depth of the exile they looked back and projected their sense of themselves back into history, already beginning with Abraham and culminating in Joshua and from there on. They based this conviction of being a special people on their collective and national memory of the Exodus, of their liberation from Exile. They 'forgot' that being a chosen people was entirely dependent on a creative act of Yahweh who can open wombs and give birth to a first-born or 'firstling' child.

As children of Yahweh they are to be a blessing to all the peoples of the earth. These stories are not historical accounts. They are expressions of faith, they proclaim. That is what they came to believe about themselves during the time of the exile. It was a vision that did not include other peoples or a land that belonged to everyone. Even though, for example, at the same time, there are accounts of Abraham, Isaac and countless other shepherds coexisting peacefully roaming around freely and exchanging with people of different towns.

This misguided understanding of their identity is one of the implications that the Bible is not a supernatural book, nor a history book. It means that visions and ways of life stand under the judgment of the whole of scripture and our understanding from our common human experience of the guidelines for life. The scriptures are the deposit of a collective confession of faith, not all of which can be accepted by us today. Special and chosen people and a land as their own possession is not part of the whole of the witness of the scriptures even though all the other nations were a part of their perspective and the scriptural witness. Throughout the ages, Christians proclaiming to be the chosen people of God at the exclusion of others have done irreparable harm and brought about untold suffering. Similarly, today Israel claiming it has the right to the Palestinians' land with an appeal to the Hebrew Scriptures is both misguided and is ending in the genocide of the Palestinian people. It is a misuse and violation of Hebrew Scriptures.

If we want to know how we are to approach other peoples and their lands we cannot just turn to Joshua. Instead we need to look elsewhere in the world at the many examples from the last decades of how indigenous people have understood themselves and their lands. For example, see the struggle of the Mozambique people during the Pro-Savana project and their ultimate victory. See also TerrAfrica's, Ripple's, UNDP's and WOCAT's reports and examples ("Where the Land is Greener' and 'Land for Life') and the Ashden projects, as well as many others. These reports and projects tell us what normative approaches to the people and the land are like today.[7] They have added to our understanding of what regenerative agriculture is like as well as sustainable fisheries and forestry. See the writings of Gabe Brown, *Earth to Soil, One family's journey into regenerative agriculture* (2018); Bob Quinn, *Grain by grain; a quest to revive ancient wheat, rural jobs, and healthy food* (2019); Darrin Qualman,

---

7. De Graaff, *The Gods in Whom They Trusted*, 124–140; 288–296.

Civilization critical; energy, food, nature, and the future (2019); and others. This is how we can picture how our understanding of 'normative societal principles' (in this case normative regenerative agriculture) grows and changes over time (Zuidervaart).

It is hard for many of us, privileged people, to understand Yahweh's sovereign dealings with Israel as a chosen people, even though there is a condition. They can only be a special people in the Promised Land by keeping their covenant obligations and following the great commandment with a calling to be a blessing to all people and all nations. The land and following the Torah are of one piece. It is the opposite of Israel's practices today in relation to the Palestinian people. Even if Joshua's conquest never happened the way it was told, it is still in the scriptures as God's word for our edification. It is proclamation.

Whether Joshua was an actual historical figure is hard to judge. He certainly exemplifies the ideal savior who brought all the people in one country around one Torah. He saved Israel through the Power of Yahweh. The questions of the historicity of Joshua and whether or not there was even a historical conquest or a gradual penetration can be left aside. The key is the prophetic role Joshua played in the redemption of Israel and taking possession of the land as Yahweh's gift to his people.

In Canada, if Joshua is taken too literally as God's revelation, colonized and Christianized indigenous people can only hear these stories about Joshua's conquests and extermination of men, women, children and animals as a sharp reminder of their own lands being taken away, their water poisoned, their forests decimated, their game and fish stocks eliminated, their children abused and ripped from their families; being reduced to living on isolated reservations without adequate services, housing, water or education.

How will they respond to the prophetic message of Joshua? Without much power or voice until recently, how are they to respond to Joshua's conquests? How are they to oppose the corporate takeovers while being seduced by some of the mining and logging companies with prospects of money and work that is poisoning their land, water and health? What are they to do with no other possibilities of employment? Now that they finally have a voice and after some "Truth and Reconciliation," can they truly negotiate? Could they be given authority to run some federal and provincial parks especially up North in their traditional way? Even having won a Supreme Court ruling for the right to fish in a sustainable way, their fishers are still being harassed and threatened.

If only our forefathers had remembered the stories of Joshua and the view of the land as God's possession for the good of all peoples of the earth and the belief of the first nations in the Creator calling for respect of all creatures, how different our, and their, history might have been.

If only the mining executives and the shareholders had remembered that the land belongs to the Creator and is not to be treated as private property. How differently would the pollution of the environment have turned out, today? Many native people across the world have little or no voice or power. Instead they see their environmental and community leaders killed year after year (over a hundred each year). Yet many courageous people risk their lives to oppose the neo-colonial powers, including Canadian mining interests in many parts of the world. How can it be a story of liberation when they don't have a voice to oppose the neo-colonialism and neo-liberal ideology which is bringing the earth and its creatures to extinction?

It is an 'abomination'. They defy Yahweh as the Landlord and the Owner of all resources at their own peril and our communal risk of environmental disaster.

Worldwide, many indigenous people can only hear Joshua's conquest as a violent extermination of a people and their culture, just as Israel today is committing genocide against the Palestinian people with an appeal to Joshua and with the acquiescence of much of the world. How are individual people to respond to this prophetic voice? For example, the mother in Asia that is washing her five year old daughter with poisoned water because that is all she has. Her daughter has big welts and sores all over her body. Or the boys that risk their lives every day going down a narrow shaft to dig up coal or gold. Or the mother, with her young daughter, pounding away at big rocks to collect a pail full of gravel to earn enough for a meal for the day. Or the garbage-picking, kids, trying to collect enough saleable plastic, to have a little bit to eat. Will they finally find the peace Joshua talks about in their own land? Examples of these individual situations are easily available online for all to see, including slavery, sexual violence, and the impact of AIDS and other health crises on families leaving countless children orphaned.

With regard to each topic, (agriculture, forestry, fishing, water allocation, land use, etc.), I have given many concrete examples in my book of what many people are doing and can do to counter the neo-colonial practices of the wealthy nations. See, *The Gods in Whom They Trusted*, chapter 11, "A Radical Alternative Way of Living."

Besides concrete alternatives, it calls for a strong testimony and protest by the Christian churches as in the ACCRA Confession. It seems like a fantasy. Yet it is not far-off from any faith community to do so. The life-giving word is not far from us. For an actual example of the wording of a united voice and proclamation consider the statement of the World Communion of Reformed Churches in its ACCRA Confession of 2004 in Ghana, further developed in 2010 in Grand Rapids Michigan (and basically rejected in favor of a weakened form by the Christian Reformed Church). Then we will realize again that it is Yahweh that gives the victory and that the future still beckons for its final fulfillment.

There are many individual and local groups that understand this challenge and calling. By way of example, the traditional teachings and traditions of the First Nations in many countries are more than adequate to counter global warming, climate change and provide food, building materials and fish in a sustainable way, as well as ways of negotiating and seeking cooperation and reconciliation.

The good earth under the good heavens will not come about solely by our protests and our alternative policies and practices. We are still called to stand as an abiding witness of what 'justice, solidarity, equality and resourcefulness' are like, or need to become. In the end we hope for a creative word/act of God as in the past. It is not our 'chariots and horses' that will gain the victory and bring peace on earth. And suddenly an angel said, 'be not afraid; for behold, I bring you good news of a great joy which will come to all the people; for to you is born this day in the city of David a Savior, who is Christ the Lord. And suddenly there was a multitude of the heavenly host praising God and saying, 'Glory to God in the highest, and on earth peace among men with whom he is pleased!'" (Luke 2:10) Peace on earth, still to come . . .

This, is the emphasis and witness of the first book of the Bible, Genesis, to the last, the book of Revelation. It is all about God's love affair with humanity and the love of his creation, our home. This is what makes the Bible such a remarkable book.

The Amsterdam school of exegesis and Biblical Theology has made this approach to understanding the scriptures serious again. They started this movement before and in the midst of WW II and the threat of Nazism with its ideology of a superior race and inferior species that led to the concentration camps. Their rediscovery of the scriptures and teachings became a powerful protest against Hitler, for which many paid with their lives. Just like the protests against the divine emperor and the refusal to sacrifice to him led to martyrdom in the amphitheatres with the gladiators and wild animals. And like the protests during the Middle Ages led to persecution and gruesome torture by the Inquisition and governments. Today it has led to the killing of more than a hundred activists, journalists, and environmentalists, each year, in the global South, not to mention the starvation and poisoning of millions of people through industrial agriculture, mining, fishing and forestry practices and the countless climate refugees. Also, more recently with the rise of neo-fascism in America with the victory of Trump, how will we respond to this new threat to God's life-saving guidelines?

7:14 Excursion: Israel and Palestine

7:14a) Introduction

It is impossible to write about the conquest of Canaan by Joshua and Israel as the chosen nation by Yahweh and not deal with the displacement and annihilation of the Palestinian people in Gaza and the West Bank today. This is even more so when writing about the rediscovery of Hebrew Scriptures and its meaning for understanding the New Testament. It is hard to grasp how a people, that have gone through centuries of anti-Semitism by the Christian church and many governments, the horrors of the Holocaust and what Jewish people continue to endure in our day, can engage in such actions. In view of that suffering, how can the Israeli government and its army annihilate and displace a whole people? The only word that fits the present situation is genocide. We can only respond in horror to the destruction and ethnic cleansing of the Palestinian people.

The aim of this excursus is to provide an overview of the scriptural witness about Israel and the land. It will make clear that the scriptures do not provide any foundation, permission or argument for the present day Israeli government's and army's actions.

Each day the death toll, 60 percent are women, children and the elderly, keeps rising above 50.000, increasing each day Meanwhile, their infrastructure is systematically destroyed: from schools, libraries, universities, hospitals to countless apartments and houses. Gaza has become uninhabitable. Many are dying of hunger which will only increase with the ongoing blockade of essential goods and medicine. Many children have had their arms or legs amputated, or both. Limited air drops of food cannot begin to remedy this situation. Gaza has become a concentration camp, walled in so that no one can go in or out without being checked by the Israeli soldiers. Israeli soldiers are accused of torture and humiliation of Palestinian prisoners, depriving them of basic necessities, starving them to death, and using unspeakable physical, sexual and emotional abuse. Netanyahu, Prime Minister, of Israel, is an irresponsible, corrupt, vengeful person, inciting hatred. How is all that possible? Over a hundred journalists have been targeted and killed by Israeli soldiers in order to prevent public awareness of the destruction. In spite of all this the U.S. and other countries refuse to stop the flow of arms to Israel.

The policies and events from before October 7, 2023 shows a litany of planned, systematic destruction, humiliation, imprisonment, harassment of the Palestinians, curtailing their supply of water, electricity, internet connection, and other services, as well as raids on individual homes and families and their destruction and displacement. Meanwhile the West Bank has been illegally infiltrated and nearly taken over by (extreme right-wing) Israeli settlers. The Gaza strip is relentlessly bombed. Where are the remaining millions of Palestinian people to go? In the desert where the Israelites in ancient times wandered for forty years? Where life is not possible without the miraculous intervention of Yahweh (water and manna), as the story goes?

How can a people, supposedly inheritors of the Torah, so blatantly ignore its instructions? Almost every page from Genesis to the later prophets, testifies against the current Israeli government and army. The Jewish scriptures constantly remind the people 'you were sojourners in Egypt', and, therefore, you ought to treat any of those among you with respect and care, loving them as yourselves. He executes justice for the fatherless and the widow, and loves the sojourner, giving him food and clothing, even within their own extended family group. They are always to remember they were slaves in how they treat others.

> Love the sojourner therefore; for you were strangers in the land of Egypt.
> Deuteronomy 10:19 (cf. Lev 19:24, 34; 20:23)

The prophet Micah puts it very distinctly, "He has showed you, O man, what is good; and what does the Lord require of you but to do justice, and to love kindness, and to walk humbly with your God?" (Micah 6:8).

In summary, the Israeli, government, and army, act in violation of their own traditions, and international law. How can religious and secular Jewish citizens live with this Holocaust of the Palestinians and justify what is happening? The U.S., and many other nations, for decades supported the Israeli government and its illegal policies, including occupations, denial of citizenship for Palestinians, and daily harassment. They have been providing them with a constant supply of missiles, weapons, tanks, jets and deadly bombs. How can they continue to support this genocide and ethnic cleansing by Israel?

7:14b) Scriptural witness: the appeal to 'the destruction of the Amalikites'

The appeal to the extermination of the Amalekites, erroneously identified as Palestinians, seems like an opportunistic distortion of history and interpretation that is not accepted by, either Jewish or Christian scholars of the Hebrew Scriptures.

The Amalikites were not Arabs, but closely related to the Edomites, which means they were also related to the Israelites. In the genealogy of Esau we read that Amalek is the son of Esau's firstborn son Eliphaz and his concubine Timan, the daughter of Seir. (Genesis 36:12–14) "So Esau dwelt in the hill country of Seir; Esau is Edom." (36:8) Together they buried their father Isaac, "and his sons Esau and Jacob buried him."

It is only later after the Edomites opposed and made war with Israel, which they were to regard as a brother nation, that they were defeated. In Amos we read, "For three transgressions of Edom, and for four, I will not revoke the punishment; because he pursued his brother with the sword, and cast off all pity." (Amos 1:11) Already in Deuteronomy 23:7 we read, "You shall not abhor an Edomite, for he is your brother . . ."

Over time Edom became the arch enemy of the Israelites. Primarily because the king of Edom, refused Israel passage through their country even though they offered to pay for the water and promised not to pass through their fields or vineyards., but "Edom refused to give Israel passage through his territory; so Israel turned away from him." (Num 20:14–21) In Deuteronomy 2:4–8, after years in the wilderness the Lord told Moses, ". . . You are about to pass through the territory of your brethren the sons of Esau, who live in Seir; and they will be afraid of you. So take good heed; do not contend with them; for I will not give you any of their land, no, not so much as for the sole of your feet to tread on, because I have given Mount Seir to Esau as a possession . . . so we went on, away from our brethren the sons of Esau who live in Seir."

Later, "I will punish what Amalek did to Israel in opposing them on the way when they came up out of Egypt. Now go and smite Amalek. (1 Samuel 15:2–3). "Remember what Amalek did to you on the way as you came out of Egypt, how he attacked you on the way, when you were faint and weary, and cut off at your rear all who lagged behind you; and he did not fear God . . . you shall blot out the remembrance of Amalek from under heaven; you shall not forget." (Deut 25:17–19) King Saul is commanded to execute this command, "Now go and smite Amalek, and utterly destroy all that they have; do not spare them . . ." (1 Sam 15:3). Saul disobeyed God's command and saved their king and all the animals. Later on David waged a sacred war against the Amalekites and destroyed them. (1 Sam 30:1–20)

The Amalekites have long since disappeared, as a distinct nation, or been absorbed by the surrounding nations. They no longer exist. Extreme right-wing nationalists and West Bank Jewish settlers like to quote these passages out of context and regardless of both Jewish and Christian scholarship. They like to quote these passages as a justification for genocide. "We have to wipe these people out." Israeli extremists view Palestinians as modern-day Amalekites. Each year on the Sabbath, before the holiday of Purim, these sections in Deuteronomy are recited, reinforcing hatred. On Purim the Jews remember that they were saved from the evil plans of Haman, a descendant of the Amalikite king Agag, to destroy all the Israelites young and old, women and children. (Esth 3:1–6)

In general, the appeal to the "promise of the land of Canaan to the Israelites" can only be understood if we go back to the very beginning, to Gen 3 through 11, before the promises to Abraham, Isaac and Jacob. The basic theme of Genesis is about the becoming of Israel in the midst of the nations (Breukelman). Before the call of Abraham much has already happened, including the flood that destroyed all people and animals, "The LORD saw that the wickedness of man was great in the earth, and that every imagination of the thoughts of his heart was only evil continually. And the LORD was sorry that he had made man on the earth, and it grieved him to his heart. So the LORD said, "I will blot out man whom I have created from the face of the earth . . . for I am sorry that I have made them." (Gen 6:5–7) The LORD was grieved in his heart, because of their wickedness and evil.

We need to go back further to the sons of God marrying the daughters of men, (Gen. 6:1–4) wanting to be God-like. "Then the LORD said, 'my spirit shall not abide in man forever, for he is flesh, but his days shall be a hundred and twenty years." This reminds us of, "then the LORD God formed man of dust from the ground, and breathed into his nostrils the breath of life; and man became a living being." (Gen.2:7) Humans are creaturely and vulnerable, subject to death.

But we need to go back even further to the original violation of wanting to be like God in Genesis 3 when Adam and Eve were tempted by the serpent to eat from the tree of life . . . and live forever. They were cursed and expelled from the Garden of Eden. Not only did they want to be like God, but Cain, their son refused to take care of his younger brother Abel. (Gen 4:1–16) These two accounts represent all humankind and all the earth in the first chapters of Genesis. It seemed like God's good intention for all humankind and the earth was thwarted by a rebellious people that did not care about brotherhood. (Gen 3, 4)

We are mindful that the earth was created for the sake of the earthlings, to live in harmony and peace forever on the good earth. The creation of the earth is for the purpose of providing a good living space for all creatures before the face of the LORD. This ideal situation is disturbed by humans breaking their relationship with the LORD. In spite of this violation they did not die but were left to wander the earth estranged from God. In spite of God's judgments, or rather, in and through God's judgments, Yahweh shows himself to be merciful, each time again. "At that time men began to call upon the name of the LORD." (Genesis 4:26) And "Noah found favor in the eyes of the LORD." (Gen 6:8) That is how the stage is set for the call of Abraham and the promise of the land and a son.

Only against this background can we understand the call of Abram to leave his father's house and to go to the land that the LORD will show him. In spite of humankind's rebellion and rejection, the LORD will maintain his good intention for the earth and humans. He does so by singling out one person and then a special nation to receive a specific land for an inheritance. "Then the LORD appeared to Abram, and said, 'To your descendants I will give this land.'" (Gen 12:7)

Later on the promise is qualified, "Know of a surety that your descendants will be sojourners in a land that is not theirs, and will be slaves there, and will be oppressed for four hundred years; but I will bring judgment on the nation which they serve, and afterward they shall come out with great possessions . . . And they shall come back here in the fourth generation; for the iniquity of the Amorites is not yet complete." (Gen 15:7–16) Only then will the Israelites inherent the land as a miraculous gift from the LORD. This promise becomes all the more significant if we remember that Genesis was written after the prophets. Even though they were in exile, this story about a return to their homeland comforted them and kept hope alive.

Still later, this promise is repeated, "Behold, my covenant is with you, and you shall be the father of a multitude of nations.... And I will give to you, and to your descendants after you, the land of your sojourning, all the land of Canaan, for an everlasting possession; and I will be their God." (Gen 17:4, 8) Then there is the promise of a child for Sarah. The promise of the land is repeated to Isaac, "Sojourn in this land, and I will be with you, and will bless you; for to you and your descendants I will give all these lands, and I will fulfill the oath which I swore to Abraham your father ... and by your descendants all the nations of the earth shall bless themselves. This promise is repeated to Jacob when he had to flee from his brother Esau and leave Canaan "... by you and your descendants shall all the families of the earth bless themselves." (Gen 28:10–22). The LORD remains the landlord; they are to be good caretakers of the land for the benefit of all, without following the abominations of the people around them.

In this way, through Abraham, Isaac, Jacob and the people of Israel, the LORD will achieve his intention for the earth and humankind in spite of their rebellion, turning away from God and their lack of solidarity. Through this particular people and nation, God's universal aim will be achieved. Finally through his first-born son, Jesus, whom he 'called from Egypt,' his purposes will realize themselves, through judgment, death and resurrection, all nations will be blessed.

Jesus had to be born from a certain set of ancestors (see Matt 1), in a particular country and city under certain rulers (the Roman occupation, elders and high priest). Only in this way could the particular become a universal again (all the people of the earth). That is the way the LORD chose to redeem his special people and all humanity and bless them. He keeps covenant forever and does not forsake the works of his own hand. The LORD takes no pleasure in the death of the wicked, but that the "wicked turn from his way and live." (Ezek 33:11; 18:23) Jewish settlers and others like to appeal to these promises, without accepting the responsibilities that go with it, or being mindful of God's judgments when they fail to do so.

7:14c) The New Testament witness

When Jesus was crucified, died and rose again from the dead, everything changed, the particular changed to the universal. The church did not replace Israel. Rather, with the coming of Jesus of Nazareth, the son of David, the son of Abraham (Matt 1:1), a fundamental change took place in God's dealing with humanity and the earth. It was a radical change as told in the scriptures that was difficult to understand for Jews at that time, even for the Christian Jews as the experiences of Paul and Peter illustrate. The promises to the forefathers were extended to all people. From the beginning it was there, 'to be a blessing to all nations'. In the gospel of John the radical nature of this change was clearly announced.

> I am the good shepherd; I know my own and my own know me ... And I have other sheep that are not of this fold; I must bring them also, and they will heed my voice. So there shall be one flock, one shepherd.
> John 10:4, 16

The old divisions between Israel and the gentiles, between the pure and the impure, the holy and unholy have been broken down. "For he is our peace, who has made us both one, and has broken down the dividing wall of hostility," (Eph 2:14)

> And you, who once were estranged, and hostile in mind, doing evil deeds, he has now reconciled in his body of flesh by his death, in order to present you holy and blameless and irreproachable before him ...
> Colossians 1:21

From here on it is clear that there is no distinction anymore,

> There is neither Jew nor Greek, there is neither slave nor free, there is neither male nor female, for you are all one in Christ Jesus. And if you are Christ's, then you are Abraham's offspring, heirs according to the promise.
> Galatians 3:28
> Here there cannot be Greek and Jew, circumcised and uncircumcised, barbarian, Scythian, slave, free man, but Christ is all, and in all.
> Colossians 3:11

It took the disciples and the early Christian community a while to understand and accept this 'new' order, as we can read in Acts 9 through

10. Ananias, a disciple in Damascus had to hear from the Lord about Paul's mission, "But the Lord said to him, 'Go, for he is a chosen instrument of mine to carry my name before the Gentiles and kings and the sons of Israel.'" (Acts 9:15) The same with the apostle Peter, he had to learn through a vision. In the vision he was instructed to kill and eat unclean animals, to which he answered, "... No, Lord; for I have never eaten anything that is common or unclean." The answer was clear, "... What God has cleansed, you must not call common." (Acts10:14, 15) Cornelius from Caesarea invited him to a gathering of followers. "He said to them, 'You yourselves know how unlawful it is for a Jew to associate with or visit any one of another nation; but God has shown me that I should not call any man common or unclean, so when I was sent for, I came without objection....'" (Acts10:28, 29) When he went back to Jerusalem, the 'circumcision party' criticized him. However when they listened to his story, they were silenced, and they glorified God, saying, "... 'Then to the Gentiles also God has granted repentance unto life.'" (Acts11:18) In view of these two events it is not surprising to read in the letter to the Galatians, "For neither circumcision counts for anything, nor uncircumcision, but a new creation." (Gal 6:15; cf. Col 2:11). As Peter states recalling the words of the prophet Hosea (Hos 2:23),

> But you are a chosen race, a royal priesthood, a holy nation, God's own people, that you may declare the wonderful deeds of him who called you out of darkness into his marvelous light. Once you were no people but now you are God's people; once you had not received mercy but now you have received mercy ... For you were straying like sheep, but have now returned to the Shepherd and Guardian of your souls.
> 1 Peter 2:9, 10, 25

Now all are to be called children of Abraham, a holy nation, sharing in all the promises to the forefathers. It puts the promise of the land in a new light. It is no longer a geographically limited area. The promise is extended to all people with the same charge, to care for the land as God's possession to be stewarded for the benefit of all, just as in ancient times, when the farmers had to leave enough grain for the poor to gather and the second pluck of the olives and the grapes for the needy. (Deut 24:20, 21; cf. Lev 19:9; 23:22) That is the mandate and abiding calling. They are to care for the land in God's name in solidarity with all people.

The reason given for this solidarity is, "for the land is mine," (Lev 25:2, 3, Exod 9:29, 19:5), or as it says in Psalm 24:1 "The earth is the

LORD's and the fullness thereof." (cf. 1 Cor. 10:26) The LORD remains the Landlord. Therefore they are to care for the land in solidarity with the poor, the widows and the orphans. The Promised Land "which the LORD your God cares for; the eyes of the LORD are always upon it, from the beginning of the year to the end of the year." (Deut 11:12) It always remains God's possession, God's land.

The first Christians were Jewish, just as Jesus and all his disciples. Later on, Greek Christians joined in. Over time it gave rise to a conflict between the 'synagogue Christians' and 'Hellenistic Christians' (including whether all gentiles needed to be circumcised, keeping the ceremonial laws and the Sabbath). It is not surprising that the early Christian church (Acts 8, 10, 15) and Paul (in his letter to the Roman church (Romans 9–15) had to come to terms with the rejection of Christ as the Messiah by the Jewish officials. They expected a royal son of David and not a lowly servant riding on a donkey. Paul too was a Jew, "educated according to the strict manner of the law of our fathers, being zealous for God as you all are this day." (Acts 22:3–5) When he was hauled before the Jewish Council in Jerusalem, "he cried out in the council, 'Brethren, I am a Pharisee, a son of Pharisees; with respect to the hope and the resurrection of the dead I am on trial' . . . the following night the LORD stood by him and said, "Take courage, for as you have testified about me at Jerusalem, so you must bear witness also at Rome." (Acts 23:6–11)

It grieved Paul deeply that his countrymen were rejecting Jesus as the Messiah. "I am not lying . . . that I have great sorrow and unceasing anguish in my heart. For I could wish that I myself were accursed and cut off from Christ for the sake of my brethren, my kinsmen by race." (Rom 9:1–5) It grieved him deeply because, "They are Israelites, and to them belong the sonship, the glory, the covenants, the giving of the law, the worship, and the promises; to them belong the patriarchs, and of their race, according to the flesh, is the Christ. God who is over all be blessed forever. Amen."(Rom 9:4, 5) That is how Paul struggled through the pain of seeing his own people turn against the Christ and his followers.

Thus the conquest of the land must be considered carefully. The Lord does not arbitrarily command the Israelites to annihilate the Canaanites. The abominations, of the seven surrounding nations, are listed in Joshua, (see the chapter on "Re-reading Joshua"). It illustrates God's judgment of the nations and their sins. Abraham engages in a daring plea with Yahweh, 'What if there are only ten righteous people left in Sodom and surrounding towns, will you destroy the righteous with the unrighteous. "Shall not the Judge of all the earth, do right?" (Genesis 18:25) The answer is a clear, 'yes', if there are only ten righteous people I will save the city. In the end only one person bears the full judgment of God and that is the Christ, the Messiah for all Israel and all peoples. The final judgment of all unrighteousness of all nations and people is shifted from the present to the future. Joshua has been destructively distorted in the present debates and conflicts.

In his booklet on Jonah, Deurloo presents a compelling picture of Jonah (as a counter-figure to Abraham who pleaded for the rescue of Lot and his family and the inhabitants of Sodom). Jonah cannot accept God's grace toward the cruel, destructive and pagan Assyrians. On a hilltop outside the city he awaits God's judgments on the people of Nineveh. He expects judgment not grace. (see: *Exposition of the Hebrew Bible, Jonah*, Baam: Callenbach), and who can blame him? See also the many other contributions in #22 of the Supplement series of ACEBT, ed. K. Spronk, *Jona*. It is a hard lesson to learn for Jonah and all of us. We want justice to be done to a people that commit such atrocities. The contrast could not be greater, "and Abraham went early in the morning where he had stood before the LORD and he looked down toward Sodom and Gomorrah and the land of the valley, and beheld, and lo, the smoke of the land went up like the smoke of a furnace," (Gen 19:27, 28) as Abraham agonized about Lot and his family.

Israel was special "Not because of your righteousness or the uprightness of your heart are you going to possess their land," (Deut 9:5) it is entirely because of Yahweh's free and sovereign choice and mercy.

> Behold, to the LORD your God belong heaven and the heavens of heavens, the earth and all that is in it; Yet the LORD set his heart in love upon your fathers . . . Circumcise therefore the foreskin of your heart . . . For the LORD your God is God of gods and LORD of lords, The great and mighty, and the terrible God, who is not partial and takes no bribe . . . He executes justice for the fatherless, and the widow, and loves the sojourner, giving him food and clothing . . .
> Deuteronomy 10:14–22

The scriptures emphasize that there is an inseparable bond between the Jewish nation and Christianity and a joint future. There is a direct line from Jesus to Genesis. That makes the present situation all the more difficult to bear. Our impulse today is to have nothing to do with 'these murderous people' that stand under the judgment of God, even though it is also our own collective history. With Jonah we want to take a boat in the opposite direction. Yet there is a future promise to Israel along with the church. How is that possible?

In these somewhat closely argued chapters from nine to eleven, Paul is trying to come to terms with Israel's rejection of the Christ and the new inclusion of Gentiles.

The judgment upon Israel is not final; the promise to Abraham, Isaac and Jacob remains. In their past history mercy has always triumphed. The Church has not come in the place of Israel, instead, it may join in and share in the riches of the promises to Israel. The promise to them remains and Christians share their belief in the coming of God's reign in the ages to come and may read along in the Hebrew Scriptures each Sabbath again, as preserved by the Jewish people and scholars.

7:14d) The promise of the land

The promise of the "Promised land" cannot be 'spiritualized', like a 'heavenly earth'. In biblical times it was a very specific, physical geographical area, the land of Canaan. Nor can the land be seen as a 'political entity', a state. The promise of the 'land' is not to be equated with a new Davidic kingship in Palestine with Jerusalem as the capital city. The promise stands, "all the land of Canaan, for an everlasting possession; and I will be their God." (Genesis 17:8) The psalmist exclaims, "... the covenant which he made with Abraham, his sworn promise to Isaac, which he confirmed to Jacob as a statute, to Israel as an everlasting covenant, saying, 'To you I will give the land of Canaan as your portion for an inheritance.'" (Psalm 105:9–11) But because of Israel's abominations there was only one conclusion in the ancient times: "into exile."

Such an 'uncontaminated' land remains a 'future' land. That is also why the land can be portrayed in ideal terms, like that of Paradise. It remains the "Promised Land," counting all the more when we realize that the land stands for all the earth, par pro toto. We get glimpses of that land wherever there are earth keepers on behalf of all.

> They shall return to the land of Egypt, and Assyria shall be their king, because they have refused to return to me.
> Hosea 11:5

If not as a' political entity', how then might we conceive of the 'land'? The reign of God, his kingship is always portrayed as a reign of justice and righteousness, where all people will dwell in security and peace, including the gentiles, the foreigners and strangers among them, who will share in the blessings of Israel. Wherever that is practiced, glimpses of the Promised Land become visible. It may be helpful to emphasize the promise of the land in all its concreteness during certain times without identifying that with a political entity today, the present state of Israel. It encourages us to hold Israel accountable to what the 'land' was meant to be, "a place where each one can sit under his olive tree and be at peace," (see the many scriptural references below).

The land remains a 'prophetic designation'; it remains the 'Promised Land', just like Jerusalem and 'the people of Israel.' The 'land' was meant to be an uncontaminated land, where righteousness and loving kindness was practiced. Very little of that became a reality for very long. The land became contaminated by the 'abominable' practices of the Israelites, like that of the previous inhabitants, which led to their exile from Canaan. The land remains the LORD's. He is the Landowner and the Caretaker. "Private property" is not a biblical concept. Land that was lost to a family was to be restored to the original family every fifty years, during the year of Jubilee.

All this does not legitimize the politics of the present state of Israel, even though all the other nations are co-responsible for how that came about. It can be judged by the norms of justice and righteousness for all the inhabitants. The evil perpetrated by Hamas and Israel and the anti-Semitism of the church throughout the ages all stand under the judgment of God.

Even if there was a Davidic king over Israel, his main task would be to establish justice as the psalmist expresses so strongly, "Give the king thy justice, O God, and thy righteousness to the royal son! May he judge thy people with righteousness, and thy poor with justice! . . . May he defend the cause of the poor of the people, give deliverance to the needy, and crush the oppressor!" (Psalm 72:1–4) The constant refrain of the books of Kings is they did "what was evil in the sight of the LORD" from chapter 12 on.

When God's kingship is established,

> It shall come to pass in the latter days . . . many nations shall come . . .
> they shall sit every man under his vine and under his fig tree,
> and none shall make them afraid.
> Micah 4:1–4 (cf. Zech 3:10; 8:12)

THE PROPHETIC CALL TO LOVE AND JUSTICE

> Therefore, behold, I will allure her,
> and bring her into the wilderness,
> and speak tenderly to her.
> and there I will give her her vineyards,
> and make the Valley of Achor a door of hope.
> ... And I will make for you a covenant on that day with the beasts of the field, the birds of the air,
> and the creeping things of the ground; ...
> and I will make you lie down in safety ...
> I will answer the heavens and they shall answer the earth;
> and the earth shall answer the grain, the wine, and the oil,
> > Hosea 2:14–22 (Isa 65:17–25)

These passages strongly emphasize the future of the land, the earth, everyone sitting under his olive tree and inviting his neighbor. It is a land where everyone is at peace and there is no threat of war. There will be shalom for all with justice and solidarity for all. The scriptures end with an end time image of the new earth under a new heaven. The Land of Promise remains for all people.

It is difficult to find words to describe an alternative to 'spiritualizing' land or seeing it as 'a political entity.' It is a 'prophetic promise' that will find its fulfillment 'in the age to come.' It is a future promise, waiting for its final fulfillment. The 'land' in these contexts is the opposite of the 'cursed earth' of Genesis 3:17, "cursed is the ground because of you." And the promise to Noah confirms this vision, "I will never again curse the ground because of man ... While the earth remains, seedtime and harvest, cold and heat, summer and winter, day and night, shall not cease." Genesis 8:21–22 The 'land' is not a past entity, but an abiding promise, where everyone can sit in peace under his vine and fig tree with plenty of wine, figs and olives, Palestinians as well as Israelites, as well as all peoples.

We suffer along with the Palestinian people. Israel can be and must be confronted with the demands of justice and righteousness. The church is called to cooperate to bring about reconciliation between Israel and Palestinians. Even in exile, "... seek the welfare of the city where I have sent you in exile, and pray to the Lord on its behalf. For in its welfare you will find your welfare ... plan for welfare and not for evil, to give you a future and a hope." (Jeremiah 29:7–12) We are all called to work toward a just political solution, which Israel presently continues to reject.

Both Israelis and Palestinians deserve a safe homeland and a humane existence for all. Is anything too hard for the Lord?! And shall the Judge of all the earth not do right? We can count on it. That is our hope and trust. Earlier we took note of the great turnabout in God, his unexpected and miraculous mercy. What was promised and took place with his special people has become a universal promise to all, to Greeks and Jews, slave and free, male and female and all genders. Already in the Hebrew Scriptures and the gospels we see the inclusion of outsiders. (Matthew. 8:5–13) "Truly, I say to you, not even in Israel have I found such faith . . . I tell you, many will come from the east and the west and sit at table with Abraham, Isaac, and Jacob in the kingdom of heaven." (Matthew 8:8–11; 15:21–28) We recall that Israel stands for all of humanity. Each day we grieve and are in anguish about what is happening in Palestine. At this point it is not Israel's security that is at stake, much more so it is that of the Palestinians.

7:14e) Christianity's anti-Semitism.

Ever since the early church there was a struggle between 'synagogue Jews' and the 'Christ following Jews and Greeks.' At first both met together in the synagogue as Luke tells us and Paul's journeys illustrate. Slowly the alienation and conflicts increased until there was a sharp division between 'synagogue Jews' and 'Christian Jews'. From there on the slogans, 'They killed Jesus', 'his blood be upon our heads,', and 'Christ murderers' took hold, along with many other derogatory slogans and persecution with annihilating pogroms and cruelties during many centuries that ended with the extermination of six million Jewish people by the Nazis. All the humiliating practices by the Nazis were pre-figured by the policies of popes and governments during the previous centuries. It is a shameful history of individual and collective guilt.

After the Holocaust any form of 'paternalism' or 'evangelism' among the Jews by Christians was looked at with great suspicion and rightly so. In the face of this horror and the remnant that survived, many Christians felt they could only be silent and listen.

7:14f) Zionism and especially American Zionism.

Zionism had early roots at the very least when in 1917 the Balfour Declaration was incorporated into the British Mandate. It stated among other things that non-Jewish peoples' rights were to be respected. Yet it came to be understood to be on an individual level not on a national level for Arabs. Certainly from an Arab perspective it was pure colonialism. As the decades ensued, anti-semitism globally increased and so did the abuse by Isrealis of the Palestinians.

Zionism is a complex and evolving movement that has a long history and includes many different groups. One key figure grappling with these issues was the American, Reinhold Niebuhr. There continues to be an ongoing discussion of his views.

From the beginning of their nationhood American immigrants (the Puritans) saw themselves as the chosen people and America as the Promised Land. Later when things changed in Europe, the focus shifted to the Holy Land as the Promised Land. This ideological nationalism as a reaction to anti-Semitism in Europe, Eastern Europe, Russia and Germany fuelled the support for a homeland for Jews. The Holocaust really politicized Zionism. Since that time the abuse of Palestinians has increased further.

A powerful Israeli lobby AIPAC (American Israel Public Affairs Committee) infiltrated all aspects of government and was able directly to influence US policy for decades. Christian evangelicals have long since advocated a homeland for Jews in Palestine, seeing in every detail of the conflict a fulfillment of biblical prophecies related to the end of times.

The ethnic Israeli does not exist anymore. The promises in Ezekiel do not relate to the establishment of a modern state of Israel that is secular by nature. The place has become a war zone. There is no argument from a prophetic position for present-day Israel. The modern state of Israel cannot be identified with the biblical Israel. The term 'the people of God' as a designation of ethnic Israel is misplaced.

Happily there are many Jewish and world-wide protests against Israel's annihilation of Gaza and the West Bank settlements. T'ruah (The Rabbinic Call for Human Rights) is one of those organizations. There are many movements and grassroots groups that oppose Israel's war on the Palestinians, "Another Jewish Sound" (EAJG) and Jewish Voices for Peace. The words of Chris Hedges' speeches and books are constantly with me and ring in my ears. As a journalist and historian his prophetic words summarize the history of the conflict and core issues. Although it is hard to write this book in view of Gaza's destruction, we are all called to continue to witness and protest against the destruction of Palestine and the genocide in whatever way we can and to speak for justice and righteousness for all.

7:14g) Deurloo's vision

Deurloo, together with Bouhuijs, provide their own extensive account of Israel and Palestine. It was written in 1974. We can only imagine how much stronger their testimony and outcry might have been today with what is happening in Gaza, and the West Bank. We will follow their extensive and inspiring account closely in the last part of their *The Voice in the Events; a messianic resumé*.[8] To summarize, they see no hope for the fulfillment of all the promises about the land in the establishment of the state of Israel. Nor do they see the geographical city of Jerusalem with its temple and centre of worship as a hope for the fulfillment of the New Jerusalem. In his characteristic way Deurloo will interconnect many scripture passages to make his point.

He starts by referring his readers to an earlier 'resurrection story' in the gospel of Matthew. Right after feeding the five thousand, Jesus sends his disciples ahead across the sea, while he went up alone into the hills to pray. Meanwhile the disciples' boat was far from land because the wind was against them. The waves were crashing against their boat, so they made little progress. In the middle of the night while struggling to reach the other shore, Jesus came toward them, walking on the sea. When the disciples saw him they were afraid and thought it was a ghost. They cried out in fear, but Jesus spoke to them and reassured them, "Take heart, it is I; have no fear." (Matt 14:23–33) This story comes right after the feeding of the multitude. The night and the sea are symbols of chaos and the power of death. It is a resurrection story.

In the middle of the night, amidst the powers of the sea, chaos, and death, he comes to them. The sea is not only a source of power in itself. It also represents the events of the people and world history. In Isaiah we read, "Ah, the thunder of many peoples, they thunder like the thundering of the sea! Ah, the roar of nations, they roar like the roaring of mighty waters! The nations roar like the roaring of many waters, but he will

---

8. Bouhuijs and Deuloo, *De Stem in het Gebeuren; messiaans resumé*, 99–119.

rebuke them, and they will flee far away..." (Isa 17:12–13) Peter plays a special role in this story. After his confession in the previous chapter, "You are the Christ, the Son of the living God," (Matt 16:16) he is speaking for all the disciples and the early church. But once he ventures out of the boat, he starts to doubt and is about to drown. This 'resurrection story' appears here right in the middle of the gospel.

We can ask ourselves, what is this small messianic movement of Christ followers expecting in the middle of the storm? They are in the middle of the sea of the roaring of nations and world powers, in which the wind is against them? What do they expect!? What do they expect at the horizon of history? What about us personally? Wouldn't you despair about the future of the Messiah? As Matthew writes later on, even at the very end, "but some doubted." (Matt 28:17) They did not doubt the resurrection took place, because out of this event the Messianic community arose. But they can doubt whether the risen Christ has such worldwide dimensions, and whether he can still the storms of the nations? Questions about the truth of the resurrection are not answered from the past but the future. If there is nothing to hope for, if Jesus is not risen and creates a new community again and again, Jesus remains a ghostlike appearance.

The images of the storm at sea are of great intensity in the Hebrew Scriptures. Compare Psalm 46:2–7 for example, "Therefore we will not fear though the earth should change, though the mountains shake in the heart of the sea; though its waters roar and foam...God is in the midst of her... the nations rage, the kingdoms totter... the LORD of hosts is with us..." or Psalm 93:4, "Mightier than the thunder of many waters, mightier than the waves of the sea, the LORD on high is mighty" or Psalm 65:5–7, "O God of our salvation, who art the hope of all the ends of the earth, and of the farthest seas... who dost still the roaring of the seas, the roaring of the waves, the tumult of the peoples..."

The symbols of nature are turned upside down to symbols of history. The earth is dislocated, mountains shake in the heart of the seas, waters foam and storms roar. Not nature does something, but the storyteller does something with nature: it is the nations, the world powers that roar and shake. God sent forth his voice and the floods subside. Israel heard this voice at times as his Voice. This reality becomes the language of the prophet Isaiah. "I am the LORD, your Holy One, the Creator of Israel, your King. Thus says the LORD, who makes a way in the sea, a path in the mighty waters...." (Isa 43:15–16)

It is a reminder of the exodus from Egypt and the path through the sea. Yes, it is that, it is also a call not to stay stuck in the past, but to discern the future history. "Remember not the former things . . ." (Isa 43:18) In Isaiah 51, he heightens this proclamation and, adds: "Awake, Awake, put on strength . . . awake, as in the days of old, the generations of long ago. Was it not thou that didst cut Rahab in pieces, that didst pierce the dragon? Was it not thou that didst dry up the sea, the waters of the great deep; that didst make the depths of the sea a way for the redeemed to pass over?" (Isa 51:9–10) The exodus is connected with very old images: the battle with the powers of chaos; in 'the beginning'. It is his battle to create space and time for humanity.

The creation is the first 'resurrection story'. The Creation story is, including today, a story of liberation. "In the beginning God created the heavens and the earth. The earth was without form and void, and darkness was upon the face of the deep; and the Spirit of God was moving over the face of the waters. And God said, 'Let there be light and there was light.'" (Gen 1:1–3) And God saw that it was good. Because of hearing the Voice, they believed that the creation was good, in spite of what they saw around them and that the creation is not yet completed. In Genesis 1, in the story of the beginning, they saw a confirmation that the crucified Christ speaks. They hear it as the story of the future. "All authority in heaven and earth has been given to me . . . and lo, I am with you always, to the close of the age." Possessing all power? Yes, in order to make humans of us wandering and lost peoples. You will see it!

There are Christians who see in the destruction of Jerusalem in 70 C.E. a judgment of God upon the people of Israel. Just as today they see the creation of the state of Israel as a new turn of events, a new hopeful sign. We are not happy with either kind of views, says Deurloo. They identify the Voice too easily with specific happenings.

To avoid misunderstanding, we believe that the state of Israel must be evaluated by the rule of law, whether the state is living up to its calling, to execute justice and care for all, especially the vulnerable. We feel deeply connected to Israel because of the 'synagogue'. We can hope for a future of this state of Israel in the midst of the Arabic states. But at the same time we know the despair of the Palestinian people. With fear in our hearts we look at the politics of Israel. This was written by Deurloo in 1974 after the creation of the state of Israel (May 14, 1948).

He was afraid that Christians that see the state of Israel as an historical re-birth of 'the book of Joshua'. When they do, they do Jews and

Palestinians a great disservice. For them the state of Israel was not a sign of 'God's power' and the fulfillment of God's promises. Instead, the words of the scriptures focus our eyes on the growing Messianic movement. Like flickering lights, here and there are events that have Messianic features. They are like fireflies in the night. Words and deeds that seem insignificant yet are not, like the breaking of bread that is shared. The storm on the sea comes immediately after this astounding event of the feeding of the five thousand. Whoever starts with the resurrection ends up right at the beginning, with the creation and the breaking of bread. You will see that it was very good.

In the last section of his account Deurloo asks about the location of Jerusalem. In contrast to the optimism of some Christians, they need to let their views be corrected by what the New Testament says about the city of Jerusalem. What do Jews mean when at the end of Passover they say, 'Next year in Jerusalem!'? Can they still say that living in the present Jerusalem? Jerusalem is located in Palestine, in the Holy Land, the centre of the earth and worship. To that city the nations will come and share in the promises to Israel.

Jerusalem is the city of the temple, but at the same time it stands under judgment. As Luke laments, "O Jerusalem, Jerusalem, killing the prophets and stoning those who are sent to you! How often would I have gathered your children together as a hen gathers her brood under her wings, and you would not! Behold, your house is forsaken. And I tell you, you will not see me until you say, 'Blessed is he who comes in the name of the LORD!'" (Luke 13:34, 35)

At the same time it is the city of the future. How and when are we on the way to this city, the centre of the real liturgy?. Where is it located, in the church, in the world, in 'nowhere land', in utopia, in heaven? The geographical concreteness of this city as we know it is a sign that we are – in search of this city – we realize we have to be 'on the way' to the city and the land of the future and be very realistic, breaking bread along the way. Present-day Jerusalem is not the city of promise, the city of peace.

This search for the future Jerusalem can be illustrated from the journey of the two disciples to Emmaus (Luke 24), which is in ruins today. The young community gives expression to the resurrected Lord in their liturgy, in their exposition of the scriptures, and in the celebration of the Lord's Supper, in which the living LORD is present. It illustrates how they experienced the LORD in their midst. Luke composes his gospel from out of the spirituality of this young community.

Especially conservative Christians, hold that Christ is only present where the gospel is preached and the sacraments are celebrated. This kind of exposition is very dangerous if with that emphasis the engagement with the world and all its political and social disasters and all future possibilities are neglected. As if there are no signals of his reign detectable in the world. In that case they can all return to a safe 'mother church'.

However this story which follows has a very different focus. Two men go away from Jerusalem to a village named Emmaus when a stranger joins them.

> While they were talking and discussing together, Jesus himself drew near and went with them. But their eyes were kept from recognizing him. And he said to them, 'what is this conversation that you are holding with each other as you walk?' And they stood still looking sad then one of them, named Cleopas, answered him, 'Are you the only visitor to Jerusalem who does not know the things that have happened there in these days?' And he said to them, 'What things?' And they said to him, 'Concerning Jesus of Nazareth, who was a prophet mighty in deed and word before God and all the people, and how our chief priests and rulers delivered him up to be condemned to death, and crucified him. But we had hoped that he was the one to redeem Israel. Yes, and besides all this, it is now the third day since this happened. Moreover, some women of our company amazed us. They were at the tomb early in the morning and did not find his body; and they came back saying that they had even seen a vision of angels, who said that he was still alive. Some of those who were with us went to the tomb, and found it just as the women had said; but him they did not see.' And he said to them, 'O foolish men, and slow of heart to believe all that the prophets had spoken! Was it not necessary that the Christ should suffer these things and enter into his glory?' And beginning wih Moses and all the prophets, he interpreted to them in all the scriptures the things concerning himself. .. When he was at table with them, he took the bread and blessed, and he broke it and gave it to them. And their eyes were opened and they recognized him; and he vanished out of their sight.
> Luke 24:15–31

They told the others how "he was known to them in the breaking of the bread" (Luke 24:35). A remarkable 'must' rules the life of this stranger, in which the Messiah could be recognized. Not the 'must' of Fate or Destiny, ('it-had-to-be') of the Greek way of thinking, but the 'must' of one that stands in the tension of the covenant. This 'must', has to do with the 'way' of him who as covenant partner takes up the battle against the powers of the world. Everything points to this one thing: the movement of God-with-us, to peace, to the Promised Land, and the city, to Jerusalem, to each one sitting under his olive tree. Along the way the scriptures are opened up. Maybe they only speak to those whose ears are 'burning along the way'.

The disciples on the way to Emmaus are going in the wrong direction. They have to go back to Jerusalem and from there to Galilee and from there to the ends of the world. "But you shall receive power when the Holy Spirit has come upon you; and you shall be my witnesses in Jerusalem, and in all Judea and Samaria and to the end of the earth." (Acts 1:8) The return to Jerusalem may be a wrong turn, but then we see from out of our faith in the resurrection, that Jerusalem is not behind us but ahead of us. That is called Eschatology: knowing that the road to Jerusalem is to the ends of the earth and to the end of the ages; it represents the road to his glory.

This road leads through death to shalom. That is the liturgy of the Christ. This liturgy is politically colored and is lived along the way. Moreover it is ecumenical and not exclusive, intolerant, or just focused on an inner religious culture. Real liturgy is inclusive and is concentrated on the life possibilities of peoples and individuals under the heavens and on the earth. How inclusive the liturgy of Jerusalem is, Luke tells us in his famous Pentecost story where tongues of fire, wind and Spirit, brings people in motion. The peoples learn to understand each other. The ends of the earth are already present in this story of the beginning in Jerusalem.

Deurloo illustrates his point from another story, in an elaborate account of Paul's shipwreck on the way to Rome as a prisoner. There is a raging storm and everyone panics, fearing they will all drown. "A day was about to dawn, Paul urged them all to take some food, saying,

> Today is the fourteenth day that you have continued in suspense and without food, having taken nothing. Therefore I urge you to take some food; it will give you strength, since not a hair is to perish from the head of any of you.' And when he has said this, he took bread, and giving thanks to God in the presence of all he broke it and began to eat. Then they all were encouraged and ate some food themselves.
> Acts 27:33–36

It is like a déjà-vu, a multiplying of the bread that preceded the other story about a storm on the sea. They celebrate the LORD Supper in the midst of the storm. With one liturgical gesture the people in distress are encouraged, 'Not a sparrow, nor a hair of your head . . .' In the midst of death, we see life . . . A stranger, in a moment, highlights with one gesture, something extraordinary that bread, life, is present in the midst of death. To celebrate the liturgy is living under God's presence. Liturgy helps us cross the threshold. Liturgy is to be on the way from Jerusalem, from the inside to the outside, from yesterday to tomorrow, from the individual to the community. Is there a city without darkness? Is there a city when the sea is no more and the sun is no longer needed?

On the way, when we are most discouraged, we are to break bread and be encouraged. The vision of the end of the ages beckons us, "Then I saw a new heaven and a new earth . . . and the sea was no more . . . and I saw a holy city, new Jerusalem, coming out of heaven, prepared as a bride adorned for her husband; and I heard a great voice from the throne saying, 'Behold, the dwelling of God is with men. He will dwell with them, and they shall be his people, and God himself shall be with them; he will wipe away every tear from their eyes, and death shall be no more . . .'" (Rev 21:1-4) And we will proclaim this again and again even in the face of our doubting, fear and despair. (Matt 28:17, "and some doubted")

Along the way when we are doubting and afraid, confronted by the powers of the nations, but on the way, from Jerusalem to the ends of the earth, bread shall be broken to comfort and sustain us. The promise is to those who go the way of Abraham, to a land that the Lord will show him.

There is no hope in a 'land' like a political state of Israel and there is no hope in a 'geographical Jerusalem' as the centre of worship. That vision leads to genocide. Our vision will be to the ends of the earth and to the end of the times, breaking bread along the way.

7:14 h) The promise of the 'land' today

How are we today to look at the Promised Land now that the barriers have been broken down? How are we to actualize and implement the age-old calling of caring for the land and all peoples today? This calling echoes the first calling to be keepers of the Garden and to reign over the earth in God's name, as it was reiterated to Noah. (Gen 9:1-7)

Certainly it is not the practices of the present Israeli government and army. Their practices can only be called "an abomination." They have 'defiled' the land. The blood of tens of thousands victims cries out to the heavens, like Abel's blood did long ago. (Gen 4:11; 9:6; Matt 23:35) What God's judgment would be today in the face of Israel's abominations we don't know and have to leave to the Judge of all the earth.

The land stands for all the earth and all are called to care for it with justice and care for all. Today, we get a glimpse of how that charge to care for the land in God's name is to be implemented or actualized by the practices of many indigenous farmers, foresters and fishers. Some of them emphasize the need for inclusiveness, cooperatives, others emphasize, relying on regional markets, community well-being, self-governance, land tenure, water rights, stewardly practices, small size farms and fisheries, shared knowledge and local teaching, egalitarian relations that are inclusive and participatory, etc. The last chapter of *The Gods in Whom They Trusted*, contains many examples and summaries of these kinds of approaches by many indigenous peoples around the world. The practices of the Cree people are a great example of such actualization. Together they are faithful responses to God's call for caring for the land with communal caretaking, justice for all, inclusiveness, stewardship and solidarity with all people and the flourishing of all creatures. They stand under the promise and blessing of the LORD God about the land being fruitful.

For a current orientation see: *The Shortest History of Israel and Palestine: From Zionism to In to Intifadas and the Struggle for Peace*, by Michael Scott-Baumann; *The Hundred Years' War on Palestine: A History of Settler Colonialism and Resistance, 1917-2017*, by Rashid Khalidi; *Finding Messiah*, and *Healing the Schism*, by Jennifer M. Rosner; *Abraham's Promise: Judaism and Jewish-Christian Relations*, by Michael Wyschogrod; and *Being Jewish After the Destruction of Gaza: A Reckoning*, by Peter Beinart.

7:14i)   Dr. Andrew Judge's account of the land

Recently (April 28, 2024), Dr Andrew Judge (an Anishinaabe scholar and land restoration specialist), moved many people in our community with his inspiring two hour talk on "Indigenous Land Based practices; Braiding together Health, Environment and Community." Over against industrial and chemical agriculture (monocultures) he presented a very different vision with an eye to the future of many generations to come. As one respondent said, "Yesterday's event did something rare in that it got us to think differently about our world and how we live in it. Dr. Judge introduced us to a worldview that focuses on a different way to look at what our species is, and how we fit in. And he assigned us all with a different range of responsibilities, all of this presented with passion and good humor." This listener had heard the voice of the Creator, and the Spirit spoke and touched many other people as well. As Andrew said,"It seems there were some people very open to receiving the message from the Ancestors."

He emphasized several key points including: the complexity of societies before colonization; the value of understanding a radically different worldview that has now been replaced by the dominant perspective of our time, which is primarily focused on profit and consumption, and how we practice industrial and chemical agriculture; the critical importance of thinking generations ahead in how we work with the land and finally how important this knowledge is for our survival in this time of climate emergency.

He urged us to take action. This requires individual and communal action to experientially learn more together by observing and tending the natural environment in which we live.[9] His speech offers a new basis for learning from indigenous people where the Christian missionaries and the government has utterly failed.

7:14j) Billy Gauthier's account of the land.

A little while after this event we saw an exhibition by Billy Gauthier in the Kitchener-Waterloo Art Gallery in Ontario. He is an accomplished sculptor from Newfoundland and Labrador. Remarkably he integrates many aspects of life in his work including the environment, spirituality, relationships, community, the aesthetic and justice. He is both an artist and activist. He continues to be inspired by his close connection to the land and culture from North West River, Labrador.

His many sculptures share stories and life experiences. "My core belief is Inuit and our lands are synonymous: when our Nunangat is

---

9. Many of his presentations are available on line. See: "Itgan Project, gardening: medicines and plants." https://www.google.com/search?q=Dr.+Andrew+Judge%27+presentations&rlz=1C1GcEA.

harmed, we become harmed and when our Nunangat heals, we begin to heal. I understand my work to be a form of activism, carrying messages about the importance of caring for the land, animals and resources." His protests are against the problems that come with neo-liberal globalization and industrialization, especially of food processes, and the community impacts of mining and forestry companies. These corporate and government efforts are not centered around the needs of indigenous populations. His intricate sculptures are entirely made from natural materials like bone, feathers, baleen, antlers, stones, etc. They are astounding in their exquisite detail. Together they make a powerful statement.

His comments about one of his sculptures, that depicts, a refrigerator speak for itself. "The absence of fresh nutritious foods in the North contributes to a diverse range of health problems in Inuit society. Traditional meals of fish, caribou and other native foods are being substituted by imported foods from the South, which are often high in sugar, salt and saturated fats. Food insecurity affects 44 percent of households in Nunatsiavut and 70 percent in Nunavut. Rates of diabetes are at least three times higher in indigenous populations than in the general population. These issues are compounded by comparatively high rates of smoking and substance abuse, the lack of access to addictions treatment, mental health care, and medical services in communities." In Northern Frigidaire Diet, he reveals these demons that haunt the daily lives of so many people, adding, 'We have the most beautiful, healthy and uplifting grocery store in this world, which is our land.'" "Food becomes your brain, it becomes your eyes, it becomes your muscles that help you move throughout the day. It gives you life."

Because of this situation he went on a hunger strike when the government threatened to flood a large area that would have devastating effects for the Labrador Inuit. The high mercury levels that would result from the flooding would threaten their health, potentially poisoning the water and everything around it. His hunger strike, together with two other activists, lasted thirteen days. He could not imagine being unable to hunt, fish and eat the marine wildlife from this waterway. He risked his life to protect their way of life.

Taking in the rich details of the exhibit also made me feel ashamed because of our complicity in the destruction of the First nations' vision and way of life, including the Inuit. As Gauthier writes. "Before the arrival of settlers in Labrador angakkut (shamans) mediated politics, performed religious ceremonies, healed the sick and maintained the Inuit belief system. With the establishment of the first missions in the 18th century most Inuit spiritual practices were forbidden and thus lost. The loss of identity amongst Inuit today can largely be blamed on this unfortunate reality." Gauthier sculpts mainly in an effort to reestablish the presence of shamanism in Labrador.

Gauthier explains that, as he was told, "the shaman is often the greatest hunter in a group, the best at predicting weather, the one who understood the way animals reacted to the seasons, the one who best understood things are connected and where we fit in this world. The shaman was the leader that gave us hope during the harshest times and I believe one of the main reasons we thrived all over the North."

The description under a piece titled "Tungamejuk in the Spirit" is a fitting inclusion: "The environment is the foundation of Inuit existence. Many of Gauthier's pieces reflect the dependence of Inuit livelihood on a healthy, functioning ecosystem. Understanding this critical relationship will help to create a more sustainable future for both Inuit and the planet."[10]

Tragically missionaries to Canada's First Nations including the Inuit clearly had not read or absorbed the change in perspective by Kraemer, Newbigin, Bavick, and many others that formulated a new vision and perspective with regard to missions. The many images of his sculptures can be viewed on You Tube.

There are similar exciting and innovative agricultural approaches in other countries and continents by non-native people. The development of school gardens, urban farming and community gardens across the globe, including Africa, offer new possibilities and hope for self-sufficiency and food sovereignty.[11]

7:14k)   Alternatives for today: regenerative agriculture, fishing, and forestry

The challenge of every cooperative and small business is to keep developing a vision that reinforces doing justice to all the dimensions of life, to give everyone and everything its rightful place. Following such a direction is a daily challenge; it means following life-enhancing and life-honoring

---

10. Gauthier, Sila Exhibit: https://kwag.ca/exhibitions/billy-gauthier-sila

11. Berkes, F. and Adhikari, T. "Development and Conservation: Indigenous businesses and the UNDP Equator Initiative." Berkes et.al. (March 17, 2006), http://pubs.iied.org/pdfs/17274IIED.pdf 3.

directions, step by step. Ultimate security can only be found in the fullness of life. When we do, as the prophets of old proclaimed, there will be shalom, everything doing what it can be expected to do, the heavens responding to the earth, and the early and late rains responding to the pastures and the flocks, the olive trees and the vineyards responding to the rains and bearing fruit, then there will be peace and abundance. As we highlighted in chapter 7, the prophets' messages are against the violation and the disintegration of life that results from deifying the powers inherent in creation. Whatever ruthless empires there may be, they are all creatures and not gods; such is the prophet's message.

There are many promising accounts of other indigenous peoples and small-scale farmers, foresters and fishers from around the world. TerreAfrica has published one such report called, "Sustainable Land Management in Practice," (SLM); "Guidelines and Best Practices in Sub-Sahara Africa" (2011), which contains 47 case studies. The *World Overview of Conservation Approaches and Technologies* (WOCAT) along with "Where the Land is Greener" (2007), reports on 42 soil and water conservation examples. In 2013 the *UN Convention to Combat Desertification (UNCCD)* published "Land for Life, Managing Land Sustainability for better Livelihoods," covering forty innovative approaches. Together these reports cover a wide range of methods reflecting both indigenous practices and knowledge and the insights of agricultural sciences and the contributions of modern technologies. The case studies in "Sustainable Land Management in Practice" cover twelve main examples of a wide variety of approaches. The Ashden project awards many winning projects about climate solution in action each year. The last chapter of *The Gods in Whom They Trusted* (freely available on line) contains many references and evaluations of these practices by many indigenous peoples around the world.

In North Amertica there are also several great examples of alternative approaches to agriculture. To mention just a few:

Gabe Brown, *Dirt to Soil; one family's journey into regerative agriculture* (2018)

Rob Quinn and Liz Carlisle, *Grain by Grain; a quest to revive ancient wheat, rural jobs, and healthy foods,* (2019)

Darrin Qualman, *Tackling the farm crisis and the climate crisis,* NFU, (2019) as well as *Civilization Critical, energy, food, nature and the future,* (2019).

Together they are faithful responses to God's call for caring for the land with communal care taking, justice for all, inclusiveness, stewardship, and solidarity with all people and the flourishing of all creatures. All stand under the promise and blessing of the LORD God about the land being fruitful.

Ultimately these different practices provide an alternative to global capitalism, not as a great new ideology and system like capitalism, Marxism or socialism. With its emphasis on cooperatives, community well-being, self-governance, land rights, small size farms and fisheries, water rights, local and regional distribution, shared knowledge and local teaching, egalitarian relations that are inclusive and participatory, etc. These are the building blocks of an alternative approach. It is a faithful response to God's good intention for life.

These are glimpses, none are perfect. It remains a constant calling and task. Together they hold the promise of a future fulfillment. Meanwhile all of us are to be on the way as earth keepers, acting, protesting, witnessing, and breaking bread along the way with all who want to join in. The promises remain, "but they shall sit every man under his vine and under his fig tree, and none shall make them afraid." (Mic 4:4), or as the prophet Zechariah put is, "In that day, says the Lord of hosts, every one of you will invite his neighbor under his vine and his fig tree" (Zech 3:10, cf. Isa 36:16, 17). Meanwhile we will protest and take action against all violation of God's earth, in hope.

CHAPTER 8

A new god image?!

8:1   Introduction: Preamble

FOR MANY PEOPLE THE perspective on Genesis and Joshua presented above calls for a very different or 'new' God image ('totally new' to me). Throughout we will pay special attention to how God presents himself and how he wants to be known. The scriptures present many images of God: God as King, Judge, Warrior, Father, Mother, Friend, Liberator, Husband, Wife and other images. The following pages contain a summary of my understanding of the God of the scriptures and the love affair of this God with all humanity and their home, the earth. It is a remarkable, often moving, and humbling story of the God of the scriptures.

In my upbringing there was a pervasive sense of doom and resignation. Although we went to church twice every Sunday and my father read from the Bible three times a day and prayed a standard prayer before and after every meal, there was no joy. The Bible sections were never discussed nor were the prayers ever personal. It was a joyless faith. Judgment was never far away nor the mystery of God's eternal council and election ('het moet je maar gegeven zijn," if you are lucky 'it will be given to you', if not . . .) There is a family secret that a second cousin of my father committed suicide because he believed he was not elected and decided there was no sense in living any longer; he was doomed anyway. It was the culture of the day in many conservative, reformed churches, full of melancholy, resignation and longing. It reminds me of the Mennonite's piano concerto by Victor Davies with its sadness and longing, incorporating some of their favorite German hymns.

The only thing I remember of all those sermons, prayers, Bible readings, was the salutation at the beginning and the end of the church services. Our tall minister had a warm and melodious voice that always touched me. "Our help is in the name of the Lord who has created the heavens and the earth; who keeps covenant forever and never abandons the works of his hands. Grace and peace be to you from Jesus Christ." It was the only thing that touched me to the core of my being as a very fearful and lonely boy without any inner connection to anyone. Of course I was aware of God's judgment and punishment that dovetailed perfectly with my overactive sense of guilt and shame. In this context faith in Jesus and salvation through his blood had no meaning for me.

In church, the Westerkerk in Delft, we had our (assigned?) regular place on the second side balcony from where we could look down on the front rows where the lawyers, business leaders, engineers and other notables were seated. I think my father suffered all his life from these class distinctions, coming from a poor working class family on one of the islands below Rotterdam. On the middle balcony in the back some of the older young people would congregate, especially during the second 'catechism' sermons and play cards to the dismay of many ministers who often had to reprimand them. I could not begin to imagine daring to be so 'disrespectful', even though I too was bored most of the time.

It highlights that a god image is not just a particular doctrine of God or a belief. It has a strong social dimension that can characterize a whole faith community and culture. It becomes the spiritual air a religious community breathes that lingers for generations. It penetrates the hymns and prayers and social values. As an example, the very first sermon I preached was about election primarily based on Berkouwer's book, *Studies in Dogmatics: Divine Election*. It gave me some comfort to think that we can never talk about election apart from Christ. ("Elect in Christ"). Looking at all the scripture passages now about God's wrath and punishment *and* God's compassion was like a great relief and comfort. It is interesting to me that many of the new studies of God's wrath come from ultraorthodox ministers and theologians. It challenges everyone to question the background of their God-image. Theologians are not always sufficiently aware of the social context in which doctrines and confessions of faith function.

Without a new God image our witness, protests, and faith will remain limited or impotent. Do we really have an alternative to the dominate religion of today, the global, neo-liberal ideology? This is a story about the god of the scriptures we hardly ever met in Sunday school, Daily Vacation Bible School or catechism. Dr. Gispen, my catechism teacher tried hard to answer all my questions and searching, but teaching twelve year old kids right after the war was not his gift, even though he was a very talented, kind man and had many other gifts.

Most of us have met the god of morality, of being good or bad, or of the confessional, admitting to 'impure' thoughts, but never the god of the Scriptures. Many have met the god of orthodoxy, of the right doctrines, like god's immutability, sovereignty, election, and so on. Many others have met the god of 'Jesus saves us from our sins'. Many have met or heard about the god of damnation and hell, the god of violence and wrath, but seldom the god of the scriptures.

The god of the scriptures is not the god of the evangelicals and the fundamentalists and literalistic interpretations (Jesus saves us from our sins); nor is he the god of the right doctrines of the Presbyterians, the Lutherans and the Reformed churches; nor is he the god of rationalistic theology, nor is he the god of being good middle class citizens, of morality and humanism.

Besides helpful insights, the history of exegesis or interpretation has deeply affected our God image. It is often a sad account of many distortions throughout the ages, fragmenting the text, often obscuring the message and its meaning. We have just come through a long period in which the 'critical historical method' dominated and distorted interpretation, dividing the text into little segments and assigning each piece to a different tradition, time and editor, losing the message and its meaning or leaving its meaning to the interpretation of ministers and priests. In spite of this history of interpretation, the word was preserved and proclaimed. This is not an anti-intellectual reaction. The history of interpretation has its own irreplaceable value and needs to be pursued academically. My reactions express my deep disappointment and frustration in reading theological studies and commentaries and my frustration with all the time I spent in the University of Toronto's library and theological colleges' libraries, trying to find an alternative to the Christianity which still surrounded me, and in which I was raised.

8:2 The god of the scriptures

The god of the scriptures is a mystery and surprise. I wrote the word "god" with a small letter, because the word "god" is a general or generic name, like any other name, which does not say anything about what particular god we are talking about. In this sense, 'god' is a general category, There are many gods, (gods by the dozen). In the language of the Scriptures, they are all idols or "non-gods," "scarecrows in a cucumber field," that do not live up to their reputation, that do not do anything. In the Scriptures this does not mean that they are not taken seriously. On the contrary, the first commandment reads, "You shall have no other gods before me."(Exodus 20:3). It is a constant refrain, in the scriptures.

But who is this God of Israel? What is special about him? Israel confesses that "Yahweh is God," for he created a people for himself out of the land of death and slavery. Out of his great mercy and moved by compassion, he calls his people to return from slavery and exile. "Yahweh, he is god." Whatever this mysterious name may mean, it says something decisive about "Yahweh. From then on "God" can only mean, "the special God of Israel." When we talk about the God of the Bible, we cannot talk about 'god' in general, but only about the "God of Israel, Yahweh" "Yahweh, he is our God" and the church may repeat it after Israel, "Yahweh, the God of Israel, he is God," also for us.

God's Name distinguishes him from all other 'gods' or powers. His Name is above all other names. ". . . in the midst of the gods he holds judgment" (Ps 82:1); ". . . O give thanks to the God of gods" (Ps 136:2); "For the Lord is a great God, and a great King above all gods. (Ps 95:3); ". . . There is none like thee among the gods, O LORD nor are there any works like thine." and ". . . unite my heart to fear thy Name." (Ps 86:8, 11) God's name is revelation. For this reason his Name is to be praised. "I will sing praise to thy Name, O Most High." (Ps 9:2) "O LORD, our LORD, how majestic is your name in all the earth" (Psalm 8:1) and many other references. God's Name stands central, "I AM WHO I AM . . . I am has sent me to you . . . this is my name forever . . ." (Exod 3:14) God is a 'human' God. Jesus Christ is the confirmation, and fulfillment of the one name of God, Yahweh. The Name expresses God's faithfulness, "and lo, I am with you always, to the close of the age." (Matt 28:20) He is approachable.

The Name is God, the true and living God, to be known to humanity. He is truly the God who entered into a relationship with humanity.

He is not an all-God, a Creator God, as the all-Powerful God, but a particular God with specific virtues. He is Yahweh Sebaoth, the LORD of hosts. As Miskotte puts it: "The Name = Revelation; the Name = Yahweh; the Name = Jesus Christ."

And again as Miskotte writes,

> Love means that God becomes involved with people to whom God is not obliged, and in such a way that God is and remains ungraspable.
>
> It is the drama of God's initiative to call humankind into the communion of divine love: to meet them, bless them, delight them, and test them. Such drama summarizes the holy history.
>
> Some say that Song of Songs was 'originally' a collection of love songs. This is doubtless true...This does not embarrass us. On the contrary, the sensuality and ardor, the passion, the sweetness of these songs assures us that the love of God is not a general idea, not a universal force of life, but a personal engagement: a personal loyalty. The holy history is a history of love. The unity of divine virtues, proceeding from the assumption that their unity is actually Love. God is Love.[1]

All the other names used of God are further explanations of God's essence, like the name Elohim, El Shaddai, the LORD of Hosts, the Father, and others. Together, they illuminate the one Name. In the fullness of time he fulfills the meaning of his name in Jesus Christ, God-with-us.

Elohim, which means 'god'; it too is a proper name. The God Yahweh, this one is Elohim, God! "Know that the LORD is God! It is he that made us, and we are his; we are his people, and the sheep of his pasture . . . bless his name." (Ps 100:3, 4)

El Shaddai is usually translated with God Almighty. It means "God of the mountain." He rules over the future by a divine miracle. His power is a very particular power, namely the power that brought about the birth of Isaac from the shriveled loins of Abraham and the barren womb of Sarah. Yahweh, the 'nameless name' is an aspect of the Name that is Revelation itself. Yahweh, the revealed and hidden Name, which is the exercise of power against death itself. This one holds all power, even death.

> . . . The LORD appeared to Abram, and said to him, 'I am God Almighty'. . . And I will make my covenant between me and you, and will multiply you exceedingly.'
> Genesis 17:1,2; cf. 28:3;35:6; 48:3; Exodus 6:3; Revelations 19:6

---

1. Miskotte, *Biblical ABCs*, 28; 46–54.

A NEW GOD IMAGE?!

The LORD of Hosts means, LORD of angels, LORD of stars, LORD of Israel's army. He is the LORD of history. He takes no rest before the final victory is won. God is not alone in this, he is surrounded and reinforced by legions of arch angels, thrones, powers, messengers. "The LORD of Hosts is with us" (Psalm 46:11), the Warrior, the Commander, the Sovereign of history. Yahweh and all other titles, proclaim that God is a particular God with specific attributes. He is the LORD of History, Yahweh Sebaoth, The LORD of Hosts.

> Who is the King of glory?
> The LORD strong and mighty . . .
> . . . The LORD of Hosts
> He is the King of glory!
> Psalm 24:8–10

Then there is the title, *Father* as he is called in many places in the Old Testament. "Father of the fatherless and protector of widows is God in his holy habitation" (Ps 68:5); "As a father pities his children, so the LORD pities those who fear him." (Psalm 103:13 The LORD is called Father as Jesus taught us to pray, "Our Father who art in heaven." And through him and his Spirit we can call God, Abba, Father, too in the same way as God can be called the Mighty One, the LORD of Hosts. As Paul puts it,

> . . . yet for us there is one God, the Father, from whom are all things and for whom we exist, and one LORD, Jesus Christ, through whom are all things and through whom we exist.
> I Corinthians 8:5, 6

> [Jesus Christ] emptied himself, taking the form of a servant, being born in the likeness of men . . . Therefore God has highly exalted him and bestowed on him the name which is above every name.
> Philippians 2:7–9

However, does the church still say something different when it confesses in the Apostolic Creed: "I believe in God the Father, Almighty, Creator of heaven and earth." Any Roman citizen could affirm those words, a Creator god, maker of the cosmos, an Al-god (Al-mighty, al-powerful, al-knowing, al-present, al-ways or time-less, etc.). But is he a Father? Again, who would object to an Al-father or Al-Mother? Over against these general references, the scriptures talk about a very special god, Yahweh, the God of Israel's becoming (genesis) in the midst of all the nations of the earth.

When the scriptures sometimes apply the word Father, and by exception the word Mother, to Yahweh (the scriptures originated in a male dominated society), then the word is totally taken up by the Name. That Name is 'explained' by stories of his Word/Deeds; stories around the exile from Egypt, the great turnabout of Yahweh and the return of a remnant from Babylon. As Isaiah 64:8 has it, "Yet, O LORD, thou art our father (cf. Isaiah 63:16; Deuteronomy 32:6; God as mother, "As one whom his mother comforts, so I will comfort you." Isa 66:13)

In Hosea 11:1 we read, ". . . out of Egypt I called my son." There, in Egypt, it all started. That is where Moses was told to say to Pharaoh, "Thus says the LORD, Israel is my first-born son, and I say to you, 'Let my son go that he may serve me; if you refuse to let him go, behold, I will slay your first-born son." Pharaoh answered, "Who is (this) LORD, that I should heed his voice and let Israel go? I do not know the LORD (this god) and moreover I will not let Israel go." (Exod 4:22, 23; 5:2)

In connection with the exile we hear the same words, ". . . for I am a father to Israel, and Ephraim is my first-born." (Jeremiah 31:9). In the Apostolic Confession the word "Father" is specified further in the second article by, "Jesus Christ, his only-begotten son." If we understand the credo (not just historically) but biblically, then our focus goes immediately to the opening of Matthew, about the "book of the genealogy of Jesus Christ, the son of David, the son of Abraham." (Matt 1:1) He is the Messianic king that represents all Israel. What typifies Israel? "Out of Egypt I have called my son, out of slavery and death." Then Matthew tells of Joseph's flight to Egypt and his return to be able to recite Hosea and apply it to Jesus.

Whenever we talk biblically about God, then we are talking about the *Father of Israel, the Father of Jesus the Messiah, his first-born Son.* Then we need to recite the story about the exodus from Egypt and at the same time about the great-turn-about (in Yahweh), the story of the return from exile. As the God of Israel, God has compassion on his exiled people when all seems lost and they are scattered among the nations. As the God of Israel, Yahweh, like a father has compassion for his children. "The LORD is merciful and gracious, slow to anger and abounding in steadfast love . . . as a *father* pities his children, so the LORD pities those who fear him." (Ps 103: 8, 13) For the apostle Paul, Yahweh is the "*Father* of our LORD Jesus Christ, the Father of mercies and God of all comfort." (II Corinthians 1:3) Anyone who prays the Lord's Prayer, by Jesus' own authority, in the first petition, prays, "Our *Father* ... hallowed be thy name." (Matt 6:9) Yahweh, he is God. Since he reveals himself in his deeds, stories need to be told, otherwise, like Pharaoh we can only say, "Yahweh? That God I do not know."

Few have met the God of the Hebrew scriptures, who has a special name, namely, Yahweh, the LORD of LORDs, the mysterious God who made himself known in his deeds in the history with his people and all mankind and the earth. Many of us have met the god of morality, of being good or bad, or of the confessional, but not the god of the Scriptures. Many have met the god of orthodoxy, of the right doctrines, like god's immutability, sovereignty, election and reprobation, and so on. Many others have met the god of 'Jesus saves us from our sins'; many have met or heard about the god of damnation and hell, the god of violence and wrath, but not the god of the scriptures.

The god of the scriptures is not the god of the evangelicals and the fundamentalists (Jesus saves us from our sins and other literalistic interpretations); nor is he the god of the right doctrines of the Presbyterians, the Lutherans or the Reformed churches; nor is he the god of rationalistic scholastic theology, nor is he the god of being good middle class citizens, of morality and humanism. The God of the scriptures is Yahweh, the God of Israel (and through them of all mankind).

8:3 *Yahweh's love affair with all people and the earth*

Who is this remarkable god according to the witness of the scriptures? To really fathom something of God's love we need to continue to listen and let the scriptures themselves speak!

The consistent witness of the Hebrew Scriptures and the New Testament is that *God is love*. His love for humanity and his earth stands central. In spite of all theological speculation about God's holiness, righteousness, wrath and judgments, even in the Old Testament God's love stands central. Let's listen to the Hebrew Scriptures first.

The mystery of God's Name is made plain by the many virtues or attributes the scriptures mention, like holy, righteous, wise, merciful, long suffering, truthful, enraged, faithful, etc. None of these adjectives can be played out against one another. Together they illuminate the Name. They clarify each other. All the key or core words elucidate the Name and all the concrete manifestations of the Name. The conquest of Canaan, for example, is a teaching, or exemplary story about the Name of a very specific God and contains all his virtues, and not just a 'horrifying', judging God. The Name includes all his other designations and must be understood in that light, as we highlighted in the previous chapter. No one adjective can be played out against the others. Together they illuminate the Name, Yahweh. Although all these adjectives are not just 'anthropomorphic' ways of talking about God, the 'Wholly Other', but in all the differences they can indicate something essential about God. For example, God's righteousness is totally different from our righteousness. Yet they communicate the essence. Compare, H. Berkhof's account of the symbolic language of revelation, in his *Christian Faith* (1993, 69–75).

In God's love, is the deepest motivation for the election of Israel, and their liberation from slavery. This love is a free choice of God and does not depend on the special worth or merit of Israel. On the contrary, God's love is not only his free choice, but also his deepest emotion. When his people do not respond to his love, God is jealous. God becomes angry when the people turn away from him and do not follow his life-giving commandments. From these emotional reactions it is apparent that God longs for his peoples' love in response. God does not only show his love in these special events, but that he, himself is loving.

> The LORD passed before him, and proclaimed, 'the LORD, the LORD, a God merciful and gracious, slow to anger, and abounding in steadfast love and faithfulness, keeping steadfast love for thousands, forgiving iniquity and transgression and sin, but who will by no means clear the guilty . . . pray thee, go in the midst of us, Although it is a stiff-necked people . . . and take us for thy inheritance.' And he said, Behold, I make a covenant. Before all your people I will do marvels, such as have not been wrought in all the earth or in any nation . . .
> Exodus 34:6–10

> The LORD is gracious and merciful, slow to anger and abounding in steadfast love.
> The LORD is good to all, and his compassion is over all that he has made.
> Psalm 145:8–9; cf. Ps 86:5, 145:8, 9

> . . . but they stiffened their neck and appointed a leader to return to their bondage in Egypt. But thou art a God ready to

forgive, gracious and merciful slow to anger and abounding in steadfast love, and did not forsake them. Even when they made for themselves a molten calf and said, 'This is your god who brought you up out of Egypt . . .
Nehemiah 9:16–18

I have loved you with an everlasting love; therefore I have continued my faithfulness to you.
Jeremiah 31:3

For a brief moment I forsook you, but with great compassion I will gather you.
In overflowing wrath for a moment I hid my face from you,
but with everlasting love I will have compassion on you,
says the LORD, your Redeemer.
Isaiah 54:7–8; (cf. verses 9, 10)

This love of God is described as "forgiving, merciful and gracious," in relation to our guilt and as "loving kindness" in regard to our suffering. They are all expressions of God's love. In his love God wants to be with all people. When God hates, it is with regard to practices God abhors and people who do such things. His hate is a reaction to peoples' unrighteousness and evil. God's anger is temporary; his love is eternal. "For his anger is but for a moment, and his favor is for a lifetime." (Ps 30:5; Mic 7:18)

The scriptures present a remarkable story about God's love affair with all humanity and his creation, the earth. The story has a lot of ups and downs, to the point where we would despair. And yet each time Yahweh comes to the rescue. He takes the initiative and breaks through our abandonment and violation of his love. He is a God of a tender love affair, a God who has compassion, but also a God that gets hurt and feels violated and rejected. People have often chosen non-gods instead of the Maker of heaven and earth. God is love and at the same time a God of justice and wrath, like the wrath and anger of a spurned lover. He presents himself as almighty and holy, but he is also vulnerable and servant-like. Each time his love wins out even in and through judgment.

This god, from the very beginning, is pictured as having a love affair with all creatures of the earth, starting in Genesis and from there on. Abraham walked with god and David was a man after God's own heart, and so on. Israel is portrayed as Yahweh's bride. It is a moving and humbling story.

8:4 Yahweh's anger and wrath

Even when God's people are unfaithful and abandon him for other gods, (like the fertility gods of ancient times; or the worship of the divine emperor of the Holy Roman Empire or the power of the pope and rulers of the holy Catholic Church during the Middle Ages; or the rationalism of the post-reformation time, or with today's neo-liberalism's religion of greed, profit and power (and its core confession of faith: 'in progress is our faith with science and technology as its servants') this God keeps his promises. Even when they abandon him, he still reconciles himself with them, even if they behave like harlots and pimps; he courts them all over again and takes them back. There are many examples of this; even though they, and we, go through judgment, (the flood, The Red Sea, the Jordan, the exile and a remnant that returned), because of god's doing, his initiative, and of his longsuffering. That is also our hope for today even in the face of the disintegration of the earth and the suffering of millions of people.

This does not mean a kind of 'universalism' or salvation of all humanity, without justice being done. It is in and through his judgments and disasters (through death) that the chosen people were changed and entered the Promised Land. Idolatry is taken seriously because it brings untold suffering and death to millions of people today and in the past. The scriptures are always on the side of 'the poor, the widow, the orphan and the stranger that is in your midst' and against empires and unjust rulers.

It is crucial to see the book of Joshua, for example, (often seen as a book of violent conquests and extermination) as an integral part of the 'former prophets' (Joshua, Judges, I, II Samuel and I, II Kings), followed by the later prophets. This is the context for understanding the reality of Yahweh's wrath. The long journey of the people of Israel ends in banishment from the Promised Land. From the beginning they stood under the judgment of Yahweh, because "they did what was evil in the sight of Yahweh." Again and again they violated their covenant relationship with Yahweh and served idols. Each time they evoked Yahweh's wrath and were punished.

They violated their deepest bond of loyalty with their Creator, Liberator, Judge and King. They betrayed their relationship time and again. Yahweh punished them as they had been warned even from before entering the Promised Land. All the curses of Deuteronomy 28:15–67 had become true. As a result they were abandoned by Yahweh and given over to their enemies, ending in exile.

The many references to Yahweh's wrath and anger must be understood first of all in this context, a context of ultimate betrayal, giving their loyalty to the idols, the no-gods instead of their Creator.

> The LORD is a jealous god and avenging, the LORD is avenging and wrathful ... Who can stand before his indignation? Who can endure the heat of his anger? His wrath is poured out like fire ...
> Nahum 1:2, 6

> I will stretch out my hand against Judah, and against all the inhabitants of Jerusalem;
> and I will cut off from this place the remnant of Baal and the name of the idolatrous priests;
> those who bow down on the roofs to the host of heavens ...
> those who have turned back from following the LORD, who do not seek the LORD or inquire of him.
>
> The great day of the LORD is near, near and hastening fast ...
> A day of wrath is that day, a day of distress and anguish,
> a day of ruin and devastation ...
> Zephaniah 1:4–6, 14, 15

In Deuteronomy 27 and 28 and the following chapters the curses of mount Ebal are clearly spelled out, as well as the blessings of keeping the covenant with Yahweh. "See I have set before you this day life and good, death and evil ..." (Deut 30:15) But again and again they

> ... did what was evil in the sight of the Lord, and served the Baals and the Ashtaroth, the gods of Syria, the gods of Sidon, the gods of Moab, the gods of the Ammonites, and the god of the Philistines; and they forsook the LORD, and did not serve him. And the anger of the LORD was kindled against Israel ...
> Judges 10:6, 7

The prophets understood the deepest reasons for Yahweh's wrath and revenge.

> Thus says the LORD God to Jerusalem: Your origin and your birth are of the land of the Canaanites; your father was an Amorite, and your mother a Hittite. And as for your birth, on the day you were born, your navel string was not cut, nor were

you washed with water to cleanse you, nor rubbed with salt, nor swathed with bands. No one pitied you, to do any of these things to you out of compassion . . .

When I passed you again and looked upon you, behold, you were at the age for love; and I spread my skirt over you, and covered your nakedness; yea, I plighted my troth to you and entered into a covenant with you, says the LORD God, and you became mine. Then I bathed you and washed off your blood from you, and anointed you with oil I clothed you . . . And I decked you with ornaments . . . You grew exceedingly beautiful . . . And your renown went forth among the nations . . . But you trusted in your beauty, and played the harlot . . . So I will satisfy my fury on you, because you have not remembered the days of your youth and have enraged me . . . behold, I will requite your deeds upon your head, says the LORD God.

Ezekiel 16:3–5, 8–11, 13–15, 42, 43 (cf. Hos 11:1–4)

Again, we cannot play out one characteristic, of God, over against his other designations. God's wrath can only be understood if we understand something of his love.

8:5 Yahweh as Father, Mother, Parent, Friend and Lover

There are four main images the scripture uses to describe Yahweh's love: that of a parent, a father and mother; a friend; and a lover; or husband and wife.

The way Yahweh relates to Israel as a young bride stands in sharp contrast to Israel's own harlotry. They look for fertility from the idols, but Yahweh is the real husband and lover that opens wombs, gives children, gives abundant lambs among the flocks and plentiful harvests. They don't have to engage in the fertility rites of the Canaanites to ensure offspring, lambs and grain. Yahweh is the real fertility god as well as the weather god, the storm god, the real estate god, and the landlord. It is hard for us twentieth century people to understand the depth and intimacy of the covenant relationship, the partnership between Yahweh and his people.

The covenant relation was not some cold, impersonal, legal arrangement between Yahweh and his people, like some legal contract. It started with Yahweh's promises to Abraham, his friend, of the Promised Land and many children. They are to be a holy people, totally dedicated to Yahweh and following his good order for life. They are to be sons and daughters of Yahweh. The profoundness of Yahweh's agreements and of

A NEW GOD IMAGE?!

loyal and trustworthy relations and promises may be difficult for us to understand. We tend to hang on to our guilt and shame, our pride and self-justifications; Yahweh's covenant love is hard for us to understand. Your sins are covered over . . . How can that be?! "Even though they are red like crimson, they shall become white like snow." How can that be!? (Isa 1:18; Ps 51:7; Rev 7:14).

The prophet Jeremiah uses the image of a distressed parent and the distress about wayward children to express the Father/Yahweh's deep love for Israel. In spite of all Yahweh's care and parenting they have turned their back on their Father,

> I thought how I would set you among my sons, and give you a pleasant land, a heritage most beauteous of all nations. And I thought you would call me, My Father, and would not turn from following me.
> Jeremiah 3:19

Instead we read,

> . . . who say to a tree, 'You are my Father' and to a stone, 'You gave me birth'.
> Jeremiah.2:27

As a crushed parent whose children have turned against their father and abandoned him, Yahweh weeps tears of sorrow and pain,

> O that my head were waters,
> and my eyes a fountain of tears,
> that I might weep day and night
> for the slain of the daughter of my people!
> Jeremiah 9:1

Even the rejection by Israel does not stop Yahweh from calling his wayward children back, again and again,

> Return, O faithless sons,
> I will heal your faithlessness.
> . . . 'Return, faithless Israel,
> says the LORD.
> I will not look on you in anger,
> for I am merciful,
> says the LORD,
> I will not be angry forever.
> Only acknowledge your guilt
> that you rebelled against the LORD your God

> and scattered your favors
> among strangers under every green tree,
> and that you have not obeyed my voice,
> says the LORD.
> Return, O faithless children, says the LORD . . .
>> Jeremiah, 3:22, 11–14

In an agricultural society with many barren areas and a harsh climate, totally dependent on early and late rains, and occasional plagues of locusts, it might have been very tempting to appeal to the fertility and weather gods for offspring and good harvests. It might have been tempting to practice fertility rites at all the high places. The many household gods (Rachel - Genesis 31:33-35; Jacob, Genesis 35:4) and many fertility images discovered by archaeologists testify to how widespread this practice might have been. Maybe it is not so surprising that many of the violent texts also have to do with sexual images. It would be illuminating to explore all the other names used of God, which would be helpful for a Bible study group.

8:6 Yahweh's forgiveness and compassion

Yahweh feels his deep love with his whole being and expects the same from his people. Yahweh has a love affair with his people. For many of us that means, we have to change our God image that we inherited from Sunday school or church. This was not a god-image I was ever exposed to. Although it is an 'anthropomorphic' way of talking about God, we nevertheless have to take in the testimony of the prophets that Yahweh's anger and wrath are very real, including his judgments. Yahweh loves with all his heart and reacts with strong emotions, both ways, with wrath and anger and with love and compassion. See Talstra's article "Exile and pain: a chapter from the story of God's emotions." (In: B. Becking and D. Human, eds. *Exile and Suffering*. (2009)

Each of the passages that talk about Yahweh's wrath and judgment is followed by promises of forgiveness and restoration.

> How can I give you up O Ephraim!
> How can I hand you over, O Israel! . . .
> My heart recoils within me,
> my compassion grows warm and tender,
> I will not execute my fierce anger . . .
>> Hosea 11:8, 9

Or as the prophet Joel confesses,

> Who is a God like thee, pardoning iniquity and passing over transgression for the remnant of his inheritance? He does not retain his anger for ever because he delights in steadfast love.
> Micah 7:18

The prophet Isaiah can put it even more strongly,

> For I will not contend for ever,
> nor will I always be angry;
> for from me proceeds the spirit,
> and I have made the breath of life.
> Because of the iniquity of his covetousness I was angry,
> I smote him, I hid my face and was angry ...
> I have seen his ways,
> but I will heal him;
> I will lead him and requite him with comfort ...
> Isaiah 57:16–18

> Come now, let us reason together, says the LORD:
> though your sins are like scarlet,
> they shall be as white as snow;
> though they be red like crimson,
> they shall become like wool,
> if you are willing and obedient
> you shall eat the good of the land ...
> Isaiah 1:18, 19

All are welcomed by this God, none are excluded, but neither is it a foregone conclusion (Ezekiel). In the doing of the commandments, in the keeping of the covenant, in repentance and mending their ways they will find forgiveness for their betrayal and be restored to their relationship with their Liberator and their covenant partner. That is the Good News of the Torah and the former and later prophets.

Our Father is a loving God. What that love means we can read and know from the surprising ways He made himself known. Two such events that stand central are choosing of Israel, their liberation from slavery in Egypt and return from Exile in Babylon and sending Jesus Christ. In love God has given his Son. It is a giving love. Many of us need to drink in deeply and absorb these words and let it cleanse our misunderstandings and indoctrination of who God is. The attributes of God are the attributes of God's actions. God's acts determine our knowledge of God's virtues (Miskotte).

8:7 Yahweh's holiness

To describe Yahweh's love, H. Berkhof in his *Christian Faith*, (1986; 1993, 121–149), felt compelled to add the word "holy," a 'holy love'. He did so to emphasize that in his loving God remains the transcendent one, the Almighty One that "dwells in unapproachable light." (1Timothy 6:16) For it is precisely in his Godly power that he can love us and far surpass the limitations and failures of our earthly fatherhood and motherhood, parenthood, partnership, and friendship. He objects to the word 'immanence' as a contrast to transcendence because it is too philosophically loaded. Instead he uses the words 'God's bending down to us, his condescending'. This description may be sufficient to describe God's love. It is precisely in his holiness, majesty and might that he loves us, with all the limitations and faults of our earthly relationships. These are the images in which the scriptures describe God's love.

Given the cultural, religious history and climate of many orthodox reformed communities, it might have been better not to add the word 'holy' to God's love, for it would be too easy once again to avoid experiencing God's love, given its traditional emphasis on God's eternal council, election and reprobation. We could hide again in God's un-approachableness and un-touchableness. For a holy God it is intolerable that people should turn away from him. When used in regard to people, it indicates that they are a separate people and dedicated to God. When used of God, it means that God is dedicated to himself. "It is not for your sake, O house of Israel, that I am about to act, but for the sake of my holy name, which you have profaned among the nations to which you came." (Ezekiel 36:22–32). As the 'wholly other' he has revealed himself. God remains LORD, the Other, and as such he reveals himself to us, God-with-us. He is "The Holy One in your midst, and I will not come to destroy." (Hosea 11:9). "I will help you, says the LORD; your Redeemer is the Holy One of Israel" (Isa 41:14; 43:3–14; 48:17; 49:7; 54:5; 57:15). In his love God bends down to us, freely, remaining himself, in his being God, in his transcendence and in his holiness. It is as transcendence, in immanence; that is how God is present.

We need to learn to say straight forwardly again, God has a love affair with humanity and his creation. As Miskotte puts it, "Revelation is the Love of the Lover, not of the beloved; but the word, the answer (the prayer, the thanksgiving, and the praise) is the love of the beloved." God is the one who loves."[2]

In his love God is also righteous and just. God hates all injustice and is grieved in his being by all violations of the other. 'God is love' and 'has a love affair with humanity' remains hard to say straight out for many of us. God wants to dwell among all people. Perhaps the words 'transcendence in immanence' can capture some of that notion. In his being with us and for us he remains the transcendent one, the Holy One and Righteous One. That is how he can be with us, as in the suffering, death and resurrection of Jesus Christ. As his Father he suffers with Christ in his defenseless overpowering might. He suffers with us. God's power and might are the power of his love and the power of his righteous deeds. It remains a divine love.

The Holy One of Israel is the same God as the Redeemer God. God is for us, not against us. The judging God is the same God as the merciful and forgiving God. (See the following chapter 9, section 1, God's surprising and unheard of 'turn about' in the return from exile, because of his mercy.)

8:8 The New Testament witness

In keeping with the whole of the Old Testament, the New Testament repeats this testimony. If we want to know who God is, Jesus says, read "Moses and the prophets." God's deeds reveal who he is for his people and the whole earth. For Jesus, the disciples and the apostles, these were the authoritative scriptures. Without the Hebrew Scriptures we cannot understand the gospels and the apostolic letters. That is why the subtitle of this book reads, 'A re-discovery of the Old Testament'.

Most well-known perhaps are the words of the letters of John and his gospel. God's love is a giving love. He loves the return of his love from all peoples. He wants to give of himself to live in love with all. He loves sinners and unrighteous people. He loves us. In Jesus Christ, God makes a choice for all people. In his love God wants to be with all people and for all. He does not want to be God without people or be against people.

---

2. Miskotte, *Biblical ABCs*, 72, 54.

> He who does not love does not know God; for God is love. In this the love of God was made manifest among us, that God sent his only Son into the world, so that we might live through him. ... We love, because he first loved us.
>
>   1 John 4:8, 9, 19 (cf. John 3:16)

The God image of the Old Testament makes the God image of the New Testament more understandable and closer to our experience. The New Testament echoes the same vision. In the doing we shall be saved. Jesus is continually moved with compassion for the people, for they are like sheep without a shepherd. (Matt. 9:36; 14:14; 15:32)

As Paul says,

> ... what a welcome we had among you, and how you turned to God from idols, to serve a living and true God,
>
>   I Thessalonians 1:9

The consistent witness is that Yahweh judges in righteousness.

> When the Son of man comes in his glory, and all the angels with him, then he will sit on his glorious throne. Before him will be gathered all the nations, and he will separate them one from another... Then the king will say to those on his right hand, Come, O blessed of my father, inherit the Kingdom ... for I was hungry and you gave me food, I was thirsty ... I was a stranger ... I was naked ... The righteous will answer him, Lord, when did we see thee hungry ... or thirsty ... or naked ... Truly I say to you, as you did it to one of the least of these my brethren, you did it to me ...
>
>   Matthew 25:31–45

This perspective on Yahweh's wrath and revenge helps to understand many of the passages in the Hebrew Scriptures. They are not about preaching 'hell and damnation' or just 'the love of Jesus'. Ultimately it is a struggle between Yahweh and the idols. For that we have to go back to the battle between good and evil at the beginning and its final resolve at the end of time. 'Holy wars' and the 'ban' can only be understood against this background. It is a spiritual struggle. Yahweh's covenantal oath to Abraham, Isaac and Jacob is about to be undone by the 'Canaanization' of Israel, a total accommodation (syncretism) between the fertility gods with the worship of Yahweh. Yahweh responds with wrath and punishment but in the end with mercy and compassion to save his people and to be true to his oath. As previously noted, one virtue of Yahweh cannot be played out against another, 'wrath' over against God's 'love'.

The world powers of the day with their overwhelming power of chariots and soldiers did not have the last word. Israel's future did and does not depend on their might and their weapons or on their alliances with the great empires. The Liberator God is also the Creator God. Yahweh would do a new thing. Maybe Yahweh will yet repent from his decision to abandon his people and the earth and do a new thing. (Isaiah 43:19) Yahweh is the God who liberated them from Egypt and Babylon and who remains faithful to his promises to Abraham, Isaac, and Jacob. We are called to stay close to our Liberator.

The birth of a great nation depended entirely on Yahweh's creating a new womb in Sarah, Rebecca, Rachel, Leah, in Hannah the mother of Samuel and, as legend has it, in the mother of Moses. Matthew takes over this legend about Moses' birth almost in its entirety to tell the story of the miraculous birth of Jesus. Lands, harvests and offspring depended entirely on the Creator, the Landlord and the Fertility God, the Weather God and the Liberator God.

The Ancient Near Eastern World was a cruel world that is reflected in the Hebrew Scriptures without comment just like other social institutions and practices (like concubines, polygamy, slavery and patriarchy). Our modern 'civilized' world is not much different: with its scorched earth policies during the German invasion of Russia in WW II and then once more when the Russians advanced; the long history of slavery and ongoing sex trafficking of women; forced labor and imprisonment of children; targeted bombing of hospitals and schools in Syria and the use of chemical weapons. Then there are cruelties committed during the Vietnam War and Afghanistan, Rwanda, Ukraine and now Palestine. As well as innumerable crimes committed globally against humanity by many corporations and governments, like the mining companies of Canada. It is a long list. In spite of these horrors, the earth endures and instances of solidarity, equality, justice and peace still endure.

In reflecting on Israel's history with Yahweh it is hard to escape the thought that Israel lived for many centuries under the wrath and pleading of God through the prophets, ending in being abandoned by Yahweh. It already started in the wilderness with the worship of the golden calf. It was only Moses' intercession that saved the people from Yahweh's wrath and destruction. Yahweh found its limits in Exodus 34.

THE PROPHETIC CALL TO LOVE AND JUSTICE

> ... The LORD, the LORD, a God merciful and gracious, slow to anger, and abounding in steadfast love and faithfulness, keeping steadfast love for thousands, forgiving iniquity and transgression and sin, but who will by no means clear the guilty...
> Exodus 34:6, 7

Moses intercedes for his people and prays, "... go in the midst of us, though it is a stiff-necked people; and pardon our iniquity and our sin and take us for thy inheritance." (Exod 34:9) And Yahweh responded and said, "... Behold, I make a covenant. Before all your people I will do marvels..." (Exod 34:10).

We too living in Western society are living under the judgment of Yahweh. Ever since the Enlightenment with its hubris of autonomous man and its ultimate faith in reason, science and technology that will bring about the Great Society with prosperity for all, civilization has been in decline. However it is not yet the Day of Judgment. Life endures with much to enjoy and celebrate in spite of injustice and violations.

For the last number of decades, the ultimate faith in the global neo-liberal ideology with its commitment to unlimited progress was the hope to bring about the good life with abundance for everyone and great profits for the rich. With the increase in neo-liberal policies since the 1960's, this Utopian vision has been tarnished. The dream about the golden age to come has turned into a nightmare. There is a slow disintegration of the environment, lack of social justice and corruption everywhere. The gap between the rich and the poor is getting wider. There is a pervasive sense of doom. Science and technology seem unable to save us. The environment is coming to a point of no return. A constant stream of refugees, are overwhelming Europe and other countries.

We live in a state of climate emergency. It seems that the Western world is bringing its own judgment upon itself. Collectively we stand under the judgment of God. The Creator and his good order for life for all his creatures are continually ignored. Nature has not abandoned us. We have abandoned nature. The very fabric of creation is unraveling. We have violated his creation. The built-in guidelines of creation and social relations keep on calling us back to come to our senses... (God's love). The blessings of the covenant keep calling us back. Yet Yahweh moves beyond hurt and anguish about spurned love and injustice and risks reconciliation, even at this late date.

> Have you not known? Have you not heard? ave you not known?
>   Have you not heard
> The LORD is an everlasting God,
> the Creator of the ends of the earth.
> He does not faint or grow weary,
> his understanding is unsearchable,
> He gives power to the faint,
> and to him who has no might he increases strength.
> Even youths shall faint and be weary,
> and young men shall fall exhausted;
> but they who wait for the LORD shall renew their strength,
> and shall mount up with wings like eagles,
> and they shall run and not be weary, they shall walk and not faint.
>   Isaiah 40:28–31

Such is the proclamation and hope of the ancient scribes and prophets, and the New Testament speaking to our hearts and calling us to join in with the prophets. This is how Yahweh has revealed himself. This is the abiding message, "Comfort, comfort my people, says your God. Speak tenderly to Jerusalem, and cry to her that warfare is ended, that her iniquity is pardoned, that she received from the LORD's hand, double for all her sins." (Isa 40:1, 2) It speaks tenderly to us as well, God-with-us, the Word becoming flesh, in this early twentieth century.

If only we had been taught and learned to read the Bible this way . . . How much agonizing and suffering would have been avoided . . . for me and countless other believing and struggling children and adults . . . Happily, through Deurloo's writings and that of many others, I have been able, vicariously, to experience something of the richness of the scripture. Surprised by joy, for it is the culmination of a lifelong journey to understand the scriptures and with it my religious background and indoctrination.

CHAPTER 9

The nature of Biblical Theology

FIRST A FEW COMMENTS about the academic discipline of theology. Different kinds of theology start from different presuppositions, many of which distort or violate the prophetic message. The Amsterdam way starts, from a faith perspective that is a belief in the God of scriptures. In some types of biblical interpretation, like an historical-cultural or literary approach they may assert that they begin without a "faith" perspective, (which some of them may consider as prejudicial, or not neutral) yet their "faith" is then in history and or literature. A simple flow chart may help to make sense of the discussion that follows, particularly for those without a background in the discipline of theology:

Scripture ← → Exegesis ← → Biblical Theology ← → Systematic Theology → Church: doctrines

Exegesis is the analysis and interpretation of the language (Hebrew, Greek, Aramaic, etc.) and is a technical theoretical academic discipline. Biblical Theology, from the Amsterdam perspective, is based on the basic structures, themes and crosscuts that the scriptures themselves indicate. It stays closer to experience than abstractions. This is in part why Deurloo's biblical theological studies, for example, are more accessible to non-theologians. This is also why it was unfairly critiqued and devalued by many theologians as non-academic or 'less than' other academic approaches. Systematic Theology focuses on the fit between Biblical Theology and Church doctrines. The object of study for Biblical Theology is the scriptures and the core structures it presents, based on a careful interpretation of many individual texts. Systematic Theology is an academic discipline that focuses on the church's confessions and teaching. In this respect it plays a critical role.

After Genesis, Joshua (with the Excursion about Israel and Palestine) and another God-image, (chapters 6 through 8), this new section on the four biblical theology books by Deurloo presents a different approach. Instead of dealing with a whole Bible book, they deal with core structures that cut across different genres and Bible books providing intriguing perspectives.

The idea of using Biblical theology as a frame of reference for exegesis deserves ongoing attention within the Amsterdam approach. In their view, a number of interconnected core structures, key words and themes form a framework for understanding the scriptures. They are like word-horizons. They are not abstractions, rather core structures, key words and themes indicated by scripture itself; they are repeated many times in different contexts in which they reveal their core meaning. Especially as more literature appears on the 'theology' or 'structure' of different Bible books, there will be more opportunity to check these studies against the whole of each Bible book and all of scripture.

In addition to Cahiers on individual Bible books, both Breukelman and Deurloo published several volumes that provide repeating crosscuts that emerge from many scriptural givens. Together they form the 'basic structures' ('grond struturen") of both the Old and New Testament and elucidate the prophetic message.

Breukelman has given an extensive account of the nature of Biblical Theology in relation to both Exegesis and Systematic Theology. He presented his most well-known account in his first *Bijbelse Theology, 1; Scripture Reading*, 9–35, (1980). A later version appeared in *Biblical Theology in Practice*, (2012). From the beginning, as an initial description, he asserts that there is an inseparable connection between Biblical Theology and Exegesis. The continued exegesis of scriptural passages shows the contours of a Biblical Theology. In turn Biblical Theology forms the hermeneutic (interpretive) horizon for exegesis. There is a continual interaction. The hermeneutic horizon is the way the prophets and the apostles, as the primary witnesses of God's great deeds, experienced the whole of reality. It forms the framework within which biblical texts need to be explained. Not the doctrines of the church, nor the history of religions, nor the neo-Protestant theology after the Reformation, can function as such a horizon. Rather, Biblical Theology focuses on the core structures of the scriptures.

After this initial description Breukelman explores the nature of theology in general as a 'speaking and teaching about God'. Over time it became the study of the 'sacred doctrines'. After the Reformation this view was maintained, even though exegesis was added, primarily as 'proof texts' of the church's doctrines. In this process Systematic Theology was narrowed to the doctrine of God (the Trinity, the divinity of Christ and the Holy Spirit). He distinguishes between Systematic theology that has the church's doctrines as its object of study, and that which serves the church in a 'critical correcting' role. Biblical theology on the other hand has as its object the testimony of the prophets and the apostles as the biblical witness to God's own speaking. Biblical theology explains the 'hidden' theology ('core structures') contained in the texts, in order to give an account of the abiding message for all people. Each generation has this task, since circumstances and times change presenting different contexts in which the scriptures are to be sounded out. This exposition of core structures undergirds their prophetic meaning and proclamation. It is the history of God's speaking in many different ways for all humanity.

The church explains the biblical witness that is addressed to all people. The witness of the 'prophets and the apostles' theology is 'totally hidden' in these texts as witness. Individual texts function in the whole of the scriptures. The different authors never add even a little explanation of what they mean, a little theology. The stories carry the message. We are called to explain this theology as present-day readers. The hearers must do the interpreting. That is the church's mandate and the hearers' task. The church can do this because the scriptures explain themselves. We must explain the words so that the hermeneutic horizon becomes clearer and clearer. As we interpret, basic patterns appear. For example, the 'toledot structure' of Genesis is such a core structure or pattern that highlights its message, or Joshua's liturgical context. In this exchange, between Exegesis and Biblical theology, the contours of a Biblical theology become more and more evident. These themes are not just repetitions but they lift up many passages to a new and often unexpected level.

Deurloo closely follows Breukelman's exposition and adds a unique feature. Deurloo describes Biblical theology not only in terms of core structures. But core structures "according to the canon of the ecclesia; in its reformation form." In following the 'canonical order' of the scriptures he does not follow the usual order of the Old Testament but according to the order of the books in the three categories of the Hebrew Bible, the TeNaK: Torah, Prophets and Psalter. His first volume of Biblical theology is a good example of this approach. In *Exodus and Exile* he goes through all the references in the Torah, then the (later) Prophets and the Psalms and finally the Apostolic witness. He traces how they refer to the exodus and the return from exile. When dealing with *Kings and Temple*, Deurloo takes note of the first mention of kings, starting with Genesis all the way to the end-time king of the book of Revelation. Likewise with regard to the third volume about mothers and their (dead) sons, he starts with Eve and then continues on to Sarah, and so on. He ends with the touching scene with mother Mary at the crucifixion and Jesus' care for her. It highlights his many references to the scriptures that at first reading just seem to tumble over each other. Instead they follow the canonical order of Moses, the prophets and the Psalms (the Writings).

> Moses and the Prophets: We have taken that primarily in the smaller sense of as the Torah and the later prophets, even if the whole of the TNK and especially the Psalter (Luke 24:44): Biblical Theology according to the canon of the ecclesia; in her reformational form.[1]

In an inspiring article by R.R.Brouwer (2020), "The issue of confessing and the 'canonical approach'" discusses article 4 of the Belgic Confession, dealing with the canon. In this article he explores first of all what it means to confess. Article 5, of the Belgic Confession, starts with: "We receive all these books and these only as holy and canonical for the regulating, founding, and establishing of our faith." 'We receive' indicates it is first of all a gift. In spite of many possible objections to this creed, we are nevertheless to read it primarily as a declaration of love. The God of these biblical writings is a loving God. God's love calls for our love in return. Love is saying "yes" to the "Other One." All historical questions become secondary. "We receive" involves our action as a part of the communion of believers. God speaks to us in these words of the many books of the scriptures.

Secondly, Brouwer discusses the question of the canon. He does so by looking at the contributions of B. Childs, R. Rendtorff and K. Deurloo. Specifically, he deals with Deurloo's question whether there is a 'middle' to the scriptures. Do the many 'theologies,' of the different Bible books, present a 'middle'? The answer is that the texts themselves present such a middle or centre.

---

1. Deurloo, *Exodus en Exile*, 140.

For example, the "Torah and the Prophets" present two focal points: the liberation of slaves, Exodus, and the turnabout of a people, the return from Exile, which dominates the Torah and the later prophets (Isaiah, Jeremiah, Ezekiel, and the 12 minor prophets). In between the Torah and the later prophets are the earlier prophets, which focus on David, the king and Solomon, the temple builder, King and Temple and from there, the decline of the kingship leading to the Exile. In Matthew 1:1–17 we find a reading of the TeNaK. In which these structures become evident, and within which the story of Jesus can be told. Brouwer published several other articles on the confession.

Finally, Brouwer asks which canon we should follow. His answer is clear, the order of the rabbinic, Palestinian canon, which is the order Deurloo follows. Deurloo does not start, as is usually done in Systematic theology, with the traditional order of creation, sin, reconciliation or redemption. According to the biblical structure (the Palestinian canon) it needs to start with the Exodus, followed by the turnabout in Yahweh, his mercy and the return from Exile. It cannot start with the doctrine of sin, (which is often taken in a 'moral', individualistic' sense as being 'bad', rather than the breaking of the covenant). For how can we reflect on what 'sin' means if we have not first reflected on the revelation of the Name of God, God-with-us, as manifested in Jesus, Yahweh liberates, Immanuel. He will liberate his people and with Israel the goyim from their sins, their abandonment of covenant obligations. That is how God-with-us happens. That is why in theology, and in preaching, we first need to talk about the Name. How else would we know what the word 'sin' means?

These four volumes on Biblical theology published by the Amsterdam tradition provide many challenging and important core structures that are crucial for understanding the scriptures in their unity and basic perspective. Deurloo called his four volumes on Biblical Theology, *Small Biblical Theology: Exodus and Exile* (2003); *King and Temple* (2004); *Our Dear Mother gives birth to a son* (2006); *Creation from Paul to Genesis* (2008). For this discussion we could add, and *Closer to Paul*, and *Humans as riddle and secret* (1980). We already made reference to his *The Beginning in our midst; aspects of the biblical faith in creation* (1977). Also with Beker, *The guidance of our existence; questions and references with respect to providence*. The Amsterdam tradition has published two volumes on biblical theology: J. Dubbink, ed., *Biblical Theology*, volume 30 (2015); and R. Reeling Brouwer, ed., *Biblical Theology in Practice*, (2012).

Breukelman has published five volumes on Biblical Theology, which he wrote during the course of many years. They existed mostly as notes and were finally published with the help and encouragement of his friends. They are all extensive studies that were decades in the making. Each one would require a separate paper, which would carry us too far afield. See the bibliography for the titles. Rinse Brouwer gave a brief introduction and summary of each of the volumes by Breukelman that have been published thus far. See, *Biblical Theology in Practice*, (2012). Joep Dubbink discusses the Systematic Theology contributions of Van den Brink and Van der Kooi in his essay, "Dogmatic, Christian or Faithful reading of the Scriptures?"). In: *volume 30* of the *Amsterdamse Cahiers*, (2015).

Together they form a frame of reference for the interpretation of individual passages and vice versa each new interpretation enriches and elucidates the main themes. In this way, biblical theologians seek to uncover the central message of each Bible book, of the TeNaK, Prophets, Psalms and the New Testament, the whole of scripture.

Theology is a 'science', or an academic discipline, but more in the sense of the humanities than the natural sciences. Even natural sciences tend to be distorted if the object of investigation is reduced to a mere 'object' without context, history, time or space. Then it becomes a restrictive, empiricistic, verifiable, experimental approach. The humanities, given their different subject matter (history; literature; cultural anthropology; theology; sociology; education; medicine; etc.), generally require their own methods; more likely, a more descriptive or phenomenological approach. H.Berkhof gives an overview and references of 'theology as a science' in his *Christelijk Geloof*, p. 34–39, (1993) that is helpful for a more theological discussion within Systematic Theology. Whether that is sufficient for understanding Systematic theology would require a separate study.

Biblical storytellers, poets, wise men, prophets and evangelists are not historians. As prophets and apostles they are witnesses to the great deeds of Yahweh. The oneness of the Name (dabar, word/deed) is central and belongs to the core structure of the biblical idiom. The Word is not a general truth. It is an encounter. God's words are deeds. He speaks and it is. This means it is a decision. And as a decision it is history. Their reality cannot be established by way of analogy from our reality. Their reality is not identical with our sensory observations and our rationality. The Bible is the witness to God's presence. In the fullness of time, it happened. It is liberated time. Time is space in which the debarim, (the deed/words) are being fulfilled, in the 'fullness of time' . . . on this earth and in our history.

It may be helpful as well to acknowledge more strongly (again) that this Amsterdam approach of a close reading of the text, as given in the scriptures, has led to a new form of 'Biblical Theology'. These biblical theological guidelines are not merely cognitive constructions. They are 'summaries' of biblical texts and recurring themes that can be challenged and re-formulated. We could say (epistemologically) that they are 'generalizations'. They do not abstract from scripture. They summarize and generalize the themes of different texts into core structures. They are based on the experiential givens the scriptures provide.

They need to be in constant interaction. This has led to a re-discovery of the importance of the Hebrew Scriptures for the church and theology and the unique voice and central place of the Old Testament in the whole of theology.

This more 'practical' approach is not in contrast or in conflict with, in many respects, the technical, academic, specialized, exegetical study of a text (aided by the computer). It was preserved during a long process over the ages especially before the art of printing. We have our printed copies and take for granted how the text was preserved earlier. It highlights even more how the Spirit preserved the Word in the worshipping, living and reading of faith communities. In the end the interpretations still need to take their start in the final text as it has been handed down to us.

This very practical approach of the Amsterdam school is the need of the hour. It certainly is the need of our hour. The message of the church does not reach large sections of the church's children, young people and even fewer of the university students. At the very least it can complement the work of the exegetes. Ideally it should be part of the task of every doctoral student in theology to indicate how his/her study can contribute to the witness and preaching of the church. Piet van Midden in his *Kingship and Brotherhood*, is exemplary in this regard, He added an example of how the story of Gideon could be told, without moralism, and intellectualism, to middle school students. Normally, Gideon is presented instead as a heroic figure and as an example for our faith.

Deurloo's courage and openness to new theological, historical and archaeological insights is heartwarming. It liberates us from an anxious defense of the faith when new insights and discoveries appear. They can all be tested against the prophetic witness of the scriptures.

From the very beginning, Breukelman, Deurloo and associates absorbed major biblical studies and commentaries in their own exegetical work. They used the exegetical situation to develop a new approach. It became an occasion to take another look at specific passages and see if a different approach would elucidate the text, instead of the assumed traditional or historical context. For example, instead of just accepting the 'fairy tale' character of the Balaam story in Numbers 22-24 or the David and Goliath story of 1 Samuel 16 and 17 (2 Samuel 21:18-21), Deurloo illustrates how these 'fairy tale' literary motifs are lifted up by the storyteller to bring out the essential meaning of the story, the prophetic proclamation.

The same is true with regard to the 'legendary-like' story of the temptations of Jesus at the beginning of his ministry (Matt 4:1-11; cf. Matt 27, 28) and how they are used by the author to bring out something essential. Rather than throwing doubt on the historical character of accounts, he illustrates how 'legendary' elements are lifted up to show the meaning and nature of Jesus' entire ministry right at the beginning and until the very end of his public appearances.

With his dry humor, Deurloo tends to say, about these 'historical' assumptions, "That may be true enough" ("Dat zal wel waar zijn"), but then he will add, does this assumed historical tradition or origin actually aid in our understanding of the text. Instead, he will highlight certain key words and inter-textual connections to show that quite a different understanding of the text is possible that incorporates these differences. Rather than ending up defending the 'historicity' of the scriptures, he offers an alternative approach. 'Fairy tale' givens, 'legendary accounts', 'mythological references', 'geographical references', 'historical data', etc. are all taken up to serve and highlight the prophetic meaning of the story. He tends to turn the 'critical historical' approach upside down and uses it to show the depth of meaning in a particular passage or unit.

Rather than seeing them as 'historical inaccuracies' that throw doubt on the trustworthiness of scriptures, they actually deepen our understanding of the basic meaning of a passage, like Jacob's epiphany at Bethel. (Gen 28:10-22) This story is not just a reminder of an ancient cultic place at Bethel, rather it is an important reference taken up in the story and given special meaning. It illustrates what is at stake in Jacob's fleeing from Esau who had threatened to kill him for stealing the blessing of the firstborn son.

There are anachronisms like camels in Abraham's story. Ur of the Chaldeans is really a reference to Neo-Babylonians, who don't appear until Jeremiah's time. At times current events are projected back into the past. Readers of the scriptures need to know that these and other stories receive their power not from their historical but from the proclaiming trustworthiness of the story. Our faith does not depend on a 'historically' based faith. Historical research has its own value and should not be mixed with 'faith assumptions'. To read biblical stories as history is a barrier to our faith. Orthodoxy carries a lot of guilt in this respect.

There is a great deal of 'biblical realism' in scriptures. The realism of many children's story Bible pictures tends to distort the actual realism, and turn the story more into a 'romantic' or 'adventurous' story. The mother of the sons of Zebedee, for example, as a particular person probably existed, but she stands for so much more. She is 'typified' with the result that there are also 'unhistorical' elements in the story. Breukelman has pointed out that we can detect these elements by comparing Matthew's account with that of Mark. (Mark 15:40 and Matt 27:55, 56) The mother presents Jesus with a request, "'Command that these two sons of mine may sit, one at your right hand and one on your left, in your kingdom'. But Jesus answered, 'You do not know what you are asking.'" (Matthew 20:21–28) Later on we read, "Then two robbers were crucified with him, one on the right and one on the left." "And the women looked on from afar." (Matt 27:55) We cannot escape the deep poignancy of the gospel writer's story and the mother's agony. But the story is about being of service and not about ruling and competition.

Jesus is crucified as the King of the Jews. That is not what she and the reader had expected. Jesus came as a humble servant riding on a donkey into Jerusalem, while the people shouted, "Tell the daughter of Zion, behold your king is coming to you, humble, and mounted on an ass . . . Hosanna to the son of David! Blessed is he who comes in the name of the Lord! Hosanna in the highest!" (Matt 21:5–11) This is not what the mother of the two sons had expected. She had to radically change her understanding of the Christ and we can only be followers of this Christ, the suffering servant whose name was Jesus, for he will save his people, and his name shall be called, Immanuel, God-with-us. (Matt 1:21–24) Only at the crucifixion, the extent of the mother's request became clear. Most of the time we do not know exactly what was said, because of the 'unhistorical' (prophetic) character of the Bible stories, which we can call biblical realism.

It is tempting to go through each of the following four volumes of Deurloo's biblical theology series. They are rich in content. Deurloo presents a rich array of passages that give rise to different themes. He follows all the ins and outs of each theme, about the exodus and return from exile, *Exodus en Exile*; the kingship and the building of the temple, *Temple and King*; barren women and sons, *Our dear mother gives birth to a Son*; and finally the creation, *Creation from Paul to Genesis*. We will highlight some key points from each volume. Deurloo's work is based upon and is built on Breukelman's rich, exegetical and biblical theological studies. He presents his own more broadly thematic aspproach.

9:1 Exodus and (return from) Exile belong together (2003)

From the very first volume of his biblical theology cycle, *Exodus and Exile*, Deurloo highlights two focal points of the Torah (the five books of Moses) and the later Prophets that are centered in the revelation of the Name, Yahweh, the God of Israel, and through them with all peoples and the whole earth. The two themes are the exodus and return from exile; they belong together. They are explored in detail and cover most of the first volume, *Exodus and return from Exile*. In chapter 7 he gives a detailed and promising account of the same themes in the books of the *Psalms*, the first of the Writings. Some of the examples may have been dealt with before, but in these studies, they are lifted up to a new and unexpected level, namely the inseparable connection between the Exodus and the return from Exile. Both give voice to Yahweh's great mercy, the liberation from slavery in a foreign land.

Right from the beginning, Deurloo asks the question about the centre of the Old Testament canon (the Torah, the early and Prophets and Writings). The Torah is centered in the Exodus, and the later prophets on the (the return from) Exile. The middle of the early prophets is focused on David, the ideal king, or king and temple. And from there the Apostolic writings can be examined.

Yahweh creates a people for himself from the land of death and slavery. Yahweh is God and being moved by compassion, he lets his people return from the land of exile. Yahweh, he is God. These are the two focal points of the scriptures and form the one centre: the Name of Yahweh.

When all seems lost again, as in Egypt with Pharaoh's attempts to kill all the male babies, and later, when they are once more enslaved in Babylon there is a second delivery. They are miraculously saved from two world powers (Egypt and Babylon). Both are based on Yahweh's hearing "their groaning" and 'their sorrowful songs' (Psalm 137 and Lamentations), and Yahweh's own 'turn about,' being moved with compassion even after they broke their relationship with him and went after other gods. Singlehandedly, as it were, he restores their relationship. Then the people too had to become fully engaged. They needed to leave Egypt and get ready for the journey ("your loins girded, your sandals on your feet, and your staff in your hand"); and actively return to Jerusalem and participate in the rebuilding of the temple and the walls of Jerusalem.

Deurloo makes the unexpected and intriguing suggestion, or hypothesis, that the account of the exodus could have its origin in the 'confession' of the great turnabout from exile. In the next volume, King and Temple, he formulates it as follows:

> The given of the Exodus could very well have its origin in the 'theology' of the turn about from exile. Nevertheless the bible makes the exodus from Egypt its point of departure, from out of which the return from exile can be understood. Even though we know that parts of the Exodus came into existence in different historical situations. We read those in the redactional order of the book ... Even in this 'canonical' constructed book the reader will encounter, sometimes implicitly, and sometimes explicitly historical references or insights.[2]

Regardless, the scriptures take the exodus as the point of departure, from out of which we are to understand the return from exile. This suggestion is still particularly helpful when considering the issues around a sudden and total conquest versus a gradual infiltration of nomadic tribes of southern and northern Palestine, as well as the gradual return of a part of the exiled people, and the issue of the early or late dating of various Bible books. It can leave these questions open; that too is a liberating perspective.

He touches on many detailed aspects of these two focal points, the exodus and the return from exile, to show how they arise out of the consistent witness of the scriptures. Because of the many details it is helpful to keep these two themes in mind, so as to not get lost in the fascinating and compelling descriptions and scriptural references. They have interest

2. Deurloo, *King and Temple*, 10.

THE NATURE OF BIBLICAL THEOLOGY

and impact in themselves, but they are taken up to elucidate this twofold theme. In this way we become immersed in the 'word-world' or 'horizon' of the scriptures, in which many passages and key words take on new meaning. Together they present a rich perspective of the scriptures.

The many passages he selects follow the canonical order: Torah, prophets, Psalms. In doing so, "Breukelman's book, about the core word, Debarim, is a constant help. Breukelman outlines the core structure that is behind the many theologies of the Bible, like the theology of Genesis or the gospel of Matthew. Deurloo wanted more and asks, "What is the middle of the Torah, (early and later) Prophets and the Psalms. The Torah is all about the exodus and the later prophets are all about the exile. The middle of the earlier prophets (Joshua, Samuel, Kings) is the person of David, or better, king and temple. This seems to me a simple canonical given from out of which the apostolic writings can be examined."[3] "The approach of this first volume of Biblical theology was indicated by the authoritative witness itself, the Torah and (later) Prophets, Biblical theology, in the manner of the canon of the ecclesia, in its reformational form." [4] This is a correction to the usual order of the Old Testament (Belgic Confession, art.4.) Instead he followed the three categories of the Hebrew Bible, the TeNaK (Torah, Prophets, and Psalm).

Yahweh creates a people from out of the land of death and slavery. Moved by compassion, Yahweh lets his people pull out of the land of slavery in Egypt and the return from exile in Babylon. These are the two focal points, exodus and return from exile, of the Torah (Genesis to Deuteronomy) and the Later Prophets, Isaiah, Jeremiah, Ezekiel, and the books of the twelve Minor Prophets. At the same time it elucidates and forms the one centre of the scriptures, the Name Yahweh. The 'being god' is totally determined by that name. Yahweh, *he* is god, says something different than, Yahweh is *God*. I, Yahweh, am your God. I, Yahweh-your-God is the one who . . .

Who Yahweh is becomes apparent in his deeds and words. The designation 'God' is not something separate or an addition to his Name. Yahweh cannot be called the Maker of the cosmos, or any other general word. To talk about Israel's God, we can only do so by telling the story of the exodus and the return from exile. Generally that does not happen in expositions, and seldom in the church.

---

3. Deurloo, *Exodus and Exile*, 7, 8.
4. Deurloo, *Exodus and Exile*, 140.

THE PROPHETIC CALL TO LOVE AND JUSTICE

To really tell can't be done without engagement and involvement in the story. The surprise of the explanation of the Name in Exodus 3:14, is that it does not really explain, "I am who I am", (I will be with you as I will be). God said to Moses, "say this, to the people of Israel, 'Yahweh, the God of your fathers . . . has sent me to you, this is my name forever.'" Instead it involves Moses and the people directly. They have to come into action and get ready for the journey.

That is how the people of Israel came to know God, responding to his voice along the way. As such Yahweh will be present to his people. Yahweh 'happens' to Israel and to us along the way as he sets us on the way to freedom, which is the way of the Torah, the commandments. Being liberated from slavery and set in the liberty of service to Yahweh by doing his commandments, that is how they came to know Yahweh. "All that Yahweh has spoken (on the mountain) we heard and we will do." (Exod 24:7) We heard with our whole being, we truly heard, with all our heart, following the life-giving directions.

Telling about Yahweh is telling about our life history, the road we have travelled from Egypt to Canaan and from Babylon back to Jerusalem. All the laws in Leviticus are marked by "I am Yahweh your God," (Lev 19:4) or it can just say, "I am Yahweh." (Lev 19:12) Liberated from slavery, you shall follow my instructions, "For I am Yahweh, who brought you up out of the land of Egypt, to be your God; you shall therefore be holy, for I am holy." (Lev 11:45) His Name guarantees it.

When we tell about the exodus from Egypt, we need to tell about the miracle of the return from exile in Babylon, and of Yahweh's own turn about, of his great compassion.

> I will tell of thy name to my brethren;
> In the midst of the congregation I will praise thee . . .
> And stand in awe of him, all you sons of Israel!
> Psalm 22:22, 23

When Moses hears the voice of Yahweh for the second time on the mountain after the golden calf episode, and the renewed promise that Yahweh will nevertheless go with his people, he exclaims,

> The LORD, the LORD, a God merciful and gracious, slow to anger, and abounding in steadfast love and faithfulness, keeping steadfast love for thousands, forgiving iniquity and transgression and sin . . .
> Exodus 34:6, 7

THE NATURE OF BIBLICAL THEOLOGY

> For he who is mighty has done great things for me, and holy is his name. And his mercy is on those who fear him from generation to generation.
>
> Luke 1:49, 50. (Song of Mary)

See Psalm 103:13 "... as a father pities his children ... "In remembrance of his mercy .." (Luke 1: 54) That is how Mary closes her song, or in Zechariah's words, "to perform the mercy promised to our fathers ..." (Luke 1:72)

The two focal points, the exodus from Egypt and the return from exile in Babyhlon belong together. In the earlier (or former) prophets the exodus achieves its goal ("the fulfilment of all God's promises"; everyone receiving their inheritance). With Joshua the people pass through the Jordan to receive the gift of the good land, their inheritance. Via the book of Judges, we are taken to the centre of the earlier prophets, the kingship of David (Samuel) and the building of the temple (Kings). In Kings we are witness to the downward spiral of the kings and the people, which ends in the deportation to Babylon, first that of the North Country and then Judah in the south.

In chapter II Kings 17, the prophet recites all the sins of Israel, the North Country, when they were led into captivity by the Assyrians to Babylon about six centuries later, and the connection to the exodus.

> And this was so, because the people of Israel had sinned against the Lord their God, who had brought them up out of the land of Egypt from under the hand of Pharaoh king of Egypt, and had feared other gods and walked in the customs of the nations whom the Lord drove out before the people of Israel, and in the customs which the kings of Israel had introduced. And the people of Israel did secretly against the Lord their God things that were not right. They built for themselves high places ... They set up for themselves pillars and Asherim ... And they did wicked things, provoking the Lord to anger ... Yet the LORD warned Israel and Judah by every prophet and every seer, saying, turn from your evil ways and keep my commandments ... But they would not listen, but were stubborn, as their fathers had been, and did not believe in the Lord their God. They despised his statutes, and his covenant ... They went after false idols ... And made for themselves molten images of two calves ... And worshipped all the host of heaven and served Baal. And they burned their sons and their daughters as offerings ... Therefore the LORD was very angry with Israel, and removed them out of

> his sight; none was left but the tribe of Judah only. Judah also did not keep the commandments of the LORD their God …
> II Kings 17:7–19

Therefore Israel was led into captivity. The kings before Josiah "did what was evil in the sight of the Lord." *Therefore* "Judah also was moved out of my sight." In spite of all Josiah's reforms, the unfaithfulness of the kings before and after him, Yahweh's judgments of Judah's idolatry continued on,

> I will remove Judah also out of my sight, as I have removed Israel, and I will cast off this city which I have chosen, Jerusalem, and the house of which I said, My name shall be there.
> II Kings 23:27

For hope of a return from exile, we have to wait for the later prophets. Here we are only told that the land, according to the Torah, that has been defiled, will vomit out its inhabitants. (Lev18:25; II Kings 25:21)

The reason why "I will take you into exile" (Amos 5:27) is elaborated in great detail by the later prophets, especially Ezekiel and Hosea,

> Hear the word of the LORD, O people of Israel;
> For the LORD has a controversy with the inhabitants of the land.
> There is no faithfulness or kindness, and no knowledge of God
>   in the land;
> There is swearing, lying, killing, stealing, and committing adultery;
> They break all bounds and murder follows murder.
> Hosea 4:1, 2

The (ten) commandments are continually violated, leading to 'contamination' of the land. Instead of 'land' we can also read 'earth', which reminds us of the creation account: Israel as representative of the adam, the earthling, the human on the earth, in the midst of all the peoples and the land, animals, birds and fishes. As the Midrash (the Rabbinic commentary on the Hebrew Scriptures) asserts, "In the beginning God created … with an eye to the Torah"; "it is for the doing of the Torah that God created heaven and earth." From a biblical theological perspective that seems to the point. Wherever the Torah is no longer followed, and is not really heard, the creation refuses to perform its services. Rather, knowledge of God is going the way of his lifegiving commandments.

Jeremiah echoes the same view and has to prophesy against the people who put their trust in the presence of the temple. He says, "Do not trust in these deceptive words: 'This is the temple of the LORD, the temple of the LORD, the temple of the LORD.'" (Jer 7:4) Jeremiah directly opposes this false security.

> For if you truly amend your ways and your doings, If you truly execute justice one with another, if you do not oppress the alien, the fatherless or the widow, or shed innocent blood in this place, and if you do not go after other gods to your own hurt, then I will let you dwell in this place, in the land that I gave of old to your fathers for ever. Behold, you trust in deceptive words to no avail. Will you steal, murder, commit adultery, swear falsely, burn incense to Baal and go after other gods that you have not known, and then come and stand before me in this house, which is called by my name, and say, 'we are delivered!' only to go on doing all these abominations? . . . I will cast you out of my sight, as I cast out all your kinsmen, all the offspring of Ephraim.
> Jeremiah 7:5–15

Jeremiah even goes so far as to say: "As for you, do not pray for this people . . . therefore, behold my anger and my wrath will be poured out on this place, upon man and beast, upon the trees of the field and the fruit of the ground, it will burn and not be quenched." (Jer 7:20) In a vision Jeremiah sees what this means,

> I looked on the earth (the land), and lo, it was *waste and void*; and to the heavens, and they had no light,
> I looked on the mountains, and lo, they were quaking, and all the hills moved to and fro, I looked and lo, there was no man, and all the birds of the air had fled. I looked, and lo, the fruitful land was a desert, and all the cities were laid in ruins before the LORD, before his fierce anger. For thus says the LORD, the whole land shall be desolation . . Yet I will not make a full end. For this the earth shall mourn, and the heavens above be black . . .
> Jeremiah 4:23–28 (cf, Hosea 4:3, 6)

Or as Hosea exclaims,

> 'I will utterly sweep away everything from the face of the earth', says the LORD.
> I will sweep away man and beast; I will sweep away the birds of the air and the fish of the sea.
> I will overthrow the wicked; I will cut off mankind from the face of the earth,' says the LORD.
> I will stretch out my hand against Judah, and against all the inhabitants of Jerusalem . . .
> Zephaniah 1:2–4

From the beginning humans and the land (crying out from the blood of Abel and of all murders) are inseparably connected. All creation suffers from the faithlessness of the people. "The whole creation has been groaning . . ." (Rom 8:22), the animals, the birds, the fishes, the mountains, the cities and the people. The people, the land, animals, birds and fishes are inseparably connected. The creation has lost its purpose and all creatures will suffer along with the earthlings. Is this the end of Yahweh's journey with his chosen people, humanity and the good earth? The exodus seems to have been in vain. Could it just as well not have happened? (Judges 18:30, 31) This is how Jeremiah's prophecies started,

> I remember the devotion of your youth, your love as a bride, how you followed me in the wilderness... 'What wrong did your fathers find in me that they went far from me and went after worthlessness, and became worthless?'... The priests did not say, 'Where is the LORD?' Those who handle the law did not know me; the rulers transgressed against me; the prophets prophesied by Baal . . .
> Jeremiah 2:2–8

'Worthlessness' or 'nothingness', or 'damp' is a play on words for Baal, the non-god, a fog. "But when you came in, you defiled my land, and made my heritage an abomination. The priests did not say, 'Where is the LORD?' Those who handle the law did not know me; the rulers transgressed against me, the prophets prophesied by Baal." (Jer 2:7–8) The question about the Name of Yahweh is no longer asked. In actual practice it is lost. In many different ways Jeremiah will elaborate on this judgment. There is only one conclusion, "Therefore I will take you into exile." (Amos 5:27)

There is no hope left. The exile means the end of the people of Israel as Yahweh's chosen people, because of their own doing, Israel will be scattered among the nations; as fortold in Deuteronomy, "And the LORD will scatter you among all peoples, from one end of the earth to the other; and there you will serve other gods, of wood and stone, which neither you nor your fathers have known . . . and there shall be no rest for the sole of your foot." (Deut 28:64) The words, "Hear Oh Israel, YHWH is our God . . . who brought you up out of Egypt, out of the house of bondage" (Deut 6:4, 12) are no longer heard. If it is heard it is not really known with the heart. Is the exodus a failed project? Is the only thing that is left, is to lament?

THE NATURE OF BIBLICAL THEOLOGY

The theme of exodus and exile is not only prominent in the *Torah* and the *Later Prophets*, but also in the *Writings*, the third category of the TeNaK. We only need to think about the Lamentations of Jeremiah (one of the Writings), or the protests of Job and scepticism of Ecclesiastes, "Vanity of vanities! All is vanity."

> How lonely sits the city
> that was full of people!
> How like a widow has she become,
> she that was great among the nations!
> She that was a princess among the cities
> has become a vassal.
> She weeps bitterly in the night,
> tears on her cheeks;
> among all her lovers
> she has none to comfort her;
> all her friends have dealt treacherously with her,
> they have become her enemies.
> Lamentations 1:1

It is because of the exile that Jerusalem, the daughter of Zion, is in this situation. Yet the widow's lament can turn into hope,

> But this I call to mind,
> and therefore I have hope:
> the steadfast love of Yahweh never ceases,
> his mercies never come to an end;
> they are new every morning;
> great is thy faithfulness.
> Lamentations 3:21, 22

> For the LORD will not cast off forever,
> but, though he cause grief, he will have compassion
> according to the abundance of his steadfast love;
> for he does not willingly afflict or grieve the sons of men.
> Lamentations 3:31–33

For this reason the widow's lament ends with a prayer,

> Why dost thou forget us for ever;
> why dost thou so long forsake us?
> Restore us to thyself, O, LORD, that we may be restored!
> Renew our days as of old!
> Or hast thou utterly rejected us?
> Art thou exceedingly angry with us?
> Lamentations 5:20–22

There is only one conclusion: deportation to Babylon. Or is there still something else that must be told about the Name of Yahweh? In the exile we hear the people say, "My way is hid from the LORD" (Isa 40:27) and "The LORD has forsaken me, my LORD has forgotten me" (Isa 49:14). The entire section of consolation (Isa 40–55) gives an answer to these questions. And Ezekiel, the great prophet of the exile, prophesies with a graphic image,

> (Yahweh) set me down in the midst of the valley; it was full of bones . . . "'Son of man, these bones are the whole house of Israel. Behold they say, 'our bones are dried up, and our hope is lost, we are clean cut off'"
> Ezekiel 37:1, 11

The first expression of 'flesh and bone', recalls that we are flesh "The Lord God formed man of dust from the ground, and breathed into his nostril the breath of life; and man became a living being." (Gen 2:7). For Israel this breath of life is cut off. The weak flesh is held up by the bones. But when one's "bones are troubled" (Ps 6:2), and one's "strength is dried up" (Ps 32:4), then that is the end, then we are near death.

The whole banishment is pictured as a valley full of dried up, dead bones. Can these lifeless skeletons come to life again? Impossible, we would say. Dead is dead. But then Ezekiel is led into the middle of the valley full of skeletons, and "there were many of them and they were very dry." He is asked by the LORD, "Son of man, can these bones live? And Ezekiel answered, 'O Yahweh, you know.' Then he is commanded to prophesy,

> Prophesy to these bones, and say to them, O dry bones, hear the word of the LORD. Thus says the LORD God to these bones: 'Behold, I will cause breath to enter you, and you shall live. And I will lay sinews upon you, and I will cause flesh to come upon you, and cover you with skin, and put breath in you, and you shall live; and you shall know that I am the LORD.
> Ezekiel 37:4–6

In this graphic image Ezekiel's mission is summarized. At the end there is a great noise, "a rattling of the bones coming together, bone to its bone" (vs. 7). The prophecy ends with,

> Behold, I will open your graves, and raise you from your graves, O, my people; and I will bring you home into the land of Israel. And you shall know that I am the LORD, when I open your graves. And raise you from your graves, O, my people. And I

THE NATURE OF BIBLICAL THEOLOGY

> will put my Spirit within you, and you shall live, and I will place you in your own land, then you shall know that I, the LORD have spoken, and I have done it, says the LORD.
> Ezekiel 37:12-14

The whole House of Israel is "stood upon their feet, an exceedingly great host." (37:10) This is exactly, what Ezekiel himself had experienced at the start of his mission. "When He spoke to me, the Spirit entered into me and set me upon my feet" (Ezek 2:1, 2) "to set them upon their feet," ready for the journey back home. Returning home from exile, that is a truly astounding miracle, like a resurrection from the dead, "I will open your graves and have you come forth from your graves and bring you to your own land." It indicates the great turn-about of Yahweh, "in his great compassion." (Ezek 37:12)

At the end of this major section, Ezekiel concludes his prophecy, saying,

> Therefore thus says the LORD God: Now I will restore the fortunes of Jacob, and have *mercy* on the whole house of Israel; and I will be jealous for my holy name. They shall forget their shame . . . When I have brought them back from the peoples and gathered them from their enemies' lands, and through them have vindicated my holiness in the sight of many nations. Then they shall know that I am the LORD their God because I sent them into exile among the nations, and then gathered them into their own land. . . . I will not hide my face anymore from them, when I pour out my Spirit upon the House of Israel, says YHWH, your God.
> Ezekiel 39:25-29

Will Ephraim/Israel, the northern part, go under in exile? Will it turn into a catastrophe like that of Admah and Zeboiim (and Sodom and Gomorrah)? And will all the nations say, "Why has the LORD done this to the land? What means the heat of this great anger?" (Deut 29:23, 24) No, not like Admah and Zeboiim (Sodom and Gomorrah) that were turned upside down, but something totally surprising is turned 'upside down', namely the heart of Yahweh.

In unexpected and unimaginable ways, the Name 'happens' in Yahweh's great turn-about. This is the only place Ezekiel uses the word 'mercy', the same way as we already heard the word in Deuteronomy 30:1-6, "And you call them (the blessings and the curses) to mind among all the nations where the LORD, your God has driven you, and return to the LORD, your God... and obey his voice... with all your heart... then the LORD your God will restore your fortunes, and have compassion (mercy) upon you." "He will gather you and He will fetch you... and the LORD your God will circumcise your heart and your offspring, so that you will love the LORD your God with all your heart and with all your soul that you may live."

Hosea proclaims, "I will love them no more," (Hos 9:15); for there is "no knowledge of God."

> They shall return to Egypt, and *Assyria* shall be their king,
> because they have refused to return to me...
> They are appointed to the yoke, and none shall remove it...
>   Hosea 11:5–7

Egypt and Babylon are mentioned in the same context. Here in the negative sense, as a judgment and punishment of their unfaithfullness. Yet, from out of the depth of his being Yahweh cannot abandon his son Ephraim,

> Who is a God like thee, pardoning iniquity
> and passing over transgression
> for the remnant of his inheritance?
> He does not retain his anger forever
> because he delights in steadfast love.
> He will again have compassion upon us
> He will tread our iniquities under foot...
> Thou wilt show faithfulness to Jacob
> and steadfast love to Abraham,
> as thou hast sworn to our fathers
> from the days of old.
>   Micah 7:18–20

> Is Ephraim my dear son?
> Is he my darling child?
> For as often as I speak against him,
> I do remember him still.
> Therefore my heart yearns for him;
> I will surely have *mercy* on him,
> says the LORD.
>   Jeremiah 31:20

Yahweh maintains his solidarity regardless of Israel's unfaithfulness. He will lure Israel like a lover into the wilderness (desert) and there speak tenderly to her. (Hos 2:14) In the desert (usually a metaphor for death),

THE NATURE OF BIBLICAL THEOLOGY

the word (dabar) can be heard. In the desert, life is near impossible. But in Jeremiah the desert is the place of the wedding feast, "I remember the devotion of your youth, your love as a bride, how you followed me in the wilderness." (Jer 2:2)

Yahweh will have compassion in spite of unfaithfulness and rejection. It is an astounding message that we cannot fathom but only embrace by faith. "The LORD will have compassion on Jacob and will again choose Israel, and will set them in their own land..." (Isa 14:1) Therefore, "Go forth from Babylon, flee from Chaldea, declare this with a shout of joy, proclaim it, send it forth to the end of the earth; say, 'The LORD has redeemed his servant Jacob!'" (Isa 48:20) When they do,

> they shall not hunger or thirst,
> neither scorching wind nor sun shall smite them,
> for he who has pity on them will lead them,
> and by springs of water will guide them.
> And I will make all my mountains a way,
> and my highways shall be raised up.
>
> Sing for joy, O heavens and exult, O earth;
> Break forth, O mountains, into singing!
> For the LORD has comforted his people,
> And will have compassion on his afflicted.
> Isaiah 49:10-11, 13. (cf. Isa 40:1-11)

Because of Yahweh's mercy the prophet can invite everyone to the feast,

> Ho, every one who thirsts,
> come to the waters;
> and he who has no money,
> come buy and eat!
> Come, buy wine and milk
> without money and without price.
> Isaiah 55:1

When my father was seriously ill with pneumonia during the war and was afraid he was going to die, he wanted me to read this passage from Isaiah. I had no idea what was troubling him so deeply. He seemed in anguish. But these verses expressed his hope and comfort. They were the spiritual issues he could not share or talk about, the "good news" according to the prophets. This gospel was not ever talked about. Looking back I wish I could have comforted him more with this total context of the Exodus and the return from Exile ("come buy and eat without money").

I trust that he is comforted now and has found peace from his troubled life (the early death of his father; being responsible for his siblings; having to quit school early as a smart kid; the first world war; the death of his brother from pneumonia during the mobilization; the struggle during the depression to build up a business, the second world war, trying hard to provide food for his kids; immigration in their old age, becoming displaced persons). But then, that was before I became immersed in the scriptures and these words took on personal meaning for me (and finally had something to say from out of the scriptures) under the guidance of Deurloo and the Amsterdam tradition of interpretation. (J. W. Dyk, *Unless someone guide me . . . Festschrift for Karel Deurloo*, 2001)

> As one whom his mother comforts, so I will comfort you;
> you shall be comforted in Jerusalem.
> You shall see, and your heart shall rejoice; your bones shall
>   flourish like the grass . . .
>   Isaiah 66:13, 14

The reason can only be found in Yahweh's mercy and encourages us to confess with the prophet.

> For thou art our Father,
> though Abraham does not know us
> and Israel does not acknowledge us;
> thou, O LORD, art our Father,
> our Redeemer from of old is thy name . . .
> Return for the sake of thy servants,
> the tribes of thy heritage.
>   Isaiah 63:16, 17

No longer will the people say that Yahweh has abandoned them, even though,

> For a brief moment I forsook you,
> but with great *compassion* I will gather you.
> In overflowing wrath for a moment
> I hid my face from you,
> but with everlasting love
> I will have compassion on you,
> says the LORD, your Redeemer.
>   Isaiah 54:7, 8

This central confession of the prophet still remains,

> For your Maker is your husband,
> The LORD of hosts is his name;
> and the Holy One of Israel is your Redeemer,
> the God of the whole earth he is called.
>> Isaiah 54:5

As Jeremiah proclaims,

> In this place of which you say, 'It is a waste without man or beast',
> in the cities of Judah and the streets of Jerusalem that are desolate,
> without man or inhabitant or beast, there shall be heard again
> the voice of mirth and the voice of gladness,
> the voice of the bridegroom and the voice of the bride,
> the voices of those who sing thank offerings to the house of the LORD.
>> Jeremiah 33:10, 11

Children are playing again in the town square; the vendors are busy; a bridal procession is going by. It is a vision of a renewed land and country life. Hearing these words can only give rise to profound surprise,

> Who is a God like thee, pardoning iniquity
> and passing over transgression
> for the remnant of his inheritance?
> He does not retain his anger for ever
> because he delights in steadfast love.
> He will again have compassion upon us,
> he will tread our iniquities under foot.
> Thou wilt cast all our sins
> into the depths of the sea
> thou wilt show faithfulness to Jacob
> and steadfast love to Abraham,
> as thou hast sworn to our fathers
> from the days of old.
>> Micah 7:18–20

The message is clear, "Therefore, says the LORD, I have returned to Jerusalem with compassion; my house shall be built in it, says the LORD of hosts . . . and the LORD will again comfort Zion and again choose Jerusalem." (Zech 1:16,17)

> I will strengthen the house of Judah, and I will save the house of Joseph.
> I will bring them back because I have compassion on them,

> and they shall be as though I had not rejected them;
> for I am the LORD their God and will answer them.
>
> Though I scattered them among the nations,
> Yet in far countries they shall remember me,
> and with their children they shall live and return . . .
> I will bring them home from the land of Egypt, and gather them
>   from Assyria . . .
>   Zechariah 10:6, 9, 10

In many different ways, using a great variety of metaphors, the later prophets, and the twelve Minor Prophets, repeat these messages over and over again. Egypt and Assyria can be mentioned in the same context. Yahweh's chosen people, liberated from Egypt, are going into captivity because of their unfaithfulness, rejecting Yahweh and worshipping other gods, and the great reversal. Yahweh nevertheless bringing a remnant of his people back, because of his unfathomable compassion that arises from the depth of his being.

Prophetic history is the history of God's love, the drama of God's searching and finding, even through the pain of his wrath and judgements. Given our state, his loving can only be by way of sacrifice. He has to 'deny' himself in order to stay with us. *In this way* God loves the world that he sent his only son, to fulfill all righteousness. It is in this context of Yahweh's turn-about, allowing the return from exile of his people that we gain a deeper understanding of John's proclamation, both in the gospel and his Letters.

This love is proclaimed or called out. It is an event, a happening. The unity of his attributes is found in this one deed, that is, in his love. That is how he loved the world that he sent his only son. His love is not some abstract virtue, quality, or romantic notion, rather it has the glow and passion of a love story as portrayed in the Song of Songs. As it says in the First Letter of John,

> In this the love of God was made manifest among us, that God sent his only Son into the world so that we might live through him. In this is love, not that we loved God but that he loved us and sent his Son to be the atoning sacrifice for our sins. Beloved, since God loved us, we also ought to love one another.
>   I John 4:9–11

These are liberating words that had no spiritual meaning for me in growing up, and even now they only have meaning against this Old

Testament setting of Yahweh's turnaround, his astounding love and mercy; liberated from Egypt and Babylon, from idolatry, because of his great compassion. Israel is Yahweh's son and Jesus his first-born son, and by giving his own son we can be children of God . . . and call God, Abba, that is, dear Father. (John 1:12; Rom 8:16; I John 3:1–2, and others). We can't help but be reminded of Yahweh's command to Abraham to offer his only son, Isaac. Such total dedication, it is like a foreshadowing. Jesus came to fulfill all righteousness.

In the course of his discussion, Deurloo will often make passing comments about the dating of Bible books. He believes that it is during the time of the rebuilding of the second temple in Jerusalem that the conditions existed for creating the five books of Moses, the Torah (and many other parts of the scriptures). Reading the account of the exodus we soon realize that it is not a 'historian' talking; it is Moses, the prophet. The story of the exodus is not 'historical' in the sense of 'ordinary', 'factual' history based on 'verified-facts-history', (with a dose of imagination to connect the facts into a meaningful account) with its underlying sense of fate or chance. There was no TV camera crew to film and record the events.

The same is true with the events around Jesus, his birth, death and resurrection. We cannot reconstruct a history of the life of Jesus, according to 'historical' research guidelines. Such 'ordinary' history cannot begin to capture the depth of the miracle of the exodus or the return from exile, or the resurrection. It is 'reductionistic' and 'one-dimensional'. It wasn't until the second temple period that the 'structural infra-structures' (Finkelstein and Silberman, *The Bible Unearthed*, 2002), were present that could give rise to the creation of the Torah and other books.

> We can assume that the five books of Moses for many reasons took form in the second temple period and conclude that the story is not 'historical'. Far more important is the conclusion that it gives words to Israel's confession.[5]

In view of the archeological evidence and the social and political situation, we can surmise that there was no sudden, total conquest, but only a gradual infiltration and that there was no established, walled city at Jericho and Ai during that period. Within this prophetic account, we can leave those questions open. That too is liberating.

---

5. Deurloo, *Exodus en Exile*, 93.

More important is the prophetic message which Israel gave expression in its confession: 'we have become the people of Yahweh when we were brought out of the house of slavery, out of Egypt, celebrating Passover; every time again, leaving Egypt, celebrating our liberation and freedom, returning from Babylon. We have become his people. We confess Yahweh who says, 'I am the LORD your God, who brought you out of Egypt, so that "you should not be their servants; I have broken the bars of your yoke and made you walk erect." (Lev 26:13) The same words are used by Jeremiah,

> And it shall come to pass in that day, says the LORD of hosts,
> that I will break the yoke from off their neck, and I will burst their bonds,
> and strangers shall no more make servants of them. But they shall serve the LORD, their God.
> Jeremiah 30:8, 9

The return from exile has 'historical' roots in the Babylonian captivity which was terminated during the Persian period. Israel certainly happened and came into existence, even if we do not know exactly 'how'. The account does not tell us much, not only because many did not leave Babylon, so that 'exile' and 'living in captivity' remained a permanent condition for many Israelites. But primarily because "returning from captivity," being exiles became a 'theological' theme, a confession; perhaps the most important theme of the entire TeNak, 'exiles in a foreign land, returning home'. We need to learn to think thematically about the exodus and the exile, and not 'historically'.

At the same time Deurloo can also state in *King and Temple*, "If someone, with good arguments, can make a plausible case for a much earlier date for Genesis, we will readily accept that."[6] More important is the question, why does this story appear at this place in the canon and what does it want us to confess?

Although the wording and formulation may be awkward at times and could be improved upon, Deurloo's intention is clear. 'Ordinary', 'secular' or 'recorded' and verifiable history cannot begin to relate the depth of the experience of the miracles of 'exodus' and 'return from exile', or resurrection. It calls for religious language. It is 'confessional or prophetic history', and calls us to return from exile, again and again, mindful of Yahweh's compassion. We are reminded of a birth announcement

---

6. Deurloo, *King and Temple*, 10, 107.

formulation, mentioned in the introduction: 'The LORD gave us a baby girl', but now to announce an equally great miracle of the exodus and return from exile. Yahweh sets us free! a people! "Bless the LORD, O my soul . . . bless his holy name." Without giving us a lot of details of 'how', 'when' and 'where' exactly; not enough to re-construct a 'history of Israel'; but nevertheless, a 'birth announcement', that calls for a confession: 'Yahweh let us return and set us free'. Maybe there are enough givens here to come to some new formulations and a confession, Yahweh, our Liberator.

'Yahweh sets us free', therefore stay close to your Liberator, that is all that counts, that is the confession and that is all we need to know to chime in with the people of old. Yahweh, He sets us free from all gods, ideologies, world powers, oppressors, rage, anguish, and despair. Let me tell you the story of the miraculous escape from Egypt, and then the return from Babylon. This is how it came about.

"Anyone who does not experience the story of the exodus, does not know who Yahweh is. Anyone who does not practice, the Ten Commandments, will not know what the Name of Yahweh means."[7] It is enough to know, what Yahweh did for his people, and through them, for all humankind.

> Many times he delivered them,
> but they were rebellious in their purposes,
> and were brought low through their iniquity.
> Nevertheless he regarded their distress,
> when he heard their cry.
> He remembered for their sake his covenant,
> and relented according to the abundance of his steadfast love.
> by all those who held them captive.
> Psalm 106:43–46

The stories of the two-fold miracle of the exodus and the return from exile are the two focal points of the Torah and the later prophets. They are the two ways of telling about the Name of Yahweh, of his compassion. We can imagine that the exodus, (by telling about the return from exile), plays the role of a 'primordial beginning' and 'background' for the later telling of the return from exile. By telling of Yahweh's mercy or compassion, they reveal something of the deepest secret of his Name. The entire book of Jeremiah stands under the sign of the exodus. Every time that beginning is recalled. ". . . I remember the devotion of your youth . . .

---

7. Deurloo, *Exodus and Exile*, 59.

how you followed me in the wilderness" (Jer 2:1). Once they had arrived, the people no longer asked, "Where is the LORD who brought us out of the land of Egypt?" (Jer 2:6) Every time the prophet reminds us of that beginning. (cf. Jer 7:22; 11:4; 32:21; 34:13)

Because of their betrayal, "I will love them no more." "They shall return to Egypt, and Assyria shall be their king, because they have refused to return to me." (Jer 11:3; 9:15; cf Amos 2:10; 3:1; 9:7; Mic 6:4 . . .).

> I will bring them home from the land of Egypt, and gather them from Assyria . . . They shall pass through the sea of Egypt, and the waves of the sea shall be smitten, and all the depths of the Nile dried up. The pride of Assyria shall be laid low, and the scepter of Egypt shall depart. I will make them strong in the LORD and they shall glory in his name.
> Zechariah 10:10–12

The two, Egypt and Assyria, are mentioned together. The exodus stands model for and forms the background for the return from exile. The specialness of the return from exile is described in terms of the exodus (Ezek 20:5 and others.). "As the LORD lives who brought up the people of Israel out of the land of Egypt, but "As the LORD lives who brought up and led the descendants of the house of Israel out of the 'north country' and out of all the countries where he had driven them." (Jer 23:7.8; cf. Jer 16:14–16) 'Egypt' and the 'north country' can be used in the same context. The exodus and the return from exile belong together. Together they tell of the depth of Yahweh's compassion, 'leading them out of the land' and 'leading them back to the land' . . . Anyone who has not yet responded to the call to come back from exile, is encouraged and challenged to,

> Seek the LORD while he may be found,
> call upon him while he is near;
> let the wicked forsake his way,
> and the unrighteous man his thoughts;
> let him return to the LORD, that he may have mercy on him,
> and to our God, for he will abundantly pardon.
>
> For you shall go out in joy,
> and be led forth in peace;
> the mountains and the hills before you
> shall break forth in singing,
> and all the trees of the field shall clap their hands.
> Isaiah 55:6, 7, 12 (cf, Ps 72:18, 19; Num 6:24–27)

And we, as gentiles, having heard the secret of the Name, may share in that blessing along with the people of old.

At the end, Deurloo raises the question about, how we can speak, in a systematic theological way about the two focal points and the secret of the Name. His answer is that we cannot start with the usual fourfold: (perfect) Creation, fall into Sin (original sin), Redemption, (the substitutionary atonement), and Fulfillment. How can we reflect on the fall into sin without first having talked about the secret of the Name, beginning with the exodus and the return from exile? Yahweh makes himself known in his deeds. God-with-us! Therefore we cannot start with the doctrine of sin in Systematic Theology and in preaching, but with the Name, the core of the message. In Yahweh's mercy with Israel, he has taken us up in his covenant. In Jesus, the Jew, Yahweh has come near to his people, including the gentiles. It is the intermezzo of sin and alienation that has obstructed the fulfillment of the covenant (Genesis 3, 4).

But, Yahweh in his faithfulness has been able to overcome our lack of faithfulness, moved by his great compassion, in and through his judgements. In Jesus, the kingdom of God has come near. Redemption is the restoration of the broken covenant. This covenant is the presupposition of redemption. Jesus came to "fulfill all righteousness," that is, he lived up to and fulfilled all the expectations of the covenant (Matt 3:15). First, the revelation of the Name, Yahweh's mercy and compassion, the stories of the exodus, then, come things that led to our exile and the miraculous return.

The greatness of his Name is the fact that God is with us in his deeds. Yahweh is with us in his Name, the God of Israel, and in that way wants to be the God of all humanity, in spite of all our resistance. This core is presented right at the beginning of Matthew, where God speaks to Joseph, that Mary will bear a son, the Emmanuel, God with us, "And you shall call his name Jesus, for he will save his people from their sins." That is how 'God-with-us' happened and happens.

9:2 *King and Temple (2004)*

9:2a) A Biblical theological perspective: King and Temple

In the next book by Deurloo, King and Temple, (2004) these two themes are elevated to say something new and unexpected about just kings and rightful temple worship. The king is responsible for the rightful worship and living by the Torah: to execute justice and righteousness. In this execution of their kingship, they stand under the judgments of the prophets. (Ps 72:1–4). It is all about the right kind of kingship in distinction from other peoples' kings. Other kings that are mentioned are representative of brute and arbitrary power, and the enslavement of their people.

Without the temple, we cannot understand the depth and surprise of "God with us." In Matthew 1:23 we read, "And his name shall be called Emmanuel (which means, God with us)." Finally, God's true identity is revealed in Jesus Christ, 'God with us', and will find its ultimate fulfillment at the end time, "Behold, the dwelling of God is with men. He will dwell with them, and they shall be his people, and God himself will be with them." (Rev 21:3)

In order to understand Deurloo's interpretation of the remarkable story of King Josiah's reformation upon finding the book of the law in the temple, it is essential to first read the account in 2 Kings 22, 23, either as a group or individually. It is also important to take note of many references to Deuteronomy. Together, King and Temple give a depth of meaning and a thematic unity that otherwise might escape us. We shall trace these themes in some detail in the pages to come.

The perspective of the Torah is the same as that of the later prophets: the Exodus and Return from Exile. Then, there is the great surprise of Yahweh's mercy and turn about, so that a remnant can return. This is the theme of Exodus and Exile. These themes that may have been dealt with in previous accounts are elevated to a new and unexpected level. The Exodus from Egypt is inseparably connected with the return from exile from Babylon.

In this volume too, Deurloo reiterates his canonical approach. "We will not follow a historical approach, but a canonical-structural . . . we try to be led by the themes of the scriptures themselves in their interconnectedness and diversity. In the first volume the key question is 'what is central in Torah and the later prophets' (exodus and exile). In this volume we ask the question, 'What is central in the earlier prophets connecting the Torah and the later prophets?" (p.9) In the last part, he includes a long section on the Apostolic writings. In the jewish-messianic witness about Jesus, the New Testament, the theme of King and Temple play a central role in the gospels, as will become evident at the end of this section.

In earlier studies, the failure of the Israelites to live up to their covenant relation was already detailed and prepared. H. Blok, et al., *No*

King in those days; about the book of Judges as prophetic history writing, (1982),; and P. Van Midden, *Brotherhood and Kingship: an examination of the meaning of Gideon and Abimelek in the book of Judges*, (1998). In 2001 *Cahier # 19, Judges*, ed. By J. Dyk, et al. eds., was published, which contained an overview of the current research on Judges by K. Spronk and eight other articles. One article, by Hoogewoud, "Samson re-visited" 'updates' the overview of the research, in honor of Aleida van Daalen who had written her dissertation on Samson in 1966. In an elaborate article she 'summarized' and 'updated' (1982) her own dissertation in *No King in those Days*, "Samson refers; Judges 13-16)" In 2001, a volume with the Hebrew text appeared with a new Dutch translation (*a translation to read aloud*), *Judges*. The *Supplement Series #7*, published van Wieringen's dissertation on, *Delilah and the others, Judges 13-16,*" 2007.

Together these studies provide a basic perspective, motifs, themes and key words for a biblical theological overview, a core structure. Especially van Daalen highlights several themes. She highlights, for example, how each of the episodes from the Samson cycle has their counterpart in secular literature. But once again these 'Hero' motifs are taken up in a different context and serve the proclamation. In contrast to the familiar hero stories, Samson is dependant on Yahweh for his power. The birth of such a hero is a miracle. "Behold, you are barren and have no children; but you shall conceive and bear a son . . . no razor shall come upon his head, for the boy shall be a Nazirite to God from birth." (Judg 13:3-5) "He (Samson) shall begin to deliver Israel from the hand of the Philistines." (Judg 13:5) The story as a whole in its context points ahead to the one real judge, Samuel, who calls Israel to repentance, to call on Yahweh, and in this way liberate Israel from the Philistines. This also points ahead to David who does not allow the living God to be blasphemed, but who as a good shepherd kills Goliath and liberates Israel from the Philistines, "After this David defeated the Philistines and subdued them . . . and the LORD gave victory to David wherever he went." (2 Sam 8:1, 6)

In an earlier article, Deurloo (1982), *Cahier # 3*, "The king listens to the Torah, 2 Kings 22 and 23," and points to the concluding words of the prophet Malachi, "Remember the law of my servant Moses, the statutes and ordinances that I commanded him at Horeb for all Israel." (Mal 4:4) Joshua starts with, "This book of the law shall not depart out of your mouth. But you shall meditate on it day and night that you may be careful to do according to all that is written in it." (Josh 1:8) The former prophets are framed by the Torah. Apart from Joshua, contrary to our expectation, the Torah is not mentioned in the earlier prophets, except at the end in 2 Kings 22 and 23. As part of finding the Torah during the renovation of the temple and the reformations of King Josiah, the Passover is celebrated again. Apparently the Passover was not celebrated since the time of Joshua 5:10–12. Thus the Torah, together with the celebration of the Passover frames all of the earlier prophets, from Joshua to Kings.

All the usual *introductory* issues (the historical questions: the when, where and how of its origin) take center stage by many exegetes and dominates interpretation. Exegetes ask themseselves, is there a dependable and historically trustworthy point for these chapters in 2 Kings and from there to trace the origin of the book of Deuteronomy? The primary interest has been on these historical questions. This preoccupation with the historical and literary questions overshadowed the interpretation of the texts. Through this process of historical analysis, they hoped to find the origin of the text and in that way find a reliable basis for their interpretation. All done was done in order to prove the historical validity of Deuteronomy and Kings. For Deurloo it is a backward approach.

The book of Deuteronomy and the story about finding the book of the Torah and the reforms by Josiah (2 Kings) do indeed belong together. There are many references to Deuteronomy. The centralizing of the cultus at a place chosen by Yahweh (Deut 12:5) and the destruction of the 'high places' to make Jerusalem the religious centre refer to each other. The book of Deuteronomy 28:15–68 contains curses that are also referred to in 2 Kings 22:16, "Thus says the LORD, Behold, I will bring evil upon this place and upon its inhabitants, all the words of the book which the king of Judah has read. Because they have forsaken me and have burned incense to other gods, that they might provoke me to anger . . ." There is also a correspondence between Deuteronomy 18:18 about raisng up a prophet and consulting the prophetess Huldah (2 Kings 22: 6). Finally the Passover celebration in Jerusalem mentioned in 2 Kings 23:21, "And the king commanded all the people, 'Keep the pasover to the LORD your God, as it is written in the book of the covenant." finds its parallel in Deuteronomy 16:1, 2, "Observe the month of Abib, and keep the Passover to the LORD your God; for in the month of Abib the LORD your God brought you out of Egypt by night. And you shall offer the Passover sacrifice to the LORD your God, from the flock of the herd, at the place which the LORD will choose, to make his name dwell there." Exegetes conclude that Deuteronomy or a previous edition have co-determined the events of the stories in 2 Kings.

This close connection between Deuteronomy and 2 Kings makes some (Wurthwein) doubt the historicity of the events related in 2 Kings. Wurthwein sees the 'Deuteronomist' giving special authority to the ordinances of the book of Deuteronomy. For Deurloo, his underscoring of the fictional character of these chapters leaves the way open for their real prophetic meaning. Then the historical question no longer needs to obstruct our understanding. In these accounts, he sees the results of a 'Deuteronomistic discussion' by the scribes during the time of the exile. The stories are not just about Josiah, or the historicity of Deuteronomy and Kings, instead they are about their present situation in exile.

For Deurloo the focus is on finding the book of the Torah and covenant making according to the Torah. If, 2 Kings is 'prophetic history' writing, it manifests an unhistorical character, but if so, how did the writers fit this account into the historical situation? How then can the historical question be dealt with? Deurloo considers that Josiah saw his opportunity to expand his territory, reform and centralize the cultus, when there became a power vacuum due to the decline of the Assyrian empire. A religious 'reformation' in connection with that situation seems likely, maybe even a 'centralization' of worship. The historical and prophetical praising of King Josiah can be presented as the figure by which a good king can be portrayed (based on listening to the Torah). He can be the outstanding king, by whom all other kings can be judged, because he turned, to Yahweh and the whole Torah of Moses. "Before him there was no king like him, who turned to the LORD with all his heart, and with all his soul and with all his might, according to all the law of Moses." (2 Kings 23:25)

Josiah is introduced in stages in the story. He took the initiative to restore the temple, which was prefigured earlier by King Jehoash's restoration. (2 Kings 12:4–16) The text does not tell us how in this process the Torah scroll was found. The important issue is that it is found in a climax of events. The key is that Josiah heard the words of the Torah and Yahweh heard him, "because your heart was penitent, and you humbled yourself before the LORD, when you heard how I spoke against this place, and against its inhabitants, that they should become a desolation and a curse, and you have rent your clothes and wept before me, I also have heard you, says the LORD." (2 Kings 22:19)

The Passover had become the feast of the exodus and the covenant. "And the king commanded all the people, 'Keep the Passover to the LORD your God, as it is written in this book of the covenant.' For no such passover has been kept since the days of the judges who judged Israel, or during all the days of the kings of Israel or of the kings of Judah; but in the eighteenth year of King Josiah this Passover was kept to the Lord in Jerusalem." (2 Kings 23:21–23)

The historical issues have been so dominant among exegetes that the real exegetical questions could hardly come to the fore. "That history in which the kingship of David stands central as a sign that points to the future is framed by Joshua and Josiah. If that is the prophetic framework of these books, the exegetes will primarily have to ask themselves with each section what its place and special function is within the whole.

> The prophetic-theological character of this way of writing history makes it clear that on the basis of the books of Joshua-Kings we can know much less of Israel's history, then we thought we knew. But even though we have to place many question marks after the assumed established results of the present-day historical critique, that same critique has been of great service to exegesis. The exegete does not have to know exactly anymore what really took place in the eighteenth year of Josiah, even though it can be helpful to know what can be known. Then he can consider if the text really enters into the flourishing of the citystate Jerusalem in the period of the Assyrian decline during Josiah's reign, or if the text uses this period to highlight the faith history. The political in Israel is supposed to get its form in the light of the Torah. From out of that history a future is born."[8]

This exegetical study by Deurloo, once more emphasizes the 'poverty' and 'limitations' of the critical historical method of interpretation, even though it can give hints for closer exegetical studies. The same can be said about the overviews of the research and commentaries of individual Bible books in the *Supplement Series*. It reminds me of how difficult it was to get a basic understanding and overview of the books of Joshua, Judges and Ecclesiastes, and others, at the University of Toronto library including the theological colleges. To do what Deurloo does in this article and the ones discussed in chapter four, "Deurloo's exegetical methods," would be hard for any individual pastor or priest to do each week in preparation for a sermon. Exegesis has become a highly specialized, scholarly undertaking primarily by those who have a teaching assignment at universities. For this reason alone, I value the Amsterdam

---

8. Deurloo, "De Koning hoort naar de Tora," II Kon.22, 23," Amsterdamse *Cahiers* #3, 69.

tradition of interpretation and its many publications. My only wish is that more of their booklets could be translated into English.

The history of the exodus and exile is framed by the Torah and Passover (the feast of the exodus). If this is the prophetic framework for these stories in 2 Kings, we have to ask ourselves at each point what the special function each episode has within the whole. Are these chapters really about the flourishing of the state of Jerusalem during a period of Assyrian decline? Or does the text use this period to highlight a religious theme that the kingship can only take form within the framework of the Torah. That is how King Josiah can rise, to the surface, because he heard the Torah and Yahweh heard him. "Before him there was no king like him, who turned to the Lord with all his heart... according to all the law of Moses." (2 Kings 23:25) These words echo Deut 6:4, "and you shall love the Lord your God with all your heart." This king, as a representative of the people, makes true the words of "Hear, O Israel: The LORD your God is one LORD." (Deut 6:4) Kings and Torah belong together.

This is how Deurloo sets the stage very early on for his Biblical Theological study of *King and Temple*. He starts with the earliest mention of kings or heroes (the non-kings) in Genesis, followed by Abraham's encounter with gentile kings. Finally he comes to David, the ideal king, who becomes the standard for all the following kings. Likewise, he follows all the references to altars and worship in Genesis. From there he explores the original Tent of Meeting that could move with the people. Then comes the blueprint of the tabernacle; Yahweh, dwelling among his people.

In a series of four articles, Smelik together with his associate, van Soest, contributes another aspect for a biblical theological perspective on the book of kings. "The dynasty of Omri and Ahab; the composition of the book of Kings" (1) in *Cahier # 6* (1985); "Opening formulas in the book of Kings"(2), in *Cahier # 12*, (1993); "Obitiaries in the book of Kings" (3), in *Cahier # 13, (1994);* "Source references in the book of Kings; the composition of the the book of kings" (4), in *Cahiers # 15*, (1996).

By means of a careful linguistic analysis, he establishes the unity of the book of Kings. Instead of breaking up and attributing parts to three different editors as is the usual approach, they propose a framework for the whole of Kings. The proposed blueprint frames the narrative parts. The supposed 'Deuteronomistic editors' are not responsible for the framework. The references to Deuteronomy are an integral part of the whole

THE PROPHETIC CALL TO LOVE AND JUSTICE

of Kings. The narrative parts are not 'historical' in the usual sense of the word. They are prophetic history that underlines the theological meaning. It is history that proclaims. The stories of the prophets Elijah and Elisha fit seamlessly within this framework. Again we can conclude that Smelik as well as Deurloo, turns the 'historical critical' approach upside down and asks instead what function each part (that are usually attributed to a different editor, source or time) plays in the total composition.

In the Torah the kingship is already anticipated. In the promise to Abraham and Sarah, kings are mentioned, "No longer shall your name be Abram, but your name shall be Abraham; for I have made you the father of a multitude of nations. I will make you exceedingly fruitful; and I will make nations of you, *and kings shall come forth from you*." (Genesis 17:5–7) Jacob is given the same promise, ". . . no longer shall your name be called Jacob, but Israel shall be your name. . . . And God said to him, 'I am God Almighty, be fruitful and multiply; a nation and a company of nations shall come from you, and *kings shall spring from you*.' (Gen 35:10, 11) About Esau it is mentioned that ten kings came from his descendants, "These are the kings who reigned in the land of Edom (where Esau had settled), before any king reigned over the Israelites." (Gen 36:31)

Outside of Israel many kings are mentioned, at the end of the journey through the desert, from the king of Egypt to king Sihon and Og, who were the kings of the Amorites and Bashan. Both kings had refused Israel passage through their territory, in spite of Israel's promises and offer to stick to the 'highway' and pay for the water for their cattle, (Num 21:21), as a result they were both defeated.

Seeing what happened to the Amorites, "Moab was in great dread of the people, because they were many; Moab was overcome with fear of the people of Israel." (Num 22:3) In desperation Balak, the king of the Moabites enlisted a diviner, Balaam, to curse the Israelites. Israel was encamped at the plains of Moab beyond the Jordan at Jericho. Their next step would be to cross the Jordan. However Balaam was unable to curse them. The Lord had forbidden him to speak against Israel, at the risk of his life. His ass had to teach him. He was only allowed to speak the words the Lord told him to prophesy. He was made into a reluctant prophet and had to bless the Israelites to the dismay of Balak, "Behold, I received a command to bless . . . The LORD their God is with them, and the shout of a king is among them. God brings them out of Egypt . . . For there is no enchantment against Jacob, no divination against Israel." (Num 23:20–23). So he prophesizes for Israel, "how fair are your tents, O Jacob

... his king shall be higher than Agog, and his kingdom shall be exalted." (Num 24:5. 7)

During his fourth prophecy Balaam even has to prophesy, "... the oracle of the man whose eye is opened, the oracle of him who hears the words of God ... who sees the vision of the Almighty ... a star shall come forth out of Jacob, and a scepter shall rise out of Israel; it shall crush the forehead of Moab and break down all the sons of Sheth. Edom shall be dispossessed ..." (Num 24:15–18). These royal words are reminiscent of Jacob's blessing of Judah. "The scepter shall not depart from Judah, nor the ruler's staff from between his feet ... and to him shall be the obedience of the peoples." (Gen 49:10)

The Torah does not only have its focus on the land but also the king, and anticipates the central theme of the former prophets. In 2 Samuel we read how David defeated the Moabites and the Edomites, (2 Sam 8:1–18; 21:15–18) in reference to the prophecy of Balaam. When Israel, blessed, enters the Promised Land, that blessing will manifest itself in the kingship. With the name of the king on their lips, people bless themselves, a psalm for the king. Psalm 72:17) In *Joshua* and *Judges* we find the transition from the Torah to the kingship. They form a 'theological' unity. The brotherhood is described in the way Joshua had exemplified it for the people. The new land becomes inhabited and everyone finds their inheritance, and when there are problems, they are solved in accordance with the Torah.

Traditionally the image of Judges is the opposite. The Torah no longer functions and with that, the brotherhood is lost. The first kings come to the fore and the author can only sigh, "Wish there was a king (like David). The course of the true king is prepared. Brotherhood and kingship are closely connected themes. The brotherhood will fall apart again and again: Cain and Abel; Abraham and Lot; Jacob and Esau; Joseph and Judah; the northern country (Ephraim and Manasseh) and the southern state of Judah. They will fight each other, but once in a while a leader rises who connects the brothers: Moses, Joshua, Judges, and Samuel, who is a transition figure toward the kingship, and finally King David, who will unite the brothers and unite the north and the south. That union comes to expression in two ways: the Davidic kingship and the temple in Jerusalem. Kingship and Temple also belong together.

Jeroboam, who started his own shortlived dynasty, broke up this union and erected two holy places in Dan and Bethel. The northern kingship is characterized as a 'non-kingship', "not right in the eyes of the Lord."

The northern kingdom ends with the conquest by the Assyrians in 722 BCE. The upper classes are deported. Only a small remnant remained. In 586 BCE the Babylonians took Jerusalem captive and ended the Judean kingship. The leaders, scribes and craftsmen are deported to Babel. The big difference is that a part of the Judeans, after the edict by Cyrus in 536 returned to Jerusalem. The walls of Jerusalem and the temple are rebuilt. The liturgy, the worship and sacrifices are reinstituted. But there is no news of a Davidic king on the throne. The kingship is ended. Or, rather, the true kingship is moved to the endtime.

During this period there is time to reflect on the brotherhood and kingship. It took on literary form. These two themes are constantly interwoven. Both kingship and temple can also become false securities and a denial of God's kingship and true worship, doing righteousness and justice. Many kings "did evil in the sight of the Lord," and led the people astray to serve other gods and become unfaithful to Yahweh. The temple became a false security to cover up their violations of the commandments. Yahweh takes no pleasure in their offerings. (Hos 6:6; 8:13; Jer 7:9–10, 21; Isa 1:12–17)

9:2b) Kingship

In the familiar story of David slaying Goliath, Deurloo clearly showed 'fairy tale' features. It could be written as: "Once upon a time there was a king who had to battle against a people that threatened his land. His armies are stationed on the hills of the valley on one side. The enemy camp was positioned on the other side. The battle has not started yet, because something shocking has taken place. The enemy has appointed a fighter who challenged and taunted the army of the king to appoint a warrior to fight him. Whoever would win the fight, his people and king would rule. That would not be a problem, if it were not for the fact that the enemy fighter was a very powerful giant. Nobody of the royal army dared to face the giant, not even when the king promised half of his kingdom and his daughter. As it happened, a youth came into the camp and offered to fight the giant. He was offered the king's armor, but he had no experience in warfare so he could not feel comfortable in the king's armor. His power seems to be in his ability to protect his sheep and in his cleverness. That is how he defeated the giant. He marries the king's daughter and they lived long and happily forever after . . ." That is how a fairy tale might go.

THE NATURE OF BIBLICAL THEOLOGY

So, is this story from 1 Sam 17 a fairy tale? No, it is about a shepherd boy, who leaves his sheep with another herdsman, to show himself, to be a true shepherd and a true king of his people. He does so with his small weapons, and the Name of Yahweh, Israel's God. David's speech is the core of the story.

> Then David said to the Philistine, 'You come to me with a sword and with a spear and with a javelin; but I come to you in the name of the LORD of hosts, the God of the armies of Israel, whom you have defied. This day the LORD will deliver you in my hand, and I will strike you down, and cut off your head; and I will give the dead bodies of the host of the Philistines this day to the birds of the air and to the wild beasts of the earth; that all the earth may know that there is a God in Israel, and that all this assembly may know that the LORD saves not with sword and spear; for the battle is the LORD's and he will give you into our hand'.
> 1 Samuel 17:45–47

That is the language of the messianic king in Israel. He presents a contrast not only against the armored Philistine but also to Saul and David's tall brothers. "But the LORD said to Samuel, 'Do not look to his appearance or on the height of his stature.'" (1 Sam 16:7) "And when he (Saul) stood among his people, he was taller than any of his people from his shoulders upward." (1 Sam 9:2) David could not move himself in Saul's armor that was offered to him. Later he did marry Saul's daughter, Michal, but they did not live happily ever after. Michal despised David when he danced like an ordinary fellow before the LORD, one with his people. (2 Sam 6:12–19)

Saul asks three times, 'Who is this youth?' Why would the author of Samuel introduce David with a story about his anointing in the previous chapter (1 Sam 16:13) and his presence at the court of Saul playing the harp and the king's armor bearer? Then in the next chapter, he appears suddenly as someone who is unknown to Saul. Did he make a mistake? On the contrary, it seems that he does not know David. He does not really know who David is. When Saul watched him to go to battle against the Philistine, he asked his commander, "Abner, whose son is this youth? And Abner said, 'As your soul lives, O king, I cannot tell.' And the king said, 'Inquire whose son the stripling is." (1 Sam 17: 55, 56) A little later Saul asked again, this time directly of David, "Whose son are you, young man?" And David answered, "I am the son of your servant Jesse, the Bethlehemite." (1 Sam 17:58)

Three times 'whose son', is it too much of a repetition? Let us assume that the narrator is not interested in telling us some anecdotal incidents, but wants us to hear 'history that proclaims'. Then the point would be that not only Saul, we too need to find out who David really is. What does David's answer mean? What does that tell us? He says, "The son of your servant Jesse the Bethlehemite" We remember that David appears suddenly in the story. The Philistines are camped over against the Israelites with Saul in command. "For forty days the Philistine came forward and took his stand, morning and evening." (1 Sam 17:16). None of the mighty warriors of Israel dared to confront him.

The story pauses at this point to switch our focus. "Now David was . . . the son of an Ephrathite of Betheleem in Judah, named Jesse, who had eight sons . . . The three eldest sons of Jesse had followed Saul to the battle . . . David was the youngest; the three eldest followed Saul, but David went back and forth from Saul to feed his father's sheep at Bethlehem." (1 Sam 17:12–15) He goes away from Saul while the three brothers follow Saul. David is a shepherd in Bethlehem. He does not belong to the sphere of Saul. But here we already have the answer to the question, 'whose son is this youth? He is the son of an Ephrathite man from Bethlehem in Judea, his name is Jesse! The teller lets us reread the story as it were with this answer in mind.

David is the shepherd of his people, who will defeat all that threatens Israel with the Name of Yahweh and not with a sword and spear. All he is, as the messianic king, is summarized in this 'unhistorical' story. In 1 Samuel 17:54 we read, "David took the head of the Philistine and brought it to Jerusalem." Historically that is impossible. At this time Jerusalem does not yet belong to Israel. It is a fortified city that David was only able to capture with a clever trick long after the death of Saul. (2 Sam 5:7–9) But the 'city of David' has to appear in this summary about David's origin, of what he is and does. This theme the storyteller embroiders in a 'fairy tale' literary account.

One of the Minor Prophets says it very directly,

> But you, O Bethlehem Ephrathah,
> who are little to be among the clans of Judah,
> from you shall come forth for me
> one who is to be ruler in Israel,
> whose origin is from of old,
> from ancient days.

> And he shall stand and feed his flock
> in the strength of the Lord.
> And they shall dwell secure,
> For now he shall be great to the ends of the earth.
> And this shall be peace...
>   Micah 5:2, 4, 5

This is how the original king of Israel was and that is how he will be: the shepherd whose power is found in the greatness of the Name of Israel's God. Whoever reads the prophets has to be prepared for surprises. In an 'unhistorical' way they can tell about things that truly happened.

Right from the beginning the risks of appointing a king are clearly described in Deuteronomy. Already in the Torah, the desire for a king is questioned, and sets out the criteria for the right king,

> When you come to the land which the LORD your God gives you, and you possess it and dwell in it, and then say, 'I will set a king over me, like all the nations that are round about me'; you may indeed set as king over you him whom the LORD your God will choose. One from among your brethren you shall set as king over you... Only he must not multiply horses for himself, or cause the people to return to Egypt in order to multiply horses... And he shall not multiply wives for himself, lest his heart turn away; nor shall he greatly multiply for himself silver and gold.
> And when he sits on the throne of his kingdom, He shall write for himself in a book a copy of this law... And he shall read in it all the days of his life, That he may learn to fear the LORD his God, by keeping all the words of this law and these statutes, and doing them; that his heart may not be lifted up above his brethren, and that he may not turn aside from the commandment... so that he may continue long in his kingdom, he and his children, in Israel.
>   Deuteronomy 17:14–20

These words are repeated by Samuel. He had appointed his two sons as judges, "but they did not walk in his ways, but turned aside after gain; they took bribes and perverted justice." Then the people demanded that he appoint a king over them,

> Behold, you are old and your sons do not walk in your ways; now appoint for us a king to govern us like all the nations...
> And the LORD said to Samuel, hearken to the voice of the people... They have not rejected you, but they have rejected

> me from being king over them . . . According to all the deeds which they have done to me, From the day I brought them up out of Egypt even to this day, Forsaking me and serving other gods, so they are also doing to you . . . you shall solemnly warn them, and show them the ways of the king who shall reign over them . . . he will take your sons and appoint them to his chariots . . . and he will appoint for himself commanders . . . and some to plow his ground and to reap his harvest . . . He will take your daughters to be perfumers and cooks and bakers. He will take the best of your fields and vineyards and olive orchards . . . He will take the tenth of your grain . . .
> I Samuel 8:4–15

Their desire for a king was a rejection of Yahweh as their king. They wanted a king like all the other nations round about them: a king that would once more enslave them. But the people did not want to listen to Samuel. A little later on Saul is anointed king over Israel and the people shouted, "Long live the king!" Once more Samuel tells the people "the rights and duties of the kingship; and he wrote them in a book and laid it up before the LORD." (I Sam 10:25)

9:2: c) Temple

The goal of the exodus was to worship Yahweh, Israel's God in the desert at the mountain, as Yahweh had promised.

> And God said to Moses, I am the LORD. I appeared to Abraham, to Isaac, and to Jacob, as God Almighty, but by my name the LORD I did not make myself known to them . . . Moreover . . . I have remembered my covenant. Say therefore to the people of Israel, 'I am the LORD . . . I will redeem you with an outstretched arm and with great acts of judgment, and I will take you for my people, and I will be your God . . . And I will bring you into the land which I swore to give to Abraham, to Isaac and to Jacob; I will give it to you for a possession. I am the LORD.
> Exodus 6:2–8

Only in the song of Moses the word 'sanctuary' is mentioned. The temple is still in the future and Jerusalem is only hinted at.

> Thou wilt bring them in, and plant them on thy own mountain, the place, O LORD, which thou hast made for thy abode, the

sanctuary, O LORD, which thy hands have established. The LORD will reign for ever and ever.
Exodus 15:17, 18

In the introduction to the building of the tabernacle the word 'sanctuary' is mentioned. "And let them make me a sanctuary, that *I may dwell in their midst*. According to all that I show concerning the pattern of the tabernacle, and all the furniture, so you shall make it." (Exod 25:8, 9)

The land is a 'holy land', not to be contaminated, because it is the place of the Lord'd presence.. "The land shall not be sold in perpetuity, for the land is mine; for you are strangers and sojourners with me. And in all the country you possess, you shall grant a redemption of the land." (Lev 25:23) Yahweh will choose a place from among the tribes to establish his name there. "But you shall seek the place which the LORD your God will choose out of all tribes to put his name and habitation there; thither you will go, and thither you shall bring your burnt offerings and your sacrifices . . . and there you shall eat before the Lord your God, and you shall rejoice, you and your households . . . and you shall not do according to all that we are doing here this day, every man doing whatever is right in his own eyes; for you have not as yet come to the rest and to the inheritance which the Lord your God gives you." (Deut 12:5-9) ". . . then to the place which the LORD your God will choose, to make his name dwell there, thither you shall bring all that I command you," (12:11) God-with-us.

The Tent of Meeting is the place where God will live among his people. His presence will be there. "Behold, the dwelling of God is with men. He will dwell with them, and they shall be his people, and God himself will be with them. (Rev 21:3, 4; John 1:14) That is the present and future vision.

This already happened during their journey through the desert. In the middle of Exodus (25-40), that is devoted to the planning and building of the House. Yahweh speaks to Moses, ". . . at the door of the tent of meeting . . . there I will meet with the people of Israel, and it shall be sanctified by my glory . . . And I will dwell among the people of Israel, and will be their God. And they shall know that I am the LORD their God, who brought them forth out of the land of Egypt that I might dwell among them; I am the LORD their God." (Exod 29:42-46) These words are repeated by Solomon. (1 Kings 6:13)

When it was completed, a great cloud covered the Tent by day and a fiery column by night. "And Moses was not able to enter the tent of

THE PROPHETIC CALL TO LOVE AND JUSTICE

meeting, because the cloud abode upon it, and the glory of the LORD filled the tabernacle." (Exod 40:34, 35) Later, when the ark was placed inside the temple, "... a cloud filled the house of the LORD, so that the priests could not stand to minister because of the cloud; for the glory of the LORD filled the house of the LORD." (I Kings 8:11, 12) Solomon questioned, "But will God indeed dwell on the earth? Behold, heaven and the highest heaven cannot contain thee; how much less this house which I have built! Yet have regard to the prayer of thy servant ..." (I Kings 8:27)

God's presence is not a foregone conclusion. Ezekiel, the prophet, has to watch in a vision how the glory of the LORD left the temple and then Jerusalem. At the beginning he was shown a vision of the glory of the LORD. "Such was the appearance of the likeness of the glory of the LORD. And when I saw it, I fell upon my face, and I heard the voice of one speaking. And he said to me, 'Son of man, stand upon your feet'... the Spirit entered into me ... I send you to the people of Israel, to a nation of rebels who have rebelled against me ..." (Ezek 10:4;11:22) Only later he sees the glory of the LORD returning to the new temple. "And behold, the glory of the God of Israel came from the east; and the sound of his coming was like the sound of many waters; and the earth shone with his glory ... and behold, the glory of the LORD filled the temple." (Ezek 43:2–5)

That was after the skeletons had come to life again and a remnant had returned to Jerusalem. (Ezek 37) That is why he can end his prophesies with, "... And the name of the city henceforth shall be, The LORD is there." (Ezek 48:35) In Isaiah, the prophet exclaims, "And the glory of the LORD shall be revealed" as the LORD prepared a way through the wilderness for the people to return from exile, "Comfort, comfort my people, says your God, speak tenderly to Jerusalem." (Isa 40:1, 5) In the fullness of time, with Jesus coming, the final prophecy is fulfilled, then and at the end-time.

"Arise, shine, for your light has come, and the glory of the LORD has risen upon you ... and his glory will be seen upon you. And nations shall come to your light, and kings to the brightness of your rising." (Isa 60:1–3). And then follows his visions of the future, "For behold, I create new heavens and a new earth, and the former things shall not be remembered ... But be glad and rejoice for ever ..."; "Then I saw a new heaven and a new earth ... Behold the dwelling of God is with men. He will dwell with them, and they shall be his people, and God himself will be with them. He will wipe away every tear from their eyes, and death shall be no more . . . (Isa 65:17; 66:22; Rev 21:1–5)

It is not surprising that Kuitert, from his earlier period, ends his 'vocabulary' booklet (of key words of the scriptures) with a chapter on "The Glory of the LORD," *Signals from the Bible* (1972). It is interesting that the Torah already carried within itself, the goal of the exodus: Yahweh living among his people." "Then the cloud covered the tent of meeting, and the glory of the LORD filled the tabernacle." (Exod 40:34)

The House or Tent of Meeting was first of all the place for the ark. ". . . You shall erect the tabernacle of the tent of meeting. And you shall put in it the ark of the testimony." (Exod 40:2, 3) The ark is the place where the Ten Commandments are kept, the 'witness'. (Exod 25:16) The core of the Torah gives meaning to the ark and the sanctuary. Wherever the commandments are kept, there Yahweh will have his house and will dwell among his people. The cover of the ark, is called, the 'mercy seat', in the ark you shall put the testimony . . . there I will meet with you, and from above the mercy seat, from between the two cherubims . . . I will speak with you of all that I will give in commandment for the people of Israel." (Exod 25:21, 22)

The mercy seat is also the place where the sins of the people are covered and atoned, during the daily offerings and especially during the celebration of the Day of Atonement. (Lev 16) Ultimately, the secret of the holy place is the word of Yahweh, the ten words, or the two tablets of the witness that were placed in the ark. (Exod 31:18) After the intermezzo of the golden calf, Moses cut two new tablets of stone to be placed in the ark. They are not only preserved but they were also hidden there to guarantee, and witness, that the tent of meeting would remain the house of the LORD: "I am Yahweh your God . . . you shall not . . ."

In as much as the worship in the temple was reality, the word became flesh in the Torah. By reading the book, the words can be heard again, and again, and taken along into the world; the visible becomes audible, into our ears to do them. In the weekly reading on the Sabbath the holy place is present. The Torah is kept in the Holy Ark in the synagogue, just as the witness in the ark of the tent, the home of the witness. For how the first and second temple functioned, we have to read in the Torah. The worship service has become the service of the word. In his song, Moses exclaims, "Thou wilt bring them in, and plant them on thy own mountain, the place, O LORD, which thy hands have established. The LORD will reign for ever and ever." (Exod 15:17, 18)

"But you shall seek the place, which the LORD your God will choose out of all the tribes to put his name and make his habitation there; thither you shall go, and thither you shall bring your burnt offerings, . . . and there you shall eat before the LORD your God, and you shall rejoice, you and your households . . ." (Deut 12:5–7) The LORD will establish when and where the temple will be built. It is not to be possessed or treated like a magical object that they could control.

When the Israelites were about to lose a battle with the Philistines, the Israelites decided to bring the ark of the covenant of the Lord from Shiloh to the battlefield, almost as a magical gesture. When the Philistines heard of it, they were very frightened. "Woe to us! Who can deliver us from the power of these mighty gods?" They had heard about what had happened to the Egyptians with every sort of plague." (1 Sam 4:3–9) But the Philistines took courage and said to the soldiers, "Acquit yourselves like men and fight." So they did and defeated the Israelites. ". . . The glory had departed from Israel, for the ark of God had been captured." (1 Sam 4:22)

But all did not go well for the Philistines, for to whatever city the ark of the Lord was taken, "a great plague broke out; all the inhabitants were afflicted with tumors." (1 Sam 5:1–12) There was a 'deadly panic' among them. The ark stayed in the hands of the Philistines for seven months. It was moved from one city to the other, but each time with the same results. The inhabitants were stricken with tumors and many died. Finally they decided to return the ark to Israel on a new cart with guilt offerings and golden replicas of the tumors. The two milk cows that pulled the cart found their way to Israel, in spite of the calves they had left behind. They came as far as the field of Joshua of Bethshemesh where the cows stopped. Many people were killed, because they looked inside the ark. They responded with, "Who is able to stand before the LORD, this holy God? And to whom shall he go up away from us?" The men of Kiriath-jearim came and took the ark. It stayed there for a long time, some twenty years.

After David was settled, had consolidated his kingship, defeated the Philistines and captured Jerusalem, his one great desire was to build a house for the LORD. He prayed,

> Remember, O LORD, in David's favor,
> All the hardships he endured; how he swore to the Lord
> and vowed to the Mighty One of Jacob,
> 'I will not enter my house

> or get into my bed;
> I will not give sleep to my eyes
> or slumber to my eyelids,
> until I find a place for the Lord,
> a dwelling place for the Mighty One of Jacob' . . .
> Let us go to his dwelling place;
> Let us worship at this foot stool!
> Arise, O LORD, and go to thy dwelling place,
> Thou and the ark of thy might . . .
> For the LORD has chosen Zion;
> He has desired it for his habitation:
> This is my resting place for ever;.
> I will satisfy her poor with bread.
> There I will make a horn to sprout for David . . .
>   Psalm 132 (cf. Ps 24)

He prayed to the LORD, "Behold, I dwell in a house of cedar, but the ark of the covenant of the LORD is under a tent." (1 Chr 17:1) He pleaded with God, but he was forbidden to build a temple and was told that his son would build it. Instead he planned to bring the ark to Jerusalem. He prepared a place for the ark of God, and pitched a tent for it. "Then let us bring again the ark of our God to us; for we neglected it in the days of Saul . . . and they carried the ark of God upon a new cart . . ." (1 Chr 13:3, 7; 1 Chr 17:16)

His first attempt had failed. Uzzah had touched the ark unlawfully when it seemed it was about to fall off the new cart and was killed. After this failure David asked himself, "How can I bring the ark of God home to me? (1 Chron 13:12) So David hesitated to bring the ark further to Jerusalem; he was angry with the LORD and feared for his life. It was temporarily parked at the house of Obededom.

Three months later he tried again when he heard that Obededom's house was blessed. " . . . So David went and brought up the ark of God from the house of Obededom to the city of David with rejoicing." (2 Sam 6:12) This time he had the Levites, after they had sanctified themselves, carry the ark as Moses had prescribed. "And David danced before the LORD with all his might; and he was girded with a linen ephod. So David, and all the house of Israel, brought up the ark with great rejoicing and with shouting, and with the sound of the horn." (2 Sam 6:14, 15) The author of Chronicles adds a whole band to the procession, ". . . to the sound of the horn, trumpets, and symbols, and made loud music on harps and lyres," (in keeping with the Chronicler's emphasis on liturgy, on singing and music). (1 Chr 15:25–28)

K.A.D. Smelik, one of the frequent contributors to the *Cahiers*, #4, ("The entry of the ark in Jerusalem," 2 Sam 6:1–23; 1 Chr 16:1–43) considered whether or not this story is based on an ancient fertility cult as many commentaries hold, and originates from a different source. Clothed only in a linen ephod, while dancing, jumping and leaping, at times David's genitals would become visible. In the ancient world, seeing the king's private parts was considered to enhance fertility for whoever caught a glimpse. Also considered to enhance fertility, were the cakes of dates and raisins that the king handed out to all Israel. Smelik translates that David handed out to all Israel "from man to woman." (2 Sam 6:19) The king symbolized the fertility of the people. After that the king turned to go to his palace to bless his own household as well. Instead he encounters Michal, Saul's daughter with her disdainful criticism. "How the king of Israel honored himself today before the eyes of his servant's maids, as one of the vulgar fellows shamelessly, uncovers himself!" (2 Sam 6:20) So instead of the event culminating in a ritual marriage with the queen, he reminds her. "It was before the LORD, who chose me above your father, and above all his house, to appoint me as prince over Israel, the people of the LORD." (2 Sam 6:21)

However correct this allusion may be, Smelik insists that considering the whole of 2 Samuel 6, this episode is not to be interpreted as Michal's protest against the feritility cults. Instead it is to be understood as the final break between Saul's house and David's. Michal, explicitly named the daughter of Saul, will remain infertile and there will be no future connection between Saul's offspring and David's. No physical descendants, but an absolute rejection of Saul's dynasty. Their marriage will not serve to strengthen the monarchy. Michal will remain childless till her death.

It is another example of how a possible reference to an ancient fertility rite is taken up in this proclamation. David shows himself as the chosen and true king over Israel. The connection between other parts of Samuel must be taken into account when interpreting this episode. It is not about an old legend of the entry of a holy object into the city, something which hardly would concern us today. It is about how this part of 1 Samuel 6 fits into the whole of Samuel. It is another part of how the people can enter into a relationship with a holy God, the God of Israel and in which way Yahweh will continue his journey with the people. "I will make merry before the Lord." His dance is first of all a sign of joy and humility before God. It calls to mind the account in 1 Samuel 4, 5 and 6. In a previous article Smelik highlights many of these same points in *Cahier #1*, "The ark in the land of the Philistines."

And they brought the ark of God and set it inside the tent which David had pitched for it. He distributed "to all Israel, both men and women, to each a loaf of bread, a portion of meat, and cakes of dates and raisins." He composed and sang a song of thanksgiving. "O, give thanks to the LORD, call on his name, make known his deeds among the peoples! . . . " (1 Chr 16:8–35) David danced with all his might. He was ecstatic, because of the miracle of the LORD dwelling among his people, in a permanent place, God-with-us. The court annals of the kings might have recorded that on December 25 in the year 586 B.C.E. that the ark of the LORD was brought to Jerusalem, but they might not have recorded what David experienced, or we.

In the apostolic writings, the themes of King and Temple play a central role, especially at Jesus' trial and crucifixion. In the oldest gospel of Mark this theme stands out strongly. (Mark 14:53–15:39). In Matthew the emphasis is on kingship and in Luke on the temple. The book of Revelation deserves special attention as it witnesses to the real Messianic King and Judge.

When Pilate asks Jesus is asked, "Are you the king of the Jews? And he answered, 'You have said so.'" (Luke 23:3). Instead the rulers mocked him, saying 'He saved others; let him save himself, if he is the Christ of God, his Chosen One.The soldiers also mocked him . . . if you are the king of the Jews, save yourself. . . There was also an inscription over him, 'This is the king of the Jews.'" (Luke 23:5–38) This is not a report or a documentary, but a proclamation story, for us to come to understand that his kingship was of a very different order. This Messianic king must suffer, be crucified, die and be resurrected. He came to serve and not to rule over. That was a difficult lesson for the disciples to learn, for they quarreled among themselves, who would be the greatest, in the kingdom of heaven. He was the Annointed One in the sense of a true king, 'anointed' by a prophet. (1 Sam 16:7; 2 Sam 7:13, 14) He is also the suffering servant of Isaiah, despised and rejected. In this way he fulfilled all righteousnes as a true king, seeking justice and solidairity for all to the very end. (Ps 72). He is a royal king riding on a donkey, and mocked by the authorities.

Paul does not mention the temple as such. Instead he highlights a fundamental change that has taken place with the crucifixion, death and resurrection of Jesus. He writes,

> Do you not know that you are God's temple and that God's Spirit dwells in you? If anyone destroys God's temple, God will destroy him. For God's temple is holy, and that temple you are.
> 1 Corinthians 3:16 (cf. Eph 2:19–22)

How did Paul come to use the image of the temple in this way and apply it to the new fellowship of Jesus' followers? This usage is based on Jesus' own testimony in the gospels, "Destroy this temple and in three days I will raise it up . . . But he spoke of the temple of his body" (John 2:19–21). "The Son of man must suffer many things, and be rejected by the elders and chief priests and scribes, and be killed, and on the third day be raised. (Luke 9:21) Before his death he instituted the Lord's Supper, "And he took a cup. ". . And he took bread, and when he had given thanks he broke it and gave it to them, saying, this is my body." (Luke 22:14–28; 1 Cor 11:17–26) In the last chapter of Luke, Jesus said, "These are my words which I spoke to you while I was still with you . . . Then he opened their minds to understand the scriptures and said to them, "Thus it is written, that the Christ should suffer and on the third day rise from the dead, and that repentance and forgiveness of sin should be preached in his name to all nations, beginning from Jerusalem'. The gospel ends with, "And they returned to Jerusalem with great joy, and were continually in the temple blessing God." (Luke 24:44, 53)

Luke writes after the destruction of the temple in 70 A.D. (Luke 19:41-48; 21:20–24). He writes, "And as some spoke of the temple . . . As for these things which you see, the days will come when there shall not be left here one stone upon another that will not be thrown down." (Luke 21:5, 6) For the new Christians living far away from the destroyed temple, these words are a comfort. In the midst of death there is life. "He took a cup and took bread."

Luke uses the word temple thirty six times. "And every day he was teaching in the temple . . . and the people came to him in the temple." (Luke 21:37, 38; 19:47; 20:1) In the temple he chased out the money changers (Luke 19:45-48). Luke's gospel starts in the temple with Zechariah. When after the Passover, Jesus' parents could not find him and questioned him, he replied, "How is it that you sought me? Did you not know that I must be in my Father's house? The books of the temple are read in the synagogue. What begins in the temple is sounded out in the synagogue?" (Luke 2:49) In his Father's house, the temple, that is where the Torah is kept in the Ark of the Covenant.

In Moses' time, the tabernacle held the Torah scroll, "And you shall put the mercy seat on the top of the ark; and in the ark you shall put the testimony that I shall give you. There I will meet with you, and from above the mercy seat, from between the two cherubim that are upon the ark of the testimony that I shall give you, I will speak with you of all that I will give in commandment for the people of Israel." (Exod 25:19–22) In chapter 29:45, it adds, "And I will dwell among the people of Israel, and be their God. And they shall know that I am the Lord their God, who brought them forth out of the land of Egypt that I might dwell among them; I am the Lord their God." The Torah scroll which was kept in the ark could go with them wherever they went, into the Promised Land (Joshua 1:8) and that can travel along, into exile. In Nazareth Jesus "went to the synagogue, as his custom was, on the Sabbath day. And he stood up to read; and there was given to him the book of the prophet Isaiah." (Luke 4:16,17; 13:10)

Just as the scriptures from the temple, the encounter with God is 'wrapped' in the Torah scroll, so Luke 'wraps up' the temple in his gospel, so that everyone can take the temple with them as the starting point of the gospel, also after the destruction of the temple "And beginning with Moses and the prophets, he interpreted to them in all the scriptures the things concerning himself . . . These are my words which I spoke to you, while I was still with you, that everything written about me in the law of Moses and the Prophets and the Psalms must be fulfilled." (Luke 24:44–49) Then he opened their minds to understand the scriptures.

The emphasis is on the scriptures, from the temple, that can travel with God's people everywhere on earth. First Jesus identifies his own body with the temple and then with all those who believe in him, the body of believers. Paul wrote. God's presence is no longer tied to a particular place. The gathering of the followers of Jesus can be called his body, the temple, where the scriptures are opened. "But the hour is coming, and now is, when the true worshippers will worship the Father in spirit and truth." (John 4:22–24) A new priesthood has emerged without King or Temple, only the TeNaK or in Jesus' words, Moses, the Prophets and the Psalms. Both the word King and Temple are lifted up to a new meaning. ". . . and you shall be my witnesses in Jerusalem, and in all Judea and Samaria and the end of the earth." (Acts 1:8)

In the book of Revelation the words King and Temple receive a new meaning in the many visions seen by John. In Revelation 1:5 Jesus is called "the ruler of the kings of the earth." In a vision John sees seven golden lampstands and in the midst of them, a figure like a son of man, (Rev 1:13), which are the seven churches. (Rev 1:20) With John we get a glimpse of heaven. The earthly and heavenly temple, are seen as each other's complement. The holy of holies mirrors the sanctuary in heaven. A door is opened in heaven, (Rev 4:1–11) different aspects of the church are shown and we become participants in the heavenly liturgy. Is it a temple or a palace? The images seem to intertwine.

The temple is the place where God resides as the King and where the Ark of the Covenant is based (Rev 11:19). What was strictly separated in the Old Testament coincides in Revelation. The focus is on the heavenly king. The one standing before his throne is in the temple cleansed liturgically (Rev 7:15). John structures his Apocalypse according to the formula seven times seven, forty nine visions in total. He ends his visions with Jesus who will be heaven on earth. The temple in Jerusalem is destroyed (Rev 11:2), but now the temple is equal to the church with Jesus at its head. (Rev 11:5, 19) God's people are made to be priests that will reign like kings. (Rev 5:10)

Kingship and priesthood become one. God's people are a kingdom of priests. The separation between the holy and the world is undone and becomes total in Revelations 21. He has power over all evil. The other kind of kingdom is that according to the model of the Dragon, followed by seven visions of Babylon and the counter-image of Jesus. After the whore of Babylon is defeated the bride of Zion is presented.

> The kingdom of the world has become the kingdom of our Lord and of his Christ, and he shall reign for ever and ever . . . Then God's temple in heaven was opened, and the ark of his covenant was seen within his temple."
> Revelation 11:15, 19

This is followed in chapter 21 by the marriage between heaven and earth.

> Then I saw a new heaven and a new earth...And I saw the holy city, new Jerusalem, coming down from heaven from God, prepared like a bride adorned for her husband; and I heard a great voice from the throne saying, "Behold, the dwelling of God (the tabernacle or the tent of meeting) is with men. He will dwell with them, and they shall be his people, and he Himself will be with them; and he will wipe away every tear from their eyes, and death shall be no more, neither shall there be mourning nor crying nor pain any more, for the former things have passed away."
> Revelation 21:1–4

The bride does not take residence in heaven but on the earth. There is no longer a temple; it has become superfluous. There will be no more candlesticks, for God himself will be the light. "And night shall be no more; they need no light of lamp or sun, for the LORD God will be their light, and they shall reign for ever and ever. (22:5). The Messianic King, even if it was David, could not accomplish this. In exile they had to do without an altar. In the New Testament it is the same, they have to do without a Temple and without a King. The new followers of Jesus, the messiah, have the TeNaK, the words of apostles and prophets. The words King and Temple have taken on a whole new Messianic meaning.

9:3 Barren Women and Unexpected Sons (2006)

9:3a) Introduction

The third volume in this Biblical Theology series *Our dear mother gives birth to a Son* is closely connected to the previous books, the same themes appear, with different images and emphases. Deurloo raises another core theme, that of (barren) mothers and the birth of their (first-born, 'first-ling') sons. Here too, the theme of the 'barren mothers and first-born sons' is raised to a new level. Those miraculous births throughout Israel's history culminate in the birth of *the Son*, Jesus," the first-born of the whole creation." (Col 1:15-20) From out of the Messiah, we gain perspective on the entire creation. It is for the sake of humans, heaven and earth were created.

In the scriptures, including the New Testament, the emphasis is not on the origin but on the presence of the Name. Again, Deurloo emphasizes the canonical, rabbinical order, guided by the designation: the *Law* (Torah, the five books of Moses) and the *Prophets* (the four books, Isaiah, Jeremiah, Ezekiel, and the book of the twelve Minor Prophets), the *Writings* (Psalms, Ruth, Job, etc.). The New Testament can only be understood in relation to the authoritative witness of Moses and the Prophets and as celebrated in the Writings. Heaven and earth are created for the sake of the gift of the Torah given on Mount Sinai to Israel. And who is Israel? Yahweh calls this people out of Egypt, his first-born son. The middle of the Old Testament reveals itself in the revelation of the Name in the becoming of Israel as Yahweh's people, Yahweh's son. In the prophets the emphasis is on the great turn-about of Yahweh and return from exile, moved by his mercy, *Exodus and return from Exile*. Again, we will closely follow Deurloo's account in this third volume of Deurloo's Biblical theology.

There are many sculptures and paintings of Madonna holding or breast-feeding her baby. It reminds us of the passage in Genesis where Sarah says, "God has made laughter for me; everyone who hears will laugh over me . . . Who would have said to Abraham that Sarah would suckle children? Yet I have borne him a son in his old age." (Gen 21:6, 7) A painting of this scene would indeed be a little comical, a very old woman (ninety years old) suckling a baby. It is almost more miraculous than a breast-feeding virgin.

In near-Eastern society, women only counted if they gave birth to sons. That infertility could also be the husband's problem, would not occur to anyone during those times. Eternal virginity was not an ideal; there was certainly no halo of holiness surrounding it. Equating sexual intercourse with sin is not a biblical notion. Not to be able to bear children was a horrible fate for a woman. Jefta's daughter was allowed to mourn her virginity for two months. The fact that she has to remain a virgin was as terrible as the infertility of the tribal mothers, the primordial mothers. The harem rivalry between Leah and Rachel finds its source in their infertility. But at least Rachel was loved by Jacob, "and he loved Rachel more than Leah." (Gen 29:18). We can understand Leah's agony even after she conceives and gives birth to a son, "surely now my husband will love me." (Gen 29:32)

When Rachel becomes envious and distressed she cries out to Jacob, "Give me children, or I shall die." (Gen 30:1). Jacob becomes angry and exclaims, "Am I in the place of God, who has withheld from you the fruit of the womb?" (Gen. 30:2) In desperation, she gave Jacob her maid, Bilhah, "Here is my maid, Bilhah, go in to her that she may bear upon my knees, and even I may have children through her." (Gen 30:3) Finally when, "God remembered Rachel . . . and opened her womb and she conceived and bore a son, she said, 'God has taken away my reproach.'" (Gen 30:23) It reflects her deep sense of shame, the injury of being childless. Such views are not normative for us today, even though it still lingers.

This theme of the barren women, however, is taken up to another level to express something new and unheard of. It serves the inauguration of the history of Israel and a new start for humanity. The mother who becomes pregnant in a surprising way can be called, 'mother Zion' ("Deborah arose as a mother in Israel" (Judg 5:7); "He gives the barren woman a home, making her the joyous mother of children" (Ps 113:9);

"You seek to destroy a city which is a mother in Israel," see 2 Sam 20:19, in which Israel may recognize itself. She may give birth to a future, a son. A miraculous birth can stand for an impossible and unheard of event and can stand for the overwhelming progression of salvation, which nobody expected anymore. It is typical for the Old Testament that this theme of mothers and sons arises at crucial moments.

Breukelman has formulated the topic of the first book of the Bible as the becoming, the genesis or birth of Israel in the midst of the peoples of the earth. Hence its name, Genesis, because it is one long genealogy, or birth announcements. After the overtures of chapters 1:1–3 and 2:4–4:26, we read, "This is the book of the generations of Adam, the earthling." (Gen 5:1). Would 'genealogy' not be a better name? No, because it is not about looking back, but looking forward. The question is not, from whom did he descend, but who came forth from Adam, namely the son, Israel.

When we read, "These are the descendants of Terah," (Gen 11:27) then what follows are the names of those born to Terah, with their life story. It also made clear that our tribal mother, the mother of Israel will have to appear in a miraculous way. Right from the beginning it is mentioned, almost in passing, "Now Sarah was barren; she had no child." (Gen 11:30) There can be no question of the birth of sons, of offspring. The future of Israel, the birth of a son, will not come about through "the will of the flesh." (John 1:13) The theme of 'mother and son' is not about natural processes, but about a powerful witness, a decisive and crucial event in history.

Through the natural impregnation of the daughters of man by the sons of God, heroes and giants will be born. (Gen 6:1–4) Not so in Israel, because their tribal mother is either old, infertile or a virgin. Nevertheless a son will be born. There will be a future for humanity. Masculine potency has no effect. It is a hopeless situation. Barrenness becomes a core theme. We are slaves in Egypt, how will we be liberated? Through Pharaoh's murder of the infants there will be no future. How will Moses be born? Without descendants will a people walking in darkness ever hear the promise, "For to us a child is born, to us a son is given . . ."? (Isa 9:6) Will something happen that will change the course of human history that will make living worthwhile and allow us to live in expectation?

Imagine that humanity is 'expecting', but not through male seed, but through the hearing of a word! Are the images metaphorical or literal? The psalms are full of such 'strong' or 'ambiguous' expressions, "For the waters have come up to my neck." (Ps 69:1; 42:8) For Jonah, however these words were all too real as he prays in the belly of the whale, in the Pit, ". . . all thy waves and thy billows have gone over me" (Psalm 42:7). For him the citations from the psalms, which no doubt he knew by heart, have become literally true. "The waters closed in over me, the deep was round about me." (Jonah 2:3) He was literally thrown into the roiling waters of the sea. He was in the belly of the fish, in the pit, in Sheol. It is a familiar image in mythology: a mother giving birth to a son (Isa 54:1, 3), the metaphorical and literal run through each other. In this way the prophetic proclamation about Zion that is barren yet receives sons, becomes narrative reality in the story about Sarah.

It is not surprising that 'being pregnant and giving birth' are frequent images used in the scriptures. In a negative sense we hear the psalmist say, "Behold the wicked man conceives evil, and is pregnant with mischief, and brings forth lies. (Ps 7:14) Or, ". . . they conceive mischief and bring forth iniquity." (Isa 59:4) There is no future in these births, "You conceive chaff, you bring forth stubble." (Isa 33:11) Yahweh will make the land childless, "I have bereaved them . . . I have made their widows more in number than the sand of the seas . . . She who bore seven has languished; she has swooned away; her sun went down while it was yet day.(Jer 15:7–9) The coming exile also affects the prophet, "You shall not take a wife, nor shall you have sons and daughters in this place." (Jer 16:1, 2) But once in exile he can say, "Build houses and live in them, plant gardens and eat their produce. Take wives and have sons and daughters; take wives for your sons, and give your daughters in marriage, that they may bear sons and daughters; multiply there . . ." (Jer 29:5, 6). A new period is in sight. (Isa 54:1, 2) There is hope a barren one will give birth to a new future.

It will be a miraculous birth that takes narrative form in Israel, in the stories about 'tribal' mothers. According to Genesis, this breakthrough to the future is also Israel's origin. This theme returns in many forms: in the birth of Moses. Israel's kingship is embedded in prophecy, which is told in the birth of Samuel out of a barren Hannah; and how prophecy creates life, is told in the mother-son stories of Elijah and Elisha. 'Our dear mother' appears as a sign in heaven in the book of (Rev 12:1–6). Then there is the 'mother Mary ideology' that must be evaluated by the New Testament itself. It is the gospel variation of the theme in the TeNaK. Each of these miraculous births is an exposition of the incarnation, the Word becoming flesh. It is the surprising gift of the future, Yahweh overcoming the unfaithfulness of his people by his faithfulness, his mercy, regardless of the cost. The Emmanuel appears in Jesus, who will save his people and the gentiles.

After this introduction Deurloo discusses each segment in detail. It is a rewarding journey. I have chosen a few parts because of their special interest and richness.

Jeremiah is told by the LORD to buy a field, even though the enemy is about to capture the city. What good is a field when he is about to go into exile? It seems like a crazy, hopeless task. Yet the prophet confesses, "Ah LORD God! It is thou who hast made the heavens and the earth by thy great power and by thy outstretched arm! Nothing is too hard for thee" (Jer 32:17). The LORD said, "Behold I am the LORD, the God of all flesh; is anything too hard for me?" (Jer 32:27) and then he makes a promise:

> Fields shall be bought in this land of which you are saying, It is a desolation, without man or beast; it is given in to the hands of the Chaldeans. Fields shall be bought for money, and deeds shall be signed and sealed and witnessed, in the land of Benjamin, in the places round about Jerusalem and in the cities of Judah . . .
> Jeremiah 32:43, 44

The piece of land Jeremiah has bought is a sign of the future that nobody expects anymore . . . The same words are used by the Lord when he speaks to Sarai, the mother of Israel. Her situation is as hopeless as those of the surrounding people of Jerusalem. Sarah is the missing link in the chain of generating which Genesis talks about. From out of Adam, the human, Israel is supposed to come forth, first-born among the nations. The line of the generations must lead to Abraham, Isaac and Jacob. With Abram it will happen. Because of his calling, everything centers round Abram. The storyteller lets Lot, the 'natural first-born' son of Haran travel along with Abram. (Gen 12:4; 13:1) It gives rise to the question, with whom will it continue, with the first-born or with the 'called' one? Sarai was barren and without a baby. Israel cannot be born. How can that be with the promise to Abram that was repeated several times, "to your descendants I will give this land?" (Gen 12:7) When Abram finally requests that his main, trusted servant be his heir, Yahweh says, "This man shall not be your heir; your own son shall be your heir." (Gen 15:4)

When Abram was ninety-nine years old the LORD appeared to him and made a covenant with him, ". . . I will multiply you exceedingly . . . no

THE PROPHETIC CALL TO LOVE AND JUSTICE

longer shall your name be Abram, but your name shall be Abraham; for I have made you father of a multitude of nations . . . As for Sarai your wife, you shall not call her name Sarai, but Sarah shall be her name. Sarah was listening at the tent door behind him. "I will bless her, and moreover I will give you a son by her . . . Then Abraham fell on his face and laughed, and said, to him self, 'shall a child be born to a man who is a hundred years old? Shall Sarah, who is ninety years old, bear a child?'" (Gen 17:5, 15, 17) Sarah is not only barren but also ninety years old, a double barrier. The writer spells out this event in some detail, because it concerns the core of the TeNaK. Before long, via Isaac and Jacob's twelve sons, we find ourselves in Egypt.

The four tribal mothers, or matriarchical mothers, have one thing in common, they are all barren. At the crucial moment the natural course of events fails; intercourse is of no effect. Isaac has to plead with the LORD to open Rebecca's womb. This given is already prepared for by the first birth of Eve, mother of all that lives.

When she has given birth to Cain, she exclaims, "I have gotten a man with the help of the LORD." (Gen 4:1). Adam mirrors Yahweh's creative deed, "When Adam had lived a hundred and thirty years, he became the father of a son in his own likeness, after his image, and named him Seth," just as Yahweh created man in the likeness of God. Male and female he created them, and he blessed them and named them Man when they were created." (Gen 5:1–5) In the Writings, the wedding wish for Boas and Ruth is,

> May the LORD make the woman, who is coming into your house, like Rachel and Leah, who together built up the house of Israel. May you prosper . . . and be renowned in Bethlehem, and may your house be like the house of Perez, whom Tamar bore to Judah . . ."
> Ruth 4:11,12

That is how Naomi is comforted,

> . . . For your daughter-in-law who loves you, who is more to you, than seven sons, has borne him. Then Naomi took the child and laid him in her bosom, and she became his nurse. And the women of the neighborhood gave him a name, saying, 'a son has been born to Naomi'. They named him Obed; he was the father of Jesse, the father of David.
> Ruth 4:15–17

The Moabite, Ruth, has joined the people of Israel. In the overture to the gospel of Matthew after the murder of the infants, the author thinks of the mothers of Bethlehem and with them about all the mothers of Israel, "A voice was heard in Ramah, wailing and loud lamentations, Rachel weeping for her children; she refused to be consoled.Because they were no more." (Matt 2:18) Ramah is identified with Bethlehem and she refuses to be comforted just like Jacob when he hears of the 'death' of his son Joseph.

Rachel's grave is on the way to Bethlehem. (Gen 35:19; 48:7) Almost in passing it mentions, "Rachel to my sorrow died in the land of Canaan on the way, when there was still some distance to go to Ephrata; and I buried her there on the way to Ephrata, that is Bethlehem . . . and Israel journeyed on . . ." The grave points to the birthplace of David, thus to the kingship. In Jeremiah the son of Rachel is called Ephraim, who just as Israel in Egypt is called God's first-born son. (Exod 4:22) Ephraim, according to this prophet is lost in captivity, but he will return them to the land, "Behold, I will bring them from the north country . . . for I am a father to Israel, and Ephraim is my first-born." (Jer 31:9) Ephraim represents every one. He is not lost forever, dispersed among the nations.

Here too with regard to the theme of 'mothers and sons' the Torah and the prophets need to be read together. They refer to and assume one another. "Look to Abraham your father and to Sarah who bore you." (Isa 51:2) This author is familiar with Genesis. He lets the miracle to Sarah happen again, without mentioning her name, "Sing, O barren one, who did not bear; break forth into singing and cry aloud, you who have not been in travail!" Exiled Israel will return and bear children. Yahweh stands behind it, ". . . you will forget the shame of your youth, and the reproach of your widowhood . . . For your Maker is your husband, the LORD of Hosts is his name; and the Holy One of Israel is your Redeemer, the God of the whole earth he is called," (Isa 54:1–5) ". . . enlarge the place of your tent . . ." (Isa 54:2)

It is time for re-building and renovation; get ready to return. ". . . The place is too narrow for me; make room for me to dwell in . . . I was bereaved and barren, exiled and put away, but who has brought up these?" (Isa 49:21) The prophet himself spells out the answer, "But now thus says the LORD, he who created you, O Jacob, he who formed you, O Israel: 'Fear not, for I have redeemed you; I have called you by name, you are mine.'" (Isa 43:1) The birth process is happening. The miracle is almost complete. "Behold a virgin shall conceive and bear a son, and his name shall be called Emmanuel, (which means, God with us)." (Matt 1:23)

Yahweh will complete the miracle. "Before she was in labor she gave birth; before her pain came upon her she was delivered of a son . . . rejoice with Jerusalem, and be glad for her . . . for as soon as Zion was in labour she brought forth her sons . . . rejoice with her in joy . . . that you may suck and be satisfied with her consoling breast; that you drink deeply with delight from the abundance of her glory." (Isa 66: 7–11) Jerusalem, Madonna with child, Israel's mother, "Sing O barren one," Comfort, comfort my people, Speak tenderly to Jerusalem . . .

Both Job and Jeremiah curse the day of their birth, because of the horror they had to face. Birth is accompanied with pain, just like the whole creation. (Rom 8:22) It reminds us of the curse in Genesis 3:16, "in pain you shall bring forth children." At the same time there is the promise, "Eve, because she was the mother of all living." (Gen 3:20) When the child is born, she no longer feels the pain but joy at the new-born child. "When a woman is in travail she has sorrow, because her hour has come; but when she is delivered of the child, she no longer remembers the anguish, for joy that a child is born into the world." (John 16:21). Not all births give rise to joy. Benjamin's birth was one of anguish. Rachel was pregnant during the crossing of the Jabbok where Jacob was touched in his 'hip', the place of his natural potency. He was born when Jacob's natural potency was gone. After Rachel gave birth to Joseph, she said, "May the LORD add to me another son." (Gen 30:22–24) She did conceive again when they journeyed on and Jacob's name was changed to Israel. Now the number of Israel is complete, twelve sons. But during the birth, she encountered difficulties. "The midwife said, 'Fear not, for now you will have another son' And as her soul was departing (for she died), she called his name Ben-o ni (son of my sorrow); but his father called his name, Benjamin. So Rachel died, and she was buried on the way to Ephratyh (that is Bethlehem . . . Israel journeyed on." (Gen 35:16–21) Rachel, mother of Israel, mother of sorrows! Her death, however, points to Bethlehem, that is, to David's kingship over the the twelve tribes of Israel. Benjamin is the tribe that connects Judah and Joseph, northern Israel. Rachel's grave monument points to the future, the birth of the king over all of Israel. Jacob remembers Rachel when he is about to die and blesses his sons. "Rachel, to my sorrow died in the land of Canaan on the way, when there was still some distance to go to Ephrath; and I buried her there on the way to Ephrath (that is, Bethlehem)." (Gen 48:7).

Ikabod, Eli's grandson, is another untimely born son. "Now his daughter-in-law, the wife of Phinehas, was with child, about to give birth. When she heard the tidings that the ark of God was captured, and that her father-in-law and her husband were dead, she bowed and gave birth; for the pains came upon her. And about the time of her death the women attending her said to her, "Fear not, for you have born a son". But she did not answer or give heed. And she named the child Ichabod, saying, 'The glory has departed from Israel!" because the ark of God had been captured . . . 1 Sam 4: 19–22) She cries out, Ikabod, without honour. Gone is Israel's glory gone in exile. This period will only end when David brings the ark back to Jerusalem. It is not a period without hope, because Hanna has given birth to Samuel. (1 Sam 1:20) Before the ark disappears in the land of the Philistines Samuel is already proclaimed a prophet. (1 Sam 3:1–21)

Deurloo mentions two more names. Sisera's mother looks out of the window for her son to return from battle. He never comes home because he has been killed by Jael. (Judg 5:27–28) Deborah was judge in Israel at that time, a mother in Israel. (Judg 5:7) These references to untimely born sons indicate how different, births can be, like Jael, who hit a tent peg through Sisera's temple while the mother of Sisera, hopes for her son's return. Jael is called the blessed one among the women "Most blessed of women be Jael." (Judg 5:24–27) And finally he mentioned David not performing the 'ritual' marriage with Michal, Saul's daughter. She had mocked him and did not want any part of the celebration of returning the ark to Jerusalem. "And Michal the daughter of Saul had no child to the day of her death." (2 Sam 6:20–23) Once more the birthpangs of a mother about to give birth returns.

The metaphor of a birth can also be applied to Israel's exodus, "You were unmindful of the Rock that begot you, and you forgot the God who gave you birth." (Deut 32:18) In your unfaithfulness you have forgotten your Maker, "The Rock, his work is perfect; for all his ways are justice. A God of faithfulness and without iniquity, just and right is he. They have dealt corruptly with him, they are no longer his children . . . (Deut 32:4–5). Moses spoke the words of his song until they were finished, in the ears of all the assembly, "Give ear, O heavens, and I will speak . . . Is not he your Father, who created you, who made you and established you? Remember the days of old . . ." (Deut 32:1, 6, 7)

That is when Yahweh found them in the desert and cared for them, washed and clothed them, fed them and taught them how to walk. In

Genesis we hear, who Israel is. It is the first-born among the nations, who is pulled, out of Egypt. They are to tell Pharaoh, "Israel is my first-born son, . . . let my son go that he may serve me . . . if you refuse to let him go, behold, I will slay your first-born son." (Exod 4:22, 3) First-born over against first-born, the future that Yahweh has in mind for his people over against Pharaoh's vision of their future: to be slaves forever.

From then on, the people stand under the proclamation of Yahweh. From then on, the people will be his son, his first-born, ". . . He found him in a desert land, and in the howling waste of the wilderness; he encircled him, he cared for him, he kept him as the apple of his eye." (Deut. 32:10) "You shall be my own possession among all the peoples; for all the earth is mine, and you shall be to me a kingdom of priests and a holy nation." (Exod 19:5, 6; Deut 7:6) Yahweh has given birth to them. Moses complains to the LORD that he cannot lead these people by himself, "Did I conceive all this people? Did I bring them forth, that thou should say, 'Carry them in your bosom, as a nurse carries a sucking child, to the land which thou didst swear to give their fathers?'" (Num 11:12–13) Hosea describes how the LORD himself took care of all the infants' needs. "When Israel was a child, I loved him, and out of Egypt I called my son . . . I bent down to them and fed them." (Hos 11:1–4)

Matthew quotes from this passage and keeps the word 'son' and not 'his children'. "Out of Egypt I have called my son." (Matt 2:15) That is exactly what he needed at that moment, so that everything written about the exodus from Egypt could concentrate on this one son. We can only write about the conception of this Messiah and messianic time that has arrived in terms of Israel's origin, "my son, my first-born."

Again a birth story has to mark the totally new event of the exodus. Yahweh calls his son Israel by Moses. We don't need the motive of 'barrenness' at this point to indicate that this birth is impossible. The descendants of the twelve sons of Israel that had come to Egypt are about to go extinct under the repression of Pharaoh. That the miraculous birth of Moses happens is because of the twelve daughters (the two midwives, the mother and daughter, the daughter of Pharaoh and the seven daughters of Reuel who kept him alive). He gave his daughter Zipporah to him as a wife and she bore him s son and he called his name Gershom, 'I have been a sojourner in a foreign land.' (Exod 2:22)

The story of Moses' birth is told very simply, without names, "Now a man from the house of Levi went and took to wife a daughter of Levi. The woman conceived and bore a son; and when she saw that he was a goodly child, she hid him three months." (Exod 2:1, 2) The description reminds us of Genesis, "she saw that he was good" just as the light was called good. The Midrash tells that the whole house was filled with light at his birth. What started in Genesis finds its goal in the birth of Moses.

After three months she was unable to hide him from the Egyptians any longer. Instead of deciding to throw him in the river as they had been commanded to do, she made a little 'coffin' for him, the same word that is used for Noah's ark, which was also an (oversized) coffin. She lined it with pitch and "placed it among the reeds at the river's brink." (Exod 2:3; Gen 6:13) With Noah the whole creation drifts across the waters of death to a new future. Moses' life is saved through the waters of death to a new life. In Genesis, at the core, it is all about the Torah of Exodus.

There floats the infant, three months old. His sister is a prophetess as she will show later on after the journey through the Red Sea. (Exod 15:20) She keeps watch and is able to suggest a woman who could nurse the infant, his mother. The child grew, and when he was weaned she brought him to Pharaoh's daughter, "and he became her son. And she named him Moses, for she said, 'Because I drew him out of the water.'" (Exod 2:6–10) She calls him her son, even though she knows she is not his mother. She knows that, ". . . this is one of the Hebrews' children." (2:6) She takes pity on him in spite of her father's command, and in doing so she becomes one of the twelve women that saved Moses' life.

As the psalmist has it, "He reached from on high, he took me, he drew me out of many waters." (Ps 18: 16) His name is "He who is drawn out." That is what Moses has to do with Israel. He, who is drawn out of he waters of death is 'made to appear,' will pull Israel through the waters of the Red Sea. It is as if the great liberation is one big birth process and Moses is the wet nurse, again a 'Madonna that nurses her infant'. Moses too has a unique and miraculous birth.

Luke reminds us, "And at the end of eight days, when he was circumcised, he was called Jesus, the name given by the angel before he was conceived" . . . and they offered a sacrifice according to the Law of Moses. (Luke 2:21, 22) "And when the time came for their purification according to the law of Moses, they brought him to Jerusalem to present him to the LORD (as it is written in the law of the LORD, 'every male that opens the womb shall be called holy to the LORD' and to offer a sacrifice according to what is said in the law of the LORD." (Exod 13:2; Num 3:13) Zipporah too saves Moses from death before he faces the LORD and goes off to Egypt and presents him ritually clean by circumcising their fist-born

Gershom and touching Moses' genitals with it ... (Exod 4:25), "the bridegroom of blood."

Birth stories announce decisive moments in Israel's history: the four tribal mothers and the birth of Moses as the beginning of the exodus. The return from exile is also pictured as a barren woman and widow who, nevertheless receives children. David's presence is 'introduced' by the birth of Samson, the judge who makes a beginning with the liberation from the Philistines. "He shall begin to deliver Israel from the hand of the Philistines." (Judg 13:1-5) David will complete what Samson had begun to do. "After this David defeated the Philistines and subdued them ... So David reigned over all Israel; and David administered justice and equity to all the people." (2 Sam 8:1, 15)

The story of the birth of Samuel introduces the reign of David. These somewhat complicated connections deserve attention with regard to the two kings Saul and David. There is a direct connection between Samson and David. The mother of Samson and Hannah are representative of the barren mothers in the house of Israel, "He gives the barren woman a home, making her the joyous mother of children." (Ps 113:9). The woman is the barren one of the house of Israel; she is a Sarah. Hannah recognizes herself in her as she acknowledges in her song, "The barren has born seven, but she who has many children is forlorn. The LORD ... brings low, he also exalts." (1 Sam 2:5–7) It required a miracle to have this happen.

In relation to David, we also need to take note of the birth story of Perez from Tamar (Gen 38). He is the ancestor of David. In the book of Ruth there is the story of the birth of Obed, the father of Jesse, the father of David. "May the LORD make the woman (Ruth), who is coming into your house, like Rachel and Leah, who together built up the house of Israel. May you prosper in Ephrathah and be renowned in Bethlehem; and may your house be like the house of Perez, whom Tamar bore to Judah, because of the children that the LORD will give you by this young woman." (Ruth 4:11, 12) It is prophetic history, the prophet Micah in a vision sees it coming, "But you, O Bethlehem Ephrathah, who is little to be among the clans of Judah, from you, shall come forth for me one who is to be ruler of Israel, whose origin is from of old, from ancient days." (Mic 5:2) It is David who will come forth from the house of Judah.

The birth of Solomon has an even more dubious origin than Tamar's courageous exposure of Judah's unfaithfulness and the birth of Perez. The child that is born becomes ill and dies. It is the result of adultery and murder by David and Bathsheba. "The LORD struck the child . . . and it became sick. David fasted . . . and lay all night upon the ground." His servants worried about David and they were afraid to tell him that the child had died, but he guessed as much. Then he arose, washed and ate. His servants were confused by this and he explained, "I fasted and wept; for I said 'Who knows whether the LORD will be gracious to me, that the child may live? But now he is dead, why should I fast? Can I bring him back again?' Then David comforted Bathsheba; they had intercourse, and she bore a son and called his name Salomon, "and the LORD loved him and sent a message by Nathan the prophet; so he called his name 'beloved of the LORD.'" (2 Sam 12:24, 25)

Both women, Tamar and Bathsheba, (she is not mentioned by name, just yet, "the child that Uriah's wife bore") are mentioned. Matthew lists both of their names along with Rahab in the genesis of Jesus. 'Our ancestral mother bears a son', Tamar arranged it. Israel, my first-born son!

With Salomon, the beloved, a new era starts. Or is this still a part of prophetic history that needs to be given new expression by the prophet Isaiah,

> For to us a child is born,
> to us a son is given;
> and the government will be upon his shoulder,
> and his name will be called
> 'Wonderful Counselor,
> Mighty God,
> Everlasting Father, Prince of peace.
> of the increase of his government
> and of peace there will be no end,
> upon the throne of David,
> and over his kingdom,
> to establish it,
> and to uphold it with justice and with righteousness...
> The zeal of the LORD of hosts will do this.
> Isaiah 9:6, 7

The great king is still to come. "Hear then, O house of David! Is it too little for you to weary men, that you weary my God also? Therefore the LORD himself will give you a sign. Behold a young woman, (who has not given birth to a child) shall conceive and bear a son, and shall call his name Immanuel (that is, God is with us)." (Isa 7:13-14) "God with us" is not a foregone conclusion, but the Lord himself guarantees

THE PROPHETIC CALL TO LOVE AND JUSTICE

it. "Immanuel" is not only a prophecy, but it can also become misused as a slogan and propaganda. Jesus comes as the miraculous, unexpected, humble servant riding on an ass, and not as a royal king, fulfilling all righteousness.

9:3b) The death and resurrection of a son

First, there is a small anecdote that closes the stories about Elisha. When he was dying, king Joash came to visit him, "Now when Elisha had fallen sick with the illness of which he was to die, Joash king of Israel went down to him, and wept before him, crying, 'My father, my father! The chariots of Israel and its horsemen!'" (2 Kings 13:14) Joash repeats what Elisha himself had cried out when Elijah was taken up to heaven by the LORD. "And Elijah went up in a whirlwind into heaven. And Elisha saw it and he cried, 'My father, my father! the chariots of Israel and its horsemen!' And he saw him no more." (2 Kings 2:1–12)

What is Israel to do without prophecy? The power of Israel is not in its military power. Elisha is aware of it. The mantle of Elijah is given to him, "And he took the mantle of Elijah that had fallen from him, and went back and stood on the bank of the Jordan. Then he took the mantle of Elijah that had fallen from him, and struck the water, saying, 'Where is the LORD, the God of Elijah?' And when he had struck the water, the water was parted to the one side and to the other; and Elisha went over. (2 Kings 2:14) He had been called to be a prophet by Elijah. (1 Kings 19:19–21)

Even after Elijah's death, stories have to keep prophecy alive, so that there may be a future for Israel. That is the meaning of another anecdote that follows the death and burial of Elijah. (2 Kings 13::20, 21) These stories need to be told just like the calling of Ezekiel. "Son of man, stand upon your feet, and I will speak with you." (Ezek 2:1) When Ezekiel prophesied (in the famous prophecy of the 'dry bones' (Ezek 37:1–14), Israel arises from the death of the exile to be ready to march back to the land in which there is life. "So I prophesied as he commanded me, and the breath came into them, and they lived, and stood upon their feet, an exceedingly great host." (Ezek 37:10)

It becomes apparent when the king asked Elisha's servant Gehazi, "tell me all the great things that Elisha has done'. And while he was telling the king how Elisha had restored the dead to life . . ." (2 Kings 8: 4–6)

Gehazi tells everything and summarized it in the one great deed of bringing the dead to life, a son for his mother.

The prophet Elijah by the LORD's command lodged with a woman from Zarephath. He asked her to bake him a cake and bring some water. There was a draught and famine. There was only a little flour left for herself, and her son and she feared that after that was gone, they would die. But Elijah could reassure her that the flour and oil would not diminish "until the day that the LORD sends rain upon the earth." (1 Kings 17:8–16).

There is a parallel story in 2 Kings 4:1–7. This time there is a wealthy woman from Shunem where Elisha lodged. She had made him a place to sleep on the roof and he called the woman and asked what he could do for her. She did not want anything, but his servant Gehazi said 'She has no child and her husband is old' . . . And he said, 'At this season, when the time comes round, you shall embrace a son', but she responded with, "No, my LORD, O man of God; do not lie to your maidservant.' But the woman conceived, and she bore a son about that time the following spring, as Elisha had said to her." (2 Kings 4:8–17) It is reminiscent of Genesis 18:15. She does not laugh like Sarah, but she does protest; 'don't deceive me'.

At the time of the harvest where the boy is present suddenly this idyllic scene turns into a disaster, the boy becomes ill, he suffers a sun stroke and was brought to his mother. ". . . The child sat on her lap till noon, then, he died." There seemed to be a bright future for her but now it has abruptly ended. These two parallel stories are two versions of the same motif. Elisha lay on the child on his bed. The child takes in the warmth of the prophet, but the spirit was not in him. The prophet stretches out once more on the boy. This time the child sneezed seven times and opened his eyes. Breath and spirit come together in a great force. Then he calls the woman and tells her, "Take up your son." She did. It is a very concrete story and also a parable.

In the same way as Elisha, Elijah in the first, story brings her son to life again. "And Elijah took the child, and brought him down from the upper chamber into the house, and delivered him to his mother; and Elijah said, 'See, your son lives.'" (1 Kings 17:23, 24)

The miracle happens, signifying that there is life, olive oil and bread in the midst of famine. Prophecy brings life! What else could it mean that there is a future for the widow of Zarephath? With her confession she becomes a proselyte in Israel, who sees a future in the light of Yahweh, the God of Israel. She confessed "O man of God" and "Now I know that you are a man of God, and that the word of the LORD in your mouth is truth." She is a counter-type to Jezebel.

Jezebel was the daughter of the king of Sidon. Ahab took for "wife Jezebel the daughter of Eth-baal king of the Sidonians, and went and served Baal in the house of Baal, which he built in Samaria." (1 Kings 16:31, 32) She threatened to kill Elijah, especially after the miraculous burning of the water soaked offering at Mount Carmel and the killing of Baal priests. (1Kings19:1–3) In the first story about a dead son that is resurrected, the emphasis is on Jezebel as a counter image of a widow who learned to confess the God of Israel. In the second story, the emphasis is on the powerful prophetic word of the LORD. The same literary motif is used for a different purpose.

In the book of Kings the storytellers come back once more to the widow of Shunem. Elijah had instructed her to go to the land of the Philistines because of a seven year famine. During that time she had lost her house and her land. She is poor and her husband is old. She wants to appeal to the king, just as Gehazi, Elisha's assistant was being questioned by the king. "'Tell me all the great things that Elisha has done.' And while he was telling the king how Elisha had restored the dead to life, behold, the woman whose son he had restored to life appealed to the king for her house and her land. So, the king appointed an official for her, saying, 'Restore all that was hers, together with the produce of the fields from the day that she left the land until now.'" (2 Kings 8:1-6) Son and land belong together. It is her lifeline, for what is she to do with a son without her land and food. Now that she has come back, the king gives her land back, so she can feed herself and her son.

The return from exile is the great sign of Yahweh's mercy. He gives them land again.

> LORD, thou wast favorable to thy land;
> Thou didst restore the fortunes of Jacob . . .
> that glory may dwell in our land . . .
> Yea, the LORD will give what is good,
> and our land will yield its increase.
> Righteousness will go before him,
> and make his footsteps a way.
>   Psalm 85:1, 9, 12, 13

Luke devotes a separate story to this event. Jesus comes to Nain, which is close to Sunem.

> As he drew near to the gate of the city, behold, a man who had died was being carried out, the only son of his mother, and she was a widow; and a large crowd from the city was with her. And when the LORD saw her, he had compassion on her and said to her, 'Do not weep'. And he came and touched the bier, and the bearers stood still, And he said, 'Young man, I say to you, arise'. And the dead man sat up, and he began to speak. And he gave him to his mother.
>
> Luke 7:12–15

With a few words, Luke recalls the stories of the TeNak. The woman is a widow. Like the widow of Zarephat, her only hope is her son. The gospel writer tells a concrete story, at the same time, is it not a parable as well? "There were many widows in Israel in the days of Elijah, when the heaven was shut up three years and six months, when there came a great famine over all the land; and Elijah was sent to none of them but only to Zarephath, in the land of Sidon, to a woman who was a widow. (Luke 4:25, 26) In the story of the widow of Zarephath from Sidon, the 'Sarah motif' is missing. We are in the land of the gojim. But what else can it mean that there is a future for the widow from Zarephath as well? No future for Sidon?! Jesus took pity upon the people.

The two stories about the essentials for life (flour and oil) frame the central pericope of the birth, death and resurrection of the son, which summarizes "all the great things Elisha has done." After this introduction of the multiplying of flour and oil, follows the story of the death and resurrection of the son. It is followed by a second story of a miraculous feeding. Smelik, in his essay, "The widow from Sarafat; the literary function of 1 Kings 17:18–24" (*ACEBT, number 10*), makes a convincing case that the first story about Elijah comes second and is modelled after the parallel story about Elisha.[9]

Once more in the theme of mothers and sons during a famine, the theme returns in a gruesome story. The city of Samaria is surrounded. The situation becomes so desperate that the head of a donkey is sold for eighty pieces of silver.

The king makes his round on the city wall and a woman cries out to him, "Help, my lord, O king!" "This woman said to me, 'Give your

---

9. van Dalen, "Vertel mij toch al het grote dat Elisha gedaan heeft," in: *ACEBT* # 1.
Riemersma, "Hoe een jong mens weer tot leven komt; een close reading van 2 Koningen 4:32–35," Cahier # 35.
Becking, "A magical ritual in Jahwistic perspective; literary structure and religious historical background of 11 Kings 4:31–38."

son that we may eat him today, and we will eat my son tomorrow.' So we boiled my son, and ate him. On the next day I said to her, 'Give your son, that we may eat him'; but she has hidden her son." (2 Kings 6:28; 7:2) This is the absolute worst. This is indeed the complete opposite of all the great things Elisha has done. The king is no longer able to perform his office to speak and do justice. He has drifted very far from David's son Solomon, who pronounced justice for the mother of the living son, which two prostitutes were fighting over. (1 Kings 3:16–28) The wise decision of Solomon is about the rescue of the 'son'. Kingship is in the service of the future.

9:3c) Mother Mary

Finally we must consider Mary the mother of Jesus. Matthew mentions her name in the beginning chapters of his gospel. She appears later on with his brothers in the middle of his teaching, asking him to come to speak to them. But he does not want to be interrupted, "Who is my mother, and who are my brothers? And stretching out his hand toward his disciples, he said, 'Here are my mother and my brothers! For whoever does the will of my Father in heaven is my brother, and sister, and mother." (Matt 12:46–50) In the birth announcement he gives particular attention to Mary, even though she stays in the shadow of Joseph. Along with Luke he gives the biblical background to the confession of the Credo, 'born of the virgin Mary.'(cf. Matt 1:23) He quotes Isaiah 7:14 and the TeNaK and the rich givens of the Midrash.

For his list of 'generations' Mathew takes his starting point in Genesis 5:1, "This is the book of the generations of Adam." As the leading sentence of his gospel, he writes, "The book of the genealogy of Jesus Christ, the son of David, the son of Abraham." (Matt 1:1) The numerical value of David's name is twice the complete number seven, which is fourteen. Matthew uses that given to order his lists of names, from Abraham to David, fourteen generations and from David to the exile, fourteen generations and from the exile to Jesus, fourteen generations. (1:17) He takes more freedom in the second series. He eliminates some kings (1 Chronicles 3) to get to the number fourteen. He changes the name Asa to Asaf to identify this king with the poet of the psalms; and he changes the name Amon to Amos, the prophet.

The kings appear not to bring forth the Messiah, but to announce him with psalms and prophecy. In the first list the line goes up, from Abraham to David. The Christ is generated in the context of all of Israel, which is highlighted, ". . . Jacob, the father of Judah and his brothers . . . . (Matt 1:2) Men generated sons in Israel, but through three women (Tamar, Rahab, and Ruth) the gojim also come to the fore. The generating does not happen without them, "Salmon the father of Boaz by Rahab, and Boaz, the father of Obed by Ruth, and Obed the father of Jesse, and Jesse the father of David the king." (Matt 1:5, 6)

The second series goes downward and ends in exile. This series is coloured by the first generating, "David was the father of Solomon by the wife of Uriah." (Matthew 1:6) Sons are born to David, but none of them is the Son of David. Therefore the history of the kings ends in exile, but from the exile the line goes up again. The return from exile is the sign of the mercy of Yahweh and compassion for his people. It is the time of the promise, a new David will appear and that is how the last series ends with the Messiah. In three clear equal periods that are not just characterized by 'before and after the king' but also by 'before and after the exile'. The word exodus does not appear here at the beginning of Mathew's gospel. The exodus coincides with the return from exile, in which the descendents of Abraham, Isaac and Jacob become God's people. He records the flight to Egypt to explain how Jesus is 'God's Son' and to recite the prophecy . . . "Out of Egypt have I (Yahweh) called my son." (Matt 2:15)

The most surprising verse is the end of the genealogy list, "Jacob the father of Joseph the husband of Mary, of whom Jesus was born. (Matt 1:16) Did Matthew want to say that all the generating of sons throughout did not happen 'by the will of a man'? But that all along it had to do with God, that it took place 'from out of heaven'. In this generating, Joseph does not play his role as a husband who can generate sons. 'Was born' is in the passive tense, just as it says in Matthew 26:6, he has risen. Matthew does not, like Luke, tell a birth story but a 'generating' story. The first part of his story closes with the words, "And he went and dwelt in a city called Nazareth, that what was spoken by the prophets might be fulfilled, 'He shall be called a Nazarene.'" (Matt 2:23)

The second account of Mathew starts with the announcement of the answer, "Now the birth of Jesus Christ took place in this way. When his mother Mary had been betrothed to Joseph, before they came together she was found to be with child of the Holy Spirit." (Matt 1:18) Matthew liberally uses the tradition about Moses birth. According to the

Old Testament pattern: a man takes a wife, comes to her, she becomes pregnant and gives birth to a son. He calls out his name. Only with the giving of the name is the birth complete. Usually the name of the place where he comes from is added, Nazareth. (Matt 2:23) It concludes the second part of this account of Jesus' birth. The many generations end with 'the father of'.

In this case, it is different. The second part of the birth story begins differently,"Now the birth of Jesus Christ took place in this way." (Matt 2:18) She became pregnant. The deed by Joseph is eliminated. They are betrothed, but the 'before they came together' has not taken place yet. She conceived by the Holy Spirit. When Joseph noticed she was pregnant, he quietly wants to divorce her. He was a righteous person and did not want to shame Mary by sending her away. He wants to do so secretly. (Check Deuteronomy 24:1-4). But Jesus' birth cannot happen in secret. It has to happen openly in Israel, in the house of David. The righteous person gets a task. Instead of taking a back seat, he gets a task. In a dream he is commanded, "Joseph, son of David, do not fear to take Mary your wife, for that which is conceived in her is of the Holy Spirit." (Matt 1:20) The second thing he has to do is to call out his name, Jesus. As a son of David, he is to be completely involved in the event. That is why after his task and "he knew her not until she had borne a son" the prophecy could be cited, "Behold, a virgin shall conceive and bear a son."

It reminds us of Isaiah, "Hear then, O house of David! Is it too little for you to weary men, that you weary my God also? Therefore the Lord will give you a sign. Behold, a young woman shall conceive and bear a son, and shall call his name Immanuel." (Isa 7:13-14; see also Isa 9:1-7; and 11:1-5) In the Greek Bible the word alma (young woman) is translated with 'virgin', which Matthew could use. If Matthew knew about the virgin-goddess in the ancient world, ('pure, unspoiled') that did not seem to bother him. In the ancient world it is a common theme: a virgin who bears a divine child, but in those instances the emphasis is on the qualities of the mother, her youth for example.

However, her purity is not what the evangelist has in mind, nor the sinlessness of Mary. It is not Mary's quality as a virgin. The fact that she is a virgin is a concentration of the barrenness of the tribal mothers, "Behold, a virgin shall conceive" points to a deed of God. "All this took place to fulfill what the LORD had spoken by the prophet." We are reminded of Genesis, "And the LORD did to Sarah as he had promised." (Gen 21:1)

Matthew is not interested in the quality of virginity. There is no question here of virginity as a quality in itself, never mind, of eternal virginity.

The birth story concludes with the magician's (wise men) actions over against the new Pharaoh, Herod. Matthew saved an essential given of the giving of the name to the end. Even though Jesus was born in Bethlehem, the city of David, the son shall be called, Jesus of Nazareth. The magician Bileam saw a star that rose within Israel. (Num 24:17) "Now when Jesus was born in Bethlehem of Judea in the days of Herod the king, behold, wise men from the east came to Jerusalem, saying, 'Where is he who has been born king of the Jews? For we have seen his star in the east, and have come to worship him.'" (Matt 2:1, 2) They are real gojim, star gazers that were already involved as soon as the conception has taken place. They were worshippers of the 'host of heaven.' They don't know the book of Genesis, so they talk about the king that has been born. The gospel in its concentration on Israel will be proclaimed to all the nations. (Matt. 28:19) How will they find the Messiah? They will by inquiring in Jerusalem of the chief priests and scribes, and because Israel's God himself will bring them there. Yahweh is the shepherd of the stars.

> Lift up your eyes on high and see: who created these?
> He who brings out their host by number,
> calling them all by name; by the greatness of his might,
> and because he is strong in power not one is missing."
> Isaiah 40:26

The star showed them the way. "And low, the star which they had seen in the East went before them." (Matt.2:9)

When Herod realized he had been deceived by the magicians, he flew in a rage and commanded all the male infants up to two years old in Bethlehem and the whole region to be killed. In Ramah, near Bethlehem, where Rachel was buried, all the mothers of Israel that are represented by Rachel wept over their infant sons and would not be comforted because they were no more. (Matt 2:16–18) Joseph's flight to Egypt reminds us of Pharaoh's cruel edict to kill all the male infants of the Hebrews in the waters of the Nile. Thus the words, "out of Egypt have I called my son." (Matt 2:15)

In Matthew, Jesus' kingship stands central. In Luke it is the temple that is central. His gospel starts and ends with the temple. "... There was a priest named Zechariah ... and he had a wife ... and her name was Elizabeth. And they were both righteous before God, walking in all the commandments and ordinances of the Lord blameless. But they had no child, because Elizabeth was barren, and both were advanced in years." (Luke 1:5–7) They are like Abraham and Sarai, barren and old. Just like Isaac had prayed for a child, so Zechariah had prayed. Zechariah was addressed by an angel, "Do not be afraid, Zechariah, for your prayer is heard, and your wife Elizabeth will bear you a son, and you shall call his name John." (Luke 1:13) What remained implicit in Matthew, the fact that virginity of Mary was an intensifying of the barrenness of the tribal mothers, Luke gives full attention. The birth of John shall be with great joy ("and you will have joy and gladness, and many will rejoice at his birth, for he will be great before the LORD." (Luke 1:14, 15) It is in preparation for the great joy of the shepherds. John will be a Nazarene, "and he will be filled with the Holy Spirit, even from his mother's womb . . . and he will go before him in the spirit and power of Elijah." (Luke 1: 15–17) But Zechariah has his doubts and asks for a sign. He will be silent and unable to speak until his son is born.

Luke's account too is reminiscent of the TeNak. Like Matthew he has chosen his starting point in Genesis, but not with the generations but with the birth of a son from the barren tribal mothers. Luke presents a birth story and not a genealogy. Therefore Mary will play a more prominent role, while Joseph stays in the background. He tells a birth story. Surprisingly, the messenger came "to a virgin betrothed to a man whose name was Joseph, of the house of David; and the virgin's name was Mary." (Luke 1:27) The virgin is addressed as the "Hail, O favored one, the LORD is with you!" which means you are blessed. (Luke 1:28) Mary is shocked by these words. Hannah too was called the favored one. She is favored like Hannah before her as well as Ruth, "and the Lord gave her conception, and she bore a son." (Ruth 4:13)

The story of Ruth also ends with 'a Madonna with child' image. "Naomi took the child and laid him in her bosom, and became his nurse. And the women of the neighborhood gave him a name, saying, 'A son has been born to Naomi.'" They named him Obed; he was the father of Jesse, the father of David." (Ruth 4:16, 17) With the son that was born to her she is like the old woman Sarah. In the visual arts Mary is always portrayed like a young woman, except in the famous variation of the pieta of Michelangelo. There she is the woman of sorrows with her dead son on her lap. In the gospels we do not find this scene. We have to turn to the TeNaK to find such a mother with her dead son, the widow of Zarephath.

THE NATURE OF BIBLICAL THEOLOGY

Luke tells of the miracle of all miracles and has Mary ask, "How can this be since I have no husband?" (1:34)The messenger answers, "The Holy Spirit will come upon you, and the power of the Most High will overshadow you; therefore the child to be born will be called holy, the Son of God." (1:35) And Elizabeth, your kinswoman "in her old age has also conceived a son; and this is the sixth month with her who was called barren. "For with God nothing will be impossible." Mary responds in faith, "Behold, I am the handmaid of the LORD; let it be to me according to his word." (Luke 1:36-38)

When Mary visited Elizabeth as soon as she greeted her, "the babe leaped in her womb; and Elizabeth was filled with the Holy Spirit and she exclaimed with a loud cry, 'Blessed are you among women, and blessed is the fruit of your womb!'" (Luke 1:41–42) Three times the words "And it happened in those days" are used. It gives a division in which the author wants us to read his story. It is not always translated with 'in those days it took place'; often it is just translated with, 'Now' or 'in those days'. Luke starts his gospel with "a narrative of the things which have been accomplished among us." (1:1–4) It is world history, especially for Mary and Joseph. The LORD's word, dabar, happened from out of heaven, the birth of a child from a virgin by the Holy Spirit. It is a world event that is announced to the entire world. The announcement, "I bring you good news of a great joy which will come to all the people; for to you is born this day in the city of David a Savior, who is Christ the LORD." (2:10, 11) It will be testified to by the wise men and the shepherds. They will bear witness to the event. As Mary had said, "let it be to me according to your word." She does not forget, but "kept all these things, pondering them in her heart." (Luke 2:19). And for no other reason than this, "all generations will call me blessed." (1:48) Then after eight days, Jesus was circumcised and given his name. (Luke 2:21)

In one sentence Luke also describes the 'mother of sorrows'. "Behold, this child is set for the fall and rising of many in Israel, and for a sign that is spoken against (and a sword will pierce through your own soul also)," (2:34, 35) Simeon tells Mary. Luke does not tell us what Mary pondered in her heart. We get a glimpse of her motherly feelings when they have lost track of the twelve year old Jesus on the way back from Jerusalem after the Passover. ". . . Son, why have you treated us so?" Jesus answered bluntly, "How is it that you sought me? Did you not know that I must be in my Father's house?" That is in the temple, searching the scriptures. They did not understand, but "his mother kept all these things in her heart." (2:48–51)

Opponents of Jesus will say, "The Jews then murmured at him, because he has said, 'I am the bread which came down from heaven,' they said, 'Is not this Jesus, the son of Joseph, whose father and mother we know? How does he now say, 'I am the bread which came down from heaven'?'" (John 6:41) "But all who received him, who believed in his name, he gave power to become children of God; who were born, not of blood, nor the will of the flesh, nor of the will of man, but of God." (John 1:12, 13; cf. John 3:1–21 about Nicodemus' question)

How must Mary be praised? Luke illustrates this with a small vignette, after the cleansing of a man of an unclean spirit. A woman in the crowd raises her voice and says, "Blessed is the womb that bore you, and the breasts that you sucked! But Jesus said, "Blessed rather are those who hear the words of God and keep it!" (Luke 11:27, 28) It is not the quality of Mary's womb or breasts, but that as a young woman she heard the Word of God and kept it that gives the reason for the exclamation. Israel was not chosen because it was such a good nation. (Deuteronomy 8:17; 9:4)

About Mary we can only speak as we do about Israel. Jesus is an Israelite 'according to the flesh', no more and no less. "Grace and truth came through Jesus Christ. No one has ever seen God; the only Son, who is in the bosom of the Father, he has made him known." (John 1:18)

Mary plays an important role during the first miracle John reports."On the third day there was a marriage in Cana in Galilee and the mother of Jesus was there; Jesus also was invited to the marriage, with his disciples." (John 2:1–12) In this parable-like story the bride is not mentioned and the bridegroom only in passing. His mother simply says, "They have no wine." She leaves it to Jesus, but he responds harshly, "O Woman, what have you to do with me? My hour has not yet come."

His hour is when they want to arrest him, "but no one laid hands on him, because his hour had not yet come." (John 7:30) And "no one arrested him, because his hour had not yet come." (John 8:20) Before the feast of the Passover, ". . . when Jesus knew that his hour had come to depart out of this world to the Father, having loved his own who were in the world, he loved them to the end." (John 13:1) That is how the story of Jesus suffering and death starts. Jesus' mother will not contribute anything to this. It will be entirely his task. The mother represents 'the flesh', the reality in which Jesus entered the world.

There were six stone jars at the wedding according to the Jewish purification laws. Jesus said, "Fill the jars with water." There stand the jars as a silent witness. Water becomes wine and there is wine in abundance. Where does the wine come from? The master of ceremonies does not know, but the servants know for they had been instructed by Mary. "Do whatever he tells you." After this he went to Capernaum, with his mother and his brothers and his disciples. In Cana "it was the first of his signs and manifested his glory; and his disciples believed in him" (John 2:11).

After that, Jesus went up to Jerusalem. Did Jesus' mother go along? It is not yet his last going up. That event is introduced by ". . . and many went up from the country to Jerusalem before the Passover . . ." (John 11:55). Shortly afterwards, Jesus made his entry (John 12:12–19). At the moment of his crucifixion Jesus' mother is there. Pilate wrote a title for above the cross, "Jesus of Nazareth, the King of the Jews." The soldiers cast lots for his garments.

Standing by the cross of Jesus were his mother ". . . when Jesus saw his mother, and the disciple whom he loved standing near, he said to his mother, 'Woman, behold your son!' Then he said to the disciple, 'Behold your mother! And from that hour the disciple took her to his own home." (John 19:25–27) It is a very moving scene where Jesus speaks about mother and son. At the wedding at Cana he was blunt with her, but now he shows his deep concern for her and commends her to his beloved disciple who takes her into his home. After these words the deed of his death follows. "'It is finished' and he bowed his head and gave up his spirit." The sonship of God is not a matter of flesh and blood, but of the Spirit. (John 2:30)

Whatever the church has said over the ages about Mary ('the Mariology') needs to have as it touchstone, 'if the same things can be said about 'mother Zion'. Mariology in the biblical sense expresses the inseparable connection of the Church with Israel. All the stories about births are about the incarnation, the Word becoming flesh. The incarnation is the miraculous gift of the future, as a gift of God's grace. Our matriarchal mother bears not 'a' son, but 'the' Son. Whenever Mary gets too much of an active role as the human partner, Deurloo opposes all such emphases on Mary by herself. In his booklet about Paul (with Bouhuijs, *Dichter bij Paulus*, 1980) he quotes Acts, "Go, for he is a chosen instrument of mine to carry my name before the Gentiles and Kings and the sons of Israel." (Acts 9:15) Mary is taken as a chosen instrument to give birth to the Son of God.

Just before his death Jesus said (to fulfill the scriptures), "I thirst." (John 19:28–30) A bowl full of vinegar stood there; so they put a sponge full of vinegar and hyssop and held it to his mouth. After that he said, "It is finished" and gave up his spirit. In Psalm 69:21 we read, ". . . for my thirst they gave me vinegar to drink." There are associations with the exodus. the people were instructed "to take a bunch of hyssop and dip it in the blood (of the lamb) which is in the basin, and touch the lintel and the two door posts with the blood which is in the basin; and none of you shall go out of the door of the house until morning." (Exod 12:22, 24)

In the first letter of John we read eight times, "born of God" (2:29; 3:9; 4:7; 5:1; 5:18). Jesus' mother says only one thing, "Do whatever he tells you." And the disciple whom he loved takes her into his home.

Madonna with child, she is honoured because she believed "Let it be according to your Word." She is like her people. She represents the people from whom the Messiah will be born. And in her song she becomes the new Miriam. As such she is favored just like the mother of Israel, Leah. The main theme is clear: the King (son of David), of Israel (son of Abraham). Jesus is crucified as the King of Israel (John 19:19) and as such, the crucified one, he is the Son of God. The New Testament is the continuation of the Jewish-messianic promise of the whole Old Testament. A miraculous event of an unexpected birth indicates the continuation of the history of redemption. Something no one had expected anymore, son of God, firstborn of the whole creation. The theme of 'mother and son' is elevated to a new level, the future of humanity and the earth, our future.

There is one more image that demands our attention, and that is the pregnant woman of the book of Revelation. "Now a great portent appeared in heaven: a woman clothed with the sun, with the moon under her feet, and on her head a crown of twelve stars; she was with child and she cried out in her pangs of birth, in anguish for delivery.(Rev12:1, 2) It echoes the words of Isa "Like a woman with child, who writhes and cries out in her pangs, when she is near her time, so were we because of thee, O LORD."(Isa 26:17; 13:8) The congregations of the book Revelation would have understood this reference. They lived in a time of persecution. They lived between the times, sometimes referred to as messianic pangs. The Messiah has appeared, but the end is not there yet. They lived toward this glorious day of the Messiah and they recognize themselves in this woman. They experienced the anguish of birth pangs. The woman of Revelation has the features of mother Zion with cosmic proportions; clothed with the sun, the moon under her feet and a crown

THE NATURE OF BIBLICAL THEOLOGY

of stars on her head, which are a reminder of the twelve tribes. She is like the 'queen of heaven' but then as the dasughter of Zion. She is a sign at the heavens. Sun, moon, stars, who would not be reminded of the fourth day of creation, to give light on the earth. This queen of heaven appears not for people to bow down to her. (Jer 8:2; 44:19) Instead, she is the mother of Israel, the daughter of Zion. In her the future is embodied by God. She is pregnant.

In the vision the moment of birth has already come. She cries out in anguish. Will she bear the son? Will she be able to call out the messianic future? Even before she can give birth, everything seems to be against that hope. Another sign appeared in heaven, 'a great red dragon ... that he might devour her child when she brought it forth;" The great dragon, the old serpent (Rev 12:9; 20:2) reminds us of Genesis 3:15. This mighty dragon is out to wage war against this woman and her child. The author of Daniel applies this vision to him, "a third of the stars is cast down." (Dan 8:10) Would the seven stars also belong to them? For their comfort and reassurance John has already said that the Son of Man holds them in his hand. (Rev 2:1) The dragon"stood before the woman, who was about to bear" to devour her child as soon as it was born. It is an unwanted child for the dragon who wanted to be the ruler of the world himself. He is an anti-Messiah. Before he could do so, "her child was caught up to God and to his throne. It is remenicient of Isaiah, "Before she was in labour she gave birth; before her pain came upon her she was delivered of a son. Who has heard of such a thing? ... For as soon as Zion was in labor she brought forth her sons ..." (Isa 66:7–11)

The daughter of Zion 'fled into the wilderness, where she has a place prepared by God." She flees to the desert where no one can survive. Did she receive manna like the people of old or did the ravens feed her like Elijah? The archangel Michael conquers the dragon in heaven and he is thrown down to earth. Heaven is safe. Until the final battle potrayed in Revelation 19–21 is over, on earth, the great deceiver persecutes the churches. The daughter of Zion does not bear a son out of her own power. The birth happens to her as a miracle of God. She has given birth to the Messiah. The dragon was intent to kill the child. Instead his birth is proclaimed. "Let us go over to Behlehem and see this thing that has happened, which the LORD has made known to us." (Luke 2:15–17) Birth and proclaiming belong together. Salvation is proclaimed in the preaching. The dragon wants to make this proclamation impossible and destroy the woman and all her offspring, "all those who keep the commandments of God and bear testimony to Jesus." (Rev 12:17) The Lamb crucified on earth (Rev 5:6), shares the throne with God in heaven. (Rev 22:1) The still hidden reality will happen, as in heaven, so also on earth. The woman bears the Son, with whom God's time starts in the fullness of time.

In the fullness of time, means that this present time is passing away and the Messianic time has started definitively. God has sent his Son under the law, because the woman is out of Israel, "according to the flesh, is the Christ." (Rom 9:5; Gal 4:4) Paul does not mention Jesus birth. Instead once more he uses the metaphor of the birth process. "For the creation is subjected to futility" and "is groaning in travail and not only the creation, but we ourselves . . . groan inwardly." This chapter forms the first high point of Paul's letter to the Romans, "Who shall separate us from the love of Christ? . . . (Rom 8:35) "For I am sure that neither death, nor life, nor angels, nor principalities, . . . nor anything else in all creation, will be able to separate us from the love of God in Christ Jesus our LORD." (Rom 8:38–39) "Subjected in futility" refers back to Adam's sin, where God said, "cursed is the ground because of you." (Gen 3:17) Humanity has tried to deify the creation by worshipping creatures. Just as the earth is personified in Genesis, so here Paul personifies the whole creation, which misses out on its destiny, God's intention for the good earth.

Nevertheless "in hope we were saved." God will fulfill his intention for the earth. We who have received the first-fruits of the Spirit and who, therefore, look forward to the harvest, to the Pentecost harvest, as we "wait for adoption as sons, the redemption of our bodies." They are children of God, who are destined to "conform to the image of his Son, in order that he might be the first-born among many brethren." (Rom 8:29) The only other place he uses this word is in the hymn to Christ, "the first-born of all creation." (Col 1:15) John can use the image of the woman in labor before she is taken up in heaven, "When a woman is in travail she has sorrow, because her hour has come; but when she is delivered of the child, she no longer remembers the anguish, for joy that a child is born into the world." (John 16:21)

Such perspectives can fill us with joy. In Genesis, Eve had already taken over the role of the primal mother. Her name is Eve, the mother of all living. "I have gotten a man with the help of the LORD." That takes on form in the figure of Sarah as the mother of Israel. They are created not on the basis of the natural creative primal power. Maria gives birth as a young woman that has not had intercourse with a man, which is an even greater miracle than Sarah's barrenness. Mary is taken up in God's service as she sings in her Magnificant. (Luke 1:46-50). She is the blessed one, "Let it be according to your word." "Is anything too hard for the LORD?" (Gen 18:14; Luke 1:45) She is called 'blessed' because she "let it be." The word has become flesh. The history of the world is not a natural birth process that leads to the incarnation, Instead it is the free gift of Yahweh, the God of Israel, in which he proves himself to be merciful. It is a miraculous birth in which the Word has complete power over the 'flesh', the human reality.

Our dear mother bears a son. The Old Testament opens up in the New Testament, the word became flesh. The apostolic writings can only be understood in terms of the TeNaK as the authoritative word of Yahweh, that the apostles are to preach to all people. In them it is all about the birth of the Son, Israel, who was born, not of blood, nor of the will of the flesh, nor of the will of man, but of God. (John 1:12) The Torah came through Moses, but grace and truth through Jesus Christ. (John 1:14) Through him the water of Moses became wine at the wedding feast and without this water no wine. (John 2:1–11) Paul can say it in this way, "But now the righteousness of God has been manifested apart from law, although the law and the prophets bear witness to it." (Rom 3:21) John starts his gospel with the first words of the creation story, "In the beginning God created the heavens and the earth" for the purpose of making a home for humanity. John begins his gospel with the same words, "In the beginning was the word . . . And the word became flesh and dwelt among us, full of grace and truth . . . we have beheld his glory, glory as of the only Son from the Father." (John 1:14–18)

9:4 Creation from Paul to Genesis (2008)

9:4a) Introduction

In the last of his Biblical Theology series, *Creation from Paul to Genesis*, Deurloo presents a unique perspective. It is different from the traditional approach to creation and 'providence', which was dominant in the community of my childhood. It usually started with the doctrine of creation, followed by a separate chapter on providence. It deals with the difficult questions of God's kingship and his care for the creation and all of humanity. 'Providence' is changed to God's 'for-seeing' by Miskotte as we will see at the end of this chapter. The universal aspect of redemption

THE PROPHETIC CALL TO LOVE AND JUSTICE

is carefully described as well as is the riddle of evil in a good creation. Together it provides a new perspective and some new themes.

Deurloo takes his starting point in the middle of the TeNaK, the revelation of the Name, which is first revealed in the Exodus story,

> And you shall say to Pharaoh, Thus says the LORD, Israel is my first-born son, And I say to you, 'Let my people go that he may serve me; if you refuse to let him go, behold, I will slay your first-born son'.
> Exodus 4:22–23

> But Pharaoh said, 'Who is the LORD that I should heed his voice and let Israel go? I do not know the LORD, and moreover I will not let Israel go.'
> Exodus 5:2

> But the LORD said to Moses, "Now you shall see what I will do to Pharaoh; for with a strong hand he will send them out, yea, with a strong hand he will drive them out of his land. And God said to Moses, 'I am the LORD, I appeared to Abraham, to Isaac, and to Jacob, as God Almighty, but by my name YHWH I did not make myself known to them. I also established my covenant with them, to give them the land of Canaan, the land in which they dwelt as sojourners. Moreover I have heard the groaning of the people Israel . . . and I have remembered my covenant, Say therefore to the people of Israel, I am the LORD . . . and I will deliver you from their bondage, and I will redeem you . . . and I will take you for my people, and I will be your God... I am the LORD.
> Exodus 6:1–8

> Come, I will send you to Pharaoh... But I will be with you; and this shall be a sign for you, that I have sent you: when you have brought forth the people out of Egypt you shall serve God upon this mountain.
> Exodus 3:10–12

It is only in the doing that Moses and the people will know who God is.

> God said to Moses, 'I Am Who I Am . . . Say this to the people of Israel, 'I am has sent me to you'.
> Exodus 3:14

At first the "people believed . . . they bowed their heads and worshipped." (Exod 4:31) But when their burdens were increased they complained to Moses and Aaron, "Because of their broken spirit and their cruel bondage." (Exod 6:9) Only after all the plagues the Egyptians suffered, and only after all the first-born sons had been killed including Pharaoh's son, Pharaoh finally consented and said, "Rise up, go forth from among my people, both you and the people of Israel and go, serve the LORD . . . be gone, and bless me also." (Exod 12:31-32) After preparing and eating the Passover, they were ready to travel, "your loins girded, your sandals on your feet, and your staff in your hand; and you shall eat it in haste. It is the LORD's Passover . . . (Exod 12:11) And Moses took the bones of Joseph with them . . . And the LORD went before them by day in a pillar of cloud to lead them on the way, and by night in a pillar of fire to give them light . . ." (Exod 13:21-22)

Only from out of this revelation, "Israel is my first-born son," necessitated by the fall, can we understand the miracle of the generating of the heavens and the earth. (Gen 2:4) It is a liberating perspective. It is for this original purpose that the heavens and the earth were created and creation was restored. "In the beginning was the Word." (John 1:1) "And the Word became flesh and dwelt among us, full of grace and truth; we have beheld his glory, glory of the only Son from the Father." (John 1:14)

Deurloo's main concern in this volume is to highlight that Yahweh's great acts of liberation are first and stand central, and only from there we can understand the beginning, the creation for the well-being of all creatures and all people, and humanity's alienation from their Creator and Liberator.

9:4b) Creation and Nature

From ancient times on and especially since the Enlightenment, nature has been separated from human culture and society. In our days this process has been intensified. Especially as a result of the ideology of 'corporate capitalism', nature has been objectified, commodified, commercialized, and consumerized as objects to be mastered, controlled, and manipulated for private gain and consumption. When used up, we move on to the next thing or service. Within this ideology, nature is no longer an integral part of the web of life, but a separate entity that can be 'objectified' (separated from its context) and used up. The big question for today is whether nature can be restored to its original purpose, that is: to serve the inter-connected well-being of all creatures, including humans.

That is the vision that awaits fulfillment. In the scriptures nature is not an independent given. Nature is not there just to look at and inspire us, because creation presupposes engagement: to practice righteousness, loving kindness, justice and truth, resourcefulness and the inter-connected well-being of all creatures.

Deurloo makes a distinction between "nature" and "creation." Nature is there; creation is first of all a deed of God and the result of his deed. 'Nature' does not exist by itself, as some independent given. The creation exists to perform a service. Nature you can see and experience. About creation, we can only tell and sing. The creation starts to shine with the creation of humans. That is why they exist. The heavens and the earth are created so that 'our earth mother can bear a son'. Creation is the beginning, which must be understood in terms of God's purpose for creation. It does not exist by and for itself. Creation exists to be of service to all creatures, including humanity. The beginning takes on light and colour when we see the reason for its purpose, the first-born in our midst to restore creation to its original purpose.

We can become ecstatic when confronted and experiencing nature. We can be moved to the depth of our being when contemplating nature. Because of the loss of our connection with nature, there has been a proliferation of nature documentaries in our time, for our pleasure and inspiration. They give the (often false) impression that all is not lost.

In *Who has Seen the Wind* by Canada's famous author W.O. Mitchell, the boy in the story is moved to his core and overwhelmed when he watches a dewdrop on a leaf glistening in the sun on a very quiet Sunday morning. He is shining shoes for all the family members before they go to church. In the stillness of that sunny morning, he experiences an overwhelming mystery. He asks his teacher, 'will I experience that feeling again?' To which the teacher responds with a clear, 'Yes'.

However, most of the time he keeps wondering about all the mysteries and perplexities around him, especially the death of his father, and other deaths and creaturely distortions: a 'crazy' person, a dead animal, etc. He listens to the blowing of the wind that whispers about the death of his father and many other creatures, but never for him. He does not understand the depth of his religious feelings. Later on perhaps, he may come to understand that this experience about the mystery of life will deepen and that he can hear it as the God of the scriptures addressing him as 'you'. The experience is part of life, but the revelation of God's creating will reveal its basic meaning to him. (The wind, God's Spirit, also blows for you, to comfort you in your loss and to make sense of your experience; the Spirit of God is with you.) Experiences like this of a boy listening to the wind blowing across the prairies and being moved to his core is a creaturely given. It is a voice which that young boy needed to hear, to be personally addressed and comforted by God's Spirit; the prairie wind also blowing for him and all other suffering creatures.

Paul in his speech to the Athenians could make use of givens like that, of a general religious sense. They believed in a Maker, a Creator, or a Cosmic Intelligence,

> Men of Athens, I perceive that in every way you are very religious, for as I passed along, and observed the objects of your worship, I found also an altar with this inscription, 'To an unknown god.' What therefore you worship as unknown, this I proclaim to you. The God who made the world and everything in it, being LORD of heaven and earth, does not live in shrines made by man, nor is he served by human hands, as though he needed anything, since he himself gives to all men life and breath and everything . . . that they should seek God, in the hope that they might feel after him and find him. Yet he is not far from each one of us, for 'In him we live and move and have our being'; as even some of your poets have said, 'For we are indeed his offspring'. . . and of this he has given assurance to all men by raising him from the dead.
> Acts 17: 22–31

Paul quotes from the Stoic poets, "for we are of his offspring." It is a daring statement, but it allowed him to come to his main message, the resurrection. At that point the Athenians reacted like Pharaoh, "Who is this God? I do not know this LORD!" They did worship the god of Heaven. Is this accommodation? Is it a belief in a general god, a Creator God that everyone can believe in? Melchizedek king of Salem could say the same thing, "Blessed be Abram by God Most High, maker of heaven and earth." (Gen 14:19, 22) Abraham 'corrects' him and changes the words to, "Yahweh, most high, creator of heaven and earth." Abraham places the name of God first, Yahweh, before Melchizedek's confession. It becomes an explanation of the name of God. In this way, the expression, "Maker of heaven and earth" takes on special meaning. It is Yahweh who is the Creator and who is behind all things and brings the creation to its fulfillment. Did the tradition accommodate itself too quickly to a general Creator God? It seems so matter of fact to believe in a Creator God. The question is not first of all, what the creation is, but the deed, the result and its purpose.

Instead of treating creation (not nature) as a separate given, Deurloo relates it directly to the core of the scriptures in both the Old and the New Testament. The fact that we are creatures generally does not evoke associations with faith, love, joy, courage and trust. Instead, we tend to associate those words with the gospel of Jesus Christ, but not with creation, Jesus instead of the Creator! Our faith in God the Creator does not have a lot of actual meaning in the Reformed tradition and in the daily lives of believers. As a result we are somewhat at a loss what we are to do with "I believe in God the Father, Almighty, Creator of heaven and earth." What are we to do with such a Fatherly, Almighty, and Creator God? If God only stands at the beginning and the end of the world, but not in the midst of our life, here and now, working, in our midst, then we hardly need such a god.

As we noted before, all of creation awaits liberation, (Rom 8) "We know that the whole creation has been groaning in travail together until now; and not only the creation, but we ourselves, who have the first-fruits of the Spirit groan inwardly . . ." Paul uses a Pentecost or harvest theme, "We ourselves who have the 'first fruits' of the Spirit, as an advance or a deposit of the great world harvest. It is a messianic perspective, ". . . to be conformed to the image of his Son, in order that he might be the first-born among many brethren." It announces what he will say more clearly and strongly in the letter to the Colossians,

> He is the image of the invisible God, the first-born of all creation; for in him all things were created, in heaven and on earth, everything visible and invisible, whether thrones or dominions, or principalities or authorities -all things were created through him and for him; He is before all things and in him all things hold together. He is the head of the body, the church; he is the beginning, the first-born from the dead, that in everything he might be pre-eminent. For in him all the fullness of God was pleased to dwell, and through him to reconcile to himself all things, Whether on earth or in heaven, making peace by the blood of his cross..
> Colossians 1:15–20

Christ is the centre, the beginning. The way God is the Redeemer, is how he is the Creator. He brings reconciliation through the Messiah with everything on earth and in heaven. In the face of all opposition and resistance, God persists in his original intention for the creation. He made "peace by the blood of his cross." That is how deep his mercy and compassion runs. In this way he is Almighty. First there is reconciliation and from there we can understand creation. Creation is for the sake of all creatures, for their well-being, including humanity. God is not an All-God, but the Father of Jesus, his first-born Son, whom he called out of Egypt. He is the Liberator and the Creator, the firstborn of creation.

Israel's storytellers, poets and prophets talk about creation as God's liberating deeds and not just about his developing a paradise-like garden, or as the beginning of everything that exists. We are not called upon to reflect on the origin of our world but only to sing about his mighty deeds of liberation and in praise of his creation.

Within this context miracles too become signs of the coming of his kingdom. The greatest miracle of all is that God in Jesus Christ can direct all creatures in their freedom to his kingdom. In all miracles it is about the fulfillment of all lawfulness. Especially in his miracles it becomes evident that God will be faithful to all his creatures and sees their destiny. Then we will not look for miracles as events that break through the 'laws of nature'.

Miracles are promises that God everywhere wants to preserve his creatures for their destination. Miracles do not just happen in a supernatural way in which we can only watch with astonishment. Rather the biblical miracles call for our own actions and responses to bear witness to God's kingdom and his righteousness. Miracles express that all of reality is focused on Jesus Christ and his kingship. In the miracles we see something of the redemption that all things highlight and carry. Miracles are not just in contradiction to 'natural laws' but carry the secret of the creation and their fulfillment. All people that are open to hearing and seeing are addressed by creation and called to act in harmony with it.

9:4c) Wisdom

All of creation speaks to us, to Israel and all humanity. All of creation is revelatory. The psalmist has used a familiar pagan hymn to the sun to express Yahweh's delight in his creation. "In them he has set a tent for the sun, which comes forth like a bridegroom leaving his chamber, and like a strong man runs its course with joy. " (Ps 19:5) "Lord, how manifold are thy works! In Wisdom hast thou made them all; the earth is full of thy creatures." (Ps 104:24)

The psalmist starts first of all by acknowledging Yahweh as the Creator, "Bless the LORD, O my soul," which is repeated at the end. (Ps 104:35) in between he lists all the phenomena of the creaturely world and calls all creatures to sing his praises. Compare Psalm 148:

> Praise the LORD!
> Praise the LORD from the heavens . . .
> Praise him sun and moon,
> Praise him, all you shining stars! . . .
> Let them praise the name of the LORD!
> for he commanded and they were created. . . .
> Praise the LORD from the earth,
> You sea monsters and all deeps,
> fire and hail, snow and frost,
> stormy wind fulfilling his command!
> Mountains and all hills,
> Fruit trees and all cedars!
> Beasts and all cattle,
> Creeping things and flying birds!
> Kings of all the earth and all peoples,
> Princes and all rulers of the earth!
> Young men and maidens together,
> old men and children!
> . . .
> Praise the LORD!
>   Psalm 148

In Psalm 104 the psalmist confesses that all creatures are under his command. "Thou hast made the moon to mark the seasons; the sun knows its time for setting. Thou makest darkness, and it is night . . ." (Psalm 104:19) All creatures are to sing his praises: "The heavens proclaim his righteousness; and all the peoples behold his glory." (Ps 97:6) All creatures pass by in one grand review: the light, the heavens, the clouds, the winds, the night, the stars, the moon, the seas, the water that brings life to all the animals, and the rhythm of time for all. They all pass by.

Even the 'demonic' creatures, like the Leviathan, are allowed to play in the sea. They are all creatures that are dependent for food and life that Yahweh gives to all creatures. It is not a 'nature' psalm, but a hymn of praise. All of creation is demythologized; they are creatures of God, not gods.

THE NATURE OF BIBLICAL THEOLOGY

"May the glory of the LORD endure for ever, may the LORD rejoice in his works . . . I will sing to the LORD as long as I live, I will sing praise to my God while I have being. May my meditation be pleasing to him, for I rejoice in the LORD." (Ps 104:31–34) The psalmist confesses, "In wisdom thou hast made them all."

The psalmist speaks about God by telling 'history'. Psalm 104 connects with Psalm 103. Both are framed by, "Bless the LORD, O my soul." He knows of no other God than the Name of Yahweh, and no other God than the One who revealed himself to Moses. As the special God of Israel, he rules universally over all kingdoms. He describes not just something that everyone can observe, but he speaks about creation in a way that only the good creation becomes visible. The shadow sides too are brought back to their limits. There is a critical note, "Let sinners be consumed from the earth, and let the wicked be no more!" (Ps 104:35)

> The LORD works vindication
> and justice for all who are oppressed.
> He made known his ways to Moses,
> his acts to the people of Israel.
>
> The LORD has established his throne in the heavens,
> And his kingdom rules over all.
>   Psalm 103:6, 7, 19

Over against them, the poet can only present himself as the one praising the Creator and his creation. "I will sing to the LORD as long as I live. I will sing praise to my God while I have being." (Ps 104:33) "Praise the LORD, O my soul." His Lordship is so great that in the midst of death he guarantees life. A poem about the living God cannot end in death. "When thou hidest thy face, they are dismayed; when thou takest away their breath, they die, and return to their dust." (Psalm 104:29) Hannah turns the order around, "The LORD kills and brings to life; he brings down to Sheol and raises up." (1 Sam 2:6) He is in charge of life and death. Death does not have the last word. Yahweh is LORD of the living and all of creation. We can only talk about God's 'providence' in hymnic ways, as do the Psalms. Given this constant testimony in the Psalms it is not surprising that God's wisdom is personified in Proverbs, like a young maiden,

> Does not wisdom call,
> does not understanding raise her voice?
> On the heights beside the way,

> in the paths she takes her stand;
> beside the gates in front of the town,
> at the entrance of the portals she cries aloud:
> To you, O men, I call,
> and my cry is to the sons of men.
>> Proverbs 8:1, 2

Not in 'nature', but in the place where people meet each other, there Wisdom is heard. Her voice is heard in public life, in the city gates. In her speech she mentions justice and righteousness, knowledge and truth. Because of wisdom, kings know what is right and just. "By me kings reign, and rulers decree what is just." Who is she? She is the first creation of Yahweh.

> The LORD created me at the beginning of his work,
> the first of his acts of old.
> Ages ago I was set up,
> at the first, before the beginning of the earth.
> Before the mountains had been shaped,
> before the hills, I was brought forth;
> before he had made the earth with its fields,
> or the first of the dust of the world.
> When he established the heavens, I was there,
> when he drew a circle on the face of the deep,
> when he made firm the skies above,
> when he established the foundations of the deep,
> when he assigned to the sea its limit,
> so that the waters might not transgress his command,
> when he marked out the foundations of the earth,
> Then I was beside him, like a master workman;
> and I was daily his delight,
> rejoicing before him always,
> rejoicing in his inhabited world
> and delighting in the sons of men.
>> Proverbs 8:22–31

We are pulled along from the threatening waters to the solid mountains. From the dependable heavens as God's abode to men's abode, the earth, to when the boundaries of the sea were established. She validates herself, Yahweh created me at the beginning of his work, the first of his acts of old, at the first, before the beginning of the earth." In all his acts , I was there, "When he marked out the foundations of the earth, then I was beside him, like a master workman, and I was daily his delight, rejoicing in his inhabited world and delighting in the sons of men." (Prov

8:22–31) When he uses the word 'beginning' was he thinking of Genesis? Lady Wisdom was there as his first creation. Heaven is full of promise, it is there for the earth. Like a skipping young girl, she was there. God created with her. He creates with great pleasure, for she was his delight. Where does she skip to? It is to the earth. That was Yahweh's intention. She is the beginning of the path that ends on the earth with humankind. As she, herself, puts it, "rejoicing in his inhabited world and delighting in the sons of men."

Is this part of Proverbs about the creation? Yes, but in connection with the main theme, Wisdom. It is about creation as the result of God's deeds. God created space for his people with and through Wisdom. "And now, my sons listen to me: Happy are those who listen to my ways . . . He who finds me finds life and obtains favor from the LORD." (Prov 8:32, 35) And where do you find her? In the midst of public life, in the city gates and the market place! She knows the way. With his creating he gave her a place, which only the LORD knows. To the human he said, "The fear of the LORD is the beginning of wisdom, and the knowledge of the Holy one is insight." (Prov 9:10) In following the life-giving ways of Yahweh we find life and peace. In Psalm 19 we read,

> The heavens are telling the glory of God;
> and the firmament proclaims his handiwork.
> Day to day pours forth speech,
> and night to night declares knowledge.
> There is no speech nor are there words;
> their voice is not heard;
> yet their voice goes out through all the earth,
> and their words to the end of the world.
>   Psalm 19:1–4

To whom do the heavens tell God's glory? To the earth! With the heavens, God sets up a tent, for the sun.

> In them he has set a tent for the sun,
> which comes forth like a bridegroom leaving his chamber,
> and like a strong man runs its course with joy.
> Its rising is from the end of the heavens,
> and its circuit to the end of them . . .
>   Psalm 19:4–6

This signal goes from the heavens to the earth, the silent speech: the glory of God. "The whole earth is full of his glory." (Isa 6:3) The heavens announce the sun to the earth. That is, Yahweh (the heavens) give humankind (the earth) the brilliance of his teaching (the Torah). "His precepts are like a shining sun to light our way." "Light is sweet, and it is pleasant for the eyes to behold the sun." (Eccl 11:7) "The law of the LORD is perfect, reviving the soul." which like the sun lights up our way. Then follow all the various ways the Torah is perfect. "More to be desired are they then gold ... sweeter also than honey." (Ps 19:7, 10)

The psalmist adds one more thought to his poem, "Let the words of my mouth and the meditation of my heart be acceptable in thy sight, O LORD, my rock and my redeemer." (Ps 19:14) As the psalmist, in Psalm 104, ends his poetic offering to the LORD, "may my meditation be pleasing to him, for I rejoice in the LORD." (Ps 104:34; cf 19:14) Or, "LORD in the morning thou dost hear my voice; in the morning I prepare a sacrifice for thee, and watch." (Ps 5:3) With the rising of the sun, the poet offers his meditation to the LORD and feels blessed by the light and warmth of the sun. As a blessed light, the rising sun is a sign of God's face, of his presence. All Israel and all peoples hear the blessing, "The LORD make his face to shine upon you, and be gracious to you: the LORD lift up his countenance upon you, and give you peace." (Num 6:25, 26) When the sun rises it promises to be a full day of light, now and in the future. Just as the light of the sun in the sky, I see the Torah that lights my way on the earth.

The creation is inseparably connected to doing righteousness and justice, to truth and loving kindness. Each creature speaks a voice that is heard throughout the whole earth, a voiceless speech. "God is our refuge and strength, a very present help in trouble. Therefore we will not fear though the earth should change, though the mountains shake in the heart of the sea ... The nations rage, the kingdoms totter ... The LORD of hosts is with us; the God of Jacob is our refuge ... He makes wars cease to the end of the earth ... he breaks the bow and shatters the spear, he burns the chariots with fire! ... The LORD of hosts is with us ..." (Psalm 46: 1–11) this is the promise awaiting its fulfillment. That is how we can also hear the prayer of Habakkuk, when wars rage and the creation is on the edge of extinction,

> O LORD, I have heard the report of thee and thy work ...
> in wrath remember mercy ...
> The mountains saw thee, and writhed,
> the raging waters swept on ...
> The sun and the moon stood still in their habitation ...
> I hear and my body trembles ...
>   Habakkuk 3:1–16

In the face of our present global injustices and disintegrating environment it is not easy to join in with Habakkuk's confession. In the midst of these impending threatening times, the prophet urges us to take heart:

> Though the fig tree does not blossom,
> nor fruit be on the vines,
> the produce of the olive fail
> and the fields yield no food,
> the flock be cut off from the fold,
> and there be no herd in the stalls,
> yet I will . . .
> Habakkuk 3:17, 18 (cf. Hab 2:18, 19)

This threat to our very existence and the earth is a call to confess anew the Redeemer and Creator of the whole earth and all humanity. Only by faith can we see and talk about God's good creation. "By faith we understand that the world was created by the word of God. (Hebrews 11:3) and John confesses,

> In the beginning was the Word and the Word was with God, and the Word was God. He was in the beginning with God; all things were made through him, and without him was not anything made that was made. In him was life, and the life was the light of men . . . and the world was made through him, yet the world knew him not. . . . And the Word became flesh and dwelt among us, full of grace and truth; we have beheld his glory, glory as of the only Son from the Father . . . No one has ever seen God; the only Son, who is in the bosom of the Father, he has made him known.
> John 1:1–18

The heavens declare God's glory. They speak of the Son, through whom all things are made, God's wisdom, his daily delight, delighting in the sons of men.

9:4d) Job

At this point Deurloo turns to the story of Job to highlight the dark side of creation. Job engages in a daring argument with God about injustice and evils that have happened to him. Who is Job? Does he stand for a righteous Israel, unjustly hit by disasters? Job is the human in protest about the mystery of evil that unexplainably hits us. But it is also the Job that remains true to the earth, when he faces the many calamities that hit his life. How can that be in harmony with the God of covenantal faithfulness and love? His conversation with God is not hopeless but it is about the meaning of his existence. He is portrayed as "a blameless and upright man, who feared God and turned away from evil." (Job 1:5) But Job is unwavering when tested. "'. . . Shall we receive good at the hand of God, and shall we not receive evil?' In all this, Job did not sin with his lips." (Job 2:10) That is not a sign of resignation, but the start of his controversy with God.

When confronted by all the disasters that happened to him, he curses the day of his birth, "Let the day perish wherein I was born, and the night which said, 'a man-child is conceived. Let that day be darkeness! . . ." (Job 3:3, 4) "Why did I not die at birth, come forth from the womb and expire?" (Job 3:11, 16) How is it possible that the righteous fare the same fate as the unjust? Job represents all those who experience undeserved disaster. After the admonitions and judgments of his friends he takes his complaint directly to God, "He crushes me with a tempest, and multiplies my wounds without cause." (Job 9:17) "But I would speak to the Almighty, and I desire to argue my case with God." (Job 13:3)

The prophet Micah turns this kind of argument upside down and talks about the controversy God has with his people, "Arise, plead your case before the mountains, and let the hills hear your voice. Hear, you mountains, the controversy of the LORD, and you enduring foundations of the earth; for the LORD has a controversy with his people, and he will contend with Israel . . . O my people, what have I done to you? In what have I wearied you? Answer me!" (Mic 6:1-3) The answer is clear, "He has showed you O man what is good . . ." (Mic 6:8) In Isaiah the controversy is initiated by, "You turn things upside down! Shall the potter be regarded as the clay; that the thing made shall say of its maker, 'He did not make the thing formed say of him who formed it, 'He has no understanding'"? (Isaiah 29:16) (cf. Isa 45:9; Rom 9:19)

People complain about what God does. It is almost as if God pulls rank because he is the Liberator, who has made you return from exile. I appointed Cyrus to liberate you and return to your home land. "Declare and present your case; let them take council together!" (Isa 45:21) The Lord is indeed the "Holy one of Israel, and his Maker: Will you question me about my children, or command me concerning the work of my hands? I made the earth and created man upon it; it was my hands that stretched out the heavens, and I commanded, all their host. I have aroused him in righteousness, and I will make straight all his ways. . . . " (Isa 45:11–13)

In spite of God's controversy with his wayward people, Job perseveres to challenge God about all the unjust calamities that have befallen him, "But I would speak to the Almighty, and I desire to argue my case with God." (Job 13:3) "Oh, that I knew where I might find him, that I might come, even to his seat! I would lay my case before him and fill my mouth with arguments." (23:3, 4) After reciting all his righteous deeds, he sighs, "Oh that I had one to hear me! Here is my signature! Let the Almighty answer me!" (Job 31:35) It is the cry of all suffering people.

How does God respond to Job's complaints? What follows is not a biology lesson. How do all these references to animals, the crocodiles or mountain goats, lions, ravens, wild asses, pelican, owl, porcupine, raven, hawk, hyenas, and ostriches, comfort or reassure Job? (Job 38, 39) To understand this imagery, we need to remember that a competent king in the ancient near east is lord of the hunt, even when the land is laid waste. "Seek and read from the book of the LORD: not one of these shall be missing; none shall be without her mate. For the mouth of the LORD has commanded, and his Spirit has gathered them." These animals are mentioned together to illustrate God's care to maintain a habitable world and his might. (Isa 34:11-16). During the first speech of his friend Eliphaz, the image of the wild animals is used to describe the wicked: the roaring of the lions, the throat of the leopard, and teeth of the young lions (Job 4:10). We have to remember this image, for it 'answers' Job's questions.

In all these images Job has to respond to, "Where were you when I laid the foundation of the earth? Tell me, if you have understanding." (Job 38:4) He has to admit, "I had heard of thee by the hearing of the ear, but now my eye sees thee." (Job 42:5) ". . . When the morning stars sang together, and all the sons of God shouted for joy?" (Job 38: 6) In our day to day reality isn't there always a sign of the future? Even the miracle of rain in the desert, which in itself as a 'natural' phenomena has no meaning, can become the promise of a flourishing culture, "the desert shall rejoice and blossom; like the crocus it shall blossom abundantly, and rejoice with joy and singing." (Isa 35:1, 2) Continually he contains the chaos of the sea, every morning anew he calls the light, and with rain he fights against the desert. Work in progress! Even more so, when it concerns the animals of the field, God's presence is in the midst of life, here and now, working, in our midst.

Job is called to see that in the battle against evil, which is still present, to also trust that God is LORD of all creation and all the animals, even the mighty sea monsters, because he is the Creator. Job has suggested that "the earth is given into the hand of the wicked." (Job 9:24) "Will you even put me in the wrong? Will you condemn me that you may be justified? (Job 40:8) With those words the bitter secret of the good creation is driven to a climax. Job is forced to admit that, "I know that thou canst do all things, and that no purpose of thine can be thwarted." (Job 42:2) Yahweh answers Job from out of the whirlwind, which does not kill him. In the end the LORD condemns his two friends, "for you have not spoken of me what is right, as my servant Job has." (Job 42:7) The first conclusion is that Yahweh daily upholds his creation and brings it to its fulfillment. He is present everywhere.

9:4e) Ecclesiastes

Job is one answer to the problem of evil in the world, in the good creation. Deurloo might have added a section on Ecclesiastes, but he does not do so. In Ecclesiastes everything seems to be futility and senseless fate. Yahweh seems absent and silent. A new god-image seems to have risen. People despair and feel hopeless. Everything is a monotonous spiral, "A generation goes, and a generation comes, but the earth remains for ever. There is no remembrance of former things, nor, will there be any remembrance of later things yet to happen." (Eccl 1:4, 11) The wise man observes and notes that, "The wise man has his eyes in his head, but the fool walks in darkness; and yet I perceived that one fate comes to all of them... What befalls the fool will befall me also, why then have I been so very wise? And I said to myself that this also is vanity... How the wise man dies just like the fool! So I hated life, because what is done under the sun was grievous to me; for all is vanity and striving after wind." (Eccl 2:14-17) All seems blind fate and chance and goes nowhere; there is no future. The wise man can't endure what he sees,

> Again I saw all the oppressions that are practiced under the sun. And behold, the tears of the oppressed, and they had no one to comfort them! On the side of the oppressors there was power, and there was no one to comfort them. And I thought the dead who are already dead more fortunate than the living who are still alive; but better than both is he who has not yet been, and has not seen the evil deeds that are done under the sun.
> Ecclesiastes 4:1-3

What are we to make of those bitter complaints, those sentiments that ring all too true in our day? Does it call for quiet acceptance and enjoying the things we still can? Yes, enjoy your bread, your wine and your partner. (Eccl 9:7, 9) Has a quiet skepticism and fatalism entered the god image at a time there was very little hope left and the horrors of life seemed overwhelming. Not so, says the wise man. In the end the message is, "Fear God, and keep his commandments; for this is the whole duty of man." (Eccl 12:13) In spite of all the evil that is happening round about us and with us, keep following the life-giving words of the LORD, for that is the way to the future and breaks through all futility and fatalism.

In this way Deurloo, primarily from out of Job, circles around the problem of evil without providing a more elaborate response to all those suffering. To see Yahweh's great works in creation and the creatures of his hands can be small comfort to someone who is suffering from evil in this world and what seems like fate or bad luck in their personal life. To see, as in Ecclesiastes, the prosperity of the rich and the powerful, the repression of the suffering ones, tends to give rise to rage and indignation and the desire for revenge and justice. More is needed. Countless theologians and philosophers during the centuries have addressed this problem of evil and God's governance. Is God the origin of evil? Does he merely tolerate it for the time being?

Our first conclusion from Deurloo's presentation is that Yahweh continually contains the chaos of the sea and every morning anew calls the light to shine and the sun to rise. Yahweh is present in the midst of our life, here and now, working, in our midst. But those two can be in conflict with each other. Is there another way to talk about evil and God's power?

9:4f) Yahweh's creating and 'maintaining' are of one piece

In his books on, *The beginning in our midst* (1977) and, together with Beker, *His governance in life, questions and references with regard to providence* (1978) does Deurloo take us further? Let's follow his argument.

What becomes apparent, from the start in understanding Genesis and Joshua, is that they present a very different picture of Yahweh's presence in life and human history than we learned from the church's teaching and preaching. As we reread Genesis and Joshua we were exposed to a very different God image. By a miraculous series of events the earth mother bears a son, the first-born son.

Right from the beginning of his discussion of God's providence in *The Guidance of our Existence; questions and referrals around providence*, together with Beker, he strongly rejects the traditional (theological) view of providence as it is articulated in the *Heidelberg Catechism*, (one of the forms of unity of the Reformed Churches). He quotes question and answer 27,

> What do you understand by the providence of God?
>
> Providence is the almighty and ever present power of God by which he upholds, as with his hand, heaven and earth and all creatures, and so rules them that leaf and blade, rain and drought, fruitful and lean years, food and drink, health and sickness, prosperity and poverty – all things, in fact, come to us not by chance but from his fatherly hand.
>
> (Followed by an array of texts)

Deurloo calls this kind of teaching a nurturing toward atheism. Biblically speaking it is not so much falsehood, but falsehood from the powerful and the rich, from the 'Bosses'. This kind of approach keeps the poor, poor and the weak, weak, and the homeless, homeless, etc.; it leads to a fundamental conservatism that keeps each person in their place, especially the poor and powerless. That is why for him it is pure paganism. Question and answer 28 is no less poisonous,

> How does the knowledge of God's creation and providence help us?
>
> We can be patient when things go against us, Thankful when things go well, and for the future we have good confidence in our faithful God and Father that nothing will separate us from his love. All creatures are so completely in his hand that without his will they can neither move nor be moved.
>
> (Followed by an array of texts)

Reading these words again some 80 years later when I first had to memorize and recite them, they do sound like 'blasphemy'. It reflects a settled and comfortable society for the upper classes, with an established and secure state to defend their private properties and livelihood. The elite sit in the front rows. But it held out very little for the dispossessed and the suffering. This kind of view of God's providence leads to atheism or life-long doubts and anger. There is no comfort here for the children that were allowed to leave school early to beg for a slice of bread from rich Christian farmers along the way home, as my father experienced as a schoolboy.

Does this kind of confession also hold for when I was eleven and looking across the canal at the desperate, emaciated people, passing by our window, pushing a cart with their grandmother or small children, on the way to the country looking for some food? Later I wondered if we should have invited them to come inside and warm up by our little stove and share some of our sugar beets and tulip bulbs. Was it God's will that my grandfather died young, leaving a wife and children, including my father to fend for themselves? Did my mother deserve the loss of her mother at an early age due to an epileptic 'fit', having to cope with a 'cold' stepmother? Did she deserve all those illnesses and operations, being on the brink of death several times, with two small children to take care of, who out of necessity, had to be farmed out to their aunts? Did all that come from God's fatherly hand?

I did not mention yet the pictures of the concentration camps that are engraved in my mind: naked boys and girls, mothers and fathers pushed inside the 'shower' rooms to be gassed and the many testimonies and eyewitness stories after the war. And today, the many pictures of Gaza turned into a heap of rubble, uninhabitable with tens of thousands dead, almost half of them children, without future, their homeland destroyed or taken over. Is this his 'fatherly hand' and a hundred other questions? It sounds more like blasphemy and a distortion of the scriptures. See the last paragraph about Miskotte's view of God's Providence *De Kern Van DeZaak*, p. 328.

Clever theological answers do not change this picture, then or now. These kind of teachings, lead to atheism. Meanwhile, many feel that a lot of God's guidance can be substituted with our belief in science and technology. We have our 'green' revolution that produces bigger yields than 'leaves and grasses'. Big yields do not come from 'God's fatherly hand' but from new techniques and knowledge, from fertilizers and genetically modified seeds. "He's got the whole world in his hands," but some things and some people a little less so; they are 'blowing in the wind'. Many are left with destroyed farms and increased suicides.

The teachings of the church enter into a specific cultural and social context, during previous ages and now. They shape the attitudes and religious experiences of an entire community. Each time again we need to ask ourselves, is that what the scriptures teach us?

When the all-good father, who conserves and guides the whole creation is unmasked as a distortion; then, as a silent presence and absent power, God has become superfluous. Such images need to be destroyed. It is a very dark image of God who holds all things in his hands, including all evil things, disasters, droughts, forest fires, floods, fatal accidents, etc. that like fate may overcome us. It is a view that is easily distorted and has led to untold suffering and many fruitless arguments. It is an individualistic and out of context understanding of God's providence, unrelated to the coming of his kingdom and the fulfilment of all things. It shows the emptiness of this kind of image of God that always takes care of everything and every person.

From the beginning, Deurloo approaches the doctrine of God's providence from the point of view of what God sees for the future of all creatures and all of humanity. To highlight his approach he starts with a reference to Genesis 22:8, "God will provide" and, "The LORD sees, as it said to this day, 'on the mount of the LORD there is vision," seeing or fore-seen? The greatest miracle of the history of Israel and its Messiah points to the destination of the whole creation.

Genesis 11:27 begins with the 'descendents of Terah', following the pattern of Genesis that is about the becoming of Israel in the midst of all peoples. The theme of the earthling on the earth (Gen 12:1–4) is concentrated in this story of Abraham in the land of Canaan. "Go from your country . . . to the land that I will show you . . . and I will bless you . . . you will be a blessing . . . all the families of the earth." (Gen 12:1–3) In contrast to his father Terah who halted at Haran, Abraham travelled on to Canaan. (Gen 12:5) He goes and sees, as the blessed one for the sake of all peoples. And God showed himself there. (Genesis 12:7) 'Going' and 'seeing,' play a special role in the Abraham cycle. Abraham does not look for the best place like Lot, to take what you can see (Gen 13:9–13).

This land full of problems is the land of promise. After their parting he is asked by God to look in every direction. "Lift up your eyes, and look from the place where you are, northward and southward, and eastward and westward; for all the land which you see I will give to you." (Gen 13:14) He is promised to become a great nation, even after they suffer slavery in Egypt, they will come back after the fourth generation: "for the iniquity of the Amorites is not yet complete." Gen 15:12–21 Later Hagar hears God speaking to her about the promises to Ishmael. Afterwards she exclaims, "Thou art a God of seeing, for she said, 'Have I really seen God and remained alive after seeing him?" (Gen 16:7–14) Later we read, "Then God opened her eyes and then she saw a well of water." (Gen 21:15–21)

The second cycle of Abraham is about the birth of a son. "You and your seed" will inherit this land. It is about the son of the promise. The words of Gen 12 return, "Take your son, your only son Isaac, whom you love, and go, you." (Gen 22:2) So Abraham went to sacrifice his only son, he "went to the place of which God had told him. On the third day Abraham lifted up his eyes and saw the place afar off." (Gen 22:4, 5) Following is the famous story of Genesis 22. Abraham learns to let go of his son as the natural offspring of himself and entrust himself to what God sees. The miracle of the birth of Isaac, of the becoming of Israel, in the midst of the nations depends on God's special care or fore-seeing. After the prevention of the sacrifice of the son a substitute stands ready. There is a special seeing or fore-seeing; God fore-sees in the un-forseen, a ram. So Abraham called the place, 'God sees'. On the mountain of the LORD it is seen. Now the blessing is more specific, "and by your descendants shall all the nations of the earth bless themselves" (Gen 22:18). What Yahweh sees is the blessed one, Israel, for the sake of all.

Only from the specific, protective care of God for the one Israel, from out of whom the one Christ comes forth, with his new community, his unique care for all becomes visible. God chooses above all to be there as the God who cares for the blessed human, who is to be a blessing for all and in this God, is glorified. From out of this choice of God to be there as the God of Israel for all, we are to talk about 'providence'. And not in some general way that is clear for everybody to see. Our faith in 'providence' is as miraculous as God's giving himself in his creation. Then our faith in God's 'providence' is in the power of Israel's God to unite heaven and earth to the glory of his name.

That is how the entire scriptures talk of his care of the blessed human and that everything, including animals and people share in this blessing. This faith, in God's fore-seeing, reaches forward to the coming of the kingship of God. Thus 'providence' is not just a matter of fact, but a matter of faith in Him and his kingship. Then God's providence reaches to its deepest fulfillment. 'Providence' is faith in expecting the liberation and blessing of all people and all things. Such faith can only give rise to a measure of skepticism when we look at the earth and humanity, also looking as a believer, and see an 'unbridgeable' gap between the reality and the promise.

It remains a miracle that God is for humanity and for all of creation. It is the miracle of the coming of his kingship. Such faith is constantly in doubt. For this reason we continue to pray, "Your kingdom come!" It only becomes a reality in the way God speaks of himself as the God of Israel in the stories of the TeNaK and the Gospels. Surrounded by these voices of the scriptures, and witnesses can we be convinced that his Kingship creates a path through life?

This faith focuses on the Lord of the kingdom to see Jesus' vision, "Repent, for the kingdom of heaven is at hand" (Matt 3:2), and "All authority has been given to me ... and lo, I am with you always, to the close of the age;" as seen from a high mountain in Galilee. (Matt 28:20) Faith in God's 'providence' is not just a general and contemplative knowledge rather it is always a faith in God's active and effective care of all things.

This is not some general knowledge of a Creator and 'Provider' that all can agree with, the Greeks of Athens and the boy listening to the wind blowing across the prairies. Such a 'provider' is great for when you are fortunate, but when things are desperate it can only lead to atheism.

Such faith is not an easily accessible belief, but is given with our faith in the God that keeps covenant forever and does not abandon the works of his hands. The words of the weekly salutation had a rich meaning and history that we only now can begin to fathom. In Sunday 9 of the Heidelberg Catechism, "That the eternal Father of our LORD Jesus Christ . . . who upholds and governs heaven and earth by his eternal council and 'providence' for the sake of his son is my God and Father." The old theology could not add that they confessed these words in the sure faith that all nations and people will confess these words. They could not believe that God's 'providential' acting was for the good of all, and not just for the predestined. Thus the unbelievers were saved and cared for only to manifest God's judgement. In this old view God can only save a few elect out of the many damned people. Even writing these words seems like blasphemy. Yet that was the spiritual climate of my family and that of many others. It was destructive of the life of the congregation and fellowship. In this individualistic view of 'providence' that does not include God's care for all and so everyone else is lost. It became a very individualistic understanding. It is an interpretation that makes suffering and questioning people despair and sometimes curse God with questions like: Everything from his fatherly hand? God foresees, really?

We could wish Deurloo had lingered a little longer with this understanding of God's 'providence'. He could have emphasized more strongly that in the scriptures God is not made into the author or origin of evil but that he constantly works to maintain his creation and people and brings all to their fulfillment. He could have emphasized more strongly that evil has no place in God's creation and ultimately will be banned and overcome. Evil cannot be placed or explained. It has no origin. His understanding that God's 'providence' can only be understood in the light of the coming of the kingdom of God and that all people and all of creation are caught up in this movement is already a strong correction of the old theology.

Deurloo/Beker might also have lingered longer with the suffering and powerlessness of countless people who cry out to God and need to hear 'I am with you, there on the cross and in the rubble of Gaza and the destruction of Ukraine and those facing torture and execution, yes, and even in all the suffering animals led to the slaughter. Baby Jesus is not just sleeping peacefully in a cradle at Christmas. He is present in the rubble and in suffering of any kind, Immanuel, God with us, wherever we find ourselves. That is what that young boy needed to hear and so did I when I was ten or twelve and as a young lost adolescent.

Above all, God's 'providence' must be understood as God maintaining his creation with an eye to its destination, namely the glorified creation or God's kingship. He conserves everything and all with a view to the great transformation that will bear the mark of his glory. He rules in such a way that each creature, according to its own nature is maintained, and free. He rules maintaining each creature's freedom.

God conserves all for the judgement of his grace; he maintains all for his kingdom. He does not judge from outside his grace, which he has proclaimed in the crucifixion and resurrection of his Son. This grace shall fully come to light at the end of days. From out of the judgement over Israel by the judge of all the earth in the past, the path goes via the early Christian congregations to all, in whom and with whom he will glorify himself. The connection between nature and history right from the beginning stands in this sign and promise. His conservation gives us a vision of the inseparable connection with the glory of his kingdom.

His rule does not stand in opposition to our freedom. The freedom of his covenant, and of the first congregations, is a freedom in covenant and in relation with each other. Each congregation is called to live that communion for all to see. In our witness, and protests, that is what needs to become evident. God's rule fully maintains our freedom, and calling, as covenant partners. God's grace does not repress or keep us dependent and voiceless but gives us freedom. This grace rules universally. It is the liberating power of the kingdom. Faith in God's providence gives the courage to oppose and struggle.

The world is conserved for the glory of the Son who has suffered for all and has risen for all and rules for their benefit. His rule implies that we can't deny that all creatures bear the mark and sign of his kingdom rule. God in Jesus Christ turns toward all things and transforms them in the dynamic course of his rule by his Word and Spirit. Such preserving never coincides with our given state of affairs, our conservatism. God wants to preserve us and all creatures for his kingdom. We misconstrue his 'providence' if we only relate it to our reality and circumstances in an individualistic and personalistic way. Only in the light of what God sees and does, can we do justice to our reality. God sees first of all the blessed earthling and not a number of elect. A God who takes us up in the dynamic of his liberation, such a view bans all fatalism and false conservatism that does not speak out against injustice and repression. We are to see all people and all creatures as called to be partners in the coming of his kingdom and its righteousness.

God's creating and maintaining are of one piece. It calls for a new reflection and searching of the scriptures about Yahweh's care of his creation and humankind. This account of God's providence and maintenance by Deurloo is a great start.

During the course of many centuries, systematic theology became ruled by rational categories, starting with the doctrine of God followed by all the other loci. As a result, the first thing I had to endure in seminary was an exposition of the "incommunicable and communicable attributes" of God, straight from the book by Louis Berkhof's *Systematic theology* and borrowed from H. Bavinck. They are: God's Omnipresence, Omniscience, Omnipotence, Immutability, Infinity, Holiness, Noncontingency, Self-sufficiency, Sovereignty, Spirit, Transcendence and Uniqueness. Even today for evangelism purposes, understanding these attributes are recommended for understanding and developing the right concept of God. (See the website of the Navigators and their campus ministry). Together these kinds of teachings made for the worst three years of my academic life. There had been a purge and a number of new professors had been hastily appointed that had limited competence in their field. Not surprising, after I graduated from seminary, I had literally and spiritually nothing to say to a congregation.

The good part was that I left for Amsterdam to learn from their great biblical scholars my father always talked about. Unfortunately the professor I was to study under, J.H. Bavinck in Practical Theology died during the first year I was there. As was the practice at that time, no one else was appointed for several years. There was no guidance. I was left on my own. For something to do, besides struggling with my dissertation, I attended lectures in Psychology, Psychotherapy, Child Development, Education and Psychiatry that was dominated by the phenomenological approach and proved extremely helpful for my future work in education and psychotherapy.

More recently, re-reading Miskotte's account of God's 'attributes' provides a radical alternative to the speculations and generalizations of systematic theologians dealing with god's attributes,[10] "The order of God's virtues and the unity of his virtues." His account is both moving and liberating. From the start he maintains that the attributes are the attributes of his deeds. He starts by emphasizing that all God's attributes are centered in his love, ". . . for God is love." (I John 4:8) God is the loving one; he is the lover. God has a love affair with humanity from the very beginning to the very end. History is the history of God's love. It is the drama of God's searching and finding, even through the pain of his wrath and judgements. Given our state, his loving can only be by way of sacrifice. He has to 'deny' himself in order to stay with us. In this way God loves the world that he sent his only son.

This love is proclaimed or called out. It is an event, a happening. The unity of his attributes is found in this one deed, that is, in his love. That is how he loved the world that he sent his only son. His love is not some abstract virtue or quality but it has the glow and passion of a love story as portrayed in the Song of Songs. As it says in the First Letter of John,

> And as for your birth, on the day you were born your navel cord was not cut, nor were you washed with water to cleanse you, nor rubbed with salt, nor swathed with bands. No eye pitied you, to do any of these things to you out of compassion for you; but you were cast out in the open field, for you were abhorred on the day you were born. And when I passed by you, and saw you weltering in your blood. I said to you in your blood, "Live! And grow up like a plant of the field."
> Ezekiel 16:4–6

10. Miskotte, *Biblical ABCs; the basics of Christian resistance*, 50–81

In this way "God so loved the world . . ." All Yahweh's attributes are grounded in this love and they take on the form of verbs. God's omnipotence, omnipresence, omniscience, etc. are only manifest in his liberating acts for his people and through them for all humanity. In his power and all-knowing, in his liberating acts he is present everywhere in life and history, and not in some general abstract way that frightens kids. His attributes become manifest in his actions for his people.

The writer of Hebrews also affirms God's creative acts, "By faith we understand that the world was created by the word of God, so that what is seen was made out of the things which do not appear (Heb 11:3). The heavens declare God's glory; they speak of the Son, through whom all things were made, God's Wisdom, his daily delight, and delighting in the sons of men.

To give one more example, in the book of Jonah, full of humor at times, the word 'arranged' or 'appointed', is used four times. Yet it is not about God as the all-Arranger, or 'proof texts' for God's providence. Very concretely he 'spoke to the fish ('arranged'), who was big enough to swallow up Jonah; and he appointed a little plant to provide shade for Jonah during the heat of the day, and then a small worm to wither the plant to Jonah's dismay. Yahweh has 'a great wind' at his disposal to whip up the sea and hurl against the ship and later he appointed a scorching east wind to kill the miracle tree.

When they were about to perish, Jonah confesses and explains to the sailors that he was running away from the LORD, "I am a Hebrew; and I fear the LORD, the God of heaven." He doesn't simply add, "The god who created heaven and earth." He uses an internationally known term "The god of heaven." As gojim, Persians, they are familiar with the highest god. Since he already used the word 'heaven' he adds "who made the sea and the dry land." There are many key words in Jonah and striking passages that point to its fundamental message. They are not prooftexts for a doctrine of divine providence. It is an exemplary story, or cautionary tale for our edification.

The words 'the dry land' play a special role. In the midst of the waters where life is not possible, God said, "let the dry land appear" (Gen 1:9), so that the humans would have a place to put their feet down. Noah too, longingly looked out of the window, "and behold, the face of the ground was dry." (Gen 8:13) And the people of Israel having left Egypt see the sea before them and the army of Pharaoh behind them. But Moses ("because I drew him out of water" from out of his little coffin floating in the water) was commanded to "lift up your rod, and stretch out your hand over the sea and divide it . . . and Moses stretched out his hand over the sea . . . and made the sea dry land and the waters were divided." (Exod 14:16–21) The people are saved right through the sea upon the dry land. Once more the expression occurs when the Israelites cross the Jordan on dry land. (Josh 3, 4, cf. 2 Kings 2:8, 14) Jonah remembers all of that, maybe even Psalm 66:6, "Come and see what God has done: he is terrible in his deeds among men. He turned the sea into dry land; men passed the river on foot." Jonah's prayer in chapter two is made up of many quotes from the Psalms, which he probably knew by heart.

Maybe 'we can guess or assume,' ('men mag vermoeden'- one of Deurloo' characteristic terms) the passing through the Sea of Reeds gave rise to the use of this special term. In Nehemiah 9:11, we read, "And thou didst divide the sea before them, so that they went through the midst of the sea on dry land." The authors of the creation story by using this expression could present the creation as liberation. 'The dry land' is a special creature that may play its role in creation as the inauguration of history. In the midst of the threat of death by the sea, the 'dry land' plays its liberating role in the scriptures, as Jonah confesses "I fear the Lord who made the sea and the dry land."

Jonah went west instead of east to Nineveh. He wanted revenge, not mercy for the people of the great city. In the face of cruel dictators and military destruction, who would not sympathize with Jonah? Will the Judge of all the earth not do right?

The sailors were so frightened that when the sea calmed down right after they had thrown Jonah overboard, they immediately became followers of the LORD, offered sacrifices and made vows. Jonah represents Israel that became God's people, "and the people feared the Lord; and they believed in the LORD and in his servant Moses" right after they crossed the sea on dry land. (Exod 14:31) The LORD spoke to the fish that spewed Jonah out on dry land. Yahweh made extraordinary creatures to play a role in history: the mountains, the sea, the rivers, the hills, and many animals. The prophet Habakkuk writes, "The mountains saw thee and writhed; the raging waters swept on; the deep gave forth its voice, it lifted its hands on high. The sun and the moon stood still in their habitations." Even then in the face of God's wrath he can write, "I will joy in the God of my salvation." (Hab 3:18, 19)

Once rescued from the raging sea, Jonah is instructed again to go to Nineveh. He had to proclaim to the people, "In forty days, and

Nineveh shall be overthrown.." (Jonah 3:4) But Jonah was still angry. He was afraid the Lord would have mercy on the people of Nineveh. So he justified himself and complained,

> ... 'That is why I made haste to flee to Tarshish; for I knew that thou art a gracious God and merciful, slow to anger, and abounding in steadfast love, and repentest of evil. Therefore, now O LORD, take my life from me, I beseech thee, for it is better for me to die than to live.'
> Jonah 4:2, 3

The LORD questioned him and asked, "Do you do well to be angry?" But Jonah persisted. After he had pronounced judgment on the city he went up a hill outside the city to watch the spectacle of Nineveh being destroyed. It is like he could not wait.

It is the opposite of Abraham's response to the LORD when in a plea, he asked for mercy for Sodom and Gomorrah. "Suppose ten (righteous people) are found there. He (the LORD) answered, 'For the sake of ten I will not destroy it.'" (Gen 18:32) In spite of his daring plea, the next morning he had to watch the smoke of the burning city. He had to trust that the LORD would not "slay the righteous with the wicked." (Gen 18:25) The story ends with, "So it was that, when God destroyed the cities of the valley, God remembered Abraham, and sent Lot out of the midst of the overthrow ...." (Gen 19:29)

Jonah responds the opposite way when he realized Nineveh was not going to be destroyed. As a result of his preaching the pople repented. The people, believed God, repented, fasted, put on sackcloth, from young to old, even the king took off his robe, covered himself with sackcloth and sat down in ashes. He commanded all people to fast and turn from their evil ways and violence.

"When God saw what they did, how they turned from their evil way, God repented of the evil, which he had said he would do to them; and he did not do it." (Jonah 3:10)

So the LORD taught Jonah a lesson. He 'appointed' a plant to provide shade for Jonah during the heat of the day. It made Jonah "exceedingly glad." But the next day the plant died, a worm had attacked the plant. God also appointed a sultry east wind that made Jonah feel faint and again Jonah asked to die, "It is better for me to die than to live." (Jonah 4:8)

> But God said to Jonah, 'Do you do well to be angry for the plant?' And he said, 'I do well to be angry, angry enough to die.' And the LORD said, 'You pity the plant, for which you did not labor, nor did you make it grow, which came into being in a night, and perished in a night. And should not I pity Nineveh, that great city, in which there are more than a hundred and twenty thousand persons who do not know their right hand from their left, and also much cattle?'
> Jonah 4:11

That is the question for all of us. It is also the message of the prophet Ezekiel, "'As I live', says the LORD God, 'I have no pleasure in the death of the wicked, but that the wicked turn from his way and live; turn back, return back from your evil ways; for why will you die, O house of Israel'?" (Ezek 33:11; cf Ezek 18:23) We have to learn that the final judgment belongs to God "He will judge the world with righteousness, and the peoples with his truth." (Psalm 96:13 cf. Matt 7:1 and Luke 6:37) We can remember the great 'turn about' in God, his great 'mercy' as highlighted in the chapter "A New God Image!?" In fact, Jesus holds up the inhabitants of Nineveh, "The men of Nineveh will arise at the judgemnt with this generation and condemn it, (Matt 12:41) "for as Jonah became a sign to the men of Nineveh, `so will the Son of Man be to this generation." (Luke 11:30–32) It remains a difficult lesson for each of us when confronted with evil. We may all be inclined to go west instead of east. We can trust that 'God will judge the world with righteousness'. We are still to call evil wherever we encounter it. "In forty days and Nineveh shall be overthrown" was the message God wanted Jonah to deliver.

What a loss if theologians can only highlight the passages that emphasize the words "appointed, which is used four times, to serve as 'prooftexts' for the doctrine of divine providence, along with passages from Genesis 22 and 45 and others, and quarrel whether God can change his mind.

Only by faith can we talk about creation. In a problematic reality full of disasters, accidents, wars, droughts, heat waves, floods, fires, and personal misfortunes, Job has an argument with God. Job is a righteous man, "blameless and upright, one who feared God and turned away from evil." (Job 1:1) He is a counter figure and counter voice. He represents righteous Israel, although innocent, that has been hit by calamities, one after the other. (Job 1:14–19) It is not right, so Job laments and complains to God. Job, the earthling, continues his protest to the mystery of evil, which hit time and again, seemingly unexplainable and undeserved. Yet in the midst of all this he remains true to the earth. He does not escape into a higher spiritual sphere of comfort and life after death. For Job a conversation or even an argument with God makes sense. That argument is about the meaning of life at its most disastrous.

In the many passages about creation the celebration of creation is directly connected to the gift of the Torah, of doing righteousness. There is no separate realm called 'nature', only creation. And the praise of all God's creatures is directly related to the Law of Moses. What we call 'nature' (abstracted from society and culture) is not a scriptural word, and any references to the creation are immediately related to following the life-giving way of Yahweh. There is no hope in just restoring 'nature' if it does not at the same time involve restoring justice, solidarity, equality and resourcefulness.

Even today reading Miskotte, Deurloo, Breukelman and many others is like a breath of fresh air, "back to the scriptures," or "the text must have its say"; *The text must have its say; reading the scriptures according to Karel Deurloo,* 2020. It feels like I have just started my spiritual journey and theological education in spite of the many theology books I have read.

Even here there are many pitfalls and remaining questions. Someone may ask in all sincerity, "Am I not part of the mystery, redemption and justice for all? And if so, how come all these things are happening in the world and to me? Is my life truly in his hand and does it truly have meaning in that great movement toward the fulfillment of all things and people? The scriptures give no answer to the mystery of evil and its presence in the world. The only promise is that it will be defeated in the end times.

We have followed Deurloo's journey from Paul to Genesis. We did not get an understanding of the origin and nature of evil in the world. In the end we can only hold on to God's care and bringing all things to their fulfillment. With a bouquet of texts in our hands and never without it, we confess that Yahweh is our Redeemer and Creator. 'Let me tell you a story...' God will provide and is anything too hard for the LORD?" (Gen 18:14; Jer 32:17, 27; Matt 3:9; Luke 1:37)

At times the references in Deurloo's account tumble over each other, like in free association and guided by a concordance, but they all have their place. If we have patience to follow the many references, they light up our world. There is no way around a close reading of the scriptures, looking up and following all the different passages he quotes, in order to get to know the scriptures in a new context and in a new way.

9:4g) Miskotte's view of God's 'for-seeing'

In relation to the Heidelberg Catechism mentioned earlier it is helpful to place Miskotte's powerful countervoice about Lord's Day 9 and 10 in his *The Core of the Issue; the happy knowledge; collected works, volume II*, 1989. Right from the beginning, he asserts that we should not talk about 'God's providence', but rather that 'God fore-sees'. (pp. 403–450) In the first instance, he says that I have to deduce who God is from my experience; in the second instance, I can start from God's revelation and acknowledge Him as the real guide of my life: God, the Father of Jesus Christ, who maintains with his power heaven and earth. In Christ, we can trust, in faith, 'all things work together for good'. We believe not first of all in God the Father, and then in the Son, but we believe first in the Son and then in God the Father.

We must understand God's care for all creatures, including humanity from out of the revelation of his Love. God does not look down from heaven, from afar, but he enters into it, goes with it. He goes under and he rises up. In this surrender He remains free and sovereign. God's leading is first of all known by his great deeds. The word "King" as a title for God means also Leader. This king is not imaginable without a royal sacrifice. His 'providence' breaks through any confusion by giving himself as a sacrifice. "Abraham said, 'God will provide himself the lamb for a burnt offering, my son.'" (Gen 22:8) Evil cannot be thought of to belong to the creation, that is, to the creative activity of God who guides everything. We may not be able to catch that view in a concept or a closed argument. In faith, the distinction between 'understandable' and 'incomprehensible' events remains. The evil in history cannot be crowned with the idea of God's 'providence'; that he allows it for a time and is not the origin of evil. If we do not keep the eyes of faith focused on the face of the Son of God, we would despair. Will God's 'providence' ever be able to protect humanity from its inhumanity? Much of God remains hidden. Likewise, so much of God's justice and righteousness remains hidden in the face of injustice. The story of the scriptures is not a tragedy, but instead all tragedies are swallowed up by the conquest. It is a holy darkness that still invites trust in the almighty and omnipresent power upholding the earth.

At this point Miskotte makes reference to the famous, often misunderstood, passage in Matthew 10:29–31, "Are not two sparrows sold for a penny? And not one of them will fall to the ground without your Father's will. But even the hairs on your head are all numbered. Fear not, therefore; you are of more value than many sparrows." Therefore, "Look at the birds of the air; they neither sow nor reap nor gather into barns, and yet your heavenly Father feeds them. Are you not of more value than they?" (Matt 6:26; Luke 12:24) No sparrow falls to the ground without God's will. How can that comfort us?

Sparrows *do* fall to the ground. People do die prematurely or in war. Tragedies do happen. Cruelty, abuse, accidents, and murders, do happen, Gaza is in ruins with the stench of death everywhere, Ukraine, remains a battleground full of explosions and dismemberments. Our comfort is not that the sparrow does not fall, but that it does not fall because of Fate. It does not fall outside God's care. We are not struck down by nameless Powers. The biblical teaching about our Father is the opposite of the pagan teaching about Fate. Nor does it teach us that everything will turn out all right sooner or later. They become a part of the unknown side of God's guidance. We are called neither to be sentimental, pessimistic or optimistic. We believe instead that all things have a meaning, a meaning that is in agreement with all God's virtues. To believe that is a huge job in the face of darkness.

Sparrows do fall to the ground, including by the light beacons of the highrises and so do powers and philosophies. But such passing taken from our experience does not prove anything for or against a history, a people, a person. Evil seems to triumph more often or at least more easily than the good and the just.

To believe in God's seeing does not mean that we believe in the facts. If that were true we could not be happy and joyful. Nor do we believe that we can discern God's guidance of all things, that we can determine the nature and intention of God's kingship. Instead we believe in the God of the covenant, of love and justice, the Leader of history. We believe in the forgiveness of sin; we believe in the assurance of all God's attributes in the final judgment. We don't have to see the final triumph over evil and yet know that evil is worthless. We are not called to conquer evil, rather not to let ourselves be overcome by it.

The word 'providence' does not occur in the scriptures. Instead they speak about 'making alive', 'carrying', 'creating', 'protecting', 'teaching', 'ruling', of 'speaking' and of 'calling us.' With these verbs we are brought back to Life, the place of meeting or encounter. We hear the apostles proclaim the great works of God. We believe that everything is one great undertaking and this way we enter through the door, which is Christ. Talking about God's fore-seeing, points us back each time to the eternal reality of the cross and the resurrection. "Was it not necessary that the Christ should suffer these things and enter into his glory? (Luke 24:26; cf. 24:44–49; Matt 16:21)

To start with this understanding, of this love-necessity of God, makes us reserved in interpreting the events around us. It also makes us courageous and determined to lift up our eyes to the end when God himself will wipe all tears from the faces and praise God for his fore-seeing in all its mystery, context and darkness. 'Providence', cannot be looked at as something by itself, but only in the light of his kingship. "God is light and in him there is no darkness at all." (I John 1:5) "Behold the dwelling of God is with men. He will dwell with them, and they shall be his people, and God himself will be with them; he will wipe away every tear from their eyes, and death shall be no more, . . . neither shall there be mourning nor crying nor pain any more, for the former things have passed away . . . And the city had no need of sun or moon to shine upon it, for the glory of God is its light, and its lamp is the Lamb." (Rev 21:3–6; 23) And, "Even the sparrow finds a home, and the swallow a nest for herself, where she may lay her young, at thy altars, O LORD of hosts, my King and my God." (Psalm 84:3)

CHAPTER 10

Conclusion
the Amsterdam way of exegesis

As has been done throughout this manuscript, there are many things to affirm about the Amsterdam way of interpreting scriptures. Its core focus on the prophetic message engages us directly today with words of liberation from the powers that be and a call to love and do justice in the world. It forms a meaningful, third alternative to liberalism and fundamentalism, rejecting literalism, historicism, moralism and intellectualism. It leaves us encouraged, with reason to celebrate and hope for the future in spite of the present state of the world.

Positively, in this context, we need to highlight the development of its own unique form of Biblical Theology in relation to Systematic Theology and Exegesis. Biblical 'Theology' does not abstract, it 'primarily' summarizes core themes that emerge from many scriptural givens, as provided in the canonical order of the Torah, Prophets and Psalms and the Apostolic, witness. As such, it makes a crucial contribution, taking its place reciprocally between Exegesis and Systematic Theology. To exegesis it offers a 'frame of reference' (or a 'word horizon') with leading structures and key words that take on their distinctive meaning in different contexts. New exegetical insights improve and illuminate previous formulations and insights. It offers a description of core structures based on many scriptural references for further systematic reflection and elucidation. (See the beginning of chapter (9) on the nature of Biblical Theology.)

The original title of the Amsterdam cahiers was 'The Amsterdam School of Exegesis and Biblical Theology'. Unfortunately the last part was

CONCLUSION

dropped later on from the title. Unfortunate only if it no longer receives the basic attention it deserves. The more exegetical studies and key structures are traced and fundamental themes accumulate, the more it calls for Biblical theological reflection and summaries. These core structures, key words and themes form the basis for the development of a 'biblical theology', according to their canonical order.

In later publications, the Amsterdam tradition has focused more on different Bible books, their place in research, specific exegetical issues, and to some extent its proclamation or theology. Whether that is sufficient in maintaining a focus on the prophetic message remains to be seen. Generally, thus far, the different summaries of research on different Bible books illustrate how unsatisfactory such an approach can be.

The summaries of the research on specific Bible books in the later publications of the Amsterdam tradition beg for further exploration and investigation. By themselves, they tend to be limited. As a result some of the research overviews by themselves, however scholarly, fail to inspire rather than serve as an inspiration to do further research. At best (or worst) they tend to bring one up-to-date on the state of present-day scholarship, which Deurloo usually turned upside down and used to further explain particular texts (like 'fairy tale', and 'legend-like' examples mentioned before).

The article by J. Dubbink on Jeremiah forms a notable exception. Instead of an overview of the research and commentaries on Jeremiah, (which would make you want to avoid the theological libraries), he discusses the main issues and core themes in Jeremiah in a more indepth way. His discussion creates intrigue and interest that stimulates further followup. See his "One book; Many visions; An overview of the state of the research on Jeremiah." In: *#16 of the ACEBT,* 1997. It illustrates how 'overviews ' of the research on a particular Bible book can be stimulating and rewarding, within the framework of the Amsterdam way of interpreting scripture.

There are two other major issues worth examining more closely. One is the influence of the Karl Barth on interpretation. The second is the historicity of the scriptures. These two issues are worth considering further so that they do not distract from the major contributions of the Amsterdam tradition.

10:1 Karl Barth's influence? (1886-1968)

What was the nature of Karl Barth's influence on the Amsterdam tradition of exegesis? In many books and articles, Breukelman, Deurloo and followers have made numerous references to the theology of Karl Barth. Their reliance on Barth gives rise to the question, to what extent the Amsterdam school has been potentially negatively influenced by Barth's view and does it actually distort the exegesis?

Many academics believe Barth held to a 'dualistic' view of the relation between Revelation and Creation, or worse, consider him to be a 'fundamentalist', or Marcionite. Even if there is a *tension* between creation and revelation in Barth's view, the question is, is that an *absolute* break? Or are his statements all part of his rejection and opposition to Nazism and all other forms of deification and paganism? Barth rejected all forms of general revelation and all other religions. To answer these questions more thoroughly would require a careful analysis of all the references to Barth in both Breukelman and Deurloo and others to determine if, or to what extent, that may be true. However, that would require a separate study. This issue has continually been in the back of my mind as I read the many publications from the Amsterdam tradition.

My own conclusion, thus far, is that upon careful reading of all the material, I found no evidence of such a dualistic view that may have distorted the exegesis. No one has a corner on the truth and particularly in describing the difficulty of how the Word became flesh and entered human history. Orthodox Christianity, with its long history of rationalism and dualism, (of natural versus supra-natural; of body and soul; of mind versus matter; etc.) certainly has little ground for critique. At times Barth's view and that of Deurloo and others may have skirted on the edge of a 'docetic' view in which revelation and creation can barely be related. It was always in opposition to a 'natural religion' or 'religious feelings' and 'morality', or a 'general sense' of a Creator God, and Provider.

Barth wrote in a very different social and political situation and addressed a very different issue that cannot be applied directly to other religions. If applied directly to other religions, his radical rejection of all natural revelation and religions in general is inappropriate and violates other peoples' beliefs.

The seeming rejection of all natural revelation by Barth and Miskotte and any natural connecting points in human nature (any innate sense of God) may be in need of reformulation in our times to avoid the danger of an absolute distinction between creational revelation and scriptural revelation, creating an outright dualism. We can perhaps come to a better understanding and description of the relation of general revelation (creational revelation) both as a 'point of contact' and a natural human possibility and another worldly spiritual sphere, and still avoid the pitfalls of the way "natural religion and mythology" was used to defend the Nazi regime. It was Nazism and liberal theologians who endorsed Nazism that called for the strong reaction by Barth and Miskotte. They felt there could not be any natural connecting points in human nature, which in turn would make the scriptures superfluous. A strong example was the Nazi foundational belief that their actions were justified by an appeal to 'land, blood and race.'

At times, Deurloo will make passing references to 'religion and culture' in a negative way. Since this issue isn't dealt with explicitly, except negatively, it leaves an open space or question mark. Neither in Barth, Miskotte, Breukelman or Deurloo, is there any discussion of other religions and especially not of some of the so-called 'nature' religions of many aboriginal people in Australia, North and South America and other parts of thw world. Can 'religion and culture' or 'religion and nature' only be talked about negatively as paganism? Whenever justice, solidarity, equality, resourcefulness, and sustainability are practiced to whatever degree, are they not signals of God's love for the earth and longsuffering with humanity?

Right from the start Deurloo opposes any form of 'general revelation', in which God becomes a 'general concept' that many people can believe in, a Creator God or an 'Intelligent-Design-God'. We can certainly chime in with Deurloo's opposition to a 'natural revelation and theology', particularly in relation to the ideology of Nazism with its deification of land, blood and race or any other ideology.

We could wish he had added a separate section on the nature of other religions, especially the so-called 'nature' religions of many indigenous peoples and the long discussions over the decades about the need for a different approach of sharing beliefs with other people, a 'non-colonial' approach, as it has emerged more and more in our consciousness today. If he had, he might have changed some of his statements, especially in the first chapter of *Schepping Van Paulus to Genesis,* but also throughout.

Each religion needs to be evaluated in terms of its own beliefs and practices. To come to terms with Canada's First Nations beliefs, for example, would require an 'insiders view' and basic respect and openness to their teachings and willingness to learn from them. Such an approach has often been in contrast to many missionary approaches (in the past?). It is particularly at this point that Barth's view and influence may become apparent, tending toward a more 'dualistic' view or 'tension' of the relation between Revelation and Creation. Barth did not directly address these issues.

The same can be said about later followers of the Amsterdam philosophy (Dooyeweerd and Vollenhoven), different from Zuidema's total rejection of Barth's theology in his, *Konfrontatie with Karl Barth*, (1963), categorizing Barth's theology as *'revelation in tension with nature'*. They are content to characterize Barth's position based on Niehbuhr's five distinctions in *Christ and Culture*. According to these distinctions Barth would be classified as basically holding to a *"Christ and Culture in Paradox"* position along with Luther and the Lutheran tradition in contrast to the Reformed tradition of *"Christ the Transformer of Culture"* along with Augustine and Calvin. Again if all that is said about Barth, having him categorized more as a Lutheran than as a Calvinist theologian, it would be a great loss. It also misses the more recent and thoughtful discussions of Niebuhr's book and distinctions. What strikes me most is that Barth's rejection of all natural points of contact in our experience or human history that is taken over by Miskotte, Breukelman and Deurloo, has been tremendously helpful in countering liberal theology and the Nazi ideology. Similarly, it could today in opposing the global ideology of unlimited growth by 'neo-liberalism', and right-wing Christian nationalism, no matter what the devastating consequences are for millions of people. Today, with the rise of Fascism in America and rightwing nationalisms in Europe, their protests seem as relevant as ever. Meanwhile, every theologian has to come to terms with Barth's rich and promising theology.

Does the Barthian emphasis on the immediacy of the scriptures distort the exegesis at times? I have not been able to find evidence of such distortions, except perhaps to suggest a different formulation in some instances that does justice both to the radical and unique nature of God's revelation and honors that "the word became flesh" and entered human history. That is how I understand Talstra's use of the term 'religious language'. H.Berkhof in his *Christelijk Geloof* (1993, 7th ed.), he maintains that "Barth acknowledged that God is also busy world-wide apart from Christ" later on in his life. (p.49) There is an intriguing article by Wolf Krotke, "A new impetus to the theology of religions in Karl Barth's thought," originally published in *Zeitschrift fur Theologie und Kirche*,

(2007), 104, pp.320–335. In it he examines the deleted paragraphs about other religions that Barth omitted from his Church Dogmatics.

Barth and Miskotte vehemently opposed any view that would lend support to the Nazi regime as in the liberal theology of Barth's time, and all 'paganism'. The Reformed confession of 'general revelation' wanted to maintain the reality of God's presence in creation. Both seem to be valid. Instead Barth emphasized the radical nature and miracle of God's revelation in Jesus Christ. An *absolute* distinction and *separation* between creation and revelation could lead to an 'otherworldly spiritual sphere' next to ordinary daily life, a new form of dualism between the supernatural and natural. Certainly all Deurloo's writings aim to do the opposite, bringing revelation close to our everyday life and experience. Since Barth played such a large role in the development of the Amsterdam tradition, it is good to be cognizant of his influence. At each point we can ask ourselves, "Does that do justice to the biblical givens?" As it is, Deurloo's sometimes 'off the cuff' remarks about religion and culture, universalism over against particularity leaves some unanswered questions. After reading most of the publications of the Amsterdam tradition, *I am content to leave an open space and at most a question mark*. I am inclined to say, is that at times it creates an unnecessary tension between revelation and creation. If it seems important over time, it must await further careful analysis.

During the last decades, there has been a constant dialogue between Barth's followers and the Amsterdam treadition. R.R. Brouwer has close contact with several members of the Karl Barth Society of North America and the center for Barth Studies at Princeton Theological Seminary; they have expressed interest in Breukelman and Deurloo. Given these on-going contacts, we will await any future developments.

All people have an ultimate faith, which must be recognized and acknowledged in order for any true dialogue to take place. True dialogue will allow Christians to join with people of other faiths to work for human freedom and justice. The key point (of some earlier missionaries, Kraemer and Newbigin, for example) is their recognition of creation (and creational revelation) and human culture and that God is present in both areas. In itself this already moves away from an individualistic form of Christianity to a more communal and cultural view. Such an emphasis radically breaks through any potential dualism between revelation and creation. It is sufficient here to highlight the potential threat of a dualistic approach. Their viewpoints dovetale remarkably well with Lambert

Zuidervaart's view of "societal principles" (like justice, solidarity, inclusiveness, resourcefulness, and others) as places, where God reveals himself, in the ongoing struggles of societies. He calls it God's gifts of love.

Dr. Lambert Zuidervaart, emeritus professor of the Institute of Christian Studies, the University of Toronto, and Calvin University, offers a welcome alternative to any onesided emphasis on God's revelation in Christ at the expense of God's presence in history and creation, that is, in ordinary life, in culture and society. He considers himself a third generation follower of the Amsterdam Reformational philosophy and advocated a radically different view of "eternal creation ordiances," 'sphere sovereignty," "the cultural mandate" and a number of other ideas of this Amsterdam philosophy and the inheritance of Abraham Kuyper. In his many publications, he engaged in a 'critical retrieval' of Dooyeweerd, Vollenhoven, Seerveld, and Hart. He wrote a widely recognized study on Adorno, which alerted him to 'human suffering' that must be recognized in the practice of philosophy. Needless to say, I have been deeply influenced by his work and many publications. His book on *Artistic Truth; Aesthetics, Discourse, and Imaginative Disclosure*, (2004) created a new interest for me in the Amsterdam philosophy that I had largely given up on earlier.

In previous writings I have emphasized how all of life impinges on us and calls us to distinguish rightly, to be just, and recognize the multidimensionality and intergrated nature of creation. This includes, ways of farming, fishing, forestry and mining that protect the interconnected flourishing of all creatures. All of life is revelatory and calls for our faithfull response in all areas of life and society. Other visions and practices, like that of many indigenous people can bring home that message more clearly. Many have an extraordinary understanding of the interconnection between their religion and their daily practices. They have a strong awareness of the inter-relation between their practices, vision of life and their experiental knowledge.

Zuidervaart engages in his Christian philosophy from out of his Christian faith, as he called it, out of his strong commitment to "scripture-within-worship," as mentioned earlier. Instead of 'eternal creation ordinances' that are given from the beginning of creation and that hold for all peoples and cultures throughout the ages, he offers a compelling alternative and presents 'societal principles' that have developed historically and are normative in character. In his *Social Philosophy after Adorno* (2007), he formulates it as follows,

> By 'societal principles' I mean historically developed, continually contested, and widely shared expectations about how social institutions should be organized, how cultural practices should be carried out, and how interpersonal relations should be configured. Justice, truth, and solidaity would be examples of such principles in contemporary Western societies. Human suffering can signal both societal evil and the violation of discrete societal principles.[1]
>
> Moreover, like Marx, Adorno sees all violations of societal principles, and perhaps even the principles themselves, as symptoms of a societal evil that resides in the structure of capitalist society as a whole ... The scope of societal evil becomes so all-pervasive that discrete societal goods cannot be distinguished nor their particular absences thematized.[2]

This distinction is crucial for Zuidervaart, for if we do not distinguish between specific "societal principles" we have no basis for alternative practices and protests. Then all that remains is a total rejection of our present society and culture as Adorno did.

> Rather God comes *to call us to justice and to gift us with justice* (emphasis added) as, within historically emergent practices and institutions, human beings work out the flourishing to which they are invited. Human responses to God's gift and call become constitutive of what justice means and what it requires.[3]

Societal principles such as political justice are historically constituted and future-oriented callings in which the voice of God can be heard and traces of a new Earth can appear. But they are not available to us without spiritual struggle amid suffering and evil.[4]

Societal principles are gifts of the Redeemer and Creator:

> ... societal principles manifest God's instruction, and invitation and guidance, God's call to love, addressed to societally constituted human beings and continually calling for their response.[5]

---

1. Zuidervaart, *Social Philosophy after Adorno*, 74.
2. Zuidervaart, *Social Philosophy after Adorno*, 75.
3. Zuidervaart, *Religion, Truth and Social Transformation*, 262.
4. Zuidervaart, *Religion, Truth and Social Transformation*, 322.
5. Zuidervaart, *Religion, Truth and Social Transformation*, 283.

> This can occur through a prolonged spiritual struggle to which our own contributions will be modest and inherently flawed.[6]

> A societal principle such as political justice is itself a continuously contested and historically unfolded outworking of the flourishing to which human beings are called within the fabric of their cultural practices and social institutions.[7]

A good example of such an ongoing struggle for justice is the efforts of indigenous communities in Canada to establish another legal system that is more just. See the report by the Department of Justice and Corrections of Ottawa Canada, co-published by the Anglican Church, called, *Satisfying Justice: Safe Community Options that Attempt to Repair Harm from crime and Reduce the Use and Length of imprisonment.* (1996). It is a book about credible alternatives to prison and why there are not more alternatives. It counters the proportionally greater number of indigenous people in jail, compared to the non-native population. The many examples, make one think, could justice, instead of being primarily 'punitive' (retributive) justice become 'restorative' justice? The many examples illustrate the pitfalls, challenges and possibilities of this new communal approach, in which the perpetrator has to face the victims of his crime and in which an admission of guilt, being sorry and reparation is required, along with community service. It is a genuine struggle that is never complete. It can be seen as a response to God's gift of justice and raising signposts of such justice, in which a sense of community can be restored. This can be a painful journey, especially when it involves crimes of rape or murder. At the same time it is full of promise and healing.

> I have qualified the disclosure of society as 'life-giving disclosure.' By this I mean a societal process in which human beings and other creatures come to flourish in their interconnections ... the principles in question are historical horizons, not timeless absolutes: they emerge from social struggles in which such principles are always already at stake.[8]

> ... I claim: to affirm *the creation of culture as a good gift entrusted to all human beings;* [my emphasis] to recognize human needs and cooperatively attempt to alleviate human suffering; and to

---

6. Zuidervaart, *Religion, Truth and Social Transformation*, 322.
7. Zuidervaart, *Religion, Truth and Social Transformation*, 324.
8. Zuidervaart, *Social Philosophy after Adorno*, 102.

CONCLUSION

> point such cultural partnering and social solidarity toward the complete liberation to which God's Spirit moves human history ... I modify, without rejecting, a traditional reformational emphasis on the goodness of creation, and I give greater weight to the eschatological promise of complete liberation. [9]

> Moreover, if one understands *creation broadly enough to include human history, culture, and Society, then God's self-disclosure can occur in other religions as well as in scholarship that either ignores or actively rejects an alignment with scriptures-within-worship.* [my emphasis][10]

God reveals himself,

> ... in creation, in scripture, and in Jesus Christ, all via the inspiration of God's Spirit. Moreover, if one understands creation broadly enough to include human history, culture, and society, then God's self-disclosure can occur in other religions as well as wel as in scholarship ... For in seeking to align one's work with scripture-within-worship, one also needs to pay attention to how *God calls and guides and inspires in the very stuff of creation and human life.*[my emphasis][11]

>> Rather the ability to distinguish, say, *between justice and injustice itself manifests something deeper.* [My emphasis] It manifests an instruction and invitation and guidance that *comes to socially constituted beings from outside themselves and continually calls for their response.* [my emphasis][12]

The key to his viewpoint is that human culture and history are included in creation. Creation is not just the physical world, but includes all creatures and human activities, all of society and culture. Creation is not just nature (the physical world). In this way, Zuidervaart avoids all potential dualisms between revelation and creation, creation and culture, society and history. It presents a genuine alternative to all dualistic viewpoints.

This open-ended journey is true for any human activity and relationship. Everything we do involves an existential encounter. It requires staying open to new situations, taking risks and trusting the signals,

---

9. Zuidervaart, *Art, Education, and Cultural Renewal*, 12.
10. Zuidervaart, *Art, Education, and Cultural Renewal*, 194.
11. Zuidervaart, *Art, Education, and Cultural Renewal*, 194.
12. Zuidervaart, *Religion, Truth and Social Transformation*, 324.

hearing the liberating voice and the voice of all those suffering from injustice. It would be tempting to think that there are absolute, universal laws or general rules or dependable procedures that we can just follow and apply. That would seem secure at first but it would turn out be an illusion and not a reality. Such false certainties soon let us down and eventually distort and disintegrate life, because situations change and call for new responses, including our limitations. We are totally dependent on God's revelation. What started as a genuine search for what things are really like, during the heydays of the Enlightenment, soon derailed into a declaration of unchanging, universal laws as an ultimate source of security. All of creation is revelatory if we listen to the voice of the Creator and Liberator to hear the call to justice, solidarity, and resourcefulness, and so on. Our joint human calling is a joyful calling, even in the midst of struggle and suffering.

Since Barth's view of other religions and points of contact played such a large role in the development of the Amsterdam tradition, it is good to be cognizant of his influence. At each point we need to ask ourselves, "Does this do justice to the biblical givens?" As in Deurloo's sometimes 'off-the-cuff remarks' about religion and culture, universalism over against particularity, it leaves some unanswered questions. I am content to leave it open.

10:2 Once more; the question of 'historicity' of the scriptures

The other major question that is worth summarizing once more is that of the 'historicity' of the scriptures. To repeat the statement from chapter four, *First Impressions*, the Bible is not a history book. This sounds like such a simple statement, but it has profound implications. It is history that proclaims.

Whatever historical references there are, they do not function independently, as historical facts. They are taken up to elucidate the proclamation of the text, or to emphasize that *there in that place* Yahweh revealed himself and at *that particular time,* (even if we cannot locate those places on a map or find any historical reference to them in a history book). They are not 'historical facts' that can be corroborated by other facts. It is similar to many geographical references and names of people. Deurloo in particular likes to play with those givens.

The stories are not historical facts, nor historical sequences that follow each other. Of course one story follows after the other, but according to different principles than historical cause and effect, like the toledot sequences of Genesis. The 'history of redemption' can easily become something of the past that no longer has much meaning for us today. From the four gospel accounts, for example, we cannot reconstruct a history of Jesus' life. The order is determined by the intent of each gospel writer. It requires a different way of thinking about history. It is a prophetic order of inter-relations, causes or sequences. Thus, it is more helpful to use other words like prophetic sequences, causes, relations, etc. instead of 'prophetic *history*', unless the word 'history' is understood as *events that proclaim*. We do not live by 'historical facts' but by the life-giving message which narratives, psalms, proverbs, prophets, gospels and letters carry. They are thoroughly grounded in our time and take place on our earth, even if we cannot locate them in our history books or on an atlas. They did not take place in some spiritual, supra-natural sphere, but in our time and on our earth. We live by faith, the same faith as that of Abraham.

> By faith Abraham obeyed when he was called to go out to a place which he was to receive as an inheritance; and he went out, not knowing where he was to go. By faith he sojourned in the land of promise, as in a foreign land, living in tents with Isaac and Jacob, heirs with him of the same promise, for he looked forward to the city which has foundations, whose builder and maker is God. By faith Sarah ... By faith Jacob...By faith Joseph ... By faith Moses ... By faith the people crossed the Red Sea ... By faith Rahab ... And what more shall I say? For time would fail me to tell of Gideon, Barak, Samson, Jephthah, of David and Samuel and the prophets ... Therefore, since we are surrounded by so great a cloud of witnesses, let us ...
> Hebrews 11:8–39, 12:1

It may take us time to change our impression of the Bible as 'religious history' and to read the scriptures as proclamation and not as 'verified historical facts', but as prophetic history that proclaims, including the 'history' of redemption. See: Nico T. Bakker, *History in Debate and Contested*.

In his article on "Key words in the Hebrew Bible," Deurloo describes 'history' in relation to the word 'debarim' as follows,

> The bible has no word for 'history', unless one takes the term 'debarim' to be such ... a 'dabar', a word, is in the biblical narrative

not merely an articulated sound with significance. A word is conceived in the heart, articulated with the mouth, and verified by deeds. A speaker must stand behind what he says and realize that he is involved through his words. The popular expression 'not words but deeds' is an odd statement in the biblical context. One is expected to say what one does and to do what one says. 'God's word endures forever,' means that he keeps his word and maintains it in spite of all opposition (Isa. 40:8). Deutero-Isaiah closes by comparing this word with rain and snow which makes the earth fruitful. When that word is sounded, real history is put into motion, a history that bears fruit. 'So shall my word be that goes out from my mouth; it shall not return to me empty, but it shall accomplish that which I purpose, and prosper in the thing for which I sent it' (Isa. 55:11) Thus it is that hearing a word is not merely an auditive matter; the word should penetrate in a way that produces results and determines behaviour . . .

According to biblical perception, history is not a report of dumb facts from some 'time (chronos) gone by, recordable in the chronicles or annals (annus 'year'). History comprises related happenings of words which were spoken and done in order to involve the hearer in its progression. From this perspecvtive, it is understandable that Luke lets the shepherds say: 'Let us go now to Bethlehem and see the thing (*rhema, dabar* 'word') that has taken place, which the Lord has made known unto us' (Luke 2:15). They go from hearing to seeing. They become involved as partners in the happenings in which God does what he says. Luke does not relate this in order to make his reader believe in the historicity of the story, but to evoke their trust in the recounted words which provide future perspective. What we call 'history' in the bible is indicated by *debarim*, this is not about cosmic, natural or historic processes, but about what takes place in dialogic encounters. These summon up a *story* as *history*."[13]

The question of historicity is even more perplexing in view of a more post-modern, secular understanding of history. A 'post-modern' view of history has found the 'big stories' wanting and have focused more on small, local histories. It tends to be more 'reductionistic' and 'empiricistic', based on observable facts, like a documentary (complete with records). The scriptures view history, as history that proclaims, that addresses us, personally.

---

13. Deurloo, *Supplement Series 1, The Rediscovery of the Hebrew Bible*, 19, 20.

CONCLUSION

10:3   A summary of the Amsterdam approach

- The most important contribution is their understanding of the prophetic nature of the scriptures that goes far beyond the 'critical historical' or 'literary' interpretations or any literalistic, fundamentalist or liberal interpretations. They are narratives, prophecies, songs, etc. that proclaim, that reveal to us the life-giving Word of God.

- The scriptures contain a surprising love story of God with all humanity and the earth. Through the crucifixion and resurrection of the Son a new order was established.

- Deurloo gives his own close translations and diagrams of the flow of the texts; key phrases that form a framework around others. Alerting us to alliterations and repetitions in the texts, highlighting key phrases and words.

- Elucidating names of places and other references as prophetic words that serve the text; they are not to be read as strictly geographical or historical references.

- Referring to many inter-textual connections. Deurloo reads the text very closely and relates it to many other passages. There is a constant back and forth flow elucidating the text, often without much further exposition. The scriptures explain themselves. Again and again he highlights how the texts assume that readers are familiar with other texts before and following.

- Making many references to Jewish interpretations and festivals. The Halleel (Psalms 113–118) were sung at different holydays in the synagogue. On Seder evening it had a special place in the celebration of the family before the Passover . . .

- Repeatedly he challenges us as co-readers how we are to take to heart the prophetic meaning of the narratives and see ourselves as people in need of being liberated from our anguish.

- The many publications provide a fundamental contribution to a biblically based environmentalism. Taking note of the scriptures' understanding of heaven and earth, days and years, creation, etc. these are fruitful perspectives to work out. Most importantly, concern for the creation is always inseparately related to doing 'justice, practicing equality, resourcefulness, freedom and solidarity'. Humans are to steward as God's representatives.

- Another issue is the idiolect translation, sentences that can be spoken in one breath; the emphasis is on the spoken word; it addresses the hearer very directly; it is interesting to compare this approach to Talstra's diagramming of sentences according to changes in speakers, audience, tense and primary and secondary sentences, providing a visual picture of the text. The English study by Young Bok Park, *Restoration in the book of Ezekiel; a text-linguistic analysis of Ezekiel 33-39, 2013,#11 of the Supplement Series,* provides an excellent and helpful example of this approach. See also Deurloo's own article in *Jona, #22, ACEBT, 2005*, "Between structure and strategy: text analysis of Jonah 1-4," in which he illustrates how he diagrams a text. Translation is always an interpretation; the same Hebrew word should be translated the same in different passages; See van Zanden's critique of potential arbitrariness.

- The new developments around the The New Bible School are both encouraging and exciting. They hold the promise of a further return to the scriptures as adult Bible classes are organized throughout the country in the Netherlands.

- To organize a Bible study group, all we need is a small number of participants that feel free to honestly express their doubt, skepticism, and hope. Participants that will read along in different Bible translations, purchase a study Bible, learn to consult a concordance, look up other references and search together for the meaning of a story, psalm, letter, etc. in their own lives and situations.

- Above all it is the primacy of the prophetic message that confronts and comforts us and re-directs our lives.

CHAPTER 11

The Psalms and Liturgy

IN HIS *AND THAT is Seven*, Deurloo mentions several new Dutch Children's Bibles and examples of Bible stories with the same aim, to let the stories speak for themselves. It reminds me of my own childhood of having to memorize a psalm a week, attend catechism classes without much meaning and suffer through endless church services. Through these writings I am able to 'relive' (like 'guided meditations, visualizations' or 'guided imagery'), my childhood in a new way. Many times it makes me tear up, tears of joy and being touched, as if I was right there. In the story accompanying Psalm 94, Deurloo mentions how a boy dreaded Monday mornings because of the chance that he would be called upon to recite a psalm verse and how he was comforted by a song his favorite teacher would have them sing full out: "Up above there is a great chorus of children exuberantly singing before God's throne, redeemed from sin and danger..."

From the beginning there has been a strong interest and concern within the Amsterdam tradition to make the scriptures more accessible to children and young people within the services and church 'school'. Deurloo has published several booklets on the Psalms, *What is wrong with you, sea, that you flee?* (1986); and with stories and songs for children, *A child may stand in the Centre, exegetical stories for small ears*, *(1982)*; and together with Hanna van Dorssen and Karel Eykman, *And that is Seven! Seven ways to tell children about the Bible*, (2003). The children's songs and plays add a delightful aspect for both children and adults. It is not surprising that Piet van Midden, together with Cees Otte (illustrator), published several volumes of what he called *Growth-bible for young people*, (1991, 2000) Already in his dissertation he had added a sample of how to tell the story of Gideon to middle school children without moralizing and intellectualizing, *Brotherhood and Kingship* (1998). In Psalm 8, he interprets the somewhat difficult phrase, "Thou whose glory above the heavens is chanted by the mouth of babes and infants ... from the mouths of infants and sucklings thou hast founded strength ... (Ps 8:1, 2), as "God's power and righteousness reveals itself 'in weakness', in the vulnerable and those who cannot speak up for themselves. The babbling and crying of infants and sucklings is not silenced, but becomes a voice of praise and power to God the liberator." [1] A child may truly stand in the centre!

In relation to Psalm 103:13, "As a father has compassion for his children, so the Lord has compassion for those who fear him." (pp 138-140) Deurloo tells the story of a widowed farm laborer. After her husband's death, with much effort and struggle she managed to buy a small farm for her eight children and escape from their severe poverty. Her oldest son became very ill. Another son, Kees would watch over him each night after a hard day's work on the land to give his mother a break. He and his girlfriend would take turns keeping watch, sharing a bed, each taking half a shift. Mother had warned him, do not get pregnant. If you do, you will have to leave the house. Sure enough, two weeks after the death and funeral of the oldest son, it came out that they had become pregnant, but his mother had compassion and said, 'we will renovate the small house and give you both a place to live'. He ends the story with, "God can take a lesson from her actions and care." In many of these stories he can be wonderfully 'irreverent'.

It reminds me of the stories documented by Kees Slager, (1981) in *Farmlaborers*, that documents the extreme poverty and inhumane conditions of many farm hands in Zeeland and Friesland before the Second World War. To my knowledge, there has never been a 'truth and reconciliation' committee or apology from the government or any of the Christian political parties for these social conditions before the war. Many experienced the 'social legislation' after the war as 'heaven on earth'. Those kids in my father's class, during the early 1900's that had to leave school early would no longer have to go and beg for a slice of bread on the way home, if they had been lucky enough to attend school in the first place.

---

1. Deurloo, *What is wrong with you sea, that you flee?* 39.

One more example, in Psalm 113:5, 6 we read, "Who is like the LORD our God, who is seated on high, who looks far down upon the heavens and the earth?" From these few lines, Deeurloo tells the story of a student from the country who had to move to the big city to a large school. He really missed the friendliness of his old school. At the new city school, the other students would often laugh at his provincial accent and tease him openly in class. One day they had punctured his bicycle tire. He struggled to repair it, but each time the tire would come off at the last moment. Then suddenly a man bent down and offered to help him. It turned out to be the principal of the school he had never met. At his encouragement he participated in reciting poems and won an honorable mention. When some students started to laugh and poke fun of him halfway through his recitation, he imitated his chemistry teacher and told them off. He got a thundering applause, including from the principal.

Because I could not do my homework after school, I volunteered to recite German poems instead of my German assignments. Apparently my German teacher had no problem with that alternative. I went to a large school in a big city (de Hague) at which I felt like a stranger. These famous poems (by Goethe, Heine, etc.) touched my core and gave expression to my deepest feelings. No one knew, I was unable to do my German grammar exercises, nor memorise vocabulary lists, because of emotional conflicts. After school I would hurry down to the bicycle parking area and bicycle home regardless of the weather. Deurloo's stories comfort me, even today. I resonate with the stream of curses he relates of the pestered school boy at the big city school. They are like pastoral gems for young people and children.

It would be wonderful to devote a separate study to Deurloo's children's Bible stories and songs. He seemed to have a special talent for relating and living into children's lives and circumstances without romanticizing or downplaying their situation. It is enough to know that the possibility is there and can inspire others. It is also a radical affirmation that the Word takes on flesh both then and now, for adults as well as children. In a special way he makes the stories present for children, very concrete and actual, culminating in the many songs and plays that he composed and wrote for these Bible stories.

The Amsterdam Cahiers published two special volumes on the Psalms, Dyk, et al. eds., (2000), *Psalms*, (*Cahier 18, Psalmen*) and van Wieringen, ed. (2010) *Psalms and their Tradition*, (*Cahier 25*, each with over a dozen articles by different authors). The last chapter of Deurloo's

Exodus and Exile (2003), is entitled, VII, "Songs of Praise and songs of Ascent." pp. 113–137.) Additionally there are numerous articles about individual psalms by Deurloo and many others.

From the beginning there was a strong emphasis on the liturgy within the Amsterdam tradition. In 2010, Dirk Monshouwer published a volume on *The Gospels and Jewish Worship; Bible and Synagogal Liturgy in the first Century C.E.* An anniversary volume was published for him in 2001, *Language in the Scriptures and Worship*, Westra, ed. He and others made a strong contribution to the one and three year cycles of reading of scripture within worship services. J.P. Boendermaker, in an article "It contains music; about exegesis and liturgy" in *The Bible makes school; an Amsterdam way in the exegesis,* (1984), In it he describes how influential this kind of exegesis can be for the liturgy, or the other way around, how we can look from out of the liturgy at a particular text or texts.(p.119).

Psalm 136, for example, recites the story of the exodus with its repeated refrain ("for his steadfast love endures for ever"). The reflection is already in the psalm that does not just tell a story or historical facts, but that celebrates the remembering and holds it up for us in the present and to chime in with the chorus. ("This psalm is known in Jewish liturgy as the Great Hallel and has been incorporated into the Passover Seder") In another example he illustrates how the scripture readings for a particular Sunday might have been reflected in the liturgy for baptism during the night of Easter. He has written several other articles in the *Cahiers*.

As Lambert Zuidervaart writes in *Art, Education, and Cultural Renewal,*

> . . . they will come like children, eager for a good story, ready to be surprised, yet again, or maybe for the first time, by the storied good news. And, like a good children's story read or told aloud, the scriptures will come alive . . . within the practice of worship, as they hear God speaking to them through the scriptures . . . In all this we expect God to address us, to call us via the stories of faith to hope and trust in God, even as we await God's appearance within the rituals of our worship. When a sensitive or dramatic reading of scripture passages or the pastoral or prophetic delivery of a sermon, speak to your heart, you hear the voice of God. When the choir's accomplished singing moves you to tears of joy or sorrow, or when a benediction delivered with compassion and conviction assures of amazing grace, you witness the presence of God in our midst . . . The scriptures are decisive because they are completely reliable in revealing who

God is and how we should respond. We find God's call to love resounding in the scriptures. We learn to follow the guidance God gives there. We inhale the inspiration the scriptures offer for a faithful walk with God. So the scriptures are decisive – not as an inert authority, but as a vibrant medium for God's call and guidance and inspiration.[2]

"Stories-in-worship" is a key phrase for Zuidervaart. The stories need to be sounded out in the context of worship and resonate in song and prayer. He has been a lifelong member of various choirs.

In his first volume on the Psalms, Deurloo presents 15 individual psalms, in which he takes note of various translations and presents his own translation. He highlights key words, and inter-textual references, as well as the different segments of a psalm. The second part is devoted to another 16 psalms exemplified by a special story. With a single anecdote he brings the psalm right into the present, into the children's lives, even very difficult and scary situations.

As he writes in relation to Psalm 113, "the past and the present are pushed into one another." In the singing we become part of the pilgrims going up to Jerusalem, the city of Yahweh, a city well-founded.

With one verse or refrain, he and his associates could bring a psalm right in the middle of a child's life situation. In a poetic rendering of Psalm 8, by Karel Eykman, titled,"God Almighty" writes in the 5th stanza, "I am just a child that lives in an ordinary street in an ordinary city, where I often play. Who is this God, who cannot resist smiling when I score a goal?"[3] It is based on vs. 4 of Psalm 8. "What is man that thou art mindful of him, and the son of man that thou dost care for him?" No doubt the boy often watched many Catholic national soccer players make a cross before entering the field or when they scored a goal. It always makes me think that 'mother Mary' must be very busy on the weekends orchestrating all those soccer games and goals and that God looks down with approval and is pleased with his achievements . . ."I am just an ordinary boy living on an ordinary street in an ordinary city, where I play soccer, scoring a goal and God is smiling at me . . . God Almighty, how is that possible, Why me?" Full of wonder and joy . . ."

---

2. Zuidervaart, *Art, Education, and Cultural Renewal*, 187–89.
3. Deurloo, *And that is Seven*,

Bibliography

Amsterdamse Cahiers:

Deurloo, Karel A. et al. *Cahier #1.* Kampen: Kok, 1980.
——. *Cahier #2.* Kampen: Kok, 1981.
——. *Cahier #3.* Kampen: Kok, 1982.
——. *Cahier #4.* Kampen: Kok, 1983.
——. *Cahier #5.* Kampen: Kok, 1984.
——. *Cahier #6.* Kampen: Kok, 1985.
——. *Cahier #7.* Kampen: Kok, 1986.
——. *Cahier #8.* Kampen: Kok, 1987.
——. *Cahier #9.* Kampen: Kok, 1988.
——. *Cahier #10.* Kampen: Kok, 1989.
——. *Cahier #11.* Kampen: Kok, 1992.
——. *Cahier #12.* Kampen: Kok, 1993.
——. *Cahier #13.* Kampen: Kok, 1994.
——. *Cahier #14.* Kampen: Kok, 1995.
——. *Cahier #15.* Kampen: Kok, 1996.
Deurloo, Karl A., et al. *#16 Jeremia.* Kampen: Kok, 1997.
Dyk, Janet.W., et al. *# 17 Hosea.* Maastricht: Shaker, 1999.
——. *#18 Psalmen.* Maastricht: Shaker, 2000.
Spronk, Klaas et al. *#19 Richteren.* Maastricht: Shaker, 2001.
van Midden, Piet J. *#20, In de woestijn, Numeri.* Maastricht: Shaker, 2002.
Delsman, Wim C. et al. *#21, Prediker.* Maastricht: Shaker, 2004.
Spronk, Klaas, ed. *# 22, Jona.* Maastricht: Shaker, 2005.
——. *#23, Deuteronomium.* Vught: Skandalon, 2007.
van Midden, Piet.J., ed. *#24, Jozua.* Vught:Skandalon, 2009.
van Wieringen,Willen C. G. ed. *#25, Psalmen en hun Traditie,* Bergambacht: 2VM, 2010.
Dubbink, Joep, ed. *#26, Ezechiel.* Vught: 1VM, 2001.
Spronk, Klaas, ed. *#27, Genesis.* Vught: 2VM, 2012.
Riemersma, Nico A., ed. *#29, Lucas & Handelingen.* Bergambacht: 2VM, 2014.
Dubbink, Joep, ed. *#30, Bijbelse Theologie.* Bergambacht: 2VM, 2015.
——. *#31, Wijsheid.* Bergambacht: 2VM, 2017.
——. *#32, De twaalf kleine profeten.* Bergambacht: 2VM, 2018.
Riemrsma, Nico, ed. *#33, Exodus.* Amsterdam: SHA.

Dubbink, Joep, ed. *#34, Ezra en Nehemia*. Amsterdam: SHA., 2021.
den Braber, Marieke and Willen C.G. van Wieringen. *#35, Elia & Elisa*. Amsterdam: SHA, 2022.
Riemersma, Nico and PietVan Midden. *#36, Het Evangelie naar Matteus*, Amsterdam: SHA, 2023.

Amsterdam Supplement series:

Dijk, Janet W. et al. *#1, The Rediscovery of the Hebrew Bible*. Maastricht: Shaker, 1999.
———. *#2, Festschrift for Karel A. Deurloo: Unless Someone Guide me . . . .* Maastricht: Shaker, 2001.
Postma, Ference et al eds. *#3, The New Thing: eschatology in Old Testament prophecy: Festschrift voor Henk Leene*. Maastricht: Shaker, 2002.
Dijk, Janet W. eds. et al. *#4, Om voor te lezen, Feestbundel voor Frits Hoogewoud*. Maastricht: Shaker, 2005.
van Wieringen, Willen C.G. *#7, Delila en de anderen*. Vught: Skandalon, 2007.
den Braber, Marieke. *#8, Built from many stones*. Bergambacht: 2VM, 2010.
Park, Young Bok. *#11, Restoration in the book of Ezekiel*. Bergambacht: 2VM, 2013.
van Leeuwen-Assink, Cornelia J. *#12, 'Wij Zouden Jesus Willen Zien'*. Bergambacht: 2VM, 2015.
Riemersma, Nico. *#14, Aan de dode een wonder gedaan*. Bergambacht: 2VM, 2016.
Hoogewoud, Frits. J. et al. *#15, Societas Hebreica Amstelodamensis 1961–2017: Jubileumuitgave* Bergambacht: 2VM, 2017.
La Rip, Marip. *#17, Intertribal Hermeneutics in the context of Myanmar*. Bergambacht: 2VM, 2018.
Visser, Marco. *#18, Pars Pro Toto*. Amsterdam: ACEBT, 2021.
Riemersma, Nico, and Bart J. Koet. *#21, Het oog op Lucas-Handelingen*. Amsterdam: ACEBT, 2024.
(All these Cahiers and Supplements (and others) are available from Societas Hebrica Amsteldalmensis either in printed form or as PDF's.)

General Bibliography (including the Amsterdam school):

Abma, R. ed. *Nog Dichterbij Genesis:Opstellen over het eerste Bijbelboek voor Karel Deurloo*. Baarn: Ten Have, 1995.
Ahlstrom, G. W. *The History of Ancient Palestine*. Sheffield: JSOT, 1993.
Anderson, H.G. et al. *Justification by faith: Lutherans and Catholics in Dialogue, VII*. Minneapolis: Augsburg, 1985.
Baarda, Tjitze. *De betrouwbaarheid van de evangelien*. Kampen: Kok, 1969.
———. "Als Christus niet is opgewekt . . . Het Nieuwe Testament in het geding." *Kerk en Theologie* 42 (1991) 3405–16.
———. *De vier evangelien en het ene evangelie*. Utrecht: VBK/Media, 1991.
Baarling, H. et al., *Vervulling en Voleinding, De toekomst verwachting in het Nieuwe Testament,* Kampen: Kok, 1984.
Bakker, Nico. *Geschiedenis in opspraak,* Kampen: Kok, 1996.
———. *Om het levende woord, deel 8*, Kampen: Kok, 1998.

———. *Een Zo'n Mannetje*. Kampen:Kok, 2004.
Bar-Efrat, Shimon. *Narrative art in the Bible*. Sheffield: Sheffield, 1989.
Barr, James. *The Semantics of Biblical language*. Oxford: Oxford University Press, 1962.
———. *The Bible in the modern world*. New York: Harper & Row, 1973.
———. *Holy Scriptures: Canon, authority and criticism*. Philadelphia: Westminster, 1983.
———. *Biblical Faith and Natural theology*. Oxford: Oxford University Press. 1993.
———. *The Concept of Biblical theology: An Old Testament perspective*. London: Student Christian Movement, 1999.
———. *History and ideology in the Old Testament*. Oxford: Oxford University Press, 2000.
———. *The scope and authority of the Bible*. London: Student Christian Movement, 1980/2002. Barstad, Hans M. *The religious polemics of Amos*. Leiden: Brill, 1984.
———. *The myth of the empty land*. Stockholm: Scandinavian University Press, 1996.
———. *History and the Hebrew Bible: Studies in ancient Israel and ancient Near Eastern historiography*. Tubigen: Mohr Siebeck, 2008.
Barton, John. *Reading the Old Testament: Method in Biblical study*. Philadelphia: Westminster, 1984.
———. *The spirit and the letter: Studies in the Biblical Canon*. London: Society for Promoting Christian Knowledge, 1997.
———. ed. *The Cambridge companion to Biblical interpretation*. Cambridge: Cambridge University Press,1998.
———. *Ethics and the Old Testament*. Harrisburg: Trinity, 1998.
———. *The Nature of Biblical criticism*. Louisville: John Knox Westminster, 2007.
———. *Oracles of God*. Oxford: Oxford University Press, 2007.
———. *Een Zo'n Mannetje*. Kampen: Kok, 2004.
Barth, Karl, Edwyn C. *The Epistle to the Romans*. Translated by Edwyn C. Hoskyns. London: Oxford University Press, 1968.
Bateson, Gregory. *Steps to an Ecology of Mind*. New York: Ballantine, 1972.
Becking, Bob. "We all returned as one!: critical notes" In K.A. Beek, et al. *Verkenningen in een Stroomgebied*. Amsterdam: University of Amsterdam, 1974.
Becking, Bob and Klass Smelik. *Een Patriachale Leugen*. Baarn: KoktenHave, 1989
Becking, Bob and Dijkstra, M. eds. *On reading prophetic texts: gender specific and related studies, In memory of Fokkelien van Dijk-Hommes*. Leiden: Brill, 1996.
Becking, Bob. "Ezra on the move . . . trends and perspectives on the character and his book". In F. Garcia Martinez & H. Noort eds. *Perspectives in the Study of the Old Testament and Early Judaism: A symposium in honour of Adam S. van der Woude on the occasion of his 70th birthday*, 154–79, Leiden: Brill. 1998.
———. "Continuity and community: the belief system of the book of Ezra." In B. Becking and M. Korpel eds. *The Crisis of Israelite religion*, 256–275. Leiden: Brill, 1999.
Becking, Bob and Korpel, M. eds. *The crisis of Israelite religion: Transformation of religious tradition in exile and post-exile times*. Leiden: Brill, 1999.
Becking, Bob and M. Dykstra, eds. *Th.C.Vriezen, Hervormd theoloog en oudtestamenticus*. Kampen: Kok, 1999.
———. "Law as expression of religion (Ezra 7–10)". In A. Rainer and B. Becking eds. *Yahwism after the exile: Perspectives on Israelite religion in the Persian era*, 18–31. Assen: van Gorcum, 2000.

BIBLIOGRAPHY

Becking, Bob. et al. eds. *Only one God?* Sheffield: Sheffield Academic Press, 2001.
———. "The exile does not equal the exile, Micah 4:1–5". In F. Postma, K. Spronk and E. Talstra eds. *The new things, Eschatology in Old Testament prophecy, Festschrift for Henk Leene*, 1–7 Maastricht: Shaker, 2002.
———. "Nehemiah 9 and the problematic concept of context (Sitz im Leben)". In M.A. Sweeney and E.B. Zvi, *The changing face of form criticism for the twenty-first century*, 253–65. Grand Rapids: Eerdmans, 2003.
———. *Between fear and freedom. Essays on the interpretation of Jeremiah, 30–31.* Leiden: Brill, 2004.
———. "Het boek Jeremia in de NBV. Zwakte en sterkte van een eigenziniege versio moderna". *Nederlands Theologisch Tijdschrift* 58 (2005) 274–85.
———. *From David to Gedaliah: The book of Kings as story and history.* Fribourg: Gottingen, 2007.
Becking, Bob and D. Human,. eds. *Exile and suffering.* Leiden: Brill, 2009.
Beek, M.A. et.al. *Verkenningen in een stroomgebied,* Amsterdam: University of Amsterdam, 1974.
Beek, M.A. *Jozua.* Nijkerk: Callenbach. 1981.
Beinart, Peter. *Being Jewish After the Destruction of Gaza: A Reckoning.* New York: Knopf, 2025.
Beker, E.J. and K.A. Deurloo. *Het Begin in Ons Midden: aspecten van bijbels scheppingsgeloof.* Baarn: Ten Have, 1977.
———. *Het beleid over ons bestaan.* Baarn:Ten Have, 1978.
Bekker,Y. W. and A.Klouwen, van Nieuwpoort, eds. *In de ruimte van de Openbaring; opstellen voor Nico T. Bakker.* Kampen: Kok, 1999.
Beresford-Kroeger, Diana. *The Green Heart: The Soul and Science of Forests.* Toronto: Random House, 2024.
Berkhof, H. *Christelijk Geloof.* Nijkerk, Callenbach, 1993, 7th ed.
Berkouwer, Gerrit. *De verkiezing Gods.* Kampen: Kok, 1955.
———. *De Herleving van de Natuurlijke Theologie.* Kampen: Kok, 1974.
———. *Studies in Dogmatics: Divine Election.* Grand Rapids: Eerdmans, 1999.
Berman, Morris. *The Reenchantment of the World.* Ithaca: Cornell University Press, 1981.
Bettelheim, Bruno. *The Uses of Enchantment:The Meaning and Importance of Fairy Tales.* New York: Vintage Books, 1977.
Blok, Hanna et.al. *Geen Koning in die dagen; over het boek Richteren als profetische eschiedschrijving,* Baarn: Ten Have, 1982.
———. *Richteren; Hebreeuwse text en Nederlandse vertaling.* Amsterdam: Societas Hedbreica Amstelodamnedsis, 2001.
Borger-Koetsier, G.H. *Verzoening tussen God en mens in Christus.* Zoetermeer: Boekencentrum, 2006.
Bouhuijs, Nico K. and Karel Deurloo. *Dichter bij Genesis.* Baarn: Ten Have, 1967.
———. *Taalwegen en Dwaalwegen; Bijbelse trefwoorden.* Baarn: Ten Have, 1967.
———. *Dichter bij de Profeten.* Baarn: Ten Have, 1968.
———. *In de ark in de kark zei de dominee.* Baarn: Bosch & Keuning, 1972.
———. *De Stem in het Gebeuren:messaans resumé.* Baarn: Ten Have, 1974 (2nd ed.)
———. *Dichter bij Paulus.* Baarn: Ten Have, 1980.
———. *Een vreemdeling in Ons Midden.* Baarn: Ten Have. 1980.
———. *Vechten voor Vrede.* Baarn: Ten Have, 1980.

———. *Gegroeide Geschriften*. Baarn: Ten Have, 1981.
Breukelman, Frans H. *Bijbelse Theologie, Inleiding: Schriftlezing, Deel 1*, 1. Kampen: Kok, 1980.
———. *Bijbelse Theologie Deel II, 2. De Ouverture van het Evangelie Naar Matteus*. Kampen: Kok, 1984.
———. *Bijbelse Theologie, Deel I, 2, De theologie van het boek Genesis*. Kampen: Kok, 1992.
———. *Bijbelse Theologie, Deel III, 2, De Koning als Richter: De theologie van de Evangelist Matteus*, Afl. 2 Kampen: Kok, 1996.
———. *Bijblische Theologie, Teil, II, Debharim*. Kampen:Kok, 1998.
———. *Bijbelse Theologie, Deel IV, 2, Theologische Opstellen*. Kampen: Kok, 1999.
Brinkman, A. *Zwijgen in all talen*, 2019 https://docplayer.nl/226302566-Zwijgen-in-alle-talen.html.
Brouwer, Rinse Reeling. *Over Dogmartiek en Marxistische filosofie: Karl Barth vergelijkenderwijs gelezen*. S'Gravenhage: Boekencentrum, 1988.
———. *Grondvormen van theologische systematiek*. Middelburg: Skandalon, 2009
———. *Bijbelse Theologie In Praktijk*. Kampen: Kok, 2012.
———. *De Man en zijn Karwei*. Gorichem: Narratio, 2012.
———. Hermeneutiek bij F.H. Breukelman. "Enige antwoorden op de vragen van J. Muis (1, 2)". *In de Waagschaal* 7 (2012) 1–7.
Brown, Gabe. *Earth to Soil, One family's journey into regenerative agriculture*. White River Junction: Chelsea Green, 2018.
Brueggemann, Walter. *Revelation and violence: A study in contextualization*. Milwaukee: Marguette University Press, 1986.
———. *Texts under negotiation: The Bible and postmodern imagination*. Minneapolis: Fortress, 1993.
———. *A social reading of the Old Testament. Prophetic approaches to Israel's communal life*. Minneapolis: Fortress, 1994.
———. *Theology of the Old Testament: Testimony, dispute, advocacy*. Minneapolis: Fortress. 1997.
———. *Deuteronomy*. Nashville: Abingdon Press, 2001.
———. *The land. Place as gift, promise and challenge in Biblical faith*. Minneapolis: Fortress, 2002, 2nd.ed.
———. *An unsettling God: The heart of the Hebrew Bible*. Minneapolis: Fortress Press, 2009.
Buber, Martin and Franz Rozenzweig. *Die Schriftund ihre Verdeutschung*. Berlin: Schocken Verlag, 1936.
Crawford, Jason. "The trouble with re-enchantment." *Los Angeles Review of Books*, Sept. 7, 2020. https://lareviewofbooks.org/article/the-trouble-with-re-enchantment/.
De Jong, C. Adam en de mensheid; Een studie naar de betekenis van het woord toledot In Gen 2, 4. 2014. Retrieved 05/06/2022. https://www.academia.edu/8610984/Adamendemensheid
DeGraaff, Arnold H. *The Educational Ministry of the Church*. Delft: Judels & Brinkman, 1966.
De Graaff, Arnold H. and Calvin G. Seerverld. *Understanding the Scriptures*. Toronto: AACS, 1968.

De Graaff, Arnold H. *The Gods In Whom They Trusted: The Disintegrative Effects of Capitalism, A Foundation for Transitioning to a New Social World.* Norwich: Heathwood, 2016.

Dekker, Cees et al. eds. *Schitterend ongeluk of sporen van ontwerp? Over toeval en doelgerichtheid in de evolutie,* Kampen: ten Have, 2005.

———. *En God beschikte een worm, over schlepping en evolutie.* Kampen: Ten Have, 2006.

Dekker, G. *De stille revolutie: De onwikkeling van de Gereformeerde Kerken in Nederland tussen 1950 en1990.* Kampen: Kok, 1992.

———. *De mens en zijn godsdienst.* Bilthoven:Aanboboeken, 1975.

———. "De ontwikkeling van de godsdienst sociologie in Nederland." *Nederland Theologisch Tijdschrift* 55 (2001) 13–30.

———. *Godsdienst en samenleving: inleiding tot de studie van de godsdienstesociologie.* Kampen: Kok, 1986.

Dekker, G., and D.A. Luidens, ed. et al. *Rethinking secularization: Reformed reactions to modernity.* Lanham: University Press of America, 1997.

Dekker, Jaap. "Profetische geschiedschrijving." *Theologia Reformata* 50/3 (2003) 267–284.

De Moor, Johannes C. *The Rise of Yahwism: the roots of Israelite monotheism.* Leuven: Peeters, 1989.

De Moor, Johannes C. ed. *Intertextuality in Uqarit and Israel.* Leiden: Brill, 1998.

De Moor, Johannes C. and van Rooy, H.F. eds. *Past, present, future. The Deuteronomistic history and the prophets.* Leiden: Brill, 2000.

De Moor, Johannes C. ed. *The elusive prophet: the prophet as a historical person, literary character and anonymous artist.* Leiden: Brill, 2001.

den Heyer, Cees J. *De messiaanse weg, 1: Messiaanse verwachtingen in het O.T. en in de vroege Joodse traditie.* Kampen: Kok, 1983.

———. *De messiaanse weg, 2: Jesus van Nazareth.* Kampen: Kok, 1986.

———. *Een bijbel - Twee Testamenten: De plaats van Israel in een bijbelse theologie.* Kampen: Kok, 1990.

———. *Een Joodse Jezus de Christus der kerken: De plaats van Israel in de Christologie,* Kampen: Kok, 1992.

———. *Kruispunten op de messiaanse we: beelden van Jesus in het Nieuwe testament,* Kampen: Kok, 1993.

———. *Verzoening: Bijbelse notities bij een omstreden thema.* Kampen: Kok. 1997.

———. *De messianse weg. Van Jesjoea van Nazaret tot de Christus van de kerk,* Kampen: Kok, 1998.

de Wit, Hans and Gerald West eds. *African-European readers of the Bible in dialogue: in quest of a shared meaning.* Leiden: Brill, 2008.

Deurloo, Karel. *Kain en Abel.* Amsterdam: Ten Have, 1967.

———. *Jozua, verklaring van een bijbelgedeelte,* Kampen: Kok, 1981.

———. *Waar Gebeurd; over het onhistorisch karakter van bijbelse verhalen.* Baarn: Ten Have, 1981.

———. *Een Kind Mag In Het Midden Staan.* Baarn: Ten Have, 1982.

Deurloo, Karel, and Zuurmond, eds. *De Bijbel maakt school: Een Amsterdamse weg in de exege.* Baarn: Ten Have, 1984.

Deurloo, Karel, and Karel Eykman ed. *Sjofele Koning.* Baarn: Ten Haven, 1984.

Deurloo, Karel, and Fritz J. Hoogewoud. *Beginnen bij de letter Beth*. Kampen: Kok, 1985.
Deurloo, Karel. and Karel Eykman. *Wat heb je, zee, dat je vlucht?* Baarn: Ten Have, 1986.
Deurloo, Karel, and Hemelsoet. *Op Bergen en in dalen; bijbelse geografie: de plaats waar geschreven staat. (Over Mountains and through Valleys; biblical geography: the place where it is written.)* Baarn: Ten Have, 1988.
Deurloo, Karel. *De Mens als Raadsel en Geheim*. Baarn: Ten Have, 1988.
Deurloo, Karel, and R. Zuurmond. *De dagen van Noach*. Baarn:Ten Have, 1991.
Deurloo, Karel. *Jona: Commentaar voor bijbelstudie, onderwijs en prediking*. Baarn: Callenbach, 1995.
Deurloo, Karel, and Kees van Duin. *Beter dan Zeven Zonen*. Baarn: Ten Have, 1996.
———. "*Liederen van opgang uit de ballingschap.*" In J.W. Dyk ed. *Amsterdam Cahiers voor Exegese van de Bijbel en zijn Tradities. No.18 Psalmen*. Maastricht: Shaker, 2000.
———. *En Dat is zeven! Zeven manieren om kinderen uit de Bijbel te vertellen*. Hilversum: NZV, 2003.
———. *Exodus en Exile: Kleine Bijbelse Theologie, Deel I*. Kampen: Kok, 2003.
———. *Koning en Tempel: Kleine Bijbelse Theologie, Deel II*. Kampen: Kok, 2004
———. *Onze lieve vrouwe baart een zoon: Kleine Bijbelse Theologie, Deel III*. Kampen: Kok, 2006.
———. *Schepping Van Paulus tot Genesis: Kleine Bijbelse Theologie, Deel IV*. Kampen: Kok, 2008.
Deurloo, Karel and NicoTer Linden. *Het Luistert Nauw*, Amsterdam: van Gennep, 2008.
De Vriese, H. and G.Gabor, eds. *Rethinking Secularization: philosophy and the prophecy of a secular Age*. Newcastle upon Tyne: Cambridge Scholars, 2009.
Dobbelaere, K. *Secularization: An analysis at three levels*. Bruxelles: P.I.E.–Peter Lang, 2002.
Dubbink, Joep. *De Tekst Mag Het Zeggen*.Kok Boekencentrum: Utrecht, 2020.
Edelman, Diana V. ed. *The Fabric of History*. Sheffield: Sheffield, 1991.
———. *The triumph of Elohim from Yahwisms to Judaism*. Kampen: Kok/Pharos, 1995.
Edelman, Diana V. *The origins of the "second" temple: Persian imperial policy and the rebuilding of Jerusalem*. London: Equinox, 2005.
Edelman, Diana.V. and C. Ben Zvi. *The production of prophecy and prophets in Jehud*. London: Equinox, 2009.
Ehrlich, Carl S. "Alle diese Worte: Impulse zur Schriftaulegung aus Amsterdam. Expliziert an der Schilfmeererzahlung in Exodus 13:17.31," In *Journal of Biblical Literature* 118/2 (1999) 340-42.
Ferrer, Hector A. ed. *Seeking Stillness or the Sound of Wings: Scholarly and Artistic Comment on Art, Truth, and Society in honor of Lambert Zuidervaart*. Eugene: Wipf and Stock, 2021.
Finkelstein, I. and N. A. Silberman, *The Bible Unearthed: Archaeology's new vision of Ancient Israel and the origin of its sacred texts*. New York: Touchstone, 2002.
Frankel, David. *The Land of Canaan and the Destiny of Israel; theologies of territory in the Hebrew Bible*. Winona Lake: Eisenbrauns, 2011.
Fretheim, T.E. *The suffering of God: an Old Testament perspective*. Philadelphia: Fortress, 1984.

Geertsema, Henk G. "Zuidervaart and Dooyeweerd: A critical retrieval? A review essay of "Shattering Silos: regaining knowledge, politics and social critique" by Lambert Zuidervaart, *Philosophia Reformata* 89 (2024) 45–79.
Goudzwaard, Bob. *Aid for the Overdeveloped West.* (1975), Toronto: Wedge.
———. *Capitalism and Progress: a diagnosis of Western Society.* Grand Rapids: Eerdmans, 1979.
———. *Toward Reformation in Economics*, Toronto: ICS, 1980.
Goudzwaard, Bob et al. *Hope in Troubled Times: a new vision for confronting global crisis,* Grand Rapids: Baker, 2007.
Graham, Gordon. *The Re-enchantment of the World: Art versus Religion.* Oxford: Oxford University Press, 2007.
Gushee, David, P. *Defending Democracy from its Christian enemies.* Eerdmans: Grand Rapids, 2023.
Hattin, Michael. *The challenge of the Promised Land,* Jerusalem: Maggid Books, 2014.
Hemelsoet, B. *Marcus.* Kampen: Kok, 1977.
Heschel, Abraham, J. *The Sabbath: It's Meaning For Modern Man.* Toronto: McGraw Hill, 1949.
———. *The Earth is the Lord's: the inner world of the Jew in Eastern Europe*, New York: Farrar Straus Giroux, 1978.
Hoek, J. "Kan God lijden? – Het evangelie van Gods bewogenheid", *Theologia Reformata* 49/1 (2006) 6–28.
Janse, Sam. "De grondtoon van de schrift in psalm 37: een agrarische lazing". In *Met Andere Woorden*, 42/2 (Oktober 2023), 19–32.
Khalidi, Rashid. *The Hundred Years' War on Palestine: A History of Settler Colonialism and Resistance, 1917–2017.* New York: Holt, 2020.
Kessler, Martin ed. *Voices from Amsterdam: a modern tradition of reading Biblical narrative.* Atlanta: Scholars, 1994.
Kessler, Martin. *Kornelis Miskotte: A Biblical Theology,* Selinsgrove: Susquehanna Univ. Press, 1997.
Kessler, Martin and K. Deurloo. *A commentary on Genesis; the book of beginnings.* New York: Paulist, 2004.
Kobes Du Mez, Kristin. *Jesus and John Wayne: How White Evangelicals Corrupted a Faith and Fractured a Nation.* Liveright: New York City, 2020.
Kuitert, Harry M. *Do you understand what you read?* Grand Rapids: Eerdmans, 1970.
———. *Signals from the Bible,* Grand Rapids: Eerdmans, 1972.
———. *I have my doubts: how to become a Christian without being a Fundamentalist.* Grand Rapids: Eerdmans, 1993.
Labuschagne, Casper. J. *Zin en onzin over God,* Zoetermeer: Boekencentrum, 1994.
Lankton, Carol H. and Stephen R. Lankton. *Tales of Enchantment.* New York: Brunner/Mazel, 1989.
Lemche, Niels P. *Early Israel: Anthropological and historical studies on the Israelite society before the monarchy.* Leiden: Brill, 1985.
———. *The Israelites in history and tradition.* Louisville: Western John Knox, 1998.
———. *The Canaanites and their land.* Sheffield: Sheffield Academic Press, 1999.
Mak, Geert. *Hoe God Verdween uit Jorwerd.* Amsterdam: Atlas, 1996
———. *De Eeuw van Mijn Vader.* Amsterdam: Atlas, 1999.
Mayes, Andrew D.H. *Israel in the period of the Judges.* London: SCM Press, 1974.
———. *Judges.* Sheffield: JSOT, 1985.

———. *The Old Testament in sociological perspective*. London: Marshall Pickering, 1989.
———. "Deuteromistic ideology and the theology of the Old Testament". *Journal for the Study of the Old Testament*, 82 (1999) 59– 82.
———. ed. *Text in context: essays by members of the Society for Old Testament Study*. Oxford: Oxford University Press, 2000.
Mazar, Amihai. *Archaeology of the Land of the Bible*. New York: Doubleday 1990.
McKenzie, Stephen L. *The trouble with Kings. The composition of the book of Kings in the Deuteronimistic history*. Leiden: Brill, 1991.
McKenzie, Stephen L. and Graham, M.P. eds. *The history of Israel's traditions: The heritage of Martin Noth*. Sheffield: Sheffield Academic Press, 1994.
McKenzie, Stephen L. and Haynes, S.R. eds. *To each its own meaning: An Introduction to Biblical- criticism and their application*. Louisville: Westminster, John Knox, 1999.
McKenzie, Stephen L. and T.Romer, eds. *Rethinking the foundations: historiography in the ancient world and in the bible (in honour of van Seters)*. Berlin: Walter de Gruyter, 2000.
McKenzie, Stephen L. and J. Kaltner, *The Old Testament: Its background, growth and content*. Nashville: Abingdon, 2007.
McNutt, Paul M. *Reconstructing the Society of Ancient Israel*. Louisville: Westminster John Knox, 1999.
Mekkes, Johan. *Scheppingopenbaring en wijsbegeerte*. Kampen: Kok, 1961. Translated by C. van Haeften. *Creation, revelation, and philosophy*.) Sioux Center: Dordt College Press, 2010.
Miskotte, Kornelis H. *Het Wezen der Joodsche Religie*. Amsterdam: Paris, 1933.
———. *Edda en Torah*. Nijkerk: Callenbach, 1939.
———. *De Kern van de Zaak*. Nijkerk: Callenbach, 1950.
———. *When the gods are silent*. New York: Harper and Row, 1956.
———. *Bijbels ABC,*. Baarn: Ten Have, 1966.
———. *De weg der verwachting*. Baarn: Ten Have, 1975.
———. *In de Waagschaal, Verzameld Werk Deel I*. Kampen: Kok, 1982.
———. *In de Waagschaal, Verzameld werk, Deel II*. Kampen: Kok, 1989.
———. *Biblical ABCs: the basics of Christian Resistance*. Translated by Eleonora Hof and Collin Cornell. New York: Lexingon-Fortress, 2022.
Mitchell, W.O. *Who has seen the wind?* New York: Macmillan, 1947.
Monshouwer, Dirk. *The gospels and Jewish worship; Bible and Synagogal Liturgy in the first Century C.E.* Vught: Skandalon, 2010.
Muilenberg, J."Form Criticism and Beyond." *Journal of Biblical Literature* (1968) 1–8.
Muis, Jan. *The implicit theology of the Lord's Prayer*, (translated by Allan Jansen), Lamham: Lexington Books, 2020.
———. "Miskotte on God", 2011, www.pthu.nl/overpthu/organisatie/medewerker j.muis.
Neusner, Jacob. *From Politics to Piety*. Englewood Cliffs: Prentice-Hall, 1973.
———. *The emergence of Judaism*. Louisville: Westminster John Knox, 2004.
———. *Judaism and the interpretation of scripture*, Peabody: Hendrickson, 2004.
Niditch, Susan. *Folklore and the Hebrew Bible*. Minneapolis: Fortress Press, 1993.
———. *War in the Hebrew Bible: A study in the ethics of violence*. Oxford: Oxford University Press, 1993.

———. *Oral world and written word: Ancient Israelite literature.* Louisville:Westminster John Knox, 1996.
———. *Ancient Israelite religion.* Oxford: Oxford University Press, 1997.
———. *Judges. A commentary.* Louisville: Westminster John Knox, 2008.
Noort, Ed. *Geweld in het Oude Testament, over woorden en verhalen aan de rand van de Kerkelijke praktijk.* Delft: Meinema, 1985.
———. "Land in zicht . . . ?" In *Tussen openbaring en ervaring: Studies aangeboden aan Prof. Dr. P. Harvelt*, 94–113. Kampen: Kok, 1986.
———. "Geschiedenis als brandpunt over de rol van de archeologie bij de vestiging van Israel in Canaan." *Gereformeerd Theologisch Tijdschrift* 78 (1987) 84–102.
———. "Omgaan met koningen, tendenzen in de exegetische literatuur." *Gereformeerd Theologisch Tijdschrift* 79 (1988) 66–81.
———. "Exegese van het Oude Testament, een zwerftocht". *Gereformeerd Theologisch Tijdschrift* 80 (1989) 2–22.
———. "De val van de grote stad Jericho". *Nederlands Theologisch Tijdschrift*, 3 (2000) 265–79.
Noort, Ed and E. Tigchelaar. *The sacrifice of Isaac.* Leiden: Brill, 2002.
Noort, Ed "Tussen geschiedenis en theologie." *Kerk en Theologie* 53 (2002) 203–7.
Olthuis, James. *A Hermeneutics of Ultimacy: Peril or Promise?* New York: University Press of America, 1987.
Oost, R. *Omstreden Bijbeluitleg.* Kampen: Kok, 1986.
Palache, Juda L. *Inleiding in den Talmoed.* Haarlem: Bohn, 1922.
Peels, Hendrik. G.L. *De omkeer van God in het Oude Testament.* Apeldoorn: Theologische Universiteit, 1997.
———. et al. "De God van het Oude Testament", *Theologia Reformata* 57/4 (2014).
Peels, Hendrik, G. L. "Tranen in Gods ogen; De keerzijde van het oordeel in het boek Jeremia", *Theologia Reformata*, 62/2 (2019) 135–48.
Perdue, Leo G. et al. *Archaeology and Biblical Interpretation. Essays in memory of D. Glenn Rose.* Atlanta: John Knox, 1987.
Perdue, Leo G. *The collapse of history: reconstructing Old Testament theology.* Minneapolis: Fortress, 1994.
———. et al. *Families in Ancient Israel.* Louisville: Westminster John Knox, 1997.
———. ed. *The Blackwell companion to the Hebrew Bible.* Oxford: Blackwell, 2001.
———. *Reconstructing Old Testament theology: After the collapse of history.* Minneapolis: Fortress, 2005.
———. ed. *Scribes, sages and seers: The sage in the Eastern Mediterranean World.* Gottingen: Vandenhoeck & Ruprecht, 2008.
Perdue, Leo G. et al. *Biblical theology: introducing the conversation.* Nashville: Abingdon Press, 2009.
Poorthuis, Mareel and Theo de Kruijf. *Avinoe: De Joodse achtergronden van het Onze Vader.* Baarn: Adveniat, 2016.
Qualman, Darrin. *Civilization critical, energy, food, nature, and the future.* Black Point: Fernwood, 2019.
Quinn, Bob. *Grain by grain; a quest to revive ancient wheat, rural jobs, and healthy food.* Washington D.C.: Island, 2019.
Rosner, Jennifer M. *Healing the Schism: Karl Barth, Frans Rosenzweig, & the new Jewish-Christian Encounter.* Bellingham WA: Lexham, 2021.
———. *Finding Messiah: A journey into the Jewishness of the Gospel.* Downers Grove: InterVarsity, 2022.

Schechter, Jack. *The Land of Israel: its theological dimensions; a study of a promise and of a land's 'holiness'*. New York: University Press of America, 2010.
Scott-Baumann, Michael. *The Shortest History of Israel and Palestine: From Zionism to Intifadas and the Struggle for Peace*. New York City: The Experiment, 2023.
Simard, Suzanne. *Finding the Mother Tree: Discovering the Wisdom of the Forest*. Toronto: Penguin, 2021.
Smelik, Klaas A.D. "De betekenis van 2 Koningen 5: een Amsterdamse benadering". *Gereformeerd Theologisch Tijdschrift* 79 (1988) 98-116.
———. *Writings from Ancient Israel*. Edinburgh: Clark, 1991.
———. *Converting the past. Studies in ancient Israelite and Moabite historiography*. Leiden: Brill, 1992.
Soulen, R.Kendall. *The God of Israel and Christian Theology*. Minneapolis: Fortress, 1996.
Spronk, Klass. *Jozua: Een praktische bibelverklaring*. Kampen: Kok, 1994.
Spronk, Klass. *Nahum, Commentaar op het Oude Testament*. Kampen: Kok. 1999.
———. "Over eerlijkheid en historisch-kritisch exegesis". *Theologisch Debat* 3 (2006) 14-22.
———. "Lekker sprinkhanen." *Interpretatie* 17 year/1 (2009) 24-5.
Spronk, Klaas and A.van Wieringen, *De Bijbel theologisch; hoofdlijnen and thema's*. Zoetermeer: Meinema, 2011.
Soggin, J.Alberto. *An Introduction to the history of Israel and Judah*. Valley Forge: Trinity, 1993.
Talstra, Eep. Clio en de agenda van de toekomst: het Oude Testament van verhaal kunstenaars, gelovigen en historici. *Gereformeerd Theologisch Tijdschrift* 89 (1989) 212-25.
———. *Solomon's Prayer: Synchrony and diachrony in the composition of Kings 8, 14-61*. Leuven: Peeters, 1993.
———. "Prediking tussen profeten en professionals: het einde van de gereformeerde exegese?" *Gereformeerd Theologisch Tijdschrift* 100 (2000) 18-30.
———. "Alle zegen komt van boven, ook als zij van beneden komt, Gedachten bij Psalm 67". In *Amsterdamse Cahiers voor Exegese van de Bijbel en zijn Tradities*, 18, 47-60. Maastricht: Shaker, 2000.
———. Actuele basisposities in de Bijbelse theologie: wijzen van lezen. *Kerken Theologie* 53 (2002) 188-201.
———. *Oude en nieuwe lezers. Een inleiding in de methoden van uitleg van het Oude Testament*. Kampen: Kok, 2002.
———. "The Rediscovery of the Hebrew Bible", In *The Rediscovery of the Hebrew Bible*. Maastricht: Shaker, 2002.
———. "Second Isaiah and Qoheleth. Could one get them on speaking terms?" In F. Postma, K. Spronk, Talstra, eds. *The New Things, Festschrift H. Leene, ACEB Suppl.* 3, Maastricht: Shaker, 2002.
———. *Zou er ook wetenschap zijn bij de Allerhoogste?* (Psalm 73:11). Amsterdam: VU Uitgeverij, 2003.
———. "Identity and loyalty. Faith and violence: The case of Deuteronomy". In D. van Keulen and M. Brinkman eds. *Christian Faith and Violence, Vol.1 Studies in Reformed Theology 10*, 69-85. Zoetermeer:Meinema, 2005.
———. "De talen van het Oude Testament." In H. Jagersma and M. Vervenne ed. *Inleiding in het Oude Testament*. Kampen: Kok, 2006.

———. " Zelfs uw houthakkers en uw waterputters. (Deuternomium 29: 10(11))". *Theologia Reformata* 51 (2008) 150-64.
Trimm, Charlie. "Recent Research on Warfare in the Old testament". *Currents in Biblical Research*, 1-46. Thousand Oaks: Sage, 2011.
van Bekkum, Koert. "De historiografie van Israels' vestiging in Kanaan". *Nederlands Theologisch Tijdschrift* 54 (2000) 295-309.
———. "Het Oude Testament als historisch document". *Theologia Reformata*. 46 (2003) 328-355.
van Bekkum, Koert. en G. Kwakkel, "Een veilige leefwereld voor de mens in dienst van God; overwegingen bij alternatieve lezingen van het begin van Genesis". *Theologia Reformata* 53 (2010) 318-335.
van Bekkum, Koert. *From Conquest to Coexistence: Ideology and antiquarian intent in the Historiography of Israel's settlement in Canaan*. Leiden: Brill, 2011.
van de Beek, A. et al. *Leidse Lezingen: Waar is God in deze tijd?: de betekenis van de geschiedenis in de theologie van H. Berkhof*. Nijkerk: Callenbach, 1994.
van Putten, Henk. *Niet te vergeten: Frans Breukelman; Kan er uit Amsterdam iets goed komen?*. Groningen: Rijksuniversiteit, 2009.
van Zanden, Gerard. *Bij het begin beginnen: Het bijbels-theologische project van Frans, Breukelman*. Utrecht: Kok, 2019.
van Niftrik, Gerrit C. *Een beroeder Israels, enkele hoofdgedachten in de theologie van Barth*. Nijkerk: Callenbach, 1949.
van den Brink, Gijsbert. "De hedendaagse renaissance van de triniteitsleer; een orienterend overzicht". *Theologia Reformata* 46/3, (2003) 210-40.
vander Kam, James C. *An introduction to early Judaism*. Grand Rapids: Eerdmans, 2001.
van der Toorn, Karel. *Sin and sanction in Israel and Mesopotamia*. Assen: van Gorcum, 1985.
———. *From her cradle to her grave*. Sheffield:Sage, 1994.
———. *Family religion in Babylonia, Syria and Israel: continuity and change in the forms of religious life*. Leiden: Brill, 1996.
van der Toorn, Karel. ed. *The image and the book*. Leuven: Peeters, 1997.
van der Toorn, Karel. *Scribal culture and the making of the Hebrew Bible*. Cambridge: Harvard University Press, 2007.
van der Woude, Adam, ed. *Inleiding tot de studie van het Oude Testament*. Kampen:Kok, 1986.
van der Woude, Adam. *New avenues in the study of the Old Testament*. Leiden: Brill, 1989.
———. *The world of the Old Testament*. Grand Rapids: Eerdmans, 1989.
van der Woude, Adam, ed. *The book of Daniel in the light of new findings*. Leuven: Peeters, 1993.
Van Dussen, Ad. "God's voorzienigheid," TSB-Lezing, 1999.
van Midden, P.J. *Broederschap en koninschap*. Maastricht: Shaker, 1998.
van Ruiten, Jacobus and J.C.de Vos. *The land of Israel in Bible history and theology*. Leiden: Brill, 2009.
van Seters, John. *Abraham in history and tradition*. New Haven: Yale University, 1975.
———. *In search of history: historiography in the ancient world and the origins of biblical history*. New Haven: Yale University, 1983.
———. *Prologue to History. The Yahwist as historian in Genesis*. Louisville: Westminster John Knox, 1992.

———. *The life of Moses: The Yahweh as historian in Exodus-Numbers.* Kampen Kok, 1994.
———. *The Pentateuch: A social-science commentary.* Sheffield: Sheffield Academic, 1999.
Von Rad, Gerhard. *Studies in Deuteronomy.* London: Student Christian Movement, 1953.
———. *Old Testament theology Vol I.: The theology of Israel's Historical traditions.* New York: Harper & Brothers, 1962.
———. *Old testament theology: Vol.II.: The theology of Israel's prophetic tradition.* Edinburgh: Oliver and Boyd, 1965.
———. *Deuteronomy: a commentary.* Philadelphia: Westminster, 1966.
———. *Wisdom in Israel.* London: SCM, 1972.
Voorwinde, Stephen, "Does God have real feelings?" *Vox Reformata*, 67 (2002) 24–51.
Vriezen, Th.C. *De godsdienst van Israel.* Zeist: Ten Have, 1963.
Vriezen, Th.C. and van der Woude, A.S. (1976 5th ed.). *De literatuur van Oud-Israel.* Wassenaar: Service, 1976.
Vriezen, Th.C. *Ancient Israelite and early Jewish literature.* Leiden: Brill, 2005.
Wallis, Jim. *The False White Gospel.* St. Martin's Essentials: New York City, 2024.
West, Gerald.O, ed. *Reading other-wise: Socially engaged scholars reading with their local communities.* Atlanta: Society of Biblical Literature, 2007.
Wiersinga, Herman. *De Verzoening in de theologische diskussie.* Kampen: Kok, 1971.
———. *Verzoening als verandering.* Baarn: Ten Have, 1972.
———. *Verzoening met het lijden?* Baarn: Ten Have, 1975.
———. *Doem of daad; een boek over zonde,* Baarn: Ten Have, 1982.
———. *Op hoogoogte; Portret van een postmodern geloof.* Zoetermeer: Meinema, 2000.
Wohlleben, Peter. *The Hidden life of trees.* Vancouver: Greystone, 2016.
Woudstra, Marten, H. *The Book of Joshua.* Grand Rapids: Eerdmans, 1981.
Wyschogrod, Michael. *Abraham's Promise: Judaism and Jewish-Christian Relations.* Grand Rapids: Eerdmans, 2004.
Zuidervaart, Lambert and H. Luttikhuizen, eds. *The Arts, Community and Cultural Democracy* London: Macmillan, 2000.
Zuidervaart, Lambert. *Artistic Truth: Aesthetics, Discourse, and Imaginative Disclosure.* Cambridge: University Press, 2004.
———. *Social Philosophy after Adorno.* Cambridge: University Press, 2007.
———. *Art in Public: Politics, Economics, and a Democratic Culture.* Cambridge: University Press, 2011.
———. "The Inner Reformation of Reformational Philosophy: Response to Geertsema and van Woudenberg". *Philosophia Reformata* 89 (2014) 1–18.
———. *Religion, Truth, and Social Transformation; Essays in Reformational Philosophy.* Montreal: McGill–Queen's University Press, 2016.
———. *Art, Education, and Cultural Renewal: Essays in Reformational Philosophy.* Montreal: McGill– Queen's University Press, 2017.
———. *Social Domains of Truth.* New York: Routledge, 2023.
Zuidema, Sytse U. *Konfrontatie with Karl Barth.* Toronto: Christelijk Perspectief, 1963.

(For a more elaborate bibliography see: "Reading the Hebrew scriptures backwards". Freely available on line: www.foundationalissues.com.)

www.ingramcontent.com/pod-product-compliance
Lightning Source LLC
Chambersburg PA
CBHW071434300426
44114CB00013B/1427